32.5$

Don't Get above Your Raisin'

MUSIC IN AMERICAN LIFE

*A list of books in the series appears
at the end of this book.*

Don't Get above Your Raisin'

Country Music
and the Southern Working Class

Bill C. Malone

UNIVERSITY OF ILLINOIS PRESS
Urbana and Chicago

Publication of this book was supported by
a grant from the H. Earle Johnson Fund of the
Society for American Music.

Library of Congress Cataloging-in-Publication Data
Malone, Bill C.
Don't get above your raisin' : country music and the southern
working class / Bill C. Malone.
p.   cm. — (Music in American life)
Includes bibliographical and discographical references (p.   )
and index.
ISBN 0-252-02678-0 (alk. paper)
  1. Country music—Social aspects. 2. Working class—
Southern States—Songs and music—History and criticism.
I. Title. II. Series.
ML3524.M344   2001
781.642'0975—dc21   2001001219

Contents

Preface

The phrase, "Don't get above your raising," may not be immediately clear to people who grew up outside the rural South. It is in fact highly complex in meaning. In one sense it is a remnant of the fatalism that once colored the thinking of many southern white people—a belief that life cannot be changed and that one should guard against the disappointment that might come from unreal expectations. It is not an injunction against wealth as such, even though riches carry the potential for corruption. Instead, it is a rebuke to pretense and snobbery, and a plea for respect for and loyalty to one's roots. This egalitarian philosophy has been a central facet of the thinking of southern working people, and it has long been a unifying, but hard to maintain, theme of the music that they have bequeathed to the world.

This book is rooted in the conviction that country music has been an art form made and sustained by working people. That deceptively simple truth has long been obscured by the tendency of both friends and foes to affix descriptions or labels that either denigrate or romanticize the music. Some descriptions, of course—such as hillbilly—were originally hatched by detractors but have been embraced by many fans and musicians as a badge of working-class pride. In other cases, we find vague terms such as "Anglo Saxon," "Celtic," "Appalachian," or "Cowboy" being used to describe the music's sources or to lend cultural legitimacy to certain styles. Such labels, in fact, have been employed to counter the hillbilly categorization, but have obfuscated more than they have explained.

The people who created the music, and who gave it its special identity, were not simply working people. Most of them, musicians and fans alike, were southerners who carried in their personalities and music the burdens of their region's history, as well as its many contradictions. I grew up as a child of these people, but have never known quite what to call them. Terms like "folk," "plain people," "poor whites," "white trash," and worse have been attached to them, but none are completely accurate, and none would be used by the people themselves. Even the term "working class" might not set too well with them, because it suggests a static station in life that seems increasingly irrelevant in our mobile society. The sense of fatalism has largely given way to the expectations of a consumer society. Generations have come and gone, and occupations, residences, and lifestyles have changed dramatically, but work remains the defining fact of their lives.

I am aware that the working people discussed in my book did not constitute a homogeneous body. They were diverse in residence, religion, occupation, ethnicity, and even in politics. They were neither Anglo-Saxon nor Celtic; in fact, they weren't all white (and a substantial number were not Protestants). Their culture and their music were remarkable blendings of ethnic, racial, traditional, and modern traits. Kentucky coal miners, North Carolina textile workers, and East Texas oil drillers worked and lived in dramatically different settings, but they nevertheless shared a rural context and social history that linked them in various ways. I am still much impressed with the insights contributed sixty years ago by W. J. Cash, who remarked in his epochal *Mind of the South* that, although there are many Souths, there is also one South.[1] This South is a product of the region's special history, its ruralism, a racism born of slavery and the belief in white supremacy, and the defeat suffered in the Civil War. A broad cluster of traits, including both memories and bloodlines, once linked the people of Virginia and the eastern seaboard to the people of East Texas. These common traits bound southerners in many ways, while their diversity lent a rich and special flavor to their musical culture.

Although the chief focus of this book is on the music made by southern working people, readers should expect neither an intensive exploration of song lyrics about work nor a class-centered study about the "struggles" waged by laboring people. Country musicians have seldom sung about labor. Marxist-oriented readers will find little satisfaction in either country music or this book. Southern working people, and their music, have been intensely class-conscious, driven often by anger and resentment and a sense of outrage concerning privileged people. Class feeling has frequently inspired expressions of united action—as in the Populist

Movement of the 1890s and the union drives of the 1930s—but, just as often, it has been diverted by individualistic responses. The problems addressed by country song lyrics are real, but their proposed resolutions often take the form of fantasy—nostalgia, machismo, escapism, religion, and romantic love. Country music deals with survival in all of its manifestations—the day-to-day problems encountered by average people as they deal with each other and an often-indifferent world.

After attempting to establish the validity of the two basic assumptions of my study—the music's southernness and its intimate relationship with working people—I then concentrate on what I perceive as the major realms occupied by country music (home, religion, rambling, frolic, humor, and politics). Each topic is treated chronologically, generally from the precommercial era to the present day. In each case, this approach permits an exploration of the degree to which the music reflected southern working-class concerns, and the degree to which such a relationship still exists. Everywhere one sees the contradictions of southern working-class life, and the struggle between the polarities of belief and conduct that establishes the tension that has made country music appealing. Here again I have been much influenced by the thinking of W. J. Cash. His famous "man-at-the-center," who was elemental in thought and impulsive in action and who moved readily between the poles of hedonism and piety (the conflicting demands of Saturday night and Sunday morning),[2] is more than a metaphor for southern contradiction. His paradoxes have also thrived in the varied styles of country music and in the lives of many of the performers—both male and female.

While country music has always borne the marks of its southern and working-class origins, it could not have survived or prospered had it remained linked exclusively to those constituencies. Even during its early hillbilly days it attracted fans in the North and around the world *because* of its presumed southern traits—whether romantically or negatively expressed—or because it seemed to fill a vacuum left by the decline of the older styles of Tin Pan Alley music. The "old familiar tunes" of the 1920s and 1930s appealed to millions of people because of their singable melodies and direct, affecting stories. One suspects that country music still captures listeners everywhere with themes that would have been familiar to fans in the 1920s—nostalgia, escape, fantasy, human-interest drama, gritty realism, and evocations of values that seem imperiled by modernity. Observing the national popularity of country music in our own time—a facet of the phenomenon described by John Egerton as the "southernization of America"—Peter Applebome declared that "country formed a visceral bond with lower- and lower-middle-class whites like no other music of our time."³

Finally, this book carries the imprint of my personal feelings. I was a fan of country music long before I became a student of it. It has been closely related to my life—as the music of my family and the culture in which I was reared. I realize the pitfalls of a personal approach, and the temptations of seeing the universal in the particular. After all, there are people who grew up under conditions very similar to mine who do not like country music at all, just as there are people who grew up in places like New York City and San Francisco, or who have known only affluence, who share my affections for the old-time, rural-based musical styles. We need all of their stories, and any kind of personal histories that illuminate the ways in which musical choices have been made. Once we admit that our assessments are often shaped by our personal histories, then we will understand the roles we play in shaping the definition and acceptance of the musical forms about which we write.

⁓ ⁓ ⁓

Many people have contributed to the shaping of my personal and intellectual growth. My introduction to country music came at home through the singing of my mother and through the little Philco battery radio that Daddy bought in 1939. The radio hillbillies became constant and beloved companions. My older brothers, Wylie and Kelly, strummed their guitars and sang the songs of Rex Griffin, Cowboy Slim Rinehart, the Carter Family, Roy Acuff, and other favorite performers. Although politics and other matters may sometimes divide us, country singing is still virtually the first thing we do and talk about when we get together.

Country music remained my obsession when I entered the University of Texas in Austin. Singing at parties could be a hindrance to proper study habits, but it kept me actively involved in the study of my passion, learning new songs and discussing their meaning. The late Willie Benson and Tom Crouch, Ph.D. graduate students in psychology and history, played guitar backup for my singing while I was learning my first chords. Tom even planted the idea of "honky-tonk" music in my mind with his references to the clubs of West Texas and Fort Worth. Kenneth Threadgill, of course, provided warm encouragement and inspiration, and a venue—his bar—in which we all could play. Stan Alexander was most often my duet partner at the now-famous Wednesday night sessions. Stan's vocal prowess was such that we could easily give him the highest praise that the "plain folk" can give to one of their talented own: "That boy ought to be on the radio." Professor Joe B. Frantz knew about my love for country music and suggested that I write the doctoral dissertation that became *Country Music, USA*.[4]

My first full-time teaching job at Southwest Texas State in San Marcos came during the final stages of my dissertation and book preparation. Again, constant immersion in country music delayed the completion of my project, but I like to think that the evenings spent picking and singing at Jeannette and Bill Pool's house in San Marcos, and at Dot and John Moore's farm in nearby Maxwell, kept me sharp and inquisitive. I was always learning new "old" songs and eager to find people to whom I could sing them. My best buddy during those years, Charlie Stephenson, did not sing, but he kept me engaged in lively political discussion, as did Bob Barton, Eddy Etheredge, and other stalwart participants in Hays County Democratic politics. Star Huffstickler, Charles Taylor, Charles Chandler, and Wayne Oakes were good musical partners, but the Pools, Moores, and Stephenson provided most of the warm emotional and spiritual sustenance that I needed during those years.

The opportunities for musical performance during the years from 1967 to 1971 proved much less forthcoming at Murray State in Murray, Kentucky, and Wisconsin State in Whitewater. Luckily, I found good colleagues and friends, such as Betsy and Don Whisenhunt in Murray, and Mary and John Hevener in Whitewater, who shared my interest in Democratic politics and Texas and southern things. The Heveners not only made their home available for picking and singing but I learned much from John, who was then in the final stages of *Which Side Are You On?* his fine book on the Harlan County coal troubles of the 1930s.[5] I regret that his untimely death prevented completion of a study of southern migration to Akron, Ohio, that we often talked about.

My involvement in music was reinvigorated after 1971 when I moved to New Orleans and Tulane University. I will be eternally indebted to Henry Kmen, professor of history at Tulane and author of *Music in New Orleans*,[6] who reviewed my book favorably for the *Journal of Southern History* and then recommended that I be hired by his history department. My first course at Tulane was taught as a visiting professor, substituting for Bennett Wall, the legendary professor of American history. By 1972 I had become the leader of a bluegrass band, the Hill Country Ramblers (named by my first wife, Ann, as a tribute to her Central Texas roots). Many good friends, such as Suzie Fitch, Jack Friedman, Patrick Flory, Jim Huey, Hazel Schleuter, Joe Wilson, Phil Breeding, Dave and Susie Malone, and Bruce Daigrepont, spent some time as Rambler musicians.

During a short stint in Washington, D.C., at the Red Fox Inn and Indian Springs Festival, a young man named Bela Fleck joined us as our five-string banjoist. June and Bob Lambert were never members of the Hill Country Ramblers, but they became the same kind of friends and mentors that I had known earlier in San Marcos. Some of my most enjoyable moments in Louisiana were spent singing old-time brother duets with Bob, sharing our mutual love for the music of the Louvin Brothers, and eating June's delectable southern cooking.

I'm also thankful for having had the opportunity to know and share musical experiences with some of the leading promoters of New Orleans and Louisiana music. Quint Davis and Allison Miner, the founders of the extraordinarily successful Jazz and Heritage Festival, invited me often to perform in various capacities as either a lecturer or singer. Mary Howell, a civil rights lawyer by trade and a fan of old-time country music by avocation, encouraged (and obtained) my active participation at the Piney Woods Opry in Abita Springs, Louisiana, a Saturday night variety show that she cofounded with Patrick Flory. WWOZ, a wonderful volunteer-run, community-sponsored radio station and a promoter of all varieties of Louisiana music, permitted me to showcase my favorite styles of vintage country music as an occasional disk jockey.

Lest my readers think that all I did in New Orleans was make music and eat, I must also recall my twenty-five years in the history department at Tulane University. Dean Joseph Gordon made my occasional sabbaticals as responsibility-free as possible, and the people in Development and Public Relations encouraged my work and publicized it often. Good Tulane faculty friends—Nancy and John Boles, Elaine and Patrick Maney, Sydney and Blake Touchstone, Janet and Clarence Mohr, Joan and Bob Hunter, Diane and Larry Powell, and Loraine and Dan Purrington—sponsored frequent picking and singing parties and lent congenial support on matters political and departmental. The friendship and intellectual stimulation provided by my graduate students, of course, will always be among the most prized memories of my years at Tulane. Stephen Ray Tucker, Bruce Raeburn, David Stricklin, Charles Chamberlain, Curt Jerde, and Kevin Fontenot all did their part to lend academic respectability to the study of American vernacular music.

The Tulane era also included a Texas interlude of four years in which I commuted weekly between New Orleans and Hide-A-Way Lake near Tyler—a distance that required an almost eight-hour drive! I learned many new songs during those lonely journeys, enjoyed the East Texas countryside and the company of family and friends, but ultimately discovered that

I could not go home again. Musically, the fondest memories of those East Texas days include getting to know Dave Rousseau, one of America's leading bluegrass disk jockeys, and getting to hear the East Texas String Ensemble (pronounced *insimbel*), the Hickory Hill bluegrass band, and Jimmy Arnold. The ensemble was an old-time string band that included four professors from Stephen F. Austin State University in Nacogdoches (Stan Alexander, Ab Abernethy, Charles Gardner, and Tom Nall). The Hickory Hill band was a funny and musically gifted group consisting of Don Eaves, John Early, Rolan Foster, Ronny Singley, and Bob Stegall. Don Eaves introduced me to Jimmy Arnold, the star-crossed musical genius from Fries, Virginia, who had somehow drifted into the Tyler area.

To my great delight and surprise, our move in 1997 to Madison, Wisconsin, where my wife Bobbie became the head of the Office of School Services at the State Historical Society, was even more productive musically and professionally. Numerous people have eased our transition from the South to the North and have contributed immeasurably to my musical sustenance: James Leary, folklorist at the University of Wisconsin, is a fount of knowledge on all aspects of American folk music (particularly midwestern), as is Richard March, a versatile musician and state folklorist of Wisconsin. Debbie Kmetz, folk musician and local history specialist at the Historical Society, put me in contact with these two scholars and friends. Paul Boyer, U.S. cultural historian at the University of Wisconsin, admitted me to his humanities seminar as a non-stipendiary fellow (a fancy way to say that I participated in the intellectual exchanges but didn't get paid for it). Chelcy Bowles and Joyce Follet, in the music and history extension programs at the University of Wisconsin, made it possible for me to teach a variety of noncredit courses on American music. Jess Gilbert, a rural sociologist at the university and a native of Louisiana, is our chief link to the South and, along with his wife Kathy, brings needed fellowship and warmth during the often bleak and cold Wisconsin winters.

My greatest Wisconsin debt, however, is owed to WORT-FM in Madison. My Wednesday morning radio show, "Back to the Country," keeps me constantly immersed in the history of country music, supplies me with the means to both enjoy and popularize the music I love, and has introduced me to a wide range of friends and fellow musicians. It is a pleasure to convey my thanks to Sybil Augustine and Norm Stockwell for permitting me to do the show, and for giving me a free hand to organize it in the way I think appropriate. James Carrott faithfully taped the shows, provided encouragement, and served as my engineer on critical occasions. Jeff Hickey worked as my substitute during the spring of 2000 while I was teaching in North Carolina, and he has graciously continued as engineer since my return. Special thanks go to Jim Mark, who served as my first engineer, hosted the show during my occasional absences, and played guitar in a band with Bobbie and me.

The music scene in Madison has been particularly rewarding. Art and Stephanie Stevenson, central members of the High Water bluegrass band, make some of the best duet music I've ever heard. The Goose Island Ramblers, an engaging blend of midwestern polka and hillbilly music, opened my eyes and ears to the wonders of a style of American rural music that I scarcely knew existed. Sadly, their career has come to an end, first with their official retirement in late 1999 and then with the death of Windy Whitford in June of 2000. The renaissance of acoustic and bluegrass music in Madison has been fostered by many people, but special kudos must be given to the irrepressible Cork and Bottle String Band, who hold forth each Wednesday night at Ken's Bar, Art and Stephanie Stevenson, the Nob Hill Boys, Wendy Brotherton, Carolyn Hegeler, and Carmen Burnett. Carmen is a friend to all bluegrass and old-time musicians, and she has been an anchor of support to me through her service as receptionist and hostess at WORT.

While the people listed above have been important to my social health, others have lent support to my intellectual growth, and especially to the research that bolstered this book. Above all, I am pleased to acknowledge the generous support of the John Simon Guggenheim Foundation, which awarded me a fellowship in 1984. During my various career moves and academic appointments, many people have lent intellectual support to my work. Archie Green, Ed Kahn, Norm Cohen, Bob Pinson, David Whisnant, Ronnie Pugh, William Ferris, Marcie Cohen Ferris, Loyal Jones, and Richard Hill have been among the most unselfish. Their contributions are noted at various points in this essay, and in the notes at the back of the book.

Visiting professorships and special lectureships also sharpened my understanding of country music, and permitted me to do research that otherwise might not have been possible. Bill Ferris invited me on several occasions to participate in symposia at the Center for the Study of Southern Culture at the University of Mississippi. Daniel Patterson and Lynwood Montel brought me to the University of North Carolina–Chapel Hill and Western Kentucky University, respectively, to give lectures and engage in music workshops. A summer appointment in 1987 at Berea College in Kentucky, teaching an undergraduate course in Appalachian music and a workshop on the same subject for teachers, was particularly rewarding. The sojourn permitted access to the Berea Archives and to the wise counsel and friendship of Loyal Jones, and made possible several trips into the southern mountains. One of the best by-products of our stay in Berea was the beginning of a lasting friendship with Debby Gray, who knows more about the National Barn Dance than anyone I've ever met. I hope that she someday writes a book on the subject.

A joint appointment during the spring semester of 2000 at Duke and UNC–Chapel Hill, as the Lehman Brady Professor of Documentary Studies and American Studies, brought rich rewards that a retired professor from Tulane University might never have anticipated. The experience provided inspiration for creative thought, a chance to hear and sing good music—most of it sponsored by Alice Gerrard, who arranged the picking sessions—and opportunities for research at the best southern history collection in the world (the Southern Folklife Collection at UNC–Chapel Hill). My seminar, "Women in Country Music," exposed me to the insights of several brilliant students, including Tes Thraves, who worked as my graduate assistant, and to the music of Betty Smith, Hazel Dickens, Alice Gerrard, Etta Baker, Murphy Henry, Tish Hinojosa, and Carol Elizabeth Jones who made guest appearances. What a dream come true! My debts are many, especially to Tom Rankin and Iris Hill, at the Center for Documentary Studies at Duke, who invited me to accept the position and then made my stay a very pleasant one. Glenn Hinson, head of the Curriculum in Folklore, and Townsend Ludington, chairman of the American Studies Department, provided comparable assistance at UNC–Chapel Hill. At both institutions talented administrative assistants, Cyndy Severns at the Center for Documentary Studies and Debby Simmons-Cahan at Chapel Hill, worked graciously and tirelessly to make my stay comfortable and productive.

Many of the conclusions and insights that appear in the present book had their origin in a series of lectures given at Mercer University in October, 1990. I had the honor to present the thirty-fourth annual Lamar Memorial Lectures in Southern History: "Romance, Realism, and the Musical Culture of the Southern Plain Folk." These presentations were eventually published, in revised form, as *Singing Cowboys and Musical Mountaineers.*[7]

Judy McCulloh and Richard Wentworth at the University of Illinois Press have exceptional qualities as editors, not the least of which has been their patience. Somehow, despite the passage of more years than I would like to admit, they have preserved confidence in my abilities, and the faith that I would eventually publish this book. Even with their support, however, the manuscript might never have been published without the additional and untiring technical assistance of Jim Sewell. Taking a manuscript written in several different versions of Microsoft Word, he miraculously converted them into uniform chapters to be mailed to the press.

I also wish to thank Nat Hentoff, James C. Cobb, and David Whisnant, who read the entire manuscript, and David Stricklin and Jack Bernhardt, who read versions of my comments on religion and country music. I hope that I have not misinterpreted or misunderstood their critical suggestions.

My indebtedness to the two major archives that deal with country music—the Country Music Foundation Library and Media Center in Nashville and the Southern Folklife Collection at Chapel Hill—should be obvious to all readers. I will pay tribute to these fine repositories again in my bibliographical essay, but I wish to give special recognition at this time to Ronnie Pugh, Bob Pinson, and Paul Kingsbury at the CMF, and to Amy Davis and Steve Weiss at the Southern Folklife Collection.

Finally, I wish to dedicate this book to the memory of my mother, Maude Owens Malone, and to my wife Bobbie. Mama was the first "country singer" I ever heard. Without her, the inspiration for this book would never have been planted. Without Bobbie, it probably would not have been written. She has been my sweetheart, musical partner, and intellectual companion. Hers was the low but firm voice that always kept saying, "Go write that book."

Don't Get above Your Raisin'

Introduction:
"I'm a Plain Ole Country Boy"

In the late 1980s, when that son of Yale and the eastern aristocracy, President George Herbert Walker Bush, announced that country music was his music of preference, no one any longer needed to be reminded that the music had become a commanding presence in the nation's popular culture. Having emerged as an industry with products consumed around the world, it had become a social force significant enough to warrant the embrace of national politicians. My personal introduction to the music, however, came in a local context untouched by power, status, or wealth. The sounds of country music suffused the world into which I was born in 1934, on our little cotton tenant farm on the western edge of Smith County in East Texas. Although we would not have described it as such at the time, the first "country music" I heard included the lonesome old sentimental tunes sung by my mother about maidens who died of unrequited love, long-suffering mothers whose love for their wandering boys never wavered, little orphans whose deaths on the bitterly cold street were but a prelude to a joyous reconciliation with Mother in Heaven, and eastbound trains that carried penniless little children to reunions with their poor blind fathers in prison.

These songs may have meant nothing more than a temporary diversion from the isolation of farm life, but when my mother sang them, she may have recalled her own orphan childhood in the little community of Primrose, where her paternal grandparents raised her from the time she was born. The songs very likely mirrored my mother's longings for her own mother, who died only three weeks after giving birth, and the love-hate relationship with her father, the railroad man who virtually abandoned his tiny daughter after his wife died. These tender songs made permanent imprints on my impressionable young mind, but none of them had as dramatic an impact as did the gospel songs my mother sang. I was too young to comprehend either the loneliness, the private anguish and frustration, and the failed dreams that underlay much of her singing or the joyousness that she often conveyed when she sang of her Redeemer or her long-promised home in Heaven. But when she sang "He promised never to leave me, never to leave me alone," while going about her domestic chores, her conviction was so powerful that it insinuated itself into my consciousness along with the words and melody of the song.

These early songs, of course, represented only one side of country music, and they reflected only one facet of the rural experience. As a child I was generally insulated from the songs that spoke about the bawdy or explicitly erotic side of life, but we loved to sing about such badmen as Jesse James and Sam Bass and about free and rambling spirits like Black Jack David. I wasn't quite sure what David's secret was, or how he could entice a young woman away from her husband, baby, and warm feather bed, but the lure of the open road was romantically appealing even to a child like me. It must have been even more compelling to people like my parents whose lives were circumscribed by poverty and the bounds of tenantry. My mother never ceased to thrill to the sight and sounds of a train, nor did she ever tire of telling stories about her father, the engineer whose job on the Cotton Belt Railroad took him all over the Southwest. She may have been thinking of him, and about his many rumored affairs and marriages, when she listened with delight to Bill Callahan's version of "Rattlesnaking Daddy," one of the few rowdy items that she admitted into her pantheon of favorite songs.

Although certain types of songs might remain unknown to me, I could not be sheltered from the seamy side of existence. We heard gossip about the "sorry" girls in our community, and about the occasional illegitimate birth, and we knew that neighbors sometimes broke the law and that violence was often the outcome of arguments or disputes. Scarcely a year after my birth the neighbor who lived across the pasture was shot to death in his backyard by a brother-in-law whose daughter had been sexually exploited by the victim. No stories were more enthralling to me than those that told about such local murders or accounts of violent family retribution or about the grisly and shameful lynchings of blacks on the courthouse square at the county seat. My little rural world had no dearth of both love and hate, nor of virtue and hypocrisy. It was a society which, at its best, was capable of warm outpourings of hospitality and kindness, and, at its worst, grim manifestations of bigotry and intolerance.

As a child I could not have known that my little community of Galena, which rested almost on the border between Smith and Van Zandt counties about twenty miles west of Tyler, was a folk community, a little outpost of that common folk culture that extended throughout the rural South. Kinship, migration patterns, cotton cultivation, evangelical religion, cultural preferences, and a belief in white supremacy linked it to the older South. We shared a history of poverty, struggle, and defeat with our fellow Southerners to the east, and too often diverted our frustration and impotence onto our black neighbors, not realizing how much we all had in common. Most important, I could not have known that our way of life was almost over—both beneficiary and victim of technological change and wartime prosperity—and that the stability that anchored my young life was a fragile one. And although I could see them played out in the day-to-day experiences of my family, I did not understand the tensions and contradictions that lay at the heart of our seemingly placid society.

A scene that recurred during my childhood provides vivid images of the two worlds occupied by my mother and father. One particular memory recalls a hot summer night, sometime in 1939, at a revival or "protracted meeting" at the Tin Top Pentecostal Church, just across the Van Zandt County line. The flickering glow of coal oil lamps illuminated the little one-room meetinghouse. The community could not afford a regular minister, but services were conducted by an itinerant preacher who alternately preached and led the small congregation in song as he strummed his guitar: "As I travel through the land, singing as I go, pointing souls to Calvary, through the crimson flow." I sat next to my mother, enthralled by her singing but frightened by the emotion so nakedly on display all around me—the shouting, weeping, praying, speaking in tongues. My mother participated enthusiastically in these church services, for they provided her rare opportunities to commune with her women friends, to express herself freely—in the joyous rapture of prayer, testimony, and music—and to gain release from the isolation, pain, and largely thankless tasks of her life as wife and mother on a luckless cotton tenant farm.

Outside, in the darkened yard that surrounded the church, a few men dressed in overalls and workshirts leaned against their wagons and traded gossip and tall tales as they passed around a bottle. My daddy was one of them, and this was as close as he ever got to the inside of a church. He sometimes accompanied my mother to religious affairs, particularly if they were outdoors brush arbor meetings, but almost always he stayed on the fringe of the gathering, talking with other farmers like himself. His resistance to organized religion always deeply troubled my mother, as did his occasional fits of temper, infrequent bouts of carousing, and general insensitivity to her emotional needs; thus, he appeared often in her prayers. Daddy's avoidance of formal church attendance did not arise from lack of belief. He was unregenerate, not atheistic. Life as a tenant farmer on the worn-out cotton fields of East Texas, working on someone else's land and under someone else's terms, did not permit much in the way of self-assertion. He was not prepared to surrender the little bit of freedom he still possessed to the discipline of church doctrine, just as he was reluctant to move to town to accept the kind of regimentation that accompanied wage earning. Like most southern rural men, he found his most comfortable communion with other men—at work, hunting and fishing, gambling, drinking, or simply lounging around. Such gatherings were always marked by the rough exchange of opinions and humor. I do not know what they talked about on this particular night. Most likely, however, the talk concentrated on local matters, the ingredients of a traditional rural society—mules, the weather, boll weevils, cotton prices, a favorite bird dog, or hunting or fishing. If they talked of politics, it was probably about President Franklin Roosevelt or about the coming of war in Europe. Few could have known in those balmy summer days of 1939 that their own sons would soon be fighting in that war, or that the conflict would permanently transform their lives and bring to an end that seemingly changeless, cotton-dependent society that they took for granted.

The two scenes enacted in and outside that little country church, and the tension represented by my parents' opposing spiritual and social needs, have not only endured in my memory but have also become part of me. The religion both attracted and repelled. I was both skeptical and accepting. Part of me was drawn by the emotion and even by the doctrine. But, mostly, I longed to be apart from it, to be free of the guilt-ridden pressure that lay so heavily upon the "sinners" who remained inside and to be part of the lounging crowd outside the church, to share their stories, jokes, and tall tales. As it turned out, I joined neither world, although I'm sure that much of those conflicting influences, both sacred and profane, remain embedded within me.

Almost nothing now remains of Galena, that little community where I was born and spent my earliest years. Weeds and underbrush now cover the sites of the cotton gin and the little country store at the old crossroads where I caught the bus to the consolidated school in Van. A half mile to the north no evidence remains of the two-room Elm Grove schoolhouse, and even farther to the south only a well curb stands at our old home site as the sole mute and lonely testimony to the lives once spent there. Only a few scattered houses and remnants of houses survive, and the original Tin Top church succumbed long ago, a victim of restless juvenile arson. Not one stalk of cotton grows in this region where the fiber was once king, and most of the farms have been converted to pasture by the absentee bankers and oilmen who now own the land. The most dramatic manifestation of change, Interstate 20, runs only a few dozen yards north of the Galena crossroads, taking people to Dallas, Shreveport, and distant points beyond. Salesmen, commuters, and shoppers now routinely make one-day return trips to those cities. During my childhood we felt fortunate if we reached Dallas once during the year. As a matter of fact, virtually up to the time of my birth, a wagon trip to Tyler, only twenty miles away, took half a day to complete and required a night's lodging in the Wagon Yard near the courthouse square. The rumble of interstate traffic is a constant reminder of the social and technological forces that have transformed rural America and lured its sons and daughters to cities throughout the nation. Nevertheless, when I return to East Texas for a visit, or for the family reunion each May, a flood of remembered impressions swirls through my imagination. Music is the fondest of these memories.

Music provides my one enduring link to that now-vanished time and place; and it is the musical moments that return often to my mind. Like biscuits and ribbon cane syrup, music was a staple in our household. Before 1939 when we obtained our first battery-powered Philco radio, my mother's repertoire consisted of songs or fragments of songs from her childhood. After the radio became the cultural centerpiece of the Malone household, we encountered a much larger range of musical options. I cannot now remember the precise origins of many of the songs that we learned and loved, because most of those that my mother sang were also in the repertoires of the radio hillbillies. Her versions of "The East Bound Train," "Little Rosewood Casket," and "Letter Edged in Black," to cite only a few examples, may have been learned from friends or relatives who had access to radio broadcasts or phonograph recordings, or they may have come from vaudeville or tent show performances, or from sheet music or other printed matter. Like many rural people who loved to sing old songs, she copied lyrics in school tablets and clipped items from magazines or newspapers that sometimes printed old and requested songs. She faithfully pasted items from the "Young People's Page" of the Dallas *Semi-Weekly Farm News* on to the pages of an old grammar book. Daddy was not a very nostalgic person, and the only survivor from this cherished collection when we moved to town was a yellowed and brittle clipping of "Little Joe the Wrangler." Now it too has disappeared.

The origin of these songs concerned us not at all. Our only criterion for acceptance was that we liked them. We similarly did not trouble ourselves much with the questions of musical definition or categorization. We thought mainly in terms of "old" and "new" songs, or, as my mother would have described certain material, of "sacred" or "worldly" songs. There was "nigger" music, of course, and we liked a good bit of it, especially when performed by someone like the Mills Brothers, the Ink Spots, or Sister Rosetta Tharpe. Only much later would I realize just how strongly "country" and "white gospel" music were indebted to black music. "Pop" music was acceptable as long as it was mellow and melodious, or not too "fancy." "High-class" music was our term for any kind of music that connoted snobbery or putting on airs, and that could include anything from Artie Shaw to opera.

Our favorite forms of music (apart from religious) were "cowboy" and "hillbilly." All varieties of white grassroots music, though, tended to become subsumed in our minds under the "hillbilly" label. Musicians might make distinctions, but we seldom discriminated between stylists with widely differing approaches. Consequently, our pantheon of favorites included everyone from such deep-dyed rural performers as Roy Acuff, Bill Monroe, and the Bailes Brothers to such smooth entertainers as Gene Autry, Tex Ritter, Jimmie Davis, Bob Wills, and the Sons of the Pioneers. Rigid categorization did not come to the country field until the late fifties when threats from rock-and-roll and pop music homogenization impelled purists to a search for "real" country music and a consequent labeling of those styles that either did or did not fit their definition. By that time, though, most of the "traditional" performers had been driven from the country mainstream, or had sought refuge in the newly developing bluegrass idiom.

Those memories of my musical coming of age, from roughly 1939 to the middle fifties, are too many to catalogue, but they are experiences that many people have shared. I would not pretend to argue, however, that everyone who grew up in the rural South responded to similar experiences as I did. After all, there are people of my age and background who detest or at least remain indifferent to country music, and still others who admitted their affection only after the music became chic in the decades after the sixties. My romance with country music, which began virtually from birth, was undisguised, ardent, and everlasting. The little battery radio did more than link me to the hillbilly and gospel programs in Fort

Worth, Dallas, Wichita Falls, Houston, Tulsa, Shreveport, Chicago, Nashville, and the Mexican border; it also transported me to the world beyond reality, to a land inhabited by singing cowboys, isolated mountaineers, hobo balladeers, and close-knit family singers. Cowboy Slim Rinehart, Tex Ritter, Gene Autry, the Carter Family, the Callahan Brothers, the Herrington Sisters, the Chuck Wagon Gang, the Stamps Quartet, Roy Acuff, and a host of others had no real personality for me beyond what I heard on their broadcasts or recordings, saw in their picture-songbooks or occasional personal appearances, or pictured in my active imagination. I knew that these performers gathered around microphones and periodically gave public concerts throughout America, and I imagined that their lives were romantic and exciting. Their performances, however, linked me to another world that was remote, enchanting, and moral. When Gene Autry sang "Empty Cot in the Bunkhouse," I pictured not only a successful Hollywood cowboy but also a group of lonesome cowboys, sitting around a campfire and recalling a heroic partner who had died. There was excitement just in the thought of the Carter Family singing over the powerful Mexican border station, XERF, but when they sang "Longing for Old Virginia," I actually did "long" for that historic old state just as I was sure they did. The hillbilly entertainers sang often of death and violence, of estrangement and unfulfilled love, of broken families and abandoned firesides, and even of rowdy or illicit behavior. But in my youthful fantasies the moral blemishes or improprieties that pockmarked Galena seldom intruded into that pristine and largely pastoral world inhabited by musicians. The performers were very close to me, almost like members of the family, and I projected onto them the same high moral code that I thought I saw reflected in my parents' and brothers' lives. Only as childhood innocence gave way to the confusions of adolescence did I become more conscious of the imperfections, and therefore the humanity, of my heroes, within and beyond our family circle.

Time and scholarship have made me aware of the enormous gap that sometimes separates image from reality in the life of a performer, and that a hint of wildness or rowdiness can actually be commercially profitable in an entertainer's career; the country music public has shown a receptivity to both "good boys" and "bad boys" (but not often to bad girls). In my years as a student of country music, I have often stressed the music's "realism" and the ways in which it accurately portrays the experiences of plain people. But fantasy and escapism have always been basic ingredients of country music, just as they have been part of the "reality" that defines the lives and culture of the music's audience. Living in Smith

County, Texas, during the Great Depression, and struggling to scratch a living from our cotton farm, was all the realism our family needed. Therefore, we seldom sought realism in our music but instead relished and cherished its capacity for deliverance.

The Great Depression reaffirmed for us one dramatic reality, that hard times had always been part of our lives. Therefore, when wartime prosperity began to open up new jobs around the state of Texas, my father went off for a short time to the chemical plants of Velasco, and by 1944 had relocated the family in Tyler, where he worked in a small plant that built prisms for bomb sights. By this time my older brother had volunteered for military service in the Navy Seabees, and cousins and other relatives by the score had gone into the army or navy or had found jobs in the defense plants and shipyards of Texas. Very few of them ever returned to the farm, although most of them exhibited the marks of their rural upbringing for the rest of their lives. In retrospect, it seems remarkable that a way of life that had seemed so changeless, and so deeply rooted in tradition, could be abandoned so rapidly.

Industrialization, of course, had been reshaping the South for a long time before we made our move to town, and we intuitively recognized its great power for social transformation in the many songs of tribute to the railroad that we took into our hearts. Even more tangible manifestations of the industrial power that would one day revolutionize the South were the oil derricks and working oil pumps that moved rhythmically on the playgrounds of my school at Van. Some people gained employment in the oil fields, either there at Van or farther to the west in Kilgore and Gladewater. Few remained untouched by petroleum's great power, but only a tiny minority won much wealth from it. In the years before World War II, most southern industrial workers toiled in settings that were distinctly rural even as they maintained residence in small towns or farming communities. Neither oil drilling, textile work, coal mining, or railroad employment really displaced the profoundly rural nature of southern folk culture. Southerners remained rural even as the processes of industrial change altered the ways they made their living.

Since World War II the southern plain folk have moved dramatically away from the world of their ancestors and have entered the world of the urban working class in both residence and occupation. While many have followed the lure of their economic dreams to far-off Detroit, Chicago, or Akron, or even a continent away to the West Coast, most have gone no farther than Dallas, Fort Worth, Houston, Atlanta, Birmingham, Memphis, or other cities relatively close to their places of birth. Some have enthusiastically embraced the change; others have never fully come to terms with life in the city. I'm sure that my father was merely jesting when he occasionally declared his intentions to buy another team of mules and move back down on the farm, but the remark did suggest the dissatisfaction that sometimes stole into his thoughts. My mother's response, while also exaggerated, was equally revealing: "If you do, you'll go without me." Town life to her meant greater ease and comfort, access to regular church participation, and an escape from the deadening isolation of the farm.

Country music remained an integral facet of our lives. It spoke nostalgically and reverentially of the rural life we had abandoned and "documented" the new society that we had entered. Those years from 1944 to 1954, or from the time of our move to town until I enrolled at the University of Texas in Austin, will always remain for me the golden years of country music history. These were the years of Roy, Eddy, Slim, Red, Marty, Rose, Kitty, the various Hanks, Webb, and Bill, Lester, and Earl, all of whom could be identified as soon as the instrumental introductions of their recordings began. I feel particularly blessed because I actually saw two of the legendary acts of country music when they appeared in Tyler— Uncle Dave Macon in a tent show hosted by Curley Fox, and Hank Williams, who appeared one night with the cast of the Louisiana Hayride on the stage of the Tyler High School Auditorium.

When I ventured off to the University of Texas in 1954, through the grace of a $35 per semester tuition and the considerable sacrifice of my parents, country music seemed not only popular but safely distinctive— an art form that still reflected the rural South as I had lived or imagined it in Smith County. If I thought the music would remain that way forever, my illusions were rudely shattered one night in 1955 at a Hank Snow concert at the old coliseum in Austin. It was bad enough to see my hero's performance shortened in order to accommodate the huge crowd that was waiting outside to attend a hastily scheduled second show. But it seemed downright repulsive to watch the antics of the other entertainer that most of the audience had come to see, Elvis Presley, and still worse to realize that those "antics"—the pelvis grinding and the sensual leer— were major reasons for his popularity. I now understand Presley's appeal much better than I did then, and in fact recognize that he and the other rockabillies were not simply rebelling against the music of their culture but were actually fusing the crucial elements of southern music—country, blues, gospel—in creating their own vital styles. The good-natured hedonism and swaggering machismo of the rockabillies were deeply rooted in southern working-class culture, not hastily donned pretensions. The city, with its burgeoning popular culture, provided new outlets for the expression of aggressive masculinity, and the appropriation of black music, or its rough approximation, gave young white men a forum to strut their stuff and display their sexual energy. Thus, the "hillbilly cat."

In the immediate aftermath of Elvis's upstaging of Hank Snow, I was not nearly so "wise" about the implications of his music as I am now. And feeling that the barbarians had entered the gates of country music, I tried to do my part to preserve and popularize the kind of styles that I grew up with. That meant scanning the radio dials for any stray recording of Webb or Kitty, retreating to bluegrass, which had become a haven for tradition-minded country fans, and entertaining at any party or gathering that wanted to hear me sing numbers like "The Knoxville Girl" or "Mary Dear." Singing inevitably led to friendship with other country partisans, and by 1960 a small group of us had begun gathering once or twice a week at Threadgill's Bar in North Austin, where we sat around the big round tables performing old-time country music and blues, and accompanying Kenneth Threadgill himself when he sang and yodeled the songs of Jimmie Rodgers. Stan Alexander, Willie Benson, Ed Mellon, and I were the first students from the University of Texas to perform regularly at Threadgill's, and we were still there a few years later when Janis Joplin first came to the bar, strumming an autoharp, and performing with a trio of young musicians called the Waller Creek Boys.

My evolution as a scholar of country music was directly affected by those cherished experiences at Threadgill's Bar, and by the fortuitous presence in the history department of Professor Joe B. Frantz, who recognized my love for the music and suggested that I write a dissertation on the subject. On one hand, my dissertation, which was eventually published as *Country Music, USA*, was delayed by the inordinate amount of time I spent picking and singing at Threadgill's, but on the other hand I like to think that my horizons were broadened by the wide variety of music that I heard during those years in Austin. After all, these years fell during the peak of the folk revival when young singers were reaching in many directions for old and interesting material, and when a handful of collectors and scholars such as Archie Green, Ed Kahn, D. K. Wilgus, and John Greenway were beginning to show the links between commercial country music and older folk styles. But as profoundly influential as these experiences may have been in shaping the slant and tone of my scholarship, no influence from those Austin years can compare with the thrilling childhood memories of waking up each morning to the broadcast of a local hillbilly band, or of hearing the sound of Bashful Brother Oswald's dobro seeping through the crackling static of WSM on Saturday night, or of hearing my mother pour out her soul through the words of the old gospel song, "Farther Along."

Since the inception of my formal research in 1961, I have tried to tell the story of country music as objectively and comprehensively as I possibly could. For better or worse, the mark of those Smith County years still permeates my scholarship, defining my perspective in certain respects but also deepening my understanding in ways that another kind of apprenticeship could not have provided. Because I equated this commercial music culture with my own family's culture, and identified personally with the musicians, they seemed no different from my own brothers and cousins— we weren't even sure that they could sing better than we could.

If I carried cultural baggage that could not easily be sloughed off, so did the music. From the beginnings of its commercial history, country music has profited and suffered from a cluster of public perceptions that have long surrounded the South, rural life, folk music, and working people. The musicians and their audience have been justifiably resistant to stereotypes about ignorant rednecks who sing through their noses (the word "twang" is still widely used to characterize the music), but other myths and half-truths have been embraced by musicians and audience alike in order to lend respectability or romance to their repertoires and performances. Terms like Anglo-Saxon, Elizabethan, or, more recently, Celtic—each suggesting antiquity and ethnic purity—have appeared repeatedly as descriptions of the music, while visions of singing cowboys and musical mountaineers have been exploited by musicians, promoters, and publicists to evoke an aura of romance. The durability of the romantic stereotypes that surround southern music was evident in the summer of 1994 when I was asked to present a program at Tulane University as part of the Summer Shakespeare Festival. The festival organizers were convinced that Appalachian folk culture was Elizabethan, and that the old mountain ballads and love songs were survivals from the days of Shakespeare. This romantic leap of faith was innocent enough, but my program was soon thereafter advertised in a local weekly newspaper with the question, "The Bard with a Gunrack?" The writer of the article went on to combine allusions to Shakespeare, "the moors of Scotland," "the hills of Appalachia," and "Elizabethan poetry" under a caption that suggested that the people I discussed were gun-loving rednecks. Appalachian culture, of course, has never been Elizabethan, although elements of that age of British history certainly moved into the southern hills along with traits from other English eras, and from Scotland, Northern Ireland, and Wales. My Tulane audience did not seem displeased when reminded of Appalachia's long and eclectic history, nor disheartened to hear that Shakespeare did not write for the Grand Ole Opry. While many cultures contributed to the making of southern folk music, it was the people of the South who fashioned it into forms that reflected their own experiences and styles of expression. As one of the greatest commercial manifestations of the South's musical culture, country music has long served as a barometer of the change that has taken place in the lives of the region's working people. The entertainers of country music have communicated easily with working folk, in both the South and elsewhere, because they and their audience share a common language and a common reservoir of assumptions. No amount of fantasizing about the freedom and romance of cowboy life, nor the identification with some remote Elizabethan or Celtic origins, can hide the central fact that country musicians have been people from undistinguished working-class backgrounds who have tried to make their way as entertainers in a society that has little respect for the working class. Understandably confused about their own identities and ambivalent about the culture that gave them birth, country musicians have created a body of music that shares the uncertainties and contradictions of its creators. In so doing, these musicians now reach out to increasingly receptive audiences around the world who recognize the universality of its themes and who find in it affirmation of their own imperfect lives.

1

"Take Me Back to the Sweet Sunny South"

Country music is America's truest music. It does not address every issue and problem in our lives, nor is it always uncompromisingly realistic. Sometimes it appeals to us through nostalgia or fantasy, the desire to go back to "the little cabin home on the hill" where we never lived, or to the life of "a happy, roving cowboy" that we never experienced. Often the music offers nothing but escape from reality—through the otherworldly promise of a gospel song, through identification with some macho hero or rambler, or through the momentary excitement of a Texas two-step or line dance. Nostalgia, fantasy, romance, and pure escapism are of course very much a part of that larger reality through which we define ourselves and learn to cope with life's vagaries. But the music does not serve simply as an escape mechanism, taking us to some imagined "country" where problems and pain do not exist; it also intimately mirrors our day-to-day preoccupations with survival. And like no other musical form in our culture, country music lays bare the uncertainties that lie at the heart of American life.

Country music expresses not only the hopes and longings of average people but also their frailties and failed dreams. At times country songs exude great confidence or even a machismo-driven boastfulness, especially when someone like Hank Williams, Jr., or Charlie Daniels sings, or when Brooks and Dunn strut their way through the rhythms of a country line dance. More often, though, the music is consumed with the fragility of relationships and the evanescence of life. Above all, the music breathes with the contradictions implicit in our lives. Indeed, the tension that gives country music its power and that defines the stylistic essence of such great singers as Hank Williams, Sr., George Jones, and Merle Haggard, arises from the struggle to voice the contending and irresolvable impulses of the human heart. Singers and songwriters deal constantly with such warring impulses as piety and hedonism, home and rambling, companionship and individualism, and nostalgia and modernity, deeply conscious that the line between these seemingly polar opposites is thin and that their ultimate resolution is unlikely. The rambling man, for instance, does not simply voice the desire for an escape from responsibility. More often than not in country music, the wanderer expresses his yearnings for a home that cannot be regained. The homebound dweller, on the other hand, just as often yearns for an open and unfettered road that will remain forever untraveled.

Although commercial country music addresses longings that are universal, while speaking to an audience whose scope is now international, the music was born in the rural South. It germinated there in a region that, though seeming to diverge dramatically from the mainstream of American life, nevertheless served as the nation's major crossroads of musical cultural exchange. Poor Anglo Americans and African Americans viewed each other with suspicion across the racial divide, but they exchanged songs and styles virtually from the time of their first encounters in the early colonial South. Out of this common crucible of poverty and pain, blacks and whites created a mélange of musical forms that eventually evolved into the nation's major popular styles.[1] From this fused musical legacy, country music emerged as the most vital voice of the southern working class and a barometer of the revolutionary changes that have marked the transition from rural to urban-industrial life. Country musicians inherited a love for frolic and dance from their British forebears, but the sustained contact with African Americans also inspired them to experiment with new rhythms and dances and to sing with full-throated intensity and bodily release. On the other hand, they inherited a British religious Calvinist tradition that left them with guilt-ridden consciences, constantly reminding them of the brevity of life and of a world of limitations. Veering between these poles of behavior and preference, the music has evolved with a sense of tension that makes it both appealing and commercially viable.

As working-class southerners struggled to survive, first in a hard and marginal rural economy and then in the blue-collar environment of an unfamiliar urban society, they learned that tradition and modernity could not easily be reconciled. Music proved to be an invaluable resource, though, in the transition from rural to urban life, serving as a source of sustenance and identity and as a medium of expression. During its early commercial venture into the mainstream of American life, when it most strongly bore the marks of its regional roots, country music functioned effectively as "the language of a subculture."[2] The insights gained from those struggles have since made the music irresistible to growing numbers of Americans everywhere who have become increasingly conscious of the inequities of life in postindustrial America.

Commercial country music entered the world, therefore, with a southern accent and a cluster of preoccupations that reflected its southern working-class identity. The entertainers who made the first recordings and radio broadcasts in the 1920s sang with the inflections and dialects of the working-class South.[3] That historical fact has forever influenced both the definition and the public perception of country music. Many fans and performers alike today judge a singer's "authenticity" by the degree to which his or her sound reflects that particular regional and working-class origin. When praising a singer's "sincerity," fans are really suggesting that the performer is communicating an emotion or response that he or she has actually experienced. That is what Hank Williams, Sr., meant when he said that "to sing like a hillbilly, you had to have lived like a hillbilly. You had to have smelt a lot of mule manure." To some people, the southern sound serves as a mark of denigration and is best described with such terms as the "twang."[4] But those who equate country music with southern working-class origins seem to know, I think, that the disappearance of traditional country music also means the passing of a way of life.

Although country music has reached out to the world, it has nevertheless preserved a special relationship with the South. Neither the existence of Japanese bluegrass bands and German rockabillies nor the remarkable popularity around the world of such singers as Garth Brooks should obscure the fact that country music and southernness have long been linked in the consciousness of most Americans.[5] The bulk of the major performers still come, overwhelmingly, from the South,[6] and they exhibit their southernness through their dialects, speech patterns, and lifestyles and through the values and themes of the music that they perform. The predominance of southerners in the early folk music collections and on early hillbilly recordings was no accident; folksong collectors and recording men traveled south instead of north or west because they believed that the South was a land of music.[7]

No one need doubt any longer that rural music was a pervasive phenomenon in the United States and Canada at the time of country music's commercial birth, or that such music shared some basic similarities whether performed in upstate New York, Canada's Maritime Provinces, Indiana, or Georgia.[8] Phonograph recording companies, however, chose to record the rural musicians of Georgia and other southern states, and devoted little attention to the performers from other regions. Southern rural musicians probably appealed to recording talent scouts, just as they had to Cecil Sharp and other collectors of folk music during the World War I era, because they came from a region of the United States that was perceived as both exotic and musical. Visions of archaic but musical mountaineers and lonesome, singing cowboys had already entered American popular culture by the time the first hillbilly recordings were made.[9] Well before that time, African Americans had introduced other versions of southern music—the spirituals, ragtime, blues, and jazz—to an enraptured American public. Recording talent scout Ralph Peer, in fact, was looking for blues performers in 1923 when, serendipitously, he found Fiddlin' John Carson in Atlanta, and inadvertently inaugurated country music's commercial history.[10]

Whether the music of the white South suited their musical tastes, once the recording and broadcasting industries actually sampled it, they found, often to their surprise, that a vast, local market was ready to buy it.[11] Above all, they discovered that this music was both different and more interesting than the rural musical forms of the North. Not simply a quaint survival of an older society (as it seemed to be in New England, for example), southern rural music appealed because of its diversity and because it truly represented the organic evolution of the southern working class. Although insufficiently understood or recognized at the time, the fusion of African American and Anglo American elements also made the music distinctive and intriguing. African American musical infusions, for instance—"the emphasis on rhythm, syncopations, blues and jazz elements"[12]—probably gave the music of the southern string bands the vitality and rhythmic punch that set them apart from other rural bands in America. Southern rural music *was* different from other styles, and the predominance of southern-born musicians on phonograph records and radio stations during these formative years created a pattern and precedent that have permanently shaped both the reality and the perception of country music. As southern men and women became radio or recording personalities, they inspired similar quests for "stardom" by people like themselves in local communities throughout the region. The southernness of country music became a self-perpetuating phenomenon.

The white folk South from which commercial country music emerged was a culture far different from the one that only occasionally evoked description in American literature and popular culture. Historically, it has been the fate of the plain folk to be most often simply ignored, except of course when their labor or firepower was needed. A long tradition of writers (and observers), extending as least as far back as William Byrd in 1728,[13] have refused to see the southern folk in their full human dimensions and have instead viewed them with contempt, condescension, or romance. While an occasional Daniel Boone, Davy Crockett, Abraham Lincoln, or Jesse James rose above the mass to become part of the nation's folklore, most plain people were ignored as individuals and instead subsumed in collectivized references to the "sturdy yeomanry," "the honest sons of toil," or "the Hunters of Kentucky."[14] When the southern plain folk appeared in the diaries of nineteenth-century travelers or in the short stories of humorists or local colorists, they seldom emerged as anything more than comic characters, and often they were described as ignorant, lazy, and vile.[15]

Few polemicists were as harsh in their judgments of southern plain folk as the acerbic Baltimore journalist H. L. Mencken. Writing in 1917, Mencken attacked the "white trash" who, after rising from the wreckage of the Civil War, had dislodged the "better elements" from their positions of power and had subjected the South to an orgy of social crudity and religious bigotry. Mencken moved a step beyond the usual tradition of vilification by introducing a racial explanation for the behavior of poor whites. They were, he suspected, not Anglo-Saxon at all, but Celts in whose veins flowed the "worst blood of Western Europe."[16]

Mencken said nothing about music, but one could infer from his general criticism that such a benighted people could never produce credible art of any kind. He was writing, of course, shortly before the rich resources of Appalachian balladry became known to the literate American public. Several years later, when the Mississippi patrician William Alexander Percy excoriated the poor whites of his own state in language similar to Mencken's, he at least could acknowledge that they "were responsible for the only American ballads." Although differing from Mencken in arguing that the southern folk were of "pure English stock," Percy was nevertheless unrelenting in his criticism, asserting that he could "forgive them as the Lord God forgives, but admire them, trust them, love them—never. Intellectually and spiritually they are inferior to the Negro, whom they hate. Suspecting secretly they are inferior to him, they must do something to him to prove to themselves their superiority. At their door must be laid the disgraceful riots and lynchings gloated over and exaggerated by Negrophiles the world over."[17]

By the time Percy wrote his diatribe in 1941, the survival of British balladry in Appalachia had become public knowledge, and a few scholars
had begun to argue that such music could be found in other parts of the
South. Percy, for example, probably knew about the scholarship of Arthur
Palmer Hudson, who had collected ballads and folksongs in Mississippi.[18]
The students of British balladry made major contributions to our understanding of the totality of American music. But while they reminded us
of the richness of America's Old World musical roots, they obscured our
vision of southern folk culture. Except for an occasional scholar like
Hudson, they concentrated too narrowly upon Appalachia; they overem-
phasized secular balladry and neglected religious music and instrumental
dance tunes; they too often insisted that southern folk music represented
an exclusive Anglo-Saxon inheritance; and, in their urgent haste to collect the remnants of what they perceived as a dying culture, they suggested falsely that folk culture was a static phenomenon. Appalachian folk
culture, they believed, was imperiled by modernity, and the old ballads
were being swept away by a deluge of inferior and modern-composed
songs. When Cecil Sharp made his pioneering song-collecting expedition
to Appalachia in 1916, he was soon impressed by the universality of singing in the region: "I found myself for the first time in my life in a community in which singing was as common and almost as universal a practice
as speaking." Sharp believed, however, that his informants too often sang
the wrong kind of songs, and that very soon "the ideal conditions" that
had fostered the survival of the ballads would disappear. Already the "simple, Arcadian life of the mountains" was being defiled by the lumber companies and other representatives of "the commercial world," and by the
"sworn enemies of the folk-song collector," the public schools.[19]

The "alien" musical forms that worried Cecil Sharp in 1916, or what
he described as "modern street-songs," were mostly the products of blackface minstrelsy, gospel hymnody, and Tin Pan Alley. After 1922 the bar-
barian that slithered through the gates of presumed cultural purity was
commercial hillbilly music. Hillbilly music did not fit the idealized version of folk music promoted by the collectors and their allies in the mountain settlement schools,[20] but it did conform marvelously to the reality
of plain-folk life in the first quarter of the twentieth century. British folksongs, or adaptations of them, appeared frequently on phonograph recordings[21] and radio broadcasts, although they were accompanied by
homegrown songs and scores of items that came from the gospel tradition or from popular culture. This music was generally ignored by the
apostles of high culture, but in 1933, about ten years after the first re-

cordings were released, an article appeared in *Etude* that was remarkable for its condescension. Written by a self-styled "dealer in sound-reproducing machines," the article informed the sophisticated readers of that music journal about a "subterranean" world of music filled with an "unnumbered inarticulate multitude" that was unknown to most Americans. Contrary to public opinion, he said, the "lowly native white folk of the South"—his customers—did not sing the romantic plantation songs of Stephen Foster; instead, these "childlike" people loved songs about "trains, wrecks, disasters, and crimes."[22] Clearly geared to the presumed biases of his culturally literate readers, the merchandiser's remarks nevertheless do convey some reality amidst their obvious distortions and half-truths. A plain-folk world of music did exist in the South and, although its brief commercial history was about ten years old when the article was written, that musical culture was largely unknown or dismissed by many Americans. Despite its dreamy southern connotations, Stephen Foster's music did not represent or reflect the musical taste and preoccupations of the southern plain folk—even though southern educators dutifully taught his songs to all southern schoolchildren. The observation that southern white folk liked outlaw and disaster ballads was also correct, but such preferences, shared by their British ancestors and by their black neighbors, did not exhaust the full range of their interests. Their musical world was far more complex than the *Etude* journalist suggested.

Early hillbilly music enjoyed a diversity that is astounding when compared to the Top 40 sounds of modern country music. One of the great ironies of country music history, and one of the major factors that makes it intriguing, is that the men and women who made the music have been simultaneously socially conservative and remarkably eclectic and absorptive in their acceptance of songs and tunes. The early hillbilly musicians drew, as we have seen, upon a rather large and floating body of music that reflected Old World, American, religious, pop, and diversely ethnic origins. Columbia Records fittingly described the old-time music listed in their 15,000-D series as "Old Familiar Tunes," while the Gennett label described theirs as "Songs from Dixie." The hillbilly musicians simply did not care where their music came from as long as it conformed to the aesthetic and social values of their community. Songs from New York's Tin Pan Alley, material from the halcyon days of blackface minstrelsy, or gospel songs born in a Dwight Moody–Ira Sankey revival crusade moved into the rural South, acquired the sounds and inflections of the people there, and found intimate companionship with "folk" songs of British and African American vintage on hillbilly recordings and radio broadcasts.[23]

The heterogeneity of the country music repertoire flowed from a similar diversity in southern folk culture. Once the layers of myth and fantasy are peeled away from what we think we know about the South,[24] we find a culture that is notably lacking in any kind of purity or homogeneity. Since folk culture is indeed alive and organic, it has never been uniform in its manifestations across the South, nor has it remained static throughout the course of southern history. Whether expressed through religion, architecture, foodways, folkways, or music, southern folk culture has exhibited marked local variations. The great frontier migrations of the nineteenth century transported elements of this culture across the entire breadth of the South, but not without altering them in significant ways. Nevertheless, as Wilbur J. Cash noted long ago in *The Mind of the South*, rural southerners shared certain overarching cultural traits and beliefs that would have been familiar to people from Virginia to Texas. (Cash was speaking, of course, about a period of time prior to the aerospace revolution, or before the post–World War II era when the Yankees began arriving in great numbers).[25]

The suggestion of ethnic or racial purity is probably the most enduring romantic myth concerning the southern folk and their music. Those historically imprecise terms, *Anglo-Saxon* and *Celtic*, have long been used to categorize the South's poor whites, and their usage has never fully disappeared. As late as 1979 historian J. Wayne Flynt, in an otherwise levelheaded discussion of the poor whites, referred to the South as the "most ethnically homogeneous" region of the country and the home of "mostly Anglo-Saxon" people. More recently, Grady McWhiney resurrected H. L. Mencken's thesis of a Celtic South, but turned the critic's conclusions on their heads by arguing that such presumably negative traits as laziness, violence, and stubbornness were actually virtues that set most white southerners apart from orderly but boring Yankees. Most crucially, McWhiney argued that the white plain-folk's culture and music formed part of a continuum that extended back at least a thousand years into the dim recesses of western European history. "Even in the late twentieth century," he said, "the continuity between the country music of Celts and Southerners is startling." Such descriptions, of course, ignore the presence of African Americans, while also obscuring the multiethnic identity of white southerners under a murky veil of romanticism that lends to them a uniformity that is impossible to document.[26]

While Flynt and McWhiney were describing the South as a whole, most writers at the turn of the century found Anglo-Saxon homogeneity most strongly displayed in the southern mountains, a region that allegedly remained isolated from the contaminating influences—religious, social, ethnic—that elsewhere infected the American body politic. The conception of a remote but reachable land and a benighted but redeemable people fueled the interests of local color writers, religious missionaries, philanthropists, educators, and ballad collectors. Remarking on his own sojourn in the southern mountains in 1915 and about the mood evoked by the old ballads, journalist William A. Bradley noted that "one now knew he might at any time meet a company of Robin Hood's men encamped in some sequestered cove." Appalachian ballad hunters spoke rhapsodically about the Anglo-Saxon or Elizabethan nature of southern mountaineers (without understanding that the two labels were not synonymous). New South propagandists, on the other hand, used similar terms to describe the poor and presumably docile whites who were being lured into the Piedmont cotton mills. The plain folk themselves and their commercial hillbilly descendants, whose lives were filled with too little of romance, were no more immune to the allure of mythmaking or to the seductive attraction of middle-class values than were the academicians or the elite patrons of folk music concerts. After lifetimes of denigration, it was highly gratifying to be told that one had a culture that was worth commemorating, and thrilling to think that elements of that culture might have been preserved from Shakespeare's or Robin Hood's England. Radio singer Bradley Kincaid, for instance, whose birthplace in Garrard County, Kentucky, was closer to Lexington than it was to the mountains, was probably trying to lend historical or moral legitimacy to his profession when he called himself "the Kentucky Mountain Boy" and asserted that his music had Anglo-Saxon roots.[27]

Although settlers from the British Isles and Ireland, and their descendants, made up the basic core of the white South, they built a culture that was neither Anglo-Saxon nor Celtic, but was instead a composite phenomenon that blended British traits with those drawn from European, African, and Native American origins. Impelled by the great social and economic transformation of England in the late sixteenth and early seventeenth centuries and by the incessant wanderings and violent strife endemic to the borders of Britain, cultural interchange had begun long before English America was settled. Music and dance flowed as freely across geographical borders and class and ethnic lines as did the restless people of the British Isles.[28]

This cultural interchange that accompanied Britain's transformation from an agricultural society to a commercially driven economy continued on the frontiers of America. White English indentured servants and

African slaves met and shared their cultures in the Chesapeake Bay region of Virginia and Maryland and in the rice fields of South Carolina. When they and their descendants eventually moved west across the Piedmont region, they encountered other immigrants from the borderlands of Britain and from Germany who were pushing down through the valley of Virginia from the important cultural seedbed of western Pennsylvania. Along with the Native Americans and Spanish and French settlers who lived on the perimeter of the South, they created a shared folk culture that spoke in varieties of the English tongue but otherwise combined the folkways of many lands.[29]

While their culture was shaped in large part by a diverse population whose common struggles for survival turned them inward toward the utilization of their own resources, neither cultural nor geographic isolation ever totally defined the lives of the southern folk. New ideas, fashions, and music filtered in slowly, but once having arrived, they endured. And music had the habit of moving frequently across racial and class lines. Southern folk culture changed over time, but nevertheless preserved a recognizable identity despite generational changes, population movements, war, and economic transformations. The traumatic stress of war, or the psychic dislocations caused by the movement from a rural environment to an unfamiliar urban scene, often reinforced the reliance on traditional habits and folkways. Like African American culture, "white folk culture" was a blending or synthesis of traditional and modern elements.[30]

It will not be surprising, or even particularly enlightening, to learn that southern folk culture emerged in a profoundly rural context, or that country musicians have been strongly influenced by that historical fact. More significantly, farming was not the all-defining trait of that rural society, nor was it the aspect that won people's loyalties or that attracted the creativity of country songwriters. When country singers voice nostalgic affection for their rural past, it is not farming itself that is most lovingly recalled. Cotton farming is certainly not remembered as one of the "precious memories" of growing up in the rural South. Singers instead commemorate the various associations linked to rural living. The southern folk valued, and were deeply influenced by, the kind of ruralism that permitted a maximum exercise of freedom and an intimate interconnectedness with nature. Digging in the soil could provide satisfaction and the feeling of a oneness with nature, and even a closeness to God, but it was best appreciated on one's own land and if done on one's own time.

Ruralism has influenced the way country entertainers talk and sing, and it has provided them with an endless array of reference points—cabin

homes, country churches, rural graveyards, creek baptizings, family reunions, swimming holes, outhouses, old gray mules, coon dogs, and so
on—through which they have constructed a common community among
themselves and with their fans. Ruralism linked country music to a broad
spectrum of Americans by providing a mythology with which all could
identify. In short, ruralism linked country singers to the nation's most
cherished myth, the deeply held belief that our country began its existence as a republic of rural virtue.[31]

At the beginning of the 1920s ruralism still lay at the center of the
nation's folklore, even as the country enthusiastically embraced the promises of urban technology. Its southern version, though, was marked increasingly by a dependency that mocked the yeoman dream and ran
counter to the traditions of plain-folk history. The southern plain folk
were far removed from the fantasy of a rural, agricultural society inhabited by either tradition-bound peasants or independent yeomen. Southern folk culture had been in the midst of a profound social transformation that dated at least to the Civil War. A lingering and deepening poverty
followed defeat on the battlefield. Reduced to tenantry and sharecropping, imprisoned by a self-perpetuating credit system, forced off the public
lands by fence and game laws, and subjected to the dictates of a steadily
encroaching market economy, self-subsistence farmers, squatters on the
public land, and a host of people like the herdsmen and drovers who had
never wanted to be farmers of any kind, now found themselves locked
in a persistently narrowing and constricting world.[32]

Paradoxically, the same period of constriction also witnessed the emergence of forces that offered, or at least seemed to promise, the possibilities of liberation and expanding economic opportunities. As the guns fell
silent at Appomattox, the whir of machinery steadily replaced them. New
South leaders spoke reverently of the passing agrarian order, but gave their
enthusiastic support to a national transportation network and a market
economy that touched and transformed the lives of all farmers.[33]

Ruralism and agriculture continued to rule the lives of most southerners during the debt-plagued years of the late nineteenth century, but some
opted for the increasingly available industrial alternatives. The railroad
played the key role in opening up new industrial possibilities and linking most rural communities to a rapidly expanding market economy.
Edward Ayers notes, for example, that by 1890 nine of every ten southerners lived in a "railroad county," and that railroad construction touched
the lives of people all along the track, providing markets for garden, farm,
and forest produce and labor opportunities for tie cutters and rail build-

ers. The railroad offered a feasible and romantic labor option for many southerners—an exciting opportunity for cash wages for young men and the chance to escape the isolation and boredom of farm life. It is little wonder that such a multitude of songs about the railroad appeared in the repertoires of country and blues singers.[34] The cotton mill industry dates from the 1840s, when regional nationalists promoted industrialization as a means of establishing southern independence, but textile employment did not become a viable option for southern workers until the 1880s. During that decade industry propagandists promoted the cotton mill as the institution that would liberate the South from colonial bondage and free poor whites from rural poverty. By 1912 railroads had penetrated the deepest recesses of the southern Appalachians, opening up the great bituminous coal regions of West Virginia, southwestern Virginia, and eastern Kentucky. In the first few years of the twentieth century the discovery of oil in Louisiana, Arkansas, Oklahoma, and Texas triggered an economic revolution that would transform forever the lives of the folk who lived there.[35]

Neither southern folk culture nor southern folk music, therefore, can be understood apart from the story of southern industrialization.[36] The communications revolution of the 1920s that brought the radio and phonograph within the reach of most rural southerners was only the most recent manifestation of an array of industrial, technological, and social forces that had been transforming the South for a hundred years or more. The remarkable confrontation of rural folkways with urban-industrial technology created the dynamic that gave country music its special character and permitted it to win an ever-widening audience.

Plain-folk southerners were well aware that the industrial revolution had intruded upon their lives. While they might bitterly resist its most oppressive and corrupting features (particularly when its promises were betrayed or unfulfilled),[37] the plain folk embraced any technological change that offered greater material comfort, leisure, independence, or contact with the outside world. And as their world expanded, hillbilly music documented their real-life experiences. The guardians of "pure folk culture," on the other hand, tended to view technological innovation with suspicion, and they generally held hillbilly music in contempt. Writing a little less than ten years after the first hillbilly records were made, and presumably well aware of the Grand Ole Opry broadcasts that originated only a few miles from his Vanderbilt office, Professor Andrew Lytle—ardent advocate of agrarianism and enemy of "machine-made bric-a-brac," told farmers what they could do to avoid the "dire consequences of industrial imperialism":

"Do what we did after the war and the Reconstruction. Return to our looms, our handicrafts, our reproducing stock. Throw out the radio and take down the fiddle from the wall."[38] Several years later, an eminent historian of the South, Thomas D. Clark, who had no doctrinaire misgivings about industrialization and who had written enthusiastically about the pervasiveness of old-time fiddling on the southwestern frontier, nevertheless contemptuously dismissed the folk musicians who had tried to build professional careers as the "hillbilly rabble" of radio.[39]

The southern plain folk never listened to Andrew Lytle's advice. In the grim years that followed publication of his essay, when economic depression stalked their land, these beleaguered southerners huddled around their radios and made heroes of the balladeers, string bands, and gospel singers whom they heard. In the most ironic twist of all, many radio listeners took down their fiddles from the walls, or ordered new ones from Sears or Montgomery Ward, after they heard the inspiring music of the radio hillbillies.

Neither Clark nor Lytle, of course, would have thought of themselves as enemies of the plain folk, but like most academicians, they maintained a static and thoroughly romantic conception of who these folk were. The distinguished southern sociologist Howard Odum was a rare exception in that he recognized the value of music as a source for understanding the folk mind, and he made no invidious distinctions between the material found on commercial recordings and that collected elsewhere. Odum noted the appeal of commercialized forms of music among his black informants as early as 1911, and in a discussion of southern white folk, in *An American Epoch,* he listed a large number of religious and secular songs that came from phonograph recordings or radio broadcasts.[40] Southern folk culture, in fact, was no more pristine than were the early commercial country musicians who emerged from that culture. The early performers are best understood as rural, working people who labored at a wide range of occupations, including coal mining, lumbering, textiles, and railroading. They also worked as sawyers, carpenters, wagoners, truck drivers, mechanics, auto body specialists, oil workers, barbers, cowboys, farmers, and occasionally as preachers, doctors, and lawyers. This was an occupational diversity that well represented the changing South—a South whose agricultural base had been gradually eroding for generations and whose people had long been reaching out for alternative or supplemental means of survival. Many sought merely to augment an agricultural income that was unsteady, while others sought to escape farming altogether. The factors that drew some people away from agriculture may have also lured them toward music, particularly after the composite influence of radio and recording in the 1920s made such a profession seem economically feasible.

A few early country musicians had some professional entertainment experience—in medicine shows, tent-repertoire theaters, or southern vaudeville—but most were talented "amateurs" who kept their "day jobs" and performed music part-time.[41] Music, though, was an escape from work, a factor that became increasingly important as the "hillbilly business" became more commercially secure in the years that followed the initial recordings. If professionalization beckoned (and it certainly did after Jimmie Rodgers demonstrated that a high lifestyle could be one of the rewards of music-making),[42] the goals of the hillbilly singers were generally shaped by middle-class ideals or by the standards set by popular professional entertainers in the early twentieth century. Early photographs of country musicians invariably show them dressed, not in rustic regalia, but in their best, Sunday-go-to-meeting clothes. When they thought of commercial "success," there are no reasons why they would not have thought of the city performers whom they had seen or read about—the blackface minstrels particularly, or the vaudeville entertainers who had appeared with great frequency in southern towns and cities in the years prior to country music's commercial birth.[43]

The hillbillies, however, were also socially conservative, and regardless of how they dressed or how they defined their ultimate goals, they exuded the sounds and values of the working-class South. Standing midway between the traditional and rural world of their forebears and the beckoning urban and middle-class society of modern America, their performance styles and musical repertoires were fraught with ambivalence. Like their African American counterparts, hillbilly entertainers learned to contend with, and actually profit from, demeaning and romantic conceptions alike about what their music should be and how it should be performed. Even though the Stephen Foster image of the South endured as a romantic conception long after the industrial capitalism of the North triumphed over the rural paternalism of the Confederacy, visions of a "benighted South"[44] also captured the thinking of a multitude of Americans. While the perception of a region clothed in darkness originated during the abolitionist crusade against slavery, it assumed a new visibility during the 1920s when the nation as a whole seemed smitten with modernity and its by-products of prosperity and urban progress. The rural South appeared to stand out in bold relief as an example of what was otherwise wrong about America—its backwardness, philistinism, bigotry, and ignorance. Well-publicized phenomena such as prison chain gangs, debt peonage, sharecropping, prohibition, religious snake handling, the revival of the Ku Klux Klan, and the Scopes "Monkey" Trial offered substantial evidence to prove the negative presumptions about the region. H. L. Mencken summed up most vividly the image of a retarded culture when he described the South as "a vast plain of mediocrity, stupidity, lethargy" and as "a cesspool of Baptists and a miasma of Methodists."[45]

Despite the preponderance of southern-born country entertainers, the borders of the South have never confined the audience for country music. Rural southerners have taken their musical tastes to every region of America and to the world, but country music could not have survived or flourished with the sole support of southern-born fans and their descendants. The music has always attracted listeners who never lived in the South or who presumably have never resided in a rural area. Unfortunately, no data exists that can confirm the size, residence, demographic contours, or presumptions of this ever-expanding audience. However, hillbilly records circulated around the world and exhibited considerable popularity in such places as New Zealand and Australia. The popularity enjoyed in the American Midwest by Chicago's National Barn Dance, heard throughout the region on powerful WLS in Chicago, and by barn dances on other stations such as WHO in Des Moines, Iowa, confirms the existence of a large and loyal audience there for country music.[46]

Abundant evidence suggests, moreover, that jazz was far from being the preferred musical fare for many Americans during the age that bore its name. Henry Ford was not alone in equating the frenzied rhythms of jazz with the alleged decline of morals among young people in the Jazz Age. Clearly oblivious to the role played by his automobile in the weakening of traditional standards and relationships, Ford agonized over the degeneracy of "Africanized" music and the alleged Jewish conspiracy that lay behind it. Inadvertently or self-consciously, his phobias corresponded to an analogous hunger for homespun music and traditional morality. In the 1920s, Ford contributed to a revitalization of the old-fashioned dance music that he had loved during his youth in rural Michigan. He financed the publication of a dance instruction book, sponsored a dance orchestra that revived old instruments and dances, and, most important, promoted through his automobile dealerships a series of old-time fiddle contests in various cities in the United States. No evidence suggests that Ford appreciated commercial hillbilly music, but he did contribute substantially to the national awareness of old-time fiddling styles while also becoming a folk hero in the rural South.[47]

At the beginning of its commercial history in the 1920s, country music probably appealed to many Americans through its fantasies of rough-and-ready independence, its evocations of nostalgia, and its suggestion that old-time ways carried with them a brand of morality superior to that of modern times. Over time, as the music established itself as a commercial force, and as "the old familiar songs" gradually disappeared from performing repertoires, the writers of country music moved beyond nostalgia—without ever abandoning it—to fashion a body of songs that spoke persuasively to the needs and concerns of working people everywhere, maintaining and yet still exploiting in new ways the traditional, conflicting preoccupations of the southern folk. The music, then and since, spoke to its listeners with many voices and with many messages—simultaneously extolling the virtues of home and the joys of rambling, the assurances of the Christian life and the ecstasies of hedonism, the strength of working-class life and the material lure of middle-class existence. In country music's subtext, one hears the hopes and fears of rural southerners struggling to balance the internalized values of a disappearing rural life with the external demands of an urban world into which they have been inexorably drawn. Increasingly, the message has resonated with those in other regions and from other backgrounds who, like their southern counterparts, have felt dwarfed by the complexities of a troublesome and uncertain future. Don't dream too high. Don't forget where you came from. Above all, "don't get above your raisin'."[48]

2

"I'm a Small-Time Laboring Man"

In 1985 the country-rock band Alabama recorded a song called "Forty Hour Week (for a Livin')" praising the contributions of a long list of generally unsung American workers.[1] Although the song was only one of several in the modern period that reaffirmed country music's image as the music of working people, when compared historically to country music's total thematic content, "Forty Hour Week" was actually a rare example of the discussion of work. No genre of American music has been more intimately intertwined with the experiences of working-class people, but few bodies of music have been less inclined to discuss the actual conditions of work.[2] Most country singers and songwriters have emerged from working-class households, but, except in rare cases, they have neither described, denigrated, nor glamorized the actual work that sustained their lives or those of their parents. The reluctance to sing about work seems to have been shared by the country entertainers' British cousins. Cecil Sharp had noted that love served as "the perennial theme of the folk singer of all lands," and that "it is not unnatural, seeing that his hours of work are long and arduous, that the labourer should find more recreation in songs of romance and adventure than in those which remind him of his toil."[3] And in his discussion of southern textile workers, I. A. Newby asserted that "plain folk were not 'economic men,' in the sense that they were not a people primarily concerned with work, accumulation, and otherwise maximizing their material condition."[4] Butcher boys, wagoner lads, lonesome cowboys, house carpenters, and other people who have been defined by their worker identities have appeared often in country songs, but usually in roles that have little to do with work itself. Country music instead has asserted its working-class credentials by concentrating on the particularities of the day-to-day lives and experiences of working people—job insecurities, marital relationships, family fragility, and mere survival.

Country music's emergence as a commercial phenomenon in the twenties was only the most recent manifestation of a process that had been under way since at least the Civil War: the gradual, but unyielding, intrusion of technology into the lives of southern rural people that consequently linked their experiences with those of urban America. It is difficult to assess the long-range consequences of this profound transformation, but its full import meant nothing less than the elimination of a way of life once prevalent throughout the rural South. Although the cotton gin may have sewed the seeds of technological revolution in the region, the Civil War provoked the most traumatic changes, disrupting people's lives, decimating their families, and destroying the traditional sources of their livelihood. Finding their herds of livestock severely depleted, and increasingly restricted from the public lands through fencing and game laws, growing numbers of people moved into cotton cultivation because it seemed to be the only viable alternative in a world of constricting options. As the cotton kingdom pressed toward the borders of the semiarid lands of West Texas, cotton production enveloped the lives of increasing numbers of reluctant former herdsmen, binding them to a life of burdensome tenantry and paltry returns for their backbreaking labor.

By the time the hillbilly music business began in the years after World War I, both the realities and popular perceptions of the country life that it supposedly represented had already changed radically in various ways. The "country" from which the performers came was pure only in song. Despite the paeans to farm life that often appeared in country songs, southern agriculture had been losing its attractiveness long before the first country recordings were made. Southern farmers had shared in the general denigration suffered by all American agriculturalists in the late nineteenth century, finding themselves described as hicks, hayseeds, yokels, and rubes. In the South terms like hillbilly and redneck joined the lexicon of humiliation,[5] and even "sharecropper" became a term of contempt that endured well into the next century.

Southern agriculture had revived slowly after the Civil War, but not without alterations that dramatically affected the lives of the men, women, and children who fell under its sway. The market economy followed the railroads into once-inaccessible regions all over the South. As increasing numbers of people moved into cotton production, the humblest farmers found themselves enmeshed in an economic system dominated by the cash nexus, and, through the crop lien, mired in a matrix of debt that extended around the world.[6]

Designed originally to organize and utilize the labor of recently freed black farmers, the system of tenantry and sharecropping inexorably enveloped the lives of most white farmers, too. Songs that graphically described the rigors of such work were still alive in the hillbilly repertoire when the first recordings were made. "Down on Penny's Farm," for example, described tobacco farmers, but farmers everywhere in the rural South shared their experiences of "chattel mortgages" and indebtedness to both landlord and merchant.[7] A virtually unyielding cycle of crop mortgages, declining prices, rising freight rates, and limited educational opportunities perpetuated the system and ensured that the farmer's children and grandchildren would also become ensnared in its clutches. The boll weevil only worsened these problems when he crossed the Rio Grande into Texas in 1892 and became the southern farmer's newest and unconquerable adversary. By 1920 the pest had devastated cotton crops from Texas to North Carolina. "The Ballad of the Boll Weevil," created presumably by black farmers in South Texas, told a story all farmers could understand when it described the "little black bug" who successfully resisted fire, flood, ice, and human invention.[8]

As railroads inched their tracks into all corners of the South, not only did they transform the nature of agriculture, they also contributed to the rise of new industries and to the accelerated pace and influence of town life. The Appalachian coalfields, the southern pine forests, the Piedmont textile mills, the Birmingham iron and steel firms, the Texas cattle industry, and the southwestern oil fields all testified to the quickening of industrial life in the New South, and to the growing demand for the region's most precious natural resource—the cheap labor of its poor white and black populations. Because of the endemic poverty, labor surplus, and educational marginality of the region, the South was already "exporting" its poor people to other sections of the nation by the time of World War I when some rural southerners began working in Henry Ford's Detroit plants.[9]

Southern industrialization proceeded in a manner and context that ensured the preservation of rural traits, or otherwise contributed to their unique fusion with industrial folkways. Industrial change came slowly to the South, and at irregular rates of growth in different parts of the region. Southern industrial workplaces tended to be located in rural settings, either in the vast open spaces traversed by the railroads, or in the remote Appalachian hollers where the massive veins of bituminous coal were found, or in the worn-out farm lands of the Piedmont where the textile industry held sway, or in the countryside of rural East Texas, Louisiana, Arkansas, and Oklahoma where the petroleum business gushed into existence in the early years of the twentieth century.[10]

As both a stimulant of song and a creator of audiences who sought musical entertainment, industrialization contributed to the transformation and commercialization of southern folk music and to the emergence of commercial country music. Although a few musicians such as Jimmie Rodgers and Roy Harvey[11] emerged from the ranks of railroading, that industry served more crucially in the making of country music through its symbolism and imagery. The arrogance and abuse exhibited by railroad corporations are, of course, well known, as is the angry response embodied in government regulatory legislation and political dissent (shown most dramatically in the rise of Populism). But examples of opposition to railroads are very rare in American folk and country music. As dozens of songs about powerful steeds, ships, and steamboats will attest, the southern folk had always been fascinated with anything that moved and suggested power, escape, or the promise of novelty.[12] The railroad, however, was far more sweeping in its impact than any other innovation in transportation, and it provided the southern folk with their most dramatic introduction to the industrial revolution. Railroad ballads extolled rambling, escape, and powerful men and machines, and they sometimes applauded the valor of engineers like Casey Jones, George Alley, and Ben Dewberry, who died with the engines they loved.[13] But except when describing the hazards that led to train wrecks, railroad songs rarely commented on the actual conditions of work. The most celebrated American ballad, "John Henry"—the story of a powerful black man who is believed to have been part of the crew that built the Big Bend railroad tunnel in West Virginia in the 1870s—does applaud the hero's prodigious skills as a laborer. But John Henry is best remembered for his manliness, fierce dignity, and refusal to surrender his individualism in the face of a threat from a steel-driving machine.[14]

Railroad employment was the most attractive available alternative to farm work, and, well into the twentieth century, it remained the most prestigious wage work that a poor white or black man could obtain. The grinding wheels and belching fire of the locomotive seemed not only to document the power of the industrial revolution but also to encapsulate the rhythm and tempo of the new society that was slowly taking shape in nineteenth-century America. The train itself, and its beckoning whistle, conjured up visions of an exciting and distant world and the possibilities of a better and more liberated life. Rural musicians, black and white, expressed their fascination with trains by imitating their sounds and rhythms on harmonicas, guitars, banjos, and fiddles, and with their voices, and by producing song after song about railroad men and railroad culture. It was altogether fitting that on the night the Grand Ole Opry received its name, DeFord Bailey inaugurated the evening's broadcast on WSM with "Pan American Blues," a stirring harmonica tribute to one of the central South's most famous trains.[15] The railroad so insinuated itself into the culture and imagination of the folk that songmakers used it often as a religious metaphor for both deliverance and warning. "God's Holy Train" and "Life's Railway to Heaven," for example, waged passionate competition with "The Hell-Bound Train" for the souls of men.[16]

Coal mines, textile mills, oil fields, or pine forests did not exert a similar romantic or poetic appeal, except perhaps as dark visions of humanity's descent from a rural Eden into an industrial hell, but they did provide employment for thousands of southern workers, and they inspired countless songs and singers. Southern workers did sometimes resort to union activity or class-based political action, but more often they confronted the newly emerging industrial system with the only major resource available to them, their culture. Mines, mills, oil fields, or lumber camps were more than workplaces; they functioned also as communities where industrial labor and rural folkways combined to create a new synthesis of existence. The authors of *Like a Family* were referring specifically to the cotton mill workers of the southern Piedmont, but they accurately described the experiences of new industrial workers everywhere in the New South: "As they made their decisions and embarked on their journeys, they did not go empty-handed. Along with the belongings piled in a horse-drawn wagon in the 1880's or a Dodge truck in the 1920's, they carried the cultural baggage of the countryside."[17] They moved often when dissatisfied with pay or treatment; they responded indifferently to the discipline imposed by their employers; they repaired to family or church resources when beset by hard times; and they clung to the remnants of their rural past as long as they could: keeping gardens, raising chickens and hogs, often commuting from farm to job, and sometimes even moving back to the farm when economic conditions temporarily suggested that rural life was feasible.

Appalachian coal camps and Piedmont textile villages encouraged a degree of social cohesion and community consciousness that was not always possible in the scattered rural or forested districts of the South nor even in the early oil fields of the Southwest. Churches, bars, and honky-tonks provided diversion where medicine shows and other itinerant forms of entertainment sometimes appeared. Many mill workers brought fiddles, banjos, and other string instruments when they relocated from their rural homes. The impetus to perform, and to learn new styles of music, was sometimes augmented by local instruction and by encouragement from mill owners. Historian Kinney Rorrer, for example, provides insight about this process through his account of R. L. Martin, a young guitar player, who organized a string band in Spray, North Carolina, in about 1896. Martin's venture was supported by the Carolina Company, the local mill corporation, which also established a music program replete with foreign-born instructors and classes in guitar, violin, and mandolin playing. The tight, almost-chamberlike style of instrumentation that became characteristic of Charlie Poole's North Carolina Ramblers and other mill town bands may owe a good deal to the influence exerted by this early example of formal music instruction.[18]

Local musicians had frequent opportunities to play with each other and for audiences who could sometimes provide them modest remuneration. String bands entertained for religious gatherings, neighborhood house dances, family reunions, fish fries, or other social events. Mine and mill workers also played their banjos, fiddles, and guitars during work breaks, between shifts, and for strikes and other union-related functions. Musicians and singers such as Dock Boggs, Dick Justice, Clarence Ashley, David McCarn, and Frank Hutchison did not simply hone their skills in front of audiences composed of their fellow workers and their families, they also learned new songs and styles from each other and from the popular media that became increasingly available in the towns and villages that grew up around the coal mines and textile factories. Quickening town life brought not only saloons, movie houses, and nickelodeons but also black workers who sometimes introduced a touch of the blues and alternative styles of performance.[19]

After World War I automobiles became widely available, permitting a broader range of performing opportunities and greater access to new musical styles and songs. When the radio and recording industries arrived in the 1920s, talented or ambitious mine and mill musicians like Charlie Poole, Kelly Harrell, Henry Whitter, Fiddlin' John Carson, and Dock Boggs were more than ready to reach out toward a wider audience.[20] The southeastern cotton mill industry has contributed an exceptionally large number of musicians to country entertainment. Performers who previously worked in cotton mills, such as David McCarn and Howard and Dorsey

Dixon, or who grew up in mill families, have in fact constituted the single largest body of occupational-derived performers in country music.[21]

The great southern pine forests and the oil industry inspired no body of songs comparable to those spawned by coal mining or textile milling, nor did they produce an array of musicians that in any way equals those who came from most other industries. Although the migratory and transient nature of early lumber and oil workers warred against the kind of cohesion found in the coal and textile camps, songs nevertheless emanated from both industries.[22] Most important, oil introduced the modern age to the South, and it contributed to the revolutionary transformation of country music. In its early stages of development, particularly in the immediate years after June, 1894, when oil was discovered in Corsicana, Texas, the oil business offered a classic example of southern industrialization.[23] Most of the early discoveries came in rural, and even remote, areas of the Southwest—Texas, Louisiana, Oklahoma, Arkansas—and the bulk of the workers were country people who moved frequently from one oil field to another. Two students of early oil-field culture noted that "more often than not, living in the oil field meant roughing it in relative isolation from large commercial centers; it meant being part of industrial life in rural, or even wilderness surroundings. No wonder country folk went to the oil field in larger numbers than their city cousins; they could get by without indoor plumbing, central heating, and a grocery store around the corner."[24] Whenever possible, oil workers continued the old southern rural practices of inviting neighbors in for an evening singing hymns and parlor songs around the little pump organ or of clearing their tents or shacks of furniture and then inviting their neighbors in for a Saturday night dance. Music was provided by local musicians, if available, or by a windup victrola or by itinerant musicians who sometimes wandered into the camps. Bars and brothels, of course, inevitably appeared in the oil-field boom communities, usually on the outskirts of town, and did lucrative business among the socially starved oil workers.[25] Itinerant oil work often exacted a fearsome toll on family life, but it put money in people's pockets and inspired a demand for entertainment.

Information is scarce, but some scattered sources allude to oil workers who became professional musicians. Bill Pruitt, for example, an Oklahoma singer and yodeler, dedicated songs in his 1930s picture-song-book to "those roughneck pals of mine" and recalled having sung "high a'loft swaying derricks." Similarly, Jerry Sloan and Frank Threadgill, described as "harmonizers of the first degree," worked in the refineries at Baytown, Texas, but also performed on KTRH in Houston and made a handful of Brunswick recordings.[26] Not until the late twenties and early thirties, however, did oil-field culture begin to shape the development of the country music business. During the days of the great East Texas oil discoveries, when such communities as Van, Kilgore, Gladewater, and Longview were bustling with energy and newfound wealth, country string bands began playing, first at root beer stands and later at the honky-tonks that appeared when Prohibition was repealed in 1933. An unnamed New Orleans reporter observed the scene during the height of the oil boom and said "the highways and byways of this new oil center are lined with taverns called 'honky-tonks,' and the music emanating from their open windows is enough to drown out the steady run of the working machinery." The galvanic combination of pocket change—a rarity in most of the South at that time—alcohol, dancing, and music contributed to the creation of the honky-tonk style of music and a breed of singers that dominated country music for at least a generation.[27]

The entertainers who created the honky-tonk style and other forms of commercial country music were working people who tried to make sense of the great economic and social forces that transformed their lives in the twentieth century. Although the "country" designation rightly suggests an art form of rural origin, virtually all of the early hillbilly entertainers, beginning with Eck Robertson, Henry Gilliland, Henry Whitter, and Fiddlin' John Carson who made the first recordings in 1922 and 1923, lived in rural settings and made their living from jobs outside of agriculture or from work that supplemented farming. They worked as house painters, carpenters, mechanics, textile workers, coal miners, cowboys, sawyers, wagoners, railroad workers, telegraph operators, oil workers, auto body men, beauticians, barbers, country doctors, lawyers, politicians and office holders, and preachers. Even performers such as Tom Ashley, Fiddlin' John, Charlie Poole, Jimmie Tarlton, and Uncle Dave Macon who played music professionally from time to time—in medicine shows, tent shows, or in vaudeville—generally found it necessary to work at other jobs. Some, like Poole and Tarlton, returned to the cotton mills periodically when funds got low. No one really made music their full-time profession until after 1927, when Jimmie Rodgers demonstrated that such a career was possible. Rodgers suggested to other country folk, through his ostentatiously lavish tastes and spending habits, that music could be a route to a better life. In the decade of the thirties, after the music had proven itself as a commercial entity, other successful musicians like Gene Autry, Jimmie Davis, Bob Wills, and Roy Acuff revealed additional proof that rural-based music could provide escape from cotton fields, coal mines, and textile mills. Ira and Charlie Loudermilk's lives were changed forever when they stood in a cotton patch near their home in north Alabama and watched Roy Acuff's band drive by in their big sleek touring car, on the way to a show at the Spring Hill School in Henagar. In later years as Ira and Charlie Louvin, the brothers could give testament to the lure and liberating power of music and the financial reward that the touring car implied.[28]

Country entertainers have been both rural and working class, but when they musically reminisce about their origins, their songs evoke, not the labor that filled much of their early lives, but the rural context in which that labor was embedded. Some songs, and much country humor, recall the painful or unpleasant aspects of rural life—the trips to the outdoor toilet, the deprivations of poverty, and even the burdensome drudgery of certain tasks—but most often country lyrics pay homage to a more wholesome country past. Country songs remember a favorite hunting dog, the joys of the old swimming hole, the warmth of the childhood home, the spiritual solace of the old country church, downhome cooking, family reunions, and, of course, the tender love of mom and dad. The men and women of country music, from Fiddlin' John Carson, who sang movingly about the honest farmer, to Willie Nelson, who has devoted much of his time and career to the crusade to save the family farmer, left farming behind at relatively early ages to go into music or to work at other occupations.[29]

Although work has not been the central preoccupation of country music, it nevertheless has made prominent appearances in the subject matter of songs. The entertainers of country music's first commercial decade preserved or inherited a large body of "old familiar" songs and tunes, mostly from the late nineteenth and early twentieth centuries, that had little relevance to the contemporary lives of the singers. It is tempting, but probably dangerous, to read too much into a performer's decision to sing such songs as "The Lazy Farmer," "Muleskinner Blues," "Brakeman's Blues," "The Wagoner Lad," "The Butcher's Boy," "Sailor on the Deep Blue Sea," "Cowboy Jack," "Jimmie Brown, the Newsboy," "Buddy, Won't You Roll down the Line" (an account of the rebellion waged by the "free labor" of Tennessee against the employment of leased convicts in the coal mines), "The Big Rock Candy Mountain" (a famous hobo song), or any one of scores of other songs that refer to occupations or labor situations. The singer may or may not have identified with the work implied by the song titles, or the songs may have appealed merely because of their melodies or rhythms or because of some other quality that had little to do with the evocation of labor. Moreover, the wagoner lads, butcher boys, millers, sailors, cowboys, and railroadmen of the early songs generally appeared, not as workers, but as lovestruck young men, macho hedonists, wanderers, or even as murderers. "The House Carpenter," for example—in the old British ballad that appeared often in the repertoires of rural singers—plays only a peripheral role as the husband of the young woman who is seduced by a demon lover.[30]

A few of the songs performed in the twenties nevertheless did speak about problems faced by working people in that decade. While most of the farm songs of the period appealed to the sense of romance or nostalgia for rural life that seems endemic to an industrializing nation, a few traveled far beyond nostalgia to capture the mood of frustration and anger that accompanied the farm depression of the twenties. "Down on Penny's Farm" and "Farmland Blues," for example, chronicled virtually the entire catalogue of tenantry, debt, poverty, weevil infestation, and social ostracization that plagued the lives of most southern farmers. "Eleven Cent Cotton and Forty Cent Meat" (written by Bob Miller, a Memphis dance band leader who successfully adapted to the new hillbilly genre), was presented as a southern farmer's complaint, but it voiced the discontent felt by farmers everywhere in America. "Stay in the Wagon Yard," a wonderfully humorous but bittersweet narrative of a cotton farmer's visit to the city, demonstrated that farm grievances encompassed much more than economic woes. The naive farmer sells his single bale of cotton, wanders out to "see the electric lights and watch the cars come in," and then is seduced into spending his hard-earned dollars on drinks for some city dudes who are clearly much wiser about the new urban age than he is.[31]

The industrial songs in the early commercial repertoire are similarly open to a variety of interpretations. Some of them, like Uncle Dave Macon's rollicking version of "Buddy, Won't You Roll down the Line," came from the late nineteenth century. While the song may have voiced a lingering sense of Populism held by Uncle Dave and many of his listeners, it said nothing about the problems experienced by workers in the twenties. Other coal mine songs did appear on recordings during that decade, but they tended either to breathe the spirit of an earlier age, or to make sentimental statements (as did the English music hall import, "Daddy, Don't Go to the Mines"), or to voice a rather generic complaint about the hard times felt by miners at all times in all places.

The cotton mill songs that enjoyed some commercial distribution, on the other hand, tended to be more contemporary than other industrial

songs, and a few of them graphically described work and shop floor dynamics. Most important, the best of them—such as David McCarn's
"Cotton Mill Colic," the Dixon Brothers' "Weave Room Blues" and
"Spinning Room Blues," and Wilmer Watts's "Cotton Mill Blues"—were
written and performed by textile workers. While it is true that a great
outpouring of textile songs came after 1929 in the wake of the dramatic
strikes that swept the Piedmont, and that the most famous cotton mill
composer, Ella May Wiggins of Gastonia, North Carolina, was apotheosized after her death by northern radicals, the textile song tradition preceded the ideological conflict of the Depression years and was a product
of indigenous conditions. Dorsey Dixon needed neither union agitation
nor radical polemics to remind him of the regimentation, overwork, and
low pay that he described in "Weave Room Blues," nor did David Mc-
Carn require anything more than his own experiences as a worker to write
his graphic trilogy of songs that documented the perils of textile life.[32]

Troubles in the textile industry dramatized the changes that since the
Civil War had been besieging a way of life that finally collapsed during
the decades of the thirties and forties. Mass disaffection swept the southern coalfields and mine villages after 1929 when wage reductions, length-
ened work requirements (described by mill workers as the "stretch out"),
and overbearing and unresponsive management provoked a series of
strikes that put to rest the myth of a docile southern workforce.[33] A return to agriculture, however, was no longer proving to be a viable option.
The tenant system disintegrated under the weight of depressed commodity
prices, mechanization, and government-sanctioned crop reductions that
effectively removed thousands of farmers from the land and agricultural production. Although this inefficient economic system had imprisoned
and impoverished many plain people, its collapse wrought terrific psychic and moral havoc on the lives of those who were displaced. This hard
but familiar existence held no mysteries for the tenants, but the survival skills finely honed in this environment were not readily transferable
or adaptable to an urban workforce. Cities were similarly unprepared
to deal with the rural immigrants who arrived in unprecedented numbers.[34] They welcomed the cheap labor offered by the rural migrants but
were unprepared or unwilling to provide the kind of housing, education,
and social services that the newcomers needed. Transplanted rural workers consequently regrouped, and they sought new forms of community
and identity at their workplaces and in the city's working-class neighborhoods. Rural folk were changed by their experiences in the city, especially as their children found new peer groups and came in contact

with postwar popular culture. But the cities also changed under the impact of these massive population shifts, exhibiting increasingly the strength and persistence of rural folkways, evangelical Protestantism, and political individualism.[35]

World War II did not simply accelerate the social transformations unleashed in the previous decade; it wrought revolutionary consequences for the southern plain folk.[36] And it marked a decisive turn in the history of country music. The war delivered the coup de grace to the tottering tenant system by presenting to beleaguered plain folk the promise of full employment and alternatives to one-crop agriculture. The sons and daughters of tenant farmers, mill workers, and other blue-collar workers moved by the thousands into the military or, along with their parents, went to work in shipyards and defense plants in the South, the Midwest, and on the West Coast. Country music had already moved to California in the jalopies of the Okies. With the huge influx of defense-plant and military émigrés in the 1940s, it became, in James Gregory's words, "the language of a subculture."[37]

Country music accompanied the move to urban-industrial America. Although recordings and live performances declined severely during the war, a casualty of military conscription and the rationing of gasoline, tires, and shellac (used at that time in the manufacture of records), the music nevertheless remained widely available. Used records, for example, appeared on jukeboxes and on hundreds of radio stations throughout the United States, and country fans seemed content to listen repeatedly to the same songs. Country entertainers also reached out to military personnel through USO shows, the Camel Caravans (touring musical troupes whose appearances at military bases were sponsored by Camel cigarettes), V-Discs ("Victory" phonograph recordings of current hillbilly hits that were distributed exclusively among servicemen), and Armed Forces Network programming aimed at military personnel in Europe and Asia. Of course, some country musicians performed in Special Services units after they were drafted into the military, or they performed as part of pickup bands in military barracks and on troopships.[38]

The music certainly moved into new civilian markets during the war, a consequence of industrial migrations, heightened radio exposure by the Grand Ole Opry and other barn-dance programs, aggressive promotion by booking agents like Foreman Phillips (who sponsored giant concerts by Bob Wills and Roy Acuff on the Venice Pier in California), and new marketing strategies by jukebox operators. Close to 400,000 coin-operated automatic music machines, known colloquially as jukeboxes, constituted a powerful market for the recording industry, while also providing an inexpensive form of entertainment for thousands of dance halls, cafés, bowling alleys, and other public centers of amusement. The beautifully decorated jukebox, with its bright chrome-and-plastic exterior, fluorescent illumination, and openly displayed record changing mechanisms, became not only a central focus for musical and social experience but also a ready reminder to displaced country folk of American capitalistic ingenuity and hegemony in the postwar era.[39]

In industrial cities around the country, jukebox operators noted the growing interest in hillbilly songs and suggested that it was a product of defense-inspired migrations. The entertainment journal *Billboard* noted for example that "the large influx of hillbillies" had left its imprint on restaurants, taverns, and other venues in Baltimore that offered jukebox entertainment. Detroit music operators had likewise described hillbilly songs as the most popular jukebox recordings in that city: "The large influx of new defense workers into the city from the South, bringing in a new taste in entertainment, is believed to be a major explanation." A letter to the journal from "A Good Old Hillbilly from Kentucky" said "I came to Detroit in 1942 and am now in a war plant. When night time comes and I get off from work I go to a place called Jefferson Inn where I find real old-time music as put on by the York Brothers."[40]

Even as country music became a national phenomenon with a remarkable commercial appeal, it continued to exhibit its southernness and working-class identity. The music that prevailed during the years that ran roughly from 1945 to 1955 was as transitional in nature as the society that sustained it. After all, rural southerners were changing their residences and occupations but were not so quickly abandoning their folkways. The crowds who attended the Renfro Valley Barn Dance or the Grand Ole Opry, or who otherwise demonstrated their affection for country music, did so for a wide variety of reasons. In some cases, they were people who had no actual experience with rural life but who nevertheless identified with musical forms that they believed were representative of an older and less perplexing America. More likely, though, they were transplanted rural people trying to come to terms with lives now spent permanently in cities while nonetheless clinging to remnants of the old home.[41]

Dramatic change in perceptions and worldviews certainly did not occur overnight. In the immediate postwar years, country entertainers, promoters, and fans shared an unspoken, and probably unconscious, assumption that the traditional social relationships that had prevailed in society and that were endorsed in the music would endure. Material conditions could be dramatically altered and improved, it was believed, without alteration of the gender, racial, generational, class, and regional relationships that had long defined American society. Traditional hierarchies, however, had been undermined during the war, and were weakened further by the prosperity and accelerated social change that came in the late forties and early fifties.[42] Ultimately, the consumer revolution did most to transform an already fragile social structure. While promising "things" at an unprecedented volume and rate, it obscured the role of class in American life by denying the need for structural change in capitalism. Increased prosperity and mass consumption also accentuated the sense of ambivalence about rural origins and encouraged, but did not easily create, homogeneity in our society. Country music could scarcely avoid being dramatically transformed by such changes, as money flowed into the hands of music purchasers and as women and young people became more assertive of their rights and needs.

Although prosperity and the desire for material consumption encouraged the embracing of middle-class values, working-class preoccupations continued to be central to country music's message, and specific allusions to work sometimes appeared in country lyrics. Class consciousness was apparent in such songs as "These Hands" and "Small-Time Laboring Man,"[43] both of which recognized the clear distinctions between hardworking people and the "gentlemen" who profited from their labor, but lyrics seldom voiced pleas for government relief or labor solidarity. Instead, these songs celebrated the loyalty, honor, and faithfulness of working people, while also emphasizing the self-reliance of the individual and the family as the ultimate source of security. It was rare to encounter a song like "By the Sweat of My Brow" that seethed with class hostility and anger at the exploitation practiced by the rich. Pro-union sentiments were also rare, but occasional songs like "Have a Heart, Taft-Hartley" (a protest against conservative efforts to curb union activities) or "The Ballad of Jimmy Hoffa," opining that the notorious labor leader was being persecuted by his enemies ("they're out to get you, Jimmy, every politician and his brother too"),[44] did appear on phonograph records.

The writing or performance of songs about labor leaders or industrial life was clearly not the chief priority of country musicians. Increasing numbers of southern folk permanently entered the ranks of blue-collar and industrial workers in the decades after the war, but if the lyrics of country songs truly reflected their thinking, working people still clung to older visions of rural independence and self-reliance. "Blackland Farmer," Frankie Miller's paean in 1958 to farmers, which described its hero as "the luckiest man ever born," probably came closest to mirroring the self-identification of most southern workers, even though neither Miller nor most of his listeners ever had any intention of living on a farm. (In 1999 Miller was working as parts manager in a Dallas–Fort Worth area car dealership.)[45] The great guitarist Merle Travis similarly had no desires to be a coal miner when he wrote two of the most graphic descriptions of mining ever encapsulated in song, "Sixteen Tons" and "Dark as a Dungeon."

Travis had no difficulty in writing such realistic vignettes because the clever lyricist had grown up in a culture of coal in Muhlenberg County in western Kentucky. The United Mine Workers *Journal* was second only to the Bible in his household. He remembered his excitement as a child when the miners went out on strike, and the sacrifices made by his family as they struggled to survive on flour and fatback. Along with the memories, he also absorbed a body of folklore from his parents and neighbors that went into the making of his songs, including the peculiar paradox of men who sometimes asserted their independence with a swaggering masculinity while also working under regimented conditions and receiving their pay in scrip.

But Travis never worked in the mines, and in fact had used his considerable skills as a guitarist and songwriter to escape the labor that had consumed the lives of his father and brothers. He was living in California in 1946 (and pursuing a successful recording career for the Capitol label), when record producer Lee Gillette asked him to record some folksongs from "back home." Travis replied that he didn't know any folksongs (which of course was not true) and couldn't write any because such songs were not newly "written." He went to work on the project, however, and emerged with a body of songs, recorded in 1946 and released in 1947 on an album called *Folk Songs from the Hills*,[46] which included adaptations of older material and two of the most powerful sets of lyrics ever written about coal mining. Often presumed to be a traditional song, "Dark as a Dungeon" recalled not only the dangers involved in coal mining but also the curiously intoxicating appeal that such labor had for many miners. These workers were addicted to coal labor, Travis noted, "like a fiend for his dope, and a drunkard his wine." As he drew upon the rich storehouse of homilies and metaphors recalled from his youth in western Kentucky, Travis remembered a phrase used often by his father that seemed to sum up the lives and expectations of most coal miners: "I owe my soul to the company store." The phrase became the recurring motif in the chorus of "Sixteen Tons," a line that attained almost universal currency after 1955 when Tennessee Ernie Ford's recording of the song sold over a million copies in twenty-one days and remained at the top of the charts for a long time.[47]

Although country songwriters most often demonstrated their kinship with working people through their preoccupation with the day-to-day concerns of survival, songs that dealt directly with work or workers were never entirely absent in the 1950s and early 1960s. A few, such as "Black-land Farmer," "Detroit City," "Busted," and "These Hands," won considerable commercial acclaim with their chronicles of working-class pride and travail. "These Hands," written by Eddie Noack and recorded by Hank Snow, was a particularly effective tribute to all hard-working people who labor at thankless jobs with the love and loyalty of family and friends as their chief rewards. Truck-driving songs, of course, emerged as a distinct genre of country music after 1963 when Dave Dudley recorded his rockabilly version of "Six Days on the Road," a swaggering tour de force that effectively captured the sense of machismo that is often associated with independent long-distance trucking. "Six Days on the Road" did comment on some of the problems and hazards of truck driving—log books, pills, truck-stop temptresses, ICC regulations—but trucking songs more often served as vehicles for expressions of masculine pride and the longing for individual liberty.[48]

Like earlier country songs, those heard in the 1950s and 1960s continued to express an ambivalence about work and worker identity. An occasional item such as "By the Sweat of My Brow" breathed with anger about class injustice and the exploitation of workers, but more often one heard a sense of fatalism about life's experiences and a conviction that relief is best attained through self-help and individual assertion. Country songwriters sometimes found themselves compared to Woody Guthrie, especially after Merle Haggard wrote his own chronicles of the Okie experience, but modern country songs contained little of the spirit of proletarian protest heard in the music of the Depression years. Songs about hard times or the Great Depression appeared frequently in the repertoires fashioned by Haggard, Johnny Cash, and James Talley, but generally as nostalgic odes to a simpler and presumably more enjoyable or more moral era, or as tributes to their parents who had survived those troubled times. The poor farmers about whom Johnny Cash sang in in such songs as "Five Feet High and Rising" generally lived in Depression-era Arkansas. Merle Haggard's, on the other hand, lived in Dust Bowl California.

Nashville's premier songwriter of the sixties, Harlan Howard, grew up in Detroit with his family who had migrated there from Kentucky. The

only song in his catalogue that refers to a Detroit worker, however—
"Watermelon Time in Georgia"—is a declaration by a homesick southerner who admits that though the money was good it could not equal
the love of his sweetheart nor the joys of country life. Howard also wrote
"Busted," a very successful song recorded by both Johnny Cash and Ray
Charles, which effectively describes the friendless predicament of a man
without money or job. Though the song was originally written about the
experiences suffered by his own father and other unemployed coal miners in eastern Kentucky, Howard rewrote the lyrics because Johnny Cash,
a son of Arkansas cotton tenantry, could not identify with them. The
revised version chronicles the life of a down-and-out cotton farmer, who
complains that "cotton is down to a quarter a pound." That history was
not only far afield from Howard's own but was a decided anachronism
in sixties America. Similarly, the most famous "work song" of the period, Mel Tillis's and Danny Dill's "Detroit City," is usually lauded as a
poignant evocation of the loneliness felt by transplanted southerners in
the industrial North. But the song strains credulity when the lonely auto
worker, who is given a voice by singer Bobby Bare, laments that he had
"dreamed about those cotton fields back home." One hears no false note
of nostalgia, however, in the version of the song "covered" by the African American singer Arthur Alexander, who omits the reference to cotton fields. The song was hardly relevant to the America of 1963, nor to
Tillis's own Florida background. Dolly Parton's "In the Good Old Days
(When Times Were Bad)" served as a refreshing antidote to those lyrics
that romanticized the past. She spoke with gentle affection about her
childhood memories, but declared that "no amount of money" could pay
her to go back and live those days again.[49]

Country singers and songwriters may have spoken for working people everywhere, but one finds no explicit public or media linking of their
music with presumed working-class values until the late sixties. Unlike
the 1930s when a national economic crisis encouraged a left-inspired
romanticization of workers and a discovery of grassroots music, the new
interrelationship was inspired by the conservative mood of the late Vietnam War era. A national backlash against Black Power, Hippies, antiwar resisters, Women's Libbers, and Gay Rights advocates inspired a
greater appreciation of Hard Hats, Blue-Collar Workers, and other Middle Americans who were presumed to be rock-ribbed in their patriotism
and commitment to traditional ideals. The blue-collar patriotism heard
in songs like Merle Haggard's "Okie from Muskogee" and Tom T. Hall's
"Mama, Tell Them What We're Fighting For" appealed to audiences

throughout the nation and encouraged the belief that country music voiced the values, aspirations, and prejudices of forgotten working people, north and south. Haggard previously had been embraced by some liberal observers because of "Mama's Hungry Eyes," "They're Tearing the Labor Camps Down," and other poignant portrayals of life in California's labor camps,[50] but he reached out to a much larger national constituency after 1970 with "Okie from Muskogee," an attack on protestors and hippies and a defense of Middle American values.

Haggard and other country songwriters remained beneficiaries of the changing political climate long after the stridency of the Vietnam era diminished. Jimmy Carter's election in 1976 seemed to signal a new period of healing and the dawn of a moderate South. The ascension to the presidency of a southerner who promoted southern styles of music and who held liberal racial views was only one factor that contributed to a more benign, and accepting, view of both the South and country music. The renewed preoccupation in country music with plain people even saw an acceptance of such once-despised terms as "redneck," "good old boy," and "hillbilly" by country singers and audiences.[51] "Redneck" seemed somehow to be overcoming the association with racial bigotry from which it suffered in the early 1960s, and instead was now being used to describe white working-class males. It became a proud self-designation for many white southerners and, by the early eighties, was appearing frequently in country songs. The word "hillbilly" also made its way back into country music, if not into songs, at least into the vocabulary and self-descriptions of many musicians. It was used in the sixties and seventies as an in-group expression, but by the nineties was being proudly and overtly accepted as a self-defining label by such singers as Marty Stuart and Dwight Yoakam.

By and large, country songs shed their militant right-wing political edge and became more broadly supportive of working people's interests. Tom T. Hall, for example, had written his angry reply to war protestors, "Mama, Tell Them What We're Fighting For," in the heated political atmosphere of the mid-sixties, but his later songs told compassionate vignettes of life as seen through the experiences of shoeshine boys, grave diggers, frustrated guitar pickers, bus station custodians, and world-weary touring musicians. James Talley similarly drew many of his musical ideas from rough-hewn working folk and identified explicitly with the tradition of his fellow Oklahoma poet, Woody Guthrie. He sometimes went well beyond comments about the day-to-day struggles and pleasures of working people to register angry protests about their exploitation. Evok-

ing the spirit of *The Grapes of Wrath*, he pondered the ominous consequences of men who couldn't feed their children and asked "Are They
Gonna Make Us Outlaws Again?" He gave one possible answer to this
question by summoning up memories of Pretty Boy Floyd who, according to popular legend, had turned to crime because of victimization by
the wealthy.[52] On the whole, country singers and songwriters, then and
since, have found it difficult to discuss workers without coupling that
preoccupation with a nostalgia for an older and presumably better America—a society where people were poor but proud, hard-working, and
resistant to welfare (forgetting the massive government support provided for the unemployed during the New Deal years), and where values were
fixed and knowable.

The explicit affirmation of the relationship between country music and
working-class culture occurred, ironically, at a time when the music was
aggressively striving for mainstream acceptance. The suburbanization of
country music's audience was already well under way by the 1960s, but
the commercial potential of this demographic shift was most dramatically displayed in the early 1980s in the aftermath of the urban cowboy
phenomenon. Country music's subsequent commercial ascent has been
fueled not only by new waves of suburbanized fans but also by young
singers who have had little or no experience with working-class culture,
or who come from working families accommodating to or embracing
middle-class values. These factors may explain Tom T. Hall's complaint
in 1996 that "young country" had learned its music from such groups
as the Eagles and the Beatles, and that "country music has always reflected
the mood of working people, so it went the way they went."[53]

Songs about working people nevertheless have continued to appear in
country music, and in the repertoires of young singers. One of the most
popular and influential "young country" groups of the modern period,
Alabama, recorded a moving tribute to working people in 1985 called
"Forty Hour Week (for a Livin')." Not only did they pay homage to their
own blue-collar origins, Alabama also reached out to many suburban fans
who worked at professional or high-tech jobs and who nevertheless felt
the compulsion to praise or identify with a less pretentious lifestyle. This
taste for "authenticity" in music may have been part of a larger quest
made by baby boomers to reconnect with the simpler, hands-on culture
that was being lost in America's rapid acceptance of technology and in
the flight to homogeneity in suburban shopping malls and neighborhoods.
Few people actually move back to the country or take up blue-collar
occupations, but increasing numbers purchase pick-up trucks and sports

utility vehicles and select rugged outdoor clothing and equipment from Land's End, L. L. Bean, or catalogues that are even more upscale and "rural." And more than a few have escaped to country music.[54]

Those record producers who had sought to give country music an urban gloss, or who had once been embarrassed by its working-class caste, must have been surprised to learn that new and young audiences sometimes wanted a harder, blue-collar edge to their music. Rednecks, good old boys and girls, truck drivers, and rodeo cowboys were only a few of the colorful working folk who often populated country songs in the 1970s and 1980s or who provided the subject matter of movies like *Urban Cowboy*. Songwriters seldom talked about the labor of such characters, however, and instead concentrated on their eccentricities or the romance that presumably surrounded them.

The most unequivocal tributes to working people appeared in the songs about hard-working and loving parents. Loretta Lynn had set the standard in 1970 with her highly acclaimed tribute to her Kentucky origins, "Coal Miner's Daughter," but Hazel Dickens demonstrated in 1995 that the theme still resonated powerfully with audiences when her poignant "Mama's Hand" won the award for Bluegrass Song of the Year. This time-tested preoccupation has inspired some of country music's greatest songs. Memories that are personal and local assume universal significance when Dolly Parton recalls her east Tennessee childhood and the sacrifices made by her mother in "Coat of Many Colors," when Doug Kershaw remembers his fishing-and-trapping father and his own Cajun boyhood in "Louisiana Man," when Tish Hinojosa lovingly celebrates the lives of her migrant parents in "West Side of Town," or when Merle Haggard commemorates an entire generation of Okies, including his own parents, in "Mama's Hungry Eyes."[55]

Modern country work songs do not dwell exclusively on nostalgia or pride; they sometimes bristle with anger and class consciousness. Country song lyrics, however, constitute no threat to capitalism. They express resentment, not radicalism. Although problems abound, the "enemy" remains ill-defined. Even in one of the angriest of the country song complaints, James Talley's "Are They Gonna Make Us Outlaws Again?" "they" are never identified. Rich men are occasionally denounced, as in Jim and Jesse's "Cotton Mill Man," Hazel Dickens's "Working Girl Blues," or Travis Tritt's "Lord Have Mercy on the Working Man," but big business seldom receives censure for its role in unemployment, plant closures, or depressed wages. The vast, impersonal world of corporate business defies understanding, so the enemy assumes local and personal dimensions. Johnny Paycheck's "Take This Job and Shove It" and Johnny Cash's "Onie," for example, remind us that the shop floor is the scene where most worker grievances are played out. But neither song promises anything more than personal response: Paycheck denounces his foreman and line boss and threatens to walk off the job. Cash declares that as soon as his retirement becomes official he will beat up Onie, his cruel foreman.[56]

Country songs are as likely to blame the government—for high taxes, meddlesome laws, welfare policies, and other seemingly onerous deeds— as they are to criticize the arrogance of big business. A form of working-class populism also surfaces in songs like Merle Haggard's "Big City" when he refers to those who "never work but they've got plenty," and in Aaron Tippin's "Working Man's Ph.D." that declares "a few more people should be pullin' their weight." Those who are nonproductive, of course, could include anyone from lawyers and intellectuals to welfare recipients. The working people described in such songs as Haggard's "Working Man Blues," George Jones's "Small-Time Laboring Man," and Alan Jackson's "Working Class Hero" (his father) are usually employed men and women[57] who express fierce pride in themselves, their families, and their country. But while they complain frequently about overwork and low pay, high taxes, the cost of living, government regimentation, and lax or declining moral standards, they remain intensely patriotic and rarely call for worker solidarity or government action.

Although since the 1930s thousands of southern rural folk have worked in factories, neither industrial labor nor labor unions receive much attention in modern country songs. Country musicians have contributed much time and money to Farm Aid, the highly publicized crusade to save family farms, but they have said virtually nothing about factory labor nor about the collapse of the steel and coal industries and other facets of America's industrial infrastructure. Consequently, the documentation of this important phase of our postindustrial life has been left to such pop singers as Billy Joel and Bruce Springsteen, or to singer-songwriters like Si Kahn, Tom Russell, and Utah Phillips who stand on the fringes of country music. The grim consequences of plant closings, and the recognition that factory work represented a sustaining way of life for many people, appear in such songs as Kahn's "Aragon Mill," Phillips's "Green Rolling Hills of West Virginia," Billy Edd Wheeler's "Coal Tattoo," Tom Russell's "Steel Town," and Jean Ritchie's "The L & N Don't Stop Here Anymore." Although such songs do appear occasionally, David Lee Murphy, a self-professed redneck and country singer from Herrin in southern Illinois, probably spoke for most mainstream country entertainers when he said, "If I had grown up in Chicago, I'd probably write about steel mill towns and those characters, like Bruce Springsteen does. But I didn't grow up there: I grew up in a small, agricultural community, so I'm going to write about going down to the lake with a bottle of wine at sunset."[58]

The yearning for a rural-based independence, the sense of manly pride, and a resignation about what is perceived as the hard reality of working-class life have endured in uneasy companionship in modern country songs. But the degree to which the assumptions of these songs are shaped by the age and origin of the singer, and the context in which they were written, is clearly shown in the repertoires of the veteran Merle Haggard and the young country singer Aaron Tippin. One finds presumptions in the repertoires of both men that have been voiced in country music since the 1920s. But Haggard sees life through a darker lens. He was born near Bakersfield, California, in 1937 as part of a poor but hard-working Okie family. The loss of his father when Merle was nine years old, a troubled youth (that included long stints in reform school and San Quentin prison), and memories of life in a struggling working-class family marked him and the timbre of his songs.

The central characters in Haggard's songs speak often with an almost-swaggering boastfulness, but like their creator, who told a television interviewer that "America isn't free unless you have money,"[59] they recognize a world of limitations and complain that "a working man can't get nowhere today." They dream of escape but generally return to the assembly line. In one of Haggard's most powerful performances (of a song he did not write), he expresses the desire to forsake his job for the allure of a fishing pole on some blue bayou, but then says "I just dream and keep on being the way I am." The narrator in "Working Man Blues" similarly declares that he sometimes thinks about leaving his job to "do a little bumming around," but he always returns to his work, finds relief in a tavern, and boasts that he's never been on welfare ("that's one place I won't be"). The central character in "Big City" complains about "too much work and never enough pay," notes that "there are folks who never work and they've got plenty," and fantasizes about a free and unencumbered life "somewhere in the middle of Montana."[60]

But if Haggard's workers sometime seem uncertain about their ability to change their lives and conditions, Aaron Tippin's exude nothing but confidence and pride. Born in 1954, Tippin was an heir to a postwar era of prosperity that seemed to promise an almost-unbounded success for those who were willing to work hard. When he made his first forays into commercial music in the 1970s, a renewed sense of working-class patriotism and redneck pride encouraged him to equate his own self-confidence with that of the nation. Unlike Haggard, who had actually spent few years as a worker during his brief stints outside of prison or professional music, Tippin had been a full-time blue-collar worker before his music career blossomed after 1991 with the success of his patriotic anthem, "You've Got to Stand for Something." The experiences garnered from his years as a professional pilot, pipe welder, heavy equipment operator, and truck driver informed the lyrics of his songs, but his aggressive stage behavior and a physique molded by professional body building made his performances viscerally compelling. The characters encountered in Tippin's songs are no strangers to the barroom, nor are they immune to an occasional interlude of masculine strutting. His "Honky Tonk Super Hero," for example, is a quiet, hard-working factory hand for five days of the week who becomes a table-dancing, drinking fool on the weekend. His workers also sometime pursue failed dreams, as is admitted in "I Promised You the World," but it is almost impossible to conceive of Tippin singing a song like "A Working Man Can't Get Nowhere Today." His "Working Man's Ph.D." does more than embody the aggressive self-confidence of the singer; it sums up the pride, machismo, and patriotism of American workers: "you build the things that really make the world go 'round. If it works, if it runs, if it lasts for years, you can bet your bottom dollar it was made right here."[61]

Tippin's tribute to American workers could just as easily be extended to country singers who, like himself, are workers who pursue the craft of music-making. Several fine songs, like Tom T. Hall's "Homecoming," have described the hazards, boredom, and excitement that punctuate the lives of touring country musicians,[62] but few so poignantly describe the dreams and frustrations of young would-be musicians as "Sixteenth Avenue."[63] Written by T. Schuyler, and recorded by Lacy J. Dalton in 1982, the song simultaneously pays tribute to Nashville's music publishing and recording district and to the young pickers, singers, and songwriters who have journeyed there seeking self-fulfillment of their talents, recognition, and fame. Arriving in "hundred dollar cars," armed with guitars and a stash of their own songs, and sustaining themselves on collect calls made to home, a few "for awhile . . . go in style" on the strength of one hit recording or published song. An even smaller contingent achieve stardom, but more often than not, the dreams remain unfulfilled, and the musicians eventually return to their former lives where they "swing a nine pound hammer" or work at other occupations to continue their passion for music. Although international in its sales, marketing, and devoted legions of fans, country music is thriving today because it remains a grassroots cultural phenomenon. For every Garth Brooks, there are a thousand country musicians who perform in local bars, taverns, and American Legion halls and who have never been able to "give up their day jobs." These are musicians whose middle-class dreams are tempered by working-class realities.

3

"I Was Dreaming of a Little Cabin"

In 1996 the International Bluegrass Music Association chose as its song of the year "Mama's Hand," written by Hazel Dickens and recorded by Lynn Morris.[1] Dickens's poignant recollection of her coming of age and departure from her working-class home in West Virginia contained virtually all of the ingredients that had always defined the impulse toward home and domesticity in country music: the willing and often eager decision to leave home, the heartaches that accompany the departure, the consequent sense of nostalgia that eventually sets in, and the centrality of mother. Although this song was identified with bluegrass music—where the persistent longing for the old homeplace has always remained intense—its themes are echoed in a variety of songs that spill across stylistic categories. "Alternative" country singer Iris DeMent and Mexican American singer Tish Hinojosa have written and recorded two of the most powerful examples. While DeMent grew up in California, "Mama's Opry" linked her to her Arkansas roots and to memories of the profound role that country music played in her own mother's life. Hinojosa's "West Side of Town," on the other hand, recalled her Mexican migrant parents and their difficult life in the barrio of San Antonio.[2] Such songs are reminders that, even as country music has reached out to envelop an audience worldwide in scope, with a musical product that has become increasingly undefinable, to a remarkable degree it still celebrates the values of home and hearth.

The home celebrated in country music has most often been enshrined as a rural or working-class abode set somewhere in the South. Such songs are more than simple yearnings for lost innocence. They also suggest that the system of moral values that surrounded that home still have relevance today even if the society that nourished them has crumbled. Since the 1920s the vision of a clean, decent, and wholesome entertainment form that drew its inspiration from the traditional rural-derived values of home and family has been central to country music's self-definition. The image has remained satisfying to country entertainers as a unifying touchstone, but it is also appealing to a large audience because such themes seem to be consonant with the way Americans view themselves and their past. That is why Chet Atkins, in ads for the Cracker Barrel restaurant chain in the 1980s, could call country music the "music of America," and why family-style restaurants in the United States invariably play country songs on their soundtracks.

Like the songs of Dickens, DeMent, and Hinojosa, country songs about home have always tended to convey a sense of loss or ambivalence. Most of them recall or celebrate a home that has been abandoned or has disappeared, and they extol values and a way of life that are fragile and under siege. Songs about "the old homeplace" (both real and imagined) have always provided emotional release and security for people who have moved into a complex world rife with uncertain loyalties and shifting moral values. The evocation of the rural or working-class home, and the suggestion that its values were both basic to and disappearing from American life, appeared in 1923 at the very beginning of country music's commercial history: as one side of the first documented recording of a southern rural musician, Fiddlin' John Carson's version of an old song, "Little Old Log Cabin in the Lane." Written originally as a minstrel piece by Will S. Hays in 1871, and burdened with a ponderous "darkey" dialect, the song became, in Carson's interpretation, an affectionate and nostalgic recollection of a crumbling rural society.[3]

Rural southerners could identify easily with such a song, for theirs was a society that had been undergoing dramatic transformation since the Civil War. To the casual observer who wandered through the rural South in the 1920s, the scattered farm houses and sleepy little towns and villages suggested a region of stability and timelessness. A closer look at this society, though, would have revealed a land dotted also with abandoned and deteriorating farmsteads, and here and there the most dramatic manifestations of a changing world—the cotton mill villages, coal camps, oil fields, and railroad lines that heralded the encroachments of the industrial revolution. The distant whistle of a locomotive signaled the advent of a new age, and though the railroad did bring people home, it more often beckoned them to new opportunities and alternative ways of life elsewhere.

The changing rural South was also a society undergoing various forms of domestication. Men did not easily give up the dominance that they had always enjoyed, but increasingly found themselves living in a society where women played new roles and exercised new moral responsibilities. Evangelical Protestantism, which made significant inroads among southern women in the middle decades of the nineteenth century, extended a sense of influence, if not power, to converted women. New ideas and fashions accompanied the railroads as they broke the geographical isolation of the rural South. Throughout the late nineteenth century, as the market culture/economy weakened old cultural standards, townways became increasingly seductive to rural folk.[4]

The work required of rural and working-class women did not diminish significantly in the late nineteenth century (most labor-saving devices became available first to their middle-class sisters in the cities), and the majority of women in mills or on farms typically performed jobs both in the house and in the fields or on the shop floor. Emma Bell Miles was speaking strictly of the people she knew in the hills of East Tennessee when she referred to two opposing spheres of life occupied by men and women, but her observations were true of men and women everywhere in the rural South during the late nineteenth century.[5] She perceptively described man's authority and the expectation of its overall prevalence, but noted that his true domain existed outdoors where he sought to exercise an untrammeled freedom. Regardless of where work obligations might take her, woman's domain was confined to the household where she acted as the conservator of domestic values.

In the late nineteenth century women played central roles in the propagation of the domestic style of music to which country music was an heir. Emma Miles spoke of women singing ballads dreamily by the loom, but even in the sparsely settled southern mountains, newer songs from the popular press and popular stage quickly replaced or accompanied the old ballads. Popular culture and the emerging system of consumer capitalism introduced new possibilities of ease, comfort, and beauty. Songs entered the South in a variety of ways: through traveling shows, sheet music, songsters, and song pages in magazines and newspapers.[6] The same Sears-Roebuck and Montgomery Ward catalogues that carried advertisements for sewing machines also conveyed the news of pianos, parlor organs, guitars, and other musical instruments, piano rolls, stereopticon slides, phonographs, and sheet music.

We cannot be sure that women were the principal consumers of the new forms of music, but there is no question that they formed the principal subjects of the lyrics. They generally fared no better in these songs than they had in the old ballads, however; at best, they died for love. At worst, they were jilted, deserted, scorned, and sometimes murdered. And, just as in real life, they received unqualified endorsement only when they appeared as innocent little girls or as saintly old mothers.

The songs of domestic sentiment that so frequently filled the repertoires of early country singers were remnants of a national flowering of romanticism and sentimentalism that accompanied the rise of the common man and the first stirrings of the industrial revolution after the War of 1812. As a musical vogue, it seems to have been inspired, in part, by a vague sense of disquietude among many intellectuals and artists who felt that America's rural-derived innocence was receding. The impulse was reinforced by a passion for the pastoral that emerged on the European continent and in England during the nineteenth century.[7] It somehow seems appropriate that "Home Sweet Home," the song that launched the musical fashion for home in the United States, was written abroad in 1809 by the American actor John Howard Payne during his extensive sojourn in Europe, and was first sung in an English melodrama, *Clari, the Maid of Milan.* The music of German family choral groups who first appeared in the United States in 1814 influenced American musicians of all stripes. Led by the Rainer Family, these Tyrolean singers popularized yodeling, vocal harmony, and the use of the word "minstrels" to describe troupes of musicians. Singing about their own native scenes of nature and pastoral bliss, the Tyrolean minstrels strongly inspired a similar interest in this country for poetic evocations of the mountains and valleys of home. Almost simultaneously, Thomas Moore's *Irish Melodies and National Airs* appeared and provided examples of song themes that influenced American writers throughout much of the century. Moore wrote often of faraway and time-dimmed scenes, investing his themes with the aura of irrecoverable innocence.

Clearly influenced by Moore, and stirred by a presentiment of the loss of rural America, American songwriters began turning out a stream of songs about the icons of this receding world—old oaken buckets, old arm chairs, and village churchyards—that found eager audiences throughout the nation. This melodic recollection of fading rural life was merely one phase of a popular culture of nostalgia that touched virtually every form of literature and art in the decades before the Civil War and became a staple of the widely distributed McGuffey readers. Here, in the misty-eyed

evocations of "Long, Long Ago," or in the anguished longings for childhood chums expressed in a song like "Forty Years Ago," one encounters
the note of melancholy that so strongly attracted Abraham Lincoln and
his generation of antebellum Americans.[8]

When country music began its commercial existence, it did not simply
draw upon a venerable preoccupation with home and the contentments
of domestic life, it also became privy to an almost-century-long obsession with the South in American popular culture. The musical exploitation of southern scenes and people that began in the antebellum era with
Stephen Foster, Dan Emmett, and the blackface minstrels did not diminish or change substantially in the decades that followed the Civil War.
When the fascination with Dixie was combined with the themes of nostalgia, home, and domesticity, the resulting potent mélange of images
proved irresistible to song-loving Americans. In musing on the abundant
number of antebellum songs that "locate felicity's domain in the American southland," Nicholas Tawa observed that "the South was what remained of the American past that was still unchanged by modern innovation." And he added, significantly, that the region remained fascinating
because it was the home of black people.[9] If Tawa had also mentioned
the southern Appalachians he would have been even more on target, and
would have touched on something that has obsessed those who look for
the roots of America's white musical traditions and the alleged original
"home" of country music.

Ironically, in this never-ending urge to "go home to the South," northern songwriters and publishers played crucial roles. Until Civil War patriotism inspired native southerners to write songs like "Maryland! My
Maryland," one finds a conspicuous absence of southern-based writers
among the multitude who exploited southern themes. The many pocket-
sized songsters that appeared in the South after 1861, carrying such titles as *Rebel Rhymes and Rhapsodies* and *General Lee Songster,* contained
lyrics that were highly derivative of the international body of genteel
songmaking that dominated American music in the mid-nineteenth century. Except for Will S. Hays, the prolific poet and composer from Louisville who identified with the South,[10] southerners remained scarce among
the many songwriters who emphasized southern topics in the decades
after the war.

The Pennsylvania-born Stephen Foster remains only the first of a long
stream of Yankees who found musical inspiration in the imagined romance of southern themes and personalities. With songs like Foster's "Old
Folks at Home" and "My Old Kentucky Home," James K. Bland's "Carry

Me Back to Old Virginny," and Charles K. Harris's "Mid the Green Fields of Virginia," northern tunesmiths satisfied the cravings of those who yearned for the simplicity, stability, or exoticism that was associated with the mythic South. Throughout the nineteenth century, and well into the twentieth, Yankee writers and at least a few Europeans poured out a steady stream of songs with titles such as "Take Me Back to the Sweet Sunny South," "Are You from Dixie?" "The Girl I Loved in Sunny Tennessee," and "Alabama Bound." The consolidation of the popular song industry in the area of New York City (described colloquially as Tin Pan Alley) in no way diminished the flow of northern-written and southern-inspired songs into the nation's musical mainstream. Hard-boiled songwriters and publishers who remained alert to public whims, fancies, and changing musical styles (while seldom if ever venturing south of Manhattan) churned out a large body of songs that reinforced the notion of a romantic South. Even as musical fashions changed repeatedly, the appeal of the South endured. Whether couched in the dreamy lilt of a waltz, the syncopated rhythms of ragtime, or the brassy swing of jazz, this faraway South was suspended in time and far different from the postbellum society emerging in the rest of the nation.[11]

The songs of domesticity remained as vital ingredients of American popular music throughout the nineteenth century, their currency enhanced by the violent displacements wrought by the Civil War. "The Vacant Chair" became more than a sentimental song about a soldier's death; it was emblematic as a permanent and poignant reminder of the war's legacy in millions of homes on both sides of the Mason-Dixon line. The affection exhibited in the South for songs like "Lorena," "Aura Lee," or "Listen to the Mocking Bird" suggest as well an acceptance of the scheme of values that permeate the lyrics. Southerners not only embraced the songs of domesticity, they kept them and other songs of genteel affectation current long after they lost favor in other parts of the nation, often simplifying melodies to conform to their own aesthetic traditions. Written in 1855 by the Philadelphia composer Septimus Winner (under the pen name of Alice Hawthorne), "Listen to the Mocking Bird" became widely popular in the South. While it is true that southern fiddlers eventually preserved only the melody of "Mocking Bird" (to which they approximated a variety of bird imitations), the region's singers also preserved the lyrics about "sweet Hallie" who lay dead in the cemetery while the mocking bird sang o'er her grave.[12]

Although such music might properly be described as "parlor music," because it was designed for the piano stand in the family parlor or living

room, it never consistently conveyed optimism or benignity but reflected realities its listeners had experienced. Many songs in fact dwelt on the
fragility of familial relationships, stressing disappointment, poverty, and
loss as the family circle was shattered by parting, abandonment, the betrayal of vows, or death. Homeless and penniless orphans appeared in
the songs with great frequency, just as they did in postbellum southern
society. The rural and small-town southerners who lovingly sang such
songs as "Little Rosewood Casket," "I'll Be All Smiles Tonight," "Ma-
ple on the Hill," "The Baggage Coach Ahead," "The Letter Edged in
Black," "Mary of the Wild Moor," "The Fatal Wedding," "Nobody's
Darling on Earth," "The Blind Child," and "Two Little Orphans" probably identified with the sentiment-laden lyrics that reaffirmed the existence of their sorrows and reinforced their belief in the evanescence of
all human relationships.

Despite the high incidence of Yankee songwriters, this scheme of values undoubtedly fit the southerners' self-definition as a home-centered
moral people. Some songwriters, such as Will Thompson and George F.
Root, wrote for both the popular and the gospel trade. Thompson's "Soft-
ly and Tenderly (Jesus Is Calling)" and "Gathering Shells from the Sea-
shore" both consequently found warm and enduring reception in the
South. "Where Is My Wandering Boy Tonight?" heard on both the vaudeville stage and in the churches of late nineteenth-century America, won
an even larger hearing in the families of rural Americans from which
young men often embarked to find a security or excitement that they
could not find at home.[13] A generation that put its anxieties about wandering boys and disappearing homesteads into both religious and popular songs also built a musical cult about Mother. The "powerful ideology of motherhood" that took shape in the early years of the nineteenth
century contributed to a great outpouring of "mother songs" later in that
century.[14] Folklorist Bill Ellis argues that "at the heart of this cultural
norm was a deep anxiety about an increasingly impersonal society and
the need to preserve human values and ideals in the face of bureaucra-
cy." Clinging to Mother, Ellis maintains, implied a "refusal to surrender
humane priorities for the sake of being part of a well-oiled machine."[15]

While Ellis centers his discussion around the idea of the growth of
impersonality wrought by corporate bureaucratization, other analysts
have suggested that the Mother cult may have arisen from a compulsive
need in American Protestantism to create a "Mary" figure. David Hoeveler, professor of history at the University of Wisconsin in Milwaukee,
argues that the emphasis on Mother at the end of the nineteenth century

represented a softening of Protestantism and a renewed commitment to domestication. Mother became an intermediary between lost and sinful sons and God.[16] Mother *did* assume a powerful religious significance in many of the songs, and Mother songs, in fact, constituted a subcategory of gospel music that posits Mother as the reverential symbol who hearkened both listeners and the American nation back to an increasingly abandoned center of moral values. "Tell Mother I'll Be There," for example, a song written by the Reverend Charles M. Fillmore in 1898, was sometimes used in revivalistic campaigns to bring straying sinners to the mourner's bench. The evangelistic song leader Charles Alexander claimed that the song had "converted more than any other song written in a decade." The song combines both popular and religious sensibilities as its narrator recalls the grief brought to his mother by his childish "folly and neglect" and then repents by promising to meet her in Heaven: "Oh Angels tell my mother I'll be there."[17] A reconciliation with Mother in Heaven was the reward and confirmation of a life redeemed.

Whatever their source or ultimate meaning, the Mother songs came south, lingered, and inspired similar songs in both the country and southern gospel traditions. Southern gospel music (discussed in chapter 4) became the chief repository of such songs precisely at the moment when northern writers began to lose interest in the genre, and in the early 1920s items like "If I Could Hear My Mother Pray Again" and "I Heard My Mother Call My Name in Prayer" became beloved and enduring ingredients of the country music repertoire.[18]

While Mother was omnipresent in the "old familiar" songs that were available to singers throughout the southern region, Daddy made only infrequent appearances. Daddy was the dispenser of discipline and the director of work, while Mother was the healer of wounds, the dryer of tears, the teacher of morality, and a refuge from the cruel world of work, pain, and authority. Unfortunately, she also provoked guilt, because not only was it easy to stray from her guidance and precepts, it was also virtually inevitable. The Wandering Boy went his way in the world, searching for employment, adventure, or identity, but he could overcome neither the memory of mama's guidance nor the guilt that accompanied his rejection of home and hearth. Consequently, he embraced those songs that memorialized his mother or assuaged his sense of having betrayed her trust.

The first generation of commercial hillbillies were men and women who had either grown up when the songs of mother and home were first introduced or who lived in a society that cherished and preserved the songs (often in altered forms) long after they were forgotten in urban America.

When they reintroduced such songs, or songs like them, in radio broad-casts, phonograph recordings, illustrated songbooks, and personal appear-ances after 1923, they found a public, North and South, prepared to embrace the melodic and social messages found in the music. Country music's commercial birth during an era of profound social and techno-logical change can be understood, in part, as a search for a "wholesome" alternative to the more frenetic urban-based musical styles that were en-gulfing America. Country music's emergence simultaneously reaffirmed values presumed to be of rural origin and indicated the ascendancy of urban America—where the music was recorded, published, and broad-cast. Cities also were home to the music's largest concentrated audiences. Ironically, Americans have enthusiastically embraced technological inno-vation but have often remained ambivalent, if not downright resistant, to the social changes inspired by technology. Henry Ford was not alone in opposing jazz and the relatively permissive society that surrounded it af-ter World War I. The fiddle contests and old-time dances that he promot-ed after 1926 were welcomed by many Americans who longed for the simpler society of their youth even as they welcomed Ford's machine that was simultaneously obliterating older conceptions of both time and space. Ford may not have reawakened in America the sense of Christian moral-ity that had prevailed during his boyhood, but he did contribute to the renewed popularization of the ancient art of country fiddling, as he in-gratiated himself and his automobiles with the nation's plain folk.[19]

Although one finds no evidence that Ford recognized any compatibil-ity between the music he sponsored and that which came to be known as "hillbilly," the emergence and popularity of commercialized strains of rural music in the 1920s suggests a hunger for homespun entertainment and village-bred morality similar to that promoted by the Detroit indus-trialist. The discovery of hillbilly music by the recording and radio in-dustries was largely an accident, and neither the early performers nor their commercial promoters were prepared initially to promote the music as a conservative cultural force. Radio stations and record companies exploit-ed hillbilly talent in the twenties because of its inexpensive availability, and few performers suspected that this kind of entertainment could sus-tain a full-time professional career. But once a potentially large and loy-al audience for the music was identified, a few enterprising promoters began trying to shape the emerging form in ways that would tap the pro-found urge for nostalgia that lay beneath the surface of a rapidly mod-ernizing America. The sense of nostalgia and the affinity for old-fashioned material, however, was not a one-sided phenomenon foisted upon the early hillbilly entertainers. The early repertoires indicate that the musicians themselves reached repeatedly for "old-familiar" songs.

The widespread use of the term "barn dance"—a term redolent with the presumed naturalness and innocence of rural entertainment—to describe contrived hillbilly radio shows emanating from cities suggests an effort to capitalize on a national mood of nostalgia for a way of life that was rapidly slipping away. "Barn dance" was used as early as 1923 to describe a short-lived program on Fort Worth's WBAP that featured old-time fiddling and a Hawaiian string band, but the description received its widest national exposure after 1924 and 1925 when it was used as the title for similar, but long-running, programs on WLS in Chicago and WSM in Nashville.[20] The downhome ambience associated with the barn dances received formal and institutionalized endorsement through the work of astute program managers, announcers, and advertisers who strived to create or evoke an easygoing, rustic atmosphere for the shows. The wearing of overalls, checked shirts, gingham dresses, bonnets, aprons, and brogan shoes, and the use of such "rustic" backdrops as hay bales and fence posts, were both cultural and business decisions made jointly by sponsors and program directors. Radio executives like WSM's George D. Hay or WLS's John Lair also gave rustic names to bands or individual performers—such as Gully Jumpers, Fruit Jar Drinkers, Possum Hunters, Coon Creek Girls, Arkansas Woodchopper, or Cumberland Ridge Runners.

Hay, of course, was the popular radio personality who created the WSM Barn Dance (now known as the Grand Ole Opry). He initially resisted a structured format for the show and the use of paid commercials. Hay's admonition to musicians, "keep it close to the ground, boys," indicated his desire to preserve a sense of family with an air of simplicity and informality. Much of what Hay wanted was an elaborate fiction that could not long be sustained. Commercials came to the show very early, and full-time professionals, with constantly replenished catalogues of new songs, soon competed with the amateurs who picked and sang on Saturday nights and then worked at other jobs during the week. The Grand Ole Opry, though, has remained famous for the "controlled chaos" that still characterizes its shows. Even in the lush and ultramodern atmosphere of Opryland Park, where the show relocated in 1974, musicians move casually and aimlessly across the stage while their colleagues perform before the microphones, and friends, relatives, or other interested spectators watch from the wings or from onstage benches. Somehow, the show always proceeds without hitch—and on time.

Hay's family emphasis has similarly proved hard to maintain. The Opry has remained passionately proud of the closeness and camaraderie of its members and of the intimate links that bind them to their fans. This relationship, built originally on shared southern and/or working-class origins and interests, has also been reinforced by company rules and regulations concerning both onstage and offstage behavior. The image of a clean, decent family show persists and is as important today as it was in Hay's time for promoting public relations and creating audience rapport, but it is created and maintained only with great difficulty—through the hiding or denial of indiscretions, or through the disciplining or dismissal of erring members.[21]

Family groups also played upon the image of wholesome, home-oriented entertainment. The Carter Family was only one of several family units, such as the Pickard Family, Jenkins Family, Deal Family, Asher Sizemore and his son, Little Jimmie, and the Massey Family, who performed in early country music. The blind Atlanta street evangelist and newspaper vendor Andrew Jenkins and his two stepdaughters apparently made the first family recordings, including the initial version of "If I Could Hear My Mother Pray Again," in 1924 for Columbia.[22] But the Carters have remained as the quintessential embodiment of the close family, marketing for public consumption songs and skills first learned at home or in church. The continuing popularity of "Carter Family Songs" and the fact that children and grandchildren of the original trio have remained in the music business lend further strength to the Carters' reputation as "the first family of country music."

The Carter Family required neither rustic moniker nor dress to demonstrate their southern rural origin, and throughout their career they seem never to have dressed in either farm or western garb. Along with Bradley Kincaid, "the Kentucky Mountain Boy," they did most to enshrine domesticity and virtue as icons in early country music. The Carters' authentic sound, their repertoire of old-time songs, their origins in the Virginia hills, and their participation as a family all combined to celebrate an aura of wholesomeness and old-fashioned morality that have remained a vital part of country music's mystique. Their famous handbill, asserting that their program was "morally good," may have been motivated by their knowledge that their fundamentalist neighbors harbored a lingering suspicion against itinerant musicians, but the assertion of moral goodness was one to which the entire country music "family" has laid claim.

Like many of the southern families to whom they sang, and whose values they professed to uphold, the Carters' unity was fragile, and the society they represented was in disintegration. If family unity was a prerequisite for survival in an unstable world, the Carters could provide little inspiration. They held together as a performing team from 1927 to 1943, even though A. P. and Sara separated in 1931 and eventually divorced. A. P.'s role as leader of the trio remains questionable. It is true that he organized the group, selected or "composed" most of the songs that they performed, and acted as their master of ceremonies. But the trio's musical strength lay in the vocal and instrumental skills of the two women, and in the stylistic arrangements that they made. Carter Family lyrics gave listeners even less reassurance about the contemporary world. Like the world in which they lived, that of which they sang was seldom idealized, for it was filled with forsaken love, abandoned dreams, departed villages and firesides, and broken family circles. Security lay generally in the remembered past, "in that little poplar loghouse on the hill," at an unrecoverable distance, "mid the green fields of Virginia far away," or in the soul's future abode in Heaven where saints were promised "fifty miles of elbow room."[23]

From 1938 to 1941 the Carters sang about those green fields of Virginia while living in San Antonio, Texas, and performing on XERA, the notorious Mexican border station whose powerful broadcasts reached out to virtually every corner of North America. The spectacle of the Carters' "mountain" sound being disseminated from the Rio Grande Valley along with seedy radio fare that promoted laxatives and goat gland transplants for sexual potency seems incongruous, but it was a mixture that in fact summed up hillbilly radio programming during the twenties and thirties. During those same years Bradley Kincaid was singing his "Kentucky mountain ballads" to radio and concert audiences throughout the Midwest and Northeast. With radically different styles of presentation, the Carters and Kincaid circulated a body of songs that celebrated a fading way of life. In simultaneously celebrating the virtues of the rural church and fireside, these seminal performers tapped a powerful fascination within the American people for the southern mountains—the sense that the mountains *themselves* embodied an ethical heritage already abandoned elsewhere. As a nexus of decency in a society apparently tottering near the abyss of moral relativism, the Appalachians have served then and since as a symbolic "home" for many Americans, and a retreat for tradition-minded musicians, who have tried to recover a sense of "purity."[24]

The Carters *were* authentic mountaineers. Although they often sang about their Clinch Mountain home, they rarely consciously promoted themselves as mountain people. Bradley Kincaid, on the other hand, could claim nothing more than the Cumberland foothills as his birthplace, but throughout his career, described himself as the "Kentucky Mountain Boy" and constantly referred to his "mountain songs" and the superior values that they allegedly represented. The clarity of his smooth tenor voice and precise articulation made Kincaid one of the finest singers of country music's early history. His career might very well have flourished on its own merits, but it clearly profited from America's love affair with the southern mountains.

Kincaid was born in 1895 near Paint Lick, Kentucky, an area marked by rolling hills but geographically and culturally as close to the bluegrass as it is to the Appalachians.[25] When he began singing on WLS in Chicago in 1926, accompanied only by his own uncertain guitar chords, his song selections similarly revealed a repertoire of rural but geographically inexplicit affinities. Like most rural singers throughout the South, Kincaid was receptive to a broad variety of songs, and he showed little resistance to any kind of "old-time" music as long as it conveyed "decency" in tone and theme. He performed old British ballads like "Barbara Allen," minstrel songs like "Sweet Kitty Wells," Tin Pan Alley tunes like "The Fatal Wedding," cowboy songs like "Bury Me on the Prairie," and religious numbers like "Mary Wore Three Links of Chain." Of the 332 songs listed in the appendix to Loyal Jones's biography of Kincaid, fully two-thirds come from published or recorded sources.

Unlike most country singers, Kincaid was aware of the varying definitions that academicians gave to such material. During his student years at Berea Academy, a school that long before had assumed the mission of educating and uplifting mountain children, he had come under the tutelage of two beloved instructors, Gladys Jameson and John F. Smith, who had encouraged him to value the oldest ballads and folksongs. During his days as a member of the WLS Barn Dance he began hawking his big-selling songbooks, the contents of which he touted as "mountain ballads and old-time songs." The most crucial legacy from his days at Berea was the conviction that mountaineers represented the purest strain of American culture. They were, he argued, "a people in whose veins runs the pure strain of Anglo-Saxon blood."[26] Although such assertions of ethnic purity have often had sinister implications, Kincaid's pronouncement seemed more designed, as folklorist Archie Green has argued, to "give American folksong a blue ribbon pedigree."[27]

The homespun style of entertainment pioneered by Kincaid and the barn dances flourished in the thirties and forties through the powerful role of radio. With direct access to parlors all across America, radio provided the cheapest and most instantly available form of entertainment,

allowing hillbilly and cowboy performers to cultivate a sense of family
between themselves and their fans (like the Grand Ole Opry writ large).
Country entertainers did not have to conjure up visions of a Kentucky
mountain cabin or a little bunkhouse on the Texas plains in order to turn
the listener's mind toward home. Hillbilly music may have profited from
the preoccupation with the mythic common man that touched every realm
of art during the Depression years. Although the music was disseminated by commercial means and for commercial purposes, it seemed to be a
profoundly homemade music. Since hard-working farmers and workers
were expected to arise early and were more likely than city people to go
home for the noon meal, hillbilly programs typically ran in the wee hours
of the morning or at noon. Shows generally were informal and lightly
scripted, and sponsored by products—like flour, syrup, work clothes, or
laxatives—aimed at working-class households. Most performers came
from rural, working-class, and southern backgrounds, and could easily
relate to their listeners with a common frame of references, associations,
metaphors, and a vocabulary familiar to everyone.

These cultural affinities were reinforced—or sometimes even engi-
neered—by the marketing strategies of both promoters and entertainers.
While such tactics were both effective and essential to ensure an entertainer's commercial growth and survival, promotional schemes also bolstered
the idea of a homemade and homey genre of music. The oft-heard and
often-burlesqued admonition addressed to radio listeners, "keep them cards
and letters coming in," signaled more than a way to simply calculate the
size, location, demography, and loyalty of the audience; it also suggested
that the performers really *cared* about the fans' interests. The picture-songbooks hawked by the entertainers on the radio, or at personal appearances,
brought in some revenue. More important, the photographs of the musicians, their families, their homes, and maybe a favorite horse or dog, along
with the words to favorite songs, recitations, and poems, became tangible
reminders of the intimate relationship between performer and fan.

Since most performers played in small venues—schoolhouses, movie
theaters, churches, tents, or small auditoriums—they tended to be highly accessible to fans. Touring entertainers frequently sat down to a lunch
or supper hosted by adoring and hospitable fans. Fans, on the other hand,
kept scrapbooks or journals devoted to their favorite shows or musicians,
organized fan clubs, and in some instances, like Floy Case in Fort Worth,
became correspondents or columnists for country music magazines. As
a pioneering country music journalist and wife of local musician Bill Case,
Floy Case became fast friends with most of the country radio talent in

the Fort Worth area. When Ernest Tubb began his career in that city in the early forties, she befriended him and worked to promote his career nationally. These local experiences eventually led to her involvement with such magazines as *National Hillbilly News, The Mountain Broadcast and Prairie Recorder,* and *Country Song Roundup.*[28] Most fans found it entirely conceivable that their favorite entertainer might be a relative or a neighbor who had embarked on a music career, and the humor, stage patter, and music heard on the shows spoke often of common dreams and complaints or of widely shared childhood recollections. Country music has traveled an immense distance since the days when Cecil Gill, performing only with guitar on WBAP in Fort Worth, proudly proclaimed himself to be "a yodeling country boy from way down on the farm."[29] The illusion of intimacy and devotion lingers, though, in today's country music scene when an entertainer gushes from the stage, "We love y'all. You're the best audience in the world."

Asher Sizemore and Little Jimmie quintessentially embodied the interconnectedness between country performers and their fans. Sizemore was born the son of a timberman in Pike County, Kentucky, but in about 1931 was working as a bookkeeper for a large coal company when he began his radio career. When his son, Little Jimmie (born on January 29, 1928), joined the act in 1933, the little tyke already knew, it was said, about two hundred songs. The immense success enjoyed by Bradley Kincaid in the selling of his songbooks on WLS in Chicago undoubtedly inspired the Sizemores to assemble a similar collection of gospel songs taken from shape-note hymnals, vintage popular sentimental tunes such as "Put My Little Shoes Away," and at least a few old songs like "Barbara Allen" that indeed might have come from mountain sources. Through advertisements run on their popular broadcasts on WHAS in Louisville and WSM in Nashville, Sizemore began marketing in 1933 the first of their widely circulated songbooks, *Old Fashioned Hymns and Mountain Ballads.* By the time the 1934 edition appeared, the number of songs included had increased, but genuine Appalachian ballads had become even scarcer.

In successive prefaces to their songbooks, the Reverend Thomas B. Ashley summoned up a trio of explanations to explain the Sizemores' popularity by dwelling on the mystique of the mountains, with their message of mystery, sorrow, and loneliness. He also noted that Asher Sizemore's "intimate contact with nature" had planted within him "the seed of song,"[30] and in a second preface maintained that Asher and Little Jimmie "sing only 'the music of the heart,' which the majority of folk, these trying days, long for—Those whose pink and purple of life's sun-

set are meeting and mingling with the golden glow of Eternity's morning, as well as the sick and sorrowing, are affectionately remembered with
songs of mother, love, home and heaven."

Rev. Ashley's analysis hit even closer to the mark when he declared that
the duo's popularity owed more to Little Jimmie than to their songs:
"Surely he's a gift from God . . . the old and the young, the learned and
the unlearned, have been taught again, how to pray, as Little Jimmie bows
his head at the microphone, leading thousands of children in front of their
own radios, in chanting his good-night, prayer-song" (1934 ed.). Ashley
was echoing, of course, one of the central tenets of Victorian home-centered theology, the conviction that little children came from God and
could be agents of earthly redemption. Little Jimmie seemed to be the
living incarnation of characters that usually assumed fictional form, such
as Little Eva in *Uncle Tom's Cabin,* or the heroines of the sentimental
ballads, "The Blind Child" and "Little Bessie." More often than not, these
characters had to suffer death before they inspired salvation among the
living.[31] Little Jimmie, on the other hand, was very much alive, and he
seems to have intuitively understood that childlike innocence could lead
to more than uplifted morality. At the conclusion of their shows, he often asked his dad, "How much dough did we make today?"[32]

Probably influenced by the exposure gained by the Carter Family, family
groups in almost every conceivable kind of combination—husband and
wife, parents and children, sisters, brothers—could be heard in the 1930s
on radio stations all over the South and Midwest. Still another contingent of Carter family singers (no relation to the Virginia group) built an
extensive following in Texas during those years, and then saw their fame
extend across the South and into the Midwest during and after World
War II. With a mixture of old-fashioned love songs and religious pieces,
Kentucky-born Ernest "Dad" Carter and three of his children (Rose,
Anna, and Jim) became radio singers in Lubbock in 1935. What began
as a family night-time diversion from cotton picking blossomed, first, into
popular entertainment for their neighbors, and then into a radio spot on
a local station. When they relocated to Fort Worth the following year and
began a long career on WBAP, the family inherited the name of the cowboy band, the Chuck Wagon Gang, whom they replaced on the station.
Despite their western sobriquet, which later versions of the group have
never abandoned, the Carters sang only a handful of cowboy songs in
an impressive career that has lasted from 1935 to the present. The Chuck
Wagon Gang has always sung gospel hymns with an understated simplicity and close, dependable harmony that suggest the shape-note singing
schools and small-town radio stations where this style first originated.[33]

Although acts like the Chuck Wagon Gang preserved and popularized the style and ambience of home-style singing, performers on powerful WLS in Chicago probably did most to nationalize those influences during the years of the Great Depression. Before he left to organize his own radio barn dance at Renfro Valley in Kentucky in 1939, John Lair had worked mightily at WLS to shape and promote singers and repertoires that embodied the twin impulses of rusticity and domesticity. He organized and named a string band called the Cumberland Ridge Runners, hired a Kentuckian named Doc Hopkins who specialized in songs similar to those sung by Bradley Kincaid, and completely redirected the career of Linda Muenich, a former nightclub singer to whom he gave the name of Linda Parker. Armed with this new identity, clad in bonnet and gingham dress, and singing vintage sentimental tunes like "Mary of the Wild Moor" and "I'll Be All Smiles Tonight," Parker became one of the most popular acts on the Barn Dance. When the young singer died in August of 1936, her passing was commemorated with a specially composed song, "We Buried Her beneath the Willow."[34]

Whether promoted directly by Lair or by George Biggar, the National Barn Dance's program director, several acts on the show embodied the campaign to manufacture and promote domesticity as a virtuous commodity. Lily May Ledford, for example, came to the show in September, 1936, after winning a talent contest in Mt. Vernon, Kentucky. Making sure that no one would mistake this genuine country girl for a city faker, Lair clothed her in a long, old-fashioned print dress and high-topped black shoes, and encouraged her to wear her hair done up in a little knot on the back of her head. The talented fiddler, banjo player, and singer even became the centerpiece of a comic strip, "Lily May, the Mountain Gal," which was used as a running advertisement for a WLS show sponsored by Pinex Cough Syrup. Lily May soon became the nucleus of the first prominent all-woman country string band, the Coon Creek Girls (consisting also of sister Rosie Ledford, Violet Koehler, and Daisy Lange), which was organized and named by Lair in 1937. The young women joined the nostalgic entrepreneur in Cincinnati where the Renfro Valley Barn Dance came into existence. Their high-spirited performances of such songs as "How Many Biscuits Can You Eat?" "Little Birdie," and "Banjo Picking Girl" evoked the old-fashioned frolics of Appalachian America. Their music seemed to be so redolent of wholesome American roots that they were invited to perform at the White House in June, 1939, for President and Mrs. Roosevelt and the king and queen of England. Lily May said often that she ceased to be nervous in front of the august assemblage when she saw King George VI tapping his foot to the rhythm of the music.[35]

The singers who became the husband and wife team of Lulu Belle and Scotty (Myrtle Eleanor Cooper and Scott Wiseman) actually came to the Barn Dance separately, in 1932 and 1933 respectively, from North Carolina, but, through George Biggar's insistence, they formed a music and comedy act that blossomed into a lifelong relationship. (They married on December 13, 1934.) With Scotty playing the part of a bashful country boy (a role played earlier by Red Foley) and Lulu Belle projecting the air of a saucy but sweet country lass, the duo became one of the most popular radio acts in the Midwest. Scotty brought an impressive array of talents to the Barn Dance, not the least of which was a gift for songwriting; he wrote two of country music's premier sentimental love songs, "Remember Me (When the Candlelights Are Gleaming)" and "Have I Told You Lately That I Love You," and, along with one of his mentors, Bascom Lamar Lunsford, was the co-writer of "Mountain Dew."[36]

Despite his talents as a writer, singer, five-string banjoist, guitarist, comedian, and student of folk music, Scotty usually found himself relegated to the role of straight man, overshadowed by the almost artless humor of Lulu Belle. Without really trying, Lulu Belle easily upstaged her husband, and everyone else on the Barn Dance, with her affecting laugh, cute smile, and altogether endearing personality. Scotty was nevertheless central to the making of what folklorist William E. Lightfoot calls "the Lulu Belle and Scotty Myth"—"the image of a beautiful and blissful Appalachian way of life." In songs like "Homecoming Time in Happy Valley," where the values of place, family, church, and reunion were stressed, Scotty celebrated the vision of "idyllic rurality" that clung to both him and his wife and to the culture that their stage presence projected.[37]

Family entertainers as a whole conveyed an aura of wholesomeness and home-centered values, even though their music often revealed a world of fragile relationships. Beautiful, heartfelt vocal harmonies sometimes masked bitter personal dissensions. Sara and A. P. Carter's separation and divorce, Charlie and Bill Monroe's violent differences, and the Bailes Brothers' problems with alcoholism and sexual indiscretions eventually broke up their acts. While the Monroe Brothers and other "brother duets" of the 1930s and 1940s did not always maintain amicable personal relationships, they somehow conveyed to their audiences a sense of family intimacy that seemed to translate into musical harmony. Students of this musical genre, in fact, argue that the brother duets' vocal harmony blend stemmed from growing up in the same household, having similar vocal timbres, pronouncing words the same way, and having the ability to anticipate and react to each other's moves and moods.[38]

Beginning in the mid-thirties, brother acts began to proliferate, not because of some inherent capacity for vocal blending but principally because the success enjoyed by the Monroe Brothers and other duos such as the Delmore Brothers and Bolick Brothers (the Blue Sky Boys) encouraged imitation and a consequent search by record companies for similar acts. In a sense, the "brother duets" were heirs to the late nineteenth-century parlor tradition and to the domestic mood introduced to country music by the Carter Family and Bradley Kincaid. Despite the affinities for the blues exhibited by some of the brother duets and repertoires that could sometimes get downright rowdy and suggestive,[39] the parlor tradition always loomed large in their song choices and performance styles. The Monroe Brothers, for instance, always balanced their supercharged breakdowns and folksongs with religious pieces and Victorian love songs such as "What Is Home without Love?" and "You Give Me Your Love." Similarly, neither the Callahan Brothers nor the Delmore Brothers, both of whom showed a particular fondness for naughty blues tunes, exhibited any qualms about also performing such songs as "Take the News to Mother," "Little Poplar Log House on the Hill," or "When It's Time for the Whippoorwill to Sing."

Although the parlor impulse and repertoire date back to the early performances of such people as Vernon Dalhart, the Carter Family, and Bradley Kincaid, the brother duets were most strongly indebted to the music of two nonbrother acts: Mac and Bob and Karl and Harty, both of whom appeared for many years on Chicago's National Barn Dance. Lester McFarland and Robert Gardner (Mac and Bob), the first influential mandolin and guitar duo in early country music, met and began performing music together as students at the Kentucky School for the Blind. Echoing the formal, mannered performances of the mandolin, guitar, and banjo clubs of early twentieth-century America, McFarland's mandolin style evoked a gentle, nostalgic, and sometimes poignant image of a quiet, family-centered society far removed from the sometimes turbulent realities of modern America.[40]

Although gentility, rather than sadness, became the chief hallmark of Mac and Bob's vocal style, a strong tinge of melancholy colored many of their songs. When they sang about those "happy childhood days down on the farm" or about the breaking of vows that had been spoken "with fond affection on the day that we were wed," they called forth the memories and language of an era whose time had passed. Definitely southern in dialect and inflection, Mac and Bob nevertheless avoided the nasal, pinched style characteristic of many of their contemporary hillbilly groups. Instead, like Vernon Dalhart, Buell Kazee, the McCravy Brothers, and Sloan and Threadgill, their sound suggested formal voice training and the rather precise and trilled-r vibrato styles associated with vaudeville singers and barbershop quartets. Mac and Bob's repertoire was as thoroughly Victorian as their vocal style. Although it included some traditional folk material such as "Pretty Polly" and "The Knoxville Girl," and even a few tunes from the twenties such as "I'm Forever Blowing Bubbles," their material came more often from the body of religious and sentimental songs introduced in the late nineteenth century. Even when they sang a prison song like "Twenty One Years," their best-selling recording, the duet used the Bob Miller–composed item as a vehicle for telling a story of faithful, but unrewarded, love. Their popular songbook of 1931 reveals more than their song preferences; above all, it demonstrates the influence exerted on the choices made by at least a generation of country singers who came after them.[41]

Sentimental "prison" songs like "Twenty One Years" also figured strongly in the careers of the two duets who did most to preserve and popularize the parlor tradition in country music. Karl and Harty (Karl Davis and Harty Taylor) and the Blue Sky Boys (Bill and Earl Bolick) formed links in a chain of musical performance that extended through Mac and Bob back to the Carter Family and Bradley Kincaid and from there back to the late nineteenth century. Karl and Harty grew up in the area around Mt. Vernon, Kentucky, where they came under the influence of John Lair, who taught them elementary education at his Red Bud School. They later followed Lair to WLS in Chicago as the nucleus of the group called the Cumberland Ridge Runners. Emboldened by the precedent established by Mac and Bob, and vigorously promoted by Lair, who supplied them with old-time songs, Karl and Harty inaugurated a career of duet singing marked by Karl's mandolin playing and tenor harmony and by Harty's guitar rhythm and baritone lead. With a rather formal style reminiscent of Mac and Bob, the duet sang songs like "Nobody's Darling on Earth" and "The House Where We Were Wed" that were products of the sentimental repertoire of Victorian America, and a growing number of items written by Karl Davis, such as "I'm Just Here to Get My Baby out of Jail" and "Kentucky." Through the wide exposure won by their recordings and performances on powerful WLS, Karl and Harty introduced a large body of songs that moved into the repertoires of most of the duets who performed during the prewar years.[42]

"I'm Just Here to Get My Baby out of Jail" (whose story line was as implausible as "The Fatal Wedding" or any parlor ballad that came out of the nineties) also marked the 1936 recording debut of Bill and Earl Bolick, popularly known as the Blue Sky Boys. Written to the tune of an old mountain ballad called "Reuben's Train," the song recounted the story of a mother who "had searched both far and wide" for her wayward son and "at last" found him "here in jail." After listening to the mother's heartrending tale of woe, the warden brought "her loving darling to her side." Finally, in a conclusion that would have made Gussie Davis proud (he was the 1890s composer of "The Fatal Wedding" and "The Baggage Coach Ahead"), "she kissed her baby boy and then she died" (but smiling!).[43]

Although the song still exerts great fascination among country entertainers who have performed it in a wide variety of styles, the Blue Sky Boys' recording gained its particular strength from the effective synchronizing of voices with the mandolin and guitar, producing an overall mood of gentle plaintiveness that perfectly complemented the lyrics of their songs. As individual vocalists, the Bolick brothers were no better nor more distinctive than most of the country entertainers of their time, but together, they were superb. They achieved a vocal blend, a juxtaposition of tenor and baritone voices against a similar backdrop of mandolin and guitar playing, never surpassed in country music. Bill Bolick was obviously influenced by both the vocal and instrumental styles of Lester McFarland, but his tenor voice did not soar like that of McFarland, nor did it faintly resemble that of the barbershop or light opera performers of the turn of the century. Mac and Bob were no less "sincere," and perhaps no less "country," than the Bolick Brothers, but they were products of a different historical and social milieu and seem to have been more receptive to popular music currents. The Bolicks grew up in a strong religious environment dictated by respect for parents, family solidarity, and the necessity of striving for personal holiness. The precepts of home and the rather narrowly circumscribed context of Cawtaba County in North Carolina governed their personal morality and general outlook on life. Delivered in the Bolicks' deadpan and emotionally controlled style, simultaneously intense and repressed, their songs captured well the sense of poignancy and loss that lay at the core of a southern rural society caught in the vortex of uncontrollable change. When they returned from military service in 1945, the Blue Sky Boys found a society in the throes of radical transformation, and a music business less and less receptive to their gentle, acoustic sound.

Wartime prosperity and a burgeoning defense industry lured rural southerners by the millions to jobs in cities all over the United States.

Although the war was a socially revolutionary phenomenon that accelerated the modernization of the South, more immediately it created tensions that reaffirmed or revitalized the old longings for home and rural certitude. The move to town, and into industry, may have been made willingly, but those in transition could hardly escape a sense of disquietude as they left the old tradition-based verities of rural life behind and as the older hierarchical underpinnings of the family became weakened. The housing shortages of the war and early postwar years seemed to undermine the very idea of home and the sense of rootedness that accompanied it. Songs like "No Vacancy" and "No Children Allowed," alluding to problems often faced by both civilians and returning veterans, documented the instability and anxieties that attended the conversion to peacetime production.[44]

Some rural southerners of course adjusted easily and even enthusiastically to town life—age and gender were only a few of the factors that influenced their decisions and adaptability—but most could not easily abandon deeply ingrained habits and assumptions born in the country. Depression-spawned anxieties, fears of failure, a loosening of traditional values, and threats to white male dominance challenged those who otherwise were experiencing heightened expectations as they changed their economic and social base. A rising generation of women and young people were ready to exercise new options introduced by the accelerated consumerism and popular culture of modern city life. While country songs of the 1940s and early 1950s tried to reassure listeners that the old social patterns and relationships would remain intact in the city, lyrics increasingly warned of situations those relationships faced. Songs summoned up women's traditional place in the household either by recalling an older world where mother had been loving and nurturing, or by complaining about women who forsook their roles as mothers and homemakers. Eddy Arnold, the most popular country singer in the immediate postwar years, inaugurated his career with a cautionary tale directed toward women called "Mommy Please Stay Home with Me."[45] Presenting the story of a child who died at home while his mother was out getting tipsy at a party, the message could hardly be misunderstood. Songs like "Don't Blame the Children" and "Married by the Bible (Divorced by the Law)," along with a rather extensive list of country jeremiads such as "Dust on the Bible," "If We Forget God," and "They've Got the Church Outnumbered," even more explicitly signaled the dangers that parental neglect and societal irresponsibility might provoke. By the early fifties such "cheating songs" as "Slipping Around," "One Has My

Name, the Other Has My Heart," "Back Street Affair," and "The Wild Side of Life" were chronicling the decline or alteration of the traditional social schemes and presenting unflattering portraits of some women.[46]

Lyrics about honky-tonk mamas and unfaithful sweethearts only reinforced the affection felt for the "little mother of the hills" or "poor old mother at home" and the conviction that "the sweetest gift" that one could receive was "a mother's smile."[47] Mother songs in fact, flourished in the late forties and early fifties as never before in country music. They reaffirmed the system of values that defined the older rural society and virtually deified the woman who had been the moral cornerstone of that vanishing world. Of course, most of the mothers who appeared in these songs were generally old or dead and rural, with attributes strikingly different from those possessed by women with whom their sons now had to deal. Mothers described as hard-working, loyal, self-sacrificing, and long-suffering constituted no threat to male dominance.

Roy Acuff, the Smoky Mountain Boy from East Tennessee, emerged during the war as the chief repository of mother and home songs, and he influenced the style and repertoire of at least a generation of country singers.[48] With his artless but emotional singing, a repertoire of old-time country and gospel songs, and the acoustic string band accompaniment of his Smoky Mountain Boys, Acuff conveyed a sense of rootedness, security, and tradition in a society imperiled by fascism and racked by massive social dislocations. When he sang "If I Could Hear My Mother Pray Again," Acuff not only paid tribute to the traditional values that underlay country music and the society that had sustained it, he also voiced a plea for their preservation. Similarly, his radio theme, "Carry Me Back to the Mountains," paid homage to his birthplace in the Tennessee hills, while also taking his listeners back to country music's ultimate and mythic beginnings, the Appalachians.[49]

The nostalgic evocations of Mother and the old homeplace were sometimes little more than concessions to perceived public tastes, but they also grew out of deeply felt private experiences. To understand the wellsprings from which the best country songs emerge, one need go no farther than to the pages of Rick Bragg's best-selling autobiography, *All Over but the Shoutin'*, his reminiscences of growing up as a poor boy on a cotton farm in northeastern Alabama. His "first and best" memory, Bragg maintains, recalled his experience as a three-year-old boy, riding the back of his mother's heavy cotton sack as she pulled it down the cotton rows on someone else's farm. He says that "it is the memory of that woman, that boy and that vast field that continues to ride and ride in my mind, not only because it is a warm, safe and proud thing I carry with me like a talisman into cold, dangerous and spirit-numbing places, but because it so perfectly sums up the way she carried us, with such dignity."[50]

Many country music performers would have identified completely with Bragg's experience. "Give Mother My Crown," written and first recorded by the Bailes Brothers (but eventually introduced by Flatt and Scruggs to bluegrass music where it became a standard), was an intensely autobiographical statement whose sentiments nevertheless could be ardently embraced by many people who grew up in working-class homes. The song lovingly recalled the Bailes Brothers' mother who had kept their family together after the death of their father ("washing and ironing on a widow's small pay") and who had resisted suggestions that would have shattered the family circle ("adoption was offered, but mother said no"). The Bailes Brothers could only win the confidence of their listeners with such lyrics, or when they sometimes told their listeners over KWKH in Shreveport that "Mommy Bailes" was with them in the studio.[51]

The songs of Mother and home appeared most often in the performances of singers like the Bailes Brothers, Molly O'Day, Wilma Lee Cooper, and the Louvin Brothers, all of whom were clearly influenced by Acuff. But such songs also appeared frequently in the music of entertainers whose styles roamed far afield from that of the Smoky Mountain Boy. Aubrey "Moon" Mullican, for example, the rollicking barrelhouse pianist from Corrigan, Texas, whose songs have attained almost mythic status among modern rockabilly enthusiasts, sang "Sweeter Than the Flowers," a loving tribute to a deceased mother, with the same emotional conviction that he gave to "Cherokee Boogie." The Nova Scotia–born singer Hank Snow, who was famous for his hard-driving train songs, gave one of his most affecting performances in a song and recitation called "My Mother." Lefty Frizzell, the quintessential Texas honky-tonk singer of the early fifties, always included his "Mom and Dad's Waltz" in his programs of laments of lost love and paeans to beer-drinking. Hank Williams's mark in country music also came as a singer of honky-tonk songs, but he always readily admitted the influence of Roy Acuff, and he routinely included such songs as "I Just Told Mama Goodby," "I Dreamed about Mama Last Night" (based on an Edgar Guest poem), and "I Heard My Mother Praying for Me" (with Audrey Williams) in his stage performances—in part because he astutely understood the tastes of his audiences but also because he paid homage to the strong role played by his own mother in his life and career.[52]

The audiences who saw Williams, Acuff, and other country music per-

formers at the Ryman Auditorium in Nashville must have had feelings
comparable to those experienced when the Mother and home songs were
sung. Home of the Grand Ole Opry after 1943, the Ryman had become
virtually the "Mother Church" of country music, and a Mecca visited
each Saturday night by thousands of people from all over the United
States. The Opry's rise to prominence, marked by the attainment of network status on NBC in 1939, accompanied Acuff's emergence as a nationally known entertainer. The Opry had been broadcast from several
locations since its inception in 1925, but when it moved into the Ryman
(originally called the Union Gospel Tabernacle when steamboat captain
Tom Ryman built it in 1892 in honor of evangelist Sam Jones, who had
converted him), it seemed to have found its most symbolically appropriate home. The addition of a Confederate Gallery in 1897 only accentuated the Ryman's singular mystique by combining the imagery of the Lost
Cause with that of evangelical religion.[53]

The Opry, of course, was not the only "radio home" available to up-
rooted country music fans during the war and immediate postwar years.
Live radio programming (or in some cases the illusion conveyed by transcriptions) brought a touch of downhome to most of the large urban
centers. Disk jockeys like Smilin' Eddie Hill in Nashville, Tennessee Ernie
Ford in Los Angeles, Randy Blake in Chicago, Hal Horton and Fred
Edwards ("the Old Insomnia Kid") in Dallas, Rosalie Allen in New York,
and Biff Collie in Houston took very personal approaches to the music
that they played and sometimes affected hayseed demeanors. To avid
radio listeners, these dj's and others like them had become indispensable
members of the country music "family." At this stage of country music
history announcers still took requests from fans, made song dedications,
interviewed performers on their shows, and often acted as booking
agents. Presented under the rubric of "frolics," "hoedowns," "shindigs,"
"oprys," "hayrides," "haylofts," "roundups," "jamborees," "jubilees,"
and "barn dances," country music variety shows actually proliferated
for about ten years or so after 1946. Although transcribed programs increasingly became the norm in most of the nation's radio markets, a remarkably large number of live shows endured, playing usually during
hillbilly "prime-time": early morning, noon, or night. Shreveport's Louisiana Hayride, Knoxville's Mid-Day Merry-Go-Round, Atlanta's Cross-
road Follies, Dallas's Big D Jamboree, Fort Worth's Saturday Night Shin-
dig, Los Angeles's Town Hall Party and Dinner Bell Roundup, and
Bristol, Virginia's Farm and Fun Time (important as a central headquarters for such bluegrass acts as the Stanley Brothers and Flatt and Scruggs)

were only a few of the country variety radio shows that thrived in the immediate postwar period.[54]

Most of these programs preserved the aura of spontaneity, downhome simplicity, and warmth that had always epitomized hillbilly radio programming. But the most explicit emphasis on home came from John Lair through his founding of the Renfro Valley Barn Dance, the show that ultimately blurred the boundaries between fantasy and reality. The barn dance extended his influence as a shaper of homespun entertainers first exhibited in the 1930s in Chicago (discussed earlier). Renfro Valley appeared as a barn dance in 1943 when Lair, Cotton Foley, and Benny Ford launched a radio show that convened, first in Cincinnati and later at a specially constructed barn near Lair's old homeplace in Kentucky.[55] Of all the entrepreneurs who became associated with barn-dance radio programming, none made a more conscious commitment to maintaining tradition, nor to the equating of old-fashioned ways with virtue, than John Lair. Quintessentially American in his nostalgia, affection for rural life, and penchant for moneymaking, he literally created a real community out of the memories of his childhood and the fantasies of his adult years. Although Renfro Creek ran near the old family home not far from Mt. Vernon, in southeastern Kentucky, the place he named Renfro Valley did not come into being until Lair built his big barn there and began holding Saturday night hillbilly shows. Since that time Renfro Valley has existed both as a distinct place, clearly delineated by a post office, highway markers, and the collection of rustic buildings that Lair and his successors constructed there, and as a mythical rural Eden in the minds and imaginations of many radio listeners who listened enthralled as Lair spoke of a "land where time stands still."

Lair conceived the show in Chicago during the mid-thirties when he worked as an announcer and leader of the Cumberland Ridge Runners on the National Barn Dance. He was not a musician, but he had a profound and lifelong affection for old-time music, and his private collection of songbooks and songsheets was one of the largest in the country. Lair also collected and preserved pioneer artifacts and architecture. In creating the Renfro Valley show and the frontier village complex that surrounded it, he effectively and seamlessly combined his love for traditionalism with old-time music.

Typical of other hillbilly radio shows of the era, Lair's Saturday night barn dance featured a variety of musical styles interspersed with comedy acts such as Aunt Idy and Old Joe Clark. Lair's personal philosophy emerged most distinctively, however, in the "Sunday Morning Gathering" (also spelled Gethering), a still-extant thirty-minute show that was broadcast nationally on CBS for many years. If only for the short duration of the show, a trip to Renfro Valley meant, to many people, a return to childhood or to Henry Ford's Middle America—a land of plain, hardworking, decent, patriotic people where most problems could be solved at Mother's knee, in the country church, or in the local town hall. Unlike the Saturday night shows, the Gatherings were totally "serious" and unrelievedly rustic in tone. All of the featured songs tended to be religious or sentimental in nature, and an old parlor organ accompanied many of the hymns. Almost always the shows centered around such themes as the coming of spring, Abraham Lincoln, Stephen Foster, flowers, or that perennial inspirer of sentiment, Mother. Lair read an appropriate tribute to the featured subject, and various members of the cast sang songs that seemed relevant to the day's broadcast theme.[56]

While the Mother and home songs provide evidence of the persistence of traditional rural elements in country music, they cannot obscure the fact that urban culture was making inroads into the music and into the society that had sustained it. Such songs, in fact, probably gained immediate currency as a way of dealing with life's stressful transitions. In many ways, the emergence of Elvis Presley and his disciples after 1954 seemed not only a marked departure from the older stylistic traditions of country music but also a challenge to the system of morality that had supposedly underscored those styles. The rise of the rockabillies suggested that a parallel youth culture was taking shape apart from, and often in opposition to, the popular culture of adult Americans. The rockabillies, whose ranks included a few "wild young women,"[57] threatened the moral dominance of home and church, and the sensuality conveyed by Presley, along with the hedonistic lifestyles flouted by Jerry Lee Lewis and others, suggested that neither mama nor daddy could restrain postwar youths' rebellion.[58] But while the rockabillies did challenge the older generational, gender, and racial hierarchies of the South, their deviance from societal norms was more symbolic than real. They were, after all, country boys and girls who grew up in an evangelical Protestant culture and under mama's watchful care, and they lost few opportunities to demonstrate their attachments to the values of home and church. More than a few aging rockabillies eventually made public professions of their religious faith.[59]

Although a few religious zealots always maintained that the rockabilly phenomenon was hatched in either hell or Moscow,[60] the resistance to the music subsided rather quickly once it was learned that these young musicians were neither hellions nor revolutionaries. Elvis Presley, above all, exhibited a remarkable ability to move from the fringe to the mainstream. National television made him a household, and even respectable, figure, and his southern "downhome" traits—his politeness, his patriotism, his fundamentalist religious identification, and, yes, his closeness to his mother—presented him as a personality who actually embodied the best in working-class culture. Elvis, in short, seemed to embody that very culture of Mother and home that country music thought it represented.[61]

Although traditionalists resented the hedonism and sexuality of rockabilly music, they tended to be more upset by the musical compromise forged by Nashville's record producers to deal with the youthful music upheaval. The emerging country-pop styles, it seemed, were diluted betrayals of country music's rural traditions. Reacting against the threat posed to country music by rock-and-roll, the makers of these newly minted urbane sounds, which were defined initially by the absence of fiddles and steel guitars from country records, argued that they were nevertheless preserving the downhome ambience of country music.[62] But the country-pop sounds, in a sense, took country music further away from "down home" than rockabilly or any previous style had done. Chet Atkins, Owen Bradley, and other Nashville record producers did not simply tap the tastes of an urban middle-class audience that had become musically homeless because of the impact made by rock-and-roll. They also found an audience that was becoming geographically homeless as it ventured into the suburbs and into the economically mobile territory of postindustrial America.[63]

The birth in 1958 of the Country Music Association (CMA) coincided with the emerging dominance of country-pop styles. As a trades organization the CMA initiated a massive campaign to enhance the music's respectability and energize its commercial potentiality that included encouraging radio stations to adopt all-country radio formats. Country listeners were soon confronted with the paradox of an increasing number of self-styled country radio stations that played a declining selection of recordings—the Top 40—and came from the nation's leading record companies. By the early sixties, country music enjoyed unprecedented commercial success and popularity, but with a product that was increasingly narrow in style and focus and blurred in identity. These stylistic and economic changes paralleled Nashville's emergence as a leading music center, and were in fact largely responsible for it. Overall, the corporatization of country music, and the passion to make records that would cross over into other fields of music, warred against the ideal of a homemade music. Not only did one hear fewer and fewer songs about Mama, Daddy, and the old homeplace in the newly developing country-pop genre but the imagined family that bound performers and fans grew even more tenuous. The "stars of country music" became less accessible to fans, and writing "cards and letters" to either disk jockeys or performers ceased to matter in the increasingly impersonal, prepackaged world of modern country music. Fans and musicians confronted these trends with ambivalence, proud of the success and newfound respectability enjoyed by a music that had always longed for them but also somewhat saddened by the music's loss of soul. When the Grand Ole Opry moved its shows in 1974 from the Ryman Auditorium to the ultramodern facilities of the new theater at the Opryland theme park, many people were confirmed in their beliefs that country music as a whole had ventured far from its traditional home.[64]

The country-pop trends have been irreversible, but simultaneous efforts to restore or preserve downhome sounds have persevered just as unceasingly. Periodically, "tradition" becomes ascendant in modern country music. In retrospect, it now seems almost inevitable that the corporate and homogenizing impulses of the Nashville industry would breed discontent and internal rebellion. Nor does it now seem surprising that the conservative record producers of that city would find ways to co-opt musical dissent and turn it to commercial advantage. The experiments that emerged sometimes ranged far beyond the bounds of country music and ventured into the realm of rock, but they also periodically assumed the shape of neotraditionalism.[65] Despite the lure of crossover cash, country musicians could not easily shed the sounds of the rural South, nor could the music establishment easily anticipate or predict the tastes of those who bought the music. Many among America's emerging suburban generations sought a sense of place, rootedness, and tradition that seemed absent in the rapidly changing society that lay around them. Their hunger for "authenticity" provided much of the fuel that sparked the urban folk music revival of the late fifties and early sixties, as well as the periodic tributes to the old homeplace that have appeared in country music since the sixties. Working-class sounds and songs, and even paeans to the long-despised redneck, sometimes intrude into the country music repertoire where they find public receptivity.

The most compelling impulse for tradition within the country music community came from those performers whose music was described as "bluegrass." Bluegrass music may have been a haven or retreat for downhome tendencies from the time its founding father, Bill Monroe, joined the Grand Ole Opry in 1939 and declared his intention to perform country music "as she should be sung and played."[66] Laboring to create a style of music that would keep the acoustic string band relevant during an age of increasing electrification, Monroe and his musicians popularized a sound that eventually came to be known as bluegrass (a term inspired by Monroe's band, the Blue Grass Boys).[67] The genre's earliest musicians, such as Monroe, Lester Flatt, Earl Scruggs, Chubby Wise, Don Reno, and Jimmy Martin, seemed content to describe their performances as country music. But as country music became threatened by rock or pop dilution, bluegrass became a repository for styles, songs, and impulses that had declined or lost favor in the larger country field: songs of rural nostalgia, gospel music, the high-lonesome style of vocal harmony, the brother duet tradition, and acoustic musicianship.[68] Well before the folk revival began, bluegrass musicians were already reviving vintage country and folk material, and were singing songs about the old country church, the old homeplace, and mom and dad. The lyrics of bluegrass songs, however, did much more than carry people back to the beloved institutions of an older and simpler rural past. When young urban folk revivalists discovered the bluegrass style in the early sixties, they linked it to country music's oldest and most-enduring myth, that of Appalachian origins, and contributed to the common misperception that bluegrass was America's truest form of country music. One of them insisted later that "bluegrass was and is *the* music of the Appalachian people."[69]

The growing popularity of bluegrass music in the fifty or more years since it first appeared can be attributed to many factors, not the least of which has been the superb musicianship and the high-energy performances of its leading practitioners.[70] Others have been attracted by the imagery that surrounds the form and suffuses its lyrics—the vision of "the little cabin home on the hill." In Bill Monroe's original song of the same title,[71] the narrator had merely sought refuge in a cabin after the failure of a love affair. Bluegrass musicians and fans have since retreated to songs about little cabin homes and country churches as sanctuaries from the highly commercial world of country music, and perhaps as symbolic escapes from modern society as well. In the mythology that grew up around the style, bluegrass was often pictured as the product of a relatively pure rural society—a world of one-room schoolhouses and mountain prayer meetings. While those influences cannot be discounted, the genre's commercial evolution was far less pristine. Bluegrass entered public consciousness through radio, recording, and other urban-based media forms, and the bars and honky-tonks of Baltimore, Washington, D.C., Dayton, Ohio, Cincinnati, Detroit, and Boston, to name only a few of the cities where bluegrass was played, were no less seamy and sordid than those shared by their country cousins. A patron could get killed in Boston's Hillbilly Ranch, where the Lilly Brothers held sway for many years, just as easily as in any southern skull orchard.[72] Generations of bluegrass fans, though, have made invidious comparisons between their beloved form of music and the larger and presumably corrupted field of country music, clinging to the vision of a pristine rural musical style and to the cherished mythology of a similarly pure culture that spawned it.

Bluegrass music reached its largest audience and its most explicit identification with Appalachian tradition through the medium of the urban folk revival. After the revival got under way in 1958, galvanized by the Kingston Trio's hit recording of an old North Carolina murder ballad called "Tom Dooley," young converts began searching for more authentic specimens of style.[73] Whether experienced through the lonesome sounds of a ballad singer, the tangy zest of an old-time string band, or the dynamic verve of a bluegrass group, the folk revival tapped some of the most deep-seated longings in American culture. Most people embraced the revival without ideological pretense, viewing it as a good and easy way to have fun and make music. To some young people, it was their first introduction to the guitar or some other instrument and, like rock-and-roll, was a vehicle for rebelling against the nation's pop mainstream (many of these people later moved easily to the Beatles and later phases of the Rock Revolution). Many fans linked the music and its joyousness to the movements for social and political change in the sixties, while still others experienced the music as the soundtrack to their rebellion against the American consumer culture. Embracing folk music could be not only part of a countercultural search for roots but also an identification with Native Americans, Asian cultures, African Americans, Appalachian people, and others who were perceived to be close to nature and its restorative powers.[74]

No "document" was more important in introducing grassroots music to revival fans than the now widely heralded Folkways' *Anthology of American Folk Music*. Released in 1952 and consisting of eighty-four recordings taken from the huge collection of Harry Smith, the *Anthology* sampled virtually the entire span of rural American music (hillbilly, blues, gospel, Cajun, cowboy, jugband) that had been recorded between 1925 and 1935.[75] Containing early performances by such hillbilly musicians as Uncle Dave Macon, the Carter Family, Tom Ashley, Frank Hutchison, Kelly Harrell, Buell Kazee, and Charlie Poole, the *Anthology* was one of the first collections to link hillbilly and folk music, and was far more widely available to young people than any of the earlier record reviews and recordings that might have suggested such an association. With appetites originally whetted by the *Anthology*, some fans and musicians began looking for original 78 rpm recordings that contained similar music, and they began urging Columbia, RCA, Decca, and other recording companies to release such material from their vaults.

The inevitable consequences of the hunger for authentic old-time music was the search for pioneer musicians who might still be alive, and the attempts by young musicians to produce their own versions of vintage hillbilly sounds. The New Lost City Ramblers (Mike Seeger, John Cohen, and Tom Paley) were the first urban musicians to re-create the sounds of hillbilly string bands and singers.[76] Through the efforts of musicians and collectors like Seeger, many of the old-timers, such as Dock Boggs, Tom Ashley, and Buell Kazee, were rediscovered and given new chances to perform for audiences at festivals and on college campuses. As a by-product of their search for the still-living hillbilly musician Clarence "Tom" Ashley (whose recording of "The Coo Coo Bird" had intrigued many listeners to the *Anthology*), collectors Eugene Earle and Ralph Rinzler journeyed in 1960 to Union Grove, North Carolina, where they also "discovered" the brilliant guitarist and singer, Arthel "Doc" Watson, who played occasionally with Ashley and other local musicians, but who made his living playing electric guitar with a rockabilly/swing band called the Country Gentlemen (not to be confused with the bluegrass band of the same name).[77]

Watson's virtuosity as a singer, guitarist, banjoist, and harmonica player fascinated his new audiences in New York City and on the folk festival circuit, but he was initially valued as much for the traditional symbolism associated with his Appalachian origins as for his musical skills. A blind man from Deep Gap, North Carolina, who was heir to an enormous reservoir of traditional songs learned from his family and neighbors, Watson seemed to fulfill the most romantic dreams of those who thought of Appalachia as the central source of American folk music. Then and since he has shown a remarkable receptivity to songs as widely varying as George Gershwin's "Summertime" and the fifties pop hit "Little Things Mean a Lot," but he also knew or was willing to learn old-time ballads and gospel songs. Immediately after his discovery by Ralph Rinzler in 1960, Watson became a fixture at folk festivals and on the Vanguard recording label, where he fulfilled the expectations of those who wanted to hear music that seemed both traditional and Appalachian.[78]

The folk revival had both immediate and long-lasting effects on country music. Bluegrass musicians found work at folk festivals and on college campuses, performing songs that they believed would be liked or accepted by folk audiences. A few country and western musicians such as Johnny Cash also found receptive audiences on the folk circuit. Songs from the revival moved into the repertoires of such country singers as George Hamilton IV, Bobby Bare, and Waylon Jennings, and country songwriters wrote folklike songs that were generally described as "saga songs" (e.g., Jimmie Driftwood, "Battle of New Orleans"). Inspired by the New Lost City Ramblers, some young musicians organized string bands (Highwoods String Band, Red Clay Ramblers, Hot Mud Family, and others) that revived the songs and styles of the hillbilly fiddle bands of the twenties and thirties. Old-time music was revitalized in certain areas of the South, largely through the popularity of festivals or fiddle contests like those in Galax, Virginia, or Union Grove, North Carolina. The area around Chapel Hill and Durham, North Carolina, has continued to be a thriving environment for old-time string bands. Older musicians like the fiddler and banjoist Tommy Jarrell were rediscovered, recorded, and newly presented at festivals. They became mentors to younger southern musicians, such as the brilliant guitarist Norman Blake, who could observe and play alongside the old-timers at festivals or at workshops like the one at Augusta, West Virginia, where instruction in traditional dancing, vocal harmony, and instrumental patterns was available. Pilgrimages to places like Mountain View, Arkansas, where Jimmie Driftwood provided inspiration, or to the Carter Fold in Hilton, Virginia—where A. P. Carter's children, Janette and Joe, sponsored weekly old-time music sessions near the site of their father's country store—permitted young musicians to learn in "authentic" contexts. The folk revival, in short, was a musical way of taking both American culture and country music back home, a way of returning to the roots.[79]

The revival's influence endured, but most of the people who now perform folk or folklike material do so on the periphery of mainstream country music—in jam sessions or other local venues, in bluegrass, or, like Nanci Griffith, Iris DeMent, or Jimmie Dale Gilmore, as singer-songwriters. The efforts to maintain a downhome or homemade flavor similarly take place in venues such as the Carter Fold in Hilton, Virginia, Grandpa Jones' Dinner Club in Mountain View, Arkansas, the Piney Woods Opry in Abita Springs, Louisiana, or at bluegrass and old-time music festivals. In these arenas electric instruments are shunned and older songs and styles predominate in homey atmospheres marked by folksy patter and humor and home-cooked meals.

The folk revival may have contributed to a greater appreciation of old-time music among many fans and musicians, but it could not retard mainstream country music's growing corporatism and suburbanization, nor could it prevent the steady erosion of its downhome qualities. Resistance to growing impersonality and corporate control, though, has not been absent among either performers or fans who have made periodic attempts to preserve a semblance of community spirit, informality, and spontaneity. The musicians who gathered in Austin, Texas, and Bakersfield, California, during the late sixties and early seventies did not necessarily evoke or promote the spirit of home, but they did foster a sense of community and self-direction that seemed absent in corporate Nashville. Journalist Townsend Miller never tired of promoting the Austin redneckrock fusion musical scene, and spoke warmly of the "colony of musicians" who seemed to gather nourishment from the surrounding Texas hill country.[80] Leading country entertainers who emerged during those years had no trouble in evoking downhome memories. No one called them "neo-traditionalists" at the time, even though they did much to counter the country-pop tendencies of that era, but singers like Loretta Lynn, Buck Owens, George Jones, Merle Haggard, Gene Watson, Dolly Parton, Vern Gosdin, Willie Nelson, and Tom T. Hall constituted virtually the last generation of performers who really had direct working-class roots or who could recall rural experiences. They paid tribute to those origins with a remarkable body of songs that included Nelson's "Family Bible," Lynn's "Coal Miner's Daughter," Parton's "Coat of Many Colors," Doug Kershaw's "Louisiana Man," and Haggard's "Hungry Eyes," usually known as "Mama's Hungry Eyes."[81]

In contrast, country music's enormous commercial growth since the sixties has been fueled by a constantly changing and expanding audience that has only the most tenuous links to either rural or working-class origins. The urban cowboy phenomenon of the early eighties—sparked by the popular John Travolta movie—attracted legions of new fans,[82] but their numbers paled in comparison with those who came to the music in the nineties in the wake of the sensation created by Garth Brooks, Clint Black, Reba McEntire, Vince Gill, and other young entertainers. Although increasingly regionless, classless, and suburban in residence and values, these young, affluent, and mobile listeners wanted a music that seemed to embody the qualities in which contemporary America seemed deficient: community, family values, and down-to-earth simplicity. Like many of his contemporaries, Garth Brooks wore cowboy jeans, hat, and boots, but neither he nor his music bore any embarrassing hayseed trappings. Eschewing haybales, overalls, and gingham dresses, the new country music spoke in increasingly suburban tones and cadences. One of the most articulate of the new fans, Bruce Feiler, a young southerner who had been won over to the music through the performances of Garth Brooks, voiced the feelings of many listeners when he said that country music now "seemed to lack the dusty old icons that made the Opry so offensive to Southerners like me, especially those of us who worked on computers, watched 'Saturday Night Live,' and tried our hands at using chopsticks."[83]

As down home receded from the memories of both fans and musicians, country music nevertheless struggled to preserve its defining signature blend of personal warmth and domesticity. Curtis Ellison came closest to capturing that spirit after traveling over five thousand miles between November, 1991, and August, 1993, observing and participating in what he calls the "country music culture" at the Grand Ole Opry and small performing arenas, and at festivals, theme parks, museums, historic sites, and tourist centers like Branson, Missouri. He concluded that "in everyday life, participants in country music culture behave something like a vast extended family at an endless church supper in a rural American small town."[84]

Ellison described two enduring "conventions" in country music culture, the impulse to pay "active homage to a living past" and the efforts made by fans to participate directly and interactively in the music's ceremonies and rituals.[85] Membership in the Grand Ole Opry is no longer indispensable to a performer's career, but such superstars as Garth Brooks and Vince Gill still gladly accept affiliation with this hallowed institution and speak reverently of the pioneers who preceded them. Induction into the show's cast remains a ritual that permits older stars to "lay hands" on young and deserving entertainers, and young country singers do not simply revere the "mother church of country music," they also generally make a point of showing respect to veteran country performers (even if most of the young stars have grown up listening to the Beatles, the Eagles, Billy Joel, or Bruce Springsteen). Articles on them are usually peppered with references to Hank, George, or Merle, or to reminders that their daddies listened to such singers when the young stars were growing up.[86]

While paying their respects to a living past, musicians and fans also labor to preserve a sense of family and connectedness to one another. Entertainers generally strive to present folksy personalities, and convey from the stage an air of sincerity that sometimes evokes parody: "We love each and every one of you."[87] Since the late sixties, country music's most-publicized display of intimacy has been pursued in the most public of settings, the weeklong extravaganza known as Fan Fair held each June in Nashville. Originally conceived by Loretta Johnson, the longtime president of Loretta Lynn's fan club and the coordinator of the International Fan Club Organization (IFCO), Fan Fair epitomizes the attempt to humanize an expanding country music industry that was becoming increasingly distant and impersonal.

Loretta Johnson's first convention in 1967 met at the Hermitage Hotel in Nashville, and was attended by 250 fans. In 1972 it began to receive the full support of the Country Music Association and the Grand Ole Opry, and after a series of moves to larger venues, it eventually settled in at the Tennessee State Fair Grounds where upwards of twenty thousand fans convene annually to commune with their favorite performers. The affair hardly re-creates the conviviality of a county fair or the warmth of an all-day-singing with dinner-on-the-grounds, but it does bring fans in close proximity to performers, while generating millions of dollars for the Music City's economy.[88] Fans visit their favorite stars' booths, literally stand in line for hours to get an autograph or to receive a kiss or embrace, purchase CD's and other mementos, and listen to lots of good music. Noting the co-dependency that fans and entertainers display for each other—"Think of Faulkner's Snopeses hanging out at the food court, eating fried chicken, and simultaneously cozying up to and smothering one another"—Bruce Feiler referred to Fan Fair as "the grand ole orgy of country music." Nevertheless, this hip journalist recognized the "remarkably enduring, even warmhearted tradition," that lay "behind this veneer of country excess."[89]

Participation in Fan Fair obviously promises commercial advantage to those country performers who choose to spend some time there, but it also offers an opportunity to renew their familial bonds with fans and to assure them that they have not strayed from their roots. By 1992, no singer in the world had achieved greater fame or commercial acclaim than Garth Brooks, and none had less reason to involve himself in the nitty-gritty search for popular approval. But at Fan Fair that year he signed autographs for nine hours a day for people who had lined up in the fair grounds' parking lot since the early morning hours.[90] Brooks had ascended to the top rungs of American popular entertainment, in part, through an exceptionally adroit business sense and skillful appropriation of theatrical rock stage mannerisms. But at Fan Fair he also demonstrated an acute understanding of the rituals of country music, the need to reaffirm his relationship with regular folks and to show them that, beneath the trappings of wealth and fame, he was still one of them.

Grand Ole Opry Audience, Dixie Tabernacle, 1936. The working-class composition of country music's constituency is evident in this earliest known photograph of a Grand Ole Opry audience. Courtesy of Douglas B. Green.

Sincere Best Wishes Lulu Belle & Scotty

Lulu Belle and Scotty, circa 1930s. Sometimes described as "the Sweethearts of Country Music," Myrtle Eleanor and Scott Wiseman worked to convey the image of wholesome, downhome America. Courtesy of Debby Gray.

John Lair and protégés (1930s). From top to bottom Linda Parker, Harty Taylor, Karl Davis, Lair, Red Foley, Slim Miller. Lair—a songwriter, promoter, and entrepreneur—sought to keep country music moored to its folksy origins. He is pictured here with some of the performers who projected his vision of old-fashioned rural values and simplicity. Courtesy of Debby Gray.

W. Lee O'Daniel campaigning in San Antonio, Texas, with his Hill-Billy Flour Band, during his first successful race for the governorship in 1938. Left to right: Mike O'Daniel, W. Lee O'Daniel, and Pat O'Daniel. Other band members are unidentified. Courtesy of the San Antonio Light Collection, University of Texas Institute of Texan Cultures (San Antonio).

Roy Acuff and His Smoky Mountain Boys and Girls (1940s). From right to left: Lonnie "Pap" Wilson, Acuff, Rachel Veach, Jimmie Riddle, Beecher "Bashful Brother Oswald" Kirby. Others unknown. Acuff's music combined traditional and modern elements, but as this staged photo indicates, he tried hard to preserve the image of an entertainer who made home-centered "mountain" music. Courtesy of Douglas B. Green.

Rod Brasfield and Minnie Pearl hamming it up at the Grand Ole Opry (1940s). Ray Price is pictured to the right of Minnie Pearl. Courtesy of the photographer, Les Leverett.

Bascom Lamar Lunsford dancing in his living room, Leicester, North Carolina. Lunsford popularized team clog dancing at his folk festival in Asheville, North Carolina (first held in 1928). From the Southern Appalachian Archives, Berea College, Berea, Kentucky. Courtesy of Loyal Jones.

Uncle Ed Mansfield and unidentified dancer at a dance in Bandera, Texas (1946). Bandera's numerous dance halls, cafés, and taverns showcase western-style dancing. Uncle Ed claimed to have originated the popular Texas hill country dance, "Put Your Little Foot." Courtesy of the San Antonio Light Collection, University of Texas Institute of Texan Cultures (San Antonio).

4

"With My Friends at the Old Country Church"

The "southernness" of country music nowhere more dramatically asserts itself than in the powerful role exerted upon its style and content by Protestant evangelical religion. Viewers who saw the syndicated television shows of Lester Flatt and Earl Scruggs in the 1950s and early 1960s can scarcely forget the "hymn time" segment when the duo and their Foggy Mountain Boys piously removed their hats before singing a gospel number. Cynics who saw those shows, or who may have witnessed a conservatively dressed Willie Nelson singing "the gospel song of the day" on Ernest Tubb's television show, may have laughed and thought they were viewing hypocrisy or, at best, quaint simplicity. What they really saw were rituals that paid homage to the strength of religion in southern culture. Flatt and Scruggs and Willie Nelson knew their audiences well, and they were well aware of the tradition that makes some sort of religious expression virtually mandatory for country musicians.

The country musician who has not included religious material in his or her performing repertoire, or who has not recorded a collection of gospel songs, is rare indeed.[1] One even finds an abundance of all-instrumental versions of religious songs on LPs and CDs—such as Billy Grammer's guitar performances and Floyd Cramer's piano renditions of standard hymns—an implication that even the melodies of such songs carry sacred significance simply by conjuring up an intimately shared cultural context. The list of country musicians, past and present, who have made public professions of their religious faith or conversions, or who have forsaken the country music business to become preachers, is as lengthy as those who have been arrested for drunkenness, drug possession, or disorderly conduct (and sometimes they are the same people). One need not doubt the authenticity of such conversions or professions of faith, or the assurance that they genuinely reflect the evangelical Protestant culture into which most of the performers were born.

The great North Carolina sociologist Howard Odum, who understood the southern plain folk better than most scholars, in 1930 noted the role played by religious music in evoking deep-seated and powerful emotions concerning home, family, community, and, occasionally, God. "Music and song," he said, "not only brought forth the sweep of social heritage and individual memories but touched deep the chords of old moralities and loyalties."[2] Odum found an abundance of southerners who had strayed far away from the old hometown church and its theology but who nevertheless could still sing, with accuracy and affection, scores of the gospel songs learned during childhood. He believed that singing these hymns brought one's "thoughts and emotions back to the old scenes and the old influences." Forty-two years later sociologist William C. Martin spoke in similar but somewhat ironic terms, when he noted that "even at meetings of learned academic societies it is not terribly difficult to find three or four good old boys who know all the words to "Gathering Flowers for the Master's Bouquet." He concluded with words that Odum would have understood well: "For all these, gospel music offers a chance to cling to their origins, or at least to give them an affectionate stroke."[3] If Odum were alive today, he would find that the language and symbolism of evangelical Protestantism, most strongly displayed in music, still permeate the culture of the working- and middle-class South, leaving their imprints upon sinners and saints alike and creating a common vocabulary and frame of reference that link many southerners to each other and to their region.

While gospel songs often evoke nothing more than memories of home and family, it is clear that they also affirm religious reality to many people and embody deeply held theological beliefs, or moral injunctions. And rare is the country entertainer whose lifestyle and philosophy have not demonstrated the influence of Protestant Christianity. The religion-shaped approach to life in fact permeates the entire country music repertoire and bears chief responsibility for the strong slices of fatalism, moralism, guilt, and self-pity unselfconsciously expressed in many country songs. The overwhelming bulk of the entertainers have always come from that region of the United States often described none too charitably as the Bible Belt—a rural South supposedly enthralled by a blind obedience to Holy Scripture or to the ministers who profess to be the infallible interpreters of the sacred writ.[4] The description is of course exaggerated, for southerners have not been immune to the liberalizing and secularizing influences that have swept over American Christendom in the last one hundred years. Nevertheless, the church continues to play an active role in the lives of southerners not quite equalled in other regions of the nation. Perhaps most crucial to an understanding of the general tone of country music, religion exerts its sway over even the most hardened non-churchgoer south of the Mason-Dixon line.[5]

The rural southerner is indoctrinated with the tenets of evangelical Protestantism from the time of birth, both in and outside the confines of an established church—from street evangelists, small-town summer revivals, and the emotional harangues of radio and television evangelists—and he or she carries the conviction well summed up in the words of a gospel song that avers that "my record started from the cradle; mother she held me close to her breast. I know she prayed for God to save me."[6] Even the most rebellious southern youngster, or the one who would roam far from the restricting influences of the family fireside, cannot forget the moral injunctions of childhood nor the sense of guilt that accompanies the violation of these precepts. Few southern country boys or girls could move easily in a life of sin while carrying the earnest plea of the departed mother who had entreated with them to "hold fast to the right, wherever your footsteps may roam. Forsake not the way of salvation . . . that you learned from your mother at home."[7]

When country music emerged as a commercial entity in the 1920s, the fires of religious enthusiasm, first ignited in the popular revivals of the late eighteenth and early nineteenth centuries, had been banked (with sporadic exceptions), and the rabid sectarianism of the early southern frontier had diminished. Nevertheless, one could still hear echoes of those distant debates in arguments around courthouse squares, and everywhere one saw or heard examples of the pervasiveness of religion in southern life. While the Scopes "Monkey" Trial of 1925 dramatically illustrated how politics and fundamentalist religion could become intertwined, more mundane examples of religiosity could be found in the crudely lettered roadside injunctions to "prepare to meet thy God" or in the wondrous if not bizarre array of churches, bearing such names as the Church of God with Signs Following After, that flourished in every southern hamlet. Above all, one could hear the songs that simultaneously reaffirmed the pervasiveness of religion and preserved traces of those doctrines that once divided the very churches that collectively converted the South to evangelical orthodoxy.

Evangelical Protestantism bequeathed to early hillbilly musicians a panorama of values and assumptions rooted in the political, social, and religious realities of the previous century, and a large body of songs and singing styles: the camp meeting spirituals of the early nineteenth century, the composed gospel hymns that flowed from the city revivals of the Gilded Age, and the songs, methods of harmony, and musical notation that emerged from the shape-note singing schools, conventions, and publishing houses. Although the commercial history of southern religious music dates back to the early nineteenth century, technological developments in the 1920s permitted a new phase of commercialization that made the gospel music field a big business. First recorded and broadcast during that same decade, the southern gospel quartets and country music enjoyed a symbiotic relationship.[8]

The white gospel quartets emerged out of the southern shape-note publishing tradition. Since 1800, when William Little and William Smith's tunebook, *The Easy Instructor,* introduced their simplified system of musical notation, singing-school teachers and publishers had roamed far and wide through the South, popularizing a method in which the pitch of musical notes was indicated by their shapes independently of the lines and spaces of the staff.[9] James D. Vaughan, a devout member of the Church of the Nazarene and community leader in Lawrenceburg, Tennessee, built one of the South's most important music publishing houses in that city. He was the first publisher to send out quartets to popularize and sell his books, and their recordings were the first of any kind that used the word "southern" to describe their musical contents. Vaughan's quartets also made broadcasts from his station in Lawrenceburg (WOAN), the first commercial radio station in the South and a central force in the promotion of his music business.[10]

Vaughan's ventures spawned competition, and such organizations as the Trio Publishing Company in Waco, Texas, the Hartford Company in Hartford, Arkansas, and the Stamps-Baxter Company in Dallas, all sent quartets on the road to sing in churches, singing conventions, or at singing schools sponsored by the publishing houses. Although Vaughan quartets were the first of these groups to appear on recordings, the Stamps All-Star Quartet in 1928 made the most significant departure from the gospel tradition when it recorded a song called "Give the World a Smile Each Day." Featuring a popular, syncopated style of call-and-response known as "after beat" (marked by a bass vocal lead that was answered by the other three voices), the song became the theme of every quartet that bore the Stamps name through World War II, and its rhythms were widely copied by rival quartets. The original Stamps Quartet also contributed to the abandonment of a capella performance by other quartets, because its jazz-influenced pianist, Dwight Brock, proved to be so popular with his colorful and innovative style and outgoing personality. Although all gospel quartets claimed to be motivated by a sense of spiritual mission, most of them moved swiftly to sever their relationships to the publishing houses that had once employed them, and all of them were quick to incorporate secular music techniques into their performances."[11]

The influence of gospel music was especially pervasive in the early years of commercial country music. Gospel songs were such an integral part of the total fabric of familiar music available to musicians that they were routinely sung as reminders of home and family and as emblems of the moral universe that country music represented. The famous Carter Family exhibited an intimate familiarity with songs from the paperback hymnals, setting the pattern among country groups of mixing hymns, morally didactic material, and secular music. Their first recorded release, in fact—"Poor Orphan Child" (originally entitled "Saviour, Lead Them")—illustrates well the difficulty of categorizing the material often heard in early country and gospel performances. Written as a tribute to "the Orphans Homes of Texas,"[12] the song was basically a compassionate and sentimentalized plea for orphan children, and only incidentally an endorsement of the benevolent and fatherly role of God. A. P.'s name appears on that song and on dozens of other hymns, such as "Keep on the Sunny Side," "Gospel Ship," "Diamonds in the Rough," and "There's No Depression in Heaven," which had actually begun their lives as the creations of shape-note publishers. In singing such songs, the Carters of course had no evangelistic intent but instead were falling back on the cherished souvenirs of a past shared with their listeners. One of the Carter Family's great contributions was to bring widely scattered songs together in one musical package and make them easily accessible to future generations of musicians and fans. Carter Family songs helped fuel the repertoires of such later country singers as Woody Guthrie, the Blue Sky Boys, Roy Acuff, Mac Wiseman, Bill Clifton, Flatt and Scruggs, and a wide array of urban musicians, such as Joan Baez and the Nitty Gritty Dirt Band, who discovered the family during the folk revival of the early sixties.[13]

As we have seen, the Carter Family's great and influential contemporary, Jimmie Rodgers, recorded only one religious song, "The Wonderful City," a duet performed with Sara Carter. Rodgers, however, sang other songs, such as "Mother the Queen of My Heart," "The Drunkard's Child," and "Hobo's Meditation," that preached moral judgments or

pleaded for the intervention of God. Uncle Dave Macon, who, like Jimmie Rodgers, loved and often sang about good corn whiskey, nevertheless frequently included religious songs in his spirited performances, or
more often made spoken comments that referred to the Bible or drew
didactic lessons. In "The Bible's True" (about evolution) he prefaced the
song with a banjo rendition of the gospel classic, "Will There Be Any Stars
in My Crown," and then made a statement affirming his belief in the
Scriptures as written: "Now I don't believe in evolution or revolution,
but when it comes to the good old Bible, from Genesis to Revelations,
I'm right there."[14] Uncle Dave's contemporary, Blind Alfred Reed, had a
brief recording career that included only a handful of explicitly religious
songs, but most of his material was suffused with a moral didacticism
that clearly flowed from religious sources.[15] Songs like "Why Do You Bob
Your Hair, Girls?" "How Can A Poor Man Stand Such Times and Live?"
and "There'll Be No Distinction There," which will be discussed more
fully in the chapter on politics, breathed with anxieties felt by fundamentalist southerners as they viewed the chaotic social changes of the 1920s.

As some of Reed's lyrics indicate, religious comment in early country
music was not all unquestioning. Songs sometimes censured religious
leaders and church members, or protested against hypocrisy (as in "The
Dollar and the Devil"),[16] although few comments were as extreme as
Reed's "most all preachers preach for gold and not for souls."[17] Early
hillbilly music preserved much of the suspicion of materialism explicit
in traditional southern Protestantism, as well as the distrust of overly
formal or luxurious churches (as in "The Model Church"). So-called
jakeleg preachers and other corrupt or hypocritical church people appear
frequently in such country songs as "The Preacher Got Drunk and Laid
His Bible Down," "Let the Church Roll On," "S-A-V-E-D," and "Deep
Ellem Blues."

A few singers did employ music as a form of evangelism, or otherwise
performed religious music almost exclusively. Andrew "Blind Andy"
Jenkins, for example, was a news vendor and street evangelist in Atlanta who won a larger constituency through broadcasts on WSB that began on August 14, 1922. In more than eight hundred songs that he
penned, Jenkins made no real distinctions between his "secular" ballads
and his gospel compositions. His most famous songs, for example, "The
Death of Floyd Collins" and "Billy the Kid" (both written on request),
were also exercises in moral didacticism that warned young listeners to
follow their parents' advice or to avoid a life that might lead to crime. In
1925, Jenkins and his two stepdaughters became probably the first of

several families who made commercial gospel recordings. They sang some of Jenkins's own compositions, such as "God Put a Rainbow in the Clouds" (which became an oft-performed number in both gospel and country music), and old standards taken from the paperback hymnals. The Jenkins Family was apparently the first group to record "If I Could Hear My Mother Pray Again."[18]

While a fairly substantial number of people performed country-style gospel music, including the Deal Family from Burke County, North Carolina (probably the first group to perform A. G. Sebren's after-beat classic, "Rocking on the Waves"), none exerted more influence than a couple of preachers from the area around Corbin, Kentucky—Alfred Karnes and Ernest Phipps. Both recorded only a handful of songs (Karnes did eight outstanding numbers, and Phipps appeared on twelve), but they made contributions that were unique and impressive. A Baptist minister, Karnes sometimes pastored as many as four churches at one time in eastern Kentucky, and his powerful singing and mastery of the banjo, fiddle, six-string guitar, and double-necked Gibson harp-guitar made him a popular entertainer in that area of the state. Karnes's style and repertoire demonstrated the crosscurrents that swept across and united southern secular and religious music. He recorded one "secular" number entitled "The Days of My Childhood Play," a nostalgic evocation of a simpler, carefree existence that aptly summed up the feelings of many Americans, north and south, during the changing twenties. In his dynamic guitar playing and full-throated swinging vocal style, Karnes demonstrated his debt to ragtime and related fields of music. When he performed the old hymn "I Am Bound for the Promised Land" to an eight-to-the-bar rhythm, he showed just how far the tendency to borrow from the devil could be taken. This and memorable versions of such songs as "Called to Foreign Fields" and "We Shall All Be Reunited" made Karnes's music almost unmatched among early country musicians.[19]

Ernest Phipps's music also provides suggestions of the strong interrelationship between country gospel music and older secular styles, while also giving us about the only auditory glimpse of early Pentecostal singing that we will ever have. Phipps, a preacher for the Free Holiness Pentecostal Church, made recordings at two sessions in Bristol, Tennessee, in 1927 and 1928. Like Pentecostal singers everywhere, Phipps exhibited receptivity to string band accompaniment and was backed up by various combinations of fiddle, mandolin, guitar, banjo, and piano. He also brought several members of his congregation to the second session and, on such songs as "If the Light Has Gone Out in Your Soul" and "Shine on Me," Phipps and His Holiness Singers captured the excitement generated in Holiness and Pentecostal churches when spirited congregational singing was accompanied by string band music and the syncopated beat of handclapping and tambourines.[20]

Both Pentecostalism and hillbilly music radio programming thrived in the 1930s, as economically deprived Americans sought relief, diversion, escape, and spiritual consolation. Hillbilly entertainers became entrenched on radio stations everywhere, and learned repeatedly that their listeners yearned to hear the musical reassurances of the old-time gospel.[21] Religious music played a crucial role in the careers of several country entertainers. Roy Acuff, for example, began his legendary career in 1936 with the recording of a rather mystical religious song called "The Great Speckled Bird," while two of the premier brother duets of the era, the Monroe Brothers and the Blue Sky Boys, became closely identified with two songs, "What Would You Give in Exchange for Your Soul?" and "Sunny Side of Life" respectively, that came directly from the gospel quartet tradition.[22] Such acts as the Blue Sky Boys, the Monroe Brothers, the Delmore Brothers, Mainer's Mountaineers, and the Dixon Brothers routinely included religious material among the diverse fare that comprised the hillbilly repertoire during those years.

The religious music circulating in the thirties, of course, came from a wide array of sources. A multitude of published gospel hymns poured from both northern and southern presses, but they were soon separated from their original composers as they became part of the anonymous possession of both singers and audiences. Consequently, older songs like "Will the Circle Be Unbroken" were sometimes dramatically reshaped,[23] and newer songs, such as "Precious Memories," "Farther Along," and "I'll Fly Away," were treated as if they were in the public domain.[24] The radio hillbillies also sang songs of their own making, such as Grady Cole's reworking of a poem that became "Tramp on the Street" and Dorsey Dixon's response to a fatal auto crash, "I Didn't Hear Nobody Pray" (best known as Roy Acuff's arrangement, "Wreck on the Highway"), or they absorbed them from the shadowy world of street evangelists and brush arbor revivalism where authorship was quickly lost, forgotten, or ignored. "When the Saints Go Marching In," "This World Is Not My Home," "The Little Black Train," "Meeting in the Air," "Something Got A-Hold of Me," and "Great Speckled Bird," to name only a few, were songs that probably arose during the early years of the Pentecostal revivals but soon lost their sectarian flavor as they became popularized by touring hillbilly singers.

The fate of Herbert Buffum's "Vacation in Heaven" illustrates the ways in which revival music, shape-note publishing, and hillbilly radio programming interacted in the thirties. Written in 1925 by Buffum for city mission work and Pentecostal revival campaigns in California, the song circulated widely after it was published by the Dayton, Tennessee, shape-note publisher, R. E. Winsett, and then picked up by hillbilly entertainers who sang it frequently during the Depression years.[25] Winsett, who was a founding member of the largest Pentecostal denomination, the Assembly of God,[26] probably became the most important conduit for the exchange between country gospel music and gospel quartet music, and for the movement of black religious songs into the country catalogue. Winsett was apparently the first white publisher to publish "Precious Lord, Take My Hand," "Peace in the Valley," and other compositions by Thomas A. Dorsey, the African American composer and musician who in Chicago launched the black gospel song movement.[27]

The country act that did most to anthologize these varying types of religious songs was the Carter Family. As we saw in the chapter on songs of home, their broadcasts after 1938 over the powerful Mexican border station, XERA, allowed them to extend their reach throughout North America.[28] Their downhome charm, old-fashioned love songs, and timeless gospel items consoled many working-class Americans, even if the Carters' message promised little ultimate hope in this world. In "There's No Depression in Heaven," written by J. D. Vaughan in 1932, the Carter Family declared that they were "going where there's no depression, to a lovely land that's free from care."[29]

Hillbilly singers such as the Carter Family crossed paths frequently with the gospel quartets during those years, for they were all itinerant musicians constantly searching for a receptive radio market and a generous sponsor. The Stamps Quartet, Blackwood Brothers Quartet, and similar groups popularized their music through live and transcribed radio broadcasts, and circulated their paperback songbooks wherever they traveled. Southern evangelical churches welcomed the quartets during the Depression years, and the Pentecostal fellowships, which always embraced spirited and innovative music, enthusiastically responded to the music of the quartets.[30] With little money available for professional entertainment during those years, touring quartets could at least look forward to a good, home-cooked meal and a friendly audience when they made their church concerts.

If partisans of gospel music cannot look back to the thirties as an economically lucrative period, they can at least take pride in the quality of the music produced at that time. The music also moved more insistently into a national arena, not through emotionally fulfilling church concerts but through radio broadcasts. The most popular group, the Stamps Quartet, broadcast its performances from the Texas Centennial in 1936, and soon thereafter began daily programming on powerful KRLD in Dallas.[31] A song written especially for them by Albert E. Brumley, "Turn Your Radio On,"[32] invited listeners to "get in touch with God," while also testifying to the importance of that great communications device in circulating popular music throughout America. Such lyrics showcased the considerable talents of Brumley, the premier example of a publishing-house composer whose songs won widespread popularity through radio exposure. Brumley maintained that he never consciously wrote a country song, and was instead committed to Christian evangelization through music. The fate of his songs, however, provides vivid confirmation of the close interrelationship of secular and sacred music in the South and of the debt that country music owes to Brumley and other gospel composers. Although Brumley's career was intimately intertwined with the historical evolution of shape-note gospel music, his success in that genre was directly dependent on radio broadcast exposure.

Born into a tenant farm family near Spiro, Oklahoma, on October 29, 1905,[33] Brumley became wedded to music after attending a singing "normal" school in about 1921 or 1922 at the Rock Island community. He began "tinkering" with songwriting almost immediately, but none of his works were printed until 1927 when the Hartford Music Company of Hartford, Arkansas, published a few of them in a "convention book"[34] called *Gates of Glory.* Brumley's association with the Hartford Music Company (which the Brumley family now owns) was lifelong, bringing him in contact with his mentor, Eugene M. Bartlett, the original owner of the company and the writer of such gospel evergreens as "Victory in Jesus" and "I Heard My Mother Call My Name in Prayer." During a career that spanned almost fifty years, Brumley wrote over six hundred songs that were published by the Hartford, Stamps-Baxter, and Stamps Quartet publishing companies. Most of the songs have been forgotten, but ten or twelve, such as "I'll Meet You in the Morning," "I Found a Hiding Place," "He Set Me Free," "Turn Your Radio On," and "I'll Fly Away," have endured as favorites in the gospel music repertoire.[35]

Virtually all of Brumley's gospel standards have found enthusiastic receptions in country music, either recorded by country musicians or familiar to them. "He Set Me Free," in fact, inspired Hank Williams's classic and often-performed "I Saw the Light." Other Brumley songs, described by their writer as "sentimental secular" songs, have become mainstays in bluegrass music. Such songs as "Rank Stranger to Me," "By the Side of the Road," "Nobody Answered Me," "Did You Ever Go Sailing? (River of Memories)," and "Dreaming of a Little Cabin," all appeared repeatedly in the gospel hymnals and, at least through the 1940s, were sung regularly by the quartets. None of them, however, can claim to be gospel songs in any real sense of the word. They apparently earned the gospel imprimatur because, like the previous century's "Where Is My Wandering Boy Tonight?" they equated home and Christian morality, and they cautioned against straying too far afield from the values and moral strength of the old homestead. They, and other Brumley songs such as "God's Gentle People," "I'll Meet You in the Morning," "The Prettiest Flowers Will Be Blooming," and "If We Never Meet Again," promised a reconciliation with loved ones in a Heaven envisioned as a pastoral retreat where "charming roses bloom forever" and "where no storm clouds ever darken the sky." These nostalgic but potent visions of a celestial antidote to a decaying rural society, combined with the hope for security and reconciliation beyond the grave, made Brumley's songs irresistible to thousands of people in the Depression and World War II–era South.[36]

Although Brumley's songs eventually found favor among a vast array of musicians, their chief entrée into country music, and probably into southern rural consciousness as well, came through the music of the Brown's Ferry Four, an assemblage of country all-stars who got together largely for recording purposes, and a Texas radio quartet named the Chuck Wagon Gang. Other singers moved in and out of the Brown's Ferry Four, but Merle Travis, Grandpa Jones, and Alton and Rabon Delmore comprised the original group that began broadcasting in 1943 on WLW in Cincinnati. The recordings made for Syd Nathan's King label after 1946, however, did most to popularize the quartet and their songs throughout the United States. Their recordings consisted exclusively of shape-note standards, but Grandpa Jones probably spoke for his fellow Brown's Ferry singers when he responded to an interviewer's questions about his favorite gospel songs: "Most of them were written by Albert E. Brumley."[37] The Chuck Wagon Gang, as we have seen, began their radio career in 1935 in Lubbock, Texas, and by 1936 were heard regularly on WBAP in Fort Worth and on their widely distributed Columbia recordings. Initially, their repertoire included old-time love songs, folksongs, and religious fare, but they soon adopted gospel music exclusively when they learned of their audience's preferences. Performing under the sponsorship of the Bewley Mills Flour Company, the Carters built their noontime radio show into one of the most popular programs in the Southwest with a warm, comfortable sound that has never changed substantially.[38] Singing to the accompaniment of Jim's guitar chords, the Chuck Wagon Gang created a style of harmony—rooted in the shapenote singing schools—that featured Rose's soprano lead, Dad's baritone, Jim's bass, and Anna's alto. They used virtually no stage patter at all, but instead made only brief announcements and let their songs speak for themselves. They brought reassurance to their listeners and popularized a wide body of songs that moved into the repertoires of both gospel and secular country singers.

Gospel singers such as the Chuck Wagon Gang were welcomed even more strongly during the World War II era, as were the songs of faith that sought the protective arm of Jesus for loved ones who were in harm's way: "Dear God, watch o'er my boy in service; help him win the victory there. And when this cruel war is over, bring him home is mother's prayer." Country war songs generally reflected public attitudes in linking America's cause with God's will. One of the most popular songs of the era, "There's a Star-Spangled Banner Waving Somewhere," spoke of Heaven as a land peopled by America's past heroes: "I'd see Lincoln, Custer, Washington, and Peary, Nathan Hale, and Colin Kelly too . . . that is where I want to live when I die." Country singers like Roy Acuff, whose popularity peaked during the war years, constantly sang the praises of home and God even as they warned our enemies about the wrath that God's justice would inevitably bring: "There'll be smoke on the water, on the land and the sea, when our army and navy overtake the enemy . . . and the sun that is rising will go down on that day."[39]

While Acuff's and other country songs promoted visions that united as a trinity America, home, and God, few institutions were as explicit in making such connections as John Lair's very popular weekly radio show, "The Sunday Morning Gathering." Since its inception on September 8, 1943, the Gathering proved to be the most popular and long-lasting program to come out of Renfro.[40] Each Sunday morning selected members of the barn-dance cast put aside the revelry of the previous Saturday night hoedown and called their listeners to a period of reflection and worship. The Gathering cast sang a number of religious songs to the accompaniment of a parlor organ, but overall the carefully scripted show conveyed a mood and vision of small-town America that had been so well encapsulated in Albert Brumley's songs, a domain of loving parents, cherished rural landmarks, and family worship—in short, a feeling that home and heaven were closely intertwined and worth fighting for.

That vision, of course, could not be sustained in the postwar years as small-town America succumbed to the allures of an urban society and as the unity of the war period gave way to the tensions and fears of the Cold War. In the mid-forties and early fifties religious-country songs often took on the prophetic and evangelistic tone of the times, viewing domestic problems as symptoms of a society that was forgetting God, or casting many of the major events of the era as portents of the end of time and Christ's Second Coming. We can now see the anxieties of those years as the conflicted marks of a society in transition and of a generation trying to understand and come to terms with lives defined by an urban-industrial civilization. But in an era marked by the presence of the Bomb, cold war suspicions, the aggressiveness of Russian Communism, and the emergence of the state of Israel, many people who grew up in an evangelical Protestant culture could easily perceive such phenomena as millennial forebodings. Pentecostalism not only survived the transition to a blue-collar urban environment, it won numerous new converts there, and in fact began making inroads into middle-class culture. Increasingly described as charismatic ministries,[41] tent evangelists proliferated, and the number of radio and television evangelists likewise increased.

The country music audience in the immediate postwar years was not yet fragmented along generational lines, and its stylistic tastes still reflected the yearnings of those who grew up in rural and evangelical households. Downhome sounds and metaphors still prevailed in country music, even though the ascendancy of pop-country styles and the Nashville sound was only a few short years away. During those transitional years, country music still had room for singers and songwriters who spoke with rural voices and who wove didactic messages into their songs as they responded to the social changes that swirled around them. The Country Music Hall of Fame will probably never acknowledge their contributions, but songwriters like Mac Odell, Grady Cole, Jim Anglin, Walter Bailes, and Ira Louvin preserved the ancient art of topical songmaking and documented the thinking of a large slice of Americans during a troubling period of national life.

Mac Odell can serve as a distinctive example of the "folk songwriters" of the era. Born Odell McLeod in Roanoke, Alabama, he built a singing career of his own in Alabama and in Benton Harbor, Michigan, but he is best known as the writer of an extensive number of songs that were recorded by others during the early fifties. Cowboy Copas alone recorded three of Odell's songs, "Purple Robe," "From the Manger to the Cross," and "Four Books in the Bible," while Roy Acuff recorded "Glo-

ry Bound Train" and Wilma Lee Cooper recorded "Thirty Pieces of Silver." Songs like "Glory Bound Train," "Life's Elevator," "Radio Station
SAVED," and his tongue-in-cheek tribute to the wonder drug, penicillin,
reveal that the old practice of using practical or technological metaphors
to indicate timeless truths had not disappeared. These items took their
place alongside such venerable songs as "Life's Railway to Heaven" and
"Hello Central, Give Me Heaven."[42]

Odell's songs reveal that the older styles and theological postures of
country religious music still won the affections of country music fans.
Predictions of the imminent end of the world appeared frequently in songs
like "Matthew 24," "This World Can't Stand Long," "That's What's the
Matter with This World," "Battle of Armageddon," and Ira Louvin's
"Great Atomic Power" (one of many songs that saw religious implications in the building of atomic and hydrogen bombs).[43]

If these topical songs breathed with evangelical passion, some of the
singers of the period sang religious material with such fervor that they
sounded like evangelists. Two of the greatest vocalists of country music's
history, for example, Wilma Lee Cooper and Molly O'Day, were impassioned singers who mixed ballads and secular songs with sacred pieces.
Singing with her husband Stoney in a group known as the Cumberland
Mountain Folk, the West Virginia–born Wilma Lee Cooper performed
the definitive versions of "Walking My Lord up Calvary's Hill," "Legend of the Dogwood Tree" and Odell's "Thirty Pieces of Silver." Molly
O'Day (born Laverne Williamson in Pike County, Kentucky) was a superb five-string banjoist who possessed a large repertoire of traditional
country songs, but she will always be best known for her rendition of
Grady Cole's "Tramp on the Street." A compassionate song that com-
pares the suffering Christ to a homeless derelict, it was Cole's adaptation
of a turn-of-the-century poem. O'Day, however, first heard the song performed by Hank Williams in 1942, and both she and Hank sang it to a
melody significantly different from Cole's. By the 1960s Molly and her
husband, Lynn Davis, had gone into full-time evangelistic work in West
Virginia (as members of the Church of God), and until her death in 1987
she recorded only religious songs.[44]

West Virginia was also the birthplace of the Bailes Brothers (Johnnie,
Walter, Homer, and Kyle). Like their contemporary, Molly O'Day, they
also sang a variety of songs but were most closely identified with religious
material. Their repertoire resembled that of the Blue Sky Boys, but unlike them, they sang with an intense emotion analogous to that displayed
in O'Day, Wilma Lee Cooper, and Roy Acuff performances. They were

at their best on religious songs or songs about Mother and home. Although Bailes Brothers' songs came from many sources—including Jim Anglin, who supplied them with one of the finest country songs ever written about the suffering wrought by war, "Searching for a Soldier's Grave"—most came from the pen of Walter Bailes, who looked at life through evangelical eyes. Such songs as "Dust on the Bible," "Whiskey Is the Devil," "We're Living in the Last Days Now," and "Building on the Sand" envisioned moral decay in the United States and prophesied the imminent return of Christ. "When Heaven Comes Down" conveyed a wondrous mixture of apocalyptic zeal and populist resentment, noting that in the earth's last days "when Heaven comes down great mansions will burn . . . and my little cabin, so close to the ground, will be a great mansion when Heaven comes down."

When Walter left the act in 1947 to become a Pentecostal evangelist, Johnnie and Homer assumed most of the vocal responsibilities. In many ways, Johnnie was the most intriguing member of the group. His impassioned tenor harmony did most to give the brothers their emotional edge, and tears almost came to his eyes when they sang a religious or sentimental Mother song such as "Give Mother My Crown." But Johnnie also fancied himself a ladies' man. His exploits got the Bailes Brothers fired from at least two shows, including the Grand Ole Opry, and he was sent to prison in Louisiana for violating the Mann Act. Homer believed that Johnnie's style came from religious guilt, or from "coming under conviction." That is, he believed that Johnnie had been called to preach but had rejected the call. The sources of Johnnie's musical power, of course, cannot conclusively be determined, but, as was the case for Jimmy Arnold, Steve Earle, Ira Louvin, and other conflicted country music entertainers, the warring elements of his personality contributed to the making of a charismatic style with wide public appeal.[45]

Ira Louvin's troubled soul inspired some of the finest songs in country music. The distinctive high-pitched, tension-filled harmony made by him and his brother Charlie set them apart from other brother acts and made them, arguably, the greatest duet in country music history. Born Ira and Charlie Loudermilk in the northeastern hill country near Henagar, Alabama, the duo began their professional radio career in 1942 but made no recordings until 1947 when they signed with Apollo. Gospel music was only one facet of their heritage, but they performed it superbly and became closely identified with the genre, particularly when their first Capitol album, *The Family Who Prays,* won commercial and critical acceptance. The Louvins, however, always longed for a mainstream country music career, and by 1955, with the success of their song of broken love, "When I Stop Dreaming," they had largely attained their desire.

Gospel songs, though, always remained basic to their repertoire, and no one in country music surpassed them in the performance of such material. The Louvin gospel songbag—composed of songs written mostly by Ira—is a repository of fundamentalist Christian theology, most dramatically portrayed by the fiery image on the album cover of *Satan Is Real.* At a time when the gospel quartet business was moving toward a soothing, nonsectarian message that eliminated all references to a vengeful God, a burning Hell, and the blood that stained the Old Rugged Cross, the Louvin Brothers and the Bailes Brothers were singing songs that recalled the fierce doctrinal battles of early southern Protestantism. Not long before they parted to attempt solo careers, the Louvins recorded a song that portended the rise of political fundamentalism. It was called "Don't Let Them Take the Bible out of Our School Rooms."[46]

As a solo singer after 1963, and as a member of a duet with his second wife, Anne Young, Ira was an undistinguished performer. But as a tenor duet singer, he was unsurpassed. A man of dark moods and eccentricities, he became a legend in country music—because of his drinking, his quick and fierce anger, his occasional rudeness to fans, his penchant for throwing an out-of-tune mandolin across the stage or walking off abruptly in the middle of a performance. Conversely, some of his songs sounded like sermons and, as in the case of Johnnie Bailes, some fans and his own brother, Charlie, were convinced that he was "under conviction" and in rebellion against a call to preach. He and his wife Anne were killed in an automobile accident in Missouri on June 28, 1965, and more than one person has noted that the force of the collision threw Ira halfway out of the car and left him in a "praying position" with his knees on the ground and his upper body leaning into the car.[47]

Hank Williams's broad-ranging repertoire cannot mask the way that religion indelibly marked his music and life. Neither Williams nor his music can be understood apart from the religious context in which he was born and raised. Although he was reared in the Baptist church and is said to have sung there when he was a boy, it is hard to know how much that influence shaped his style. After all, he also listened to Roy Acuff and other commercial singers, and was performing in honky-tonks by the time he was fourteen. His style revealed major ingredients of the southern blue-collar milieu: poverty, indoctrination by mother, and the underlying influence of the church. Religious songs always appeared with regularity in Hank's performances. In his early career he and his wife Audrey often sang duets of such songs as "I'll Have a New Body" and "Calling You." On his "Health and Happiness" transcriptions made for Dudley LeBlanc and the Hadacol company in 1949, he sang a religious song, either solo or with Audrey, on each show. As Luke the Drifter, Hank recorded mostly moralistic songs and recitations such as "Too Many Parties and Too Many Pals," "Be Careful of Stones That You Throw," "Pictures from Life's Other Side," and an item called "The Funeral" that had originally been done in black dialect. He (or Fred Rose) even exhibited some familiarity with the sentimental poetry of Edgar Guest when he transformed the popular poet's verses into "I Dreamed about Mama Last Night." All of Hank's religious material was deep-dyed fundamentalist fare, basically no different from the songs favored by the Louvin and Bailes Brothers.[48]

When Hank Williams died on January 1, 1953, bedeviled by drugs and drink, his life was a mess. We can never know whether he battled with God, or whether he ever fell "under conviction." Hank's final recordings do not reveal the personal devils that troubled the young singer, even though one of them was prophetically entitled "I'll Never Get out of This World Alive." His voice sounds strong and controlled. People who knew Hank Williams only through his recordings could not have known of his drunken bouts and canceled shows, nor of the spiritual anguish that seems to have colored the famous and chilling remark made to Minnie Pearl one night that "there just ain't no light."[49]

As the fifties wore on, country gospel songs tended to lose both their evangelical edge and their sectarian passion. Although the Soviet Union remained strong, a third world war did not erupt, and the United States assumed the role of protector of the free world. Nor did an economic depression occur, and the United States entered an era of expansion marked by affluence, an increasingly suburban society, and burgeoning growth of the middle class. As someone who would neither dismantle the government protections of the past nor embark on new and untested experiments, President Dwight Eisenhower, by his remarkable World War II leadership and by his very presence, offered reassurance. He had said, too, in his first inaugural speech, that everyone ought to adopt some form of religion (presumably Christian), but he didn't care what kind.[50]

The tone of country religious songs in the early fifties seemed to reflect the easy optimism and the benign nonsectarianism of Eisenhower Republicanism. As in no other period of country music history, gospel songs often appeared on the country "charts," with such singers as Hank Snow, Hank Williams, Jimmie Davis, Cowboy Copas, Stuart Hamblen, Martha Carson, and Clyde Julian "Red" Foley recording songs that were heard frequently in concerts and on radio broadcasts and jukeboxes. Reviving from a bitter divorce from James Carson, with whom she had recorded several fine gospel duets (such as "Budded on Earth" and "Man of Galilee"), Martha Carson wrote and recorded a spirited, Holiness-style song called "Satisfied" that in 1951 competed favorably with the honky-tonk songs of the day. Cowboy singer Stuart Hamblen, who overcame a powerful attraction to alcohol after his well-publicized conversion in a Billy Graham crusade in Los Angeles in 1949, also moved to the exclusive performance of religious music. Such songs as "It Is No Secret" and "This Ole House" moved beyond the country charts and won widespread play in pop music. As the son of a Methodist minister in Texas, Hamblen's conversion was not very surprising, but his campaign for the presidency on the Prohibition ticket in 1952 may have astounded those friends who remembered his former fondness for Demon Rum.[51]

The former two-time governor of Louisiana, Jimmie Davis, never stopped singing his signature song, "You Are My Sunshine," but he otherwise moved in the fifties to the performance of religious songs, such as "Someone to Care," "Supper Time" (with recitation), and "One More Valley." His marriage to Anna Carter, of the Chuck Wagon Gang, simultaneously forged a union of two important musical traditions. They organized an act that sang frequently in churches and at music festivals. As late as 1999 the near-centenarian Davis was still managing to sing a few verses of "You Are My Sunshine" and his standard religious numbers to entranced audiences.[52]

The most popular singer of religious songs in country music during the fifties was Red Foley, one of the most versatile performers in country music history. Foley had no trouble at all in moving from a song like "Pinball Boogie" (where he declared that "you rattle and you shake it 'til it gets in the hole") to "Just a Closer Walk with Thee." He exhibited a knowledge of and fondness for material from the black gospel tradition, including "Steal Away" (complete with recitation), "He'll Understand and Say Well Done," and the two classics by Thomas A. Dorsey, the "father" of black gospel music, "Peace in the Valley" and "Precious Lord, Take My Hand."[53]

Gospel quartet style continued to exert considerable influence on country singers down through the sixties. Choral backing, in fact—as performed by such groups as the Anita Kerr Singers and the Jordanaires— was a defining ingredient of the country-pop sound that developed in the late fifties and early sixties. As the first country singer to make regular use of such quartets as the Sunshine Boys as backup singers, Red Foley, again, played a crucial role. The gospel quartets, of course, were also changing in style and were making themselves much more visible in American popular culture. The Blackwood Brothers of Memphis, Tennessee, won an Arthur Godfrey Talent Contest in 1954, and placed their winning song, "Have You Talked to the Man Upstairs," on the popular music hit parade. The title and content of the song tells us a good deal about the changes that had been taking place in gospel music: the awesome Judge described by the Louvin Brothers was being metamorphosed, it seemed, into a Friend and Confidant. Songs no longer carried denominational identity, contained or conveyed no explicit theological content, and, secular enough to describe God as the Man Upstairs, remained only vaguely "Christian." Albert Brumley had once proudly declared that "I may be a little old-fashioned, but my Saviour was old-fashioned too," but Stuart Hamblen demonstrated just how far country music had moved from that rustic philosophy when he sang "My religion's not old-fashioned, but it's real genuine."[54]

Elvis, of course, was the man who made the quartets broadly respectable. His affinity for gospel music is well known, and visitors to Graceland can still see his gospel LP collection on display in his music room. Not long after he joined RCA, he began recording with the assistance of the Jordanaires (the gospel quartet that supplied much of the vocal backing for country-pop records in the late fifties), and later he was linked closely to other groups such as the Stamps Quartet (headed by the great bass singer, J. D. Sumner).[55]

Although the country hit parades became almost completely secular by the 1960s, religion continued to be a pervasive and shaping phenomenon in the lives of country entertainers and religious songs occasionally made their way into the commercial charts. Recordings like Ferlin Husky's "Wings of a Dove," Christy Lane's "One Day at a Time" (skillfully marketed through television), Johnny Paycheck's and Jody Miller's "Let's All Go Down to the River," and Kris Kristofferson's "Why Me, Lord" still earned widespread commercial acceptance. Obviously, audiences still responded well to such choices. Throughout the sixties country television, catering to the tastes of loyal fans, preserved religious music as part of the general fare presented to viewers. Fans of Porter Wagoner, the Wilburn Brothers, Flatt and Scruggs, and Ernest Tubb, for example, could generally expect to hear one or more religious songs or an inspirational recitation before the program ended. Ernest Tubb, as we have seen, frequently called on Willie Nelson to sing the "sacred song of the day."

Country singers continued to record occasional albums of religious material, and in 1959 Tennessee Ernie Ford inaugurated his career as the most prolific performer of gospel material with an album called *Hymns.* By 1963 it had become the biggest-selling album in the Capitol catalogue, and was only one of over eighty albums that Ford eventually contributed to the genre. The immense appeal of the familiar hymns was still apparent as late as 1998 when television icon Andy Griffith ventured into the realm of hymn singing and marketed (largely through television merchandising) a CD that is believed to have sold over a million copies.[56]

The most important barometers of religious influence in modern country music, though, have been the high incidence of country singers who have proudly spoken of a "born again experience" and who express an eagerness to "witness for Christ," and the prevalence of religious material in the field of bluegrass music. As the performance of religious music receded in the realm of mainstream country music, many religious-minded entertainers sought new venues in which to express their faith. Some found a forum on the syndicated radio show "Country Crossroads," sponsored by the Southern Baptist Radio and Television Commission, and cohosted by the singer-songwriter and disk jockey Bill Mack. Joined first by Leroy Van Dyke, and later by Jerry Clower, Mack played the top hits of the day and encouraged entertainers to talk about their religious experiences.[57]

The Christian Country Music Association debuted in 1990 with such singers as Paul Overstreet, Ricky Skaggs, Ricky Van Shelton, Barbara Fairchild, and Lulu Roman who appealed to both gospel and country radio audiences. The emergence of the Christian Country format was, in part, a facet of the national drift toward social conservatism and the hunger for positive moral messages, and also a reaction against what was considered to be the seamy side of country music. Paul Overstreet, a native of Antioch, Mississippi, soon became identified as the premier singer-songwriter of the emerging "Christian Country" genre. Overcoming an addiction to alcohol, Overstreet had become a successful writer of such upbeat, life-affirming songs as "Forever and Ever, Amen" and "On the Other Hand" (both recorded by superstar Randy Travis, who himself had overcome a youthful strain of wildness). The critical success in 1990 of an album of songs called *Sowin' Love,* which won widespread distribution in both country and gospel formats, prompted RCA producer Joe Galante to describe Overstreet as "a perfect example of somebody who has a real value system in his songs. He writes and sings what he believes in and, hopefully, will make the world a better place when people hear it."[58]

Except for Ricky Skaggs, who endorsed and campaigned for presidential candidate Pat Robertson, Christian Country singers tended to steer clear of partisan politics or explicit denominational identification. As intended, theirs was a positive, pro-family message that resonated strongly with a wide spectrum of listeners. These entertainers were, above all, professing Christians who felt the compulsion to minister or "witness" to their public. Soon after Skaggs began his highly successful career as a country singer in 1981 (after an earlier immersion in bluegrass music), he became aware that public visibility also carried public responsibilities. Feeling a special concern as a role model to children in his audiences, he vowed to set an example in both his songs and personal life that would inspire positive emulation. In response to his belief that teenagers were under greater stress from "the dark side" than any age group, he and his wife Sharon (daughter of the assertive Christian and bluegrass musician Buck White) founded an organization called "Teens in Trouble" to raise money for youth threatened by drugs, alcohol, and sexual abuse. He asserted that "I never walk on stage without thinking about my platform and my life." A similar motivation inspired the work of Marty Stuart, a Philadelphia, Mississippi, native, who had followed a similar path through bluegrass—including a formative stint with the Sullivan Family, a Pentecostal bluegrass group—before settling into his rockabilly style of country music. Stuart was the coproducer of a video called *Silent Witness* that featured religious songs and testimonies by himself, Skaggs, Tammy Wynette, Marty Raybon, and other country entertainers who yearned to make their professions of faith public.[59]

The public confession of religious faith was an inconsequential facet of country music life until the music experienced its dramatic growth after World War Two. Since that time—probably beginning with Stuart Hamblen's well-publicized conversion in 1949 during a Billy Graham crusade in Los Angeles—country musicians, consciously or unconsciously, have discovered that the testimony of a changed life can increase both their public visibility and commercial potential. It is difficult to think of anything analogous to this in any other area of American music. The explosion of interest in country music, too, has created a veritable subindustry of drugstore rack biographies and autobiographies of country entertainers. In these books, religious inspiration almost always plays a central role.[60]

Cowboy singer Roy Rogers and his wife, Dale Evans, inspired the first of these books when Elise Miller Davis wrote about them in *The Answer Is God*.[61] Rogers had embraced religion through the influence of his wife, Dale, who had made her own personal religious decision when she was ten years old. That commitment grew as the couple sought healing after the death of their retarded daughter, Robin. The Rogerses specifically dedicated their ministry to children, which Roy initiated by singing "Peace in the Valley" on September 24, 1952, at the rodeo in Madison Square Garden in New York. He assured the children there that they should go to church, because a real cowboy needs real faith. For the remainder of his public career, Rogers viewed performance as a form of Christian ministry, and he and Dale met regularly in prayer sessions with other actors and actresses in California.[62]

The roster of country entertainers who have "gotten religion" is quite extensive, as is the list of those who have written or testified about their conversions.[63] Tommy Collins, Johnny Cash, Wanda Jackson, Jeannie C. Riley, Connie Smith, Skeeter Davis, Billy Grammer, Billy Walker, Slim Whitman, Glen Campbell, Ricky Van Shelton, comedian Jerry Clower, and even Kris Kristofferson,[64] are only a few of the country music personalities who have testified about their redemption. In almost every case, however, redemption means a return to a faith that was implanted in childhood. And several entertainers, like Jeannie C. Riley, Reba McEntire, Barbara Mandrell, and Dolly Parton, lovingly recall grandparents or some other relative who had been preachers or who otherwise had provided religious inspiration in their lives. While a few musicians, such as Dale Evans and Barbara Mandrell, speak of childhood conversions, most of the country confessors return to Christ after years of transgression or during a time of profound physical or emotional suffering. In the often-tortuous quest for spiritual consolation, country entertainers have been helped along by loving friends and relatives or by charismatic evangelists, such as Bob Harrington, Walter Bailes, Jimmie Rodgers Snow, and Will Campbell, who have understood the temptations of the flesh and the demons that often bedevil the souls of entertainers because they themselves had sometimes succumbed to them.[65]

Snow, a musician and son of country singer Hank Snow, according to his own testimony, had led a highly debauched life filled with wild women, drugs, whiskey, and suicide attempts. After the third attempt in 1957, he threw his gun down and ran wildly until he fell to his knees in desperation by the side of his father's front-yard mailbox. There he gave his heart to Christ, found peace, and vowed to become a preacher. After several years of itinerant evangelism, during which he became notorious for his sermons against rock-and-roll, Snow settled down in 1965 as the minister of his own Pentecostal church in Nashville, the Evangel Temple Assembly of God. A Friday night radio show on WSM, the Grand Ole

Gospel Hour, followed in 1972, from the stage of the Ryman Auditorium, and made his name well known throughout the country music industry. Such entertainers as Eddie Miller (the writer of "Release Me"), Billy Grammer, Billy Walker, Connie Smith, Kris Kristofferson, and Johnny Cash became publicly identified with Snow's ministry.[66]

The most highly publicized member of the Evangel Temple was the man in black, Johnny Cash. In classic redemptive fashion, Cash first descended to the depths of despair and degradation, almost succumbing to the destructiveness of prescription medications, before finding personal salvation through the loving devotion and support of his wife June Carter Cash. Cash noted that when he and June were married in 1968, he "had just come off seven years of addiction to amphetamines and other prescription drugs . . . and had been a devastated, incoherent, unpredictable, self-destructive, raging terror at times during those years."[67] Cash insisted, though, that when he walked down to the altar of the Evangel Temple on May 9, 1971, his public profession of faith was actually a recommitment of a decision made for Christ when he was about twelve years old.[68] In the years that followed this renewal, and before the onset in 1998 of a debilitating disease falsely diagnosed as Shy-Draeger, Cash somehow managed to maintain an active performing career while also appearing frequently as a guest and performer in Billy Graham's revivalistic crusades, producing a movie about Jesus called *The Glory Road,* and writing a novel about St. Paul called *The Man in White.*[69]

Jimmie Rodgers Snow may have experienced a remarkable success ministering to the spiritual needs of the reprobates of country music, but no one made more dramatic confrontations with evil, nor was more forthright in his efforts to reach the neglected and despised poor people of the world, than Will Campbell. Born and reared in Mississippi, and introduced to fundamentalist Christianity through the Southern Baptist Church, Campbell actually honed his maverick brand of thinking and theology in the racial battlegrounds of the civil rights–era South. Campbell became chaplain at the University of Mississippi in 1954, but soon incurred the wrath of most white southerners and ostracization by the Southern Baptist hierarchy when he joined the crusade for black equality and racial justice. If that unorthodox stance was not enough to brand him as an unpredictable individualist, his defense of the Ku Klux Klan and rednecks seemed even more perverse. The universality of his compassion, and the recognition that any kind of stereotyping obscures the humanity that dwells in all of us, is summed up in his oft-repeated aphorism: "We're all bastards, but God loves us anyway."

Campbell's origins in the despised southern redneck class partly ex-
plains his defense of them, but his arguments also arise from his profound
commitment to justice and his belief that poor whites and blacks had been
similarly victimized in a society that exploits them economically and ig-
nores their basic social needs. His affection for country music likewise
reflected a personal love for the idiom, and the knowledge that the music was a way of communicating with working folk. Campbell's picking
and singing (and "Rednecks, White Socks, and Blue Ribbon Beer" was
one of his special favorites), and his belief that country music was honest, liberal, and "theologically sound," brought him in contact with country singers and into an intimate and affectionate friendship with some
of them. Largely through the influence of Jessi Colter, the wife of Waylon Jennings, who was deeply impressed by Campbell's forgiving nature
and openness of spirit, he became virtually the guru of country music's
Outlaw contingent.[70]

If religious influence has touched every corner of the country music
experience, the flame of the old-time religion has burned most brightly
in the realm of bluegrass, which remains the chief repository of traditional
forms of gospel music. As a musical genre that has attracted hordes of
fans and musicians who came from neither the working-class South nor
a background of Protestant fundamentalism, the performance of gospel
songs has become a virtually required way of affirming one's legitimacy
or authenticity and a means of celebrating the culture of bluegrass and
the older styles that anticipated it. Jerry Wicentowski, for example, a
devoutly observant Orthodox Jew whose soulful bluegrass singing has
been confined largely to Milwaukee, routinely sings such gospel songs
as "Old Daniel Prayed" and "By the Side of the Road" (with references
to Jesus deleted).[71]

The fascination with tradition is not the only motivation that attracts
some bluegrass musicians to the older hymns and styles; many fans and
musicians have embraced religious styles in order to surround their music with a decent and almost reverential aura that sets it apart from mainstream country music.[72] The bluegrass community originally retreated to
the festival style of performance because their music was being shut out
of many of the venues frequented by country musicians,[73] but it is difficult
to avoid seeing a similarity between the festivals and the religious camp
meetings of the nineteenth century. Like the camp meetings, festivals
usually convene in clearings in wooded areas that are surrounded by tents
and campers. The chief "pulpit" of the festival is the central stage where
touring professional musicians play, but jam sessions can be heard in

scattered areas throughout the campgrounds all through the night (an almost-spiritual way of renewing oneself in the company of other believers). Many bluegrass fans have a central guiding faith, the conviction that the true foundation of their music lies in the original performances made by Bill Monroe, Flatt and Scruggs, and the Stanley Brothers back in the sacred days of the late forties and early fifties. The true believer, they feel, must not stray from the original sound—even if the founders themselves had sometimes strayed! Whether committed to the traditional sounds of Bill Monroe or to the progressive sounds of other bluegrass musicians, fans who have felt alienated from less pure forms of country music have found both spiritual and musical solace in the festival environment.

Gospel songs have remained central to bluegrass performance. All bluegrass bands include large numbers of gospel songs in their repertoires, and some of them, usually performing as family units, sing nothing but religious music. Pure entertainment remains the hallmark of many of the gospel-oriented groups, such as the Lewis Family, a Baptist group from Georgia, whose "spirituality" is generally overshadowed by the zany stage humor of their banjo player, Little Roy. But the performances of other groups, such as the Pentecostal Sullivan Family from St. Stephens, Alabama, sometimes assume the aura of a revival service. The deceased founder of the group, Arthur Sullivan, was a Pentecostal preacher, as is his talented daughter-in-law, Margie Sullivan, whose heartfelt singing provides central focus for the organization. Jerry and Tammy Sullivan, a father and daughter singing act, and a contemporary offshoot of the original Sullivan Family, give concerts that assume the overtones of worship services, complete with shouts and testimonies. Reflecting upon their music and their unselfish dedication, Jack Bernhardt said "Jerry and Tammy have taught me that the Spirit stirs as fervently in the southern soul today as it has at any time since the Great Awakening."[74] Bluegrass gospel concerts as a whole are often given as adjuncts to church services, and the music is accompanied by the raising of hands, speaking in tongues, and altar calls. In the music of such groups as the Sullivan, Lewis, Forbes, Isaacs, Marshall, and Spencer families, one can hear almost the full range of southern religious musical performance, from spirited Holiness singing to the austere cadences of the Old Regular Baptist church.

It is true that the songs and mellifluous sounds of Christian contemporary music can often be heard in modern bluegrass music, but many performers, young and old, still adhere to the tradition of the paperback hymnals, where Albert Brumley reigns supreme. A few musicians, such as Ralph Stanley and the Spencer Family, often reach back to the performances of the Primitive Baptists, Old Regular Baptists, and Holiness Christians, or to the folk hymns of rural America. Inspired probably by the singing of the Chestnut Grove Quartet, a group of Methodist singers who were popular in his region of southwest Virginia,[75] Ralph Stanley became the first bluegrass musician to introduce regular performances done in a capella fashion. Today, the a capella performance of at least one gospel song in a concert is virtually mandatory for bluegrass bands. Two of the most important exponents of the style, Doyle Lawson and Quicksilver and the Nashville Bluegrass Band, have expanded the parameters of bluegrass performance by dipping frequently into the repertoires of Sister Rosetta Tharpe, the Fairfield Four, and other African American gospel singers.[76]

If bluegrass gospel performance is heavily indebted to "traditional" forms of southern religious music, singers in the old-time evangelical Protestant churches also exhibit a marked fondness for songs introduced by bluegrass and other country musicians. Old Regular Baptist, Primitive Baptist, and Pentecostal congregations regularly perform songs learned from the Stanley Brothers, Flatt and Scruggs, and other bluegrass singers, while storefront services, radio ministries, and street preachers also sing songs borrowed from professional entertainers. Such examples of interchange of course are not novel; they are part of a process that began long before America was settled, and they vividly illustrate the democratic nature by which the South's religious musical heritage was built.[77]

The omnipresence of religious material in the bluegrass repertoire is only one of many factors that reaffirm the enduring popularity of gospel songs. Their appeal, however, springs from much more than religious devotion or spirituality. For many singers and fans songs like "I'll Fly Away," "I Saw the Light," and "Amazing Grace" are simply fun to sing, or they are ways of reaffirming the traditions of country music culture. Religious songs, for example, did not figure in the middle-class upbringing of Emmylou Harris, nor do they serve any evangelistic purpose when she sings them in concert. Such songs as "The Darkest Hour," "Angel Band," and "Wayfaring Stranger," which she learned through the influence of Ricky Skaggs and the Stanley Brothers, permit her to pay homage to the total culture of the musical tradition that she has so lovingly and effectively adopted.[78] The Nitty Gritty Dirt Band similarly made a cultural and not a religious statement in 1972 when they chose an old Carter Family gospel song, "Will the Circle Be Unbroken," as the title cut and centerpiece of their historic album.[79] Like the Carter Family and other country acts who had preserved the old-time gospel numbers, the

Nitty Gritty Dirt Band perceptively viewed religious material as part of the seamless but intricately interrelated web of music that had defined the culture of working-class southerners.

That insight was intuitively, and powerfully, understood by two singers who did emerge from evangelical Protestant backgrounds, but who realized that the gospel songs tapped wellsprings that went far deeper than institutional religion. Iris DeMent and Merle Haggard grew up in California, a generation apart from each other but as heirs to an Okie tradition that instilled within them both pride and a consciousness that they stood on the margins of mainstream culture. Their well-known admiration for each other's music may derive, in large part, from this sense of common cultural kinship.[80] DeMent parted, intellectually, from the Pentecostal church when she was sixteen years old; Merle Haggard seems never to have questioned the theological tenets of the Church of Christ but nevertheless resisted its moral authority. But while DeMent and Haggard departed in significant ways from their parents' churches, they preserved essential psychological and emotional components of the faith that had underpinned those associations. DeMent said "even though I grew up in Southern California, inside the house it was very much Arkansas. I was always very aware that there was this other place that we came from."[81] Pentecostalism was a crucial ingredient of that inherited Arkansas culture, and it endures in her impassioned musical style and in some of the songs that pay tribute to her parents' religious beliefs: "I Don't Want to Get Adjusted," "Fifty Miles of Elbow Room," and "Higher Ground" (which she performs with her mother).[82]

Oklahoma lives similarly in the life and culture of Merle Haggard, the first member of his family to be born in California. This "one and only rebel child" paid little heed to his mother's warnings or to the strictures of her church, but he nevertheless absorbed, and preserved a profound respect for, the basic values that defined his parents' world. He paid tribute to them, while also recalling the religious traditions of country music, in two collections of gospel songs, *Land of Many Churches* and *Songs For the Mama That Tried*.[83] In *Land of Many Churches*, recorded in four different religious settings (the Big Creek Baptist Church in Millington, Tennessee, the San Quentin Prison Garden Chapel, the Nashville Union Rescue Mission, and Assembly of God Tabernacle in Keyes, California), Haggard dug deeply into the paperback hymnal tradition to present songs by fellow Oklahoman, Albert Brumley, and other gospel stalwarts. While singing in the Big Creek Baptist Church, Haggard clearly revealed the personal and emotional connotations that gospel music conveyed for him when he recalled his father, who died when Merle was nine years old. Before singing Brumley's "If We Never Meet Again" Haggard shared some tender recollections with his church audience: "I can remember him playing fiddle and singing certain songs. My mother has told me many times, with tears in her eyes, that this was my daddy's favorite song."[84] Songs like "If We Never Meet Again" had brought reassurance and the promise of reconciliation in Heaven to working folk like Haggard's mom and dad. And while we should not deny the possibility of some kind of spiritual dimension in Haggard's choice of songs, his performances are best understood as tributes to his parents and their world, and as celebrations of those "precious memories" of childhood when virtue and innocence prevailed. When we listen to DeMent, Haggard, and other country entertainers sing gospel songs, we may not be borne away to the realm of the old country church, either real or imagined, but we are often transported to an otherwise unarticulated place of innocence or spiritual yearning where we are free from preoccupation with the daily concerns of life. That special quality of religious music, which connects us to our own private domain of spirituality, also preserves country music's link to its own origins in the evangelical Protestant South.

5

"When the Lord Made Me, He Made a Rambling Man"

> When a woman gets the blues, she hangs her little head and cries,
> But when a man gets blue, he grabs a train and rides.[1]

The last time I saw Jimmy Arnold was on the evening that I refused to drive him to the Gregg County line so that he could buy a pint of whiskey. Becoming increasingly morose and uncommunicative, he soon walked out of our house and out of our lives. I heard about him a few years later when news came of his death at the age of forty. Although the man of gentle spirit and superb musicianship is the Jimmy Arnold I remember best, I also recall the fully tattooed man with mutual attraction to biker culture, Jesse James, and the Lost Cause, who seemed fatally drawn to violence and the underworld and who could not overcome his addiction to drink. More than anyone I've ever known, Jimmy Arnold embodied W. J. Cash's "divided" southerner,[2] the simple man torn between the poles of hedonism and piety.

Jimmy was a musical prodigy from Fries, Virginia—a bluegrass banjoist by the time he was a teenager and, eventually, a master of all the country string instruments. He grew up in a family of devoutly Pentecostal cotton mill workers, and he often talked of having been "saved"— many times, only to be lured back to the bottle for the inevitable backslide into oblivion.[3] As a matter of fact, salvation and backsliding seemed to define his life. Unfortunately, Jimmy discovered alcohol virtually as soon as he found Jesus and music. Like Hank Williams and Jimmy's friend, Keith Whitley, Jimmy became an alcoholic when he was a teenager. A weakness for drugs followed soon thereafter, and an involvement in this illicit traffic led to a prison sentence when he was still in his twenties. Once his prison term was over, he resumed his profession of music, playing in a succession of bluegrass bands and recording a handful of brilliant solo albums. But he could never overcome the demons that ravaged his life, nor the penchant for self-destruction that eventually consumed him.

Jimmy recovered more than once from physical infirmities that led him to death's door, married a sixth time to a loving nurse in Tyler, Texas, who bore him two sons, often forswore the consumption of strong drink, and returned again and again to the church (both Pentecostal and Baptist) where he often served as a missionary. He regularly spoke of God, but gravitated just as often to the biker culture that had earlier won his allegiance, and by the time he died, he was covered almost totally by garish and brightly colored tattoos.

Jimmy left behind a recorded body of beautifully performed music, including one album that speaks volumes about the fantasies that have lured southern country boys to fields of valor and sometimes to reckless acts of death. As a musical event, *Southern Soul*[4] was a tour de force, with Arnold playing guitar, fiddle, banjo, and harmonica (he was joined by dobro player Mike Auldridge) and singing all the songs. As a concept album it effectively captured the romance of the Lost Cause as imagined by a son of the southern plain folk, and it presented poetic vignettes of the ways in which the Confederate spirit has been used to rationalize individual rebellion or hedonistic behavior. In some of the album's songs, Jimmy reworked older folk material or adapted Civil War love songs (like "Lorena"), or interpreted new versions of recent pop songs, such as "The Night They Drove Old Dixie Down." The most interesting songs, however, were Arnold's own creations in which he not only captured the undying defiance of neo-Confederates but also insinuated himself and his values into the personalities of the historical figures whom he described. "Jesse James," for instance, emerges as more than an outlaw; he becomes a man victimized by Yankees who continues his rebellion long after the Civil War and therefore "wins his name in the Rebel Hall of Fame." In lyrics set to an old fiddle tune named "Sally Ann," Arnold becomes simultaneously the "son of a Pentecostal cotton-mill man" who reminisces about the Civil War and a dying Confederate soldier whose spirit he has inherited. Defying the more than one hundred years separating the two, Arnold helps us see clearly through this dual character that "Dixieland lives forever" in the rebel spirit of Arnold himself.

Unlike Jimmy Arnold, the rambling men of country music have not always gone to early graves, but instead have most often been fortunate to resolve their dreams in the realm of fantasy. "Rambler" in this chapter is used as a metaphor for the man who defies or otherwise tries to live apart from the conventions of society. Country musicians have exhibited a fascination for the rambling man since the beginnings of their music's commercial history, and a few of them have self-consciously absorbed and projected lifestyles that seem to mirror the rambler and his flight from responsibility. No term, in fact, has been more popular as a descriptive label for country bands than "rambler," and country entertainers and songwriters have extolled this historic character through scores of songs about gamblers, drifters, rounders, boasters, conmen, brawlers, hoboes, outlaws, convicts, railroadmen, cowboys, and rogue lovers. The rambling impulse most often assumes a relatively benign posture in country song—with singers boasting about the joys of getting drunk, about their prowess as lovers, or praising the joys of the open road and the unfettered freedom that it promises. Historically, rambling has been an intensely masculine preoccupation, with the unbridled desire for freedom at its core. But not surprisingly, the yearning for the open road in country music nevertheless springs as often from a sense of failure and insecurity as it does from the facade of swaggering sense of confidence that seems to envelop many songs. In the 1923 recording that introduced the genre to country music, "Lonesome Road Blues,"[5] Henry Whitter (also a product of Fries, Virginia) described the woes of an ex-convict who was going where the climate suited his clothes and who opined that "I ain't gonna be treated thisaway."

Rambling is an ancient impulse in the western European tradition that gave rise to southern folk culture, and one that may have lured some men into the performance of music in the first place. In Europe, professional musicians were often viewed or defined as rambling men by legal statute or church prohibition. That is, they were viewed as irresponsible or "masterless men" who posed threats to society. Even older superstitions holding that fiddling was a black art, and that, in fact, the Devil himself was a fiddler (hence the description of the fiddle as "the devil's box"), reinforced these "official" views in the public mind.[6]

The expansiveness and abundance of the rural South and the slow growth of legal institutions there simultaneously permitted the survival of many British folkways and contributed to the creation of new behavioral norms. Masculine dominance and patriarchal hegemony survived. Immigrants from the British Isles brought certain concepts of honor to the South that endured at all levels of society. Men strove to preserve the honor of their name and of their family.[7] Whether expressed in upper-

or lower-class terms, the concept of honor rested on the concept of patriarchal dominance, and it assumed that certain questions of personal honor took precedence over the law. In a sense, men were always involved in competition with each other or, at the least, they felt compelled to preserve the aura of masculinity at all costs. The ability to demonstrate skill in physical feats was important—(hunting, fishing, shooting, riding, drinking, fighting, dancing, fiddling), but oral displays of masculinity (boasting, tall-tale spinning, lying) were always expected, and sometimes even these relatively harmless pastimes could cross the line into violence.[8]

Immigrants to the South brought not only certain concepts of honor but also a fascination with the rambling man that endured in folk and popular culture—ballads and songs, tales, and folklore concerning outlaws, badmen, rogues, and rakish lovers. Whether as heirs to the experience of black slavery or of the social dislocations that radically transformed the lives of plain folk in western Europe during the late Middle Ages, or as recipients of a Calvinistic worldview, southern plain folk were acutely aware of the impermanence of earthly institutions and of the fragility of human life. Perceiving man as a pilgrim in a hostile and irredeemable world,[9] religion reaffirmed realities that economic scarcity and political oppression seemed to suggest about the human potential: life was destined to be brief, hard, and materially unfulfilling. America held out to new arrivals the promise of a more rewarding life, and conditions in the newfound land gradually reshaped the attitudes of settlers, lending to them an optimism that was scarcely realistic in the Old World. Nevertheless, a bleak and fatalistic view of human existence lingered among many southerners long after the plain folk gained "liberty" and economic sustenance. In a world of limited options, where humble folk saw little chance for improvement, that person who exhibited the ability to live independently, apart from the establishment or outside the law, was often admired.

The plain-folk relationship with ramblers, of course, was not simply a matter of imaginative speculation or vicarious identification. Plain people had always had an intimate, and generally love-hate, relationship with ramblers and, of course, had produced many such characters from their own ranks. Poor people often suffered from the wiles, schemes, or brutality of sharpies, hustlers, gamblers, bandits, highwaymen, thieves, and assorted con artists on the lonely roads of the British Isles where robbers lay in wait, or at the county fairs and other public gatherings where such characters preyed upon the gullible and ignorant.[10] Musicians, likewise, could sometimes be rascals who used their art, or were used by others, to deceive or ensnare naive listeners. Muriel St. Clare Byrne, in her study of Elizabethan social history, notes that rogues sometimes posed as balladmongers in order to gain public confidence, and musicians sometimes seduced or beguiled country folk while their pickpocket accomplices practiced their cunning art.[11]

Songs about bold highwaymen or wily rascals nevertheless provided dramatic relief or escape to people whose own constricted lives seemed devoid of romance. The most innocent, and probably most appealing, example of the rambler, and the one who appeared most often in songs, was the rogue lover. One of these, "Black Jack David" (the Gypsy Laddie),[12] endured as an example of the handsome, footloose lover who could not be resisted. As a gypsy, he is also an early example of the tendency to attribute certain exotic traits (usually sexual) to outsiders. Other songs like "The House Carpenter" (whose wife is lured out to sea by another "outlander"—perhaps the devil) or "Little Matty Groves" warned about the consequences of giving one's heart to a rambler.[13] Such characters were simultaneously appealing and dangerous.

Other songs had more overt political overtones, with outlaws viewed as social bandits, that is, as men who warred against the rich and privileged or who redistributed their purloined wealth among the poor. Few Robin Hood ballads made the transit across the Atlantic Ocean, but this centuries-old romance contained stock conventions that appeared in American outlaw songs and stories. As an unwilling convert to outlawry, Robin Hood had been driven into a life of banditry through injustice, but he remained religious, with a strong compassion for the poor.[14] Similar characters in America, from Jesse James to Pretty Boy Floyd and Bonnie and Clyde, have fueled the content of stories and songs. Jesse James became the quintessential example of the southern "good outlaw," and we are assured in at least one song that "before every raid Jesse James prayed."[15] He was also more than an enemy of the rich and a patron of the poor; he was, in his war against banks and railroads, an unreconstructed battler against Yankee capitalism. In Jimmy Arnold's musical depiction of Jesse James, one finds no reference to James's career as an outlaw. Instead, James is treated solely as a rebel whose life was permanently transformed by Yankee violence and treachery. The song's refrain alleges that "Jesse James, you won your name in the rebel hall of fame."[16]

Although certain attitudes exalting manly independence were inherited from the Old World, they were reaffirmed and given new meanings in the culture of the South. The spirit of machismo endured among working-class males but, fortunately for society, was usually diverted or sublimated into generally "harmless" expressions in religion, entertainment, sports, music, and popular culture. Such historians as Frank Owsley, Grady McWhiney, and Steven Hahn[17] are probably right in arguing that the South once provided an environment that, through its openness and abundance, permitted plain-folk men to exercise an extraordinary degree of freedom. Although hierarchical stations characterized a social order dominated by class and wealth in which men were divided and governed by unwritten rules of deference, patriarchal order also existed in the plain-folk world. Men governed that society and exercised a competitive liberty in that world outside the traditional enclave of the woman whose place in the home, as described by Emma Bell Miles, was to "preserve tradition." She felt that the man had "the adventures of which future ballads will be sung. For him is the excitement of fighting and journeying, trading, drinking and hunting, of wild rides and nights of danger."[18] Respect in the eyes of other men came through physical displays of excellence, and sometimes through the use of violence—acts that, simultaneously, allowed men both to bond and to compete with each other.

Security in this masculine society, it seems to me, was always fragile. The migration west weakened the stability of families, even as it encouraged a stronger exertion of freedom among western males. The Civil War hastened the demise of plain-folk well-being, first by killing 250,000 men and then in demonstrating to them that they could not always protect their homesteads, women, and children, and finally in disrupting that open, stable environment that had permitted the exercise of individualism and freedom.

In the decades after the Civil War the southern plain folk witnessed the persistent narrowing of the liberty of that older civilization even as a newer world with fresh opportunities opened up to them. First came the closing of the open range through fence and game laws; next came the imposition of sharecropping that gradually pulled most southern farmers into its orbit of dependence and debt;[19] and finally came a renewed upsurge of evangelicalism in the late nineteenth century that sought to tame the passions of the folk. Ted Ownby declared that "evangelicals constantly worried about the sinfulness of male culture": "It was the tension between the extremes of masculine aggressiveness and home-centered evangelicalism that gave white southern culture its emotionally charged nature." Ownby also noted that the evangelicalism of that era received its most passionate support from women and that most of the targeted sins were committed by men.[20]

Southern violence certainly did not disappear. Unfortunately, much of it was directed at black people in the late nineteenth century. Sometimes poor men whose frustrations could not be assuaged through blows at their "real" enemies (the rich, the landowners, the corporations) aimed their violence at wives and children or animals. Some men joined farmer alliances and then sought relief through Populism. Others became religious converts. The Holiness movement of the late nineteenth and early twentieth centuries, in fact, seems to have attracted the same kind of dislocated and frustrated people who experimented with Populism.[21]

Even in an economy increasingly characterized by tenantry, sharecropping, or other restrictions on plain-folk liberty, men still sought ways to let off steam or to prove themselves to other men—through hunting, fishing, the use of firearms, wrestling, fighting, elaborate practical jokes, certain rituals such as anvil shooting and shivarees, or prowess with a horse. Examples of wanton brutality continued to appear in the years around the turn of the century, when the old and savage practice of "gouge and bite" flared up in casual encounters,[22] and reckless young men continued to cross the threshold into violent mayhem or murder. In one famous ballad the narrator finds his sweetheart walking at the side of "Wild Bill Jones." When Jones is told to leave the young woman alone, he replies with a rash bluster that leads to his destruction:

"My age it is twenty-one,
Too old to be controlled."
I pulled my revolver from my side,
I destroyed that poor boy's soul.[23]

Although men like Wild Bill Jones, and songs about them, did flourish, more often such violence was sublimated and redirected as humor or verbal jousting. Above all, boasting and tall tales continued to circulate on the front porches of the country stores, during hunting and fishing trips, at horse races, trades days, or anywhere that men gathered. The house parties and frolics could also be arenas for physical display, but the presence of women encouraged some degree of civility or social restraint—unless drinking was part of the scene. Organized sports of all kinds—including high school, college, and professional football—and patriotic participation in the armed forces eventually drained off much of the excess energies of young southern men. As automobiles proliferated in the rural South, they literally became vehicles for the demonstration of manly excellence, and southern rural men exhibited a remarkable receptivity to cars and trucks of all kinds, and a marvelous command of them. Journalist Dave Hickey, however, provides some insight as to why stock-car culture may have taken root in the South: "'Good old boys' try to disguise the fact they are going nowhere by driving stock cars around in circles and, contemptuous of self-pity, transform their frustration into prejudice."[24]

Early hillbilly musicians inherited from their regional culture a cluster of presumptions that extolled the idea of aggressive masculine independence, and a body of songs that chronicled the exploits of manly men. Emerging from the British tradition, southern folk experience, African American music, the vaudeville stage, and Tin Pan Alley, such songs as "Black Jack David," "Rake and Rambling Boy," "Sam Hall," "John Henry," "The Roving Gambler," "Wild Bill Jones," "Jesse James," "Stackolee," "John Hardy," "Frankie and Johnny," "Ragged but Right," and "Bully of the Town" emerged as integral components of the country music tradition. It is no accident that "John Henry," presented in a wide array of stylistic arrangements, became one of the most performed songs in early country music. While the song commands attention as a graphic commentary on work, it also stands as a great example of the powerful man who dies while trying to preserve his manhood and individuality. Consequently, its lyrics tout John Henry's prowess as a worker, lover, and free man: "a man ain't nothing but a man, but before I let this steam drill beat me down, I'll die with this hammer in my hand."[25]

From the time Henry Whitter recorded "Lonesome Road Blues" in 1923 to Merle Haggard and Willie Nelson in our own time, who voice their exhilaration in "Rambling Fever" and "On the Road Again," country singers and songwriters have vocally extolled the freedom associated with flight from responsibility. Several entertainers in early country music embodied the rambler personality in their personalities and lifestyles. That is, they tended to be restless spirits who moved from place to place and who were reluctant to work at a steady job.

As noted earlier, musicians encountered ambivalent responses in their communities. While people appreciated their talents and rewarded them in certain ways, they were also often looked upon with disfavor as ne'er-do-wells or irresponsible types. Some musicians, of course, rambled from place to place because of handicaps or infirmities—these were the ubiquitous blind and crippled musicians who had already become familiar figures on southern streets, in railroad stations, or at county fairs and other public gatherings long before the first commercial country recordings were made. A few of these entertainers, such as Charlie Oaks, Peg Moreland, George Reneau, and Dick Burnett, made the transition to commercial hillbilly music. The Kentucky musician Dick Burnett, for example—famous for his performances of "Man of Constant Sorrow," "Willie Moore," and "Short Life of Trouble"—abandoned the printed songsheets and cards that he had sold to his listeners when he began making Columbia phonograph recordings in 1926. Some men, however, became almost as famous for their lifestyles as for their music. Like Jimmie Tarlton, Harry McClintock, and Goebel Reeves, their wanderlust led them all over the country and into a succession of occupations. McClintock's wanderings, in fact, took him from his boyhood home in Knoxville, Tennessee, to journeys around the world as a merchant seaman and civilian freight hauler for the army, and eventually to the Northwest and into the radical Industrial Workers of the World, where he laid claims to the authorship of "Hallelujah, Bum Again" and "Big Rock Candy Mountain." These experiences provided him a storehouse of stories and songs which he put to good use when he became a cowboy singer in 1925 on KFRC in San Francisco.[26]

Other musicians, like the Texas fiddler Prince Albert Hunt, and Charlie Poole, a legendary five-string banjo player and singer from western North Carolina, lived life too hard and too recklessly. Hunt's escapades led to his death outside a Dallas, Texas, tavern where a jealous husband gunned him down. Poole led a trio appropriately known as the North Carolina Ramblers and was admired throughout the southeastern hills for his three-finger method of banjo playing and for a gruff style of singing that seemed patterned after that of Al Jolson. Poole avoided a violent death but was cut down at the age of thirty-seven by years of excessive drinking and sleepless nights.[27]

By the early 1930s, when the emerging country music field had demonstrated its commercial viability, most full-time country entertainers tended to be itinerant performers who moved from radio station to radio station, or who otherwise barnstormed frequently, playing in schoolhouses, movie theaters, and other widely separated venues. They were literally "rambling men" who moved from territory to territory in their quests to be independent and professional. Paradoxically, they also sought "community" with their audiences and other musicians. Traveling brought musicians in contact with experiences that were largely unknown to their working-class audiences, and it introduced them to songs and musical styles that were rare in their home communities. Their travels set them apart and gave them a touch of glamour that made them appear to be men who had seen and tasted the temptations of the world. Consequently, these musicians brought a touch of "exoticism" to country audiences with only limited exposure to what lay beyond their everyday lives. By identifying with the performer or with his songs, listeners could safely and vicariously sample the temptations they otherwise resisted or rejected, or never had the chance to pursue.

Although Charlie Poole had been calling his band "ramblers" several years before Jimmie Rodgers began his professional career, Rodgers seems to have been the first country singer who consciously cultivated the persona of a rambler and built his reputation around that identity. The vision of the rambling man expressed in his stage persona and general demeanor, however, was relatively benign. It was that of the worldly-wise man-about-town, the gay and breezy young man who kept abreast of current fashions and who had seen and tasted thrills that the average yokel could only imagine. When Rodgers ventured beyond the jaunty image suggested by his apparel of straw sailor hat and dapper suit, he exploited the romance that surrounded his longtime profession of railroading. He toured widely as "the Singing Brakeman," seldom stressing the danger and backbreaking labor of that profession but instead promoting the sense of freedom that seemed integral to railroad life.

Rodgers truly had been a wanderer most of his life, having grown up in a motherless household and as the son of a railroad construction worker who was gone from home most of the time. His principal biographer, Nolan Porterfield, said that if Rodgers's life could be "characterized by a single element, it would be impermanence. His early home life, continually subject to flux, was followed by a nomadic adolescence and the erratic rambles of an itinerant railroader."[28] Rodgers was familiar with cities, industrial workers, bums, hoboes, gamblers, saloons, and prostitutes. Very much the boaster, he sometimes exaggerated the events of his rambling past, once telling a newspaper reporter in New Orleans that he had sung all over the world and had given a performance for the king of England in Buckingham Palace.[29] Though the ravaging disease of tuberculosis drained his strength and left him with little time, energy, or money for a dissipated lifestyle, he nevertheless bequeathed to country music the legacy of a hard-living, free-loving, free spirit who died young.

While cultivating the image of a man who had seen the world and tasted both its dangers and pleasures, Rodgers also contributed to country music a repertoire of songs about rogues, rascals, boasters, rounders, convicts, hoboes, railroadmen, cowboys, and other ramblers that still beguile us today. Some of Rodgers's rambling songs, or fragments of them, probably came from his wanderings. He may have heard versions of songs like "Frankie and Johnny" and "Rounder's Luck" in the saloons, speakeasies, and brothels that catered to railroaders and other traveling men. His famous blues verses, in some cases, may have been absorbed from direct experience with black railroad workers. When he sang "Hey, little water-boy, bring that water 'round" (in "Muleskinner Blues"), he may have been recalling his boyhood days as a water carrier for the men who worked on his dad's extra gang crews repairing the tracks. But songs also came from minstrel shows and tent-repertoire and vaudeville performers, or from phonograph records of which he was very fond. These in turn inspired his own writing and that of others who supplied him with material. Whatever the source, verses like "I can get me more women than a passenger train can haul," "Any old place I hang my hat is home sweet home to me," or "It's better on down the road" contributed to the image of untrammeled freedom and hedonism that supposedly accompanied the rambling life.

Through his long experiences as a wanderer and railroad worker, Rodgers intimately understood that rambling did not flow solely from optimism or bravado, and that many men took to the road in industrial America to find employment (these were the true "hoboes"), or because of heartbreak or disappointment, or simply because they sought to avoid responsibility. Violence and death were often the companions of the lonely men who hopped the trains, and many found that life was not better on down the road. As a brakeman, Rodgers was very familiar with hoboes, and had even been one himself. These migratory workers had been part of the public discourse since the last third of the nineteenth century, when the depressions of 1873 and 1893 threw many men onto the highways and railroads looking for work. When Rodgers sang "Hobo Bill's Last Ride," "Hobo's Meditation," or his signature song, "Waiting for a Train," he recalled private experiences and communicated them to a receptive audience.[30]

The hedonism suggested by the rambling metaphor received its strongest statement in the blues fashioned by Rodgers and his disciples. Well before Rodgers's ascendancy, however, country musicians had exhibited a fascination with the blues, and the word itself had appeared frequently in the titles of country songs, usually expressing pain or loneliness but often conveying moods of joyousness (as in the fiddle tunes, "Carroll County Blues" or "Florida Blues") that seemed far afield from the classic African American form.[31] Some white country singers, such as Jimmie Tarlton, Frank Hutchison, Dick Justice, the Allen Brothers (Dewey and Austin), and Cliff Carlisle, demonstrated not only a knowledge of black blues tunes but also an ability to mimic the vocal and instrumental sounds of African American musicians that was superior to that of Jimmie Rodgers. Songs like "Do Right Daddy Blues" (sung by Gene Autry) and "Red

Night Gown Blues" (performed by Jimmie Davis) suggest that the retreat to black culture—even if nothing more than an idealized or distorted version of it—could also seem like an excursion into an alternative and often-forbidden cultural zone. Blues music permitted experimentation, the breaking of rules, and the entrance into stylistic territory far different from familiar white music forms. The appropriation of the blues style, after all, was only the most recent manifestation of a larger fascination with black culture, the parameters of which extended at least as far back as the blackface minstrels of the mid-nineteenth century. The blues provided examples of men and women who flaunted social rules. Like the donning of the black mask, the affecting of a black lifestyle and the performance of music that purportedly came from the black sexual underground permitted white men either to express a natural bent for hedonism or to rebel in a nonthreatening way against their own inhibited culture. Stereotypical conceptions of black culture, presuming the exaggerated sexuality or violent tendencies of black men and women, or the flirtation with tabooed subject matter gave white people license to do or say things lacking in their own culture.[32]

The sexual content found in many of the blues songs performed by white country musicians, however, certainly did not come exclusively from the black tradition. Much of it was nothing more than a heavy-handed attempt to simulate what the singer perceived to be a black style or approach. Other sexual forays represented an exploitation of material that, though often suppressed, was endemic to white working-class culture. Most white rural bluesmen grew up in cultures of masculine dominance and boastfulness where broad humor and sexual wordplay had been common but not often displayed in the presence of women. Some white entertainers too, like Rodgers, Tarlton, Carlisle, and Buddy Jones, had traveled widely around the country and had sampled much of life's rowdy experiences in barrooms, brothels, flop houses, and railroad shop houses. They did not have to listen to phonograph records to come up with ideas for songs, even though such items were widely available. When Cliff Carlisle noted musically that "Sal's got a meatskin hid away," and that he was going to get it someday, he was actually reaching far back beyond the American experience to a bawdy tradition that his British ancestors had known and relished. His listeners similarly did not have to spend much time guessing what he was really saying when, in "Tom Cat Blues," Carlisle asserted, "man, he's quick on the trigger; he's a natural-born crackshot. He's got a new target every night, and he sure does practice a lot."[33]

The popularity of songs like "High Behind Blues," "Red Night Gown Blues," and "Rattlesnaking Daddy," along with the raft of songs that appeared in the 1930s on western swing and honky-tonk recordings—"Milk Cow Blues," "It's Tight Like That," "Pussy, Pussy," and "She's Sellin' What She Used to Give Away"—demonstrated the enduring appeal of naughty blues tunes and suggested that home and Mother were not the only popular icons in the developing country music tradition.

These songs also suggested an alternate pattern of conduct among country entertainers, involving drugs, prostitution, and promiscuous relationships, that ran counter to the overall message that country music has always labored to convey. The country music business as a whole has tended to ignore or deny the indiscretions of its performers, clinging to the image first promoted in the Carter Family's famous handbill—"This program is morally good." Fans, though, were free to speculate about the presumed foibles of their favorite entertainers, and it was fun to think about Jimmie Rodgers and his many women, or about the debauched lifestyles that some country songs seemed to suggest.

Some students of country music have taken great delight in exposing the hypocrisy of country singers, particularly when professions of morality are piously made. Writing about the music made in the 1930s by such singers as Cliff Carlisle, Gene Autry, and Jimmie Davis, Nick Tosches entitled his chapter "Stained Panties and Coarse Metaphors" and declared that "country music is less sexy, less vulgar than it ever has been."[34] But even when the paradoxes present in the musical career of Jimmie Davis are revealed—the disclosure that this former governor of Louisiana, famous in recent years for his pious performance of gospel songs, was once a prolific performer of bawdy songs—it still remains difficult to prove an explicit correlation between Davis's repertoire and lifestyle. His blues tunes seem little more than a musical foray into forbidden territory, a lyrical rendering of a body of experiences that, in all likelihood, he had never had.[35] Several of his contemporaries, however, had ample opportunities to sample the wilder side of life in their careers as itinerant entertainers. Davis's sometime companion and protégé, Buddy Jones (Oscar Bergan Riley), had even worked in the brothels of Port Arthur, Texas, before he recorded a batch of songs that were rawer than those of his mentor. But by the time he sang his rowdy songs of being "staggering drunk, living off street women, and nights in jail," he had become "a soft-spoken, model husband and parent and a career policeman" in Shreveport, Louisiana.[36]

References to drugs appear occasionally in early country lyrics, sometimes in "covers" of black blues tunes, such as Dick Justice's "Cocaine," but also in traditional tunes like the Skillet Lickers' "Soldier's Joy," where morphine is praised. It is now virtually impossible to know how often marijuana, cocaine, or other drugs were used by early country musicians, or even when benzedrine and other kinds of pills became staples in the gear of constantly touring performers. We do know, though, that alcohol has always been the country entertainer's drug of preference, and a seemingly inexhaustible source of songs. Charlie Poole, who had an inordinate fondness for Demon Rum, made the cocaine song "Take a Whiff on Me" more consonant with southern working-class tastes by renaming it "Take a Drink on Me." In country music, and the culture from which it came, the consumption of whiskey and other alcoholic drinks has been a way of asserting masculinity, of competing with other men, and of showing fellowship with them.[37] Drinking was clearly a way of exhibiting freedom but, ultimately, it was also a sign of weakness, a measure of desperation, and a signal of personal defeat. It has also been a source of great personal pain for many country musicians and their families, and the cause of death of more than a few. A long list of country entertainers—including Charlie Poole, Uncle Dave Macon, Jimmie Rodgers, Bob Wills, Gene Autry, Hank Williams, Ernest Tubb, Red Foley, the Delmore Brothers, Carter Stanley, Jimmy Martin, Lefty Frizzell, Don Gibson, Willie Nelson, George Jones, Charlie Moore, Jimmy Arnold, and Keith Whitley—have more than convinced us that one drink is never enough and that the ultimate goal of drinking is to get drunk. As Willie Nelson noted in one song, "I gotta get drunk, and I sure do dread it."[38]

If the blues boaster provided glimpses of the wild side of life, the cowboy conjured up an alternative and more respectable vision of freedom, that of the free and untrammeled existence lived far beyond the pressures of home, family, or urban civilization. The cowboy has proved to be a symbol of almost infinite plasticity but, until the emergence of the Austin Outlaws in the 1970s, with their contrived desperado looks and hints of booze and cocaine, he has generally been treated as a benign and respectable representative of freedom and individuality. The cowboy image that country singers embraced came not from the gritty reality of cowboy life but from the realm of popular culture—a domain shaped by Wild West shows, novels, dime novels and other pulp literature, and silent movies.

The cowboy of popular culture carried little of the grime, sweat, and manure of the cattle kingdom but instead appealed to Americans as fearless, independent, moral, and a White Knight of the Plains. Even though John Lomax published his famous book *Cowboy Songs and Other Fron-*

tier Ballads in 1910, such songs had played only a minor role in building the cowboy myth prior to the emergence of commercial country music. Music did appear prominently in the performances of the Wild West shows, but the songs played by their brass bands tended to come from ragtime, John Philip Sousa, and other city show sources.[39] At least one song learned from the Lomax collection, "The Dying Cowboy," appeared on a phonograph recording in 1919 (performed by vaudeville singer, Bentley Ball), but the book otherwise appears to have had only limited circulation or influence outside of a small circle of educated readers.[40]

In 1927 Blind Andy Jenkins, the evangelist and ballad maker from Atlanta, Georgia, provided an example of the way in which the romance generated by popular culture could influence the shaping of hillbilly music. He wrote a ballad that was inspired by Walter Noble Burns's romantic book about the boy bandit king, *The Saga of Billy the Kid*. In this song, which is presumed by most people to be a traditional product of the late nineteenth century, Blind Andy reaffirmed the idea of western masculine individuality by saying that in the West "a man's only chance was his own 44."[41]

While the cowboy had appeared frequently in country songs since 1925, when Carl Sprague recorded his version of "When the Work's All Done This Fall,"[42] this romantic American hero did not come into his own in American music until the 1930s. During that Depression decade, when Americans sought escapist relief from economic anxieties and reassurance that heroes still survived, songs about cowboys began to appear in virtually every realm of American music—from Tin Pan Alley to the classical concert halls. Bearing names like the Lonesome Cowboy, the Texas Ranger, the Drifting Pioneers, Red River Dave, Montana Slim, the Girls of the Golden West, Cowboy Slim, and the Sons of the Pioneers, cowboys appeared on radio shows all over the United States and in Canada, on a multitude of recordings and, after 1934, in Hollywood movies. Stuart Hamblen's "Out on the Texas Plains," declaring that "these city lights and city ways are driving me insane," became virtually the theme of cowboy singers everywhere,[43] even though most of its performances came from city studios and were delivered to city audiences.

The romantic conception of the cowboy derived from the belief that he was a man of courage, presumably Anglo-Saxon, who had cut loose from the shackles of urban civilization and who lived a life close to nature and in communion with the expansive landscape that surrounded him. The presumed attributes of the cowboy were so powerfully appealing that they filled the lyrics of song after song and provided country musicians with

irresistible imagery that still pervades the music. Older cowboy songs continued to appear, but the great majority of those performed were newly
written. And most of them presented depictions of cowboy or western life
consonant with the romantic ideal. Jimmie Rodgers had begun to popularize this emerging genre of cowboy songs as early as 1930 when he recorded "Land of My Boyhood Dreams" (about his adopted state of Texas) and "Yodeling Cowboy." In these and other songs such as "Prairie
Lullaby," "When the Cactus Is in Bloom, "The Cowhand's Last Ride,"
and "The Yodeling Ranger" (written in 1933 after he had been made an
honorary Texas Ranger), he contributed powerfully to the building of both
the western myth and the western music genre. Even earlier in his most
famous "railroad" song, "Waiting for a Train," Rodgers had evoked the
magic of the expansive West, when his "railroad bum" said "he put me
off in Texas, a state I dearly love. Wide-open spaces all around me, the
moon and stars up above."[44]

Cowboy identification, then and since, provided country musicians a
body of symbolism that could be used to deny or avoid the taint of hillbilly culture and its southern fundamentalist overtones. Some writers and
musicians have in fact argued that western swing, the jazz-influenced
music made famous by Milton Brown and Bob Wills, was a unique product of the West. Charles Townsend, the principal biographer of Bob Wills,
actually strove to link Wills to two important traditions that fostered
freedom and creativity in country music: the West and African American culture. Since Wills grew up in "one of the largest and most famous
ranching areas in the world" (in Hall County, near Memphis, Texas), his
music, Townsend argues, "was for the most part western, that is, aimed
at cowboys, cattlemen, and people influenced by that way of life." But
Townsend also notes that the young Bob Wills had worked in that region's
expansive cotton fields with African Americans and that he "learned
much of his music and style directly from blacks."[45]

The cowboy mystique touched the lives of country singers everywhere
in America. Only four years after Rodgers's death, fourteen-year-old
Hiram (Hank) Williams set out to build a career as a hillbilly performer,
singing in the rough honky-tonks of South Alabama but dreaming of a
free and unfettered life out on the Texas plains. This son of a log train
operator, with roots deep in Alabama soil and a vocal style that bore the
marks of Roy Acuff and the Southern Baptist church, wore cowboy
clothes, used "Happy Roving Cowboy" as his theme song, and described
himself as the Drifting Cowboy. But if cowboy romance did much to
shape his perceptions, the far grittier reality of South Alabama honky-

tonks contributed more to the molding of his music. In this aggressive masculine environment Hank easily fell into a tradition of performance that gave voice to an assortment of drifters, cowboys, railroad men, and boastful lovers. The themes of such songs may not have always reflected his personal feelings; on the other hand, Hank's life had been no bed of roses, and he was already well positioned by the time he was a teenager to think in terms of alienation. He was born into a poor family in 1923 near Mt. Olive, Alabama, with a father often domiciled in a V. A. hospital and a mother who was very much the dominant and domineering presence in his home. Hank already had a drinking problem by the time he was a teenager, as well as a chronic back affliction—spina bifida occulta—that kept him in almost constant pain. The indoctrination absorbed from his boyhood Baptist church reaffirmed the message of life's bleakness and brevity, while holding out the promise of security only in another world.[46]

Hank's songs explored and evoked virtually every human emotion, and joy and delight figured prominently in his music.[47] But a fascination with ramblers, both innocent and tragic, permeated his repertoire. He sang railroad songs that both reveled in the freedom of the open road (like "Pan American") and bewailed its loss (as in "Lonesome Whistle"). He excelled in the performance of blues tunes and rowdy songs, either bemoaning his sad fate or bragging about his exploits. He sang love songs like "Hey, Good Looking" and "Baby, We're Really in Love" that joyously affirmed the relationships between men and women, but more often spoke of estrangement, betrayal, or loss—"Why can't I free your doubtful mind, and melt your cold, cold heart?" Even Hank's gospel songs spoke of flight or alienation from the world. With a repertoire reeking of alienation, it was easy for him to communicate with his plain-folk listeners, because a similar frustration and sense of dislocation lay just beneath the surface of their culture. No one in country music had ever sung quite like Hank. Neither of his two musical heroes, Ernest Tubb with his deadpan style nor even Roy Acuff with his plaintive wail, sang with the straining intensity that Hank Williams conveyed. Hank sang "hard," pushing his light, expressive voice to its limits. When he did, he brought the listener into his confidence and communicated his feelings in a more direct, personal way than any country singer before him. Hank's style led directly to people like George Jones and Ray Price who sang with similar emotional intensity.

When viewed against the backdrop of his early death at the age of twenty-nine, his pathetic last years—when divorce, drugs, physical pain,

and whiskey brought anguish to his life and instability to his performing career—contributed to the making of the Hank Williams legend, one
aspect of which has been described as the Hank Williams syndrome. In
essence, the syndrome refers to the younger singers who followed in his
wake. They believed that they should live as intensely as possible, walking in Hank's footsteps, living a similar lifestyle and even courting an early
and presumably romantic death. Paul Craft was referring to Hank's ability
to capture feelings of universal import when he wrote "Hank Williams,
You Wrote My Life," but Waylon Jennings delivered a more somber
message in a song called "The Hank Williams Syndrome." As one of those
who had chosen Hank as his mentor, Jennings delivered a musical message to his hero, saying "it's no thanks to you that I'm still living today."[48]

The Hank Williams legend has been further embellished by assertions
from such entertainers as Jennings, David Allan Coe, and Hank Williams,
Jr., that Hank was an early country music renegade and virtually the
godfather of the so-called Outlaws who thrived commercially in the 1970s
(many of whom were associated with the music scene in Austin, Texas).
Journalist Mark Humphrey notes that Williams's early death almost
ensured that he would become "all things to all people," and that his
abuse of chloral hydrate, morphine, and other drugs and the "unproven
notion" that he had died from an overdose contributed to his being seen
as "sort of a proto-rocker."[49] Such arguments are clearly self-serving ploys
designed to provide legitimacy and historical precedent for the rebellion,
both in music and lifestyle, promoted by some modern musicians. In
reality, Hank Williams seemed more lost than rebellious, more confused
than hedonistic, and perhaps more pathetic than tragic. He was a young
country boy from Alabama, talented but limited in education, thrust too
early into an environment of hard living and heavy drinking, and wealthy
and famous too young in life. He won the world but could not overcome
his personal devils. Sometime in early 1952 during a tour in California,
while being driven around between shows by Minnie Pearl and other
friends who tried vainly to sober him up, Hank abruptly stopped while
they were singing his famous hymn "I Saw the Light" and said "Minnie,
I don't see no light. There ain't no light."[50]

Hank Williams's choice of songs often exhibited his fascination with
ramblers, but even though his style of performance diverged in significant ways from his predecessors, he remained closely moored to the older
rural foundations of southern music. A major cultural gulf separated his
music and that of Elvis Presley, the man who ushered in a real revolution in style only a few scant years after Hank's death. Greil Marcus called

Hank "a poet of limits, fear, and failure" who had pushed toward the outer zones of hillbilly culture but could not go beyond them.[51] Elvis, in contrast, shoved, almost effortlessly, beyond those borders and, along with other rockabillies like Jerry Lee Lewis and Carl Perkins, forged a new musical subculture that celebrated sensuousness and physical abandon. Elvis's experiments with black music, as we have seen, had abundant precedents in the white country tradition, and his country predecessors had performed material like "Tom Cat and Pussy Blues" that was far sexier than his song choices. His open display of sexuality, however, set him apart from all other white performers who had come before him. His fusion of boyish vulnerability and sexual daring did not simply appeal to women of all ages; it also brought to the surface the contending urges that lay at the core of southern masculine culture, the contest between piety and hedonism.[52]

Before they ventured into the larger stream of American music, Elvis and his fellow rockabillies swam in the milder tributaries of mainstream country music. Virtually all of them, from Presley to Buddy Holly and the Everly Brothers (Don and Phil), came from southern working-class families who loved country music. And most of them began their careers as country singers (several of them, in fact, expressed a particularly strong fascination with Bill Monroe and bluegrass music).[53] As products of southern working-class homes, and as heirs to the country music tradition, these young musicians were certainly no strangers to the hedonism, swaggering masculinity, and individualism that had sometimes erupted in the music of Charlie Poole, Jimmie Rodgers, Cliff Carlisle, and other pioneer hillbillies. While they could draw easily on such cultural resources, and on the music of such "liberated" hillbillies as the Maddox Brothers and Rose, the Delmore Brothers, and Bob Wills's Texas Playboys, the driving force and energy of their performances came from black music and from the sense of liberation that ensued from the crossing of racial and cultural boundaries.

If rambling is a metaphor for breaking free from convention and asserting a robust manhood, then the rockabillies were the first "country" musicians who collectively broke from the restraints of southern rural culture and its traditional music limitations. To be sure, some of the rockabillies, such as the Everly Brothers and Buddy Holly, exuded boyish charm and innocence, and even Elvis brought out the mother instinct in many women. But rockabilly music as a whole suggested a hedonism, in both song and performance, that had only been hinted at earlier in the music of Jimmie Rodgers, Jimmie Davis, Bob Wills, or Hank Williams.

In short, the rockabillies were the first white musicians to put their whole bodies into their musical expression.

Elvis Presley's stage antics may have elicited gasps of repulsion from musical and moral conservatives, but his theatrics were mild compared to those projected by Jerry Lee Lewis, the swaggering wild man and quintessential rockabilly from Ferriday, Louisiana. While Elvis's hedonism resided primarily in his music, Jerry Lee's enveloped both his lifestyle and his musical performance. Elvis reserved his famous leer and pelvic thrust for the concert stage, and kept his personal hungers private from his adoring public, while Jerry Lee's indiscretions were always front-page items. In Jerry Lee's case, the music and the public man seemed much the same. In a manichean struggle similar to that waged by Jimmy Arnold, Lewis veered often between the poles of religious salvation and fleshly damnation and, strangely, managed to survive an early grave. Nick Tosches said of him, "Of all the rock-and-roll creatures, he projected the most hellish persona. He was feared more than the rest, and hated more, too. Preachers railed against him, mothers smelled his awful presence in the laundry of their daughters, and young boys coveted his wicked, wicked ways."[54]

While Jerry Lee Lewis paraded his hungers before an enthralled (or appalled) public, another sometime-rockabilly, Johnny Cash, merely hinted at indiscretions, imagined and real, but nevertheless managed to build an alluring mystique around them. Among his imagined sins was the myth of prison incarceration, a phenomenon that seemed irresistibly appealing to the country music public. Cash began his musical career on the same Memphis Sun label that introduced Presley and Jerry Lee Lewis to the world. Less than a year after his first recordings, Cash recorded "Folsom Prison Blues," a song that has remained one of his most popular numbers, and is a key to the bad boy legend that once surrounded him.[55]

Prison songs, of course, have always played crucial roles in the evolution of country music, and one of the earliest, Vernon Dalhart's "Prisoner's Song" (1924) had been a giant seller that contributed to the music's commercial acceptance in American entertainment. Most similar songs, such as "Birmingham Jail," "Columbus Stockade Blues," "Twenty One Years," "Roy Dixon," and "In the Hills of Roane County," were actually love songs that said very little about the actual conditions behind bars. By and large, country prison songs tend to paint sympathetic portraits of convicts, implying that they were falsely convicted or suggesting that they were good men who had stumbled into an act of crime. Condemned prisoner songs also showed up frequently, especially the "goodnight songs" in which prisoners said their farewells and left words of advice before going to their death.[56]

As we have seen, the folk fascination with badmen and outlaws is very old, and songs about them have been plentiful. But although some country singers like Charlie Poole, Jimmie Rodgers, and Hank Williams had carried the reputation of rounder or wastrel (and a few, such as Lefty Frizzell, Johnnie Bailes, Spade Cooley, Buzz Busby, Dave Evans, Freddy Fender, and Jimmy Arnold, have actually spent some time in jail), until the 1960s no one in country music had ever borne the reputation of "badman." Certainly, no one earlier had exploited the image for commercial reasons. The prison aura that arose around Johnny Cash and Merle Haggard was influenced by preoccupations in American popular culture, such as the cult of the antihero and the notoriety of the Hell's Angels in the 1950s, and even by occasional books and movies that concentrated on convicts and prison life. Johnny Cash, for example, has disclosed that his popular song, "Folsom Prison Blues," written during his military service in Germany during the early fifties, was actually inspired, not by personal experience, but by a movie called *Inside the Walls of Folsom Prison*.[57]

The fascination with convict life, however, has been fed by much more than the ephemeral whims of popular culture. Country music tapped into a feeling that may be universal, the suggestion that we can see a little bit of ourselves in the sins and sufferings of convicts, and a hint of our own potential for evil in the actions of outlaws. Our fascination may also be tinged with jealousy or even a bit of pride when we see someone defy the "system." And when we recall that some badmen historically have been class heroes, and that blue-collar boys of all colors get sent to prison more often than do white-collar criminals, we may inch closer to an understanding of the prevalence and the cultural significance of such songs in country music.

Johnny Cash appears to have been the first country singer to be identified as a bad boy, a perception that he did not always discourage. We can't be sure about the origins of this identification, but we can be sure that he skillfully exploited the image. If no precedents existed in country music, the powerful black folk singer from Louisiana, Huddie "Leadbelly" Ledbetter, had certainly established one in the realm of African American music. A product of both the Texas and Louisiana prison systems, this singer and twelve-string guitar player had been a prominent participant in the New York folk music scene in the late thirties and early forties, when he introduced such songs as "Goodnight, Irene," "Cotton

Fields Back Home," and "Rock Island Line."[58] Like most Americans who
evinced an interest in folk music, Cash would have known about these
songs even if he had no intimate awareness of the singer. His knowledge
would have been augmented in the early sixties when the songs and legend of Leadbelly were revived. Cash was the first country singer to identify with the folk revival of the early 1960s, and the first to participate
in concerts and festivals with the urban folkies. Harry Belafonte may have
inspired Cash's penchant for black costumes (despite Cash's avowal that
such costuming constituted a penance for the injustices of the world), and
Cash's sense of stage drama and identification with "downtrodden" elements came likely from similar sources. Referring to Cash's performance
on an album that came out not long after his revival debut at the Newport Folk Festival in 1964, an unidentified reviewer said "it's an Actor's
Studio performance all the way, reeking of melodrama" and that "everything comes out as artificially dramatic as the liner photo of Cash in
hobo's costume atop a boxcar."[59]

At some point in the 1960s rumors spread that Cash had served time
in prison, and that the scar on his face allegedly came from a prison beating. Although his "Folsom Prison Blues" seemed to reinforce the idea of
a prison record, Cash had never been to prison, and instead has spent
only two short stints in jail, once when a spark from his RV set off a forest
fire and again after he was arrested with a large supply of illegal pills.
On the other hand, Cash did have the reputation in his early career of
being a hell-raiser who got drunk, trashed hotel rooms, and played violent practical jokes. His problems with pill addiction, of course, have been
real. Convicts have often identified with him, probably because he has
given concerts in prisons and has been genuinely committed to the cause
of prison reform. Sometime between 1955, when he first recorded "Folsom Prison Blues," and 1968, when he recorded the song a second time,
Cash emerged as a full-blown spokesman for convict rights. The 1968
recording, performed in Folsom prison before an enthusiastic audience
of inmates, hints at the kind of dark bonds that linked Cash and the
convicts. When he sings that he "shot a man in Reno just to watch him
die," some of the convicts shout with glee.[60]

When Johnny Cash sang at San Quentin, one of his most ardent fans
was inmate Merle Haggard. Deprived of the love and support of his father, who died when Merle was nine years old, this "one and only rebel
child" proved resistant to the loving care and concerned supervision of
his mother. He served several stints in reform school before graduating
to San Quentin. Nevertheless, one finds no hint of this past, and certain-

ly no glorification of it, in Haggard's early career as a professional country singer. His prison record was never mentioned in early publicity material and no songs detailing his criminal career were recorded, and his promo photos showed him in a very clean-cut guise.[61]

Possibly because of Cash's emphasis on prison songs and concerts, or perhaps through accident, Haggard turned toward an exploitation of his own prison past and found the identification commercial and highly appealing. In 1967, about three years after he began making records, he recorded his first number one hit, a song written by Liz Anderson called "I'm a Lonesome Fugitive"[62] (inspired by the television series and later film, and still another example of the powerful role played by popular culture in the creation of stereotypes). There may be no connection at all between the success of this song and Haggard's later compositions and recordings of "Branded Man" (the problems of adjustment encountered by ex-convicts), "Sing Me Back Home" (a condemned convict's desire to be transported home on the wings of song), or "Mama Tried" (a partly autobiographical account of a young man who turned bad despite the earnest efforts and prayers of his Christian mother). "Mama Tried" was actually written for a movie called *Killers Three*,[63] indicating that the interrelationship between popular culture idioms can be a two-way street.

Whatever the origins of the exploitation of his convict past, Haggard found a media that was eager to talk about it and a country music public that was intensely curious about his criminal history. No comparable publicity campaign had preceded this one in country music history, and it was made palatable by Haggard's "reform," if not salvation. Country music's core Christian audience has always been ready to forgive and accept the wayward sinner who changed his ways.

Prison/convict songs actually make up a tiny portion of Haggard's repertoire, and he has more often displayed his longing for the open road in railroad songs (he is a railroad buff); in his love for Jimmie Rodgers (even though his knowledge of the Blue Yodeler's songs may have come through Lefty Frizzell's performance of them); in songs like "Rambling Fever"; and in such macho songs as "The Fightin' Side of Me" and "Working Man's Blues,"[64] where he links individual toughness to blue-collar patriotism. Haggard's autobiography, *Sing Me Back Home*, is saturated with a potpourri of rambling poses—his restlessness with middle-class convention, his womanizing and avowal that any woman who links up with him must accept his extramarital sexual needs, his militant patriotism, and, of course, his exploitation of his convict past. It is hard to resist the conclusion that Haggard is somewhat proud of some of his bad-boy exploits—and that he is a lonely man who has never found real satisfaction.

Other entertainers who followed hard on the heels of Haggard's prison exploitation stressed their own experiences in jail or otherwise became notorious for their hell-raising (a few ex-convicts, like Glenn Shirley, made unsuccessful attempts at country music careers). Johnny Rodriguez came to country music in the early seventies with a novel bilingual style of singing and the looks of a choirboy. His early promotional material, however, presented him as a delinquent who had been saved by his exceptional vocal talents. He or his publicity managers took the materials of an actual event—participating with friends in the stealing and barbecuing of a goat in a state park in Uvalde, Texas, and his consequent incarceration in a local jail—and distorted them into a story of redemption and stardom. In their story, Texas Ranger Joaquin Jackson "accidentally" heard Johnny strumming his guitar in the cell, recognized his talent, and took him to Alamo Village in Brackettville where he was discovered and hired by country singer Tom T. Hall. The truth, though, was not quite so romantic: Johnny's talents were already known to the Ranger before the goat incident, and he had previously found the young man in jail sleeping off a drunk.[65]

Johnny Paycheck (né Donald Lytle) and David Allan Coe, who both came from Ohio, were "hard cases" who had spent time in prison before their professional music careers blossomed. Both were remarkably gifted singers, but each won recognition as much for his lifestyle and bad reputation as for his singing. Paycheck's prison experience began in 1956 when, as a navy enlisted man, he hit a superior officer and was sentenced to two years military prison. Over thirty years later, in 1989, he went back to prison after shooting a man in a 1985 bar incident. (He has lived a straight life since his release in 1991.)[66] Each singer seemed to enjoy the reputation of being a rebel, and Paycheck included in his repertoire such songs as "Pardon Me (I've Got Someone to Kill)" and "I'm the Only Hell that Mama Ever Raised."[67] Coe is the only country singer who has gone to elaborate lengths to convince people that he had killed a man in prison (in the Ohio state prison, he claimed). He came to Nashville in 1967, garbed in a black cape and mask, described as the Mysterious Rhinestone Cowboy, and surrounded by an extraordinary amount of publicity that stressed his prison record and general "badness." Coe had served time in prison but had never killed anyone. Nevertheless, with Merle Haggard's songs making listeners conscious of convicts, Coe was well positioned to capitalize on the growing public fascination with badmen. In 1976, during the hoopla surrounding the "Austin Outlaws," Coe carefully identified with the major leaders of that group, ostentatiously calling attention to "Willie, Waylon, and me." Generally accompanied by menacing-looking bikers, Coe used rough and vulgar language during his concerts, surreptitiously recorded albums with pornographic content, made demeaning comments about women, and often conveyed an air of violent nihilism that overshadowed his impressive talents as a singer and songwriter.[68]

The fascination with country music outlawry, best represented by David Allan Coe, emerged in the early seventies as a facet of the resistance to Nashville's "conservatism," and it borrowed its defining forms from rock-and-roll and media-generated publicity. When Willie Nelson was still in Nashville, he became friends with a group of musicians and songwriters such as Tompall Glaser, Billy Joe Shaver, and Kris Kristofferson who were on the fringe of the Nashville establishment or, like Waylon Jennings and Johnny Cash, were perceived as rebel figures within the Nashville music community. Jennings, for example, starred in a movie in 1967 called *Nashville Rebel.*[69] Altogether, they were often pictured as mavericks, or even as "hillbillies" (a term they used to describe themselves), because they experimented with musical forms and lifestyles that diverged from the wholesome image that Nashville liked to convey.[70]

Willie Nelson moved to Austin, Texas, in late 1971, where he became part of an already-thriving musical community.[71] The young musicians who played in the numerous clubs there easily combined blues, rock, and country in their performances, just as Willie did. Willie changed more than just his residence; as he reached out to this new audience, he also changed his physical appearance and costuming in dramatic ways. His new affectations of long hair, beard, earrings, Indian headband, and sandals demonstrated his recognition of the fusion of countercultural sensibilities and country music performance that prevailed in the city. Musicians in Austin also resurrected the cowboy as a symbol of their independence from Nashville and the corporate mentality that it supposedly embodied. Unlike the benign personalities represented earlier by Gene Autry, Roy Rogers, and other Hollywood stars, the cowboy seen and heard in the new Austin musical scene was basically a countercultural figure—a "cosmic cowboy" as he was termed by Michael Martin Murphey—surrounded or emblazoned by such stereotypical Texas symbols as longhorn steers, longneck beer bottles, cactus, and armadillos.

Texas music stood in dramatic contrast to that of Nashville's, it was alleged, because the Texas style was as liberated as the environment that gave it birth. Texas musicians supposedly played for the freedom that music conveyed, and not for the money.[72] Jerry Jeff Walker (born Ronald Clyde Crosby in upstate New York) moved to Austin in 1971 after several years of residence and music in New Orleans and Greenwich Village. His sojourn in New Orleans, where he made his living singing on the streets, included an experience in the local jail where he wrote "Mr. Bojangles," a major hit in 1971 for the Nitty Gritty Dirt Band. Although "Mr. Bojangles" was a compassionate and bittersweet portrait of an aging but irrepressible dancer that Walker encountered in an adjoining cell, raucous songs like "Up against the Wall, Redneck Mother" were more representative of his Austin years. Walker cultivated, and seemed to revel in, an aura of arrested adolescence—similar to that conveyed by Jimmy Buffett—marked by heavy drinking, rowdiness, and a laid-back demeanor that virtually defined the Austin style.

A world-weary cynicism and childish irreverence marked the music and persona of still another Austin personality, Richard "Kinky" Friedman, the self-styled "Texas Jewboy," who participated actively in the Austin musical scene before he relocated in about 1976 to the Lone Star Café in New York City. Throughout his musical career, and even during his later phase as a writer of detective novels (which starred a wise-cracking hero named Kinky Friedman), he often came across as an irreverent brat bent on shocking the people around him with naughty words and outrageously expressed opinions. Kinky's brash exterior, however, masked a genuine iconoclasm, born of being a Jew in a Christian society, a finely honed wit (similar to that of Lenny Bruce), and a low level of tolerance for hypocrisy, self-righteousness, and bigotry. Refusing to sublimate his Jewishness in the interests of finding acceptance in a musical world dominated by "Anglo-Saxon Christians," he instead combined elements of both Jewish and Texas culture to produce the ultimate outsider, the Texas Jewboy. He wore cowboy clothes adorned with stars of David and other Jewish symbols, and sang his own compositions to the beat of a honky-tonk band. His first commercial hit, "Sold American," a sensitive portrayal of a fading country star, was squarely within the country music tradition. But songs like "Ride 'Em, Jewboy" (a Holocaust memorial set to the cadences of a cowboy ballad) and "They Ain't Makin' Jews like Jesus Anymore" seemed inspired by the heightened consciousness aroused by Israel's Six-Day War. The hero of the latter song, after averring that it was Santa Claus and not Jews who had killed Jesus Christ, flattens an abusive and bigoted drunk who had spewed out a stream of vile references to blacks, Jews, Chicanos, and other ethnic groups.[73]

Waylon Jennings did not relocate in Austin but was nevertheless a habitual participant in the city's musical clubs and a major contributor to the cult of the outlaw. He willingly exploited the public fascination with outlaw culture by releasing albums (inspired by song titles) called *Lonesome, On'ry and Mean* and *Ladies Love Outlaws*. In 1976 RCA repackaged a collection of old hits by Waylon, his wife, Jessi Colter, Willie Nelson, and Tompall Glaser in a package called *Wanted: The Outlaws*. Few of the million or more record buyers who purchased the album and made it country music's first platinum recording seemed troubled by the irony that powerful RCA, the quintessential embodiment of corporate Nashville, was contributing to the perception that a group of country musicians were defying both Nashville and middle-class convention.

Waylon Jennings may have been more of a team player than his outlaw image suggested, but his personal behavior and that of his musical companions did seem far different from the lifestyles publicly presented by other country entertainers. Drug usage among country musicians, in fact, began to be a topic of public discourse in the mid-eighties. In an Associated Press story Rick Blackburn, of Columbia Records, said that there had been "a significant jump in the last six years in cocaine use in the country music world" and that the practice had become "a nightmare." In his revealing autobiography Jennings declares that "almost everybody in Nashville took pills," but few were as forthcoming as this self-described outlaw who said that "the music, the pills, and the women—that was our life on the road. Sometimes I'd screw two or three a night." Jennings is not the only country musician who has admitted an addiction to drugs far more dangerous than pill popping, but few have had careers successful enough to support such an expensive habit. Discussing his addiction to cocaine, Jennings commented, "I was buying it for twenty thousand dollars a pop. My intake was reaching fifteen hundred dollars a day."[74]

In the open admission of drug usage and other forms of hedonistic behavior, some country musicians were exhibiting their close affinity to rock culture. The history of southern rock music, in fact, cannot be separated from the evolution of country music. The country music scene of the late 1990s was thickly populated with musicians who cut their teeth on either the country-rock sounds of groups like the Eagles, Poco, or the Flying Burrito Brothers or on the harder rhythms of such bands as the Allman Brothers, the Marshall Tucker Band, and Lynyrd Skynyrd.[75] The southern-born music journalist Chet Flippo captured the enthusiasm felt by many southern youth when he spoke of his delight in knowing that people like him had a body of homegrown music that they could truly call their own (that is, the rock music made by the Allman Brothers, Lynyrd Skynyrd, the Marshall Tucker Band, Wet Willie, Charlie Daniels, and other southern-born musicians).[76] Southern rock seemed simultaneously a forum for dissent against certain societal standards and a reaffirmation of those southern grassroots musical styles, such as blues and country, from which it borrowed. One can argue about whether these bands had distinctive styles that set them apart from rock bands in other parts of the country, or about whether the term "southern" refers to anything more than an identification with the aggressive symbols of Confederate nationalism. These musicians did borrow heavily, though, from southern blues styles, while being aggressively southern in their rhetoric and in the symbols with which they surrounded and adorned themselves. But southern rock bands stressed regional rather than racial identity.[77] Their use of the Confederate battle flag and other rebel symbols as costume adornments and stage decor, and even Ronnie Van Zandt's well-publicized defense of Alabama governor George Wallace (in "Sweet Home Alabama"), did not necessarily connote racism or ethnocentric bigotry. Most southern rock musicians distanced themselves from country music, but a few, such as Charlie Daniels, consciously forged links between southern rock and country. Daniels identified proudly with his fellow rock performers and was a prime mover behind the Volunteer Jam held annually in Murfreesboro, Tennessee, that showcased their music. But he also played a hot, western-style fiddle (as well as a high-decibel guitar) and spoke often of his close associations with Roy Acuff and other pioneer country performers.[78]

Singers such as Travis Tritt and Marty Stuart have enthusiastically carried the banner of southern rock alongside the country standard, but among modern country singers, Hank Williams, Jr., has most clearly demonstrated the influence of the southern rock genre. Only moderately successful in his fledgling years as a country singer, his career really boomed when he linked his style to that of the Allman Brothers and their musical kin. Long before making that identification, though, Williams had projected a lifestyle and ambience of freewheeling hedonism, with a body of music that usually conveyed the image of the "don't give a damn" hellraiser. If one perceives the man as the embodiment of his music (an assumption that is always dangerous to make about a popular artist), then Williams appears as a hard-drinking, pot-smoking, sexually uninhibited, intensely macho, and jingoistic individual. The Good Old Boy writ large. Not even a headlong plunge from a Montana mountain in 1979, which almost took his life and required massive plastic surgery (including the virtual rebuilding of his face), could chasten him or alter his general approach.[79] Hank has been very clear about his likes (whiskey, women, guns, hunting, professional football, the South) and dislikes (New York City, liberals, the Nashville music establishment). Confederate imagery and militantly southern songs such as "If the South Woulda Won" and "Dixie on My Mind"[80] have played prominent roles in his career. While religious expression almost never appears in his songs, womanizing, the utility of violence (as in "A Country Boy Can Survive" and "Attitude Adjustment"), rugged individualism, and references to Jim Beam whiskey appear frequently.[81] An all-out hedonism pervades his music, as well as the suggestion that a man can make it on his own without government interference (the government is necessary only to destroy enemies like Saddam Hussein).

Even as he resists government intervention or any kind of outside control, Hank embraces the collective action of associates, seeking camaraderie among people whom he once described as his "rowdy friends."[82] Above all, Hank has tried to link his style and personality to those of his deceased father, while at the same time paradoxically expressing displeasure at those who tried to push him into a re-creation of his father's music. He spoke of "a family tradition," for example, in a song with that title,[83] and suggested that his behavior was little different from that of his famous father. In this case, he seemed above all to be describing the country music industry as the "family" that, while forgetting its own transgressions, was concerned with public image and pressuring him to behave. Hank Jr., of course, was only one of several performers—including Waylon Jennings and David Allan Coe—who tried to link their lives and styles to the tradition of Hank Williams, Sr.

In the almost-twenty years since he first described them in song, Hank Jr.'s rowdy friends have not only grown older and more subdued, they have also virtually vanished from mainstream country music. Hank still commands a large and passionately loyal concert audience, but his recordings receive little or no airplay on commercial stations, and his television exposure is confined largely to his widely seen commercials for Monday night football.[84] His loud-boasting colleague, Charlie Daniels, still speaks out strongly when manliness or patriotism seem threatened, but after "getting religion" in the early nineties, Daniels began to show signs that his hedonism was abating. He told an interviewer in 1997 that he felt amused by the image of the "hard-drinking, carousing, good ol' boy" that still clung to him and that he felt "more like an altar boy than a good ol' boy."[85]

Waylon Jennings had noted as early as 1978 that "this outlaw bit" was getting out of hand (although he was talking mostly about perceptions of his lifestyle), but by 1992 he was asserting, in "Hank Williams Syndrome," that after years of trying to walk in his hero's footsteps he was lucky to be alive.[86] Willie, Waylon, and the Boys, and other aging country stars, complained often about the handsome young singers of the nineties who had crowded them off of the Top 40 charts. Shel Silverstein, who had contributed many great songs to the older singers, reminded them that they too had been the "pretty young boys" that the record companies had once promoted. He then wrote a series of songs for four of his old friends—Waylon Jennings, Bobby Bare, Jerry Reed, and Mel Tillis—that spoke humorously and affectionately about their ebbing masculine powers. Waylon Jennings probably voices the mood of all of them, when he says in one of these songs, "if you're thinkin' of partyin' strong, I'm sorry to say you can't take me along. I don't do it no more."[87]

Whether viewed as a consequence of an aging and tired outlaw movement or as an effort made by the music establishment to create a more respectable product, mainstream country music had become a highly sanitized phenomenon at the end of the nineties. Singers sometimes resurrected old songs, such as "Don't Give Your Heart to a Rambler," that extolled the virtues of the open road or of unfettered masculinity, but new songs of this nature appeared only infrequently. Travis Tritt and Marty Stuart sometimes decked themselves out in skintight leather pants and strutted to the beat of a rousing song like "The Whiskey Ain't Working," but when Tritt invoked the names of Hank Jr. and Waylon and declared that "There's lots of room for old outlaws like us,"[88] it was hard to take him seriously. He was in fact singing to an audience that, increasingly, had little recollection of the singers he described. Still another group of entertainers, Confederate Railroad, who, like Tritt, represented a fusion of southern rock and country sensibilities, basked in a kind of working-class hedonism and saw their version of "Trashy Women" receive airplay on Top 40 radio.[89]

Increasingly, though, those who wished to hear country music with an air of raucousness or a hint of rebellion had to reach out to the fringes of mainstream country, to the music of those singers variously described as "alternative," "no depression," or "insurgent."[90] The "alternative" description has been applied to the musical styles of a wide range of performers, some of whom, like Dale Watson and Iris DeMent, have adhered to tradition-based country sounds. Others like Son Volt, Dave Alvin, the Waco Brothers, and Jason and the Scorchers have produced music suffused with the volatility and style-bending flavor of rock. All of them, however, have shared a refusal or inability to compromise with the Top 40 compulsions of Nashville. Few, though, have expressed their disgust as graphically as Robbie Fulks, who vented his feelings about Nashville in a tune called "Fuck This Town."[91]

At the time Fulks made this recording in 1997, he was performing his fusion of country-rock for a little storefront recording label in Chicago called Bloodshot. Fulks, the Waco Brothers, Neko Case, Alejandro Escovedo, and other "insurgents" who recorded for the Bloodshot label, did country music with an edge or attitude. When the Scottish-born artist and musician Jon Langford—the central force in the Waco Brothers— told of first hearing country music back home, he also provided insights about the ways in which these older styles gave voice to a pent-up rebellion in many young fans like himself. Hard country music, he said, "was a total eye-opener; confirmation of something dark, sinewy and beer-drenched that lurked beneath. These stripped down tales of lust and loneliness, sex and death, struck a chord . . . and connected our alienated, drunk, commie souls to a strident tradition we barely knew existed."[92]

The Bloodshot company occasionally paid tribute to the veterans of country music—by producing anthologized tributes performed by its young artists or by releasing older music taken from radio transcriptions.[93] But contemporary Bloodshot artists performed with the energy and defiance of rock-and-roll, and their promotional material, like that presented by Langford, suggested an affinity for the self-indulgent side of country music. The notes for the *Boone County* collection, for example, asserted that "more than anything perhaps, country music embodies the fact that a two-week drinking binge, getting used up and tossed away in the game of love, and longing for the 'better days' of some misremembered past are simply equal parts in a well balanced life." The brochure that accompanied a Spade Cooley reissue noted that the recordings came from "country music's seminal glory days back when 'outlaw country' came from real murderous outlaws" (recalling, of course, that Cooley had served a prison sentence for murdering his wife). The advertisement for a Kansas bluegrass band, Split Lip Rayfield, described them as "three pissed-off bonafide farmboys" and noted that they were "about to boil out of the Kansas prairie like a force of Mother (fucking) Nature."[94]

Steve Earle's stage vocabulary is, arguably, more colorfully profane than anything found in Bloodshot literature, but his checkered career has been pursued independently of the insurgents and other alternative performers. Earle's music has straddled the worlds of rock, country, folk, and insurgent music but, unlike the other young rebels of country music, he has flirted with mainstream success. His personal and professional history (including brazenly displayed tattoos) bears a close, and chilling, comparison to that of Jimmy Arnold. Earle was born in Fort Monroe, Virginia, in 1955, but grew up in Schertz, Texas, just northeast of San Antonio and the Randolph Field air force base. Like too many country performers, Earle acquired at an early age an addiction for both music and drugs. A heroin habit, eventually displaced by a craving for methadone, began when he was only thirteen and eventually led him, in 1994, to jail and to substance abuse treatment.

Earle had entered the music business as a young teenager when he moved to Houston and became a regular participant in the coffeehouse folk music scene, learning the craft of songmaking and hell-raising from Townes Van Zandt, an extraordinarily talented but doomed singer-songwriter whose bad habits ultimately took his life in January, 1997. Earle experienced mainstream country success with his debut album of 1986, *Guitar Town*,[95] a highly praised synthesis of gritty working-class reality, rock-and-roll fury, and downhome country sensitivity. Quarrels with Nashville producers about his future stylistic directions followed immediately, and he veered away from country music toward the hard-edged and metallic rock found in such collections as *Copperhead Road*.

Since his release from jail and drug rehabilitation in 1995, Earle has returned to the performance of roots-oriented country music, including some dynamic recordings and concert tours with the Del McCoury bluegrass band.[96] The many fans who thrill to Earle's music applaud his personal and artistic survival but nevertheless probably do not want him to "reform" completely. The restless energy, arrogance, passion, and rebellion that have defined his life, for good and ill, have also shaped his music, endowing it with pulsating vitality, experimentation, and creativity, attributes that have been in short supply in recent country music. The untameable quality that clings to Earle's life and music simultaneously repels and attracts, suggesting both the perils that lie outside the prescribed boundaries of our culture and the possibilities of renewed strength and excitement that lie hidden in those forbidden zones.

6

"Stay All Night, Stay a Little Longer; Dance All Night, Dance a Little Longer"

Don't tell my heart, my achy breaky heart;
I just don't think he'd understand.
And if you tell my heart, my achy breaky heart,
He might blow up and kill this man.[1]

In contrast to the music discussed elsewhere in this book, "Achy Breaky Heart" drew its appeal, not from its lyrics, but from its rhythm, beat, and tune. Its singer, Billy Ray Cyrus, was virtually unknown until he and the tune were marketed in 1992 on a widely shown video. Performed to the accompaniment of a line dance choreographed by Melanie Greenwood, the song was first distributed to dance clubs and then was shown frequently on television before its release as a record. The resulting Polygram album was number one on the *Billboard* Top Albums chart for seventeen weeks in the summer of 1992. By ensuring that the song was well known before reaching the airwaves, its promotion marked an innovative way of marketing country music. "Achy Breaky Heart," along with similar examples of the combining of country music and dance, such as Brooks and Dunn's "Boot Scooting Boogie," fueled country music's great commercial surge during the 1990s.[2] Such songs remind us that dance has served as a powerful engine of change in folk and country music history.

As the oldest tradition from which country music has drawn, dance music is probably the most vital in shaping its stylistic patterns. Dancing has always linked musician and audience in ways that not only encouraged but virtually demanded experimentation and innovation in performance style. When pipers, fiddlers, banjoists, or string bands played in a dance setting, they were by their very nature "public performers." They learned to respond to their listeners, and while doing so, they perfected their skills and learned from other musicians in their midst. In pleasing their audience, they built reputations and thereby found their services welcomed at other functions and in other communities. Audience approval usually carried commercial reward: popular musicians received compensation (money, drink, food, shelter, sex) for their performance, reinforcing the impulse to play publicly.

Dances and the tunes that accompanied them came to the American South in the memories of immigrants from the British Isles, continental Europe, and Africa, and in the repertoires of dance instructors and stage entertainers. Dances that have endured can claim neither stylistic purity nor certainty of origin because they had mixed and interrelated often in the Old World, just as they continued to do in this country. Some dances certainly originated among the country folk of Europe and Africa, who incorporated them into celebrations of feast days, seasonal changes, the end of harvest, and secular and religious holidays. The passion for dancing and the eager and allied acceptance of drink and other hedonistic pleasures were universal throughout the British Isles. Fiddlers and pipers abounded, playing in taverns or at any secular public gathering.[3] They, and the pastimes where their music held sway, served as sources for the descriptive term "Merrie Ole England," which neither the Puritan revolution nor the commercial and industrial revolutions could obliterate from the plain folks' memories nor from their customary practices.

Of course, no one believes any longer that the Puritans, on either side of the Atlantic, were humorless and prudish enemies of music.[4] While they did try to eliminate secular and "popish" practices from their churches, they did not abandon the performance or enjoyment of music in other settings. Cromwellian restrictions, which deprived musicians of courtly and church patronage, ironically encouraged them to seek outlets in taverns, on the streets, and in other secular spaces. The Puritan era, in fact, saw the appearance in 1651 of a publication that played a profound role in the development of country dancing, John Playford's *English Dancing Master*. This very popular book went through numerous editions, and the 104 dances originally found there eventually swelled to 918. Although aimed at a middle- and upper-class clientele—those who had the leisure and wealth to cultivate dancing skills—the book apparently made extensive use of rural and peasant dances.

The fascination exhibited by the European elites for presumed peasant or pastoral amusements has a very old history. Queen Elizabeth I was probably not the first monarch to find intriguing the peasant dances she observed in 1591 at the Cowdray House in Essex.[5] The people who purchased Playford's book several decades later, and kept it in print for many years, were part of the vogue that Elizabeth helped to make respectable. They were probably already familiar with many of the dances anthologized in the book. The Playford items included a variety of "longways" dances in which men and women faced each other in two lines, as well as dances where couples were arranged in square and circular formations. According to Richard Nevell, "Playford's book did more than introduce country dancing to the urban public. It changed the very nature of the country dance, by turning it into a commodity. For the first time in history this simple part of rural English folk life became salable."[6]

Dance history of the seventeenth and eighteenth centuries provides wonderful examples of the myriad ways in which diverse cultures, social classes, and nations have intersected to shape the musical evolution of our country. Many of the dances collected by Playford became fashionable among the French elites after the Stuart restoration normalized relations between the upper classes of France and England. The longways dances were described in France as contredanses, because of the opposed positions of the dancers. Then the term contredanse gave rise to the mistaken opinion that "country dance" was an English corruption of the French term and, consequently, an English borrowing of a French dance. These dances, or adaptations of them, were reexported to England along with a new vocabulary of French terms that described their movements. The dances came to America soon after the War for Independence, but became especially prized during the early years of the French Revolution, when popular enthusiasm for French culture was at its height in the United States. One of the longways dances, often described as the "Sir Roger de Coverley," became the basis for America's famous Virginia reel.[7]

Even more crucial for the development of country dancing in the United States were the quadrilles, dances that involved four couples arranged in square formations. The cotillon, which was anglicized as cotillion, appears to have been a type of quadrille. Since cotillon was a peasant girl's petticoat, the likelihood that the dance was of rural origin seems rather strong. French dancing masters brought the dance to the American colonies, along with a language of instruction that is still a basic part of the square dance tradition. Words like allemande, promenade, dos-a-dos, and chassez (sashay) still direct the movements of square dancers today, while also preserving remnants of the dances' aristocratic French origins.[8]

Although at least thirty dance instruction books were published in the United States between 1794 and 1800, Americans soon dispensed with printed instructions and the necessity for memorization, and instead performed the steps to the accompaniment of ongoing and rhythmic oral direction. Their basic innovation was the introduction of the caller, a role played by the fiddler or someone else who shouted out the movements of the dance and led the dancers through their paces. The introduction of the practice cannot be precisely dated, but S. Foster Damon, the leading authority on square dancing, asserts that the first published reference to calling came in 1828 when Bernard, duke of Saxe-Weimar-Eisenach, recounted hearing a fiddler call the dance figures a few years earlier at a dance in Columbia, South Carolina.[9]

We will never completely understand the process by which these group dances entered American life, nor the means by which they became integrated into the lives of the southern rural folk. As we have seen, dances came to America in a variety of ways, in the cultural baggage of both plain people and professional dancers. In 1917 Cecil Sharp observed a country dance performed by the students at Pine Mountain Settlement School in Kentucky, and referred to the "wildness and the break-neck speed of the dancers" as they responded to the "even, falsetto tones of the caller" who "calmly and unexcitedly" directed them. He described the dance as a "running set" (because of the flowing steps of the dancers) and theorized that it was a folk survival of a rural dance that preceded those anthologized by John Playford.[10] But long before 1917, dances in American folk communities had been described as cotillions and quadrilles. In his diary of March 2, 1842, William Bollaert described a ball somewhere in South Texas that celebrated the new republic's independence, and said that "country dances, cotillons and waltzes followed each other in rapid succession."[11] Sharp's suppositions that the "Kentucky Running Set" was an organic reflection of local community life and that the dance rituals he observed were preserved from the remote British past may be accurate (although we cannot be sure about how much input was made by settlement-school teachers). Nevertheless, from the earliest beginnings of southern history, folk and cultivated dance traditions had often intersected, just as they had done earlier in the Old World.

Throughout the southern frontier people used terms like "quadrille" and "cotillion" interchangeably to describe group dances. If we could know the specific process by which these terms (and perhaps the dances themselves) traveled from aristocratic French origin into the possession of the American folk, and how the people transformed them into something that was distinctively their own, then we could come close to understanding the dynamics through which folk culture is constantly being revised. The dance masters advertised their skills in the newspapers, and then held classes in towns and cities mostly along the Atlantic seaboard but also at plantations where the roles of dance instructor and tutor might be combined. Neither the dance classes nor the instruction books that the masters sometimes compiled would have been easily accessible to working people in the cities or to plain folk in the countryside. If the dance masters were unlikely to have ventured into the rude huts and dogtrot cabins of the plain folk, or to have rubbed shoulders willingly with farmers or drovers, fiddlers tended to be a peripatetic lot who purveyed their art among a wide spectrum of people. Clason Wheeler, a fiddler and indentured servant in the late seventeenth century, was probably not the only musician of humble origin who accompanied dance masters as they made their rounds.[12] Calling out the basic moves and positions of the dance, the teachers and fiddlers introduced square dancing (and perhaps other dances as well) to country folk who in turn transmitted the skills to their children and neighbors. Whether organically evolved by the folk themselves or introduced to them by those outside their culture, the square dances have become basic ingredients of the rural musical culture of America.

Other rural dances have displayed a similar evolution, and our knowledge of their origins, and of their "movement" into folk culture, remains similarly hazy. The various "step dances," for instance—distinguished by individual foot or body movements rather than group interaction—have been the products of both folk creativity and borrowings from popular culture. Exhibiting a wondrously cyclical nature, material inspired by or copied from the folk was refashioned by popular stage entertainers who, in turn, circulated it anew in grassroots culture, albeit in altered form. In much the same fashion, dances introduced on the stage have been copied or appropriated by the folk who have reintroduced them to popular culture. While it is true that southern rural dances have also moved freely across racial lines, the step dancing that was popular among black and white people may also have arisen from similar yet independent origins.

Unfortunately, early references to dancing among the plain folk, in both Europe and America, share the same imprecision, vagueness, and loose terminology that have been applied to folk music as a whole. Most often, observers made no attempt to describe precisely the dances they saw but instead made generalized references to cotillions, reels, quadrilles, jigs, double shuffles, or breakdowns. The English traveler Charles Lanman and the German tourist Frederick Gerstaecker were typical, but hardly enlightening, when they referred to "a series of fantastic dances" and "extraordinary movements" that they saw, respectively, in Black Mountain, North Carolina, and backwoods Arkansas in the antebellum South.[13]

Used indiscriminately in the British Isles to describe various forms of solo dance steps, as well as the tunes used to accompany them, the term "jig" came to America burdened with a haziness and inconsistency of definition that have ever since made it next to impossible to visualize what was being described when the word was used.[14] In America observers spoke of both "Irish jigs" and "Negro jigs." Similarly, blackface minstrels danced, and popularized, jigs, clogs, hornpipes, and other step dances that may have been borrowed from folk sources or that may have been the original and artistic creations of the dancers themselves. Consequently, to be told that someone "danced a jig" is hardly revelatory; the expression might describe a professionally executed series of steps, a folk survival of some forgotten ethnic past, or nothing more than an individual improvisation.

In the folk history of the rural South, jig has been merely one of several terms, such as clogging, flat-footing, hornpipe, buck-and-wing, double shuffle, hoedown, and breakdown, used to describe step dances—movements that might be done in solo fashion or that might be executed while going through the motions of a circle or square dance. The precise techniques that differentiate such movements as the buck-and-wing, double shuffle, clogging, or the hornpipe, and that usually can be recognized only by a dance historian or dance instructor, were not always discerned by the folk themselves. Minstrel dancers popularized the buck-and-wing even though it may have been based on earlier folk dances (a composite of buck dancing and the pigeon wing). Clogging was a British cousin of the jig, and often was performed by minstrel entertainers who would have been well known to the folk. Barney Fagan, for example, best known as the writer of "My Gal Is a High Born Lady," was described as "one of the fanciest clogdancers" in the blackface profession.[15]

Although country dancing evolved in many arenas—around the Maypole, on the village green, in barns, in the courtly salons of France and England, in those places where the dance masters held sway, and even at the festivals, YMCAs, public school gymnasiums, settlement house recreation halls, and other arenas where square dancing, clogging, and other folk dances were "revived"—the phenomenon found its most "natural" habitat in the community setting once known universally as a "frolic." Originating in the British Isles as an event of social merriment accompanied by food, drink, and dancing, the frolic was often associated with some kind of communal work project. The men might gather for a corn shucking, house raising, or other project; the women would quilt; and at the conclusion of their labors a feast with dancing would be held.

Contemporary accounts tell us little about the dance steps or accompanying instrumental styles heard and seen at the frolics, but they do provide descriptions of the social context of the dances that remain remarkably similar from the early nineteenth to the early twentieth centuries. Whether described in a newspaper such as the *Spirit of the Times,* in the fictional essays written by the antebellum southwestern humorists, in the diaries recorded by travelers, or in the recollections of ex-slaves found in the *WPA Narratives,* the dances emerge as community events marked by conviviality, drink, food, and dancing. A. B. Longstreet's depiction of a country dance, published in *Georgia Scenes* in 1835, is not only the classic account of such an affair, it also presents descriptions that would have been familiar to observers one hundred years later. Longstreet evokes the rough democracy of the frontier South when he recalls dancing "the good old republican reels" in the home of a country magistrate, and he informs us of the community nature of such events.[16] Frolics evolved in a logical sequence: invitations were sent to neighbors; furniture was removed from one or more rooms; and fiddle music accompanied the dancers through the night. Often, as in the scene remembered by Longstreet, only one lonely fiddler (a black man) kept the music going throughout the evening, but rhythmic accompaniment might come from any one of several sources—from someone beating a straw or knitting needle against the unfretted strings of the fiddle, or from a banjo, guitar, French harp, perhaps even a piano. The fiddle and banjo, however—with their "hint of fusion" between Europe and Africa[17]—together seem to have formed the earliest type of string band found in the rural South, one that could have been heard at house parties from the Appalachians to the Texas plains. Any kind of social gathering that attracted young and competitive men, or where strong drink was available (as was often the case at the country dances), could degenerate into violence. Most frolics, however, were convivial, high-spirited, and harmless diversions where friendships were renewed, loneliness dissipated, and courtships initiated.

Precise information about the dances, tunes, and styles of performance seen and heard at the frolics is hard to come by,[18] but eclecticism formed the essential hallmark of both dancers and musicians. If we could be transported to a pre–World War I southern rural community, we would not see a classic rural dance preserved unchanged from its Old World origins. Neither would we see a clear expression of an Irish or Scottish step dance, nor any other kind of dance "classically" presented. We would see instead representations of the eclecticism that defined folk culture—dances that reflected both Old and New World influences: African, British, minstrel, vaudeville. Or we would see nothing more than the high-spirited, free-wheeling improvisations of the dancers who had forgotten the classic movements of the past and who could care less about tradition or formality. A correspondent to the *Spirit of the Times* in 1843 revealingly described this freedom and spontaneity when he described an East Tennessee rural dance: "The music sounds high, and the wild woods ring; the feet of the company fly thick and fast; reels, cotillions, and waltzes, are all so mingled and blended together that it is a dance without a name."[19]

Dancers performed square dances, reels, waltzes, polkas, and other couples dances, and they did solo steps that could have been the preserved remnants of Old World folk dancing, imitations of stage dancing, or nothing more than zestful improvisation. The famous landscape architect and traveler Frederick Law Olmsted encountered a bit of the latter when a backcountry Mississippian described "plank dancing" to him. Standing face to face, dancers cavorted on a plank that had been placed on two barrel heads so that it might spring. Dancing as fast as they could, the participants responded to shouts like "keep it up, John. Go it, Nance. Old Virginny never tire. Heel and toe, Ketch a-fire!"[20]

Solo performance often came at the end of an evening of square dancing, during the "breakdown" when dancers felt emboldened or were encouraged to demonstrate their individual talents.[21] Fiddlers and string bands likewise were receptive to a broad spectrum of songs and styles, and they repeatedly reshaped and renamed the inherited tunes of Europe and linked them to melodies that came from blackface minstrelsy, African American performance, brass bands, vaudeville, Tin Pan Alley, or even from classical settings. When the legendary Norwegian violinist Ole Bull visited the United States, he often attracted the patronage of plain rural southerners, and the curiosity of country fiddlers, when he gave concerts in the South. When he appeared in places like Memphis or New Orleans, "the roads into town were crowded with whole families traveling by ox-cart to hear him."[22] Whatever the source of the dances or instrumental tunes, the frolics were the birthplaces of rural secular public performance, places where music and styles of performance were preserved and transmitted throughout the rural South, and where musicians learned to ply their trade in a quasi-commercial environment. That is, they could expect some kind of remuneration for their performances.

At the dawn of commercialization in the 1920s, house parties still thrived in the South. Increasingly, though, the popular tunes were now divorced from the dances that once sustained them. Fiddlers played "Sailor's Hornpipe," "Fisher's Hornpipe," "Durang's Hornpipe," "Rickett's Hornpipe," or "The Virginia Reel," for instance, without knowing that the tunes had once been indispensable accompaniments of dances that bore the same names.[23]

As important as the house parties may have been in providing experience for musicians, the equally venerable fiddle contests had a more direct impact on the new forms of commercialization that emerged in the twenties. These contests have been documented as early as November 30, 1736,[24] in Hanover County, Virginia, where the patrons of a St. Andrews Day celebration promoted a number of contests that included both dancing and fiddling. Toward the end of the nineteenth century country fiddling had become identified as an old-time art that represented the defeated but still-proud South. Confederate reunions became popular sites for the contests, and old soldiers were prominently involved as participants, judges, and listeners.[25] With Atlanta's city fathers and business spokesmen leading the way, apostles of the New and progressive South often seized upon the romantic imagery of the Lost Cause to lend dignity and a sense of tradition to the new society that they were striving to bring into existence. Atlanta's sponsorship of a fiddle contest in the spring of 1913 musically linked the city's growth to the presumed innocence and virtue of Georgia's rural past. In the years that followed subsequent Atlanta contests, along with similar events broadcast on local radio, played host to such fiddlers as Lowe Stokes, Clayton McMichen, Gid Tanner, John Carson, and others who later played prominent roles in the early commercial history of country music.[26]

If city boosterism in the South sometimes represented a blending of Old and New South imagery, the new technologies of radio and recording facilitated the widespread dissemination of southern rural musical sounds. Confederate symbolism, once again, contributed significantly to the newly won exposure of rural music. In 1922 fiddler Eck Robertson, from Amarillo, Texas, played at a contest sponsored by Confederate veterans in Richmond, Virginia. At the end of the contest he and an old friend from Oklahoma, Henry Gilliland (both a fiddler and veteran of Company H,

2nd Texas Cavalry), traveled to New York where they made test recordings for the Victor Talking Machine Company. Gilliland was one of a contingent of former Confederate soldiers—including Mose J. Bonner, Matt Brown, Jesse Roberts, and James Knox Polk Harris—who participated in fiddle contests around the turn of the century and who had been instrumental in the creation in April, 1901, of the Old Fiddlers Association in Fort Worth. Gilliland was still wearing the Confederate uniform that he had sported at the Richmond event. His and Robertson's renditions for Victor often are described as the first documented commercial recordings of southern rural musicians.[27] Approximately one year later, an ex-Confederate captain, Mose J. Bonner, played a variety of fiddle tunes on WBAP in Fort Worth, inspiring an avalanche of telegrams and telephone calls, and demonstrating the far-flung appeal of the ancient art of fiddling. Garnering responses from listeners as far away as Haiti and Hawaii, the tunes inspired the creation of the first radio show in America that bore the name of "barn dance."[28]

Old-time fiddling everywhere formed the core of what was soon described as barn-dance radio programming. WLS in Chicago inaugurated its barn dance in 1924 with the fiddling of Tommy Dandurand and the square dance calls of Tom Owen being alternated with the pop dance band music of Isham Jones.[29] During the next year WSM in Nashville introduced a similar show that featured the fiddle playing of Uncle Jimmie Thompson, who claimed that he knew a thousand tunes. Even earlier, at WSB in Atlanta, Fiddlin' John Carson had been popularizing tunes and an archaic style of fiddling that he had introduced at fiddle contests and house parties many years before. In June, 1923, Polk Brockman, a local furniture dealer and record seller, saw a newsreel of a fiddle contest and was immediately reminded of Fiddlin' John. Well aware of Carson's popularity among the working folk of Atlanta, Brockman urged Ralph Peer, a talent scout for Okeh Records, to record the old-time fiddler and singer. Carson's recording of "Little Old Log Cabin" and "The Old Hen Cackled" marked the real beginning of country music's commercial history.[30]

An old-time fiddling renaissance, powered by new methods of dissemination, was already well under way when, motivated by a hatred of jazz and the fear that it would corrupt the morals of American youth, Henry Ford launched his campaign to revive the old-fashioned dances of his childhood. He organized a dance band that could play traditional dance tunes on fiddles and period instruments, published a dance instruction book, and promoted a series of fiddle contests that brought musicians to Detroit in 1926 for a national competition. The eventual winner, Uncle

Bunt Stephens, was a Tennesseean who made a handful of commercial recordings the following year.[31] Ford's campaigns lent renewed respectability to the art of old-time fiddling and encouraged rediscovery of traditional group dances that would, in Ford's opinion, revitalize a spirit of wholesome and nonsensual entertainment that could effectively serve as an antidote to the Jazz Age.

While Ford pursued a moral and political agenda largely oblivious to what was happening in the world of commercial phonograph recording, the early hillbilly entertainers were doing their own part to preserve fiddling and rural dance tunes. The bulk of the songs heard on the earliest commercial country recordings, that is, in the period from 1923 until 1927 when Jimmie Rodgers and the Carter Family appeared, were instrumental tunes that summoned up memories of rural dances or play parties and of the colorful pastiche of songs heard there. Singing was generally only incidental in the pioneer string bands, or was shared by various members of the groups. In most string bands, too, from Virginia to Texas, the fiddlers carried the lead. These fiddle bands varied widely in the overall mood they conveyed, ranging from the rather structured predictability of the North Carolina Ramblers to the abandoned zestfulness of Georgia's Skillet Lickers, but most of them recalled the house parties where the bands had once held sway. In the Skillet Lickers' famous recording of "Soldier's Joy," for instance, fiddler Clayton Mc-Michen's spirited spoken introduction not only establishes the character of that band but also evokes the atmosphere of a North Georgia house party: "Here we are, the Skillet Lickers, red hot, and raring to go. Don't let 'em mess up your rug; make 'em roll it up."[32]

When early country bands took to the road, they of course often played for dances, or they featured dance exhibitions on stage. Singer and guitarist Sam McGee recalled traveling out of Nashville and into the Midwest in 1925 with a WSM Barn Dance troupe that included Dr. Humphrey Bate and his daughter Alcyone. The group often played in movie houses for square dancing between films.[33] Individual members of bands occasionally added a touch of novelty to their concerts by performing a spirited buck-and-wing or flatfoot dance, and performers who were well known for their dancing skills sometimes shared the bill with fiddle bands and other country groups. Lew Childre, for example, honed his talents as a singer, steel guitarist, comedian, and buck dancer on the tent-repertoire circuit, and then became an active participant in country music road shows by the middle of the thirties.[34]

The 1930s was a period of innovation in dance, and a consequent time of expansion and stylistic change in country music. Dance provided a welcome release for those trying to escape the grim realities of the Great Depression, while the back-to-the-roots consciousness of the era contributed to the revitalization of folk dancing of all types. Square dancing had already profited from the allied vogues for folk dancing and public recreation that began in the early years of the century, largely as a consequence of efforts made in this country to emulate the work done by Cecil Sharp and the English Country Dance Movement. The campaigns launched in New York between 1903 and 1905 by Luther Gulick and Elizabeth Burchenal to incorporate European folk dances into the recreation programs of that city's settlement houses and public schools were widely copied throughout the nation.[35] The cultural nationalism of the World War I era, when the American Folk Dance Society was organized, lent further encouragement to the revival of square dancing and other old-time forms, but they received even greater encouragement from the folk festivals that emerged in the thirties as the creations of a rather unlikely coalition of folk revivalists, economic developers, chambers of commerce, and other civic improvement groups.[36] Between 1928 and 1934 four large festivals appeared at Asheville, North Carolina, Ashland, Kentucky, White Top Mountain in southwest Virginia, and St. Louis (where the first National Folk Festival convened). The sword and morris dances that were introduced to audiences at the White Top Festival in 1935, and at some of the mountain schools, were so alien to local tastes and sensibilities that they found few adherents. Other dances that seemed rooted in American folk culture, however, won permanent acceptance. The cultivation of what seemed to be indigenous southern rural dance styles began in 1928 when the Asheville, North Carolina, chamber of commerce asked Bascom Lamar Lunsford—lawyer, musician, and amateur folklorist—to organize some folk music contests as part of the city's Rhododendron Festival. The competitions, which involved both musicians and dancers, evolved into the nation's first and most enduring event of its kind, the Mountain Dance and Folk Festival.[37]

One of the competitive acts featured at the first festival, Sam Queen's Soco Gap Square Dancers, popularized a form of ensemble dancing that soon influenced the style of dancers throughout the southeastern United States. They were square dancers with a difference: they performed individual buck dance or clogging steps as they went through the motions of the group dance. Although individualistic in execution, the step dancing performed by Queen and his dancers was eclectic in origin, having been influenced by the buck dancing of a local African American, Bob Love, and by the tribal dances of Cherokee Indians who lived in western North Carolina. The presence of the Soco Gap Square Dancers at the White House in 1939, where they performed for President and Mrs. Roosevelt and the king and queen of England, lent both publicity and prestige to this form of vigorous grassroots dancing. "Clogging" had been used to describe this form of group dancing at previous festivals in Asheville and Galax, Virginia, but the the term received greater publicity when the queen asserted that it looked like the clog dancing she had seen back home.[38]

While the folk dance movement gained strength throughout the country, most dancers in the thirties found diversion in the dance halls and taverns that proliferated after 1933 with the repeal of Prohibition. Here, in an expanding environment marked by the confluence of dance, drink, music, and electrical amplification, country music strived to come to terms with an audience simultaneously trying to cling to its rural roots and to adapt to an emerging urban-industrial existence. The relationship between music and strong drink, of course, is ancient, and dancing in one form or another always maintained a presence, first in the taverns of the British Isles, and later in America's saloons and bars. A rare sketch of one such performance appeared in an 1873 edition of *Scribner's Monthly* showing a fiddler and guitarist sitting on a platform and playing for dancers in a Denison, Texas, saloon. According to the correspondent, "men drunk and sober danced to rude music in the poorly lighted saloons and did not lack female partners."[39]

The term "honky-tonk" was being used at least as early as 1894 to describe low-life drinking establishments in certain towns in the United States. Generally used as a catchall description, or as an adjective (as in "honky-tonk theaters" or "honky-tonk halls") honky tonk in 1900 had been appropriated by at least one dive in New Orleans as its official title.[40] New Orleans usage and early published song titles (such as "Everything Is Hunky Dory down in Honky Tonk Town," 1918) suggest an African American connotation, and it was not until some undetermined time in the thirties that "honky-tonk" became a commonly used designation in the South for bars and taverns where white people gathered to drink, dance, and listen to music. The term was common enough in 1936 for Texas singer Al Dexter to ask James Paris, who was, ironically, best known as a gospel composer, to write a song about it, "Honky Tonk Blues."[41] Some establishments were too small to permit dancing, but in the dance halls music was provided by bands or by coin-operated record-playing machines known as jukeboxes. One finds little evidence that the term "honky-tonk" was ever affixed to a style of country music until the mid-sixties,[42] but "honky-tonkin'," referring to an evening of drinking, conviviality, and dancing, was in common parlance among working-class southerners long before 1949 when Hank Williams musically popularized the term.[43]

The most crucial innovations made in the realm of honky-tonk dancing came in Texas and Oklahoma where string bands, whose music is now described as western swing or honky-tonk,[44] flourished. Famous bands such as Bob Wills's Texas Playboys, Milton Brown's Musical Brownies, and the Light Crust Doughboys played for dances at places like Cain's Academy Ballroom in Tulsa, Crystal Springs Ballroom in Fort Worth, and Mattie's Ballroom in Longview, Texas, offering a diverse mix of country hoedowns, ragtime, blues, and jazz melodies. Bob Wills's Texas Playboys won wide exposure through their daily broadcasts on powerful KVOO in Tulsa, but their real bread and butter came from the dances for which they played constantly throughout Oklahoma, Texas, and Kansas. Wills's longtime steel guitarist, Leon McAuliffe, spoke of dancing as the key ingredient that distinguished the music west of the Mississippi from that of the East: "We played for dancing. East of the Mississippi they played a show . . . just for people to sit and listen." Still another Wills musician, pianist Al Stricklin, remembered the first dance that he played with the Playboys: "When I said Glen Oak was out in the country, I mean it was out in the country. There was maybe two families living there. One of them owned the dance hall." Nevertheless, by 8 P.M. "cars were piling up outside. Some people were coming on foot. Some were riding horses. By nine, they were having to turn them away."[45] Although their increasingly youthful audiences mildly pressured the groups by asking for the pop hit songs of the day—particularly those done by Glenn Miller, Benny Goodman, and other swing musicians—innovation came primarily from the musicians themselves, many of whom had served apprenticeships in jazz groups or who freely admitted their fascination with the sounds of hokum and swing music.[46] Benny Goodman's famous guitarist, the Dallas-born Charlie Christian, and the inventive Gypsy guitarist Django Reinhardt influenced many of the western swing musicians with their fluid, single-string improvisations. From the thirties until his death in 1997, Stephane Grappelli, the French jazz violinist, fascinated many country fiddlers with his hot rhythms.[47]

Group dancing occurred often in the dance halls, in such routines as the Cotton-Eyed Joe or in "mixers," such as the Paul Jones (which were designed to encourage dancers to mix and get to know each other), but couples dancing predominated. Usually circling in counterclockwise fashion around the entire dance floor—with men leading and women typically moving backwards—dancers did waltzes, polkas, schottishes, "put your little foot," "herr schmidt," and the two-step. Of all the dances encountered in the honky-tonks, the two-step ("generally done with two long steps and a step-close-step to two-four time") was, and has continued to be, the preferred dance of working-class Texas.[48]

Dance hall culture has thrived in country music since the forties, even though it has not always dominated the scene. During the years of sacrifice and scarcity in the World War II period, musicians could no longer maintain bands as large as the sixteen-piece organization that Bob Wills headed in the late thirties. The intensely dance-oriented style of western swing also declined in the forties, and vocalists began to predominate. Even in those states where the swing style had prevailed—Texas and Oklahoma (where the style was introduced) and California (to which many of the principal bands emigrated)[49]—smaller bands headed by featured vocalists became the norm. Typically, bands became identified with and subsumed by the singers—for example, Ernest Tubb and the Texas Troubadours, Hank Williams and the Drifting Cowboys, Ray Price and the Cherokee Cowboys, Hank Thompson and the Brazos Valley Boys, Buck Owens and the Buckaroos, Merle Haggard and the Strangers—who led them.

But even in a musical form where lyrics are said to be central—the great jazz musician Charlie Parker, who had an affinity for country music, advised skeptics to "listen to the stories"[50]—and in which the vocalist is supreme, it is the dance beat that has energized and propelled the song. Influential singers such as Ernest Tubb, Hank Williams, Ray Price, and Buck Owens have justly won admission to the Country Music Hall of Fame, but the crucial dance beat that was central to their music was created by largely unsung musicians who borrowed their riffs from jazz, swing, blues, and rock-and-roll. During intermissions, when the star vocalist stepped off the stage, or when he permitted his musicians to play an all-instrumental number, "sidemen" such as Jimmy Day, Buddy Emmons, Roy Nichols, Johnny Gimble, and Buddy Spicher chose material that was generally far more complex than the featured vocal offerings.

The eruption of rock-and-roll in the mid-fifties temporarily drove the older country styles off the jukeboxes and radio playlists, and, in the quest for a more urban and youth-oriented sound, the fiddle was silenced. But the honky-tonk country dance beat never disappeared. It flourished especially in the dance halls of Texas and California where working folk continued to let off steam on weekends as they danced the two-step to the insistent commands of the fiddle, electric guitar, and steel guitar, and the throbbing beat of drums and electric bass. During those years Ray Price's Cherokee Cowboys set down an infectious rhythm, a 4/4 shuffle beat marked by drum brush strokes and a walking bass that contributed mightily to their leader's success in the music charts and was widely imitated by other musicians.[51]

The honky-tonk style popularized by Price and the Cherokee Cowboys and other modern bands, however, differed substantively from the music played earlier by the bands of Tubb, Tillman, Williams, and Frizzell. This new country dance band style fused elements born in the recording studios, on the bandstand, and in the electronics laboratories. Bands were now more heavily eclectic and electric. Every instrument, including the fiddles, took advantage of electrical amplification, and the musicians reached well beyond the parameters of country, jazz, and rhythm-and-blues and into the competitive territory of rock-and-roll. The younger musicians, after all, grew up during the heyday of rock-and-roll enthusiasm, and they played for audiences that increasingly cut their teeth on the music of rock performers who emerged in the sixties and beyond. The periodic resurgences of "traditional" country music that have occurred since the early sixties have been powered, for the most part, by musicians like Buck Owens, Merle Haggard, Willie Nelson, Ricky Skaggs, and Dwight Yoakam who have freely mixed sounds and styles that represent the broad spectrum of American popular music.

Buck Owens's emergence in the early sixties was widely hailed as representative of a resurgence of "hard" country music, and he even made a widely publicized pledge to perform only real country music.[52] His music more precisely exemplified the blending of styles that has characterized the music's modern commercial ascendancy. Owens's early recordings sometimes featured the fiddle, and his songs, performed with duet harmonies and to the accompaniment of a shuffle beat, occasionally echoed strains of music made earlier by Ray Price's Cherokee Cowboys. The music made by Owens's Buckaroos, though, was preeminently a music molded in the clubs of Bakersfield and southern California—part honky-tonk and part rockabilly—and made distinctive by a propulsive, high-pitched, and thoroughly electronic energy produced by the guitar stylings of Owens and his talented sidekick, Don Rich.[53] Owens's sound reached beyond the country audiences that had sustained the music of Ray Price and other fifties' traditionalists, and captivated a new generation of listeners who wanted their country music spiced with the bounce and energy of rock-and-roll. Manifestations of the revolution wrought by Buck Owens first appeared, appropriately, in California, in the music of Chris Hillman and Gram Parsons who founded the Flying Burrito Brothers and, later in Los Angeles among the "cowpunks," young musicians who brought the aggressive edge, attitude, and high-volume sounds of rock-and-roll to the music.[54] Today, a host of young acts who combine swing, rockabilly, boogie, and country—such as Dwight Yoakam, Big Sandy and the Fly-Rite Boys, BR 5-49, and the Derailers—proudly acknowledge the influence and legacy of Owens and his Buckaroos.

The passion for dancing has never abated among the fans who have gravitated toward country music in all of its forms. Many of the older varieties of group and solo dancing attained renewed popularity through the influence of the folk revival in the early sixties and through the back-to-the-roots vogue that has prevailed since that time. The popularity of square dancing of course had never really diminished since the forties, with its network of clubs, colorful costumes, and instruction books offering constant renewal and reinvigoration. Square dance clubs, in fact, had done much to keep fiddling alive in the late fifties, largely through their use of dance recordings that featured such well-known fiddlers as the Grand Ole Opry's Tommy Jackson. The Grand Ole Opry itself lent widespread exposure to both traditional square dancing and team clogging through the featured stage performances of Ralph Sloan and the Tennessee Travelers, who had been on the show since 1952, and Ben Smathers and the Stoney Mountain Cloggers, who came in 1957. Audiences could see the dancers not only as they did their steps during the Friday and Saturday night Opry shows but also on the widely syndicated television shows of Opry performers produced by Al Gannaway.[55]

The square dance clubs appealed largely to adult Americans whose interest in country music was sometimes only incidental, while the Opry dancers catered to fans whose chief interest was the music itself. The dances and dance music seen and heard at folk-revival festivals, on the other hand, encompassed another audience, a generation of young people who were searching for simpler pleasures that lay outside the mainstream of middle-class culture. Festivals in Newport, Rhode Island, and on the Smithsonian Mall in Washington, D.C., introduced folk culture to many people, provided models for similar functions that have since been held elsewhere in the United States, and inspired a rediscovery of older grassroots musical gatherings.

Established in 1972, Rod Kennedy's Kerrville Folk Festival (located in the heart of the Texas hill country) has become the premier affair in the United States, typically running for over two weeks in late May and early June.[56] Traditional fiddle contests, like those held at Union Grove,

North Carolina, since 1924, or at Galax, Virginia, since 1935, almost
became countercultural events[57] as thousands of youth with free and easy
lifestyles brought their fiddles, banjos, and guitars, or only the desire to
have a good time in communion with nature and down-to-earth people.
To most participants, festival attendance provided a temporary diversion.
To others, it began a lifelong commitment to old-time music. Dancing
of course was a secondary or even unessential consideration for most of
the people who came to the fiddle contests, even though they typically
heard hundreds of old-time tunes that were once integral accompaniments
for dances. The folk music workshops and summer camps, on the other
hand, which have flourished since the sixties, generally offer courses in
dancing along with instruction in instrument playing and singing. The
festival at Elkins College in Augusta, West Virginia, to cite only one instance, has weeklong workshops throughout the summer providing instruction on swing and folk dancing, vocal harmony, ballad singing, and
other traditional music arts, as well as quilting, instrument-making, and
other traditional crafts. String bands committed to old-time dance music
similarly have flourished, and clogging, flatfooting, buck dancing, contredanses, square dances, and other traditional styles have won thousands
of ardent devotees.[58]

Within the world of professional country music itself, the resurgence
of dancing has been accompanied by the revitalization of older styles of
musical performance, such as western swing and rockabilly, that had
fueled earlier explosions of dance interest. Western swing had never been
completely dormant, even in the days of rock and country-pop ascendancy, but had been kept alive by singers such as Hank Thompson, Red
Steagall, and Ray Price,[59] who tended to mix the style with honky-tonk,
cowboy, and other forms of music, or by bandleaders like Hoyle Nix, of
Big Spring, Texas, who adhered faithfully to Bob Wills's songs throughout the broad swath of territory covered by his band in West Texas. Wills,
though, did not become a cult figure for many young people, nor an influence on their music, until 1970, when Merle Haggard began paying
his own special tribute.

Haggard never forgot the youthful thrill he had felt as a boy when he
rode his bicycle to the Beardsley Ballroom in Bakersfield and then stood
on the seat in order to look through the window to both see and hear
his musical heroes, Bob Wills and Tommy Duncan.[60] His tribute album,
which included some of Wills's original musicians, was followed by a
reunion in December, 1973, of the Texas Playboys (along with guests
Hoyle and Jody Nix), who recorded their own album for United Artists.

Wills was too ill to perform, but he added his famous holler to some of the songs and provided emotional and symbolic leadership as he sat and listened to the recording sessions. These events, in turn, generated a widespread enthusiasm for western swing, as well as a metamorphosis in the style of certain musicians. A rejuvenated group of Texas Playboys embarked on a series of concerts and recordings, and a growing number of younger musicians, such as Alvin Crow, Red Steagall, and the band known as Asleep at the Wheel, began dispensing their own brands of western swing. Asleep at the Wheel had been playing mostly rock-and-roll and country-rock until its members heard Haggard's tribute album. Led by guitarist and singer Ray Benson (Ray Benson Siefert) they transformed themselves into a western swing unit, lured the Texas Playboy fiddler Jesse Ashlock out of retirement, and became, after 1974, one of the central showpieces of an emerging Austin music scene.[61]

The exciting musical culture that evolved in Austin in the 1970s was a mélange of rock, blues, country boogie, folk, cowboy, honky-tonk, and western swing, all held together by cowboy imagery and presented to the world with typical Texas hyperbole as a liberated and revolutionary phenomenon that could have emerged only in that state. During these heady days of high oil prices and unbridled musical enthusiasm, dozens of clubs with names like Armadillo World Headquarters, the Broken Spoke, and the Split Rail provided steady employment for musicians and diversion for dancers. Texas music, it was argued, was freer and more inventive than other southern styles because it expressed the ethnic and cultural pluralism of the state and the openness of the southwestern "frontier." At a time when mainstream country music seemed to be settling into a predictable and money-driven mode, the musicians of Austin were creating refreshingly hybrid styles that reflected liberated living and the joys of such an existence. Allegedly less inhibited by religious strictures than other southerners (astigmatic observers somehow managed to overlook the deep-dyed Protestant fundamentalism that lingered even in Bob Wills's West Texas),[62] Texans loved to dance and were drawn inexorably toward lively fiddle music. A popular song recorded later by the group Alabama declared that "if you're gonna play in Texas, you gotta have a fiddle in the band." Considered to be the godfather of this expressive and innovative musical culture, Bob Wills had bequeathed a legacy as expansive as the landscape in which it was born. Waylon Jennings, who actually knew better, got caught up in the euphoric commingling of Texas nationalism and Bob Wills lionizing that erupted in the early 1970s. He wrote and recorded a song that exhibited no discernible influence gathered from either Wills or western swing but that nevertheless declared, "When you cross that old Red River, hoss . . . Bob Wills is still the king."[63]

Although proponents may have exaggerated its uniqueness, the Austin musical culture did contribute to the commercial reinvigoration of country music as a whole, while also reinfusing it with vigorous stylistic elements that had been in danger of being forgotten. The city's dance club scene, and the related festivals sponsored at nearby Dripping Springs and elsewhere by Willie Nelson,[64] lured thousands of new young listeners to country music and encouraged musicians everywhere to tap into the music's traditional wellsprings.

Right at the peak of Austin's musical flowering, an even more strongly hyped phenomenon emerged, with the crucial help of Hollywood, that presented still another version of the Texas musical myth. Building on an article in *Esquire* magazine,[65] a popular movie called *Urban Cowboy* apotheosized a club in Pasadena (near Houston) called Gilley's that was described as the largest honky-tonk in the world. Starring in the role of a frustrated Houston oil worker who acted out his manhood each Saturday night trying to ride a mechanical bull and otherwise playing cowboy at Gilley's, actor John Travolta almost achieved for country music what he had done earlier for disco in *Saturday Night Fever*. Dancing with athletic majesty, Travolta and other cast members performed the two-step, the Cotton-Eyed Joe, and other country dance steps to the rhythms of country-pop songs.

While ostensibly a movie about failed working-class dreams, *Urban Cowboy* both anticipated and hastened country music's dawning suburbanization. In the wake of the movie's success, singers Johnny Lee and Mickey Gilley (the proprietor of the club) won widespread commercial exposure, and clubs similar to Gilley's—such as Billy Bob's in Fort Worth—bedecked with mechanical bulls, pinball machines, cowboy decorations, and even restaurants and rodeo arenas, began to appear in cities and suburbs all over the country. The Cotton-Eyed Joe, the most prominently featured dance in the movie,[66] became the rage in country dance clubs everywhere, with dancers shouting "bull shit" as they swung their legs. With designer blue jeans, cowboy shirts, hats, and boots touted as the proper attire, America had succumbed to country chic, all part of the largest infatuation with country music in which it had ever been engaged.

When the urban cowboy craze collapsed in the early eighties, some critics thought they saw the economic demise of country music as a whole. If clothing designers could not anticipate the ubiquity of denim over the decades that followed, neither did music critics reckon with the staying power, and adaptability, of country music. Nor did they bargain for the undying urge for nostalgia in the American psyche—the back-to-nature urge inherent in a suburbanizing society. Above all, they seemed to forget about the revitalizing power of dance. When Billy Ray Cyrus appeared in 1992 with his widely circulated video, "Achy Breaky Heart," he entered a scene populated with urban cowboys and "hat acts" (singers like Garth Brooks, Clint Black, and Mark Chesnutt who wore cowboy hats and other western attire).[67] He also sang to an increasingly suburban society that was already expressing its desire to go back to the country through its flirtation with outdoor life, RV's and sport utility vehicles, designer jeans, and other commodities promoted in the L. L. Bean and Eddie Bauer catalogues and scores of magazines that bore "country" in their titles. Cyrus wore no cowboy costume when he sang his way to fame (he instead wore a body shirt and conveyed the aura of a male stripper)— Travis Tritt complained that Cyrus had turned country music into an "ass-wiggling contest"[68]—but he lured thousands of would-be cowboys and cowgirls to the dance floors of America with a physical and emotional demeanor that seemed to come directly from Elvis and the urban working-class world he represented.

Line dancing, as we have seen, dates from at least the sixteenth century, and the dances that became popular in country music in the nineties, such as "the Electric Slide," were often nothing more than recycled dances introduced earlier in Harlem or other urban centers. The country line dance craze that Cyrus launched was made possible by the revolution in visual technology, but it was grounded culturally in the urban cowboy phenomenon of the early eighties and the later suburban cowboy vogue represented by such singers as Garth Brooks and Clint Black. The multitude of enthusiastic fans who filled the dance clubs of the nineties, or who swelled the enrollment in the newly created dance courses, invariably sported the standard uniform: tight-fitting blue jeans, cowboy hats, and boots.

Billy Ray Cyrus may have initially triggered the enthusiasm, but the duo that best represented the fusion of urban cowboy élan with line dance culture was Kix Brooks and Ronnie Dunn. The contrasting physical postures of the two singers only added to their visual and musical appeal. Brooks wore smartly tailored cowboy clothes and strutted across the stage, while Dunn wore modish slacks and shirt and sang with restrained but soulful passion. Their high-powered "Boot Scootin' Boogie" (first recorded by Asleep at the Wheel) became one of the most popular line dance songs, and it did most to launch a highly successful career that regularly keeps the duo among the finalists in the Country Music Association's annual awards for Entertainer of the Year. They and a long list of other performers, such as Tim McGraw with "Indian Outlaw," Tracy Byrd with "Watermelon Crawl," and Mary Chapin Carpenter with "Down at the Twist and Shout," popularized a string of dance-oriented songs and popular dances that lured people to the dance floor and filled the coffers of country music.[69]

At the end of the nineties hopeful dancers could buy any one of a host of instruction videos, pick up pointers from dance columns in country music magazines, or attend one of the thousand or more dance clubs that proliferated in the United States. Television's Nashville Network (TNN) presented two dance shows, "Wildhorse Saloon" and "Club Dance," which consisted almost exclusively of dancers of all calibers scurrying around the dance floor against the backdrop of the newest recordings in country music. Country and western dancing was accompanied by a comparable vogue for Cajun dancing, a conglomerate of jitterbugging, two-steps, and waltzes that owed as much to the creativity of dance instructors as they did to folk survival. Dancing nevertheless contributed mightily to an enthusiasm for Cajun music that has spread around the world and has not yet run its course.[70]

The expanding network of dance clubs and music videos that promote dancing have been both a cause and evidence of the commercial burgeoning of country music in the nineties. Since the popularity of dancing depends on neither vocal style nor the lyric content of songs, country line dancing has attracted throngs of people from all walks of life who previously had little experience with country music and who in fact may profess no liking for it. They come to dancing through boredom, the quest for exercise, the search for a pleasant diversion, the desire to meet other people (especially important for singles who need no partner to line dance), or for any number of reasons that may have little to do with music itself (Eddie Rabbitt's recording of "I Love a Rainy Night" was widely used as an accompaniment for aerobic dancing long before the country dance craze began). Whatever the reason, the dance sells the song, and country music insinuates itself into the mind of the dancer or passive listener. It is impossible to determine the ultimate effects that the line dance craze will have on the style, content, and quality of country music, but this fusion of dance and song has taken the music into the farthest reaches of suburbia, where it was already headed, and has contributed to the greatest commercial growth that country music has ever experienced.

Red Foley and Hank Williams (early 1950s). Hank offered a model that has been eternally popular with country singers: "When the Lord made me, he made a rambling man." Courtesy of Douglas B. Green.

Louvin Brothers (Ira and Charlie), 1950s. Ira is on the left, and Charlie is on the right. Country music's greatest "brother duet" drew heavily on both secular and gospel roots. Courtesy of Douglas B. Green.

Hazel Dickens, Alice Gerrard, Florence Reece, and Mike Seeger, 1973. Courtesy of Earl Dotter <http://www.earldotter.com>.

Bill Monroe (1975). Rehearsing in his Grand Ole Opry dressing room, Monroe displays the power and dignity that earned him the title "Father of Bluegrass Music." Courtesy of the photographer, Les Leverett.

Tim O'Brien and John Hartford at MerleFest, 2000. Pictured here with fellow neotraditionalist John Hartford, O'Brien creatively reinterprets traditional material and produces his own stunning variations. Courtesy of the photographer, Becky Johnson.

Merle Haggard at Renfro Valley, 1995. As a writer, performer, and personality, Haggard embodies the best that has been, and should be, in country music. Courtesy of the photographer, Loyal Jones.

Willie Nelson at MerleFest, 2000. Sometimes a rambler or outlaw, sometimes a gospel singer or storyteller, Nelson stamps his own personality on any style of music that he chooses to perform. Courtesy of the photographer, Becky Johnson.

Hazel Dickens. Hazel Dickens still sings "hard-hitting songs for hard-hit people." Photo by Nobuharu Komoriya (Tokyo, Japan). Courtesy of Hazel Dickens.

Arthel "Doc" Watson at MerleFest, 2000. A superb instrumentalist and singer, Doc Watson is simply America's best traditional musician. Courtesy of the photographer, Becky Johnson.

Austin Lounge Lizards. Humor, politics, and splendid musicianship define the performances of this Austin band. From left to right, Conrad Deisler, Hank Card, Lex Browning, Boo Resnick, and Tom Pittman. Photo by Wyatt McSpadden. Courtesy of the Austin Lounge Lizards.

Iris DeMent at MerleFest, 1994. Totally unscripted, and disarmingly sincere in style and personality, Iris DeMent creates music that evokes the best in the country music tradition. Courtesy of the photographer, Becky Johnson.

Dale Watson. God bless Dale Watson. He has never tried to get above his raising. Courtesy of Dale Watson, 1990s.

7

"How-dee, I'm Just
So Proud to Be Here"

I had to move to Madison, Wisconsin, to find a survival of the kind of stage shows that once characterized country music. For several decades a wonderful trio of musicians named the Goose Island Ramblers have delighted midwestern audiences with a marvelous blend of solid musicianship, a wide variety of songs, and zany stage humor.[1] The Ramblers do not simply perform a concert of songs; above all, they present a program of "entertainment." Founding member and singer Windy Whitford, who died June 10, 2000, soothed the audience with old-time sentimental and nostalgic songs, but while they were still savoring the poignance of the moment, accordion player Bruce Bollerud, in an exaggerated German accent, followed with "The Milwaukee Waltz," singing with slurred diction and growing progressively more tipsy as the song continues. George Gilbertson, master of several instruments, would then don a grass skirt and, with waving hips and appropriate hand gestures, sing "The Beach at Waunakee," a small town in Wisconsin that lies far from any major waterfront. Since two of the Ramblers are of Norwegian extraction (and the third a lifelong resident of a Norwegian community near Madison), Gilbertson might follow his "beach song" a few minutes later with the "Norwegian War Chant," improvising guttural phrases while wearing a colander to which simulated Viking horns have been attached. The Ramblers presented variations of the same routine each time they performed, but their fans would have been deeply disappointed if they had not done so. The humor that country stage shows presented was similarly predictable, but it bound audience and musicians in an affectionate community, providing restorative relief from the cares and frustrations of life.

Country music's reputation for crying-in-your-beer songs obscures the fact that humor has always been a staple of country entertainment, just as it had been a survival mechanism for southern rural folk culture. Its presence reminds us that although often fraught with sorrow and pain, the world of country music is also a world of laughter. Country humor at its best asserted the humanity of working people's lives, exposed the hypocrisies that lay around them, brought the pompous and mighty down to size, served as a painless way of calling up bittersweet memories of the past, eased the pain of lives that were often hard and lonely, and, of course, added the healing balm of laughter to spirits in need of relief. Humor served as a populistic defense mechanism in southern folk culture, attacking pretension and sham, and striving to keep people from becoming too self-important—admonishing them with the unspoken command not to get above their raising.

Except for the routines seen in reruns of television's "Hee Haw" or in the act of an occasional "hayseed comedian" like Renfro Valley's Bun Wilson or those seen in Branson, Missouri, the rustic, baggy pants comedian has almost disappeared and the comic skit, replete with entertainers in drag or old men's attire and reminiscent of the tent-repertoire circuit, no longer appears in country entertainment. Comedy, however, has remained as an integral component of the country music business, still appearing in the work of such monologuists as Bob Murphey, Justin Wilson, Jerry Clower,[2] and Jeff Foxworthy, in the stage routines of such groups as the cowboy revivalists Riders in the Sky and the bluegrass satirists the Austin Lounge Lizards, and of course in scores of songs performed by country musicians.

As eclectic in origin as country music itself, country humor flowed into the cultural reservoir of the southern folk from a variety of sources.[3] The original European settlers carried jokes, tall tales, and funny songs to the South as part of their cultural baggage. Some of the early comic songs reflected the ribaldry and lusty atmosphere of Elizabethan England, although the bawdiest among them, for obvious reasons, never made their way on to commercial recordings.[4]

Rural southerners, of course, did not rely solely on comedy preserved from their European heritage. They found plenty of humor in the rugged life that lay around them, while also absorbing comic material from minstrel, circus, vaudeville, burlesque, and other forms of professional entertainment. The proof of the popularity of such material among the folk can be found in the printed folksong collections and in the recorded repertoires of early hillbilly musicians. Such songs as "Old Dan Tucker," "Little Black Mustache," "Riding on the Elevated Railroad," "The Cat Came Back," "Baldheaded End of the Broom," and "Ain't We Crazy," which had their births in urban entertainment, appeared with regularity in the performances of such musicians as Uncle Dave Macon, Vernon Dalhart, Charlie Poole, Bradley Kincaid, and Lew Childre.

When country entertainers began to tour in the mid-twenties, they appropriated jokes and styles of comedy that had long been staples of blackface minstrelsy and other forms of stage entertainment, as well as a vogue for "rube humor" that was already entrenched in American popular entertainment.[5] Before Uncle Dave Macon began his long tenure on the Grand Ole Opry, he had already appeared as a "rube comedian" in vaudeville houses in New Orleans and Birmingham, and in fact had been censured by at least one critic who dismissed his act as little more than a pale reflection of a long-standing show-business tradition.[6] Hillbilly musicians needed few incentives to play roles that had already demonstrated widespread popular appeal, but they received additional encouragement from promoters, sponsors, radio executives, and record producers. Consequently, male performers occasionally appeared in blackface; in the attire of stage rubes (false whiskers, blackened teeth, ill-fitting clothes); as wizened and salty old men with goatees; or as red-wigged country boys ("Tobys"). Early female comics typically donned the attire and demeanor of granny ladies or dour, sharp-tongued old maids.[7] The task of country comedians since the twenties has been to overcome the "hillbilly burden" without discarding the genuine humor in rural life, and particularly that inherent in the relationship between country and city people.

Largely through the inspiration of their recording directors, a few early country acts such as Ernest Stoneman, Buell Kazee, the Skillet Lickers, and even Jimmie Rodgers and the Carter Family, recorded lengthy "rural dramas" or skits that focused on moonshining, hunting, beekeeping, hog-killing, fiddle contests, and other rural social practices.[8] Both humor and dialogue tended to be improvised (with suggestions offered by Frank Walker and other recording men) and interspersed with brief snippets of music. The Georgia string band, Gid Tanner and his Skillet Lickers, were the most prolific in the recording of such material. With such skits as "Bee Hunting on Hell-for-Sartin Creek" and "Corn Licker Still in Georgia," which ran to fourteen parts, they provided schematic documentation of many of the social rituals of rural North Georgia.

One enduring medium of country comedy has fused elements of the monologue or recitation with musical accompaniment. An early example of this genre was the "talking blues," a style heard in country music since at least 1926 when Chris Bouchillon, from South Carolina, recorded the first of such songs for Columbia. Performed in a humorous, self-deprecatory style and with a wry but deadpan delivery, Bouchillon's pieces generally chronicled the trials and tribulations of the singer. The "lyrics" of his "songs" may have been extracted, for the most part, from the broad corpus of black folklore, although one suspects that the more immediate source of such lines as "down in the henhouse on my knees, I thought I heard a chicken sneeze" came from blackface minstrelsy and its derivative, the "coon songs." Bouchillon's best piece, "Born in Hard Luck," sounds like something that the black vaudevillian Bert Williams might have done: "I was born on the last minute of the hour, in the last hour of the day, on the last day of the week, in the last week of the month, and in the last month of the year. To tell you the truth, I almost didn't get here."[9]

Bouchillon's pieces were droll, bluesy chronicles of woe, punctuated by the accompaniment of his brother Uris's hot guitar runs. Since that time, musicians have experimented with varied forms of accompaniment for the talking blues and other monologue styles. Most singers, however, have used the simplest of accompaniment, preferring to let the lyrics alone carry the message and mood. Ernest Tubb, for example, used only bass guitar runs in "Talking Guitar Blues" when he effectively summed up the mortification felt by most aspiring guitarists when confronted by a hostile and unappreciative family.[10] Before World War II Robert Lunn gained the sobriquet of "the talking blues boy" while showcasing the genre consistently on Grand Ole Opry broadcasts. Performed by Lunn, often with the accompaniment of Roy Acuff's Smoky Mountain Boys, the form was humorous, apolitical, and probably derivative of Bouchillon. His most popular verse declared that "if you want to get to heaven let me tell you how to do it. Grease your feet in a little mutton suet . . . Go easy . . . go greasy."[11] But Woody Guthrie demonstrated, in "Talking Dust Bowl Blues," where he commented on the Okie migration to California, that the style could be both comic and socially conscious.[12]

Except for an occasional revival by such "urban folk" singers as Bob Dylan, Jack Elliott, and Arlo Guthrie, the talking blues form defined by Bouchillon and Lunn did not survive the World War II period. Country singers, however, have continued to produce humorous recitations with musical accompaniment. Lazy Jim Day, a product of Grayson County, Kentucky, and a fixture for many years at the Grand Ole Opry, was known for his renditions of "the singing news," a wryly delivered commentary on largely fictional events that began with "Howdy, everybody, here comes the news with a little music to chase away the blues," and ended with the refrain, "I don't reckon that'll happen again in months and months and months."[13]

Most of the postwar monologues, both serious and comic, generally served as fillers for stage, radio, and television shows, but a few experienced considerable commercial success. Two popular recordings from 1948 and 1957, both intensely rural in theme and presentation, seemed to signal country music's farewell to its rural past. Carson Robison's "Life Gets Teejus, Don't It," told the story of an obviously aging bachelor acutely conscious of the physical deterioration of both his body and his surroundings but too lazy to improve his conditions. Gene Sullivan's "Please Pass the Biscuits," originally written for Jimmie Dickens, was the pathetic tale of a man who sat at a big dinner table and slowly watched the coveted biscuits disappear as he vainly sought to make his appetite known to the other eaters.[14]

Show-business personality Andy Griffith, who has since excelled in a wide range of performing venues, made his professional debut in 1953 with a monologue called "What It Was, Was Football." The Mt. Airy, North Carolina, native introduced his recitation on a small label in Chapel Hill, and then saw it become a major hit when it was rerecorded on the Capitol label. Capitol was so impressed by Griffith's potential that they put him on a salary with the stipulation that his earnings from lectures and other public appearances were to be shared with the company. Playing the part of a drawling and naive country preacher who had witnessed his first football game, Griffith described in wonderment the mayhem and seeming chaos of the scene without ever understanding what he had seen: "I don't know to this day what it was that they was a-doing down there but I have studied about it. And I think that it's some kindly of a contest where they see which bunch-full of them men can take that pumpkin and run from one end of that cow pasture to the other without either getting knocked down or stepping in something."[15]

Imitations of other performers or of well-known personalities have long appealed to country entertainers, and were probably inspired by the impressionists of popular entertainment. Country singers, of course, have long imitated each other (as in the case of Jimmie Rodgers and the legion of country vocalists whom he inspired), but the precise moment when entertainers began consciously imitating, or parodying, the styles of others for comic purposes is impossible to determine. Dave Landers experienced at least a modicum of success in the late forties and early fifties by imitating the vocal mannerisms of people like Ernest Tubb, Tex Ritter, Gene Autry, and Roy Acuff (the quartet of veteran singers whose individualistic styles have most often lent themselves to imitation).[16] When audiences applauded Landers, they were applauding not only his talent for mimickry but also the performers he chose to portray. Several of the modern country and western performers, such as Johnny Cash, Merle Haggard, Del Reeves, and Ferlin Husky, often do impressions of other performers on both their recordings and personal appearances. In addition to his country routines, Reeves also imitates well-known show-business personalities like John Wayne and Walter Brennan, while Husky, acting through his hayseed comic alter ego, Simon Crum (a role that he now plays infrequently), occasionally does impressions of people like the one-time radio rustics Lum and Abner. In a recording made in 1958, called "Country Music Is Here to Stay," Husky even did a passably good imitation of Kitty Wells, a type of impression that virtually no other male performer would dare to attempt.[17]

As our society becomes increasingly media-dominated and culturally homogenized, the subjects and themes of country music have become less unique. The country entertainer, though, once worked from a perspective that was significantly different from that of most other entertainers: the consciousness of being a product of a way of life, rural and southern, presumed to be different, if not inferior, when compared to national norms. Like other "minorities" in American culture, hillbilly comedians employed humor as a survival mechanism. Country humor has often functioned as a form of "ethnic" humor, an expression of the lifestyles or shared memories of southern rural whites, a style of reminiscence and identification that permits country people, or "ex"-country people, to share experiences that only they fully understand. Humor permits them to poke good-natured fun at themselves. Parody, or exaggeration, of one's self, is therefore a major ingredient of country humor, a quality of self-satire, or in-group humor that is not readily accepted if imposed by outsiders. Alternately defensive and boastful, both embarrassed by and proud of their culture, aware that they and their culture were perceived as exotic, half believing all the stereotypes and more than willing to play the roles expected of them, the hillbilly comedians made their way through American show business. The audience for country humor, of course, extended far beyond the parameters of southern rural culture, but many fans found in the comedy reminders of a common bond of memories and cultural presumptions. Even as they rapidly retreated from their rural past, fans and entertainers alike nevertheless recalled those memories with humor.

Much of the humor in country music can be described as a bittersweet reflection or recollection of the rural past; it is both nostalgic and humorous, a comic re-creation of experiences that were often painful. Like a remembered hymn, comedy elicits camaraderie as people recalled humbling experiences (like a midnight visit to the outdoor toilet during the dead of winter). A song like "Y'all Come," written in 1953 by a Texas singer and disc jockey named Arleigh Duff (described as the "Singing School Teacher") and recorded by many people, tells of big rural family gatherings and "grandma's" mutual delight and chagrin in the face of a crowd that greedily consumes all the food she has labored to cook and then fails to help with the dinner dishes. But despite her chagrin, when the kinfolk begin to leave, she ushers them off with the customary southern rural farewell, "y'all come." An older country song, often identified with the Canadian singer Montana Slim but perhaps best known through performances by Bradley Kincaid, is "The Little Shirt My Mother Made for Me," a plaintive recollection of a childhood filled with numerous embarrassing situations that found him wearing only "the little shirt." More recently, Billy Edd Wheeler, a sensitive portrayer of rural life from West Virginia, has captured well the ambivalence felt by many people toward their rural past in his tongue-in-cheek "Ode to the Little Brown Shack Out Back," a seriocomic lament about an outhouse doomed by a health department decree. When Wheeler spoke of the hours spent reading the Sears-Roebuck catalogue while sitting in the little house decorated with quarter moons, he evoked images that were once well known to virtually every country boy and girl.[18]

These bittersweet recollections of rural life are becoming increasingly rare in country music, but such songs were quite common at least until the fifties. The premier performer of such material was another West Virginia–born singer named Jimmie Dickens, a man of diminutive size (he is only 4'11") but the possessor of a powerful voice and one of the most dynamic styles in country music. By the 1950s, Dickens was almost alone in doing songs that described unashamedly the rural past; most other country singers offered songs that reflected the urbanizing process that was transforming American life. He recorded a long string of comic rural songs in the late forties and early fifties (many of them written by the team of Boudleaux and Felice Bryant) and gained a reputation as a singer of novelty songs, when in fact he has always been one of the most effective interpreters of "heart" songs in the country music field. This comic repertoire, however, evoked a wide range of rural and farm experiences. "Galvanized Washtub" told of those agonizing bath nights out in the country alternately freezing from the bath water and then roasting while standing in front of a roaring fire. "Out behind the Barn" described both the forbidden pleasures (smoking, lovemaking) and the punishment (whippings administered by dad) associated with experiences back of the barn; "Sleepin' at the Foot of the Bed" discussed the fate that often befell young people when company came visiting; "Country Boy," although ostensibly a paean of praise concerning farm life, recalled the rigors as well as the pleasures of that existence; while "Take an Old Cold 'Tater and Wait" (written by the gospel composer, Eugene Bartlett) depicted the plight of rural children who had to wait patiently while visiting adults (including the preacher) gobbled up every morsel of the customary Sunday chicken dinner. When Dickens sang these songs, his audiences, many of whom were rural or only shortly removed from such an existence, could shake their heads, chuckle, and say knowingly, "that is just the way it was."[19]

Some of the best comic country songs reflect the rural-urban tensions of American life, the conflicts that rage both within the individual and between Americans. The "classic" song in this category, of course, is "The Arkansas Traveler," a piece dating back to at least the 1840s and now best known as a fiddle tune.[20] A city traveler gets lost in the Arkansas backwoods, comes up on a country fiddler who is sitting on his front porch sawing on a fiddle tune, and then proceeds fruitlessly to inquire about the directions to Little Rock. One question after another is answered with a smart-aleck remark by the country person: "Can you tell me where this road goes to?" "I've lived here all my life, and it ain't gone nowhere yet." "How deep is that river?" "I don't know, but there's water all the way to the bottom of it." The country man constantly gets the better of the city person, but, in some versions, the farmer's hostility melts when the stranger picks up the fiddle and adroitly finishes the tune that the farmer has been painstakingly trying to figure out. The city person wins the confidence of the rustic, but only by demonstrating a proficiency that the latter finds socially acceptable, that is, fiddling.[21]

"Stay in the Wagon Yard," however, a song of more recent vintage than "Arkansas Traveler," is probably a much more accurate portrayal of the reality of rural life, particularly in the South, after the Civil War. Everywhere, the farmer was made conscious of his declining status, and in the South, tenantry was robbing him of his independence. The farmer's self-consciousness sometimes assumed the form of militant protest, as in the case of the Populists, or it provoked a desire for physical escape from agriculture or was internalized in various ways. As in the case of "Stay in the Wagon Yard," self-consciousness sometimes revealed itself in comic songs. The song described the plight of the country yokel who ventured too far from the safe confines of the wagon yard and fell into the clutches of a city slicker who offered to buy him a drink, then rooked him of all his hard-earned cash. He no doubt spoke for many country folk when he opined, "I wish I'd-a bought me half a pint and stayed in the wagon yard."[22]

While "Stay in the Wagon Yard" warns farmers to stay away from city dudes who are "slick as lard," other songs are used as vehicles for self-parody or self-deprecation. "Fifteen Cents Is All I Got," a vaudeville song and monologue performed by Grandpa Jones, is about a naive bumpkin who goes into a fancy home and commits innumerable faux pas while remaining blissfully ignorant about the nature of his actions. When the haughty host exhibits a piece of furniture that "goes back to Louis the 14th," our hayseed hero announces that he has an item that "goes back to Sears-Roebuck on the 15th" (if he can't come up with the next payment). Eventually, the country guest wanders into the bathroom and mistakes the commode for a footwash. Delighted by the ingenious contraption, he asserts that "you wash one foot and pull a little lever, and then you wash the other one."[23] It is clear that, along with the presumed self-deprecation, the song conveys a note of derision concerning affected or pretentious ways. This characteristic is more strongly displayed in Roy Acuff's "Stuck Up Blues," a complaint not against city people as such but against "self-important" people who would mask their rural roots or try to "get above their raising." The song reminds one uppity person who begins to high-hat his neighbors that "I know where you came from, and your pappy used to use the words 'by cracky' and 'by gum.'"[24]

A large body of comic country songs enthusiastically endorse country folks and ways or weave nostalgic webs around them with little of the bittersweet reflection noted earlier. Several songs, for example, recall animals that made vivid impressions. "Old Shorty," recited and sung by Tex Ritter, and "Old Rattler," performed enthusiastically by Grandpa Jones, tell the story of good-for-nothing but lovable old dogs. "Bessie the Heifer," still another Boudleaux Bryant composition recorded by Jimmie Dickens, describes a cow of legendary qualities who "gave more milk than any law allows." Some cowboy songs, such as the famous "Strawberry Roan" and "Midnight the Outlaw," pay awed tributes to horses that could not be broken or rode. "Old Slewfoot," first recorded by Johnny Horton but now a bluegrass standard, describes still another animal that was remembered with respect and no affection. Slewfoot was a wild bear that had never been cornered and never been "treed," and the singer admits, "some folks say he looks a lot like me."[25]

In addition to memorable animals, certain types of country characters are often humorously recalled in song. The lazy farmer, for example, is described in an old song called "The Young Man Who Wouldn't Hoe Corn," as well as in those of more recent vintage like "He Went to Sleep and the Hogs Ate Him" (the ultimate in laziness), and in the previously discussed "Life Gets Teejus." The awkward or unattractive country girl, who sometimes develops into the stereotyped old maid, appears often in both comic song and monologue. None of these songs would today pass the test of political correctness, but country audiences have often guffawed at the thought of "charming Betsy," when they are told that "My girl don't wear no perfume at all, but you can smell her just the same," or when Merle Travis talks about his "fat gal." "Get Along Home Cindy," known by virtually every country entertainer, is about a pretty but clumsy country girl who "got so full of glory, she knocked the preacher down." "That Cross-Eyed Gal," by Gene Autry, and "The Old Maid and the Burglar" (recorded by Henry Whitter and several others) are about homely country girls. In the latter song a burglar is terrified when he sees an apparently attractive old maid gradually dispel the illusion by removing her wig, glass eye, false teeth, and wooden leg.[26]

In country music's early commercial period, performers seldom hesitated to burlesque themselves or to exaggerate their rural characteristics. Many of the early string band titles, though sometimes admittedly coined by talent scouts or promoters, were delightful examples of self-parody (as evidenced by the Skillet Lickers, the Fruit Jar Drinkers, Dilly and the Dill Pickles, Dr. Smith's Champion Hoss Hair Pullers, and the Gully Jumpers). Although their songs often exaggerated the facts of rural existence, the most stereotypical material came from outsiders who seized on "mountain" or "rural" material as a means of eliciting laughs from urban and/or sophisticated audiences. Beginning as early as the 1920s, with songs like "I Like Mountain Music," and continuing through the 1950s with such songs as "Knock Her Down Again, Pa" (sung by a performer who called herself Esmereldy), "Feudin' and Fightin'" (performed by Dorothy Shay, "the Park Avenue Hillbilly," who sang similar songs before nightclub audiences), and "I Didn't Know the Gun Was Loaded" (written by Hank Fort, a woman composer from Nashville), Broadway and Tin Pan Alley writers contributed to the creation of what might be termed "the Little Abner conception" of rural society: a self-contained world composed of occasionally lovable but basically simple and violent cultural degenerates.[27]

The Little Abner stereotype, often accepted and utilized by country entertainers (sometimes with great commercial profit), was not necessarily malevolent in design, although it did perhaps contribute to a baleful public attitude toward the needs and aspirations of rural people (particularly those residing in the Appalachian districts of the South). Quite often when country performers affected the rube or simpleton image, they actually employed the characterization as a device to demonstrate the native wit of the rural person as opposed to the artificiality of the city dweller. The motif had appeared in "Arkansas Traveler" routines in the 1840s, but drew upon stereotypes that dated from the beginning of American history ("Yankee Doodle," in fact, provides an early example).[28]

No country entertainers were more effective as parodists of urban ways than Homer and Jethro (Henry Haynes and Kenneth Burns), yet none were more sophisticated and urbane than these two "hip hillbillies." They inaugurated their career in Knoxville in 1932, as part of a country swing group called the String Dusters, but by 1944 were performing as a rube comedy duet who dressed in hayseed costumes and burlesqued the pop hits of the day. Until Homer's death in 1970, they attracted an ever-widening audience, first on the popular radio country shows the Renfro Valley Barn Dance and the National Barn Dance, but also on the nightclub circuit, on national television, and in Nashville, where most of their thirty-five albums were recorded. At Renfro Valley, John Lair had advised them to abandon hillbilly attire if they ever ventured into other show-business settings, surmising correctly that the duo's comedy and musical skills alone would sustain them before urban audiences. Wearing business suits or casual sports attire and singing songs like "Baby, It's Cold Outside" and their Grammy-award winning "The Battle of Kookamonga," Homer and Jethro took their act to the "Tonight Show," "The Perry Como Show," and other formats where country acts had seldom ventured. Jethro was probably correct when he noted their effects on country comedy: "I think Homer and I may have helped to phase out that baggy-pants stuff." Their musicianship, of course, did not hurt them either. Homer, for example, was considered to be one of the best rhythm guitarists in the country music field, and Jethro could play everything from classical music and jazz to hillbilly on the mandolin. Their song lyrics, though, made few pretenses at sophistication: "You know what a basketball nose is; it dribbles all over the floor."[29]

Other rube country parodists, although sometimes obviously inspired by the success of the Homer and Jethro duet, have generally shied away from put-ons of pop material and have instead been content with burlesques of earlier country songs and singers. Sheb Wooley, probably best known for the writing and singing of the smash pop hit of 1958, "Purple People Eater," could boast of a long and varied career that included stints as a country radio singer, television performer (he played Pete on the "Rawhide" series), and Hollywood character actor (he was one of the outlaws in *High Noon*). He won still another following as a country parodist, portraying a country drunk named Ben Colder who irreverently satirized "serious" songs like "Almost Persuaded."[30] The team of Lonzo and Oscar profited from the success won by Homer and Jethro, but they made no pretensions at urbanity and never tried to take their act on to the nightclub circuit. The team was conceived in 1944 by Eddy Arnold as part of his touring act. Rollin Sullivan, who has always played the role of Oscar, and Lloyd George, who was the first of three Lonzos (the others have been Johnny Sullivan and Dave Hooten), donned clownlike clothes and backwoods hillbilly dialect to perform an act of pure rural slapstick. On the strength of the immense success of "I'm My Own Grandpa" (a complicated song inspired by a Mark Twain story), Lonzo and Oscar broke free from Arnold's patronage and maintained a career of uncompromising hillbilly comedy that endured until the mid-1970s. Accompanied often by steel guitarist Clell Summey, who performed as Cousin Jody—complete with toothless mouth and country clown costuming, the duet usually satirized well-known country songs like Hank Snow's "Moving On," to which they affixed comedy lines like "the old Tom Cat was feeling fine, til' he fell in a barrel of turpentine; he's moving on." Not until 1974, when they recorded a sentimental love song called "Traces of Life" and began tailoring their style to the likings of bluegrass audiences, did they depart in any sense from their time-tested hillbilly style.[31]

By the decade of the seventies the rube parodist had virtually vanished from country music. Homer Haynes's death ended the career of the Homer and Jethro duet; Lonzo and Oscar could seldom be heard outside of occasional Grand Ole Opry performances; Ben Colder appeared only infrequently; and Simon Crum disappeared from recordings altogether. Sandy Pinkard and Richard Bowden resurrected a semblance of the rube parody act in the eighties, but although their jokes were delivered in downhome country dialect, they were of the blue nightclub variety—crude, sophomoric, and only mildly funny.[32]

Almost the only true rural-oriented parodists who have remained active, and they seldom appear outside of Texas, are the Geezinslaw Brothers, a duo from Austin, who had begun their careers during the fifties singing for campus functions at the University of Texas. The nucleus of the group has always been their mandolinist and tenor singer, Sam Allred, who was sometimes called "Ring-Eye" (because of his eyeglasses). The role of the other "brother," Son, the guitarist and lead singer who never talks or smiles, has been played by various people down through the years. They adopted the name Geezinslaw after seeing a listing for a family named Giesenslagh who lived in the tiny town of Snook, Texas. They are rather hip country singers whose inspiration came probably from Homer and Jethro. They sing their own creations and do parodies of well-known songs. They were known only locally until they appeared on the Arthur Godfrey show and then were "discovered" by Lady Bird Johnson, the wife of President Lyndon Johnson, who asked them to perform at barbecues and social functions at the Johnson ranch. Although the duo entertained often in nightclubs and on national television, they have remained primarily regional attractions, with Sam Allred spending most of his time as a funny and outspoken disc jockey in Austin.[33]

A very old and continuing theme in country humor has been the war between the sexes. The tradition of spirited male-female repartee, first heard in old folk songs like "Reuben, Reuben," "No Sir, No Sir," and "Buffalo Boy," has been preserved and revitalized by entertainers like Lulu Belle and Scotty, Charlie Louvin and Melba Montgomery, Porter Wagoner and Dolly Parton, Conway Twitty and Loretta Lynn, and Johnny Cash and June Carter Cash. This genre was especially significant because it was one of the few phases of modern country music, at least until the late eighties, in which the woman unqualifiedly asserted her own prerogatives and challenged the supremacy of the male. Numerous songs, though, explored marital conflict in a humorous fashion from both the male and female points of view. One of the oldest, "Every Day Dirt" (an American version of "Will the Weaver") tells of a philandering man smoked out of his chimney hiding place by an irate husband. In hillbilly versions of the Child ballad "Our Goodman"—with such titles as "Drunkard's Special" and "Three Nights Drunk"—a husband comes home drunk repeatedly and finds on his pillow an object which his wife alleges to be a cabbage head, but to the husband it looks suspiciously like a human male head. In "Hang Out the Front Door Key" a wife finally grows tired of coddling her playboy husband; she turns the tables on him, stays out late, and uses phony excuses identical to his ("I'm with a poor sick friend, dear, who would do the same for me"). Much more recent songs, such as "Divorce Me, C.O.D." and "She Got the Gold Mine; I Got the Shaft," are self-explanatory.[34]

The feisty and uncowed woman has become more common in country music's modern period. Loretta Lynn, for example, has written and performed a number of songs that chronicle the battles between man and woman, and the respective campaigns made to hold on to their partners. While Loretta can advise her husband that his drink-inspired passion will not be appreciated (as in "Don't Come Home a-Drinkin' with Loving on Your Mind"), she is just as decisive in her warnings to flirtatious women that she will go to "fist city" to hold on to her man. And in a very popular song of the sixties, Nat Stuckey sang as if he were the man that the heroine of "Fist City" was talking about: in "Sweet Thang," he told of a woman who went from bar to bar looking for her husband and striking terror in the hearts of "barroom floozies" who were too attentive toward her "sweet thang." Earlier in the fifties Hank Williams, who was best known for his songs of heartbreak, wrote a number of comic songs, usually from the man's point of view, which told what sometimes happened when a man strayed from the path of marital fidelity. In "Dear John, I Sent Your Saddle Home" and "Move It on Over," Williams tells of a husband spurned by his wife, locked out of the house, and, as described in the latter song, literally forced to seek refuge in the doghouse. But in another recording, "Mind Your Own Business," Williams reminded censorious neighbors and gossipmongers that "me and that sweet mama's got a license to fight," an attitude that most other country entertainers, and probably their fans, would appear to endorse.[35]

Southern country people, and their Old World ancestors before them, relished jokes about natural bodily functions and sexual conduct. Barnyard, or bathroom, humor has been a constant of country comic routines, just as it has been among the people who comprise the basic country audience, and within Jewish, African American, and other ethnic communities. Reminiscences concerning the old outdoor privy, and the Sears-Roebuck catalogues and corncobs that were necessities before toilet paper was available or affordable, have been staples in the repertoires of numerous comedians. Country audiences guffaw when references are made to those artifacts of a vanished, or vanishing, way of life. Much of the humor is elemental, to say the least, and sometimes is little above the level of the childish prattle and horseplay of the playground: for instance, bluegrass singer Jimmy Martin cannot resist pointing toward a restroom when a lady gets up to leave one of his performances and saying, "it's that way, lady." Although this kind of treatment can clearly be embarrassing to a person, the most skillful comedians establish rapport between themselves and their audiences as they share these bittersweet memories or associations.

Country entertainers could scarcely avoid the dangerous ground of sex and, in fact, a song like the aforementioned "Don't Come Home a-Drinkin'" explores the relationship between alcohol and other "hungers of the flesh." Country music may be, in part, the product of a pietistic, evangelical culture, but it has also been the province of earthy men and women who knew that their Bible advised them to be fruitful and multiply. The subject of sex, though never absent from country humor, has seldom received explicit treatment (as is befitting a business which describes itself as "family" entertainment); jokes dealing with homosexual or deviant behavior are rare, four-letter words are seldom used outside of nightclubs (although they do show up frequently in the music of "alternative" bands),[36] and sexual indiscretions are generally accompanied by humiliation or embarrassment (i.e., a would-be Casanova is sent scrambling nude into the night by an enraged husband). Sex-escapade jokes, however, are never used as vehicles for moralizing; one often finds, in fact, a strong tinge of admiration for the rascal who moves from one embarrassing situation to another.

The bawdy humor of the Elizabethan tradition surfaced occasionally in some of the older songs, but many of the "newer" ones, particularly from the late twenties and early thirties, reflected the risqué and double-entendre influence of the blues. Repressed white southerners found in black music and black culture vehicles for expressing deep-rooted longings that their own culture did not condone, but the impulse toward "broad" and biological humor had always been present in southern rural culture; the blues tradition merely supplied a vocabulary of metaphors and symbols to express old inclinations. For example, Homer "Bill" Callahan's famous version of "Rattlesnaking Daddy" drew upon similar material done by black blues performers, but it also reflected the boastful spirit of the "rounder" tradition: "I rattled last night and the night before, got up this morning, gonna rattle some more."[37]

Since World War II the double-entendre type of blues song has declined in country music, but the allusion to sex, often couched in a different kind of double meaning, remains strong. The desire among men for permanent sexual vigor, or consciousness of its decline, occasionally appears in country songs, especially since the wonder drug Viagra appeared on the market in the nineties.[38] Back in the fifties Lefty Frizzell had recorded "I'm an Old, Old Man" (since revived by Merle Haggard), and argued that "I'm not too old to cut the mustard anymore." On the other hand, in the same period Bill Carlisle (Cliff's brother) complained that he was indeed "Too Old to Cut the Mustard." Girls of easy virtue, or those with erotic appeal, also have appeared frequently in country songs—as in "Sally Let Your Bangs Hang Low" ("I saw Sally changing clothes; she was in a perfect pose"), "Sally Was a Good Old Girl," "The Girl Most Likely," and "The Girl on the Billboard" (who wore nothing but a smile)—as well as a few that celebrated the delights of sexual encounter such as Tennessee Ernie Ford's "Shotgun Boogie" and "Blackberry Pickin'" that described more than the usual rustic virtues.[39]

The supermasculine hero in country music is a man known for his excesses, not the least of which is his penchant for the bottle. The humorous endorsement of strong drink has a very old history in American folk music, a tradition that country singers still perpetuate in songs like "Good Old Mountain Dew," "White Lightning," "Rocky Top, Tennessee," and "Six Pack to Go." Jay Webb indicated one consequence of excessive drinking, though, when he sang "She's Looking Better by the Minute," and in an older song, "The Intoxicated Rat," the Dixon Brothers explained how the imbibing of spilled whiskey contributed to the confidence of a rat ("bring on that dadburned cat!"). In "Ten Little Bottles," Johnny Bond describes the steady (or unsteady?) progression of a man into inebriation. Bond's effective use of drunk dialect was not the only example of the device in country music. As noted earlier, Sheb Wooley built a successful commercial characterization around a rustic inebriate named Ben Colder. The "classic" example of drunk dialect in country music, and perhaps praise for alcohol as well, was Tex Ritter's version of "Rye Whiskey," one of the great performances of country music history. Ritter's performance, complete with hiccoughs and slurred phrasing, proclaims that if the ocean were whiskey and the narrator was a duck, "I'd swim to the bottom and never come up."[40]

From the earliest beginnings of recorded country music its singers and songwriters have persistently used humor to chronicle and criticize the events of the day. The writing and performing of humorous topical songs, evident in the work of men like Uncle Dave Macon, Blind Alfred Reed, and Carson Robison during the early commercial period, has not slacked off in the decades that have followed. The Watergate scandal of the 1970s, as might be expected, inspired a rash of songs, including Red River Dave's "Watergate Blues." Even the grim business of war has provoked comic responses. In the 1920s Red Patterson and the Piedmont Log Rollers recorded the "Battleship of Maine," telling the story of a naive country boy who didn't relish fighting Spaniards in a war whose origins he only dimly understood, and many years later, Roger Miller voiced similar confusions about "Private John Q" who found difficulty adjusting to the regimentation of military service. Henry Ford fascinated country singers and songwriters during the twenties (as in Uncle Dave Macon's "On the Dixie Bee Line"); as late as 1974 the Detroit industrialist was still inspiring the making of country songs. Jerry Reed used "Please Mr. Ford" as a means of cataloguing the manifold problems associated with automobile ownership in the modern age of highway congestion, fuel scarcity, and air pollution.[41]

Country songs generally have taken a rather bemused if not jaundiced attitude toward innovative dress and lifestyles, and the positions taken range from the sternly moralistic to the satirical. Blind Alfred Reed was serious in 1928 when he asked American women "Why Do You Bob Your Hair, Girls?" but Lester Flatt seemed more tolerant in the sixties when he acclaimed that "I Can't Tell the Boys from the Girls," and Ray Stevens was clearly tongue-in-cheek in 1974 when he satirized the then-current fad of streaking. When Tex Williams made his hit recording of "Smoke, Smoke, Smoke" in 1946, he was probably more accurate about the dangers of nicotine than he or most anyone else realized at the time. Williams, in fact, had been concerned primarily with the irritations visited upon innocent bystanders by the chronic smoker ("a nicotine slave is all the same, at a petting party or a poker game"), and in his remake of the song in 1968 he noted, perhaps accurately, that few people would abandon the smoking habit despite governmental or medical warnings. Habits in country songs, too, are slow to change, and the humorous critique of society's foibles and pretensions, always a major ingredient of the country repertoire, survives today in the music of such people as the Geezinslaw Brothers, Robert Earl Keen, and the Austin Lounge Lizards.[42]

When one turns from the humor in country songs to the country comedian—the individual who is known for his comic monologues or who divides his time equally between singing and joke-making—we find sources that are as ancient and varied as those underlying the music. Country comedians extract material from their own experiences, and from the repertoires of other professional laugh-makers, past and present. Benny Ford, who performed for many years as the Duke of Paducah, claimed to have half a million jokes catalogued under 455 different subjects.[43] Some of the successful "hillbilly" comedians, in fact, began their careers in other show-business formats, such as vaudeville or tent repertoire. And if we listen closely to the situations of country humor, we often find that only the rural dialect and the context in which it is placed mark it as different from other styles of humor.

Some of the folk humor that made its way into early country music began its life among the tall-tale spinners of frontier America. From there it had moved into the repertoires of the southwestern humorists and local colorists of the nineteenth century, and then into the contrived folk humor of men like Artemus Ward and Mark Twain.[44] A great deal of this material, or imitations of it, lingered in short stories, novels, and plays, and eventually wound up in such radio shows as "Lum and Abner" in the twentieth century. In these formats the chief character was usually the "country bumpkin," a naive but innately wise figure whose prototype first appeared as Jonathan in Royall Tyler's play, *The Contrast,* in 1787. The character appeared often in American fiction and popular culture, and very popular manifestations appeared at the turn of the century in characters like David Harum, from a popular novel of the same name; Uncle Josh Whitcomb, the hero of a long-running play called *The Old Homestead;* and another Uncle Josh, a salty rustic humorist played by Cal Stewart, who appeared in numerous comic monologues on stage and on cylinder and disc recordings. Characters like Uncle Josh appealed in part because they appeared quaint and droll to modern urbanites but also because they seemed to embody an innocence and directness that was vanishing from American life. One could simultaneously make fun of and extol our disappearing rural ways.[45]

Although much of the humor discussed above appeared in printed sources such as books, newspaper columns, and jokebooks (such as the widely circulated *Slow Train through Arkansas*), and although abundant evidence reveals that country comedians sometimes studied such material (as acknowledged by Pat Buttram, the Duke of Paducah, and Archie Campbell),[46] this kind of humor more likely moved into the possession of country people via traveling forms of entertainment. Blackface minstrel humor, for example, disseminated in the South by traveling troupes as late as World War I, became one of the nuclei around which country stage humor developed. Large-scale organizations, such as those led by Lew Dockstadter and Al G. Fields, visited the major cities of the South well into the twentieth century, while smaller, local-based units carried minstrel entertainment into the hamlets and rural areas.[47] Minstrel jokes and comic stage routines were absorbed by itinerant entertainers who performed in tent and medicine shows, and thus they were dispensed among rural audiences that had little access to more professional forms of entertainment. Country comedians heard and preserved much of the material and incorporated it into their own routines. Some country comedians, in fact—such as Greasy Medlin, Kentucky Slim (Charles Elza), Jake Tindell, and Tommy Millard—easily made the transition from blackface to baggy pants rural humor.[48] Blackface comedy itself appeared periodically in country shows as late as the early stages of the civil rights revolution in the early 1960s.[49]

Jokes, skits, and stage costumes were also borrowed from other show-business sources. Two of the most popular country comedians of the post–World War II period, the Duke of Paducah and Rod Brasfield, were both reminiscent of baggy pants' burlesque comics in their costuming and stage patter. Many of the "vaudeville" jokes found in country humor came, not directly from urban stage entertainment, but from little fly-by-night tent operations or from radio and television comedians, many of whom, like Bob Hope, Milton Berle, and Red Skelton, had begun as vaudeville or burlesque comics.

Of all the traveling entertainment units that contributed to the shaping of country humor, while also incidentally providing occasional employment for country musicians, none were more successful in penetrating the most remote regions of rural America than the medicine and tent-repertoire shows. The patent medicine industry, which was among the first businesses in the United States to recognize the potentiality of advertising, has always shown an amazing ability to adapt to technological change. The patent medicine people, for instance, very shrewdly recognized the utility of radio advertising when the broadcasting medium was still in its infancy. The era of Mexican border broadcasting began in 1932 when Dr. John R. Brinkley established XERA in Villa Acuna as a forum for claims that male sexual rejuvenation could be achieved through his goat gland surgical implants.[50] The hillbilly entertainers and gospel singers who populated XERA and other radio stations were only the most recent examples of the union of patent medicine and entertainment. Since the Middle Ages, patent medicine vendors had recognized the power of entertainment (music, dance, and humor) in attracting audiences and in breaking down sales resistance. Little was unique about the humor used in medicine show come-ons; the comedy tended to be an adaptation or composite of folk-minstrel-vaudeville humor (some of the medicine show comedians, incidentally, performed in blackface). But these itinerant shows were important disseminators of comic and musical material throughout rural America, and they often provided formats in which potential comics could perfect their routines, develop show-business techniques, and learn how to establish rapport with their audiences. In the 1950s Dudley LeBlanc's Hadacol Caravan, featuring a star-studded cast of entertainers, including Hank Williams, criss-crossed the United States advertising a beverage that would allegedly cure most any ailment known to man. Even into the 1990s Rambling Tommy Scott, who had recorded at least one popular song during an earlier country music career ("Rose-buds and You"), was touring with an act called the Last Real Medicine Show, presenting over 150 shows a year.[51]

While a medicine show might consist of no more than a self-proclaimed "doctor" and his assistant hawking bottles of a mail-order concoction spread out on a portable stand, or perhaps a one-horse wagon driven by the "professor" and his banjo-playing sideman, the tent-repertoire show at least had pretensions to show-business legitimacy. Tent-repertoire units, working out of cities in the Midwest and South, carried homemade dramas and variety entertainment into towns and villages at least as late as the onslaught of the Great Depression. These dramatic skits and their performances came about as close to being "folk theater" as anything ever produced in the United States. The melodramas were suffused with bathos, and the comedies were characterized by slapstick and broad humor. Tent-repertoire theater profited, above all, because it glorified the basic American theme of rural innocence and innate wisdom—a message of reassurance in an era of rapid and uncontrollable urban growth.

Although the tent-repertoire shows had much earlier antecedents, their heyday appears to have been in the years between 1917 and 1930, when groups like the Rosier Players, Murphy's Comedians, Bisbee's Comedians, the Paul English Players, the W. I. Swain show, Harley Sadler's group, and many others roamed the countryside dispensing their brand of American culture. Musical accompaniment might be provided by no more than an energetic pianist, but some of the more successful organizations traveled with a small orchestra. Variety shows often followed the dramatic presentation or were interspersed between acts. We as yet do not know enough about the identities and performing characteristics of tent-repertoire variety entertainers to justify specific conclusions, but there is evidence that some country performers traveled with the shows. Lloyd "Hank" Jones, a veteran country musician and comedian who has performed for about fifty years in New Orleans and along the Gulf Coast, served his show-business apprenticeship as a Toby in the late thirties with a tent show headed by the cowboy singer and politician Glen Taylor (a later U.S. senator and running mate with Henry Wallace in the presidential campaign of 1948). The only published account of Harley Sadler's popular tent show makes no mention of country music, but it presents a group picture of the organization showing Lew Childre and Everett Stover, a longtime member of Bob Wills's Texas Playboys. Other sources confirm that Childre—a singer, clog dancer, and storyteller for many years

on the Grand Ole Opry—traveled with Sadler in the thirties, as did Wiley
Walker, a sometime associate of Childre but better known as the fiddling
half of radio's hillbilly duo, Wiley and Gene. Rod Brasfield, a longtime
comic mainstay of the Grand Ole Opry, had traveled with Bisbee's Comedians. As is well known, Jimmie Rodgers was a headliner before his
death in 1933 for tent shows headed by J. Doug Morgan, Leslie Kell, and
Paul English.[52]

The tent-repertoire groups, of course, did not think of themselves as
either "folk" or "country," even though they carried their cultural offerings to the most backwater regions of the nation. They undoubtedly had
a more exalted conception of their role; it would probably be unlikely
then to find a pure rural type performing in the repertoire companies.
However, the tent-repertoire groups drew upon the folk for inspiration
and sustenance, and in turn fed their ideas into the folk communities. The
tent-repertoire theater, for example, was instrumental in perpetuating the
stereotype of the naive but lovable country bumpkin, a character generally known as "Toby" whose genesis has been traced to Fred Wilson's
portrayal in 1911 of Tobe Haxton in "Clouds and Sunshine."[53] Wilson
played the role so often, and in play after play, that he became popularly
known as Toby Wilson, a characterization that was imitated by other tent-
repertoire actors. Toby characterizations generally took on the colora-
tion of the regions in which they were presented—Harley Sadler, for
example, sometimes played a cowboy Toby in his appearances in the
West—but Toby appeared most often in one-gallus overalls or baggy
pants, and sported freckles and a red thatch of hair. In this guise Toby
became a model everywhere for similar portrayals of simple but deceptively dumb country boys. Although it is difficult to prove a direct link
between the Toby character and the rube comedians who appeared with
great frequency in country music entertainment during the following
decades, it is clear that he and the hillbilly comedians occupied the same
mythological milieu and satisfied the same psychological needs.

In the decades since country music began to take shape as a commercial force in the twenties, country comedians have in most cases come
directly out of rural society, while others have been merely skillful interpreters of rural people and situations. Many of the early entertainers, like
Gid Tanner and the Skillet Lickers, wore exaggerated "hillbilly" garb,
adopted outlandish names, and "acted a fool" during their performances.
The tendency to parody their country ways, or to act as they thought they
were expected to, was present from the beginning. Occasionally, recording men, radio station managers, and sponsors encouraged the playing

of "hillbilly" roles. Individual gifted entertainers, like Bob Shelton (of the singing Shelton Brothers of Texas), fiddling Slim Miller, and Lulu Belle Wiseman on the National Barn Dance; Hank Penny, an Alabama boy who took his natural comedic ability to the West Coast, and Uncle Dave Macon, Bashful Brother Oswald (Beecher Kirby), Marshall Louis "Grandpa" Jones, and Stringbean (David Akeman) on the Grand Ole Opry, all demonstrated a natural flair for comedy along with their musical abilities. The ability to tell a funny story, make grotesque facial expressions, or to dance a buck-and-wing greatly enhanced the musician's ability to build up a large following.[54]

It would be difficult to pinpoint the exact moment when comic monologuists began to appear on country radio shows and personal appearances, but it must have been very early. The Weaver Brothers and Elviry, a group that deserves special study,[55] were an established and popular vaudeville "hillbilly" group during the twenties and early thirties. At a time when most country acts were ignored by the world of show business or were confined to the schoolhouse and movie theater circuits of the South, this Springfield, Missouri, troupe—Frank, Leon, and June Weaver (who performed as Abner, Cicero, and Elviry)—played on the vaudeville circuits in the North and in Europe. Although the Weaver Brothers were talented actors and song-and-dance men, their "sister" Elviry was the most memorable and influential member of the troupe, playing the highly caricaturized role of an unsmiling and tart-tongued old maid. June Shipp Weaver was a professional actress from Chicago who was married, at one time or another, to both brothers. Her characterization of Elviry appears to have been the prototype for many of the female rustic comedians, such as Judy Canova, Sarie and Sally, Aunt Idy, and Minnie Pearl, who emerged in the two decades before World War II. Lulu Belle told folklorist William Lightfoot, "I'll tell you who I think John Lair patterned me after: Elvira Weaver, of the Weaver Brothers and Elviry," and she went on to say that Lair had sent Lulu Belle and her father down to the theater in Chicago to see the vaudeville group in action. Sarah Ophelia Colley, who later became famous in her role as Minnie Pearl, saw a Weaver Brothers movie long before she made her own entrance into show business, and was impressed by the stern facial impressions and sense of timing shown by June Weaver.[56]

Aunt Idy, born Margaret Lillie, began her career as a trooper in her uncle Pawnee Bill's wild west show. Her style of comedy, that of the salty, plainspoken, downhome type of philosopher, was plainly modeled upon that of Elviry. Her career began as a member of the cast of the National

Barn Dance in Chicago, but through the urging of John Lair, who named her Aunt Idy, she moved to the Renfro Valley Barn Dance where she did a single act and occasionally worked as part of a duo with Harry Mullins, who played the role of an overgrown brat.[57] Sarie and Sally were sisters who appeared in rustic skits on the Grand Ole Opry in the early thirties. Attired in bonnets and long country dresses, Sarie and Sally gossiped and philosophized in homely fashion the way country women would over the back fence or during a quilting bee. Their style of humor was laconic and low-key, and appealed to their listeners primarily because it struck a nostalgic note and reminded people of similar situations, or a neighbor, grandmother, or aunt back home.[58]

Many of the comedians, then, were people like Sarie and Sally, entertainers who projected a plain, down-to-earth rural quality and who gave the impression that, like Grandpa Jones, Jerry Clower, Stringbean, Pete Stamper, and Junior Samples in our own time, they were merely playing themselves and were conducting a dialogue with an audience that understood them well. Other comedians, however, used styles that, though basically rural, nevertheless reflected years of show-business experience. With the decline of minstrel entertainment after World War I, some of the blackface performers gravitated toward the country radio and barn-dance shows. Lasses White and Honey Wilds, for example, had joined WSM with the Dixie Minstrels in late 1932. By the end of 1938 an off-shoot of the Lasses and Honey team, Jamup and Honey, were doing their Amos-and-Andy-style routines three evenings a week on the same station, and were performing in blackface each Saturday night on the Grand Ole Opry. Tom "Jamup" Woods and Lee "Honey" Wilds played the roles of proprietors of the Second-hand Sporting Goods Store, with a show described in one press release as "a humorous story of every-day life among the Southern darkeys." By 1941, with Bunny Biggs now playing the role of Jamup, they became the nucleus of the first touring tent show sent out under Grand Ole Opry auspices, supported by an extensive road crew and performing in an 80- by 200-foot tent.[59]

Lew Childre seems to have had little if any blackface experience, but he was a reservoir of musical styles and comedy that dated at least to the late nineteenth century. This song-and-dance man from Opp, Alabama, performed for years on radio stations on the Mexican border and in the South, and was a long-time fixture on the Grand Ole Opry with routines that were merely continuations of acts performed earlier in vaudeville and tent repertoire. Performing often with Stringbean Akeman, Childre conveyed an image that has been a continuing one in country music, that of the "slick rube," a wise-cracking boy from the country who was a bit too green to make it in the big city but who had been there and was therefore perceived as more "sophisticated" than the "hayseeds" back home. In a fast-talking style of lingo Childre cracked jokes, danced the country buck-and-wing, and, accompanied by his dobro-style guitar, sang old songs like "Riding on the Elevated Railroad," "Hang Out the Front Door Key," "Put on Your Old Grey Bonnet" and the one for which he was best known, "I'm Alabamy Bound."[60]

Some country-style comedians, after years of experience in vaudeville, tent shows, and on radio barn dances, gravitated toward Los Angeles, hoping for roles in movies or seeking employment in the city's active musical organizations. The Birmingham, Alabama, native Herbert Clayton "Hank" Penny, famous for both his style of comedy and his brand of western swing, went to California in early 1945 and obtained a job in a Charles Starrett western called *Headin' West*. He soon became actively engaged as a singer and bandleader in the burgeoning postwar musical scene in California, but never abandoned his career as a comedian.[61] After Gene Autry demonstrated in 1934 that the singing cowboy was a highly salable item, the movie industry latched on to other singers like Roy Rogers, Tex Ritter, and Rex Allen, who had already developed followings as radio and recording performers, to continue the trend established by Autry. Country comics soon followed in the wake of the singers. A few entertainers, like Johnny Bond—an immensely talented musician and songwriter from Oklahoma who was named to the Country Music Hall of Fame in 1999—seem to have drifted into humor only after they moved to Hollywood. Others, like Pat Buttram and Smiley Burnette, moved into the movie business carrying comic credentials that had already been well honed in radio and other performing venues. Lester Alvin "Smiley" Burnette was performing on WDZ in Tuscola, Illinois, in December, 1933, when Gene Autry hired him as part of his touring entourage. Probably the most beloved of all "cowboy comedians," Burnette played the role of Autry's sidekick, Frog Millhouse, in eighty-one movies and in scores of personal appearances. Burnette's enduring persona is that of the fat, bumbling, but lovable person who was always falling off his horse and yelling "Gene! Gene!" when he got into trouble (which was often). His flair for comedy, however, was only one facet of a multidimensional career that included singing, the ability to play many instruments, and songwriting (he wrote good and popular songs such as "Riding down the Canyon," "Hominy Grits," and "It's My Lazy Day"). At the end of his career in the late sixties he was playing the role of a railroad engineer on television's "Petticoat Junction."[62]

Gene Autry was the medium through which several other country performers, both singers and comedians, made their way into the movie industry. Johnny Bond, as we have seen, played many roles in Autry's troupe. Pat Buttram, on the other hand, did little singing. After a successful stint from 1934 to 1949 as a popular comedian on WLS and the National Barn Dance, this Winston County, Alabama, boy traveled to Hollywood to take up a career as Autry's sidekick in many movies and on the CBS Sunday night show, "Melody Ranch."[63] His trademark, like that of Andy Devine, was a wobbly, grating voice that would have prevented a singing career had he chosen to pursue one. After his tenure as a member of Autry's Melody Ranch Gang, he remained in big-time show business and sloughed off much of his downhome cast. He appeared in television serials, such as the "Green Acres" show where he played the role of Mr. Haney, a rustic flimflam man, and, in the last years of his life, was a popular toastmaster. He obviously moved far beyond his original hayseed image, and his comedy, in fact, always reflected wide reading and intensive study in the works of such well-known humorists as Artemus Ward, Mark Twain, and Will Rogers.[64]

The three outstanding radio or barn-dance comedians of country music history have been the Duke of Paducah (Benny Ford), Rod Brasfield, and Minnie Pearl (Sarah Ophelia Colley). The Duke of Paducah had one of the longest careers in American entertainment, actively participating in country road shows until the late seventies. Born in DeSoto, Missouri, he began his long apprenticeship in vaudeville and related fields of entertainment in 1922 as a member of a jazz group, singing and playing the tenor banjo. Before joining the Grand Ole Opry in 1942, Ford had worked with Otto Gray's Oklahoma Cowboys, as emcee and comedian for Gene Autry on the National Barn Dance and public appearances, and on such radio shows as the Plantation Party and the Renfro Valley Barn Dance. As a country comic he played a role similar to that of Lew Childre, as a yokel who had pretensions to urbanity. His olive-drab suit was too short and outdated, and his shoes, purchased in 1933 from a sidewalk cart in Chicago, were the high-button type. He talked in a loud, boastful manner, but he was easily taken in by the city types who were "slicker" than he. Borrowing a line which he had heard used by a tired country boy in Hazen, Arkansas, way back in 1924, he invariably ended his act by saying, "I'm going to the wagon, boys, these shoes are killing me." Ford's rise to prominence as a country comedian began in 1938 when he moved to Cincinnati with John Lair as both a partner and a participant in the then-new Renfro Valley Barn Dance. He reached his largest audience during a stint on the Grand Ole Opry from 1942 to 1958,

but he continued to perform with his own road show and on other touring packages, including that of Hank Williams, Jr., on into the 1970s.[65]

Rod Brasfield served his apprenticeship with tent-repertoire shows, such
as that of Bisbee's Comedians, and as an understudy of his older brother, Boob Brasfield, who gained prominence in the fifties as half of the team
of Uncle Cyp and Aunt Sap on Red Foley's Ozark Jubilee. Although actually born in Smithville, Mississippi, in August, 1910, Brasfield played
the role of a seedy, ignorant country boy from Hohenwald, Tennessee,
who had somehow wound up in the city. His dress (a floppy hat and baggy
pants), style, and comic routines reflected vaudeville-burlesque humor.
He would not have been at all out of place following a girlie routine on
the stage of the Gaiety Theatre. He became one of the best-known, and
best-loved, comedians in country music because of exposure gained during the late forties and early fifties on the NBC segment of the Grand Ole
Opry, the Prince Albert Show. He won additional national recognition
through a supporting role in Budd Schulberg's critically acclaimed movie, *A Face in the Crowd*. Described as the Hohenwald Flash, Brasfield did
short monologues but was best known for his repartee with NBC host
Red Foley and with Minnie Pearl.[66] With an expressive, rubbery face that
easily ran the gamut of emotions, or with nothing more than a wry comment on the weather—"By Ned, it ain't so hot tonight" when Nashville's
temperature had plunged below the freezing mark—Brasfield simultaneously entertained and reassured his audiences with routines that were
familiar and comforting.

Rod Brasfield won the affections of his colleagues and millions of fans
before his death in 1958, but this acclaim paled before that won by his
long-time associate, Minnie Pearl. Minnie Pearl was not simply present
during country music's first great commercial surge during and immediately after World War II, she played a central role in the music's popularization. As a regular participant each Saturday night in the nationally
disseminated NBC segment of the Grand Ole Opry, and through her frequent appearances on other popular radio shows, Minnie Pearl became
known to millions of people who had only a vague familiarity with such
singers as Roy Acuff, Red Foley, or Hank Williams. Her contributions
were ironic in a sense because she did not listen to country music when
she was young, even though her father, who was a lumber dealer in Cen-
terville, Tennessee, was an ardent Opry fan.

Growing up in a relatively prosperous home in rural Tennessee,[67] Sarah Ophelia Colley nourished dreams of becoming a serious stage performer and was fortunate enough, despite the ravaging effects of the Great

Depression, to receive two years of training in speech and dramatic arts at Ward-Belmont College in Nashville. Obtaining employment in 1934 as an actor, dramatic coach, and agent for the Wayne P. Sewell Producing Company, an organization that employed local talent in small towns throughout the upper South to present theatrical productions, Miss Colley unconsciously began building the character of Minnie Pearl.

Although Minnie was a composite of many country girls whom she encountered in her traveling and teaching experience, the character was inspired most directly by an elderly mountain lady with whom she had resided in Baileyton, Alabama. Sarah was charmed by the dialect, good humor, and generosity of this lady, and always felt that in her persona of Minnie Pearl, she was not making fun but was instead paying tribute to the simple and decent culture that sustained such people's lives. Appearing often before civic groups to publicize the Sewell productions, Miss Colley devised the Minnie Pearl character as both a promotion and entertainment relief. In 1938 Minnie Pearl first appeared before a small audience at the Pilot's Club in Aiken, South Carolina. By the time she made her first appearance at the Grand Ole Opry in 1940, the long, ruffled dress, flower-bedecked hat, country dialect, roster of familiar characters—such as Uncle Nabob, her boyfriend Hezzie, and the sibling who was known simply as "Brother"—and basic routines were already engrafted into her characterization. When she added the $1.95 price tag that dangled conspicuously from her hat, the persona of the simple, naive, and good-hearted country girl known as Minnie Pearl was largely complete.

As the girl from Grinder's Switch (the uninhabited railroad junction from which Sarah's father had shipped his lumber), Minnie Pearl achieved an almost-instant rapport with her audience when she began her first performance with what became her internationally known trademark, "Howdy, I'm just so proud to be here." Through national broadcasts carried on NBC, and as a member of the "Camel Caravan," a country-music package show that visited military installations during World War II, the character of Minnie Pearl was implanted in the consciousness of the American people (in fact, a special type of army truck bore her name).

Although the character changed somewhat down through the years (the original "howdy" was rendered in a shy, quiet manner rather than in the loud, brash, and prolonged style—"how-dee"—used in later years),[68] Minnie Pearl remained a good, down-to-earth, naive country girl, full of wonderment at the world around her, nostalgic about her home and people, and consumed with the desire "to have a feller." Her regular boyfriend, Hezzie, though a convenient companion, was hardly marriage-able material. One day when Minnie noted that it was about time that the two of them got married, he replied incredulously "Why, who would have us?" Minnie Pearl was the embodiment of most of the strains of country comedy described earlier in this chapter, but, above all, she was the seemingly naive but innately shrewd rustic character who has ap-peared often in American popular culture. Never vulgar, but occasional-ly mildly risqué, and always the eternal optimist, Minnie Pearl possessed infinite faith in the goodness and potentiality of humankind.[69] Her ca-reer after 1940 coincided with the worldwide growth of country music, and almost exactly paralleled the tenure of the Grand Ole Opry in the Ryman Auditorium. Minnie Pearl's tears, shed during the last appearance of the Grand Ole Opry in the old building in 1974 before it moved on to new and more sumptuous accommodations, are indeed understandable.

Although the old-time country comedians have virtually disappeared from stage shows and have instead retreated to Branson, Renfro Valley, and other regional barn dances, humor has nevertheless remained as an indispensable ingredient of country music. Country humor, in fact, was central to country music's commercial resurgence after 1969 when the national television series "Hee Haw" became one of the nation's most popular shows.[70] A weekly production that combined music and "hill-billy" humor, the show seemed little more than a pale, but rustic, reflec-tion of "Laugh In," a very popular and zany program starring Rowan and Martin. Both shows had formats filled with rapid-fire jokes and vi-gnettes, slapstick humor, stock and continuing situations (such as a fence plank tilting up and hitting a bad punster or jokester in the seat), and beautiful, scantily clad girls.

"Hee Haw"'s performers, for the most part, dressed in hillbilly cos-tumes that made the stage look like a set from a "Li'l Abner" produc-tion. The hillbilly theme, which seemed purely a caricature of "country" characters and lifestyles, or some adman's idea of what rural life was like, was appalling to many viewers and, in fact, projected an image that most country entertainers had been trying to slough off for decades. Few coun-try performers, however, could resist the temptation to appear on national television; therefore, if any of them had any significant opposition to the rube image, the feeling never surfaced.

Most country comedians enthusiastically welcomed the emergence of the show, and rightly recognized that it provided a widely visible forum for their art. Jethro Burns, in fact, revived his act in 1976 with a new "Homer" (the original Homer Haynes had died in 1971) because of the renewed popularity that "Hee Haw" had engendered for corn-pone humor. He later described the show as the "greatest on the network," and opined that he had "tried every way in the world to get on that show."[71] The general public, on the other hand, needed little conditioning to accept such a show; it had demonstrated its receptivity to hillbilly stereotypes for many years by making shows like "Beverly Hillbillies," "Green Acres," and "Petticoat Junction" nationally popular. Many people no doubt watched the show in order to hear the music, performed by the regular hosts Buck Owens and Roy Clark, or by big-name guests. The series was one of the few showcases on which country music could be displayed nationally, so some viewers may have suffered patiently through the humor until their favorite singer appeared. One of the ironies of the show's formats was that the "country" music performed on the show was considerably more removed from its rural roots than was the "country" humor.

Despite its stereotypes (or more likely because of them), "Hee Haw" proved to be one of the surprises of national television. From the beginning it maintained consistently high ratings, a popularity that endured even after CBS adopted an anti-rural policy in 1971 and canceled it and most of its other "homefolks" programs (including the Lawrence Welk Show). "Hee Haw" maintained a wide popularity when it moved to independent syndication and reruns. Many of the show's critics, particularly those from the ranks of country music, learned to tolerate the hillbilly cliches and recognized the production for what it essentially was, a self-parody, or a burlesque of outsiders' conceptions of rural society.

"Hee Haw" was a composite of comic styles, drawn from recent professional origin and from earlier traditions of folk and popular entertainment, and its performers represented a variety of approaches to country humor. Every show featured a modified version of the "Arkansas Traveler" routine, when Buck Owens on guitar and Roy Clark on five-string banjo played fragments of a hoedown tune, stopped suddenly, did a comic dialogue, and then resumed the tune. Archie Campbell, who actually came from a little town in the mountains called Bull Gap, Tennessee, recalled one of the venerable social occasions of rural and small-town America when he played the role of a barber who regaled "the boys in the shop" with funny stories about people whom they all knew. Jimmie Riddle and Jack Phelps re-created one of the scenes of blackface minstrelsy with their hambone routine, keeping a rhythmic pattern going by slapping their legs and stomachs. They also created, simultaneously, a vocal rhythm that they called "eephing," by making nonsense sounds with their mouths.

Usually during the show a "hayseed radio announcer" murdered the English language but kept his listeners aware of all the local gossip. In fact, the cherished American habit of gossiping and tall-tale spinning, loved by rural folk and city dwellers alike, was depicted in several formats, as in scenes around the old cracker barrel in the general store, in Minnie Pearl's description of her "latest feller" to her assembled girlfriends, and in David "Stringbean" Akeman's reading of his "letter from home" when the exploits of his relatives and old friends from "down home" were described to his amused companions.

Some scenes, of course, catered to the general stereotype of the lazy, or humdrum, hillbilly family. One segment, for example, called "the Culhanes," appeared to be a hillbilly satire of "One Man's Family." The Culhanes appeared week after week sitting on the same couch, staring stuporously, and drawling out comments about completely inconsequential matters (one wonders if the producers of the "Seinfeld" show received inspiration from the Culhane skits). The segment was reminiscent of a similar scene heard years before on the Judy Canova radio show when Ma Canova, in an incredibly long drawl, persistently, show after show, said to Pa: "Get up, pa. Get up you lazy critter."

Apart from its perpetuation of country comic styles, "Hee Haw" was more important as a showcase for country comedians, men and women whose styles in some cases showed the polish of many years of professional entertainment, and in others reflected "natural" but uncultivated comic gifts. Archie Campbell, for example, came to the show after a long career as a country band leader, singer, and comedian. Sometimes described as the "mayor of Bull's Gap," Campbell was essentially a country comedian with the looks and manner of a city slicker. However, the type of "sharpie" he portrayed looked like someone out of the twenties, a well-dressed con artist with a Tom Dewey mustache. Campbell played the type of personality that one would have found in the small towns of the rural South, rather than on the farms—an undertaker, perhaps, a merchant, a banker, a barber, maybe a dentist or a church deacon. In short, Campbell projected the image of a rustic who affects city ways.[72]

Roy Clark, of course, could not lay claim to the many years of experience that Archie Campbell had, but his expertise was apparent. As he is fond of telling interviewers, Clark came not from the country but from Washington, D.C., where his father worked as a federal government employee. But as anyone knows who saw the Clark Family perform when Roy invited them on the show, his family is still deeply rooted in the Virginia soil from which they migrated. Clark is one of the outstanding instrumentalists of country music (and can play virtually every string instrument known to the genre); he is an effective interpreter of country-pop ballads; and he has one of the greatest natural wits in the music business. His multitalented approach, which earned him recognition as country music's Entertainer of the Year in 1973, enabled him to fit in easily in either the hillbilly atmosphere of "Hee Haw" or the urbane milieu of something like the "Tonight Show" or Dean Martin's show.[73]

Grandpa Jones and Stringbean, on the other hand, fit in somewhere between the sophisticated rustics like Archie Campbell and Roy Clark and the untutored country types like Junior Samples who will be discussed later. These men, as well as the female comedian Veronica Loretta "Roni" Stoneman (who occasionally appeared as a snaggletoothed backwoods type), came to the show with many years of show-business experience but continued to display authentic old-time rural styles. These performers never displayed any pretensions to urbanity. Marshall Louis "Grandpa" Jones, one of the most beloved entertainers in country music history, was born on a Kentucky farm, but grew up in Akron, Ohio, an industrial center that lured thousands of displaced southerners. His show-business experience, which began in 1929, took him into radio work with "Lum and Abner" and into roadshow appearances with Bradley Kincaid. At Kincaid's suggestion Jones began creating the character of "Grandpa," a personality that at first required makeup and a false mustache, but one which he later naturally embodied. Before death terminated his long professional country music career, Grandpa Jones held sway as an expert five-string banjoist, a singer and yodeler of both humorous and sentimental songs (often performed as part of a duet with his wife Ramona), and an accomplished comic storyteller. His repertoire of songs, jokes, and instrumental styles came, at least indirectly, from folk, vaudeville, and minstrel sources. "Hee Haw" audiences seldom heard him sing, but they were amused by his Kentucky twang and his droll stories. When Grandpa responded each week to the question "Grandpa, what's for dinner?" by answering something like "possum, collard greens, and blackberry cobbler" (the list changed each week), the audience was reminded that soul food was not the monopoly of any one racial group.[74]

David Akeman, christened "Stringbean" by Asa Martin because of the comedian's lean and lanky physique, was also a "natural" country comic character who made people laugh by merely being himself. Before his tragic death in early 1974 (he and his wife were shot to death by robbers), Stringbean had used the "Hee Haw" show as a vehicle to gain the commercial success that had largely eluded him in his long prior career.

As a five-string banjo player, a singer of old-time songs (including many learned from Uncle Dave Macon, whom he considered his idol), and a teller of droll tall tales, Stringbean was an unaffected rural type, a quality that no monetary success or performing career could diminish. He first came to the Grand Ole Opry in 1940 as a member of Bill Monroe's Blue Grass Boys and was, in fact, Monroe's first banjo player. He remained on the Opry for over thirty years and became known for his traditional songs, his deadpan delivery, and his trademark expression, "Lord, I feel so unnecessary." The expression was seldom used on the "Hee Haw" show (he replaced it with "how sweet it is"), possibly because his new-found popularity gained there through such formats as his "letter from home" demonstrated to him that he and his style of humor were indeed "necessary."[75]

The careers of at least two "Hee Haw" performers, Jerry Clower and Junior Samples, displayed the old American myth of rags to riches as a literal reality. Clower, who appeared only occasionally on the show, and Samples, who was a regular from the beginning, moved into their professional comedy careers in the late sixties with no prior show-business experience. No adman or writer could have created more credible examples of the Deep South rustic, dripping with downhome dialect and aphorisms, than these two comedians. Unlike Junior Samples, Jerry Clower earned a college degree in agriculture while playing football at Mississippi State (he had never previously played a down of the sport). After his graduation he found employment as a salesman with a fertilizer corporation, a profession that took him all over the United States and eventually led to his emergence as a popular convention and after-dinner speaker. Clower discovered early that humor would enliven even a dull subject like fertilizer, and that no humor was more appealing to his listeners than that which centered around his rural boyhood on a Mississippi farm. When he ventured into professional entertainment—on the strength of a best-selling album taken from a tape of one of his live convention speeches—Clower found there a seemingly inexhaustible hunger for his variety of southern rural nostalgia. In his skillful comic hands the Mississippi countryside emerged, not as a locus of embarrassment that an aspiring bourgeois urbanite might best forget, but as a scene of warm and enduring human relationships. The incidents that Clower recalled or fictionalized, although not always inherently humorous, were made so by his genius for embellishment. He maintained that he did not tell funny stories but instead told stories funny. As a "rural nationalist," Clower never permitted his listeners to forget that he was "pure country," a man who could still pull a rope and bucket up and down a well without letting the bucket hit either side and without spilling a drop of water.[76]

Junior Samples could not boast of a college career but instead was known around his Cumming, Georgia, home as a local "character," a semiliterate country hedonist who preferred drinking, hunting, and fishing to the sawmill work at which he had been long employed. It was another talent, however, a propensity for the tall tale, which got him into show business. Self-proclaimed as the "world's biggest liar," Junior could not resist the temptation one day to tell a game warden that he had caught a record-breaking fish that in fact had been caught by someone else. The warden collected the story on tape for his report, was amused by it, and subsequently turned it over to a disc jockey who, in turn, got the dialogue between Junior and the warden released on a Chart recording.[77] The recording was only moderately successful, but when heard in Nashville it impressed industry people sufficiently to cause them to recall his name when casting for "Hee Haw" took place.

With his 300-pound frame encased in a pair of overalls, and stumbling over the words held up on cue cards, Junior Samples proved to be one of the most popular "Hee Haw" performers. The show's producers decided very early that Junior's mistakes were as potentially funny as any of the polished routines done by the veteran actors. Consequently, Junior's successive attempts to read a line, or to pronounce a particularly big word, were often shown to the television audience without editing. One day on the set, wearing a Roman toga and stumbling over the lines from Hamlet's soliloquy, Junior supposedly asked who had written the skit. After being told that it was Shakespeare, he said "Well, I don't like to be ugly, but I sure do hope you all don't hire that fella to write for us again next year." He sometimes played the role of a car salesman, and his mock phone number, BR-549, was later adopted as the name of a young revivalist country band. As in the Shakespeare skit, Junior was sometimes deliberately given a complicated line to say, and if this obvious exploitation of his lack of education troubled him, he never showed evidence of it. Like Liberace, Junior no doubt cried all the way to the bank.[78]

The "Hee Haw" show continued to be a popular feature of television syndication throughout the seventies, but it had already become one of the few remaining venues for old-time country comedy. Jerry Clower continued to regale listeners with tales of the Ledbetter clan who inhabited the imaginative landscape of rural and small-town Mississippi. His style, though, was far removed from the burlesque or tent-repertoire circuits that had shaped much of the older humor and was instead that of a genial country Baptist preacher or small-town story teller.

The emergence of Jeff Foxworthy in the nineties spoke volumes about the evolution of southern rural life and the mating of southern and northern folkways. More and more, the children of southern working folk (like Foxworthy) live in suburban areas and preserve their rural contacts by purchasing from the L. L. Bean and Lands' End catalogues, by taking occasional camping trips in state or national parks, or by driving Land Rovers or other SUVs. The son of an Atlanta IBM executive, Foxworthy was a graduate of Georgia Tech and a product of the nation's proliferating comedy clubs where comedians hone their talents with an eye, not toward the Grand Ole Opry, but toward the Johnny Carson, David Letterman, or Jay Leno television shows. He did not at first think of himself as a country comedian, but he gradually became known to the country audience because of his use of a series of one-liners known as "You Might Be a Redneck If . . . " Foxworthy spoke with a strong southern accent, but in his interpretation, the redneck lost much of his regional identification and became anyone characterized by "a glorious lack of sophistication." An identification with Foxworthy's humor seemed to be a way for southern working folk to laugh at themselves and to assert identity, while at the same time being assured that they were like everyone else. His style also seemed singularly appropriate for a musical genre that was similarly losing its regional and class associations.

Most contemporary country comics, like Jeff Foxworthy, also illustrate the growing marriage of city and country in the South and nation as a whole. Although southern rural affectations still color the style of some comedians, such as Ron Thomason, the sensibilities of most tend to be more urbane and sophisticated—the consequence of college training and lives constantly assaulted by the glow of television and other homogenizing forces. Modern country jokesters rarely dwell on their rural past— "the good old days when times were bad." Instead, satire, burlesque, and irreverence have become the standard fare of contemporary country comedy. The songs of Ray Stevens, an Atlanta singer-songwriter, have roamed freely across the categories of American humor. "The Streak" satirized the brief vogue of public nude flashing in the 1970s, while "The Mississippi Squirrel Revival" and "Would Jesus Wear a Rolex?" ventured into the generally forbidden zone of religion. Stevens's satires of religious practices were bold and original, something that few public entertainers have before or since undertaken to do, but reminiscent of some of the digs taken at preachers and religious groups in the 1830s and 1840s by the men associated with the literary genre known as southwestern humor. "Would Jesus Wear a Rolex?" was clearly inspired by some of the television evangelists of the 1980s, with their ostentatious wealth and personal corruption. "Mississippi Squirrel Revival" was a hilarious account of a revival in Pascagoula, Mississippi, which was thrown into pandemonium when a boy's pet squirrel got loose and began slithering in and out of women's skirts. Viewers of the scene thought that the power of the Holy Spirit had been unleashed.[79] Terry Ree and Bruce Williams (who perform as the Indian and the White Guy) exhibit a similar indifference to political correctness with an act that humorously exploits their cultural and racial differences. In a self-written ad in *Music City News*, Bruce Williams (the White Guy) said "after twenty years trying to regain huge chunks of land, the Indian is now able at least to experience the exhilaration of actual wheels on a car so that he may visit the land stolen from him." He then advised fans not to offer the Indian any alcoholic beverages or government cheese products. Building on routines that began privately in 1968 during their college days at Black Hills State College in Spearfish, South Dakota (they both claimed to be majoring in draft dodging), Ree and Williams utilize stereotypes that nevertheless generally keep the white man on the defensive.

Just as it preserves a traditional country-music repertoire, bluegrass also showcases traditional forms of humor. Ron Thomason (the leader and mandolin player of the Dry Branch Fire Squad) built his comedic reputation through the seemingly incongruous blending of backcountry twang and worldly-wise liberal commentary. Born in Honaker, Virginia, but reared in Ohio among transplanted southerners, Thomason grew up with ardent attachments to Appalachian culture and an acute understanding of the larger world that threatened to subsume that culture and its values. Thomason gave well-rehearsed monologues delivered in a dry, hillbilly dialect that were both funny and compassionate. His characters sometimes initially appeared to be slow, and even dim-witted, but ended up—as in "The Arkansas Traveler"—offering insightful observations of contemporary issues.[80]

Unlike Thomason, the Austin Lounge Lizards were city boys who ventured into the performance of bluegrass music initially as a diversion from busy professional careers in Austin, Texas. The group's genesis can be traced to 1976 when Hank Card and Conrad Deisler, two history majors at Princeton University, discovered a mutual talent for songwriting and fondness for satirical songs. Enrolled later at the University of Texas Law School, they became immersed in the vigorous musical scene of

Austin and began a musical collaboration with Tom Pittman, a five-string banjoist and pedal steel guitar player from Georgia. As the seat of state government, with a large university population, Austin served as a perfect locus for the biting liberal criticism and social satire dispensed by these talented musicians. Adding a bass player and mandolinist/fiddler (consisting in 1999 of Boo Resnick and Richard Bowden), the Lizards began playing at local clubs and at the nearby Kerrville Bluegrass Festival. A first-place award in the "Best Band" competition at the Kerrville Folk Festival in 1983, and an album in 1984, gradually introduced them to a larger Texas audience, but they did not become a full-time performing unit until 1987 when their schedules took them to festivals and concerts throughout the nation and to Canada.[81]

As they move effortlessly from bluegrass to honky-tonk to Beach-style rock and gospel, with smooth and satisfying harmonies and eclectic instrumental styles that defy precise definition, the Lizards present (with the possible exception of Kinky Friedman) the most uncompromising body of satirical social criticism ever heard in country music. But one encounters neither twang nor hillbilly parody in their performances. Instead, the Lizards apply their thoroughly urbane, irreverent, but humane sensibilities to a wide range of social institutions and sacred cows. Religious hypocrisy and self-righteousness are confronted in "Jesus Loves Me, but He Can't Stand You" ("God loves his children, but that don't mean he won't incinerate some"); domestic virtues in "That God-Forsaken Hellhole I Call Home"; the pangs of divorce in "The Dogs, They Really Miss You"; political extremism in "Gingrich the Newt"; Texas chauvinism in "Another Stupid Texas Song" and "Dallas, Texas" ("Most cities have soul, but Dallas must have been at the bank when they passed it around"); a popular president in "The Ballad of Ronald Reagan" ("at least he's not Nixon, he's even worse"); and the myth of aged and besotted wisdom in "Old Blevins." The value of the homely philosophy dispensed by Old Blevins, the town drunk, is appropriately summed up in the song's refrain: "Blah blah blah."[82]

Some of country music's satirical humor has dealt with or paid tribute to older forms of country music, catering to an audience that generally has some knowledge of the material that is being satirized. The Statler Brothers, for example, recorded a classic, but condescending, spoof of amateur country shows in an album called *Alive from Johnny Mack Brown High School.*[83] Playing the roles of earnest but inept country musicians, Lester "Roadhog" Moran and His Cadillac Cowboys, the Statlers re-created the off-key singing, clumsy rhythms, and out-of-tune

musicianship that sometimes characterized the music of hometown jubilees. With dialogue confined largely to "all right" and "mighty fine,"
the wheezing Roadhog presided over the discordant show until it disintegrated into a violent melee replete with the sounds of anguished voices
and broken bottles.

The Hot Rize bluegrass band (named for a widely advertised ingredient in Martha White flour), usually took time out in their concerts to pay
tribute to 1950s-style honky-tonk music by transforming themselves into
another group called Red Knuckles and the Trailblazers. Wearing dark
glasses and outdated cowboy attire, the Trailblazers took the stage during a Hot Rize "intermission," claiming to have been patiently waiting
in the dark and hot confines of the stars' touring bus. They sang vintage
country tunes, supposedly learned from the only existing jukebox back
home, to the accompaniment of steel guitar and other electric instruments.
Like the Lounge Lizards, the humor lay not in their music, which was a
competently performed and authentic representation of earlier styles, but
in their stage dress and antics, and comic titles. Waldo Otto (Pete Wernick in real life) typically "showed off" by bouncing the steel bar off the
neck of his 8-string lap steel guitar, and Slade (Charles Sawtelle) spoke
monosyllabically and affected a silent and slightly menacing demeanor
as he played the electric Fender bass.[84]

If burlesque was only an occasional ingredient of most country performances, it was central to the act of the popular trio Riders in the Sky.
One finds no condescension, and certainly no ill will, in their good-
natured parodies of the singing cowboy tradition. Performing with an un-
abashed love for the music of Gene, Roy, the Sons of the Pioneers, and
other musical heroes of the silver screen, Douglas B. "Ranger Doug" Green
(who styled himself "the idol of American youth"), Fred "Too Slim"
LaBour, and Woody Paul ("King of the Cowboy Fiddlers") breathed life
into a seemingly moribund tradition with a marvelous blend of superb
musicianship and off-beat humor. Funny songs, such as "Always Drink
Upstream from the Herd," appeared frequently in their repertoire, but
the Riders relied more often on romantic love songs, replete with the best
yodeling (performed most often by Ranger Doug, but occasionally by the
entire trio) heard since the forties. Their humor came instead from their
repartee, monologues, and skits. Each musician contributed to the humor of the act, but Too Slim has been the central core of their comedy.
Whether delivering an impression of the veteran western comic Gabby
Hayes, tapping melodies on his face with the palms of his hands, carrying on a dialogue with a steer skull, rolling a tumbleweed across the stage,

peddling his cac-tie (a necktie made in the shape of a cactus), or merely
making droll and irreverent comments, Too Slim contributed vitally to
the making of an act that brought both young and old people into the
Riders' family of fans.[85]

Unfortunately, the most satisfying glimpse of humor in country music
may be the kind that most fans seldom get a chance to see or hear. It
emerges in the entertainers' small talk and gossip during moments of
relaxation or retirement, or during times of reunion, when they recall the
old times on the road—both good and bad—eccentric or beloved colleagues, shady booking agents, embarrassing stage moments, or merely
the context in which a favored song was written. One of my most cherished memories is that of listening to Hank Thompson and Merle Travis
exchange stories offstage at a festival in July, 1978, in Kerrville, Texas.
The stories flowed freely, with each tale being funnier than the last. Travis,
for example, remembered an incident involving a notoriously inept California booking agent known to both of the musicians. Following the
agent's instructions, Travis had traveled to Yuma, Arizona, to do a show,
only to find out that the program had really been scheduled for Yuba City,
California. When informed about that mix-up, the agent drew on a pat
response he had reserved for such situations. He simply flicked the ashes
from his cigar and said, "That must have been partly my fault." By investing the memory of this frustrating event with the warm glow of humor, Travis had reaffirmed the community of experiences that bind entertainers to each other.

Some of this impromptu humor, of course, is chronicled in published
reminiscences or autobiographies, but fans otherwise have to be content
with the occasional televised special or interview (such as those seen on
the "Ralph Emery Show"). When fans are brought into this circle of
warmth and nostalgic camaraderie, they too become part of country
music's extended family. Watching the George Jones television show,
which typically begins with Jones and his guests sitting in easy chairs in
a casual living room setting conversing informally and listening to each
other sing a new or standard song, fans virtually become guests witness-
ing a kind of familial banter. In this type of setting, memories of missed
show dates, quirky habits, and even drunken binges can become the stuff
of humor and the vehicles for asserting the humanity that links performers
and fans. This sense of intimacy, and the feeling that one is being drawn
into and made part of a family reunion, have been recaptured in a number of recorded events, including the appearances made by Johnny Cash
and Willie Nelson on "VH-1 Soundstage," and in the series of videos

called *Country Legends* (released in 1998) that feature a host of veteran Grand Ole Opry performers seated in a format similar to that seen on the George Jones show.[86] Serious moments certainly abound in these presentations, and viewers cannot escape the poignance that arises when now-deceased entertainers such as Grandpa Jones and Justin Tubb appear on the screen. The overall mood, though, is one of conviviality as the performers gently poke fun at each other and themselves and recall the bittersweet incidents of their careers. Humor once again combines with music to evoke a sense of family interrelationship among musicians and fans, to make memories of the past more bearable, and to remind them all of the music's humble origins.

8

"We Still Wave Old Glory down at the Courthouse"

We don't smoke marijuana in Muskogee
We don't take our trips on LSD
We don't burn our draft cards down on Main Street
We like living right and being free.[1]

With country musicians being prominently displayed at the Republican national conventions in 1992 and 1996, and with President George Bush asserting that country was his music of choice, no one could be faulted for thinking that the music had become a citadel of political conservatism. Although much of the South supported Bush in 1992, the presidential victory that year went to Democrat Bill Clinton, a son of southern working-class parents. That his musical tastes ran toward jazz and sixties pop rock only underscored the irony of the South's shift toward political conservatism and of country music's growing identification with right-wing causes. This late twentieth-century political posture, however, went against the grain of the music's historic populistic stance.

The roots of country music's identification with political conservatism lay in the religious and cold war fervor of the 1950s, but its first dramatic manifestation came in 1969 with the release of Merle Haggard's "Okie from Muskogee." This song made Haggard a national superstar and contributed to the perception that country music, as an art form, defended establishment values. A rash of popular magazines, and at least a few academic journals, portrayed country music as conservative, ultrapatriotic, and jingoistic. In short, it quickly became identified as the music of Middle America or as the voice of the once quiet "Silent Majority." The late 1960s and early 1970s saw the appearance of a large number of songs that defended American involvement in Vietnam or that otherwise "protested against the protestors." The prevalence of these songs, along with others commenting on the alleged moral decay of the nation, aroused the curiosity of journalists, political pundits, and media publicists. This conservative political identification lent to country music a public notoriety, and an image, that have ever since remained with it.

While country music has demonstrated a clear and audible conservative voice, the music nevertheless has historically defied explicit political categorization or ideological identification. Like the southern folk culture that produced it, country music has exhibited eclectic and contradictory traits. Simultaneously southern and American, out of the mainstream yet striving for acceptance within it, often complacent but sometimes angry, religious and hedonistic, and always individualistic (sometimes to the point of violent contrariness), the music has been as unpredictable in its manifestations as has the culture that gave it birth.

Ideological consistency has been rare among country musicians, but political involvement has been omnipresent. The music has been consistently topical, and its performers have exhibited social consciousness, if not always social conscience. If any political label fits the music, it would be "populist," with both its positive and negative connotations. Since the days of Andrew Jackson, and at least to 1968 or so, the majority of the white plain folk tended to be Democratic (except for those significant exceptions, the mountaineers of Appalachia).[2] They valued hard work and those who struggled and survived against adversity; they were suspicious of monopolies and nonproducers—bankers, lawyers, speculators, or, at the other end of the spectrum, people who lived on welfare or who otherwise lived off the labor of others.[3] Southern working folk were usually warm, comforting, and hospitable to those who lived within or who fit the social confines of their circle of familiarity. They were prejudiced against "strangers" or "outsiders," non-Christians, foreigners, blacks, gays, or social deviants—but they were generally accepting of the unfortunate people within their midst (the crippled, blind, deaf, mentally ill) and could even accept the occasional religious freethinker. Prejudice against Jews was rare, largely because so few of them lived in southern communities but also because the Jewish merchant had a very close relationship with plain folk in the small towns of the South, and also because as people of "the book," Jews were deemed to have a very special relationship with God.[4]

Because of their struggle and their ability to survive, the southern plain folk tended to think of themselves as the "true" Americans. This kind of "Americanism" could make them both patriotic and resentful of those who seemed to embody opposing values. These attitudes could also lead them toward political positions that seem contradictory, depending on the context in which they were found. Indeed, the political postures of the plain folk created a dynamic tension, summed up, historically, by an intense individualism and clannishness, a fierce sense of liberty, and a deference toward their "betters." Their political attitudes led many of them into the southern alliances of the 1880s, and from there into the radicalism of the Populist Party. While many resisted trade unionism, others ignited the first fires of labor militance during the textile strikes of the late twenties and early thirties. Too many times, however, anger, frustration, and prejudice lured them into the loathsome lynch mobs of the turn of the century or into the Ku Klux Klan. And through good times and bad, and during both their benevolent and malevolent periods, country music endured as their music.

The close association of music and southern politics probably dates from the political barbecues of colonial Virginia, when the elites had begun to recognize and reckon with the power of the small farmers.[5] Planters sometimes invited the yeomen to balls and other social functions in order to promote a particular candidate. Since the colonial era, candidates for public office had either employed musicians to attract and amuse crowds or, quite effectively, had performed music themselves. The Good Old Boy politics of the South—a politics that has stressed personality over issues and style over substance—has often depended on music to ease or disguise bitter class feeling. Historian Thomas D. Clark was referring to frontier Kentucky in the early 1800s when he noted that "barbecue always bore the stamp of politics,"[6] but that kind of public celebration prevailed throughout early America and was used everywhere as a forum for political campaigning and for the often-allied art of the fiddler. George Washington may have won fame as a military commander, but his early political career was built in the convivial atmosphere of the barbecues of colonial Virginia, where even aristocrats were forced to rub shoulders with common men and potential voters. It is a tribute to the rough democracy of the early nineteenth century that politicians so often saw the need to sponsor barbecues, or at least to appear at them on such festive occasions as the Fourth of July. Liquor, punch, and lemonade flowed freely; people consumed great quantities of beef, pork, mutton, venison, and assorted other delicacies; candidates and officeholders glad-handed their constituents; and fiddlers played their merry tunes.

Although this kind of folksy electioneering was probably endemic to the frontier, it gained additional vigor during the Age of the Common

Man which followed in the wake of Andrew Jackson's rise to fame after 1815. Jackson's exploits at the Battle of New Orleans were commemorated in song and verse. "The Hunters of Kentucky," written by Samuel Woodworth and introduced by thespian Noah Ludlow to a howling theater audience in New Orleans in 1822, became a major campaign song in Jackson's subsequent races for the presidency. A rousing fiddle tune, "The Eighth of January," written and named in honor of the famous battle's date, is still known by every fiddler in the South.[7]

From the 1820s through the 1840s, music-making seems to have been pretty common among southern politicians. Judges, governors, congressmen, and state and local officials sang or took up the fiddle in order to portray themselves as common men. The employment of musicians obviously benefited politicians, but the demonstration of a musical skill gave even greater advantage to an office seeker. Indeed, musical talent was held in higher esteem than most personal attributes. When Reuben Davis ran for circuit judge in Mississippi in 1836, a confidant told him that he could not defeat his popular opponent, who "is a good fellow, tells a capital story, and plays the fiddle."[8] Davis did in fact win the election, but scattered references attest to the fact that antebellum southern frontiersmen often rewarded musically talented politicians. The *Spirit of the Times* in 1837 refers to an unnamed Virginia lawyer (described as HHM) who some years earlier had experienced hard times in the Arkansas territory until he ventured into a grog shop and impressed the customers with the "Scotch reels and strathspys" which he played on a borrowed fiddle. He soon attained prominence as a lawyer and was elected to several important offices in the state.[9] The identity and locale are also omitted in a similar story told by Rev. Hamilton W. Pierson of his experiences in the Old Southwest several years before the Civil War. While campaigning at a barbecue dance, a judge filled in for a fiddler who had gotten drunk. The judge declared that "when the election returns were announced, every vote in the precinct had been cast for me. That night's work with the fiddle secured my election."[10]

In the years that followed Jackson's presidencies, few political candidates could escape the necessity to cater to the plain folk's presumed love of theater and emotional flamboyance. The urge to play the role of a common man was particularly strong, and candidates strove to speak the rhetoric of plain people, to voice their values and prejudices, and to identify with their cultural diversions. The eccentric Williamson Robert Winfield Cobb, a Tennessean by birth but a longtime resident of northern Alabama, served his hill-country constituency in Congress from 1847 until his reluctant resignation from that body during the secession crisis of 1861. Cobb appears to have been a genuine champion of the common man, particularly in his support of cheap public lands, but his "undignified" electioneering tactics probably offended the Alabama "aristocracy" as much as his ideas. In his first campaign, for example, Cobb went among the people chewing on an onion or a piece of corn pone, rattling tin pans and crockery, and singing homely songs which he had composed for the election.[11]

Homespun music proved even more fortuitous in the political career of Linn Boyd. Like Cobb, Boyd was a Tennesseean who won political office in another state. He served first in the state legislature in Kentucky, but later, in 1835, was elected to Congress as a Democrat from the First District in the western part of the state. His long congressional tenure was capped off by his election as Speaker of the House in 1851. Boyd had undoubted talents, including good looks and a winning personality, but fiddling may have been his greatest asset. One of his constituents noted that Boyd "always carried his fiddle with him, and made very indifferent speeches to the people in the daytime, but played the fiddle, greatly to their admiration, for their dances by night."[12]

While they may not have been the first southern politicians to use music in political campaigns, those two fiddlin' brothers from Happy Valley, Tennessee, Bob and Alf Taylor, demonstrated the power of rural music in the late nineteenth and early twentieth centuries when they campaigned for office as members of rival political parties (Bob as a Democrat and Alf as a Republican). While campaigning against each other for the governorship of Tennessee in 1886 (in what local people called the War of the Roses), the Taylor Brothers often debated each other by day (they held forty-one debates) and then serenaded their audiences at night in hotel lobbies. Although Bob won that election, as well as other races for the United States Congress and Senate, Alf was considered to be his superior at playing the fiddle. Hoedown fiddling was a prominent and winning feature of Alf's successful campaigns to the United States Congress from 1888 to 1892 and in his victorious march to the governorship in 1920, in what was then a rare feat for a Tennessee Republican. After the conclusion of his political career, Alf lectured and fiddled on the Chautauqua circuit, and made at least two recordings with a group called the Old Limber Quartette, named in honor of his favorite hunting dog. During an interview in 1924 Alf spoke with sentiments similar to those voiced by Tom T. Hall many years later in "Old Dogs, Children, and Watermelon Wine" (Mercury 73346). Commenting on the reasons for the Taylor

Brothers' success, Alf said "we played the fiddle, were fond of dogs, and loved our fellow man."[13]

The fiddling prowess of the Taylor Brothers is well known; that of the colorful Georgia Populist Tom Watson has generally been obscured by the controversial politics of his stormy career. The fiery Watson, who served one term in the U.S. Congress before becoming a national leader and vice-presidential candidate of the Populist Party in 1896, was also a fiddler. He was already a popular musician at country dances while a teenager, just as his father had been before him, and in his first campaign for the Georgia state legislature in 1882 he put his fiddling to effective use. Watson inspired at least two hillbilly recordings, "Tom Watson Special," written and recorded by Fiddlin' John Carson in November, 1923 ("Got a Watson dog and a Watson cat. I'm a Tom Watson man from my shoes to my hat"), and a eulogistic piece written by Rev. Andrew Jenkins but recorded by Vernon Dalhart under the pseudonym of Al Craver ("There is a grave in Georgia, where silent willows weep / In a little town of Thomson, our mighty statesman sleeps; / In old McDuffie County, Tom Watson lies at rest, / and in that fallen hero our Georgia lost her best").[14]

Tom Watson was remembered, not only because of his flamboyance and colorful rhetoric, but also because of the battles he had waged against economic and political privilege. Echoes of those economic clashes that had emboldened Watson and embodied the Populist critique that underlay them still remained when hillbilly music was first recorded in the twenties. By that time the Populist Party was long dead, and much of its spirit lay crushed and battered as white men moved back into the "white man's party," the "Democracy." Populism was weakened partly by its own internal divisions but more so by the power, ostracization, and intimidation of the ruling classes, and by the blighting racism that blinded voters to their best economic interests. Populism occasionally reappeared with some of its old strength and militance, as in the case of Huey Long's movement in Louisiana, but in the twenties it generally appeared as only a pale reflection of its former self—exploited by unscrupulous demagogues, men who posed as the farmer's friend while they obscured the real issues with violent, often racist, rhetoric and "the politics of style." The old passions nevertheless still stirred the hearts of many men, especially those who had come of age during the turbulent eighties and nineties. Blind minstrel Charlie Oaks, for example, noted in his tribute to William Jennings Bryan in 1925 that Bryan had been "a friend to the poor and to the working man" but that his campaigns for the presidency had been failures because "capitalists wouldn't let him win."[15]

Incidents in the life of the famous Fiddlin' John Carson, the seminal entertainer from Georgia who made the first hillbilly recordings in 1923,[16] vividly illustrate the political uses to which country music has been put, while also warning us about the dangers of attaching a specific political label to the form. Carson's own personal odyssey, from his birth in 1868 in the Blue Ridge Mountains of Fannin County to eventual residence in a working-class section of Atlanta called Cabbage Town, reflects the larger transformation that had swept across the South in the decades since the Civil War. He worked in the Exposition Cotton Mill for many years but was best known as a fiddler in innumerable contests and community functions in the Atlanta area. Intimately involved in Georgia politics until his death in 1949, Carson was a direct link to both the Taylor Brothers' fiddling legacy and to the politics of Tom Watson.

When he was about twenty-two, Carson played in Copper Hill, Tennessee, where Bob Taylor praised him and bestowed upon him the sobriquet of "Fiddlin' John." Carson supported Tom Watson during the political battles at the turn of the century, but after Tom Watson's death in 1925, he shifted his political allegiance to another presumed "champion of the woolhats," Eugene Talmadge, for whom he played in Talmadge's race for commissioner of agriculture in 1926. Carson remained in the Talmadge camp for the next twenty-three years, shifting easily to the support of Eugene's son, Herman. At the time of his death, Carson was running an elevator in the state capitol building, the political payoff he usually received from the Talmadges. It was enough for Carson that the Talmadges identified with the farmers, and he seems not to have worried about substantive differences between the Talmadges and his earlier hero, Tom Watson.[17]

As an ardent Democrat and a repository of the wide category of songs that circulated in the Deep South in the late nineteenth century, Uncle Dave Macon often sang about social events. His "Buddy, Won't You Roll down the Line," for instance, commented on a series of incidents that must have been well known to him: the rebellion of free labor against the use of convict labor in the coal mines near Briceville, Tennessee, in 1892.[18] The contemporary fervor that underlay the Populist crusade is documented in several recorded hillbilly songs, particularly in Fiddlin' John Carson's "The Farmer is the Man" and "Honest Farmer." The severe unemployment provoked by the depressions of 1873 and 1893, which set many men on the road looking for work or trying to escape it, inspired such songs as "The Poor Tramp Has to Live," "The Last Ride," "Danville Girl," "Little Stream of Whiskey," and "Wabash Cannon Ball."

The last-named song, which was destined to play a major role in the commercial history of country music—a version of it became one of Roy Acuff's great recording successes—was about a mythical railroad that would take the tramp to a land of milk and honey. The hobo's paradise was also the subject of "Big Rock Candy Mountain," a tune written or collected by Harry McClintock. McClintock, or "Haywire Mac" as he was often called during his radio-singing days in California, was a Tennesseean whose rambles led him through much of the United States and into the famous Industrial Workers of the World, the radical singing union that was unique in its appeal to hoboes and migratory workers. McClintock also claimed credit for "Hallelujah Bum Again," a parody of the religious song "Revive Us Again" and a tune popular among unemployed migratory workers.[19]

Some of the songs merely reflected memories of earlier days in the South, but many commented on the economic conditions of the twenties and thirties. Although hillbilly music's commercial birth was largely attributable to the economic experimentation and expansion of the Golden Twenties, few of the musicians prospered through their art. And the southern society from which most of them came also remained a stranger to prosperity. The depression that came to American agriculture after 1921 had little impact upon the lives of most southern farmers. Most were already accustomed to being poor, and by 1930, 55.5 percent of all southern farms were operated by tenants.[20] "Down on Penny's Farm," recorded by the Bentley Boys in 1929,[21] came from an earlier period of southern history, but it told a story that most southern farmers had experienced intimately:

> You move out on Penny's farm,
> Plant a little crop of tobacco
> and a little crop of corn.
> Come around to see you,
> gonna plit and plot,
> Til you get a chattel mortgage
> on everything you got.
> It's hard times in the country
> Down on Penny's farm.

The best-known farm song of the twenties, "Eleven Cent Cotton and Forty Cent Meat," expressed one of the most crucial problems of American agriculture in its title and queried, "How in the heck can a poor man eat?" Blind Alfred Reed asked the same question for all working people in "How Can a Poor Man Stand Such Times and Live?" Farmers were intensely conscious that they suffered from more than simply economic problems and that the gap between their prices and expenses was paralleled by a similar gap between their own self-image and that accorded to them by the public. "Stay in the Wagon Yard," a reference to the lot where farmers stationed their wagons and provisioned their mules and horses on market days, depicts a farmer's unhappy experiences with a sharp city slicker:

> Oh listen to me farmers.
> I'm here to talk some sense.
> If you want to see those electric lights,
> Just look right o'er the fence.
> Don't monkey with those city ducks;
> You'll find they're slick as lard.
> Just get yourself a half a pint
> And stay in the wagon yard.

As unhappy as the farmer's experiences with city life might sometimes be, the lure of the city remained irresistible. "Farmland Blues" prophesied a movement that became overpowering after World War II: "Gonna sell my farm, gonna move to town. Not another furrow will I plow."[22]

Ironically, seeds of radicalism had also been sown by that most conservative of forces, southern evangelical Protestantism. Early evangelical Protestants preached not only an otherworldly doctrine but often an antiworldly doctrine as well (against the world of artificial distinctions and social discrimination in which plain people often found themselves). Evangelicalism held out the promise of a better life beyond the grave, but it also promised a new sense of community and augmented self-esteem in this world. Religious songs that were cherished and sung by country and gospel singers alike often commented on the social inequities of the world, or on the empty cravings for material gain: "Farther Along," "What Would You Give in Exchange for Your Soul?" "I'd Rather Have Jesus," "We'll Understand It Better By and By," "Leave It There." Southern religious historian Donald Mathews argues that "the evangelical call to come out of the world, a call to create new social distinctions on the basis of religious commitment, was clear and unmistakable."[23]

In seeking intimate relationships, informal rituals, and plain dress, the evangelicals were not only hearkening back to primitive Christianity but were also rebelling against the formal, established churches that were controlled by elites. Theirs was not just an economic rebellion, it was also a status rebellion. Prohibitions that seem merely narrowly puritanical—opposition to dancing, card playing, racing, fancy dress, and the like—also reflected a rebellion against the social elites who often marked themselves off from the hoi polloi by such practices. Mathews believes that the evangelicals "were trying to replace class distinctions based on wealth and status—they called it worldly honor—with nonclass distinctions based on ideological and moral purity. They tried, if they did not succeed, to go outside the social system by rejecting its claims upon them. Their ideology emphasized their radical but nonpolitical perception: it was radical for its rejection of traditional authority and deferential habits; it was nonpolitical in its rejection of political means to attain authenticity and influence."[24] Some of the homiletic songs that frequently appeared in country music seem on the surface to be merely straitlaced denunciations of Modernism or endorsements of the Fundamentalist position. But Blind Alfred Reed's "Why Do You Bob Your Hair, Girls?" was as much an indictment of vanity and preoccupation with fashion as it was a call for revival of puritanism.[25]

Like the Good Old Boy himself, country music has neither embodied nor projected any consistent political ideology. Assaying the songs that comprise the current repertoire of country music, or which constitute its folk inheritance, one can marshal evidence to prove almost any point of view. Much of the ideological content of the material, however, conveys ambivalence because some of the folk music from which country music drew its sustenance, and which often appeared on early commercial records, reflects the centuries-old presumptions, fears, and biases of British American Protestants in their struggles against Catholics, Anglicans, and monarchs, traits that have often been submerged in the subconsciousness or preserved in folklore.

Singers often sing matter-of-factly about issues that were explosive to their ancestors centuries ago. The emotional content and, often, the meanings of these lyrics have been defused or obscured by the passage of time, and they persevere not so much because they reflect a deeply held philosophy but because they comprise a cherished portion of folk cultural inheritance. "The Romish Lady" (which seems not to have appeared on commercial recordings) and "The Dying Nun," which was recorded at least once, reflected the folk prejudice of Protestant southerners, a bias brought from the Old World. They used such songs as warnings—admonitions to the young to avoid dying in sin, and popery was one of many mortal sins—and to stir up hatreds against Roman Catholics. Nevertheless, for a people so intensely Protestant, the songs of explicit anti-

Catholicism are exceedingly rare. Songs expressing anti-Semitism, either overt or veiled, are even rarer. The most famous of all anti-Semitic songs in British American folklore, "Sir Hugh, or the Jew's Daughter," is one of the few of such songs to appear on hillbilly recordings. A duo from the Mobile, Alabama, area, called Nelstone's Hawaiians (Hubert A. Nelson and James Touchstone), recorded the song under the title of "The Fatal Flower Garden."[26] In this much-abbreviated version of a ballad that described the Jewish ritual murder of a Christian, the word "Jew" is never used; the villain is called "a gypsy lady." Indeed, the recorded version reveals not even a veiled allusion to either Jews or Judaism.

Likewise, "Little Mary Phagan," composed and first performed by Fiddlin' John Carson (but first recorded by his daughter Rosa),[27] never refers to the Jewishness of Leo Frank, even though Tom Watson stirred up hatred against the accused man by printing a heavy barrage of anti-Semitic stories. The song is, in fact, sometimes interpreted as an anticapitalistic tract: an indictment of a pencil-factory manager who supposedly exploited and killed a defenseless little mill girl when "she went to the pencil factory to draw her little pay." But if populist protest was Fiddlin' John's intention, such motive cannot be discerned in the lyrics of his song. "Little Mary Phagan" differs little from scores of other murder ballads in southern folklore in its evocation of sympathy for the victim and its call for retribution for the guilty (Fiddlin' John, though, did not demand lynching).

Despite the pervasive racism of the South, surprisingly few such songs appear in either the folk music heritage or in early commercial country music. In fact, few racist songs came from indigenous southern sources; rather, most had their origins in northern minstrel and ragtime music and were absorbed by rural southerners along with other forms of popular music. Gross stereotypes created in the North resonated in the South. Early hillbilly songs often made references about "niggers," "darkeys," and "coons," as did the stage humor and comic skits of professional hillbilly music. Most of the songs painted pictures of absurd coon figures, buffoonish, brawling, oversexed creatures with affinities for razors, watermelons, and chicken-stealing. Some songs that had blackface minstrel origins and that were originally couched in an approximation of black dialect lost their original "Negro" connotations as they became part of the repertoire of country music. "Watermelon on the Vine," for instance, originally described what northerners construed as a unique "darkey delight," but rural southern whites preserved the song and divested it of its racial connotations because they knew that watermelon-eating was a trait shared by all southerners.

Quite a few of the early commercial country songs drew sympathetic portraits of pathetic or heartbroken "darkeys"—"My Pretty Quadroon," "Away down upon the Old Plantation," "Darling Allalee," "Yellow Rose of Texas," "Little Old Log Cabin in the Lane"—and southerners responded to them as much for their sentiment and morality as for their racial content. "Little Old Log Cabin in the Lane," once intended as a lament of an ex-slave, became metamorphosed through time into a piece of nostalgia for the rural past. The coon songs were usually performed to ragtime accompaniment, so they were often appealing because of their catchy rhythms and melodies. The lyrics of "Bully of the Town," for instance, portrayed a swaggering "buck," but today the piece is rarely sung, except for its nonracial chorus, and is instead performed as a fiddle or banjo tune. No songs commented on racial mixing, and even during a decade of fierce Ku Klux Klan activity, country songs rarely referred to that racist organization. Although a famous and oft-used photograph exists of a group of hillbilly musicians standing in front of a KKK poster in Mountain City, Tennessee, in 1925 (the musicians were there for a fiddlers' convention), little evidence exists that such musicians played very often for Klan rallies. The KKK was as likely to use a dance band or a barbershop quartet as it was a hillbilly unit. The Klan, after all, had much strength in the cities, North as well as South, and was actively involved in many places in building for itself a reputation as a service or chamber-of-commerce type organization. In its quest for national respectability, the best interests of the Klan lay in avoiding the hillbilly image.[28]

The topicality of country music, as well as the fundamentalism of its audience, is well displayed in the handful of anti-evolution songs that appeared in the wake of the 1925 Scopes "Monkey" Trial. But even here, on an issue where rural southern feelings can easily be gauged, it is dangerous to make facile generalizations about the political stance of the music itself. One writer who has commented on the songs asserts that they "offer an interesting example of the attitudes of the southern mountain folk toward evolution."[29] Yet he presents no evidence that the songs were any more popular in the mountains of the South than in the flatlands, and of the musicians he cites, only Charlie Oaks came from the mountains. The songs, in fact, probably reflect the attitudes of a majority of Americans in 1925. The best song inspired by the furor aroused by the Dayton trial was Uncle Dave Macon's hilarious but pointed ode, "The Bible's True." After a banjo prelude of the gospel song "Will There Be Any Stars in My Crown," Uncle Dave announces that he doesn't believe in "revolution or evolution," but "when it comes to the good old Bible, I'm right there."

And then he sings "God made the world and everything that's in it; He made man perfect, and the monkey wasn't in it."

The first person to hit the market with a song about the Scopes trial was Kansan Carson J. Robison, the event songwriter par excellence, who asserted that "oh, you must not doubt a word that is written by the Lord / for if you do your house will surely fall; / and Mr. Scopes will learn that wherever he may turn / the old religion's better after all." Robison's song, "The John T. Scopes Trial," was recorded by Texan Vernon Dalhart, who had long lived in New York and who had presumably picked up some sophistication in his lengthy previous career as a singer of light opera. He and Robison teamed for another piece dealing with the evolution controversy in August, 1925, soon after the hero of the fundamentalists, William Jennings Bryan, suddenly died. Their innocuous little song was couched in moralizing generalities and completely avoided any reference to the "Great Commoner"'s controversial earlier career as a politician. In the same month, however, the blind singer from Richmond, Kentucky, Charles O. Oaks, wrote his own tribute called "The Death of William Jennings Bryan," which came much closer than the Robison composition to summing up the real reasons for Bryan's great popularity in the South. Oaks forcefully attacked those "who are trying to ruin the minds of children in our schools," but he also reminded his listeners of Bryan's great powers as an orator and his reputation as "a friend to the poor and to the working man."[30]

No issue better illustrates the divided mind or impulses of rural southerners than the topic of Prohibition. Most southern states, it is true, had enacted prohibition laws before Congress passed the Volstead Act, but many southerners could not abandon their old fondness for strong drink nor the propensity to manufacture their own. The stereotype of the moonshining southerner was as strong in the twenties as that of the total abstainer, and the recording men and promoters of hillbilly music exploited the image because of its commercial potential. Polk C. Brockman, the Atlanta record dealer who had discovered Fiddlin' John Carson, fastened the moniker of Moonshine Kate upon Rosa Lee Carson, the fiddler's daughter. Other hillbilly groups were encouraged to do moonshining or bootlegging routines in recorded skits, such as the Skillet Lickers' "Corn Licker Still in Georgia." It is tempting to argue that the wet and dry forces in the South represented two totally different elements in the community, but conflict over the issue tore families apart and often created havoc within troubled individuals themselves. Consequently, hillbilly songs dealing with Prohibition fell on both sides of the issue,[31] reflecting an ambivalence still strongly displayed in the South, in country music, and in many of the singers who sing passionately of the evils of alcohol while maintaining a loyalty to the bottle.

Hillbilly songs could warn of "the drunkard's hell," or tug at the heartstrings with a revived nineteenth-century temperance song like Henry Clay Work's "Father Dear Father Come Home," or ridicule one of the more grotesque consequences of illicit brew in "Jake Walk Blues," but they could also advise people to "stick to that good old mountain dew" or to "pass around that long-necked bottle and we'll all go on a spree." Prohibition is popularly associated with the mindset of the rural South, and it had its defenders in song, but rural southern singers also attacked the venality and brutality of prohibition agents in songs like "Prohibition Is a Failure" and "How Can a Poor Man Stand Such Times and Live," described the wet candidate for president, Al Smith, as "a mighty good man," and rejoiced that Franklin Roosevelt's later ascendancy meant "legal wine, whiskey, beer, and gin."[32]

Despite country music's recent identification as jingoistic, the genre's historic stance on patriotism and war cannot be neatly categorized or placed firmly within any part of the political spectrum. Southerners have had well-documented affinities for violence and militarism,[33] but surprisingly few prowar songs can be discerned in the early hillbilly repertoire. One similarly finds few antiwar items, but a multitude of songs deal with the context and consequences of war—the reality facing all families of the region and nation.

War songs in fact did not constitute a particularly large percentage of the total hillbilly repertoire prior to World War II. Even though World War I provoked bitter dissent in the United States and unleashed strong nativistic sentiments that spilled over into the twenties, the hillbilly songs that began to appear on recordings after 1922 were largely free of references to the Great War or to the nativistic animosities that flared in the following decade. Between 1922 and 1942 one finds almost no propagandistic intent in the songs dealing with war. At least one song in fact—"The Battleship of Maine"—alluded to the lack of heroics shown by one farmer-turned-soldier during the Spanish-American War, and commented on the class dimensions of military service: "What kind of shoes do the poor farmers wear? / Old brogans, cost a dollar a pair. / What kind of shoes do the Rough Riders wear? / Buttons on the side, cost five and a half a pair."

A very large percentage of the early recorded war songs were actually nothing more than sentimental love songs, some of which came from the nineteenth-century storehouse of parlor material. "Just before the Battle Mother," for example, was a Civil War song, while "Faded Coat of Blue," "Just as the Sun Went Down," "Take the News to Mother," "Mary Dear," and "When the Roses Bloom Again" came from the Spanish-American War period. Such songs seldom dealt with battle scenes or the heroics of men but instead were used as vehicles to deal with the perennially appealing themes of parting, reconciliation, betrayal, loyalty, death, and mother's love.[34]

The economic crisis of the thirties brought major changes to the developing hillbilly industry and promoted new thinking about folk music in the United States. Southerners moved into the Great Depression with almost a century of experience with hard times. Submarginal agriculture and languishing industry contributed to the region's being labeled in 1938 as the "nation's number one economic problem."[35] Economic distress inspired a multitude of responses, not the least of which included efforts made by politicians to capitalize on the music's popularity among working people.

Dr. J. R. Brinkley, of Milford, Kansas, may have inspired the renewed union of hillbilly music and politics at the state level in this century. In his nearly successful campaign for the governorship of Kansas in 1930 he used the services of, among others, Roy Faulkner (the Lonesome Cowboy), who had often played over Brinkley's popular radio station, KFKB. Brinkley, a doctor of questionable credentials and a master huckster, used his station (the first one in Kansas), to promote his hospital and sensational goat gland transplants. By 1929, a *Radio Times* poll proclaimed KFKB the most popular station in the United States, and Brinkley had become one of the best-known men in the Midwest. Fighting back against efforts to revoke both his medical and radio licenses, Brinkley waged campaigns for the governorship of Kansas in 1930 and 1932, losing the second time to Republican Alfred Landon.

When the Federal Radio Commission refused to renew the license for his Kansas station in 1930, Brinkley began negotiations for the purchase of a station across the Mexican border. In 1931 his station XER (later XERA) began its transmissions from Villa Acuna across the river from Del Rio, Texas. Brinkley campaigned once again for the Kansas governorship, using this time the powerful voice of XER, which by 1932 reached out with a transmission of about 150,000 watts and could be heard distinctly throughout a major portion of the United States. The little town of Del Rio welcomed the revenue and payroll that Brinkley's relocated hospital brought into the area, and the doctor won the influence there that he had earlier enjoyed in Kansas. During the thirties XERA, and other imitative stations such as XEG, XEPN, XENT, and XELO, poured out a steady stream of gospel and hillbilly music, fundamentalist evangelism, right-wing politics, and a seemingly interminable avalanche of advertising.[36]

Wilbert Lee "Pappy" O'Daniel could not have been unaware of Brinkley's financial success nor of his political activities on both KFKB and XERA. These two hucksters had quite a lot in common, though one was a patent medicine pitchman and the other was a flour salesman. Both masterfully manipulated the developing medium of radio, and both recognized the power and appeal of rural music. Born in Malta, Ohio, and reared in Kinsman, Kansas (although he had left the state before Brinkley became such an influence there), O'Daniel came to Fort Worth, Texas, in 1925, where he became affiliated with the Burrus Mill and Elevator Company. He experienced a rapid rise until he became general manager of the organization. He also became the first person in this century directly associated with commercial country music to be elected to a major political office.

O'Daniel was no hillbilly, however. Although he had a penchant for folksy chatter and downhome homilies, he was an urbane businessman who successfully cultivated the image of a populist. He recognized the popularity of hillbilly music in 1930 when he hired the fiddle band of Bob Wills, Herman Arnspiger, and Milton Brown. They had been performing locally on Fort Worth radio stations as the Aladdin Laddies (sponsored by the Aladdin Mantle Lamp Company) and worked for the Burrus Mill Company, played for dances and on the radio, and made one recording for Victor under the name of the Fort Worth Doughboys. One of the seminal bands of western swing, a later version of the group, the Light Crust Doughboys (named for a Burrus Mill's product), became one of the most popular bands in the Southwest.[37]

O'Daniel previously had shown no particular affinity for hillbilly music, and at first seemed little interested in the music of the Doughboys. But when reports of their growing popularity filtered into his office, his business acumen overcame whatever aesthetic reservations he might have had. To say that O'Daniel became interested in the Doughboys would be an understatement. He became their radio announcer, served as master of ceremonies during their personal appearances, and wrote poems and songs for the group, two of which became standards in the country music of the Southwest: "Put Me in Your Pocket" and "Beautiful Texas" (which to many people was virtually the state song). O'Daniel's name was commonly used as part of the title of the band, and many people assumed that he was a musician or singer.

By 1935, O'Daniel had severed his connections with Burrus Mill and the Light Crust Doughboys and had launched his own very successful Hillbilly Flour Company and band called the Hillbilly Boys. No one doubted the high recognizability of his name throughout Texas, but the political establishment, the analysts, and the media of the state could only have been astounded by his rapid rise to political power. After receiving an estimated fifty-four thousand affirmative responses to his query about whether he should enter politics, O'Daniel announced for the governorship in 1938 before a large and enthusiastic crowd in Waco. As he predicted, he won the Democratic primary without a runoff and subsequently won the first of two elections to the governorship of Texas. The Hillbilly Boys included his own children, Pat, Mike, and Molly, but also featured one of the finest singers and yodelers of the thirties, Leon Huff. The group was indispensable to his campaigns. While the Hillbilly Boys warmed up the crowds with their songs, Molly passed through the throng with a miniature barrel with a sign saying "Flour, not Pork." O'Daniel then alternately soothed and amused his listeners with attacks on the "professional politicians," promises of a $65 a month pension for old people, and pleas for a return to the old-fashioned virtues of home, mother, and God. Behind this carefully calculated populist veneer and the mellow, reassuring tones lay the reality of a super salesman and ultraconservative businessman. Although the Doughboys could record in 1933 a song called "On to Victory Mr. Roosevelt"—presumably written by O'Daniel—he became one of the most consistent and reactionary opponents of the president after his 1941 election to the U.S. Senate over Lyndon B. Johnson.

The whole nation seemed intrigued by the election of the man generally described in the press as "the hillbilly governor." O'Daniel's successful uniting of music and politics was quickly emulated. The year 1938 was definitely the banner year for hillbilly politics. In California the Texas-born cowboy singer Stuart Hamblen capitalized on the popularity and exposure gained on broadcasts over KHFE in Los Angeles to win the Democratic nomination for Congress. One magazine said that his campaign was waged in "true hillbilly style," but Hamblen lent a western flavor to the race by renting the Pasadena Rose Bowl to stage a gala affair replete with roping, fancy riding, bulldogging, and pistol shooting, as well as politics.[38] In Texas, Jerry Sadler began his long career as a salty "man of the people" and professional redneck with his successful campaign for a seat on the Texas Railroad Commission. Along with a supporting cast of hillbilly musicians, and a violent rhetoric which involved him in several fist fights, Sadler solidified his reputation as a champion of the rural folk with his habit of snuff dipping. Sadler allegedly declared that "smoke is the ghost of tobacco; chewing tobacco is the body; but snuff is the soul."[39]

In Louisiana James Houston "Jimmie" Davis, a farm boy from Beech Springs who already had ten years of local entertaining behind him, became clerk of the criminal court in Shreveport. Born in the Protestant hill country of North Louisiana to very poor sharecroppers, Davis became the first member of his large clan to finish high school and then to attend college (earning a B.A. degree from Louisiana College in Pineville, and an M.A. degree from Louisiana State University). Music was always a part of his life, and he was singing on the streets of Shreveport by the time he was a teenager. Inspired largely by the music of Jimmie Rodgers, Davis began his own recording career in 1928 for Victor, singing and yodeling an interesting variety of risqué blues, novelty tunes, sentimental love ballads, and hobo songs. After his stint as criminal court clerk, Davis served four years as a city commissioner and then became public service commissioner for twenty-eight parishes. In the fall of 1943, backed by a hillbilly band that included pianist Moon Mullican, mandolinist Joe Shelton (a longtime member of a Texas group called the Shelton Brothers), and steel guitarist Charles Mitchell, Davis opened his campaign for the governorship of Louisiana in Jonesboro. Courting the voters with a sincere and homey patter that united them all in the common bond of rural nostalgia, and always singing his hit song, "You Are My Sunshine" (whose authorship has been attributed to many people, Davis included), Davis surmounted the opposition of both New Orleans and the Huey Long machine to win the election. His political style was obviously influenced by that of Pappy O'Daniel, but, unlike O'Daniel, Davis was an authentic hillbilly, a bona fide product of the woolhat South.[40]

The rich repertoire of country music, from the bawdy blues of Jimmie Davis to the gospel chants of the Chuck Wagon Gang and the cowboy ballads of Gene Autry, served many needs during the Great Depression. The music preserved its penchant for topicality, and numerous songs dealing with the Great Depression, FDR, and the New Deal appeared.[41] The predilections of these songs were shaped principally by two important facts, the poverty of the South and the overwhelming Democratic preference of its people.

Songs produced or favored by rural southerners during the bleak Depression years ran the gamut from bitter protest and revolutionary rhetoric to fatalistic resignation and easy optimism. The most militant protest, as will be noted later, came from trades-union people and did not appear on commercial recordings until picked up by urban interpreters of folk music. Woody Guthrie, it is true, was singing on KFVD in Los Angeles in the late thirties, but his dust bowl ballads did not appear on Victor until 1940. Most commercial hillbilly songs did not venture beyond the limits of moderate protest, and the palliative most often proposed as an antidote to the Depression—election and reelection of the Democratic Party—was the solution favored by most of the American people. Few of the songs reacted to hard times as blithely as "My Million Dollar Smile," a W. Lee O'Daniel composition recorded by the Light Crust Doughboys, which advocated what might be called the "Hoover Solution" to hard times: smiling the Depression away ("we've got depression on the bum with our million dollar smile").

Jimmie Rodgers's attitude in "No Hard Times Blues" was equally as confident—"I got a barrel of flour. . . I got a bucket of lard. I won't be bothered with all these old hard times"—but then his income was such that economic distress was never a problem for him. Rodgers, however, did have an empathy for homeless people, and his songs brought comfort to Depression-era dwellers. As an ex-railroad man he had often seen drifters and hoboes, and had a touch of their wandering spirit as well. After 1929 he saw many more. Rodgers's hobo songs, like those of the Texas Drifter, Goebel Reeves (who wrote or arranged the well-known "Hobo's Lullaby"), came out of the older tradition of railroad and tramp lore. The incidents of "Hobo Bill's Last Ride," "Hobo's Meditation," and "Waiting for a Train" could have happened at any previous period of railroad history, but they assumed a special significance for Americans during the 1930s when thousands of men and boys (and a few women) rode the rails in a desperate search for work.[42]

Some of the Depression songs painted grim portraits of American life, but they differed as to what kind of response should be made. Slim Smith's "Breadline Blues," for instance, called for action no more radical than the election of the Democrats in 1932. The Carter Family's "No Depression in Heaven" (written by the gospel composer J. D. Vaughan), on the other hand, pointed to no earthly solution at all but held out the promise of security beyond the grave. When the New Deal legislation began to pour out of Congress after 1933, country songs and blues tunes appeared to chronicle their existence and to comment on the new president who sponsored them. Even the young Hank Williams, as a fourteen-year-old country singer in Alabama, wrote as his first composition "WPA Blues," which he used to win a talent contest at the Empire Theater in Montgomery.[43]

Franklin Roosevelt received much of his most implacable opposition in the South, from politicians like Senators Carter Glass and Cotton Ed Smith and from conservative planters and businessmen. But this patrician Yankee was also idolized in the South, as few politicians had been, principally by the plain people, men and women of the farming and working classes. Many of them would have responded the way one North Carolina textile worker, George Dobbins, did when asked why he supported FDR: "I do think that Roosevelt is the biggest-hearted man we ever had in the White House. Roosevelt is the only president we ever had that thought the Constitution belonged to the pore man too." Fiddlin' John Carson sang in similarly benign terms about this warmhearted president whose occasional residence at Warm Springs made him no stranger to Georgia's agricultural population:[44]

> Hurrah for Roosevelt,
> With heart so brave and true.
> He's doing everything within his power
> To pull the farmer through.

In terms no less heartfelt than those used by Dobbins, Billy Cox, a West Virginia hillbilly singer, nevertheless spoke directly to the needs of coal miners and cotton mill workers when he praised Roosevelt's National Recovery Administration in "NRA Blues":[45]

> When we all join the NRA,
> Sweet thing, oh sweet thing,
> When we all join the NRA,
> We'll work shorter hours
> and get the same pay.
> Sweet thing, oh baby mine.

Almost no songs skeptical about or hostile to FDR or the New Deal appeared on commercial records. Even "Old Age Pension Check," which paints a humorous picture of the paradise awaiting elderly people who hitch a ride on the Washington gravy train, is silent on FDR. The song seems to have been inspired by the Townsend Plan—Dr. Francis Townsend's scheme to pay each American over sixty years of age a monthly pension of $200 ("there's a man who turned this country upside down / with his old age pension rumors going around").[46]

Roosevelt's landslide reelection in 1936 provides the most dramatic evidence of his appeal. Only a few weeks after the election the partisan Democrat Billy Cox again demonstrated his enthusiasm for the New Deal, this time with his recording of "The Democratic Donkey's in His Stall Again" and "Franklin D. Roosevelt's Back Again." Along with a celebration of the repeal of Prohibition, the latter song exulted in the thought that the donkey's victory meant "no more bread lines" in the United States. Roosevelt may have been unaware of the musical tributes penned in his honor by the hillbilly singers, but he and his wife did open the White House to folk and country entertainers. Wade Mainer, the Coon Creek Girls, Red Rector, and other musicians performed in 1941 at a special concert for the king and queen of England. Eleanor Roosevelt lent encouragement to folk music and folk art, and she attended the White Top and National Folk Festivals.[47]

In that age of "folk rediscovery" in the United States, the Roosevelts' patronage of country musicians is not surprising. The Great Depression inspired a new nationalism, based ironically on a renewed consciousness of the strength of regionalism, a desire to return to American roots and find a new unity in the nation's cultural diversity. The New Deal legislation dealing with farmers and working-class people, the rural documentary photography of the Farm Security Administration, the renewed excitement concerning regionalism in the visual arts, "proletarian" novels, and the upsurge in the collecting of folklore and folk music all demonstrated the awakened interest in the folk. American intellectuals began to rediscover the richness and variety of the nation's folk experience as they renewed a long-dormant commitment to making the American dream a reality. The "lost generation" of intellectuals who despaired of American materialism and philistinism after World War I began "finding" themselves and their country during the grim years of economic decline. Not only did they revitalize their traditional role as critics of American life but, under the encouragement of Roosevelt and the New Deal, intellectuals also found themselves increasingly drawn toward public service, a role that they had previously played only occasionally, as in the Progressive Era.

If the New Deal period was marked by an air of excitement about the new society that might be rebuilt from the wreckage of the old, it was marked equally by a compulsion to preserve and reinvigorate those qualities and traditions considered best in the older America. Nowhere was this revitalistic urge more strongly exhibited than in what was then a unique American experience in government sponsorship of the arts, the Works Progress Administration and its cultural programs. As has been well documented elsewhere, the WPA Music, Theatre, Arts, and Writers Projects promoted the collection and utilization of folksongs and lore,

and did much to awaken the national consciousness to the largely un-
tapped cultural substrata of American existence. WPA fieldworkers and
state guidebook compilers, as well as the researchers for the Library of
Congress's Archive of American Folk Songs, roamed the byways and
backwaters of the nation foraging for folk material in places where few
of the earlier academic folklorists had dared to tread.[48]

Since about 1928 the Archive of Folk Song had been recording folk
music under the direction, first, of Robert Gordon, who traveled with a
wire tape recorder through extensive sections of the United States, and,
later, John and Alan Lomax.[49] The Lomaxes probably did most to encourage the collecting of economic and occupational-oriented material
such as prison and coal-mining songs.[50] In a society preoccupied with
economic distress, industrial unemployment, farm dispossession, and
rumblings of class conflict, the definition of "folk" was destined to assume a stronger socioeconomic cast than in the earlier days of folklore
collecting. Although this emphasis had been anticipated by a few early
folklorists, such as John Lomax in his study of cowboy songs and George
Korson in his collection of mining material, it was not until the decade
of the thirties that the thrust of folkloristic endeavor began to shift significantly toward the consideration of the folk informant as a functioning
member of a group defined by more than place or ethnic composition.
This "broadening" of folk definition, which encompassed the industrial
laborer as well as the tenant farmer, the lowlander as well as the mountaineer, and the convict as well as the church member, ultimately did much
to diminish the folklore establishment's antipathy toward hillbilly music. For after all, if the hillbilly and his music were worth studying once
he became a worker in a Kentucky coal mine or in a North Carolina textile mill, or once he became a convict singing into John Lomax's portable recording apparatus, then why should he not be accorded similar
scholarly attention when he functioned as a member of a professional
radio entertaining group? Such recognition, as a matter of fact, has been
a long time coming. Only rarely in the thirties did a professional folklorist recognize, as did Alan Lomax, that the "radio hillbillies" were preserving folk material and breathing new life into the old traditions.[51]

Although events in the Great Depression contributed to a greater understanding and acceptance of hillbilly music, they also inspired a pre-
sumption that was as misleading and romanticized as any earlier literary theory suggesting Elizabethan origins—the belief that true folk music
functioned essentially as a vehicle of protest, and that the protest song is
a weapon in the struggle for social change (one is reminded of an asser-

tion made in 1968 by Joan Baez that she had never heard of a good Republican folksinger).[52]

Although music, historically, often has been linked to radical causes, the uniting of left-wing politics and rural folk music did not come until the years of the Great Depression. Even before the dawning of the Popular Front in 1935, American Communists gave the South a high priority in their efforts to organize farmers and workers, and they stressed the utilization of folksongs as weapons of social change and as vehicles for promoting revolutionary consciousness among the masses. Beginning as early as 1929, during the protracted and bloody strike at the Loray Mill in Gastonia, North Carolina, radical activists attempted to forge a rather unlikely alliance with black and white workers and farmers. Promoting a policy of "dual unionism," the refusal to cooperate with "bourgeois unions" such as those of the AFL, the Communists sent organizers into the southern textile country (National Textile Workers' Union) and the Kentucky coalfields (National Miners' Union). Radical activism and southern economic distress produced a temporary coalition between Yankee radicals and southern workers, but given the vast cultural gap that lay between the two groups, this social experiment was probably foredoomed to failure, even had the political establishment not mounted a powerful campaign of repression against it. The radicals had moved into a culture where singing and ballad-making were commonplace, and even though they emerged from the encounter beaten and bloodied, they had absorbed a cache of songs from their southern working-class brethren that later fueled the incipient urban folk music movement of the North.[53]

The folk balladeers absorbed much of their radical allies' rhetoric, but the melodies of their songs came from the storehouse of folk, gospel, and commercial hillbilly tunes that were a common inheritance in the southern hill country. Sara Ogan (from Bell County, Kentucky) sang "I Hate the Capitalist System" to the melody of "Sailor on the Deep Blue Sea"; her half-brother Jim Garland, a Holiness lay preacher and labor organizer, sang his widely circulated "I Don't Want Your Millions, Mister" to the tune of "Greenback Dollar"; another half-sister and the most famous minstrel of the Kentucky coalfields, Aunt Molly Jackson, wrote her gripping song of coal-camp poverty, "Dreadful Memories," to the melody of the sentimental gospel song, "Precious Memories." The most famous of all southern labor-protest songs, "Which Side Are You On?" came from the pen of Florence Reece, the wife of a Harlan County labor organizer, who attached her lyrics to the melody of an old Baptist hymn.[54]

Southern folksingers began making an impact on northern radicalism and music as early as 1929 when the *Nation* and *New Masses* ran short articles (both written by Margaret Larkin) and a sampling of songs of the first martyr of southern labor radicalism, Ella May Wiggins, the balladeer of the Gastonia workers who was shot to death in 1929.[55] After the crushing of the strikes in Bell and Harlan counties, Aunt Molly Jackson was blacklisted in Kentucky and soon made her way to New York City where she became active as a singer before labor and radical groups. American radicals had long hoped for a "new Joe Hill," a folksinger who would project the same kind of militant spirit and class consciousness of the famous earlier IWW radical. When Woody Guthrie came to New York in 1940, their prayers appeared to be answered.[56]

Guthrie was born in Okemah, Oklahoma in 1912, but spent much of his youth drifting through the Southwest doing odd jobs and oil-field work, and living for much of his time with relatives in Pampa, Texas. He picked up hundreds of songs from relatives and friends and from the hillbilly records to which he was fond of listening. The Carter Family were particular favorites, and they influenced both his guitar style and choice of songs. He moved to California in 1936 where he teamed first with his cousin Leon "Jack" Guthrie and later with Maxine Crissman (who sang under the stage name of Lefty Lou) on KFVD in Los Angeles. Guthrie was a hillbilly singer in every sense of the term, and he found a faithful audience in his fellow Okies who were beginning to be a significant portion of the population of southern and central California.

Guthrie is now best known for his ballads about the Dust Bowl, but he seems not to have experienced the storms himself and was not a part of the Okie migration that reached its peak in 1936–37. Guthrie, however, quickly identified with the migrants, and his moral outrage radicalized him. Unlike the other hillbilly singers of the thirties, once Guthrie got the radical spirit, it stayed with him. With the encouragement of actor and traveling companion Will Geer, Guthrie moved to New York in 1940 where he became part of that city's radical-intellectual circle. His Will Rogers's style of philosophizing, his plain-folks speech and demeanor, and, above all, his topical songs endeared him to radical activists and literati. Guthrie referred to himself as a communist, wrote a column for the *Daily Worker* called "Woody Sez," tried his hand at fiction and autobiography, and sang his increasingly radical songs at labor rallies and political gatherings. He met and inspired young singers like Cisco Houston, Pete Seeger, and Jack Elliott, and circulated songs like "Do Re Mi," "So Long It's Been Good to Know You," "Talking Dust Bowl Blues," "The Good Reuben James," and "This Land Is Your Land." With Guthrie as its patriarch, and virtually its founding father, the urban folk music movement was on its way.

In New York Guthrie was identified, for the first time, as a "folksinger" rather than as a hillbilly singer. Most of the people who idolized and idealized him never bothered to learn about the sources of his songs or the names of the hillbillies who had influenced him. Later generations of urban folksingers borrowed from Woody, but only rarely acknowledged, or even realized the existence of, the sources from whom he borrowed. Not only did those singers who followed in his footsteps commemorate Guthrie, they also grafted their conception of politics onto the music they performed. "Protest" came to be equated with "folksong," and many people came to view folk music as the vehicle of leftist social action; conversely, hillbilly music was generally denigrated as the commercialized projection of conservative rural southerners. Elie Siegmeister, composer and classical musician, became a collector and performer of folk music after hearing Aunt Molly Jackson sing a Kentucky mountain song. In an interview in *Etude* magazine Siegmeister voiced an attitude toward hillbilly music that tended to be typical of views held by the urban singers of folk songs: "It is a somewhat watered-down kind of folk music—most of the original rough edges have been smoothed away and 'improvements' have been added, in line with cheapened commercial tastes."[57]

Increasingly after 1940 the gulf widened between Woody Guthrie and the hillbilly culture from which he emerged. Thereafter, he sang about the folk while removing himself from them. His audience in these years was a rather small coterie of urban radicals and intellectuals, and his songs did not gain wide popular currency until they were performed by urban folksingers during the sixties. Apparently blinded by ignorance of his background, or by political prejudice, the country music world generally shunned this genuine country boy from Oklahoma, even if it sometimes made hits out of such songs as "Oklahoma Hills" and "Philadelphia Lawyer." It was not until 1978, after time and death had dulled the memory of Guthrie's controversial politics, and after songs like "This Land Is Your Land" had become patriotic standards, that he was named to the Nashville Song Writers' Association Hall of Fame. Alan Lomax, in 1960, had described Guthrie as our greatest folk composer but gave no criteria as to why Guthrie was superior to, say, Hank Williams, Floyd Tillman, Blind Andy Jenkins, Carson Robison, or Cindy Walker, composers who aimed their music at the folk and who communicated with them far better than did Guthrie. Guthrie's politics apparently made him more acceptable than those hillbilly writers who either shunned the subject or who projected a far more conservative posture. To Alan Lomax, Guthrie was "Shakespeare in overalls."[58]

Once the economic trauma of the Great Depression was past, and the entire nation, South and North, settled down to the business of winning World War II and rebuilding a dynamic economy, many of the economic preoccupations of the American people, along with the militant politics that accompanied them, ebbed. During the years of the war and in the first half of the fifties, country music left its regional base in the South and began making itself heard in the popular culture of the nation. Politically, the music did not diverge significantly during these years from the thinking that was paramount throughout the nation. The unity that was typical of the World War II period was paralleled by a similar impulse in country music, and though the songs of that period conveyed a strong patriotic tone, they did not differ markedly from attitudes held by the general public or from expressions heard in other forms of music.

Neither the dawning of the cold war nor the hardening of relations with the Soviet Union provoked much of an immediate change in the music's political posture. Like Americans everywhere, country musicians were reluctant to gird themselves for a new war after so recently coming out of another and were slow to perceive that their recent allies, the Russians, had become new and implacable enemies. Carson Robison's "1942 Turkey in the Straw" had spoken glowingly of the heroics of the Russian army, and the Sons of the Pioneers' "Old Man Atom," recorded in the early fifties, called for international cooperation to prevent a nuclear holocaust.[59]

A nearly simultaneous convergence of events—communist expansion in Europe and Asia, fears of communist subversion in the United States, and Russian acquisition of the atomic bomb—weakened the consensus that had prevailed among Americans and our former ally. By the mid-fifties country singers were opining, as did Little Jimmie Dickens, that "They Locked God outside the Iron Curtain," or were declaring, as did Elton Britt, that "The Red We Want Is the Red We've Got (in the Old Red, White, and Blue)." The new red scare exploited by Senator Joe McCarthy created a compulsion among some people, as in the case of Lulu Belle and Scotty, to declare fervently in song, "I'm No Communist." Despite the existence of such material, a monolithic political view did not yet prevail in either the country music business or in the nation at large. Cactus Pryor, for instance, a radio personality in Austin, Texas, recorded a hilarious spoof of Joe McCarthy and his tactics in "Point of Order." And while Jimmie Osborne could applaud the life and career of the conservative Republican senator Robert A. Taft in "Ballad of Robert A. Taft," Jimmy Renfro and Larry Dean, recording for a small label in Bristol, Tennessee, could sing "Estes Is Bestes," a tribute to the liberal Democratic senator from Tennessee, Estes Kefauver. The Prairie Ramblers expressed displeasure at one of Senator Taft's pet legislative measures, in "Have a Heart, Taft-Hartley," and Smokey Stover, in "The Ballad of Jimmy Hoffa," defended that powerful and controversial labor leader with the oft-repeated line, "they're out to get you, Jimmy, every politician and his brother too."[60]

The frustrating Korean War, with its limited objectives and truce without victory, placed severe strains on the patience and unity of Americans and provoked bitter debate. The enthusiasm of Harry Choates's "Korea, Here We Come," recorded very early in the war, and Jimmie Osborne's "Thank God for Victory in Korea," recorded before the Chinese Communists entered the war, faded quickly as the United States bogged down in a protracted stalemate. And when General Douglas MacArthur was removed from his command in Korea by President Truman, the frustration spilled over into songs like Roy Acuff's "Douglas MacArthur" ("a hundred million hearts will always love him") and Gene Autry's country version of "Old Soldiers Never Die." These songs anticipated the militantly nationalistic stance that many country singers would take in the late sixties and early seventies during the much more frustrating Vietnam War. During the fifties, however, the country music repertoire was not markedly jingoistic nor dramatically different from positions taken in other sectors of American life. For all of its frustrations, the Korean War was generally supported by the American public (at least, there was no particularly large or vocal dissenting group), and American youth presented little resistance to it. Furthermore, no body of music protested our involvement; therefore, no musical position of dissent emerged against which country music could be contrasted.

While cold war tensions and the Korean War weakened the national accord, the integration controversy shattered the North-South consensus that had prevailed since Reconstruction. Nothing on major record labels suggested southern displeasure or resistance among country musicians to racial integration, but a sizable body of racist underground material did develop, much of it recorded in Crowley, Louisiana, and distributed covertly through mail-order or "under the counter" purchases. Distinguished by its lack of subtlety, this material was crude in its tone and vicious in its content. Blacks were invariably described as "niggers," and the singers almost always sang or recited in an exaggerated Amos-

and-Andy dialect. Few were as moderate in tone as Happy Fats LeBlanc's recitation, "Dear Mr. President," which, under the guise of a farmer talking to the president, asked, "Will I have to mix black and white peas?" and "Must I let my black and white cattle run together?" "Old Uncle Joe," performed by The Dixie Guys on the Conservative label, featured a recitation by an "Uncle Tom" character who opposed Martin Luther King, Jr., and expressed pride in what "Mr. Charlie" had done for him, while the strains of "Old Black Joe" played plaintively in the background. Much more malevolent, and typical of the racist songs, was "Move Them Niggers North" (by Colonel Sharecropper on the Reb-Time label); "Nigger, Nigger" (by the Coon Hunters on the Reb-Time label) which referred to the monkey lips of blacks and advocated the tarring and feathering of Martin Luther King, Jr.; and "Kajun Klu [*sic*] Klux Klan" (by Johnny Rebel on the Reb Rebel label), which talked about the torturing of a "nigger" named Levi Coon by the KKK after he refused to leave a café.[61]

After 1965, when the black movement became more radical and riots rocked the ghettoes of the North, much of the glare of national publicity moved away from the South. The deepening of American involvement in Vietnam, the flaring of student protest, and the violence that accompanied the Democratic convention in Chicago in 1968 revealed a widening gulf in American attitudes. This polarization lacked regional identification, but instead reflected differences in generations and lifestyles. Historian Howard Zinn, in fact, asserted in *The Southern Mystique* that the South was no different from the rest of the country, and that the South was merely a mirror in which Americans could see their own imperfections in glaring and exaggerated form. George Wallace's growing popularity at the end of the sixties among many northerners suggested a nationalization of problems that were once assumed to be uniquely southern. His ascendancy, in fact, seemed to be a facet of the "southernization" of America.[62]

Racial politics had played little role in Jimmie Davis's election in 1959 to a second term as governor of Louisiana (from 1960 to 1964), but the hillbilly governor—who had once been fond of singing African American blues tunes and who in the 1930s had recorded with black musicians from Shreveport—soon lent his support to a rash of legislation designed to maintain racial separation in his state. But, he reminded one interviewer, unlike some of Louisiana's sister states, "We closed no schools. We shed no blood."[63] Although Davis's election proved to be the last southern political campaign in which country music played a decisive role, the music has not been absent from political campaigns. The George Wallace phenomenon, in fact, and its identification with country music, was one of the crucial factors prompting the national "discovery" of country music in the sixties. No presidential campaign, and certainly none with such a national basis, had ever been so closely associated with country music. Nevertheless, Wallace seems to have been a reluctant convert to the idea of using country entertainers for political purposes. In his first race for the Alabama governorship, he reportedly scoffed at the idea, but after singer Webb Pierce drew a large crowd at Wallace's opening rally, Wallace began making regular use of Grand Ole Opry and gospel performers. Alabama voters were certainly receptive to the allure of grassroots entertainers. Almost all of the fourteen candidates for the Democratic nomination imported country or gospel musicians, and only one aspirant, a Montgomery businessman and pianist, openly ridiculed the practice: "Can't you just imagine the confusion of a lot of voters when they go to the polls on election day and won't be able to find the names of their favorite gospel-singing quartet on the ballot."[64]

After 1958 every Wallace rally, whether for governor or president, contained its country music component. It became fashionable in the early seventies to refer to Nashville as a "command post" for George Wallace, but his support actually came from entertainers in all subgenres of the music—from old-time performers like Bill Bolick and Grandpa Jones to "country-pop singers" like Tammy Wynette and Roy Clark. The ideology of the Wallace movement, with its populist-tinged contempt for intellectuals and social planners and its resolve to preserve the older racial hierarchies, undoubtedly attracted many of the performers who shared its fears and presumptions. But Wallace's appeal among country musicians also came from the fact that he actively courted their support as no other candidate had done. This was important for a musical form that was self-conscious about its alleged inferiority and anxious for acceptance. Wallace and the country musicians shared a common ground, apart from ideology, in their origins in the southern working class with their common accents, religion, food tastes, and social memories. Although he played the role to the hilt, Wallace's cultivation of the Good Old Boy image rested on legitimate working-class foundations, and he communed easily with men and women in the workplace and with country entertainers who shared both his background and his aspirations.

The resurgence of protest music in the United States provided the soundtrack for the polarization of American life. The phenomenon that is often described as the urban folk music revival—the singing of folk or folk-style songs by city-bred pop singers—became increasingly politicized after the election of John F. Kennedy. Following his death, and especially after the frustrations accompanying our failures in Vietnam, the music became increasingly strident and radical.[65] Although this music was largely indebted to the southern folksingers of the thirties, most of its best-known singers came from white, urban, middle-class backgrounds.[66] When Johnny Cash appeared at the Newport Folk Festival in 1964, he became one of only a handful of mainstream country singers who participated in the revival. A substantial contingent of older performers, though, like Maybelle Carter, Dock Boggs, and Clarence Ashley, who were rediscovered during the folk boom, and some younger tradition-based musicians like Doc Watson became active participants in folk concerts held in colleges, clubs, and festivals. Bluegrass music also experienced its first national expansion as a result of association with the folk revival.

The association between urban folksingers and hillbilly singers was always an unsteady and perhaps unnatural one. Buell Kazee and Bascom Lamar Lunsford, for example, were repelled by much of what they saw among the "folkies." More than politics turned them off; resistance was also generated by differing lifestyles and moral postures. The dress, language, hair styles, lifestyles, and politics of the young folkies disgusted many of the hillbillies who joined them in the "revival." Kazee, for instance, was aghast at the shabby attire of the singers who seemed to be condescending to the working class. Kazee, on the other hand, commented that he and the plain folk he had always known tried to look and act their best when appearing in public or formal occasions.[67]

In the late sixties and early seventies, for the first time in its history, country music began to be identified with a specific political position, gaining a reputation for being a jingoistic and nativistic music. As we have seen, the support for George Wallace cut across all genres of country music, from the most traditional to the most progressive. In the presidential campaign of 1968 virtually all country singers who made endorsements, or otherwise made their preferences known, supported either Wallace or Nixon. If the Democratic candidate Hubert Humphrey was the preferred choice of any country musicians, such support was not publicly announced.

The conservative tenor of country music in the late sixties was generated by a complex set of factors. The musicians, in part, were voicing attitudes that, though deeply rooted in their culture, were only now being provoked by the groundswell of organized dissent in the nation.[68] Conservative reaction also emerged as an aspect of the country music industry's efforts to legitimize itself through an attachment to the American mainstream or the establishment. Like Kazee, the country music world (performers, audience, industry) found the manners, values, dress, and lifestyles of the dissenters offensive. The political stances of the country performers, whatever their sources, were neither deviant nor eccentric; they reflected what a large segment of Americans believed (the so-called silent majority). Nixon's overwhelming victory in 1972 should have brought home to everyone—political pundits, young radicals, and cultural critics as well—that there would be no "greening of America" and that the counterculture, the new radicalism, and the new politics had little support among most Americans.[69]

One of the first songs that set the mood for country music's aggressive display of nationalism was "Day for Decision." This recitation, written by a recording executive in Nashville and recorded in 1966 by Johnny Seay, spoke of America's disintegrating morality.[70] The song was a perfect foil for Barry McGuire's earlier "Eve of Destruction," an indictment of American imperialism and racism. Such industry-inspired songs certainly existed, but they were few compared to the scores of similar songs written by entertainers and disc jockeys, many of which were recorded for small labels where little "industry" pressure existed. The patriotic songs, for good or ill, accurately vocalized a grassroots urge.[71]

Country singers and composers did not defend the Vietnam War so much as they protested against the protestors. Very few songs actually defended the war, and only an occasional one, such as "The Ballad of the Green Berets" (written by an ex-member of that elite corps) even applauded the exploits of our fighting men. Tom T. Hall's "What We're Fighting For" (recorded by Dave Dudley in 1965), one of the first country songs that attempted to defend the war from a soldier's perspective, could really go little beyond saying that "we're fighting for the old red, white, and blue." Rather than defending American policy in Southeast Asia, the country songs defended what were perceived as "traditional" values: service to one's country, deference to authority, unquestioning patriotism, or, better yet, loyalty to a policy even if one questions it.

The most extreme manifestation of the defense of unquestioned obedience was the rash of songs, many of them marketed as country items, defending Lieutenant William Calley after the My Lai incident (the massacre of Vietnamese civilians ordered by Calley). The composers of the biggest-selling number among the group, "The Battle Hymn of Lt. William Calley," professed to be horrified at what had happened at My Lai, but they defended Calley on the grounds that he was just a loyal soldier trying to do his duty. The songs about Vietnam never referred to the enemy as "gooks," but worst of all, America's adversaries remained face-less or anonymous as befitted the increasingly impersonal wars of the twentieth century.[72]

An occasional song actually showed some reservations about the war or about wars in general. Some singers even indicated that if a left-lean-ing protest song was commercial enough, they would record it. Glen Campbell, for instance, recorded "Universal Soldier," written by Native American protest singer Buffy St. Marie, despite his well-known right-wing convictions. Ambivalence or confusion, however, did creep into some country songs. Bobby Bare, whose best-known contribution to the political debate was "God Bless America Again," a complaint against disruptive dissenters, also composed, along with Billy Joe Shaver, "Chris-tian Soldier." The lyrics depicted an American soldier who found it im-possible to be a Christian soldier in Vietnam where uncertainties abound-ed. The few country songs that expressed doubts about the wisdom of war, therefore, either conveyed ambivalence or were couched in gener-alities that left them meaningless. The typical attitude held by most coun-try singers toward the Vietnam War was probably that of Johnny Cash. Cash had recorded a few songs such as "Man in Black" and "What Is Truth?" that demonstrated a rather vague brand of tolerance toward dissent, but he made his brand of uncompromising patriotism very clear in "Ragged Old Flag." He also publicly expressed his support for Nix-on's war policies, thereby winning the applause of conservative pundit Al Capp, who quoted Cash's statement that "if you're not going to sup-port the president, get out of my way so I can stand behind him."[73]

The outcry against protestors peaked after 1970—ironically, after the volume of protest songs had diminished and after the level of dissent had declined. It was this wave of anti-protest music, however, that did most to provoke the national discovery of country music and the equating of it with the silent majority. The singer most identified with anti-protest—Merle Haggard—seems to have stumbled on to the idea and initially underestimated and underappreciated the market for such music. He and a few fellow band members wrote "Okie from Muskogee" almost as a joke one day while riding through Oklahoma and seeing a Muskogee road sign. One of his musicians said, "Boy, I bet they don't smoke marijuana in Muskogee." In writing this paean of praise to Middle America—a society where kids still respected their teachers, where drugs were taboo, and where Old Glory still waved proudly down by the courthouse—Haggard tapped an enormously large audience throughout the nation whose rage against hippies and student protestors ("bums," as Nixon called them) had been welling up for years. He later said that he didn't realize just how potent the song was until a short time later, at an NCO club at Fort Bragg, North Carolina, when he had to sing the song three times before an aroused audience. But civilian audiences were no less tumultuous when they heard the song. Although he had been building a large catalogue of superbly crafted songs since 1965, "Okie" was Haggard's biggest hit and his ticket to all of the major Country Music Association awards in 1970. The song was cleverly worded and set to a rousing melody, but its success owed more to the political meaning that people saw in it than to any inherent musical quality. It evoked atavistic responses and standing ovations far afield from the South in cities like Duluth, Boston, and Philadelphia.

If the reception accorded to "Okie from Muskogee" was a surprise to Haggard, his next song consciously exploited the mood of political reaction. "The Fightin' Side of Me" breathed with a macho spirit as its narrator boasted, "When you're running down my country, hoss, you're walking on the fightin' side of me." It was almost poetic, in a perverse sort of way, that Haggard should be the singer who unleashed the new wave of anti-protest songs. As the California-born son of Okie migrants who had suffered discrimination from the California establishment, he had earlier attracted considerable praise from those who hoped for the emergence of a new Woody Guthrie and thought they heard the echoes of one in songs like "Hungry Eyes" and "They're Tearing the Labor Camps Down." In the years that have followed the first public performances of "Okie," Haggard has never been able to escape the political debate triggered by the song. Typecast as a right-wing redneck poet laureate, Haggard himself has presented mixed messages about the original intent and meaning of the song, usually claiming it was a joke, but also reaffirming his distaste for the hippie lifestyle against which the lyrics were aimed. Critics and commentators have been similarly mixed in their attempts to categorize Haggard's politics, never describing him as a liberal but differing widely in their assessment of the kind of populism that he and his music represent.[74]

Second only to "Okie" in its impact on popular tastes was Bill Anderson's "Where Have All Our Heroes Gone?" a recitation that decried the nihilism and cynicism of today's youth and deplored their tawdry heroes. The song lamented the passing of "real" heroes like Joe DiMaggio and Charles Lindbergh, but it included the two deceased Kennedy brothers and Martin Luther King, Jr., as if to show that no conservative bias was intended. Other songs played on public fears and neuroses, but few had the kind of success enjoyed by "Okie," "Fightin' Side of Me," or "Where Have All Our Heroes Gone?" Some were too strong even for commercial tastes and had a mercifully short life or, like Marty Robbins's "Ain't I Right" or Tex Ritter's proposed defense of Lieutenant Calley, were never released to the public. Ernest Tubb's "It's America (Love It or Leave It)" was an attack upon hippies and war protestors and is significant because Tubb had been an outspoken Democrat at least up to the mid-sixties. The cultural conflict of that decade generated an identity crisis among many old-line Democrats that has still not been resolved.[75]

The remarkable resurgence enjoyed by country music since the seventies is attributable to many factors, but the presumed ideology surrounding the music certainly riveted national attention. Paul Hemphill's book, *The Nashville Sound,* written prior to the recording of "Okie from Muskogee," had a larger sale than any previously published book on country music and was reviewed in several major periodicals including *Life* magazine. Much of the reason for the book's appeal to non–country music fans came from Hemphill's exploration of the link between George Wallace and country music. But by 1970, many country musicians and fans had made an even larger political leap, moving beyond George Wallace to open support of Republican causes.

At a time when urban folk and rock singers were excoriating Richard Nixon and his policies or projecting images that seemed subversive to national interests, Nixon was delighted to hear of musical expressions compatible with his own philosophy or potentially exploitable for political purposes. Although he had not previously demonstrated an affinity for country music, preferring instead music of the easy listening variety, he began to invite country entertainers to the White House. In March, 1970, a brief flurry of media interest ensued when Johnny Cash reportedly refused to sing two of Nixon's requests at his White House concert. The songs were "Okie from Muskogee" and Guy Drake's satire on alleged welfare abuses, "Welfare Cadilac [*sic*]." Media coverage suggested that Cash was reluctant to sing the songs because of political reasons; *Time* magazine, for instance, asserted that the songs "did not agree with Johnny Cash's pro-underdog sympathies." Actually, a Nixon aide, not Nixon, had requested the songs, and Cash had rejected them because he did not know them. Liberal writers had attempted to create a conflict of interests where none existed. Shortly before he resigned, and at a time when his political constituencies were narrowing, Nixon made a visit to Nashville where he appeared on the stage of the Grand Ole Opry. With his administration crumbling around him, Nixon stood before what he must have considered to be one of the last constituencies available to him. With the encouragement of Roy Acuff, he played the piano and pathetically tried to yo-yo before an approving audience (trick yo-yoing was one of Acuff's stage specialties).

The newfound political notoriety of country music encouraged major media coverage. Popular magazines like *Newsweek* and *Time* ran feature stories on country music and almost invariably stressed its silent majority or hard hat associations. Some of the coverage bristled with disgust or recoiled in horror at the alleged illiberality of the music and its performers. CBS commentator Tom Braden in 1972, for example, attacked the intellectual vacuity of the Nixon administration and said that it was "headed by a man whose taste in music runs to country-and-western and Lawrence Welk." Richard Goldstein, writing in *Mademoiselle,* saw something far worse in the music, and was particularly appalled by the evidence of interest in country music shown by some of his urban intellectual friends. To Goldstein the music was more than just the predictable outcome of southern bigotry; it was also the "musical extension of the Nixon administration" and something that should instinctively horrify every Jew and liberal. Florence King, described in an accompanying author's blurb as a writer for erotic magazines, demonstrated in *Harper's Magazine* just how ludicrous such political analyses could be. Ms. King came up with an interesting twist when she indicted country music not only for being the expression of reactionary discontent but for also being a cause of it. Country music encouraged working-class alienation, she said, feeding the masses a steady diet of depression and disillusionment. She accused the music of being a major cause of the truckers' strike of 1972 because it bred discouragement among the drivers who listened to it constantly.[76]

With the winding down of the war and the reduction of political tensions in the United States, country music's flirtation with politics diminished. The seventies found the music solidly entrenched in American popular culture and performed in a variety of forms only faintly reminiscent of its hillbilly beginnings. The obsession with "crossover" records that would appeal to the broadest possible assortment of listeners encouraged the creation of a musical product that carried no class, political, or regional identification. As the industry reached out to build a larger audience, particularly among the young, it consequently sought to downplay its identification with political reaction.

Still, some strange things happened to country music along the road to respectability and national acceptance. While many country entertainers (and their promoters) sought to create a musical form that bore no overt regional, rural, or working-class roots, they ironically encountered a growing interest in the traditions they were trying to leave behind. Attempting to be "American" and majoritarian, in the sense of trying to project both a sound and a set of values presumed to be broadly appealing to the greatest possible number, the industry in the mid-seventies found itself in a national context that was becoming obsessed with things southern.

The election to the presidency of Jimmy Carter, a southerner and a reputed country music fan, along with the publicity surrounding the alleged rise to power of the Sunbelt, contributed further to the renewed fascination with the South, a region that had endured such bad press during the fifties and early sixties. Although a negatively charged exotic aura still clung to the region, it was becoming possible to embrace the South without guilt or embarrassment. Now that racism had been supposedly checked by national legislation or, at worst, shown to be a national rather than southern phenomenon, rednecks and good old boys could be pictured as lovable simpletons. Carter's brother Billy, typecast as a professional redneck and promoted by a Nashville agency, did even more than his brother to awaken interest in the downhome South. Rednecks and good old boys became staples of movies, television series, stand-up comedy, and other forms of popular entertainment, and they even became central, without apology and even with pride, to many country songs and comedy routines. Some songs, like "Up against the Wall, Redneck Mother" and "Redneck in a Rock and Roll Bar," made playful fun of the stereotypes, while others, such as "Redneck! The Redneck National Anthem" and "Rednecks, White Socks and Blue Ribbon Beer," proudly embraced the label.[77]

Industry representatives and musicians also discovered, often to their surprise, that while the public taste for political songs may have diminished, working-class songs could sometimes exhibit commercial appeal. As discussed earlier in the chapter on work, a few entertainers, such as James Talley, John Conlee, Johnny Cash, Tom T. Hall, and Merle Haggard, were described as working-class poets. The Oklahoma-born James Talley won considerable critical acclaim for his songs, as well as much public attention when Jimmy and Rosalynn Carter described him as their favorite country singer. Talley was virtually alone among country music's singer-songwriters in identifying with Woody Guthrie, and his lyrics sometimes bristled with anger at class privilege, corporate abuse, and racism, and in one of his songs he asked, "Are they gonna make us outlaws again?" Most lyrics in country music, however, concentrated on the day-to-day problems of common people and seldom delved explicitly into politics. Class consciousness did appear frequently in songs, in the form of militant pride, invidious comparisons with unproductive or effete people ("Rednecks, White Socks and Blue Ribbon Beer," for example, noted that "we don't fit in with that white-collar crowd"), but Marxists or old-line political radicals could find little in them with which to identify. Sociologist Richard Peterson argues convincingly that in country music "class consciousness is evoked and then explicitly dissipated in individual gestures of defiance and Cinderella dreams."[78] These songs nevertheless carried political import because they revealed the frustrations and desires that fueled political conduct, and they disclosed the ways in which many working people defined themselves in modern American society. Shaped by a cluster of values that included the sense of individualistic pride, patriotism, and machismo, the songs tended to suggest a suspicion of both government and trade union remedies.[79]

Except for the Carter interlude in 1976, few country entertainers have displayed much public affection for Democratic presidential candidates in the last thirty years. Republican national conventions, in fact, have rung with the voices of people like Tanya Tucker, the Gatlin Brothers, the Judds, and George Bush's special favorites, the Oak Ridge Boys. Lee Greenwood's "God Bless the USA," introduced during the campaign of 1984, has become virtually the anthem of the Republican Party and is carted out at each national convention and major party event.[80]

Aggressive displays of patriotism, such as that heard in Greenwood's song, or belligerent criticisms of certain public policies or personalities have frequently peppered contemporary country music. Charlie Daniels continued to be good copy for those who valued outspoken positions. He told one journalist, for example, that he could not "articulate the contempt" he had for Congress for its failure to remove President Clinton from office during the impeachment proceedings of 1998, and he contended that "the morals of this country have been lowered so far it's unbelievable."[81] When performed by singers such as Daniels or Hank Williams, Jr., jingoistic songs tended to be as much vehicles for manly boasting as for social criticism. Hank Jr.'s "Dixie on My Mind" and "A Country Boy Can Survive" combined harsh and explicit criticism of New York City with an implicit indictment of the liberal politics that prevailed there. Ostensibly a comment on urban crime, "A Country Boy Can Survive" sounded like a survivalist hymn with its plea for personal retributive justice against murderous street violence. The Persian Gulf War similarly inspired both personal expressions of masculine bluster and jingo-istic impulses in country songs. Even though Williams's defiant challenge to Iraq's Saddam Hussein, "Don't Give Us a Reason," threatened the dictator with the massive retaliatory power of the United States, one got the impression that a successful resolution of the Gulf crisis could have been attained with an expeditionary force led by Hank and Charlie.[82]

The only economically based crusade that has attracted the support of a broad range of country singers in the last twenty years is Farm Aid, the program designed to awaken Americans to the plight of family farmers and to elicit corrective political legislation. Most closely identified with Willie Nelson, a child of Central Texas cotton farmers, Farm Aid pro-vides a forum for country entertainers to renew their commitment to a cherished past and to harness their energies to a campaign that carries no negative baggage. Unlike the resistance to war or support for gay rights or AIDS awareness, the defense of the family farm is a "safe" issue that not only mobilizes the country singer's overpowering sense of nostalgia but also attunes him or her to the nation's central founding myth: the idea of America's virtuous beginnings as a rural society. Songs like Charlie Daniels's "American Farmer" and Charley Pride's "Down on the Farm" correctly described everyone's dependence on the farmer's labor as well as the human costs that accompany the disappearance of the family farm, but one finds no comparable campaign among country entertainers to save the jobs of beleaguered automobile or steel workers.[83]

Farm Aid may have come closest to encompassing the sympathies of country singers, but, from time to time, other issues appear in songs that capture essentially populist passions. The sense of social outrage that motivated Woody Guthrie in the thirties has not totally disappeared from country music, but its boldest expressions come from singers and song-writers like John Prine, Steve Earle, or Tish Hinojosa (whose music strad-dles stylistic categories), or from country singers like Hazel Dickens and Iris DeMent who voice their messages from outside the Top 40 main-stream. Steve Earle's "Christmas Time in Washington," an end-of-the-year reflection in 1996 on public apathy and political vacuity in the na-tion's capital, invoked the names of Emma Goldman, Joe Hill, and Martin Luther King, Jr., and concluded with the plaintive plea, "Come back Woody Guthrie." Several singers have commented on the wreckage wrought by progress as corporate America bought and reshaped the land-scape of rural America. The veteran folksinger Jean Ritchie, in a song called "Black Waters," poignantly described the ravages to land and streams made by strip mining in eastern Kentucky. Ray and Melvin Goins noted the human costs of unregulated industrial labor in "Black Lung Blues," while Billy Edd Wheeler graphically portrayed the consequences of mechanization in "Coal Tattoo," a song about the closing of the mines in Appalachia. John Prine carried this dismal story even further in "Paradise," describing the elimination of his parents' home community in western Kentucky by the powerful shovels of "Mr. Peabody's" coal mines; and the bluegrass duo of Vern and Ray put all of these various abuses into proper perspective in a song that summed up the arrogance of corporate America—"To hell with the people, to hell with the land."[84]

Contemporary country singers exhibit concern for social problems but, like a growing chorus of fellow Americans, rarely call for explicit governmental action. Mirroring a cynicism about politics on the rise in American life since at least the period of the Watergate scandals, country entertainers instead lend their support to private humanitarian projects or to individual acts of compassion. Sensitivity to the plight of the poor, homeless, abused, or neglected elements of society has never been absent from country music,[85] but one now finds increased empathy for other social issues, such as women's needs, racial differences, and tolerance of alternative lifestyles, that had not often been dealt with in country songs. Occasionally, a song like "Kids of the Baby Boom" does win extensive airplay on commercial radio stations (it in fact reached the number one position on the *Billboard* country charts in 1987). Written and performed by Howard and David Bellamy (two self-described "Old Hippies"), this well-crafted song described the awakening, and growing sense of alarm, of a generation that had grown up with affluence, indifference, and a false sense of security. Alhough acutely critical of American societal flaws, the song's message could hardly be described as radical. The rarity of such songs on Top 40 country radio is not surprising, but even public radio formats, with their dependence on government and community support, are sometimes resistant to controversial musical material. Garth Brooks found out that superstar status could not guarantee exposure on many country music radio stations for his plea for racial brotherhood, "We Shall Be Free," and Iris DeMent discovered that public radio was not always a safe haven when a Republican legislator in Florida threatened to block public funding for a station that had played her hard-hitting critique of American corruption and hypocrisy, "Wasteland of the Free."[86]

Women like DeMent have contributed significantly to the broadening of perspectives in country music. Heightened social consciousness, though, did not become prominent among women until the 1980s, and only after a couple of decades of national feminist activism had raised the consciousness that aroused young women everywhere. Earlier singers such as Dolly Parton and Loretta Lynn had sometimes written and performed songs that questioned the older hierarchies of patriarchal dominance, but most women country entertainers had not conspicuously supported women's rights issues. Representative Myrtle Eleanor Wiseman, for example, who had performed as Lulu Belle with her husband Scotty, voted against the Equal Rights Amendment in the North Carolina legislature, even though she privately supported the measure. The women's liberation movement nevertheless has touched the thinking of both male and female country singers. Not only are the women of contemporary country music more boldly assertive than their predecessors but male singers tend to be more aware of and resistant to the old double standards that demanded unquestioned submissiveness by women. Garth Brooks, however, confronted the problem of spousal abuse more dramatically than most singers with his recording of "The Thunder Rolls," a song about a deadly response made by a battered woman to her husband.[87]

Most important, a host of women singers, such as Mary Chapin Carpenter, Kathy Mattea, Martina McBride, the Dixie Chicks, Rosanne Cash, Iris DeMent, Tish Hinojosa, Nanci Griffith, Deanna Carter, and k. d. lang (the first acknowledged lesbian country singer), have actively supported abortion rights, AIDS awareness, protection for battered wives and abused children, and programs to combat hunger and homelessness. These social concerns sometimes appear in the lyrics of their songs. Nanci Griffith spoke for all of them when she sang, "If we poison our children with hatred, a hard life is all that they'll know."

This broadened vision of social concern flowered among a generation of singers who grew up in suburban America, sometimes with college degrees but armed more often with sensibilities shaped by the media, the norms of rock culture, and the lingering assumptions of the sixties cultural revolution. Several of the best of them served apprenticeships in the coffeehouses of the folk revival. Singer-songwriters such as Emmylou Harris, Nanci Griffith, Iris DeMent, Mary Chapin Carpenter, and Tish Hinojosa performed in this highly competitive urban environment, where facile verbal skills and social consciousness were equally prized. Some of these singers, like Mary Chapin Carpenter (a graduate of Brown University), ventured into country music carrying neither a southern nor a working-class heritage, and have never strayed very far from a folk-rock sound. Others, such as Lucinda Williams and Tish Hinojosa, range far and wide in their experimentation with musical styles and reach out to audiences that transcend the country music field. Hinojosa's vignettes about life in the barrio of San Antonio ("West Side of Town"), the hopes and dreams of Mexican workers who set out on the perilous journey to the United States ("Joaquin"), or about the specter of death from dangerous toxins sprayed on crops and the discrimination that accompanies migrant workers ("Something in the Rain") are nevertheless some of the most powerful examples of social commentary and protest that have appeared in American music since the days of Woody Guthrie.[88]

The most vital performers are those who, like Hinojosa, are able to address the urgent problems of their own gender without losing sight of larger questions such as hunger, discrimination, and militarism that confront all mankind. Growing up a generation apart, in different areas of the country, and under vastly different economic circumstances, Hazel Dickens and Iris DeMent have fashioned the dissimilar materials of their lives into some of the most compelling and socially conscious songs in modern country music. Together, they represent the best that modern country music has to offer. Dissimilar though their experiences may have been, Dickens and DeMent share certain attitudes and attributes: they are daughters of the rural South (Dickens in West Virginia, and DeMent in Arkansas) who have preserved fierce loyalties to family and home even though both have spent most of their lives far away from their places of birth. Dickens was working in a factory in Baltimore, and living in a hillbilly ghetto, by the time she was sixteen. And DeMent was taken to California by her parents when she was only four years old. Nostalgia figures prominently in their music, with mama and daddy and the old homeplace putting in frequent appearances, but neither of them seek salvation in a retreat to the past or to fantasy, nor do they often look for the escape routes that have been so alluring to country entertainers—the bottle, the church, the open road. Learning from Roy Acuff, George Jones, Merle Haggard, and other traditional performers, they have gone well beyond them, just as they have transcended the worlds of their fathers and mothers in many ways. They have taken their own autobiographical circumstances and convictions, and have subtly fashioned them into aesthetic statements that retain the profoundly personal while rendering it universally meaningful.

Hazel Dickens was well ahead of all of the women singer-songwriters in her fusion of women-sensitive songs and class-conscious working-folk's songs. She sternly admonished insensitive men for their treatment of women, in songs like "Don't Put Her Down, You Put Her There," and also issued clarion calls for social justice for all people in the musical soundtracks of the powerful labor movies, *Harlan County, USA* and *Matewan,* and in songs about mining disasters, industrial layoffs, abandoned communities, and the everyday concerns of working people.[89]

Iris DeMent's commitment to songs of social commentary emerged more slowly. Her first two CDs dealt mostly with intensely personal experiences, nostalgic and contemporary, that nevertheless insinuated themselves into the private domains of her listeners. But on her third recording, *The Way I Should,* she moved strongly into the area of social commentary. One of her most powerful songs, "Letter to Mom," dealt with child sexual abuse. Another, "There's a Wall in Washington," spoke with great passion about the lingering and unresolved consciousness of the Vietnam War. "Quality Time" was a searing indictment of parents "who would sell their kid's soul to keep up with the Joneses no matter the toll." "Wasteland of the Free" was a jeremiad aimed at many of the social ills that troubled America in the 1990s. No country song since Blind Alfred Reed's "How Can a Poor Man Stand Such Times and Live" had spoken so eloquently, and with such broad-ranging anger, about the corruption, avarice, and hypocrisy that befoul the body politic: preachers who dispense hatred, politicians beholden to corporate cash, CEO's who make "two-hundred times the workers' pay" but who "fight like hell against raisin' the minimum wage," high school kids in Calvin Klein and Guess jeans who can scarcely read but who can identify "every crotch on MTV."[90]

In the notes to the album, she said "Some of what I've said will make some people mad. It might even make some people hate me . . . but if I hid the truth about how I think and feel . . . I would hate myself." Merle Haggard's response to the song and album has not been reported. But if we recall the lyrics of "The Fightin' Side of Me," we know that he had reacted angrily, and with more than a hint of violence, to those "squirrelly guys" who were "talking bad about the way we have to live here in this country." On the other hand, we also know that he and Iris admired each other's music, a consequence perhaps of their common cultural kinship, though a generation apart, as children of the southern diaspora. Differences in age, gender, and, of course, the social contexts in which their varying critiques were issued may help to explain the contrasting nature of their political ideologies (if they can be so termed), but they should not blind us to the fact that these two great singer-songwriters spoke from perspectives that are deeply rooted in country music and working-class history.

Haggard's and DeMent's songs share the impulse toward social commentary, if not always social consciousness, that has always been present in country music, as well as a populist rationale that undergirds the thinking of most country musicians. From Uncle Dave Macon in the 1920s, to Dorsey Dixon and Woody Guthrie in the 1930s, and on to Haggard, DeMent, Hank Williams, Jr., Hazel Dickens, and Steve Earle in our own time, country singers have asserted the wisdom and nobility of plain hardworking people, while also alleging that they are sometimes victimized by certain powerful interests or marginalized by social elitists. Historically, country musicians have identified the "enemy" in different ways, and they have differed widely in the "solutions" that they have proposed or championed (often, one finds only frustration and resentment, and no solutions at all). But we should be warned anew against the temptation to link either southern working-class culture or country music to any specific political agenda. After all, it is the tensions and conflicting postures found in this great music, and not its alleged simplicity, that make it eternally appealing.

Conclusion

Someone killed country music
Cut out its heart and soul.
They got away with murder,
Down on Music Row.

Larry Cordle really struck a chord in the hearts of many tradition-mind-ed country music fans in October of 1999 when he introduced "Murder on Music Row"[1] at the International Bluegrass Music convention in Louisville. It immediately provoked reactions from musicians and fans alike. When Alan Jackson and George Strait recorded a duet cover,[2] most Top 40 stations refused to play it. Cordle's version, though, reached number one on the "National Bluegrass Survey" published in *Bluegrass Unlimited,* and Eddie Stubbs, the popular announcer on powerful WSM in Nashville, said "Murder on Music Row" generated more requests on his shows than any song he had ever played.[3] It's hard to resist a song that alleges that "the almighty dollar and the lust for worldwide fame slowly killed tradition."

The song raises a number of questions about the state of contemporary country music, and about the theses proposed in this book. Is country music, as heard on contemporary country radio—what is often described as Top 40—still "country"? Is it "southern"? Is it still linked to "work-ing-class" people? And is it relevant to the concerns of people today? I think that most fans, like Stubbs and myself, who identify with the song realize that "traditional" is a relative and changing term, and that music has to adapt in order to survive. We easily accepted Merle Haggard and Buck Owens, even though their brand of "honky-tonk" music diverged significantly from the styles pioneered by Ernest Tubb and Hank Williams. We have also responded positively to the smooth, supercharged, and highly arranged styles now current in bluegrass music, although they differ dramatically from the sounds introduced in the 1940s by Bill Monroe, Lester Flatt, and Earl Scruggs. We easily see them all as part of the linked and interwoven fabric of country music. But where does one draw the line of "acceptable," and why do we have misgivings about the varieties of country music that now rule the airwaves and the popular imagination?

I do not pretend to speak for all tradition-minded country fans, but as I have tried to make clear in this book, "southernness" and "working-class identity" have been closely linked in my mind to "real" country music. Those associations began over sixty years ago when I first heard the music over our little Philco battery radio. When I listen to Top 40 country radio today, I hear almost nothing that even faintly resembles the music that came into our household during my growing-up days in East Texas, or that suggests the working-class society that originally nurtured this music. It's hard for me to admit that my sense of alienation may be little more than a consequence of growing older and seeing a familiar world slip away, but I know many people much younger than I who feel a similar sense of estrangement from contemporary country music. What thoughts went through the minds of superstars Strait and Jackson when they recorded their version of "Murder on Music Row" and then saw it briefly reach the number 38 position on the *Billboard* charts? What did the song's lyrics say to them about their own successful careers within the country music establishment?

First, I will try to give Top 40 its due. As I have said elsewhere in this book, the percentage of native-born southerners who perform country music remains remarkably high. The "twang" is still there. Country singers and songwriters still make songs that comment explicitly on the South, or they lace their lyrics with references to scenes, habits, or topics that could be associated only with the region and its people. Identification with working-class culture, including tributes to working people, also appear frequently in country songs. Such references, in fact, seemed to crop up more frequently during and after the 1970s, lending an ironic cast to a music and culture that have in fact become more middle-class since that decade. Working-class poses may have become merely symbolic for a generation of entertainers who grew up in suburbia. Johnny Cash spoke eloquently on this point when he noted that "back in Arkansas, a way of life produced a certain kind of music. Does a certain kind of music now produce a way of life?" He then went on to ask, "Are the hats, the boots, the pickup trucks, and the honky-tonking poses all that's left of a disintegrating culture?"[4]

Occasional voices, though, like those of George Strait, Alan Jackson, Dwight Yoakam, Travis Tritt, Marty Stuart, Patty Loveless, Lee Ann Womack, Montgomery Gentry, Wade Hayes, and Brad Paisley do awaken echoes of that working-class society that once underpinned country music. My friend Jim Cobb, the noted historian of the South, referred accurately to a "recurring dialectic wherein country music seems ready to fade completely into the enveloping blandness of the pop-music scene only to have a 'new traditionalist' movement emerge."[5] If you can train your ears to reach beyond the pop-rock instrumentation and vocal styles that mark most of the songs, you can still hear lyrics that speak meaningfully about the problems and dreams of average people. A few of them, such as Alan Jackson's "Little Man" and Montgomery Gentry's "Daddy Don't Sell the Farm," have defended small people against corporate interests while also managing to garner extensive radio airplay.[6] In a perverse way, even a song like the Dixie Chicks' "Goodbye Earl" proves satisfying when it sanctions violence as a means of righting personal wrongs (in this case, the sins of an abusive husband).[7] It's good to hear a revival of a traditional theme—especially a good ole murder ballad—and the expression of strong feeling in a body of music that's too often slick in execution and lacking in passion.

The musicianship heard in modern country music is staggering. Top 40 musicians may be lacking in passion and originality, but they are masters of their craft. Modern country music is also brilliantly recorded and disseminated with state-of-the-art technological expertise (Nashville's recording engineers will not permit the distribution of anything short of perfection). Furthermore, these musicians *do* communicate with millions of listeners here and around the world, and they project a message and sound that *are* different from other forms of popular music. Modern country music often sounds like refurbished 1980s-style rock music, but it presents easily singable tunes and understandable lyrics that are appealing not only to a wide spectrum of Americans but also to increasing numbers of people around the world. In many respects, country music has become the nation's new pop music, offering a sound and a thematic package that resonate with a diverse audience of listeners, not all of whom are old and socially conservative. This evokes my most sobering admission—the suspicion that Top 40 songs may be more "realistic" than any other form of country music, in that they more completely meet the needs of a majority of today's fans. The music that I and other "traditionalists" yearn for may have more truly reflected the values, hopes, and dreams of those who lived in the past, or how we *think* they lived.

Many observers of course dismiss my fears concerning country music's loss of identity, a concern that I have voiced in varying ways since 1968 when my first book was published. Jim Cobb, for example, sees nothing new in the music's current flirtation with popular sounds and styles and says that it "reflects the manner in which southern culture at large has survived by accommodating rather than resisting the forces of change."[8] And it is true, too, that country entertainers always exhibited the influence of "outside" forces, whether it was Charlie Poole trying to sing like Al Jolson, Jimmie Rodgers aping the sounds and mannerisms of vaudeville stars, Uncle Dave Macon presenting banjo styles pioneered by minstrel performers, or an entire generation of hillbillies donning the attire of dude cowboys.

But when Jimmie Rodgers sang a pop song from the early 1920s, he still sounded like he could be an ex-railroad worker from Mississippi. Or when the Carter Family sang their adaptation of the Tin Pan Alley song "Are You Lonesome Tonight?" they still sounded like backcountry people from Virginia. No matter how many ragtime songs Charlie Poole sang, no one would have been surprised to learn that he was a cotton mill worker from the North Carolina Piedmont. Bob Wills dressed himself and his musicians in fancy "western" suits, experimented with blues and jazz tunes, but still sounded like a country boy who was aware of a big wide world of music. Hank Williams was and sounded like a boy from rural Alabama even when he did his version of the Tin Pan Alley tune "Lovesick Blues." The list could go on and on. What made these musicians so vital and exciting is that they fused their rural, working-class sensibilities with the styles and songs borrowed from "outside" sources to create something that seemed both familiar and innovative. But no one could ever doubt that they were "country."

But today, even when the young country entertainers sing their occasional songs about blue-collar life, they sound like what they are—suburban men and women interpreting those experiences through middle-class lenses and sensibilities. When asked about influences, they speak more often of Led Zeppelin, Bruce Springsteen, Billy Joel, and the Eagles than they do of Hank, George, Loretta, or Merle. After all, given the nature of Top 40 radio, young people grow up with little opportunity to hear the sounds of country music's pioneers, or even anyone who recorded as recently as 1975. Listeners to Top 40 radio stations do not hear the full range of today's country music, and I think that they are all the poorer for it. The narrow, formulaic playlists have little room for "classic country" songs or for the often-exciting "alternative" music that lies out on the fringe. I think it's tragic that mainstream listeners are given little chance to hear the genuine country voices and perspectives of people like Iris DeMent, Lucinda Williams, and Jimmie Dale Gilmore, and that music purchasers have to go to the "folk" bins in record stores to find their CDs (in fact, I could not find John Prine's fine album of vintage country songs, featuring duet performances with a few women singers, until I rummaged through the rock collections in a local store).[9] In a June, 2000, concert at the Annex Club in Madison, Jimmie Dale Gilmore remarked bemusedly about being too country for country radio. His reedy tenor voice is one of the most distinctive in country music—begging comparison with Jimmie Rodgers, Hank Williams, and Willie Nelson—and it cuts through the din of a honky-tonk crowd with a clarity and emotional edge that are rarely heard in any form of music. Few singers can communicate with the individual heart as effectively as he.[10]

As Top 40 country abandons the music of such veteran performers as Merle Haggard and George Jones, it also eliminates or smooths out the rough "edges" that made country music believable and appealing. To be sure, smooth and even pop-style voices—like those of Vernon Dalhart, Bradley Kincaid, Red Foley, Leon Payne, Eddy Arnold, Jim Reeves, Sonny James, and Patsy Cline—were always present in country music, but the total package of sound—their repertoire, instrumentation—presented by such singers generally conveyed a sense of unpretentious "downhome" intimacy. That homemade quality has virtually disappeared from mainstream country music, along with the rugged and natural voices of people like Ernest Tubb, Molly O'Day, Rose Maddox, Kitty Wells, Roy Acuff, and Johnny Cash who spoke and sang with the cadences and dialects of the rural or working-class South. And one hears few songs that reflect experiences lived close to the margins of economic insecurity or social unrespectability. Where are the drinking and cheating songs? Or the songs that speak of religious retribution? One does not have to condone the morality of the former, or even make a spiritual identification with the latter, to regret the disappearance of songs that actually mirrored and voiced visceral responses to life. It was a decided understatement when Merle Haggard called the homogenized and predictable sound of modern country music "a little short on soul and substance sometimes,"[11] a sentiment with which many of us would agree.

My definition of country music is still obviously rooted in the circumstances of my East Texas youth. (The passionate predilections of the fan contend with the wary skepticism of the scholar.) It is consequently difficult for me to entertain the possibility that today's mainstream country music may be the inevitable product of an organic process that I have always seen as central to the music's evolution. That is, its evolution may reflect more than the acquisition of new fans who have had no experience with rural or working-class life; it may also be the kind of music that logically emerges when southern men and women grow up in environments, and under influences, that are dramatically different from that of their forebears.

Like most of today's musicians and disk jockeys, many fans who came to country music after an immersion in rock still listen for a musical sound that is aggressive, high-decibel, and energy-driven even when the accompanying lyrics project downhome feelings. The urban cowboy phenomenon, the line dance craze, and the clever merchandising of Garth Brooks won hosts of new fans to country music. But country's current partisans are not all recent converts, by any means. Many have followed the music through every successive change of the last forty years, and are as easily reconciled to Garth and Shania as they were to the stars that preceded them. No demographic study has ever accurately measured the country music audience, but I suspect that most fans are suburban-dwelling Middle Americans, the children and grandchildren of working folk from my own generation. Their speech patterns and dialects, tastes in food, and religious backgrounds may not diverge very far from mine. They are the people who swell the attendance each year at Nashville's Fan Fair and who bravely confront the heat of a Tennessee summer for a chance to shake Garth Brooks's hand or to get John Michael Montgomery to sign their tee-shirts. Even larger numbers hear country music only when they turn on their local radio stations, or watch the Nashville Network on television. They are also the people who usually get ignored or, at best, are treated condescendingly by observers like me. The unspoken, but elitist, assumptions that seem to govern such responses to Top 40 listeners are that they are too stupid to know what "real country" music is, or that they are manipulated or seduced into patronizing a mediocre body of music that does not represent their true interests.

Whatever the value of Top 40 radio, it does not present the only form of country music that is available to us. We may grouse about the lack of soul and working-class identity in the music heard on commercial country stations, but such offerings do not exhaust the country music catalogue. Today's country music extends far beyond those narrow playlists and beyond the glib and predictable repartee of disk jockeys who don't know and couldn't care less about what they play, and who in any case don't bother to tell their listeners what they've heard. *Real* country music is alive and well in America's honky-tonks (particularly in Texas and California), at bluegrass festivals across the nation, in the small town oprys and jamborees that have proliferated in the last thirty years, at house concerts that are becoming popular in various parts of the country, and in the countless jam sessions and picking parties held in private homes, VFW halls, or other public settings.[12] If one wants to retreat to the realm of country music's past, as I sometimes do, you can listen to reissued recordings (many of them available on European labels), or you can tune in to the music of a small but dedicated cluster of radio stations that program "classic country music." For example, WOJB-FM, a Native American station owned and operated by Ojibwe Indians near Hayward, Wisconsin, features a variety of popular music styles but plays mostly country songs, none of which were recorded after 1975. Elsewhere, classic country radio disk jockeys range from Tracy Pitcox (who holds forth on KNEL, a small FM station in Brady, Texas) to Eddie Stubbs on Nashville's WSM, or to people on community and college radio stations who host shows like my own "Back to the Country" on Madison's WORT. Stubbs dips down often into what he calls "deep catalogue" to play old songs never heard on contemporary radio stations. His is one of the few programs available on commercial radio in the United States where one can hear three straight hours of Webb Pierce's music.[13]

One can even learn or imbibe "tradition" by watching instructional videos or by participating in the workshops, festivals, and government-sponsored folk apprentice programs that have flourished in the wake of the folk revival. While the apprentice programs place neophytes under the guidance of authentic rural musicians, many of the festival and workshop instructors come from neither southern, rural, nor working-class backgrounds. The phenomenon of "outsiders" encouraging the performance of "traditional" music has not only been present throughout country music's history, it in fact has been a defining paradox. While I have always liked to think of myself as an "insider" who was preserving, commemorating, and documenting the music of my own culture, I now realize that these activities have made me an observer as well as a participant and have perhaps so distanced me that I have inadvertently become an outsider too.

After all, I couldn't wait to escape the social milieu into which I was born, even though I have since spent most of my life writing about it. My refusal to be a farmer, a cowboy, or a blue-collar worker, or even a small-town office clerk, was as firm as my resistance to my mother's prayers that I become a Pentecostal preacher. I nevertheless preserved a love for

the music that issued forth from that expressive faith. I still secretly rejoice when learning that a favorite singer came up in the Holiness tradition. Like my good friend Ronnie Pugh, who wrote so convincingly about
the honky-tonk culture of Ernest Tubb, I also resisted the allure of the
barrooms, even if I could not resist the music that emerged from them.
Falling outside the two extremes of the "Saturday night/Sunday morning" syndrome, I found that my natural "place" lay in documenting the
richly textured working-class world that I fled both personally and professionally. In interpreting this world, I feel that I honor the dignity of
my parents and others like them who have been too long ignored or held
in disrespect.

And that is what I look for in country music today. I listen for singers
and musicians who value the music's roots and traditions, and who honor
the work, the sacrifices, the blood, tears, and sweat that went into its
making. If I'm unable to believe that the performer has actually "lived"
the life that is sung about, I want to believe that he or she respects the
culture that surrounded the music. Consequently, I welcome the music
of entertainers like Mike Seeger, Bill Clifton, John McCutcheon, David
Holt, Alice Gerrard, Jim Watson, Laurie Lewis, Doug Green, and Tim
O'Brien, middle-class city folk whose affection for old-time music mirrors a similar reverence for the people who originally created it. My favorites among this group, Tim O'Brien and Doug Green, have demonstrated better than most people that traditional styles can be both
appreciated for their own sake and adapted as the bases for new and vital
forms. O'Brien, an alumnus of the popular, progressive bluegrass band,
Hot Rize, is the consummate contemporary musician, moving easily from
one style to another—incorporating phrases and ideas from everyone
from Bob Dylan and Stephane Grappelli to Bill Monroe and Tommy Jarrell. But above all, it is his grounding in traditional forms, and his respect
and admiration for those on whose shoulders he stands, that wins my
ardent appreciation. Green, familiar to millions as "Ranger Doug" of the
cowboy trio Riders in the Sky, displays a wide-ranging versatility not
nearly so well known. He is a student of American grassroots music who
served several years as oral historian for the Country Music Foundation,
a skilled guitarist, a one-time member of Bill Monroe's Blue Grass Boys,
and one of the best yodelers that ever sang a country or cowboy song.[14]

Despite my respect for O'Brien and Green, and the music they make,
my strongest affection, ideally, goes to those performers whose music does
more than simply commemorate or represent working-class culture. I
identify most with the music of those people who emerged from the south-

ern working class and who still carry the imprints of that background in their styles. Not only do these singers evoke warm family feelings, the sense that they could be brothers or cousins, but they also live out the personal fantasy that I never had the nerve to pursue—the decision to be a country singer (my closest friends know that I would have given up tenure for one night on the Opry). I am thinking of singers and musicians like Marty Stuart, Jimmie Dale Gilmore, or Don Walser, the iron-lunged yodeler and tenor singer from Austin, Texas, who made a commitment to full-time country performance at the age of sixty, and only after he had retired from forty-five years of service with the Texas National Guard.[15] Or Dale Watson, another Austin-based singer who learned his music and working-class values from his Alabama-born, truck-driving father (isn't it funny how Texans keep showing up in my list of most favored singers). The nights spent listening to his father, Don Watson, in the clubs of West Tennessee are lovingly remembered in "Jack's Truck Stop and Cafe." When I see and hear Dale Watson, I get no visions of placid mountain cabins, country churches, or windswept western plains. Nor do some misty glimmers of an ancient Celtic past seep into my imagination. What I see instead is a small but muscular man, dressed in black jeans and white tee-shirt, sporting black swept-back hair and a profusion of tattoos—one arm's artistry commemorating his Texas home and the other remembering his father. Watson's songs, conveyed in a rich, expressive baritone, carry no ideological message, unless it's hillbilly nationalism. Several of his songs bristle with attitude and defiance. He is proud of his origins, quick to praise the exploits of truck drivers and other working folk, generous in his tributes to Merle Haggard, Dave Dudley, and other heroes, and contemptuous of the music purveyed by Nashville. In one of his best songs, Watson recalls the radio stations of his youth—such as KIKK in Houston—and the heartfelt music they played, and then lectures contemporary Top 40 stations: "Play me a real country song." God bless Dale Watson; he has never tried to get above his raising.[16]

Notes

Preface

1. Wilbur J. Cash, *The Mind of the South* (New York: Alfred A. Knopf, 1941), p. viii.

2. Ibid., chap. 2, esp. pp. 44–47 and 57–58.

3. John Egerton, *The Americanization of Dixie: The Southernization of America* (New York: Harper's Magazine Press, 1974); Peter Applebome, *Dixie Rising: How the South Is Shaping American Values, Politics, and Culture* (New York: Random House, 1996), p. 244.

4. Bill C. Malone, *Country Music, USA*, rev. ed. (1968; Austin: University of Texas Press, 1985).

5. John Hevener, *Which Side Are You On? The Harlan County Coal Miners, 1931–39* (Urbana: University of Illinois Press, 1978).

6. Henry Kmen, *Music in New Orleans: The Formative Years, 1791–1841* (Baton Rouge: Louisiana State University Press, 1966).

7. Bill C. Malone, *Singing Cowboys and Musical Mountaineers* (Athens: University of Georgia Press, 1993).

Chapter 1: "Take Me Back to the Sweet Sunny South"

1. See chap. 1, Bill C. Malone, *Southern Music/American Music* (Lexington: University Press of Kentucky, 1979).

2. This term was first used by James N. Gregory in his discussion of country music in the Okie subculture of California (*American Exodus: The Dust Bowl Migration and Okie Culture in California* [New York: Oxford University Press, 1989], 222–49).

3. Malone, *Country Music, USA*, pp. 31–77; Archie Green, "Hillbilly Music: Source and Symbol," *Journal of American Folklore* 78, no. 309 (July–Sept., 1965): 204–29.

4. The Hank Williams quote was first cited in Rufus Jarman, "Country Music Goes to Town," *Nation's Business* 41 (Feb., 1953): 51. I first encountered the "twang" usage in the early 1980s when I taped a couple of shows on early country music for Smithsonian Radio. They were labeled as "Birth of the Twang."

5. Foreign observers, too, tend to associate either cowboys or southern scenes with American country music. For example, Toru Mitsui, the leading Japanese scholar of country music, does not hesitate to equate country music with the South. See Mitsui, "The Reception of the Music of American Southern Whites in Japan," in *Transforming Tradition: Folk Music Revivals Examined*, ed. Neil V. Rosenberg (Urbana: University of Illinois Press, 1993), pp. 275–95.

6. Any encyclopedia or popular listing of country entertainers will support the accuracy of this observation. See, for example, the most recent and best compilation, *The Encyclopedia of Country Music: The Ultimate Guide to the Music*, compiled by the Country Music Hall of Fame and Museum in Nashville, ed. Paul Kingsbury (New York: Oxford University Press, 1998). But for scholarly verification, see Richard A. Peterson and Russell Davis, Jr., "The Fertile Crescent of Country Music," *Journal of Country Music* 6, no. 1 (1975): 19–27; George O. Carney, "Spatial Diffusion of the All-Country Music Radio Stations in the United States, 1971–74," *JEMF Quarterly* 13, no. 46 (Summer, 1972): 58–66. In 1996 Bruce Feiler argued that country music had become the music of suburban America. Most of the performers listed in his article, however, came from the eleven Confederate states or from Oklahoma; see "Gone Country," *New Republic* 214, no. 4 (Feb. 5, 1996): 19–26.

7. The romantic linking of the South and music is discussed in Malone, *Southern Music/American Music*, pp. 1–3, 18–22; and in Malone, *Singing Cowboys and Musical Mountaineers*, pp. 8–9. For confirmation of Tin Pan Alley's preoccupation with the South, see Earl F. Bargainneer, "Tin Pan Alley and Dixie: The South in Popular Song," *Mississippi Quarterly* 30, no. 4 (Fall, 1977): 527–65.

8. The better studies of northern country music include Simon Bronner, "Country Music Culture in Central New York," *JEMF Quarterly* 13, no. 47 (Winter, 1977): 171–82; and Neil Rosenberg, "Folk and Country Music in the Canadian Maritimes: A Regional Model," *Journal of Country Music* 5, no. 2 (1974): 76–83.

9. John Lomax's *Cowboy Songs and Other Frontier Ballads* (New York: Sturgis & Walton) had appeared in 1910, and Olive Dame Campbell's and Cecil Sharp's *English Folk Songs from the Southern Appalachians* (New York: G. P. Putnam's Sons) had been published in 1917. The music of the vast interior rural South, however, had been totally neglected prior to the first commercial recordings in the early twenties. See Malone, *Singing Cowboys and Musical Mountaineers*, chap. 1.

10. Eileen Southern, *The Music of Black Americans* (New York: W. W. Norton,

1971). The complicated story of Ralph Peer, Fiddlin' John, and country music's commercial beginnings is discussed in Archie Green, "Hillbilly Music: Source and Symbol," pp. 208–10; and in Gene Wiggins, *Fiddlin' Georgia Crazy: Fiddlin' John Carson, His Real World and the World of His Songs* (Urbana: University of Illinois Press, 1987), pp. 73–76.

11. Archie Green, "Hillbilly Music: Source and Symbol," p. 210; Wayne W. Daniel, *Pickin' on Peachtree: A History of Country Music in Atlanta, Georgia* (Urbana: University of Illinois Press, 1990), pp. 69–70.

12. Norm Cohen, review of Malone, *Southern Music/American Music*, in *Western Folklore* 40, no. 4 (Oct., 1981): 350.

13. Byrd began compiling the diary of his surveying expedition along the North Carolina–Virginia boundary in 1728, but the resulting *History of the Dividing Line* remained largely uncirculated in his lifetime. See Kenneth A. Lockridge, *The Diary, and Life, of William Byrd II of Virginia, 1674–1744*, published for the Institute of Early American History and Culture, Williamsburg, Virginia (Chapel Hill: University of North Carolina Press, 1987), pp. 128–40.

14. "The Hunters of Kentucky" was a song written in 1822 in commemoration of the southwestern backwoodsmen who had fought with Andrew Jackson against the British at the Battle of New Orleans. The classic account of the song's relationship to Jackson's political career is John William Ward, *Andrew Jackson: Symbol for an Age* (New York: Oxford University Press, 1955).

15. The most useful studies of the literary treatment of southern poor whites are Shields McIlwaine, *From Lubberland to Tobacco Road* (Norman: University of Oklahoma Press, 1939); Merrill Maguire Skaggs, *The Folk of Southern Fiction* (Athens: University of Georgia Press, 1972); and Sylvia Cook, *From Tobacco Road to Route 66: The Southern Poor White in Fiction* (Chapel Hill: University of North Carolina Press, 1976).

16. H. L. Mencken, "Sahara of the Bozart," *A Mencken Chrestomathy* (New York: Alfred A. Knopf, 1949), quoted in Thomas D. Clark, ed., *The South since Reconstruction* (New York: Bobbs-Merrill Co., 1973), p. 554.

17. William Alexander Percy, *Recollections of a Planter's Son* (1941; Baton Rouge: Louisiana State University Press, 1973), pp. 19–20.

18. Arthur Palmer Hudson, *Folksongs of Mississippi and Their Background* (Chapel Hill: University of North Carolina Press, 1936).

19. O. Campbell and Sharp, *English Folk Songs from the Southern Appalachians*, pp. viii, xxii. Sharp's comments about the public schools ignored the fact that the U.S. Bureau of Education had actually encouraged teachers to collect old songs from their students.

20. Settlement-school teachers generally tended to value only the rarest and most polite expressions of native-grown folk music (e.g., dulcimer playing or British balladry) or to encourage the acceptance of imported material. Folklorist D. K. Wilgus argued, in fact, that a "settlement-school tradition" of folk music had come into existence; see *Anglo-American Folksong Scholarship since 1898*

(New Brunswick, N.J.: Rutgers University Press, 1959), p. 169. For a withering and controversial study of the settlement-school teachers, see David Whisnant, *All That Is Native and Fine: The Politics of Culture in an American Region* (Chapel Hill: University of North Carolina Press, 1983).

21. Donald Knight Wilgus, "A Catalogue of American Folksongs on Commercial Records" (M.A. thesis, Ohio State University, 1947).

22. Arthur Smith, "Hillbilly Folk Music," *Etude* 51, no. 3 (Mar., 1933): 154, 208.

23. Lawrence Levine spoke similarly about the irrelevance of song origins in his discussion of African American spirituals. His arguments are appropriate for an understanding of the music of white folk: "We have only gradually come to recognize not merely the sheer complexity of the question of origins but also its irrelevancy for an understanding of consciousness. It is not necessary for a people to originate or invent all or even most of the elements of their culture. It is necessary only that these components become their own, embedded in their traditions, expressive of their world view and life style" (*Black Culture and Black Consciousness* [New York: Oxford University Press, 1977], p. 24). Norm Cohen's notes to the record collection *Minstrels and Tunesmiths: The Commercial Roots of Early Country Music* (JEMF recording 109) provide a good reminder of the late nineteenth-century pop origins of early country music, as does his essay, "The Folk and Popular Roots of Country Music," in *The Encyclopedia of Country Music,* pp. 188–92. For the Columbia 15000 series, see Charles Wolfe, "Columbia Records and Old-Time Music," *JEMF Quarterly* 14, no. 51 (Autumn, 1978): 118–25, 144.

24. Myth, of course, has played a powerful role in the making of the South, and white southerners have generally been happy with their myths. The illusion of a homogeneous and pure South is not likely to die any time soon.

25. Cash, *Mind of the South,* p. viii.

26. J. Wayne Flynt, *Dixie's Forgotten People: The South's Poor Whites* (Bloomington: Indiana University Press, 1979), p. xv; Grady McWhiney, *Cracker Culture: Celtic Ways in the Old South* (Tuscaloosa: University of Alabama Press, 1988), p. 120. The most trenchant criticism of McWhiney's thesis is Rowland Berthoff, "Celtic Mist over the South," *Journal of Southern History* 52, no. 4 (Nov., 1986): 523–46.

27. The best discussion of the origins of the southern Appalachian myth is Herbert D. Shapiro, *Appalachia on Our Mind: The Southern Mountains and Mountaineers in the American Consciousness, 1870–1920* (Chapel Hill: University of North Carolina Press, 1978). For an example of the romantic view of mountain music culture, see William Aspenwall Bradley, "Song-Ballets and Devil's Ditties," *Harper's Monthly Magazine* 130 (May, 1915): 905.

28. Carl Bridenbaugh declared that "the beginnings of American mobility are in Stuart England" (*Vexed and Troubled Englishmen, 1590–1642* [New York: Oxford University Press, 1968], p. 25); David Hackett Fischer argues that white

rural southerners were descended, in large part, from "borderlanders" of the British Isles (*Albion's Seed* [New York: Oxford University Press, 1989]); An excellent study that demonstrates the free-floating nature of folk music between regions and classes in Britain is A. L. Lloyd, *Folk Song in England* (New York: International Publishers, 1967).

29. One of the best discussions of the early interrelationship among blacks and whites is Mechal Sobel, *The World They Made Together: Black and White Values in Eighteenth-Century Virginia* (Princeton, N.J.: Princeton University Press, 1987). Excellent accounts that describe the Pennsylvania cultural seedbed are Samuel Bayard, *Hill Country Tunes: Instrumental Folk Music of Southwestern Pennsylvania*, Memoirs of the American Folklore Society, no. 39 (Philadelphia: American Folklore Society, 1944); and Don Yoder, *Pennsylvania Spirituals* (Lancaster: Pennsylvania Folklife Society, 1961).

30. Lawrence Levine reminds us that "culture is not a fixed condition but a process: the product of interaction between the past and present. Its toughness and resiliency are determined not by a culture's ability to withstand change, which indeed may be a sign of stagnation not life, but by its ability to react creatively and responsively to the realities of a new situation" (*Black Culture and Black Consciousness*, p. 5).

31. Richard Hofstadter's chapter on "the rural myth" is still the best discussion of the influence exerted by ruralism on American thinking; see *The Age of Reform* (New York: Alfred A. Knopf, 1956). Another relevant interpretation is Peter Schmitt, *Back to Nature: The Arcadian Myth in Urban America* (New York: Oxford University Press, 1969).

32. The social and economic transformation of the rural South in the late nineteenth and early twentieth centuries has evoked a splendid body of historical literature, including Steven Hahn, *The Roots of Southern Populism: Yeoman Farmers and the Transformation of the Georgia Upcountry, 1850–1890* (New York: Oxford University Press, 1983); Thomas D. Clark, *Pills, Petticoats, and Plows: The Southern Country Store* (Norman: University of Oklahoma Press, 1944); Edward L. Ayers, *The Promise of the New South: Life after Reconstruction* (New York: Oxford University Press, 1992); Ronald D. Eller, *Miners, Millhands, and Mountaineers: Industrialization of the Appalachian South, 1880–1930* (Knoxville: University of Tennessee Press, 1982); Crandall Shiflett, *Coal Town: Life, Work, and Culture in Company Towns of Southern Appalachia, 1880–1960* (Knoxville: University of Tennessee Press, 1991); Jacqueline Hall et al., *Like a Family: The Making of a Southern Cotton Mill World* (Chapel Hill: University of North Carolina Press, 1987); Pete Daniel, *Breaking the Land: The Transformation of Cotton, Tobacco, and Rice Cultures since 1880* (Urbana: University of Illinois Press, 1985); Jack Temple Kirby, *Rural Worlds Lost: The American South, 1920–1960* (Baton Rouge: Louisiana State University Press, 1987); and Ted Ownby, *Subduing Satan: Religion, Recreation, and Manhood in the Rural South, 1865–1920* (Chapel Hill: University of North Carolina Press, 1990).

33. The indispensable account of the post-Reconstruction South is C. Vann Woodward, *The Origins of the New South, 1877–1913* (Baton Rouge: Louisiana State University Press, 1951), but an excellent companion study is Ayers, *Promise of the New South.*

34. Ayers, *Promise of the New South,* p. 9; The best study of railroad songs is Norm Cohen's masterful *Long Steel Rail: The Railroad in American Folksong,* 2d ed. (Urbana: University of Illinois Press, 2000).

35. The cotton mill industry has inspired some of the best scholarship by southern historians. Edward Ayers's bibliography in *Promise of the New South* is a good place to find material on both cotton textile and coal-mining history. Some of the most important books have been listed in n. 32 of this chapter. The oil industry has not been nearly so well documented by historians, but useful books dealing with the social life of oil workers will be mentioned in nn. 23 through 25 of chap. 2.

36. The best collection of songs dealing with industrial labor in the South is Mike Seeger, *Tipple, Loom, and Rail* (Folkways Records FH 5273), notes by Archie Green.

37. The best accounts of southern populism, which was the most dramatic example of plain-folk response to the betrayal committed by New South propagandists, are Lawrence Goodwyn, *Democratic Promise: The Populist Moment in America* (New York: Oxford University Press, 1976); Robert C. McMath, Jr., *Populist Vanguard: A History of the Southern Farmers' Alliance* (Chapel Hill: University of North Carolina Press, 1975); and, of course, C. Vann Woodward's *Tom Watson: Agrarian Rebel* (New York: Macmillan, 1938) and *Origins of the New South.*

38. Andrew Nelson Lytle, in Twelve Southerners, *I'll Take My Stand: The South and the Agrarian Tradition* (1930; New York: Harper and Brothers, 1962), p. 244.

39. Thomas D. Clark's discussion of frontier fiddling is in *The Rampaging Frontier: Manners and Humors of Pioneer Days in the South and Middle West* (Bloomington: Indiana University Press, 1939). His dismissal of hillbilly musicians is in *The Kentucky* (New York: Rinehart & Company, 1942), p. 128.

40. Howard Odum, *An American Epoch: Southern Portraiture in the National Picture* (New York: Henry Holt, 1930), pp. 201–18.

41. "Day job" seems to be a fairly recent term that would-be country musicians use to describe the work that supports their musical avocation or that keeps them from pursuing a full-time career in music. In earlier days, the term "public work" was most often used by rural southerners to indicate wage jobs that supplemented their farm income or took them away from farming. See Jacqueline Hall et al., *Like a Family,* for attitudes about public work among Piedmont textile workers.

42. The best discussion of Rodgers's remarkable influence among working-class southerners is Nolan Porterfield, *Jimmie Rodgers: The Life and Times of America's Blue Yodeler* (Urbana: University of Illinois Press, 1979).

43. For a discussion of "middle-class attitudes" among early country musicians, see Malone, *Singing Cowboys and Musical Mountaineers*. Norm Cohen's edited and annotated collection of popular recordings made at the turn of the century, *Minstrels and Tunesmiths*, suggests by inference that these musicians were well-known to early hillbilly entertainers.

44. See George B. Tindall, "The Benighted South: Origins of a Modern Image," *Virginia Quarterly Review* 40 (Spring, 1964): 281–94.

45. Frank Tannenbaum catalogued a compendium of southern iniquity in *Darker Phases of the South* (London: Putnam's, 1924). Mencken, "Sahara of the Bozart," quoted in T. Clark, *South since Reconstruction*, pp. 547–56.

46. The famous and influential Australian collector of American country music, John Edwards, is discussed by Archie Green in *Encyclopedia of Country Music*, p. 162. Lewis Atherton talks about the popularity of the National Barn Dance in *Main Street on the Middle Border* (Bloomington: Indiana University Press, 1954). James F. Evans provides additional insight about the show in *Prairie Farmer and WLS: The Burridge Butler Years* (Urbana: University of Illinois Press, 1969). See also Wade Hall, *Hell-Bent for Music: The Life of Pee Wee King* (Lexington: University Press of Kentucky, 1996), which discusses a Polish boy from Milwaukee who became a country music star. Midwestern country music deserves a serious study. The Madison, Wisconsin, folklorists Jim Leary and Rick March have done most to document its existence, while also collecting an abundance of material on polka-related styles and other northern "ethnic" musical forms. Their radio show, "Downhome Dairyland," has been broadcast for many years in Wisconsin. For an example of their scholarship, see Leary and March, "Farm, Forest, and Factory: Songs of Midwestern Labor," in *Songs about Work: Essays in Occupational Labor for Richard A. Reuss*, ed. Archie Green (Bloomington: Folklore Institute, Indiana University, 1993), pp. 253–87.

47. In his spoken preface to his recording of "The New Ford Car" (Vocalion 5261), Uncle Dave Macon says that he had sent a copy of "On the Dixie Bee Line" (BR-112-B)—his earlier song about Ford's Model-T—to the industrialist and had received a favorable reply. The two recordings have been anthologized, respectively, in *Uncle Dave Macon, Vol. 2* and *Uncle Dave Macon, Vol. 1*, Vetco LPs 104 and 105. A discussion of folk attitudes toward Ford is found in Reynold M. Wik, *Henry Ford and Grass-roots America* (Ann Arbor: University of Michigan Press, 1972). Roderick Nash stresses Ford's ambivalence about modern society and the ways in which it mirrored public thinking among Americans in *The Nervous Generation: American Thought, 1917–1930* (Chicago: Elephant Paperbacks, 1990). Although it exhibited great appeal among many Americans during the Jazz Age, and does much to document the "nervousness" that Nash talks about, commercial hillbilly music is never discussed or even mentioned in his or other books about the 1920s.

48. "Don't Get above Your Raisin'" was written by Lester Flatt and was first recorded in 1951 by the bluegrass team of Lester Flatt and Earl Scruggs (Colum-

bia 20854). The song also played an important role in the commercial ascent of the modern neotraditionalist Ricky Skaggs, who recorded it in 1981 as "Don't Get above Your Raising" (Epic 02034).

Chapter 2: *"I'm a Small-Time Laboring Man"*

1. Alabama, "Forty Hour Week (for a Livin')" (RCA 14085). The song has also been anthologized on a useful CD collection called *Working Man's Blues* (Hip-O-40046).

2. Stephen A. Smith and Jimmie N. Rogers assert that "even the casual observer knows that the working poor are the predominant dramatis personae in the rhetorical vision of country" ("Saturday Night in Country Music: The Gospel According to Juke," *Southern Cultures* 1, no. 2 [Winter, 1995]: 229).

3. Cecil Sharp, *English Folk-Song: Some Conclusions* (London: Simpkin and Company, 1907), p. 97.

4. I. A. Newby, *Plain Folk in the New South: Social Change and Cultural Persistence, 1880–1915* (Baton Rouge: Louisiana State University Press, 1989), p. 7.

5. Archie Green wrote the first discussion of the use of the hillbilly metaphor in country music, in "Hillbilly Music: Source and Symbol." Anthony Harkins has written more recently on the topic; see "The Significance of 'Hillbilly' in Early Country Music," *Journal of Appalachian Studies* 2, no. 2 (1998): 311–22. Albert Kirwan grounds the term "redneck" in the economic realities of the late nineteenth century in *Revolt of the Rednecks: Mississippi Politics, 1876–1925* (Lexington: University Press of Kentucky, 1951), while David Hackett Fischer argues that the word had a pejorative usage in northern Britain, as a description of dissenting Protestants, at least as early as 1830 (*Albion's Seed*).

6. The historical literature concerning the transformation of agriculture in the post-Reconstruction South is vast, but good places to start are Hahn, *Roots of Southern Populism*, and T. Clark, *Pills, Petticoats and Plows*.

7. "Down on Penny's Farm," originally recorded in 1929 by the Bentley Boys (Columbia 15565-D), is also anthologized in the *Anthology of American Folk Music*, Folkways FA 2951 (rereleased on CD by the Smithsonian Institution).

8. Huddie "Leadbelly" Ledbetter's version of "The Boll Weevil Song" was first recorded in Shreveport in 1934 for the Library of Congress. See Charles Wolfe and Kip Lornell, *The Life and Legend of Leadbelly* (New York: HarperCollins, 1992). Tex Ritter's version can be heard on Capitol Collectors Series (CDP 7950362). One consequence of the insect's invasion of the South is discussed by Robert Higgs, "The Boll Weevil, the Cotton Economy, and Black Migration, 1910–1930," *Agricultural History* 50 (Apr., 1976): 335–50.

9. The human and economic consequences of these transformations are ably evaluated by James Cobb, *Industrialization and Southern Society, 1877–1984* (Lexington: University Press of Kentucky, 1984); Margaret Jarman Hagood,

Mothers of the South: Portraiture of the White Tenant Farm Woman (Chapel Hill: University of North Carolina Press, 1939); Jack Temple Kirby, "The Southern Exodus, 1910–1960: A Primer for Historians," *Journal of Southern History* 49, no. 4 (Nov., 1983): 585–600; and Nicholas Lemann, *The Promised Land: The Great Black Migration and How It Changed America* (New York: Alfred A. Knopf, 1991).

10. Edward L. Ayers presents a masterful survey of the South's integration into the national economy during the late nineteenth century in *Promise of the New South*. Other fine studies of southern industrialization and economic change are listed in n. 32 of chap. 1.

11. Rodgers of course was the famous ex-brakeman who recorded for RCA Victor, while Harvey was a former engineer and guitar player in Charlie Poole's North Carolina Ramblers.

12. Useful books that comment on the lore of water transportation include Michael Allen, *Western Rivermen, 1763–1861: Ohio and Mississippi Boatmen and the Myth of the Alligator Horse* (Baton Rouge: Louisiana State University Press, 1990); Leland D. Baldwin, *The Keelboat Age on Western Waters* (Pittsburgh: University of Pittsburgh Press, 1941); Byrd Douglas, *Steamboatin' on the Cumberland* (Nashville: Tennessee Book Co., 1961); William Lynwood Montell, *Don't Go up Kettle Creek: Verbal Legacy of the Upper Cumberland* (Knoxville: University of Tennessee Press, 1983); Louis Hunter, *Steamboats on the Western Rivers: An Economic and Technological History* (Cambridge: Harvard University Press, 1949); Phillip Graham, *Show Boats: The History of an American Institution* (Austin: University of Texas Press, 1951); and, of course, Mark Twain, *Life on the Mississippi*.

13. All of these railroad heroes, and the musical lore that they inspired, are discussed by Norm Cohen in *Long Steel Rail*. Another useful compilation is Katie Letcher Lyle, *Scalded to Death by the Steam* (Chapel Hill, N.C.: Algonquin Books, 1983).

14. Country musicians have had an enduring affection for the John Henry saga and, from Uncle Dave Macon to Merle Travis, Bill Monroe, and Johnny Cash, have performed variants of the song in a wide array of styles. See Norm Cohen's exhaustive listing of John Henry material in *Long Steel Rail,* pp. 61–89.

15. Famous vocal approximations of train whistles include Jimmie Rodgers in "Waiting for a Train" (Victor V-40014) and Roy Acuff in "Wabash Cannon Ball" (Vocalion/Okeh 04466). One of the most popular of all fiddle tunes, "Orange Blossom Special," owes much of its appeal to its simulation of a surging locomotive. Written by Irvin Rouse and Chubby Wise as a tribute to a train with the same name on the Seaboard Air Line, the tune has entered every fiddler's repertoire. Early and influential recordings include those made by the Rouse Brothers (RCA BS-037358) and Bill Monroe and the Blue Grass Boys (heard on the CD *Muleskinner Blues*, RCA 2494-2-R). DeFord Bailey's version of "Pan American Blues" was recorded on Brunswick 146 and Vocalion 5180, and has been anthol-

ogized on the LP *Nashville: Early String Bands, Vol.* 2 (County 542). George D. Hay was responsible for the story about Bailey's performance on the original Grand Ole Opry show; see *A Story of the Grand Ole Opry* (Nashville: copyright by George D. Hay, 1953), p. 10. Charles Wolfe says that "newspaper documentation cannot verify Hay's version of the story," but that "it does not seriously challenge it" (*A Good-Natured Riot: The Birth of the Grand Ole Opry* [Nashville: Country Music Foundation Press and Vanderbilt University Press, 1999], p. 22).

16. As noted in the previous chapter, Edward Ayers in *Promise of the New South* provides the best account of railroad influence in the late nineteenth century, and Norm Cohen has the best discussion of railroad songs. The railroad as religious metaphor in American literature extends at least as far back as Nathaniel Hawthorne's "The Celestial Railroad." "Life's Railway to Heaven" appears to have been a reworking of Will S. Hays's poem of 1886, "The Faithful Engineer." See his *Songs and Poems* (Louisville: Courier-Journal, 1886). The first country recording of the song was apparently Ernest Thompson, "Life's Railway to Heaven" (Columbia 158–D).

17. Jacqueline Hall et al., *Like a Family*, p. 43.

18. Kinney Rorrer, notes to the record album, *Cotton Mills and Fiddles* (Flyin' Cloud FC-014). This album has an excellent selection of songs recorded by Poole, Red Patterson's Piedmont Log Rollers, Kelly Harrell, Kid Smith and Family, and other Piedmont village bands.

19. Gregory Waller's study of silent and sound films in Lexington, Kentucky, is a model for investigations that should be made for other southern towns in the early twentieth century; see *Main Street Amusements: Movies and Commercial Entertainment in a Southern City, 1896–1930* (Washington, D.C.: Smithsonian Institution Press, 1995). The music of Dock Boggs and Frank Hutchison, hillbilly entertainers who were influenced by local black musicians, has been well documented. Both musicians were introduced to folk revival audiences by the *Anthology of American Folk Music*. Boggs was subsequently given further exposure through the tireless promotion of Mike Seeger: *Dock Boggs: Legendary Singer and Banjo Player* (Folkways FA 2351); and *Excerpts from Interviews with Dock Boggs* (Folkways FH 5458). He has also been the object of a CD reissue (with notes by Jon Pankake), *Dock Boggs, Country Blues: Complete Early Recordings, 1927–1929* (Revenant CD 205). Hutchison is anthologized in *The Train That Carried My Girl from Town* (Rounder 1007).

20. Archie Green is the preeminent student of American laborlore and music. His published works include "A Discography of American Coal Miners' Songs," *Labor History* 2, no. 1 (Winter, 1961): 101–15; "The Carter Family's Coal Miner's Blues," *Southern Folklore Quarterly* 25, no. 4 (Dec., 1961): 226–37; *Only a Miner: Studies in Recorded Coal-Mining Songs* (Urbana: University of Illinois Press, 1972); *Wobblies, Pile Butts, and Other Heroes: Laborlore Explorations* (Urbana: University of Illinois Press, 1993); and *Calf's Head and Union Tale:*

Labor Yarns at Work and Play (Urbana: University of Illinois Press, 1996). It was largely through Green's urgings that Mike Seeger recorded his important LP of labor-oriented songs, *Tipple, Loom, and Rail: Songs of the Industrialization of the South* (Folkways Records FH 5273).

21. John Greenway, though, argues that more songs came out of mining; see *American Folk Songs of Protest* (Philadelphia: University of Pennsylvania Press, 1953), pp. 147–48.

22. Alton C. Morris speaks of songs that emerged from the experiences of turpentine workers and lumbermen in *Folksongs of Florida* (Gainesville: University Press of Florida, 1950), pp. 10–11. Archie Green provided me an unpublished list, "Oilfield Songs on Records," that includes items spanning the period from 1934 to 1982.

23. John O. King, "The Early Texas Oil Industry: Pipelines and the Birth of an Integrated Oil Industry, 1901–1911," *Journal of Southern History* 32, no. 4 (Nov., 1966): 516–29.

24. Roger M. Olien and Diana Davids Olien, *Life in the Oil Fields* (Austin: Texas Monthly Press, 1986), pp. 4–5.

25. Esther Briscoe Stowe, *Oil Field Child* (Fort Worth: Texas Christian University Press, 1989), p. 138; Roger M. Olien and Diana Davids Olien, *Oil Booms: Social Change in Five Texas Towns* (Lincoln: University of Nebraska Press, 1982), pp. 129, 148, 154.

26. The Pruitt quote comes from a picture-songbook, *Bill Pruitt: The Oklahoma Yodeler* (privately printed, early 1930s), located in the Southern Folk Life Collection, University of North Carolina, Chapel Hill. The Sloan and Threadgill reference comes from *Radio Digest* 26, no. 1 (Nov., 1930): 79. Interview with Frank Threadgill, Austin, Tex., July 7, 1976. He was an older brother of Kenneth Threadgill, who became known in the 1970s as "the father of Austin country music."

27. The New Orleans reporter is quoted in James A. Clark and Michel T. Halbouty, *The Last Boom* (New York: Random House, 1972), p. 129. I have provided a fuller discussion of honky-tonk music's origins in the East Texas oil fields in chap. 5 of *Country Music, USA*. Additional material is provided in the frolic chapter of this book.

28. Charles Wolfe, *In Close Harmony: The Story of the Louvin Brothers* (Jackson: University Press of Mississippi, 1996), pp. 22–23.

29. Fiddlin' John recorded "The Honest Farmer" in 1934 (Okeh 40411). It can also be heard on Rounder 1003.

30. One of the classic commercial recordings of "The House Carpenter" is Clarence Ashley's version, originally recorded in 1930 (Columbia 15654-D), and included also in the *Anthology of American Folk Music*.

31. The Bentley Boys' "Down on Penny's Farm" and the Carolina Tarheels' "Got the Farmland Blues" are included in the *Anthology of American Folk Music*. "Eleven Cent Cotton" was recorded by its composer, Bob Miller, under the name

of Bob Ferguson (Columbia 15297-D), and by Vernon Dalhart (Victor V-40050), and on an anthology of Dalhart's recordings, *On the Lighter Side,* vol. 2 (Old Homestead OHCS-5166). "Stay in the Wagon Yard" (also called "Wish I Had Stayed in the Wagon Yard") was often performed, as in the case of Peg Moreland's Victor V-40008 version, but Lowe Stokes's rendition (Columbia 15557-D) has been the most accessible through its inclusion in an LP, *Mountain Songs* (County 504).

32. The cotton mill songs are part of the recorded collections *Poor Man, Rich Man: American Country Songs of Protest* (Rounder 1026), *Singers of the Piedmont* (Folk Variety FV 12 505), and Dorsey Dixon, *Babies in the Mill* (Testament T-3301). Doug DeNatale's and Glenn Hinson's essay, "The Southern Textile Song Tradition Reconsidered," in Archie Green's collection, *Songs about Work,* pp. 77–107, is the best available discussion of the subject, but Archie Green's "Born on Picketlines, Textile Workers' Songs Are Woven into History," still merits attention (*Textile Labor* 21, no. 4 [Apr., 1961]: 3–5).

33. The southern labor conflicts of the 1930s have been well described in Hevener, *Which Side Are You On?;* John Liston Pope, *Millhands and Preachers: A Study of Gastonia* (New Haven: Yale University Press, 1942), and Jacqueline Hall et al., *Like a Family.*

34. George B. Tindall explores the relationship between government policy and tenant evictions in *The Emergence of the New South, 1913–1945* (Baton Rouge: Louisiana State University Press, 1967). See also Kirby, "Southern Exodus"; and Pete Daniel, "Going among Strangers: Southern Reactions to World War II," *Journal of American History* 77, no. 3 (Dec., 1990): 886–911. Daniel notes that 3.2 million people left southern rural areas during the war to seek new opportunities: "By 1960, only 7 million people were left on the land, a statistical indication of the human displacement in the transition from sharecropping to seasonal wage labor, from hand labor to mechanization, and from farm to city" (p. 886).

35. Pete Daniel has done the best job of explaining the consequences of the collapse of the southern rural/agricultural way of life, and their effects on American music, in "Rhythm of the Land," *Agricultural History* 68, no. 4 (Fall, 1994): 1–22. David R. Goldfield is similarly provocative in "Why Southern Urbanization Hasn't Worked That Way," *American Historical Review* 86 (Dec., 1981): 1009–34. As noted previously, James Gregory provides an acute discussion of the transplantation of Okie culture in California in *American Exodus.* Harriet Arnow's *The Dollmaker* is a classic fictional account of a Kentucky family's migration to wartime Detroit. Although its time period is World War II, it provides suggestive descriptions of the varying reactions to urban life made by children and adults.

36. Martin Sosna, "More Important Than the Civil War? The Impact of World War II on the South," in *Perspectives on the American South: An Annual Review of Society, Politics, and Culture,* ed. James C. Cobb and Charles R. Wilson (New York: Gordon and Breach, 1981–87). Numan V. Bartley, *The New South, 1945–*

1980: The Story of the South's Modernization (Baton Rouge: Louisiana State University Press, 1995); Bill C. Malone, "The Rural South Moves to the City: Country Music since World War II," in *The Rural South Since World War II*, ed. R. Douglas Hurt (Baton Rouge: Louisiana State University Press, 1998), pp. 95–122.

37. Gregory, *American Exodus*, pp. 222–49.

38. For a fuller discussion of the war years, see chap. 6 of *Country Music, USA*. Richard S. Sears provides insight about the way in which country music exposure broadened during those years in *V-Discs: A History and Discography* (Westport, Conn.: Greenwood Press, 1980). The best account of a country musician who made music as a soldier is that of Louis Marshall "Grandpa" Jones, with the assistance of Charles Wolfe, "The Munich Mountaineers," *Everybody's Grandpa: Fifty Years behind the Mike* (Knoxville: University of Tennessee Press, 1984), pp. 84–95.

39. Bert "Foreman" Phillips is discussed throughout Gerald W. Haslam's *Workin' Man Blues: Country Music in California* (Berkeley: University of California Press, 1999), but his role as promoter is described on pp. 87–89. Good discussions of coin-operated music machines are Vincent Lynch and Bill Henkin, *Jukebox: The Golden Age* (Berkeley: Lancaster-Miller, 1981); Christopher Pearce, *Vintage Jukeboxes* (Secaucus, N.J.: Chartwell Books, 1988); Lewis Nichols, "The Ubiquitous Juke Box," *New York Times Magazine*, Oct. 5, 1941; and John Morthland, "Jukebox Fever," *Country Music* 6 (May, 1978): 35–36.

40. The relevant *Billboard* sources are July 24, 1943, 68; and Sept. 11, 1943, 63. The York Brothers (Leslie and George) were Kentucky-born singers who lived and worked in Michigan during the war. They broadcast on WJLB in Detroit four times a week.

41. A fine case study of a Virginia mountain family who moved to Washington, D.C., and whose members made country music over a period of seventy years is Ivan Tribe, *The Stonemans: An Appalachian Family and the Music That Shaped Their Lives* (Urbana: University of Illinois Press, 1993). The inauguration of "The Prince Albert Show," the NBC Saturday night segment of the Grand Ole Opry, is described by C. Wolfe in *Good-Natured Riot*, pp. 261–65. Harry S. Rice has written a very good account of the founding of the Renfro Valley show—"Renfro Valley on the Radio, 1937–1941," *Journal of Country Music* 19, no. 2 (1997): 16–25.

42. George Lipsitz's *Rainbow at Midnight: Labor and Culture in the 1940s* (1981; Urbana: University of Illinois Press, 1994), presents a finely nuanced analysis of the ambivalence felt by men and women after the war.

43. Hank Snow, "These Hands" (RCA 6379); George Jones, "Small-Time Laboring Man" (Musicor 1297).

44. Bill Carter, "By the Sweat of My Brow" (Republic 7126-F) and Smokey Stover, "The Ballad of Jimmy Hoffa" (Ol' Podner OP-104) have been anthologized in a two-volume compilation of recordings gathered by Archie Green, *Work's Many Voices* (JEMF 110 and 111).

45. Frankie Miller, "Blackland Farmer" (Starday 424), is also anthologized in a CD called *50 Years of Country Music*, vol. 1 (Starday SD-6301-2). See Kevin Coffey, "Frankie Miller: Texas Honky Tonker of the 50's and 60's," *Journal of Old Time Country Music* 28 (Aug., 1995): 17.

46. *Folk Songs from the Hills*, Capitol AD 50. The songs are also included in the immense Bear Family collection of Merle Travis material, *Guitar Rags and a Too Fast Past* (BCD 15637 E1), edited and annotated by Rich Kienzle.

47. Archie Green, *Only a Miner*, pp. 279–329; Rich Kienzle, notes to the Merle Travis Bear Family CD collection. Ford's version of "Sixteen Tons" was recorded on Capitol 3262. At the Kerrville (Texas) Country Music Festival in July, 1978, Travis prefaced his performance of "Sixteen Tons" with the statement that he had not cared much for the song until Tennessee Ernie recorded his best-selling version. "Now I just love it to death."

48. "Six Days on the Road" (Golden Wing 3020).

49. The best discussion of Harlan Howard is in Nicholas Dawidoff, *In the Country of Country: People and Places in American Music* (New York: Pantheon Books, 1997), pp. 23–37. "Watermelon Time in Georgia" can be heard on Lefty Frizzell's *Twenty Golden Hits* (CBS P 15595), while "Detroit City" was recorded by Bobby Bare (RCA 8183). Arthur Alexander's performance can be heard on the collection produced by the Country Music Foundation, *From Where I Stand: The Black Experience in Country Music* (Warner Brothers 9 46428-2). Dolly Parton's "In the Good Old Days (When Times Were Bad)" is on RCA 9657.

50. Merle Haggard, "Okie from Muskogee" (Capitol 2626); Dave Dudley, "What We're Fighting For" (Mercury 72500); Haggard, "Mama's Hungry Eyes" (Capitol 2383). "They're Tearing the Labor Camps Down" is in *Let Me Tell You about a Song* (Capitol ST-882). Haggard's Capitol releases can be heard in the box set *Down Every Road, 1962–1994* (Capitol Cap 7 2438 35711 2). Alice Gerrard Foster wrote a discerning and sympathetic article on Haggard, "Merle Haggard: I Take a Lot of Pride in What I Am," *Sing Out!* 19, no. 5 (Mar./Apr. 1970): 11–17.

51. In an article called "Redneck!" Larry L. King had accepted the distasteful stereotyping associated with the term, and had claimed to have come from such an origin; (*Texas Monthly* 2, no. 8 [Aug., 1974]: 50–64). "Good Old Boy" was a term that had been around for a long time, but it was given wider circulation by Tom Wolfe in his essay on the North Carolina stock-car racer and former bootlegger Junior Johnson, in *The Kandy-Kolored Tangerine-Flake Streamline Baby* (New York: Farrar, Straus & Giroux, 1965).

52. Tom T. Hall's best work is found in the LPs *In Search of a Song* (Mercury SR 61350) and *Tom T. Hall's Greatest Hits* (Mercury 824 143-2). Additional material, taken from four other early Hall LPs, has been released on two double-album CDs (Bear Family BCD 15658 and BCD 15631). Insights concerning Hall's inspiration as a songwriter are found in his book, *The Storyteller's Nashville* (New York: Doubleday, 1979). James Talley's best work also appears on a

Bear Family CD, *Got No Bread/Tryin' like the Devil,* a compilation of material taken from his Capitol albums of 1975 and 1976.

53. Tom T. Hall in *Country Weekly* 3, no. 16 (Apr. 16, 1996): 12–13.

54. Curtis W. Ellison, in *Country Music Culture: From Hard Times to Heaven* (Jackson: University Press of Mississippi, 1995), speaks of "shifting cultural attitudes . . . that opened public taste to the themes of hard times, broken hearts, domestic turmoil and salvation" (p. 230).

55. Loretta Lynn, "Coal Miner's Daughter" (Decca 32749); Hazel Dickens, "Mama's Hand" in *A Few Old Memories* (Rounder CD-11529); Dolly Parton, "Coat of Many Colors" (RCA 0538); Rusty and Doug Kershaw, "Louisiana Man" (Hickory 1113); Tish Hinojosa, "West Side of Town," in *Homeland* (A & M CD 5263).

56. Jim and Jesse, "Cotton Mill Man," in *The Jim and Jesse Show* (Prize Records PRS 498-04); Hazel Dickens, "Working Girl Blues," in *A Few Old Memories* (Rounder CD-11529); Travis Tritt, "Lord Have Mercy on the Working Man" (Warner Brothers 18779); Johnny Paycheck, "Take This Job and Shove It" (Epic 50469); Johnny Cash, "Oney" (Columbia 45660).

57. Merle Haggard, "Big City" (Epic 02686); Aaron Tippin, "Working Man's Ph.D." (RCA 62520); Merle Haggard, "Working Man Blues" (Capitol 2503); George Jones, "Small-Time Laboring Man," in *Burn the Honky Tonk Down* (Rounder Special Series 15); Alan Jackson, "Working Class Hero," in *Don't Rock the Jukebox* (Arista ARCD 8681).

58. Hazel Dickens made the best recording of "Aragon Mill," in *Hard-Hitting Songs For Hard-Hit People* (Rounder 0126). Emmylou Harris sang a nice version of "Green Rolling Hills of West Virginia," in *Quarter Moon in a Ten Cent Town* (Warner Brothers BSK 3141), and Billy Edd Wheeler wrote and performed one of the best modern songs about industrial unemployment, "Coal Tattoo," heard in *Wild Mountain Flowers* (Flying Fish FF 085). Tom Russell wrote and recorded "Steel Town." My favorite version of Jean Ritchie's "The L & N Don't Stop Here Anymore" is the New Coon Creek Girls, in a CD with the same title (Pinecastle PRC 1027). The David Lee Murphy quote is from Geoffrey Himes, "David Lee Murphy: Genuine Redneck Stuff," *Country Music* no. 183 (Jan.–Feb., 1997): 44.

59. Heard on the "Ralph Emery Show," the Nashville Network, Sept. 2, 1998.

60. Merle Haggard, "A Working Man Can't Get Nowhere Today" (Capitol 4477); Haggard, "The Way I Am" (MCA 41200); Haggard, "Big City" (Epic 02686).

61. Aaron Tippin, "You've Got to Stand for Something" (RCA 2664). Other Tippin recordings relevant to this essay can be found in *Call of the Wild* (RCA CD 66251-2) and *Tool Box* (RCA CD BG 266740).

62. Tom T. Hall, "Homecoming" (Mercury 72951). Other examples of songs that comment on the experiences of barn-storming musicians include Bill Monroe, "Heavy Traffic Ahead" (in the Columbia box set, *The Essential Bill Mon-*

roe and His Blue Grass Boys, 1945–1949, two discs, Columbia C2K 52478) and Willie Nelson, "On the Road Again" (heard in Nelson's movie, *Honeysuckle Rose,* and on Columbia 11351).

63. Lacy J. Dalton, "Sixteenth Avenue" (Columbia 03184).

Chapter 3: "I Was Dreaming of a Little Cabin"

1. Hazel Dickens, "Mama's Hand," in *A Few Old Memories* (Rounder CD-11529); Lynn Morris (Rounder 0328).

2. Iris DeMent, "Mama's Opry," in *Infamous Angel* (Philo CD Ph 1138); Tish Hinojosa, "West Side of Town," in *Homeland* (A & M CD 5263).

3. Will Hays published the song as "Little Log Cabin in the Lane" in 1871. Fiddlin' John's recording of June 19, 1923 (Okeh 4890), has been reissued on Rounder 1003.

4. Edward Ayers concentrates on emerging southern town life in two chapters, "In Town" and "Dry Goods," of *Promise of the New South* (pp. 55–103).

5. Emma Bell Miles, *Spirit of the Mountains* (1905; Knoxville: University of Tennessee Press, 1975), pp. 66–70.

6. See chap. 2 in Malone, *Singing Cowboys and Musical Mountaineers.*

7. E. Douglas Branch has argued that "nature-sampling is the common self-indulgence of the first generation of an urban middle class. It eases the transition, by glorifying the farm as it recedes down the path of experience" (*The Sentimental Years, 1830–1860* [New York: Appleton-Century, 1934], p. 146). Jan Marsh, *Back to the Land: The Pastoral Impulse in England from 1880 to 1914* (London: Quartet Books, 1982), describes a comparable phenomenon in that country.

8. S. J. Adair Fitzgerald describes the genesis of "Home Sweet Home" in *Stories of Famous Songs* (Philadelphia: J. B. Lippincott Co., 1901), pp. 19–30. The song was recorded frequently in early country music, first in 1927 by Frank Jenkins (Gennett 6165). "Home Sweet Home" eventually became best known as a bluegrass banjo instrumental piece. Ken Emerson discusses the Rainer Family's contributions in *Doo-Dah! Stephen Foster and the Rise of American Popular Culture* (New York: Simon and Schuster, 1997), pp. 75–76, 88, 93. He also provides trenchant commentary on Thomas Moore (pp. 45–47). For further discussion of nineteenth-century popular music and the Genteel Tradition, see Nicholas E. Tawa, *The Way to Tin Pan Alley: American Popular Song, 1866–1910* (New York: Schirmer Books, 1990); Gilbert Chase, *America's Music: From the Pilgrims to the Present,* rev. 3d ed. (Urbana: University of Illinois Press, 1987), esp. chap. 9; Charles Hamm, *Yesterdays: Popular Song in America* (New York: W. W. Norton and Co., 1979); and Michael R. Turman, ed., *The Parlour Song Book: A Casquet of Vocal Gems* (New York: Viking Press, 1972). See also John Lair, *Songs That Lincoln Loved* (New York: Duell, Sloan & Pearce, 1954).

9. Nicholas E. Tawa, *A Music for the Millions: Antebellum Democratic Atti-*

tudes and the Birth of American Popular Music (New York: Pendragon Press, 1984), pp. 66–67; Hans Nathan, *Dan Emmett and the Rise of Early Negro Minstrelsy* (Norman: University of Oklahoma Press, 1962); Emerson, *Doo-Dah!;* William W. Austin, *"Susanna," "Jeanie," and "The Old Folks at Home": The Songs of Stephen C. Foster from His Time to Ours,* 2d ed. (Urbana: University of Illinois Press, 1988).

10. Songsters have been deposited in many libraries, but most useful to me were those found in the Harris Collection, Hay Library, Brown University, Providence, R.I. Bill C. Malone, "William S. Hays: The Bard of Kentucky," *Register of the Kentucky Historical Society* 93, no. 3 (Summer, 1995): 286–306; Malone, *Singing Cowboys and Musical Mountaineers,* pp. 60–67.

11. Bargainneer, "Tin Pan Alley and Dixie."

12. *Minstrels and Tunesmiths,* edited by Norm Cohen, includes a recording made in 1915 of "Listen to the Mocking Bird," complete with whistling by Billy Golden and singing and banjo playing by James Marlowe. Some of the most influential fiddle recordings of the tune—featuring bird imitations—are by Arthur Smith (Bluebird B-5843)and Curly Fox (Decca 5213).

13. "Where Is My Wandering Boy Tonight?" was written by the Reverend Robert Lowry and recorded, in its most affecting version, by Vernon Dalhart (Columbia 15072-D). This version can also be heard on an album, *Vernon Dalhart, Vol. III* (Old Homestead OHCS-167). The song's use in the popular turn-of-the-century melodrama, *The Old Homestead,* is described by David Ewen, *The Life and Death of Tin Pan Alley* (New York: Funk & Wagnall, 1964), pp. 74–75.

14. Jack Larkin, *The Reshaping of Everyday Life, 1790–1840* (New York: Harper and Row, 1988), p. 70.

15. Bill Ellis, "The Sentimental Mother Song in American Country Music, 1923–45" (Ph.D. diss., Ohio State University, 1978), p. 41.

16. David Hoeveler, letter to me, May 15, 1997.

17. The story of "Tell Mother I'll Be There" is in J. H. Hall, *Biography of Gospel Song and Hymn Writers* (1914; reprint, New York: AMS Press, 1971), p. 287. Roy Acuff made one of the best recordings of the song (Columbia 37006).

18. "If I Could Hear My Mother Pray Again" was written by James Rowe and J. W. Vaughan. It was first recorded in 1926 by Jake Pickell (Columbia 15117-D) but won its greatest circulation through recordings by the Andrew Jenkins Family (Okeh 40214) and Vernon Dalhart (Edison 51883). "I Heard My Mother Call My Name in Prayer" was written by Eugene M. Bartlett and has since been recorded many times (e.g., Mac and Bob, Okeh 05488).

19. Wik, *Henry Ford and Grass-roots America;* Nash, *Nervous Generation.*

20. Malone, *Country Music, USA,* pp. 33–34; C. Wolfe, *Good-Natured Riot.*

21. See Colin Escott, with George Merritt and William MacEwen, *Hank Williams: The Biography* (Boston: Little, Brown, 1994), for details about Williams's dismissal from the Opry (pp. 208–13). Skeeter Davis describes her dismissal in

Bus Fare to Kentucky: The Autobiography of Skeeter Davis (Secaucus, N.J.: Carol Publishing Group, 1993), pp. 261–66.

22. Information on Andrew Jenkins has been garnered from Wayne Daniel, *Pickin' on Peachtree*, pp. 60, 84, 191, 233; D. K. Wilgus, in *A Good Tale and a Bonnie Tune*, ed. Mody C. Boatright (Dallas: Southern Methodist University Press, 1964), pp. 227–37; and Charles Wolfe, "Frank Smith, Andrew Jenkins, and Early Commercial Gospel Music," *American Music* 1, no. 1 (Spring, 1983): 49–59. Archie Green comments further on Jenkins's early recordings in "Hear These Beautiful Sacred Selections," JEMF Reprint no. 26 (originally published in the *1970 Yearbook of the International Folk Music Council*), pp. 52–70.

23. Bear Family has reissued the complete Carter Family collection: *In the Shadow of Clinch Mountain* (BCD 15865). "Little Poplar Log House" (Okeh 06078); "Mid the Green Fields of Virginia" (Victor 23686); "Fifty Miles of Elbow Room" (Bluebird B-9026).

24. Bill C. Malone, "Appalachian Music and American Popular Culture: The Romance That Will Not Die," in *Appalachia Inside Out: A Sequel to Voices from the Hills,* ed. Robert J. Higgs, Ambrose N. Manning, and Jim Wayne Miller (Knoxville: University of Tennessee Press, 1995), vol. 2, pp. 462–70.

25. Loyal Jones, *Radio's "Kentucky Mountain Boy": Bradley Kincaid*, rev. ed. (1980; Berea, Ky.: Berea College Appalachian Center, 1988).

26. Kincaid's "Anglo-Saxon" quote came from his first songbook but is described on p. 4 of Loyal Jones's biography (ibid.).

27. From Archie Green's introduction to Loyal Jones's *Radio's "Kentucky Mountain Boy,* p. 4.

28. Interview with Floy Case, Fort Worth, Tex., Nov. 26, 1984.

29. Interview with Cecil Gill, Arlington, Tex., Aug. 7, 1977. Gill's music was recorded on two LPs, *The Yodeling Country Boy,* nos. 1 and 2 (Bluebonnet 113 and 114).

30. *Old Fashioned Hymns and Mountain Ballads,* 1933 ed. (Louisville, Ky.: Asher Sizemore), p. 2.

31. "Little Bessie" began its existence as a poem of antebellum vintage. See Thomas Ireneus Prime, *Thoughts on the Death of Little Children* (New York: Anson D. F. Randolph, 1852), where it is printed as "Little Bessie: And the Way She Fell Asleep" (pp. 89–91).

32. My information on Asher Sizemore and Little Jimmie comes from their picture-songbooks; see the 1933 and 1934 editions of *Old Fashioned Hymns and Mountain Ballads* (Louisville: WHAS) and the 1935 edition of *Hearth and Home Songs* (Louisville: WHAS).

33. Much of my information on the Chuck Wagon Gang came from taped interviews with Rose Carter Karnes, Azle, Tex., May 10, 1979, and Anna Carter Davis, Baton Rouge, La., Nov. 17, 1978, and a telephone interview (from Fort Worth) with Roy Carter, Oct. 23, 1979. I wrote an article on them, "The Chuck Wagon Gang: God's Gentle People," *Journal of Country Music* 10, no. 1 (1985):

2–13. Harold Timmons, a lifelong student and fan of the Chuck Wagon Gang, wrote the notes for an important album, *Chuck Wagon Gang*, Columbia Historic Edition (Columbia 7464-40152-1).

34. The flavor and thrust of John Lair's preoccupation with old-time ways and old-time music can be discerned from the columns that he wrote for *Stand By* magazine (issued by WLS in Chicago). Much insight concerning Lair can be obtained from Loyal Jones's interviews with him (Apr. 30, 1974, and July 20, 1976, in the Berea Archives, Berea, Ky.). "We Buried Her Beneath the Willow" was written by Karl Davis. Linda Parker recorded "I'll Be All Smiles Tonight" (Conqueror 8164), and can be heard singing the song on a reissue LP, *Karl and Harty and the Cumberland Ridge Runners* (Old Homestead OHCS-137); her memorial service was reported in *Stand By* 2, no. 29 (Aug. 29, 1936): 6.

35. Lily May Ledford, *Coon Creek Girl* (1980; Berea, Ky.: Berea College, Appalachian Center, 1991); *Stand By* 2, no. 36 (Oct. 17, 1936): 7; ibid. 3, no. 8 (Apr. 3, 1937): 12; Charles Faurot, notes, *The Coon Creek Girls* (County 712); Ivan M. Tribe, notes, *The Coon Creek Girls: Early Radio Favorites* (Old Homestead OHCS-142).

36. Lulu Belle and Scotty, "Remember Me" (Okeh 05863). The best recorded version of "Have I Told You Lately?" was that of Gene Autry (Columbia 37079). Recorded by many people, "Mountain Dew" has been most identified with Grandpa Jones (King 624). The stories of how the three songs came to be written are in Dorothy Horstman, *Sing Your Heart Out, Country Boy*, 3d ed. (1975; Nashville: Country Music Foundation Press, 1996), pp. 115, 135–36, 190.

37. William E. Lightfoot, introduction to the reprint of Scott G. Wiseman, *Wiseman's View: The Autobiography of Skyland Scotty Wiseman*, in *North Carolina Folklore Journal* 33, nos. 1 and 2 (1985–86): 2, 7–8; and Lightfoot, "Belle of the Barn Dance: Reminiscing with Lulu Belle Wiseman Stamey," *Journal of Country Music* 12, no. 1 (1987): 2–16. "Homecoming Time in Happy Valley" is included in Lulu Belle and Scotty, *The Sweethearts of Country Music* (Starday SLP 206).

38. Good anthologies of duet singing are *Are You from Dixie? Great Country Brother Teams of the 1930s* (RCA 8417-2-R), notes by Billy Altman; and *Duets* (Time-Life TL CW-05).

39. Brother duets that performed bluesy or risqué material included the Allens, the Callahans, the Sheltons, and the Delmores. In the hands of such musicians as Bill Monroe, Bill Callahan, and Joe Shelton, the mandolin could be an aggressive instrument capable of playing ragtime, jazz, and the blues. Other instrumental combinations heard in duet performances, such as the six-string and tenor guitars of the Delmore Brothers, the six-string and Hawaiian guitars of the Dixon Brothers, the kazoo and tenor banjo of the Allen Brothers, the fiddle and guitar of Wiley Walker and Gene Sullivan, and the five-string banjo and guitar of Wade Mainer and Zeke Morris, permitted these musicians to venture into the whole broad range of country stylistic performances.

40. The first mandolins apparently came to the United States before the Civil War, but their numbers increased during the big immigration from Italy at the end of the century, and were "bowl back," "gourd," or "tater bug" in shape. They were first produced in the United States in quantity in the 1890s, by Lyon & Healy in Chicago. Mandolins could be heard on Edison recordings at the turn of the century. By 1897 Montgomery Ward was marveling at the phenomenal growth in their catalogue mandolin trade. Mandolin ensembles toured the vaudeville circuit, and "mandolin orchestras" emerged in schools and colleges. Flat-backed mandolins were introduced in the early twentieth century, and by 1922 engineer Lloyd Loar was making the Gibson Company the leading manufacturer of mandolins through such distinctive innovations as the F-5. See Charles Hunt, "History of the Mandolin," *Mandolin World News* 6, no. 3 (Autumn, 1981); also the notes to Tony Rice's and David Grisman's *Tone Poems: The Sounds of the Great Vintage Guitars and Mandolins* (Acoustic Disc ACD-10).

41. *Mac and Bob's Book of Songs, Old and New* (Chicago: Agricultural Broadcasting Co., 1931); *Mac and Bob's Newest and Greatest Collection of Songs* (New York: Bob Miller, 1935). Mac and Bob have not been well served on CDs but can be heard in the LPs *Great Old Songs,* vol. 1 (Old Homestead OHCS-158) and *Mac and Bob* (Birch 1944).

42. *Doc Hopkins and Karl and Harty* (Chicago: M. M. Cole, 1936); *Dave Minor's Collection of Karl and Harty's Favorite Songs* (Chicago: Dave Minor Co., 1936). The duo can be heard on the Time-Life *Duets* collection and on *Karl and Harty and the Cumberland Ridge Runners* (Old Homestead OHCS-137).

43. Blue Sky Boys, "I'm Just Here to Get My Baby Out of Jail," (Bluebird B-6621-B) and on *The Blue Sky Boys,* two-record set (RCA AXM2-5525). Their recording can also be heard on other anthologies, such as *Are You from Dixie? Great Country Brother Teams.*

44. Merle Travis, "No Vacancy" (Capitol 258), and on Travis's Bear Family collection; Wesley Tuttle, "No Children Allowed" (Capitol 321).

45. Eddy Arnold, "Mommy Please Stay Home with Me" (Bluebird 330520 and Victor 20-1871) and on *Eddy Arnold: The Tennessee Plowboy and His Guitar* (Bear Family BCD 15726 E1). Biographies of the Tennessee Plowboy include Don Cusic, *Eddy Arnold: I'll Hold You in My Heart* (Nashville: Rutledge Hill Press, 1997), and Michael Streissguth, *Eddy Arnold: Pioneer of the Nashville Sound* (New York: Schirmer Books, 1997).

46. Big Slim McAuliffe, "Don't Blame the Children," in *Old Favorites* (Arc A 544); Hank Snow, "Married by the Bible" (RCA 4733); Bailes Brothers, "Dust on the Bible" (Columbia 37154); Louvin Brothers, "If We Forget God" and "They've Got the Church Outnumbered"—both are in the Louvin Brothers, *In Close Harmony* (Bear Family BCD 15561 HI). Floyd Tillman, "Slipping Around" (Columbia 20581); Jimmy Wakely, "One Has My Name" (Capitol 15162); Webb Pierce, "Back Street Affair" (Decca 28369); Hank Thompson, "Wild Side of Life" (Capitol 1942).

47. Blue Sky Boys, "Little Mother of the Hills" (Victor 21-0108-A). The "poor old mother at home" line comes from "Pictures from Life's Other Side." This song has been recorded many times in country music, including versions by the Blue Sky Boys (Bluebird B-8646-B) and Hank Williams under the name of Luke the Drifter, *Beyond the Sunset* (Polydor 831 574-1 Y-1). The best recording of "The Sweetest Gift (a Mother's Smile)" is by the Blue Sky Boys (Victor 21-0034-A). The best known version, though, is that of Emmylou Harris and Linda Ronstadt, in Ronstadt's *Prisoner in Disguise* (Asylum 7E-1045).

48. These include Molly O'Day, Wilma Lee Cooper, the Bailes Brothers, the Louvin Brothers, the Wilburn Brothers, Kitty Wells, Esco Hankins, Hank Williams, and George Jones.

49. Elizabeth Schlappi has written the best biography of Acuff, *Roy Acuff, the Smoky Mountain Boy* (Gretna, La: Pelican Publishing Company, 1978). Available Acuff CDs include *Columbia Historic Edition* (Columbia CK 39998), *The King of Country Music* (AJA 5244), *The Essential Roy Acuff, 1936–1949* (Columbia CK 48956), and *The RC Cola Shows,* 3 vols. (RME Music, no numbers given).

50. Rick Bragg, *All Over but the Shoutin'* (New York: Pantheon Books, 1997), pp. 23–24.

51. Flatt and Scruggs, "Give Mother My Crown," is in *Songs of Glory* (Columbia CL 1424). Homer Bailes first informed me of the autobiographical nature of the song in an interview, Roanoke, La., Aug. 16, 1974. Johnnie Bailes can be heard commenting about the presence of "Mommy Bailes" in the radio studio at KWKH in an album made up of radio transcriptions (*The Bailes Brothers* [Old Homestead OHCS-103], notes by Ivan Tribe).

52. Moon Mullican, "Sweeter Than the Flowers" (King 673); Hank Snow, "My Mother" (RCA V 20-4632); Lefty Frizzell, "Mom and Dad's Waltz" (Columbia 20837); Hank Williams, "I Just Told Mama Goodby" (MGM 10401); Hank Williams, "I Dreamed about Mama Last Night" (MGM); Hank Williams, "I Heard My Mother Praying for Me" (MGM 10813). Hank Williams's songs can be heard on *The Original Singles Collection,* three CDs (Polydor 847 194-2), or on the impressive box set *The Complete Hank Williams* (Mercury 314536077-2). The recitation that accompanied "I Dreamed about Mama" originally had been a poem written by Edgar Guest, "The Mother Watch," which was included in one of his books of poetry, *The Path to Home* (Chicago: Reilly & Lee Co., 1919), pp. 20–21.

53. Kathleen Martha Minnix, "God's Comedian: The Life and Career of Evangelist Sam Jones" (Ph.D. diss., Georgia State University, 1986), pp. 78–79; Charles Reagan Wilson tells of the addition of the balcony as a Confederate memorial in *Baptized in Blood: The Religion of the Lost Cause, 1865–1920* (Athens: University of Georgia Press, 1980), p. 31.

54. Linnell Gentry, in the original edition of *A History and Encyclopedia of Country, Western, and Gospel Music,* attempted to list and describe most of the

radio barn dances in America (Nashville: McQuiddy Press, 1961). This edition is now out of print, and his revised work does not contain similar material. Charles Wolfe's history of the Grand Ole Opry, *Good-Natured Riot,* carries the story only to 1939. Stephen Ray Tucker, "The Louisiana Hayride, 1948–1954," *North Louisiana Historical Association Journal* 8, no. 5 (Fall, 1977): 187–201); Horace Logan, with Bill Sloan, *Elvis, Hank, and Me: Making Musical History on the Louisiana Hayride* (New York: St. Martin's Press, 1998); Ivan Tribe discusses the Wheeling show and more in *Mountaineer Jamboree: Country Music in West Virginia* (Lexington: University Press of Kentucky, 1984); Pete Stamper, *It All Happened in Renfro Valley* (Lexington: University Press of Kentucky, 1999). Harry Rice presents a good introduction to the show in "A Close Look at the Renfro Valley Barn Dance," *Journal of Country Music* 19, no. 2 (1997): 16–26. Joe Wilson gives a brief overview of an important mountain show in "Bristol's WCYB: Early Bluegrass Turf," *Muleskinner News* 3, no. 8 (Oct., 1972): 8–12; Gerald Haslam provides much information of the California radio shows in *Workin' Man Blues.*

55. Rice, "Close Look at the Renfro Valley Barn Dance"; Wayne W. Daniel, "The Renfro Valley Barn Dance—the First Fifty Years," *Old Time Country* 8, no. 3 (Fall, 1992): 4–8.

56. At one time, I had planned to do a history of Renfro Valley, and I obtained an extensive number of interviews with such personalities as Old Joe Clark, Patty Fly, Pete Stamper, and Jim Gaskin. I apologize to them for my failure to complete the project, but I believe that the Barn Dance's story is in good hands with Wayne Daniel. John Rumble, of the Country Music Foundation in Nashville, also conducted interviews, copies of which are in the Kentucky State Museum. I also listened to numerous tapes of Renfro Valley Shows that are deposited at the Appalachian Center, Berea College, in Berea, Kentucky.

57. Some of these singers are anthologized on an album called *Wild, Wild Young Women* (Rounder 1031), notes by Mary A. Bufwack and Robert K. Oermann; such women as Wanda Jackson and Janis Martin are featured in an article by Randy Fox and Michael Gray, "Hillbilly Boogie! All Mama's Children Are Doin' the Bop," *Journal of Country Music* 20, no. 2 (1998): 16–25.

58. Nick Tosches, *Hellfire: The Jerry Lee Lewis Story* (1982; New York: Grove Press, 1998). The best introduction to the first generation of rockabilly singers is Colin Escott, with Martin Hawkins, *Good Rockin' Tonight: Sun Records and the Birth of Rock 'n' Roll* (New York: St. Martin's Press, 1991). Patrick B. Mullen, "Hillbilly Hipsters of the 1950s: The Romance of Rockabilly," *Southern Quarterly* 22, no. 2 (Spring, 1984): 79–93; Craig Morrison, *Go Cat Go! Rockabilly Music and Its Makers* (Urbana: University of Illinois Press, 1996). Michael Bertrand, *Race, Rock, and Elvis,* explores the relationship between rock-and-roll, southern youth, and social change in the late fifties and early sixties (Urbana: University of Illinois Press, 2000).

59. Jerry Lee Lewis, of course, expressed religious convictions on many occa-

sions, even going so far to say that one could not sing rock-and-roll and go to Heaven. See Tosches, *Hellfire,* for an account of a "religious debate" in the Sun Studios between Lewis and Sam Phillips (pp. 129–32). See also Carl Perkins, with Ron Rendleman, *Disciple in Blue Suede Shoes* (Grand Rapids, Mich.: Zondervan Publishing, 1978).

60. David A. Noebel, *Rhythm, Riots, and Revolution: An Analysis of the Communist Use of Music* (Tulsa: Christian Crusade Publications, 1966).

61. Peter Guralnick's two-volume biography of Elvis is probably the best study of any American popular singer, *Last Train to Memphis: The Rise of Elvis Presley* and *Careless Love: The Unmaking of Elvis Presley* (Boston: Little, Brown, 1994, 1998).

62. The best explanation of the Nashville Sound is in Patrick Carr, ed., *The Illustrated History of Country Music* (New York: Random House/Times Books, 1995), pp. 266–94. See also Malone, *Country Music, USA,* pp. 245–67.

63. It is now clear that the demographic and social transformations later discussed by Bruce Feiler actually began to appear in the mid-fifties. See *Dreaming Out Loud: Garth Brooks, Wynonna Judd, Wade Hayes, and the Changing Face of Nashville* (New York: Avon Books, 1998).

64. John Hartford spoke for many when he wrote and sang "Tear Down the Grand Ole Opry," in *Turn Your Radio On* (Warner Bros. WB 1916).

65. The *Journal of Country Music* commented on the "neo-traditionalists" in a special issue, "The Old Sound of New Country" (11, no. 1 [1986]: 2–25).

66. Richard D. Smith has written the best biography of Bill Monroe, *"Can't You Hear Me Callin'": The Life of Bill Monroe, Father of Bluegrass* (Boston: Little, Brown, 2000). *The Bill Monroe Reader,* edited by a former Blue Grass Boy, Tom Ewing (Urbana: University of Illinois Press, 2000), presents an eclectic, richly illustrated compilation of writings about Monroe. Other good short accounts of his life and career include Ralph Rinzler, "Bill Monroe," in *Stars of Country Music,* ed. Bill C. Malone and Judith McCulloh (Urbana: University of Illinois Press, 1975), and Jim Rooney, *Bossmen: Bill Monroe and Muddy Waters* (New York: Dial Press, 1971).

67. Neil V. Rosenberg, "From Sound to Style: The Emergence of Bluegrass," *Journal of American Folklore* 80, no. 316 (Apr.–June, 1967): 143–50; Rosenberg, *Bluegrass: A History* (Urbana: University of Illinois Press, 1985, 1993), esp. pp. 68–95.

68. John Cohen claims to have "invented" the description "high lonesome sound" when he documented the music of the Appalachian singer Roscoe Holcomb in a film documentary and in a record album called *The High Lonesome Sound* (Folkways FA 2368).

69. Robert Cantwell, *Bluegrass Breakdown: The Making of the Old Southern Sound* (Urbana: University of Illinois Press, 1984), p. 143.

70. Those factors contributed, in fact, to Elvis Presley's seminal recording of Bill Monroe's "Blue Moon of Kentucky" (Sun 209) in 1954. Elvis was only one of several rockabillies (such as Carl Perkins, Sonny Curtis, and Buddy Holly) who

acknowledged the influence of Bill Monroe. The essential collection of Elvis's material is *Elvis: The King of Rock 'n' Roll* (RCA 07863 66050-2), the complete 50s masters on five CDs.

71. Bill Monroe, "Little Cabin Home on the Hill" (Columbia CCO 4877-1), in the box set, *The Essential Bill Monroe and His Blue Grass Boys, 1945–1949* (Columbia C2K 52478).

72. Hillbilly Ranch was located right on the edge of the notorious "Combat Zone" in Boston, a haven for prostitutes and pimps. "Skull orchard" and "fightin'-and-dancin' clubs" are terms often used to describe honky-tonks that have reputations for violence.

73. The Kingston Trio's version of "Tom Dooley" appeared on their first album, *The Kingston Trio* (Capitol T 996).

74. Robert Cantwell, *When We Were Good: The Folk Revival* (Cambridge: Harvard University Press, 1996).

75. *Anthology of American Folk Music* (Folkways FA 2951-53), notes by Harry Smith. This invaluable collection was rereleased by the Smithsonian Institution in 1997. Greil Marcus explores the influence of the Harry Smith collection in *Invisible Republic: Bob Dylan's Basement Tapes* (New York: Henry Holt and Company, 1997). See also Peter D. Goldsmith, *Making People's Music: Moe Asch and Folkways Records* (Washington, D.C.: Smithsonian Institution Press, 1998).

76. The New Lost City Ramblers' recording career began with *New Lost City Ramblers* (Folkways FA 2396). Their most influential album, however, is probably *Songs from the Depression* (Folkways FH 5264).

77. There is as yet no full-scale biography of Doc Watson. His music was first recorded in *Old-Time Music at Clarence Ashley's* (Folkways FA 2355). Other early recordings that demonstrate his affiliation with the folk revival are *The Doc Watson Family* (Folkways FA 2366) and *Jean Ritchie and Doc Watson at Folk City* (Folkways FA 2426).

78. Watson has recorded many albums. In order to sample his diversity, however, one might listen to these compilations: *Doc Watson on Stage, Featuring Merle Watson* (Vanguard VSD-9/10); *Docabilly* (Sugar Hill SHCD-3836); *Bill Monroe and Doc Watson* (Smithsonian Folkways CD 40064); *Doc and Dawg*, with David Grisman (Acoustic Disc ACD-25); and *The Essential Doc Watson* (Vanguard VCD 45/46).

79. The grassroots enthusiasm for traditional music, and the tireless labor of Archie Green who lobbied valiantly in Washington, resulted in the passage of the American Folklife Preservation Act in January, 1976. The legislation established the American Folklife Center, and Alan Jabbour became its first director.

80. Townsend Miller was a stockbroker by trade, and a country music enthusiast by choice. His columns in the *Austin American-Statesman* touted the local musicians and kept readers aware of new developments in the music scene. The Austin musicians are described in Jan Reid, *The Improbable Rise of Redneck Rock* (Austin: Heidelberg Press, 1974). The Bakersfield musical colony is chronicled

in Haslam, *Workin' Man Blues,* and Carr, *Illustrated History of Country Music,* pp. 295–304.

81. The first and biggest recorded version of "Family Bible" was that of Claude Gray in 1960 (D 1118). Loretta Lynn, "Coal Miner's Daughter" (Decca 32749); Dolly Parton, "Coat of Many Colors" (RCA 0538); Rusty and Doug Kershaw, "Louisiana Man" (Hickory 1137); Merle Haggard, "Hungry Eyes" (Capitol 2383).

82. The movie was inspired by an article written by Aaron Latham, "The Ballad of the Urban Cowboy" (*Esquire* 90 [Sept. 12, 1978]: 21–30).

83. Feiler, *Dreaming Out Loud,* p. 36.

84. Ellison, *Country Music Culture,* p. xvii.

85. Ibid., pp. xvi, xix.

86. Tribute albums suggest the reverence toward, if not actual indebtedness to, the older entertainers: Merle Haggard has been the subject of two tributes, *Tulare Dust: A Songwriters Tribute to Merle Haggard* (Hightone HCD 8058), and *Mama's Hungry Eyes: A Tribute to Merle Haggard* (Arista 07822-18760-2). Other good collections include *True Life Blues: The Songs of Bill Monroe* (Sugar Hill SHCD 2209); *Real: The Tom T. Hall Project* (Delmore 4344-31039-2); and *Tribute to Tradition* (Columbia CK 69073), fourteen songs by assorted mainstream singers.

87. Woody Paul, the fiddler in the Riders in the Sky trio, performs a skit that burlesques the overly sincere country-and-western entertainer.

88. Ellison's references are scattered throughout *Country Music Culture,* but especially on pp. 183–87; Feiler's most cogent remarks are found in *Dreaming Out Loud,* on pp. 289–91 and 294–98. Laurence Leamer devotes the first section of his book to Fan Fair, 1996, in *Three Chords and the Truth: Hope, Heartbreak, and Changing Fortunes in Nashville* (New York: HarperCollins, 1997).

89. Feiler, *Dreaming Out Loud,* pp. 291, 294.

90. Ellison, *Country Music Culture,* p. 263.

Chapter 4: "With My Friends at the Old Country Church"

1. Jimmie Rodgers recorded several moralistic songs, but only one purely religious song, "That Wonderful City" (Bluebird BB 6810), which he sang with the Carter Family. Since the 1970s, the percentage of religious songs in country music has declined dramatically, and clearly sectarian songs have virtually disappeared—a consequence perhaps of the music's efforts to become mainstream.

2. Odum devotes an entire chapter to hymns and religious songs in *An American Epoch: Southern Portraiture in the National Picture* (New York: Holt, 1930), pp. 180–200. The quotations are from p. 180.

3. Ibid. Martin's quotes come from his article on modern southern gospel music; see William C. Martin, "At the Corner of Glory Avenue and Hallelujah Street," *Harper's Magazine* 244, no. 1460 (Jan., 1972): 95–99.

4. The term "bible belt" is usually attributed to H. L. Mencken, but I must confess that even though his famous article, "Sahara of the Bozart," conveys all of the negative references mentioned above, I cannot find his explicit use of the phrase.

5. John Shelton Reed, *The Enduring South: Subcultural Persistence in Mass Society* (Lexington, Mass.: Lexington Books, 1972),

6. Ralph Stanley, with Larry Sparks, "I Want a Clear Record," in *Over the Sunset Hill* (King 1032).

7. "Hold Fast to the Right" has been recorded many times, first in 1928 by Mac and Bob (Vocalion 5259), and in 1937 by the Carter Family (Decca D 5494), and more recently by such singers as Ray and Ina Patterson, in *Songs of Home and Children* (County 737) and the Nashville Bluegrass Band in *To Be His Child* (Rounder CD-0242).

8. The scholarship that has informed my understanding of southern religious music is vast. Most useful to me have been George Pullen Jackson, *White Spirituals in the Southern Uplands* (1933; Chapel Hill: University of North Carolina Press, 1965); Richard Hulan, "Camp-Meeting Spiritual Folksongs: Legacy of the 'Great Revival in the West,'" Ph.D. diss., University of Texas, Austin, 1978; Dickson Bruce, Jr., *And They All Sang Hallelujah: Plain-Folk Camp-Meeting Religion, 1800–1845* (Knoxville: University of Tennessee Press, 1974); Timothy Alan Smith, "The Southern Folk-Hymns, 1802–1860: A Historical and Musical Analysis, with notes on Performance Practice," Master of Music Thesis, California State University, Fullerton, 1981; James Downey, "The Music of American Revivalism," Ph.D. diss., Tulane University, 1969; Phil Kerr, *Music in Evangelism* (Glendale, Calif.: Gospel Music Publishers, 1939); Otis J. Knippers, *Who's Who among Southern Singers and Composers* (Lawrenceburg, Tenn.: J. D. Vaughan, 1931); J. H. Hall, *Biography of Gospel Song and Hymn Writers;* William G. McLoughlin, Jr., *Modern Revivalism* (New York: Ronald Press Co., 1959); McLoughlin, *Billy Sunday Was His Name* (Chicago: University of Chicago Press, 1955); William R. Moody, *The Life of Dwight L. Moody* (New York: Fleming H. Revell, 1900).

9. The beginning place for any understanding of the southern shape-note tradition is Jackson, *White Spirituals in the Southern Uplands*. Other indispensable studies include Harry Eskew, "Shape-Note Hymnody in the Shenandoah Valley, 1816–1860" (Ph.D. diss., Tulane University, 1966); Buell Cobb, *The Sacred Harp: A Tradition and Its Music* (Athens: University of Georgia Press, 1978).

10. Jo Lee Fleming, "James D. Vaughan, Music Publisher" (S.M.D. diss., Union Theological Seminary, 1972). For an understanding of the commercial history of southern shape-note publishing that preceded, and shaped, the work of Vaughan, see Weldon T. Myers, "History of Kieffer-Ruebush," *Gospel Singing Journal* 1, no. 2 (Summer, 1977): 1, 9. (This article was originally published in *The Musical Million* in 1908.) See also Paul M. Hall, "*The Musical Million*": A Study and Analysis of the Periodical Promoting Reading Music through Shape-

Notes in North America From 1870 to 1914" (D.M.A. diss., Catholic University of America, 1970); Grace I. Showalter, *The Music Books of Ruebush and Kieffer, 1866–1942* (Richmond: Virginia State Library, 1975); Joel Francis Reed, "Anthony J. Showalter (1858–1924): Southern Educator, Publisher, Composer" (Ed.D diss., New Orleans Baptist Theological Seminary, 1975); David W. Music, "Ananias Davisson, Robert Boyd, Reubin Monday, John Martin, and Archibald Rhea in East Tennessee, 1816–26," *American Music* 1, no. 3 (Fall, 1983): 72–84; and Paul G. Hammond, "Jesse B. Aikin and 'The Christian Minstrel,'" *American Music* 3, no. 4 (Winter, 1985): 442–51. James Goff, a historian at Appalachian State University in Boone, North Carolina, is writing a full-scale study of the southern gospel quartet business, tentatively entitled "The Gospel Jubilee." Very little of the music of the Vaughan Quartets is available today, except for a cassette of sixteen songs produced by the Tennessee Folklore Society—*The Vaughan Quartets, 1927–1947* (TFS 111).

11. "Give the World a Smile" was written by Paul Yandell and John Otis Deaton, and was recorded in October, 1927, on Victor B-6038. No full-scale history of the Stamps Quartet exists. My information came from interviews with Dwight Brock in Dallas, Tex., June 20, 1973; Palmer Wheeler, Dallas, Tex., July 5, 1973; and Marion Snider, Dallas, Tex., Aug. 10, 1977; from an untitled biographical sketch of Virgil O. Stamps in *Precious Memories of Virgil O. Stamps* (Dallas: Stamps-Baxter Music and Printing Co., 1941); and from *Stamps Quartet Souvenir* (Dallas: Stamps Quartet Music Co., 1946). According to Otis J. Knippers, Thomas Jefferson Benton of Grandview, Texas, was the "first writer to have used afterbeats in sacred songs" when he wrote "On to Battle" in 1923 (*Who's Who among Southern Singers and Composers*, p. 22).

12. "Saviour, Lead Them" was written by H. W. Elliott and Emmett S. Dean, and copyrighted in 1898. My copy of the song is in a paperback hymnal entitled *Gospel Songs*. The title page is missing, but internal evidence suggests that its publication date was approximately 1908. The Carter Family recorded the song as "Poor Orphan Child" (Victor 20877) in July, 1927.

13. Studies of the Carter Family include Ed Kahn, "The Carter Family: A Reflection of Changes in Society" (Ph.D. diss., UCLA, 1970); the notes to *The Carter Family on "Border Radio"* (JEMF 101), by Archie Green, Norm Cohen, and William H. Koon; Archie Green, "The Carter Family's 'Coal Miner's Blues,'" *Southern Folklore Quarterly* 25, no. 4 (Dec., 1961): 226–37; and John Atkins, "The Carter Family," in Malone and McCulloh, *Stars of Country Music*, pp. 95–121. Bear Family has produced the complete collection of Carter Family recordings: *In the Shadow of Clinch Mountain* (BCD 15865).

14. Uncle Dave recorded the song on Apr. 14, 1926 (Vocalion 15322). My copy of the song is found on *Uncle Dave Macon: The Dixie Dewdrop*, Victor LP 101 (notes by Bob Hyland).

15. These songs, and others such as "Walking in the Way with Jesus" and "The Prayer of the Drunkard's Little Girl," are included on the important LP *How Can*

a Poor Man Stand Such Times and Live? The Songs of Blind Alfred Reed (Rounder Records 1001).

16. Archie Green commented on one song that ridiculed commercialized religion, "The Dollar and the Devil," in *Hear Those Beautiful Sacred Selections*, reprinted from the 1970 *Yearbook of the International Folk Music Council* (Los Angeles: JEMF, 1970), pp. 28–50.

17. "How Can a Poor Man Stand Such Times and Live," in *How Can a Poor Man Stand Such Times and Live? The Songs of Blind Alfred Reed* (Rounder Records 1001).

18. Wayne Daniel, *Pickin' on Peachtree*, p. 60; D. K. Wilgus was the first academic folklorist to recognize the folk nature of Jenkins's compositions, in *Anglo-American Folksong Scholarship since 1898*, pp. 283–84. Archie Green also discusses Jenkins in "Commercial Music Graphics: Eight, *JEMF Quarterly* 5, no. 13 (Spring, 1969): 23–26; as does C. Wolfe in "Frank Smith, Andrew Jenkins, and Early Commercial Gospel Music."

19. The Deal Family are discussed in Clarence H. Greene, "The Deal Family: Carolina Gospel Singers," *JEMF Quarterly* 19, no. 69 (Spring, 1983): 9–11. Karnes and Phipps's music has been anthologized in a fine CD collection called *Kentucky Gospel* (Document DOCD-8013), with notes by Charles Wolfe. Donald Lee Nelson has provided additional information on the two singers and others who were associated with them in "The Life of Alfred G. Karnes," *JEMF Quarterly* 8, no. 25, part 1 (Spring, 1972): 31–34; and "McVay and Johnson," ibid. 10, no. 35 (Autumn, 1974): 92–95.

20. Phipps's "Shine on Me" is included in the Folkways anthology and in the *Kentucky Gospel* CD. Pentecostal-influenced music deserves a full-scale study. Paul Oliver devotes a chapter to the African American Holiness/Pentecostal musical tradition, "Saints of the Sanctified Churches," including such important singers and musicians as Arizona Dranes, F. W. McGhee, and Mother McCollum, in *Songsters and Saints: Vocal Traditions on Race Records* (Cambridge: Cambridge University Press, 1984), pp. 199–229.

21. Bill Bolick made these observations to me when I was preparing the notes (circa 1976) for *The Blue Sky Boys* (Rounder 0052).

22. Elizabeth Schlappi, "Roy Acuff," in Malone and McCulloh, *Stars of Country Music*, pp. 187–88. "What Would You Give in Exchange for Your Soul" was written by F. J. Berry and J. H. Carr, and was copyrighted in 1912 by the Trio Music Company. The Monroe Brothers recorded it for Bluebird in 1936 (Bluebird B-6309-A). "The Sunny Side of Life" was written by a Church of Christ songwriter, Tillit S. Teddlie, and recorded in 1936 by the Blue Sky Boys (Bluebird 6457A), who learned it from a Church of God (Anderson, Indiana) hymnal, *Reformation Glory*.

23. "Will the Circle Be Unbroken" was written by Ada Habershon and Charles H. Gabriel. The McCravy Brothers made one of the earliest recordings of the song in country music (Conqueror 7794). Except for the chorus, the Carter Family's

version is strikingly different with its graphic comments about the death of a mother and the earnest pleadings to the undertaker to "please drive slow" (Carter Family, "Can the Circle Be Unbroken," recorded in 1935 on several labels, including Banner 33465 and Oriole 8484).

24. Anne and Frank Warner, respected collectors of folksongs, printed a version of Albert Brumley's "If We Never Meet Again" only six years after it was first published, but Anne Warner remarked in the headnote, "I have found no other sources for this mountain hymn" (*Traditional American Folk Songs from the Anne and Frank Warner Collection* [Syracuse University Press, 1984], p. 216). Studies of folk gospel songs are needed. Cheryl Thurber discusses the African American origins of one of the most famous, "Old Time Religion," in *Rejoice!* 1, no. 4 (Winter, 1989): 23. Al Stewart wrote an intriguing and plausible article suggesting that Sarah Dillon Workman, from Webb, West Virginia, had originally written the poem that became "The Great Speckled Bird." It had been written in about 1926 as a defense of the Church of God (Cleveland, Tennessee); see Al Stewart, "On the Trail of the Great Speckled Bird," *Appalachian Heritage* 6, no. 1 (Winter, 1978): 67–80. Grady and Hazel Cole's version of "Tramp on the Street" appeared on Bluebird BB 8262. Jeff Van Dyke, a UPI reporter, referred to "I'll Fly Away" as a Pentecostal hymn, in *Kingsport Times-News*, July 5, 1987.

25. Wayne Warner, director of the Assembly of God Archives in Springfield, Missouri, provided me with some information about the life and career of Herbert Buffum. See Warner, "Herbert Buffum," *Assembly of God Heritage* 6 (Fall, 1986): 11–14, 16; *Dictionary of Pentecostal and Charismatic Movements*, ed. Stanley M. Burgess and Gary B. McGee (Grand Rapids, Mich.: Zondervan, 1988), p. 101. Additional material includes Kerr, *Music in Evangelism*, p. 212; and Charles H. Gabriel, *The Singers and Their Songs: Sketches of Living Gospel Hymn Writers* (Chicago: Rodeheaver Co., 1916), p. 63.

26. James Goff told me about Winsett's connections to the early Assembly of God. Otis J. Knippers provides a short sketch of Winsett in *Who's Who among Southern Singers and Composers*, pp. 158–59.

27. Michael W. Harris, *The Rise of the Gospel Blues: The Music of Thomas Andrew Dorsey* (New York: Oxford University Press, 1992).

28. For the origins and significance of border radio, see Gerald Carson, *The Roguish World of Dr. Brinkley* (New York: Rinehart & Company, 1960); and Gene Fowler and Bill Crawford, *Border Radio* (Austin: Texas Monthly Press, 1987). Some of the Carter Family's radio transcriptions have been rereleased as recordings by the John Edwards Memorial Foundation (*The Carter Family on Border Radio* [JEMF 101]) and by Old Homestead Records in Brighton, Michigan (*The Original Carter Family in Texas*, vols. 1–4, OHCS 111, 112, 116, 117).

29. "There's No Depression in Heaven" was published in the hymnal *Sweet Heaven* (James D. Vaughan, Lawrenceburg, Tenn.), and was recorded by the Carter Family (Decca 5242). The song was revived in the 1960s by the New Lost City Ramblers and included in their *Songs from the Depression* (Folkways FH

5264). Recorded again in 1990 by the rock-country band Uncle Tupelo on a CD *No Depression* (Rockville Rock 6050-2), the song ultimately inspired the emergence of an alternative music magazine, *No Depression* (published in Seattle), and a Web site where articles and other information about alternative country acts can be found.

30. Palmer Wheeler, a member of the original Stamps Quartet of 1928, told me that Pentecostal churches were among the most receptive of all groups for gospel quartet concerts during the Depression years (interview with Palmer Wheeler, Dallas, Tex., July 5, 1973).

31. *Precious Memories of Virgil O. Stamps*, pp. viii–ix; Lois Blackwell, *The Wings of the Dove: The Story of Gospel Music in America* (Norfolk, Va.: Donning, 1978), p. 50.

32. "Turn Your Radio On" was originally published in the Stamps-Baxter book, *Guiding Star*, in 1938. A caption beneath the title says "Dedicated to the Stamps Quartet."

33. Interview with Albert Brumley, Powell, Mo., Apr. 5, 1972; Bill C. Malone, "Albert E. Brumley: Folk Composer," *Bluegrass Unlimited* 21, no. 1 (July, 1986): 69–78; interviews with Eugene M. Bartlett, Jr., Ardmore, Okla., July 12, 1978, and Bill Brumley, Powell, Mo., July 13, 1978.

34. Convention books were designed for the all-day singing events held periodically in a church, county courthouse, or some other community building.

35. Interview with Albert Brumley, Powell, Mo., Apr. 5, 1972.

36. *The Best of Albert E. Brumley* (Powell, Mo.: Albert E. Brumley and Sons, 1966). Several fine tributes to his work have been recorded (most of them, however, are out of print). These include the Blackwood Brothers, *Turn Your Radio On* (Arto LPG 106 L); Albert E. Brumley, Jr., *Albert E. Brumley* (Artist Recording 780725); Cathedral Quartet, *Albert E. Brumley Classics* (Eternal 760635); Chuck Wagon Gang, *God's Gentle People* (Columbia LE 10071); the Shelton Trio, *Unforgettable Songs of Albert E. Brumley* (Shelton Brothers Records LPS 1001), and the Statesmen Quartet, *I'll Meet You by the River* (Victor LPM-2065).

37. Alana White, "Grandpa Jones and the Hee Haw Gospel Quartet," *Bluegrass Unlimited* 22, no. 11 (June, 1988): 22–26. Information on the Brown's Ferry Four can be obtained from Grandpa Jones, *Everybody's Grandpa*, pp. 99–102. Rich Kienzle refers briefly to the Brown's Ferry Four in his notes to Merle Travis's Bear Family collection, *Guitar Rags and a Too Fast Past* (BCD 15637 E1), pp. 12, 24.

38. The Chuck Wagon Gang still exists at the beginning of the twenty-first century. No one named Carter, however, now sings in the quartet.

39. The references to "my boy in service" comes from "A Mother's Prayer," written by Wally Fowler and recorded by Eddy Arnold (Bluebird 33-0520). "There's a Star Spangled Banner Waving Somewhere" was recorded by Elton Britt (Bluebird B 9000). Two popular versions of "Smoke on the Water" competed for the hillbilly jukebox trade—Red Foley (Decca 6102) and Bob Wills, with Tommy Duncan (Okeh 6736).

40. "The Sunday Morning Gathering" is still a popular component of Renfro Valley Barn Dance entertainment today.

41. David Harrell, *All Things Are Possible: The Healing and Charismatic Revivals in Modern America* (Bloomington: Indiana University Press, 1975); Paul Boyer, *When Time Shall Be No More: Prophecy Belief in Modern America* (Cambridge: Belknap Press of Harvard University Press, 1992); Peter J. Boyer, "Miracle Man," *New Yorker* 75, no. 7 (Apr. 12, 1999): 64–83.

42. Ivan M. Tribe, "Mac Odell: The Ole Country Boy," *Bluegrass Unlimited* 11, no. 4 (Oct., 1976): 30–36; Ivan Tribe, notes to Mac Odell, *Wild Rose of the Mountains* (Folk Variety FV 12017); Odell McLeod, notes, *Be on Time* (Folk Variety 12016). M. E. Abbey and Charles Tillman were the writers of "Life's Railway to Heaven" and Charles K. Harris was the composer of "Hello Central, Give Me Heaven."

43. Molly O'Day, "Matthew 24" (Columbia 20534); Roy Acuff, "This World Can't Stand Long" (Columbia 20454); Wilma Lee and Stoney Cooper, "What's the Matter with This World" (Columbia 20631); Louvin Brothers, "If We Forget God" (Capitol 2852); Louvin Brothers, "Great Atomic Power" (MGM 11277); Bailes Brothers, "We're Living in the Last Days Now" (Columbia 37583); Karl and Harty, "When the Atom Bomb Fell" (Columbia 36982); Buchanan Brothers, "Atomic Power" (Victor 20-1850); Riley Shepard, "Atomic Power" (Musicor 15070). Charles Wolfe, "Nuclear Country: The Atomic Bomb in Country Music," *Journal of Country Music* 7 (Jan., 1978): 4–21. The atomic bomb songs are placed in a larger perspective by Paul Boyer, *By the Bomb's Early Light* (New York: Pantheon, 1985).

44. Wayne W. Daniel, "Wilma Lee Cooper, America's Most Authentic Mountain Singer," *Bluegrass Unlimited* 16, no. 8 (Feb., 1982): 12–18. Ivan Tribe and John Morris, "Molly O'Day and Lynn Davis: A Strong Influence on Bluegrass," *Bluegrass Unlimited* 9, no. 3 (Sept., 1974): 10–16; Wayne W. Daniel, "Grady and Hazel Cole and the Tramp on the Street," *Rejoice!* 4, no. 3 (June/July, 1992): 8–11. Molly O'Day's complete Columbia sessions have been reissued in a box set, *Molly O'Day and the Cumberland Mountain Folks* (Bear Family BCD 15565).

45. Interview with Homer Bailes, Roanoke, La., Aug. 16, 1974; Ivan Tribe, "The Bailes Brothers," *Bluegrass Unlimited* 9, no. 8 (Feb., 1975): 8–14. This article includes a discography of the Bailes Brothers Columbia recordings.

46. C. Wolfe, *In Close Harmony*. This book grew out of the set of notes by Wolfe that accompanied the CD collection, *In Close Harmony* (BCD 15561 HI), eight compact discs issued by Bear Family Records in 1992. Howard Miller wrote a fan-oriented account, *The Louvin Brothers* (n.p., 1986).

47. The photograph is in Miller's *Louvin Brothers*. He talks about Ira rejecting the call from God on pp. 38 and 39.

48. Hank Williams, *Health and Happiness Shows,* two compact discs, with notes by Colin Escott (Mercury 314 517 862-2). Most of Hank's moralistic songs and recitations were issued under the name of Luke the Drifter (twelve of them were reissued on an LP, *Beyond the Sunset* [Polydor 831 574-1]).

49. Hank has been the subject of three important biographies: Roger Williams, *Sing a Sad Song: The Life of Hank Williams,* 2d ed. (1970; Urbana: University of Illinois Press, 1981); Chet Flippo, *Your Cheatin' Heart: A Biography of Hank Williams* (New York: Simon and Schuster, 1981); Escott, with Merritt and Mac-Ewen, *Hank Williams: The Biography.* Don Cusic purports to present all of Hank's song lyrics in *Hank Williams: The Complete Lyrics,* ed. Cusic (New York: St. Martin's Press, 1993), but readers should not be misled by the title.

50. Godfrey Hodgson has presented a provocative interpretation of those years in *America in Our Time* (Garden City, N.Y.: Doubleday, 1976).

51. Rachel Goodman, "From Neon to Nashville: The Story of Martha Carson," *Bluegrass Unlimited* 26, no. 5 (Nov., 1991): 30–32. Carson's recording of "Satisfied" (Capitol F 1900) apparently did not make it into the popularity charts, but it was widely known and performed. The standard reference to the *Billboard* charts is Joel Whitburn's *The Billboard Book of Top 40 Country Hits, 1944–1996* (New York: Billboard Books, 1996), which surveys country music's chart makers from 1944 to the present. Both of the above-mentioned Stuart Hamblen recordings did become chartmakers: "It Is No Secret" (Columbia 20724) was a number 8 selection, and "This Ole House" (RCA 5739) reached the number 2 position.

52. Kevin Fontenot, of the history department of Tulane University, is writing a doctoral dissertation on the life and career of Jimmie Davis. Davis's religious songs did not reach the top ten popularity charts, but were played frequently on country radio shows during the late fifties and early sixties. Everyone knew, for example, "Supper Time," "Taller Than Trees," and "Someone to Care." Davis's blues material has been highly prized by modern collectors and record producers, but his gospel repertoire has been largely ignored. For example, MCA's "Country Music Hall of Fame Series" recording, *Jimmie Davis* (MCA MCAD-10087), includes only "Supper Time" among the sixteen songs that are anthologized. Davis is featured prominently in one of the segments of the Smithsonian's 1999 documentary, *The Mississippi—River of Song,* part 4: "Louisiana: Where Music Is King."

53. Foley has not been well served by CD reissues, but can be heard on *Red Foley* in MCA's "Country Music Hall of Fame" series (MCA MCAD-10084). The anthology includes three gospel songs, "Just a Closer Walk with Thee," "When God Dips His Love in My Heart," and "Peace in the Valley." Joel Whitburn's listing of Top 40 Country Hits demonstrates the commercial viability of Foley's music in the 1950s. Foley placed over sixty songs on the country charts from 1944 to 1959 (*Billboard Book of Top 40 Country Hits,* pp. 111–13).

54. James Blackwood, with Dan Martin, *The James Blackwood Story* (Monroeville, Pa.: Whitaker House, 1975); Kree Jack Racine, *Above All: The Blackwood Brothers Quartet* (Memphis, Tenn.: Jarodoce Publications, 1967); Doc Horsley, *Gospel Quartet Music: Then and Now* (Carbondale, Ill.: Cultural Press, 1989), pp. 13–14; Blackwood Brothers, "The Man Upstairs" (RCAV-20-5781).

Brumley's "I Guess I'm Just a Little Old-Fashioned" was published in Stamps-Baxter's *Brightest Beams* (1938). Stuart Hamblen, "My Religion's Not Old-Fashioned" (Columbia 21190).

55. Don Cusic, "Singing with the King: The Groups That Performed with Elvis," *Rejoice!* 1, no. 3 (Summer, 1988): 10–13. Peter Guralnick refers to the Blackwood Brothers and other gospel quartets throughout his two-volume biography of Elvis.

56. Ferlin Husky, "Wings of a Dove" (Capitol 4406); Christy Lane, "One Day at a Time" (United Artists 1342); Johnny Paycheck and Jody Miller, "Let's All Go down to the River" (Epic 10863); Kris Kristofferson, "Why Me, Lord" (Monument 8571); Tennessee Ernie Ford, *Hymns* (Capitol ST-756); Andy Griffith, *I Love to Tell the Story: 25 Timeless Hymns*. Gerald Smith, Jr., concentrates on the religious side of Ford's musical repertoire in "Tennessee Ernie Ford," *Rejoice!* 2, no. 1 (Summer, 1989): 16–19.

57. Bill Mack is best known for his trucker-oriented radio shows on WBAP in Fort Worth and for being the writer of the song that launched LeAnn Rimes's career ("Blue"). "Country Crossroads" won worldwide coverage through its syndication on the American Forces Radio Network and the Canadian Forces Radio network; see "LeRoy Van Dyke 'Sells' Jesus," *Country Sky* 1, no. 5 (June, 1971): 9.

58. Sandy Smith, "Country Gospel Artists Help Form New Musical Genre," *Music City News* 27, no. 10 (Apr., 1990): 28. *Music City News* published a "Christian Country Countdown" each issue listing the top twenty records as compiled from a select number of radio stations that programmed such music.

59. Unsigned article, "Ricky Skaggs," in *CMA Close Up* 27, no. 10 (Oct., 1992): 11. The video and accompanying CD are both called *Silent Witness: A Tribute to Country's Gospel Legacy* (Columbia CK 66974). See Lorie Hollabaugh, "Touching, Personal Stories Make 'Silent Witness' a Work of Love," *Country Weekly* 1, no. 20 (May 16, 1995): 55–57.

60. Ken Griffis, "I've Got So Many Million Years": The Story of Stuart Hamblen," *JEMF Quarterly* 14, no. 49 (Spring, 1978): 4–22. Jac L. Tharpe discusses eight of these accounts in "Homemade Soap: The Sudsy Autobios of the Linsey Crowd," *Southern Quarterly* (special issue on country music) 22, no. 3 (Spring, 1984): 145–57.

61. Elise Miller Davis, *The Answer Is God: The Inspiring Personal Story of Dale Evans and Roy Rogers* (New York: McGraw-Hill, 1955).

62. Dale Evans, assisted by Carlton Stowers, has told her own story in *Happy Trails: The Story of Roy Rogers and Dale Evans* (Waco, Tex.: Word Books, 1979).

63. S. Davis, *Bus Fare to Kentucky;* June Carter Cash, *From the Heart* (New York: Prentice-Hall, 1987); Jerry Clower, with Gerry Wood, *Ain't God Good!* (Waco, Tex.: Word Books, 1975); Charles Paul Conn, *The New Johnny Cash* (New York: Family Library, 1973); Jeannie C. Riley, with Jamie Buckingham, *From Harper Valley to the Mountain Top* (New York: Ballantine Books, 1981);

Barbara Mandrell, with George Vecsey, *Get to the Heart: My Story* (New York: Bantam Books, 1990); Reba McEntire, with Tom Carter, *Reba: My Story* (New York: Bantam Books, 1994); Naomi Judd, *Love Can Build a Bridge* (New York: Fawcett Crest, 1993).

64. Kristofferson has since cast considerable doubt on the authenticity of his "conversion." It seems that he did have a profoundly emotional experience in Jimmie Rodgers Snow's Evangel Temple in Nashville, but he suggests that he may have been embarrassed or pressured into making a commitment that did not necessarily connote being "saved." The experience, however, did lead to his writing of the great song "Why Me, Lord" (Monument 8571); see Jack McClintock, "Just a Good Ole Rhodes Scholar," *Playboy* 22, no. 3 (Mar., 1975): 93, 95, 122, 170, 171–75.

65. Bob Harrington was long known for his ministry on Bourbon Street in New Orleans. Walter Bailes, of course, had been a mainstay of the Bailes Brothers before becoming a Pentecostal evangelist.

66. Lee Rector, "Star's Son Is Music City Chaplain," *Music City News* (Oct., 1979): 42, 53; Wesley Jackson, "The Grand Ole Gospel Hour," *New Orleans Times-Picayune,* May 25, 1980, sec. 1, p. 35; Bob Battle, "Church of the Stars," *CountryStyle,* no. 23 (Aug. 11, 1977): 32–33.

67. Johnny Cash, *The Man in White* (San Francisco: Harper & Row, 1986), p. 4.

68. Conn, *New Johnny Cash,* pp. 33–40; Cash has referred to other spiritual turning points in his life. For example, he told the journalist Dotson Rader that he had made a recommitment to Christ sometime in 1967 after seeking refuge in a cave near Chattanooga; see "I Can Sing of Death, but I'm Obsessed with Life," *Parade Magazine,* June 11, 1995, pp. 4–5.

69. The best introduction to Cash's thinking is his autobiography (written with Patrick Carr), *The Man in Black* (Grand Rapids, Mich.: Zondervan, 1995).

70. Lawrence Wright, "The First Church of Rednecks, White Socks and Blue Ribbon Beer," *Rolling Stone,* Dec. 13–27, 1990, pp. 133, 135–37, 142, 228; Waylon Jennings, with Lenny Kaye, *Waylon: An Autobiography* (New York: Warner Books, 1996), pp. 366–70.

71. Wicentowski's CD of 1998, *Lucky Break* (Wizgrass CD 00001-2), which introduced his music to the larger bluegrass public, received generous critical praise from David Freeman in his highly respected and widely circulated catalogue, *County Sales Newsletter* no. 228 (Oct., 1998).

72. Howard Wight Marshall, "Keep on the Sunny Side of Life: Pattern and Religious Expression in Bluegrass Gospel Music," *New York Folklore Quarterly* 30 (1974): 3–43.

73. Claims of having inaugurated the first bluegrass festival have been made by both Bill Clifton and Carlton Haney. Haney has adamantly denied Clifton's claim in Barry Willis, *America's Music: Bluegrass* (Franktown, Colo.: Pine Valley Music, 1989), p. 473.

74. Interviews with Enoch Sullivan, Pollock, La., July 23, 1976; and Margie Sullivan, Walker, La., July 12, 1975, and Coushatta, La., July 26, 1976. All of the Sullivan Family recordings have been released on small southern labels or have been self-produced. Marty Stuart, though, produced an album by Jerry and Tammy Sullivan, *Tomorrow* (Ceili CD 2005). The Jack Bernhardt quote is in the album notes.

75. Joe Wilson, "The Chestnut Grove Quartet," *Bluegrass Unlimited* 30, no. 1 (July, 1995): 54–58. One compact disc of their material is available, *The Legendary Chestnut Grove Quartet* (County CD 1709). It contains their influential recordings of "Just Over Yonder" and "The Great Beyond."

76. John Wright asserts that Stanley's first recorded foray into a capella singing came in 1971 with the singing of "Bright Morning Star" on the LP *Cry from the Cross* (Rebel SLP 1499); see *Traveling the High Way Home: Ralph Stanley and the World of Traditional Bluegrass Music* (Urbana: University of Illinois Press, 1993), pp. 16, 253. Doyle Lawson's first gospel album, *Rock My Soul* (Sugar Hill SH-CD-3717), included an African American a capella piece, "Jesus Gave Me Water." The Nashville Bluegrass Band regularly presents some of the finest examples of a capella performances, particularly in their borrowings from black gospel tradition; see *To Be His Child* (Rounder CD-0242).

77. Loyal Jones made available to me copies of two paperback songbooks from the Hollybush Regular Baptist Church in eastern Kentucky. Both have the same title, *Some of Our Favorite Songs,* but they contain slightly different sets of songs.

78. Emmylou Harris, "The Darkest Hour" and "Wayfaring Stranger" are on *Roses in the Snow* (Warner Brothers BSR 3422), and "Angel Band" is on an album with the same title (Warner Brothers 9 25585-2).

79. The Nitty Gritty Dirt Band, *Will the Circle Be Unbroken* (EMI E22V-46589).

80. DeMent and Haggard collaborated on the writing of "This Kind of Happy," heard in her *The Way I Should* (Warner Brothers 9362-46188-2). DeMent sang Haggard's "Big City" on *Tulare Dust: A Songwriter's Tribute to Merle Haggard* (Hightone HCD 8058), and he sang her "No Time to Cry" on his album, *1996* (Curb D 2-77796).

81. Bob Allen, "The Spellbinding Music of Iris DeMent," *Country Music* no. 192 (July–Aug., 1998): 50.

82. "Fifty Miles of Elbow Room" and "Higher Ground" are included in DeMent's *Infamous Angel* (Philo CD PH 1138). Charles H. Gabriel said that when "Higher Ground" was written in 1898, it "at once took high rank among holiness people" (*Singers and Their Songs,* p. 22).

83. Merle Haggard, *The Land of Many Churches* (Capitol SWB 0-803); *Songs for the Mama That Tried* (MCA-5280).

84. "If We Never Meet Again" was also Elvis Presley's mother's favorite song. It was no. 115 in the Stamps Quartet's *Divine Praise,* their convention book of 1945.

Chapter 5: "When the Lord Made Me, He Made a Rambling Man"

1. Jimmie Rodgers, "Train Whistle Blues" (Victor 22379): released on June 5, 1930.

2. W. Cash, *Mind of the South*, pp. 44–47, 56–58.

3. Interviews with Jimmy Arnold in Tyler, Tex., Mar. 1 and 8, 1986. Eddie Dean wrote an outstanding essay on Arnold that captures the essence of the man, his genius, and his tragedy; see "Lost Soul," *Journal of Country Music* 16, no. 1 (1993): 20–32.

4. Jimmy Arnold, *Southern Soul* (Rebel REB 1621); also released on CD in 1983 with the same title and number.

5. Henry Whitter, "Lonesome Road Blues" (Okeh 40015). Most people probably know the version popularized by Woody Guthrie, rereleased on *This Land Is Your Land*, the Asch Recordings, vol. 1 (Smithsonian Folkways CD 40100-2), or the instrumental versions played by bluegrass banjo pickers. Earl Scruggs's rendition of the tune has been most influential among other musicians.

6. Charlie Daniels's recording, "The Devil Went down to Georgia" (Epic 50700), was based around a fiddle contest between a good old boy and the Devil. The good old boy won, and the record went to number one on the charts.

7. The most ambitious study of these persistent values is Bertram Wyatt-Brown, *Southern Honor: Ethics and Behavior in the Old South* (New York: Oxford University Press, 1982). See also Fischer, *Albion's Seed*, and Elliott Gorn's brilliant account of violence and masculinity among lower-class whites, "'Gouge and Bite, Pull Hair and Scratch': The Social Significance of Fighting in the Southern Backcountry," *American Historical Review* 90, no. 1 (Feb., 1985): 18–43.

8. Rhys Isaac has described the colonial roots of these manly competitions in *The Transformation of Virginia, 1740–1790* (Chapel Hill: University of North Carolina Press, 1982). Other important studies that concentrate on the rural South as a whole are Edward L. Ayers, *Vengeance and Justice: Crime and Punishment in the Nineteenth-Century American South* (New York: Oxford University Press, 1984); Dickson D. Bruce, Jr., *Violence and Culture in the Antebellum South* (Austin: University of Texas Press, 1979); Newby, *Plain Folk in the New South;* and Ownby, *Subduing Satan.* The WPA interviews of southern workers during the Depression years convey good descriptions of rough expressions of masculinity among poor men; see *These Are Our Lives*, interviews collected and written by members of the WPA Federal Writers' Project (Chapel Hill: University of North Carolina Press, 1939; reprint, New York: W. W. Norton, 1975); Tom Terrill and Jerrold Hirsch, *Such as Us: Southern Voices of the Thirties* (Chapel Hill: University of North Carolina Press, 1978; reprint, New York: W. W. Norton, 1979).

9. Few books were more popular in eighteenth- and nineteenth-century America than John Bunyan's *Pilgrim's Progress* (first published in 1678).

10. Rosemary Gaby, "Of Vagabonds and Commonwealths: Beggars Bush, a Jovial Crew, and the Sisters," *Studies in English Literature, 1500–1900* 34, no.

2 (Spring, 1994): 401–24; J. J. Jusserand, *English Wayfaring Life in the Middle Ages*, 3d ed. (1889; London: Adelphi Terrace, 1925); Frank Aydelotte, *Elizabethan Rogues and Vagabonds* (London: Clarendon Press, 1913); Arthur V. Judges, *The Elizabethan Underworld* (London: George Routledge and Sons, 1930); Muriel St. Clare Byrne, *Elizabethan Life in Town and Country*, rev. ed. (1925; London: Methuen, 1934).

11. Byrne, *Elizabethan Life in Town and Country*, p. 90.

12. "The Gypsy Laddie" (Child 200) has been recorded in country music in a variety of versions, usually as "Black Jack David"; for examples, see the Carter Family (Decca 5732); Cliff Carlisle (Okeh 06313); T. Texas Tyler (Four Star 1052); and Dave Alvin (Hightone HCD 8091). Nick Tosches wrote an intriguing account of the ballad's country music life, in *Country: The Biggest Music in America* (New York: Stein and Day, 1977), pp. 6, 8–19.

13. "The House Carpenter" is a descendant of "The Daemon Lover" (Child 243). An interesting account of its American history is Alisoun Gardner-Medwin, "The Ancestry of 'The House Carpenter,' a Study of the Family History of the American Forms of Child 243," *Journal of American Folklore* 84, no. 334 (Oct.-Dec., 1971): 414–27. The most influential version of the ballad has been Clarence Ashley's performance (Columbia 15654-D, and in the *Anthology of American Folk Music*). "Little Matty Groves" has been collected and recorded under many names, but it is ultimately traceable to "Little Musgrave and Lady Barnard" (Child 81). The most powerful country rendition of the song is by Doc Watson, on *Home Again!* (Vanguard VSD-79239).

14. Eric Hobsbawm, *Social Bandits* (New York: Delacorte Press, 1969); Maurice Keen, *The Outlaws of Medieval Legend*, rev. ed. (1961; London: Routledge and Kegan Paul; Toronto: University of Toronto Press, 1977); Frederick W. Turner III, "Badmen, Black and White: The Continuity of American Folk Traditions" (Ph.D. diss., University of Pennsylvania, 1965), esp. pp. 67–96; Gamini Salgado, *The Elizabethan Underworld* (London: J. M. Dent, 1977).

15. Kent Ladd Steckmesser, *Western Outlaws: The "Good Badman" in Fact, Film, and Folklore* (Claremont Calif.: Regina Books, 1983); Robertus Love, *The Rise and Fall of Jesse James* (New York: G. P. Putnam's Sons, 1926); Homer Croy, *Jesse James Was My Neighbor* (New York: Duell, Sloan and Pearce, 1949); William A. Settle, Jr., *Jesse James Was His Name* (Columbia: University of Missouri Press, 1966); Ralph Stanley's version of "Jesse James Prayed" is on *Over the Sunset Hill* (King 1032).

16. Jimmy Arnold, "Jesse James," on *Southern Soul*.

17. Frank Owsley, *Plain Folk of the Old South* (1949; reprint, Baton Rouge: Louisiana State University Press, 1982); McWhiney, *Cracker Culture*; Hahn, *Roots of Southern Populism*.

18. Miles, *Spirit of the Mountains*, p. 68.

19. Hahn, *Roots of Southern Populism*.

20. Ownby, *Subduing Satan*, pp. 14–15.

21. Mickey Crews, *The Church of God: A Social History* (Knoxville: University of Tennessee Press, 1990).

22. Gorn, "'Gouge and Bite, Pull Hair and Scratch.'"

23. It is at least mildly interesting that this great ballad and other songs about bad men were frequently recorded by women. For example—Eva Davis, "Wild Bill Jones" (Columbia 129-D); Roba Stanley, "Railroad Bill" (Okeh 40295); and Eva Davis, "John Hardy" (Columbia 167D). Roba Stanley, "Little Frankie" (Columbia 167D), is about a murderous woman. Maybe ladies *do* love outlaws!

24. Dave Hickey, untitled article, *Country Music Magazine* 3, no. 5 (Feb., 1975): 10.

25. Norm Cohen's listing of songs and recordings devoted to John Henry is exhausting and exemplary; see *Long Steel Rail*, pp. 61–89. The classic early books on this legendary railroad worker are Guy B. Johnson, *John Henry: Tracking Down a Negro Legend* (Chapel Hill: University of North Carolina Press, 1929), and Louis W. Chappell, *John Henry: A Folk-Lore Study* (Jena, Germany: Frommannsche Verlag, 1933). Good recorded samplings of outlaw music are *Bad Man Ballads*, vol. 5 in Alan Lomax's *Southern Journey* collection (Rounder 1705), and *My Rough and Rowdy Ways: Early American Rural Music*, vol. 2: *Badman Ballads and Hellraising Songs* (Yazoo 2040).

26. Charles Wolfe, notes to Burnett and Rutherford, *A Ramblin' Reckless Hobo* (Rounder 1004). McClintock's incredibly rich and varied life as a worker and singer is summarized by Lou Curtiss, notes to Harry McClintock, *Hallelujah! I'm a Bum* (Rounder 1009). Curtiss compiled his notes from letters and occasional magazine pieces written by McClintock. McClintock can also be heard talking about his days as an IWW ballad maker on the CD *Don't Mourn—Organize! Songs of Labor Songwriter Joe Hill* (Smithsonian Folkways SF 40026).

27. Kinney Rohrer has written an excellent account of the influential Piedmont musician; see *Rambling Blues: The Life and Songs of Charlie Poole* (London: OTM Booklet 3, 1982). He also wrote the liner notes for the three CDs of Poole's music issued by the County label. See also his notes to the recorded anthology of Piedmont musicians, *Cotton Mills and Fiddles* (Flyin' Cloud FC-014).

28. Nolan Porterfield, *Jimmie Rodgers: The Life and Times of America's Blue Yodeler* (Urbana: University of Illinois Press, 1979, 1992), p. 7

29. *New Orleans Item-Tribune,* June 30, 1929.

30. George Milburn, *The Hobo's Hornbook* (New York: Ives Washburn, 1930); Nels Anderson, *The Hobo* (Chicago: University of Chicago Press, 1961); Kenneth Allsop, *Hard Travellin'* (London: Hodder and Stoughton, 1967). "Hobo Bill's Last Ride" (Victor 22421). "Waiting for a Train" (Victor V-40014); "Hobo's Meditation" (Victor 23711). As in all areas of railroad lore and song, Norm Cohen's discussion of hoboes and hobo music is indispensable; see *Long Steel Rail,* "In a Boxcar around the World," pp. 343–400.

31. The word "blues," as in the term "blue devils," had appeared in British cultural discourse as a description of melancholia long before it became identified with music.

32. "Do Right Daddy Blues" is in Gene Autry, *Blues Singer, 1929–1931* (Columbia/Legacy CK 64987); "Red Nightgown Blues" can be heard on *White Country Blues, 1926–1938: A Lighter Shade of Blue* (Columbia/Legacy C2K 47466) or on the huge Jimmie Davis box collection, *Nobody's Darlin' but Mine* (Bear Family BCD 15943). For a discussion of early exploitation of black stereotypes by white musicians and audiences, see Robert Toll's important study of blackface minstrelsy, *Blacking Up: The Minstrel Show in Nineteenth-Century America* (New York: Oxford University Press, 1974).

33. The music of most of the white country blues singers mentioned in this chapter can be heard on the collection *White Country Blues: A Lighter Shade of Blue*. Other important collections include Cliff Carlisle, *Blues Yodeler and Steel Guitar Wizard* (Arhoolie Folklyric 7039); Darby and Tarlton, *On the Banks of a Lonely River* (County CD-3503); Frank Hutchison, *The Train That Carried My Girl from Town* (Rounder 1007); the Allen Brothers, *The Chattanooga Boys* (Old Timey LP-115); Buddy Jones, *Buddy Jones: Louisiana's Honky Tonk Man* (Texas Rose TXR 2711); *Mister Charlie's Blues, 1926–1936* (Yazoo L-1024); and of course, the Gene Autry anthology, *Blues Singer, 1929–1931*. A recent reminder that black singers also absorbed material from white performers is *From Where I Stand: The Black Experience in Country Music* (Warner Brothers 9 46428-2).

34. Tosches, *Country: The Biggest Music in America*, p. 118.

35. Although I had an interview with Jimmie Davis in Baton Rouge, Louisiana, my understanding of the Singing Governor has been most enhanced by Kevin Fontenot, who is preparing a doctoral dissertation on the former governor at Tulane University. Nick Tosches did most to rivet attention on Davis's blues material in *Country: The Biggest Music in America*, pp. 118–28 and passim.

36. Donald Lee Nelson, notes to to the LP, *Buddy Jones: Louisiana's Honky Tonk Man* (Texas Rose TXR 2711).

37. Dick Justice, "Cocaine" (Brunswick 395), can be heard on *Mister Charlie's Blues, 1926–1936* (Yazoo L-1024), and on the CD *My Rough and Rowdy Ways*, vol. 2 (Yazoo 2040). The Skillet Lickers' "Soldier's Joy" (Columbia 15538-D) has been often recorded, and is available on *Classic Country Music*, 4 CDs (RD 042). Charlie Poole, "Take a Drink on Me" (Columbia 15193-D). Ted Ownby concentrates on the popularity of alcohol among men in the late nineteenth-century South, and argues that "drinking and drunkenness were the most popular recreations in Southern towns" (*Subduing Satan*, p. 50). Grady McWhiney argues that the penchant for whiskey and heavy drinking began among the ancestors of white southerners in northern England, Scotland, Ireland, and Wales (*Cracker Culture*, pp. 90–92, 131–32).

38. Willie Nelson, "I Gotta Get Drunk (and I Shore Do Dread It)," in *Redneck Mothers* (RCA AYL 1-3674). The song was also a hit in 1963 for Joe Carson (Liberty 55578).

39. See Michael Lee Masterson, "Sounds of the Frontier: Music in Buffalo Bill's Wild West" (Ph.D. diss., University of New Mexico, 1990).

40. Nolan Porterfield has written the definitive biography of Lomax, *The Last*

Cavalier: The Life and Times of John A. Lomax, 1867–1948 (Urbana: University of Illinois Press, 1996). Bentley Ball's recording of "The Dying Cowboy" (Columbia A 3085) is included in Norm Cohen's collection, *Minstrels and Tunesmiths.*

41. The story of the writing and recording of "Billy the Kid" is told by Jim Bob Tinsley in *He Was Singin' This Song* (Orlando: University Presses of Florida, 1981), pp. 181–82. Walter Noble Burns, *The Saga of Billy the Kid* (Garden City, N.Y.: Doubleday, Page, 1925). See also D. K. Wilgus, "The Individual Song: 'Billy the Kid,'" *Western Folklore* 30, no. 3 (July, 1971): 226–34. The earliest recording of the song was by Vernon Dalhart (Okeh 45102), but the Sons of the Pioneers had the finest version, recorded for a variety of labels (including Vocalion 04136).

42. The Sprague recording of "When the Work's All Done This Fall" (Victor 19747) has been anthologized in *Authentic Cowboys and Their Western Folksongs* (RCA Victor Vintage LPV-522), notes by Fred Hoeptner; in *Back in the Saddle Again: American Cowboy Songs* (New World Records NW 314/315-2), notes by Charlie Seeman; and in *The Smithsonian Collection of Classic Country Music,* notes by Bill C. Malone. John White wrote the history of the song in *Git Along, Little Dogies: Songs and Songmakers of the American West* (Urbana: University of Illinois Press, 1975).

43. Stuart Hamblen, "The Texas Plains" (Decca D 5001). References to cowboy singers abound in the periodical press of the 1930s and 1940s that was devoted to radio programming or hillbilly music (*Radio Digest, Broadcasting, Rural Radio, National Hillbilly News, The Mountain Broadcast and Prairie Recorder, Stand By,* and, of course, *Billboard*). Most of these magazines are on file, although not always complete, in the Country Music Hall of Fame and Museum in Nashville or in the John Edwards Memorial material at the Southern Folk Life Collection, University of North Carolina, Chapel Hill.

44. "The Land of My Boyhood Dreams" (Victor 22381); "Yodeling Cowboy" (Victor 22271); "Prairie Lullaby" (Victor 23781); "When the Cactus Is in Bloom" (Victor 23636); "The Yodeling Ranger" (Victor 23830); "The Cowhand's Last Ride" (Victor 24456); "Waiting for a Train" (Victor V-40014).

45. Charles Townsend, *San Antonio Rose: The Life and Music of Bob Wills* (Urbana: University of Illinois Press, 1976, 1986), pp. 25–26.

46. Escott, with Merritt and MacEwen, *Hank Williams: The Biography;* R. Williams, *Sing a Sad Song;* Flippo, *Your Cheatin' Heart.*

47. Cusic, *Hank Williams: The Complete Lyrics; The Complete Hank Williams,* a boxed collection of 10 CDS (Mercury 314536077-2).

48. Moe Bandy, "Hank Williams, You Wrote My Life" (Columbia 10265); Waylon Jennings, "The Hank Williams Syndrome," is in *Too Dumb for New York City, Too Ugly for L.A.* (Epic EK 489820).

49. Mark A. Humphrey, "Hillbilly Heaven," *Guitar World Acoustic* no. 29 (1998): 27–34.

50. Songs asserting a link between Hank and modern country singers include Waylon Jennings, with Hank Jr., "The Conversation" (RCA 13631); Hank Jr., "Hank" (MGM 14550) and "A Family Tradition" (Elektra/Curb 46046), and Stoney Edwards, "Hank and Lefty Raised My Country Soul" (Capitol 3671). The quote, "There ain't no light," is found in Escott, with Merritt and MacEwen, *Hank Williams: The Biography,* p. 193.

51. Greil Marcus, *Mystery Train: Images of America in Rock 'n' Roll Music,* 4th rev. ed. (New York: Penguin, 1997), p. 131. As noted earlier (n. 60 to chap. 3), the definitive biography of Elvis Presley is Peter Guralnick's highly praised two-volume study.

52. I have described Presley's relationship to country music in "Country Elvis," in *In Search of Elvis,* ed. Vernon Chadwick (Boulder, Colo.: Westview Press, 1997), pp. 3–19. W. J. Cash's famous *Mind of the South* is the source of the influential idea concerning southern piety and hedonism. A provocative testing of the idea is Ownby, *Subduing Satan.*

53. Sam Phillips captured Elvis, Jerry Lee Lewis, and Carl Perkins on tape singing an impromptu mix of songs in the Sun Studio in December, 1957. Bluegrass and vintage country songs appeared prominently. The session is discussed by Peter Guralnick in *Last Train to Memphis,* pp. 365–68, and by Tosches in *Hellfire,* pp. 115–17. Craig Morrison's *Go Cat Go!* is a good overview of the relationship between this music and youth culture. A work that sets Elvis and the Rockabillies in the context of a changing southern youth culture and its adaptation to the revolution in racial relations that occurred in the 1950s is Bertrand, *Race, Rock, and Elvis.*

54. Tosches, *Country: The Biggest Music in America,* p. 65. Good biographies of Jerry Lee Lewis include Tosches, *Hellfire;* Robert Palmer, *Jerry Lee Lewis Rocks* (New York: Delilah Books, 1981); and Myra Lewis, with Murray Silver, *Great Balls of Fire! The Uncensored Story of Jerry Lee Lewis* (New York: St. Martin's Press, 1982). Stephen Ray Tucker discusses the role of Pentecostal religion in the lives of Jerry Lee and Elvis in "Pentecostalism and Popular Culture in the South: A Study of Four Musicians," *Journal of Popular Culture* 16, no. 3 (Winter, 1982): 68–80.

55. Johnny Cash, "Folsom Prison Blues" (Sun 232). Cash has elicited several biographies, including a short essay by Fred Danker in Malone and McCulloh, *Stars of Country Music,* and Christopher Wren, *Winners Got Scars Too: The Life and Legends of Johnny Cash* (New York: Dial Press, 1971), but the best insight into his thinking is Johnny Cash, with Patrick Carr, *Johnny Cash: The Autobiography* (New York: HarperCollins, 1997).

56. Vernon Dalhart, "The Prisoner's Song" (Victor 19427); Tom Darby and Jimmie Tarlton recorded "Birmingham Jail" and "Columbus Stockade Blues" (Columbia 15212-D) in 1927. "Twenty One Years," written by Bob Miller, was first recorded in 1930 by Miller and Barney Burnett (Gennett 7220) and, in its most successful version, by Mac and Bob (Brunswick 483); "Roy Dixon" was recorded by Jimmie Tarlton (Columbia 15629-D). The Blue Sky Boys recorded

"In the Hills of Roane County" (Bluebird B-8693-A), and the Stanley Brothers did it as "The Hills of Roan County," in *Folk Concert* (King 834).

57. Horstman, *Sing Your Heart Out, Country Boy,* p. 291.

58. C. Wolfe and Lornell, *Life and Legend of Leadbelly.*

59. *Sing Out!* 15, no. 4 (Sept., 1965): 91. Cash comments on his reasons for wearing black costumes in his autobiography (Cash, *Johnny Cash: The Autobiography,* p. 86).

60. Johnny Cash's second recording of "Folsom Prison Blues" is on Columbia 44513 and on the CD *Johnny Cash at Folsom Prison* (Columbia/Legacy CK 65955). Jay Orr wrote a good review of the recording session in the *Journal of American Academy for the Preservation of Old-Time Country Music* 2, no. 4 (Aug., 1992): 25.

61. The best evidence of Haggard's youthful, clean-cut image are the album covers of his early Capitol releases: *Strangers* (Capitol 3273); *Just between the Two of Us* (Capitol 2453); and *Branded Man* (Capitol ST 2789). The written material on Haggard is enormous. His autobiography, though, is a good place to start: Haggard, with Peggy Russell, *Sing Me Back Home: My Story* (New York: Times Books, 1981). Also recommended are Peter Guralnick, "Merle Haggard: In the Good Old Days (When Times Were Bad)," *Journal of Country Music* 8, no. 1 (1979): 39–46, 63–64; A. Gerrard, "Merle Haggard: 'I Take a Lot of Pride in What I Am'"; Bryan DiSalvatore, "Profiles: Merle Haggard," *New Yorker* 65, no. 52 (Feb. 12, 1990): 39–77; Paul Hemphill, "Merle Haggard," in Malone and McCulloh, *Stars of Country Music,* pp. 357–73, and Dawidoff, *In the Country of Country,* esp. pp. 249–62.

62. The original title was "The Fugitive" (Capitol 5803).

63. "Branded Man" (Capitol 5931); "Sing Me Back Home" (Capitol 2017); "Mama Tried" (Capitol 2219).

64. Haggard's Capitol recordings have been released in a box set, *Down Every Road, 1962–1994,* with extensive notes by Daniel Cooper (Capitol Cap 7 2438 35711 2). "Working Man's Blues" (Capitol 2503); "Fightin' Side of Me" (Capitol 2719); "Rambling Fever" (MCA 40743).

65. Ann Malone and Bill C. Malone, "Johnny Rodriguez," in Malone and McCulloh, *Stars of Country Music,* pp. 377–97.

66. The best short account of Paycheck's life and career is Daniel Cooper's notes to *Johnny Paycheck: The Real Mr. Heartache* (Country Music Foundation CMF-023D). "I'm the Only Hell That Mama Ever Raised" (Epic 50391).

67. "Pardon Me (I've Got Someone to Kill)" is one of twenty-four songs anthologized in *The Real Mr. Heartache* compact disc. It is also included in the aptly named CD anthology *Rebels and Outlaws: Music from the Wild Side of Life* (Capitol 72435-20014), notes by Colin Escott.

68. Rich Wiseman, "David Allan Coe's Death Row Blues: Rhinestone Ripoff?" *Rolling Stone,* Jan. 1, 1976, p. 16; Larry L. King, "David Allan Coe's Greatest Hits," *Esquire* 86, no. 1 (1976): 71, 73, 142–44; Martha Hume, "David Allan

Coe's Strange Saga," *Country Music* 5, no. 6 (Mar., 1976): 14; Michael Bane, "David Allan Coe's Long Hard Ride," *Country Music* no. 111 (Jan.–Feb., 1985): 31–34. David Allan Coe, "Willie, Waylon, and Me" (Columbia 10395).

69. Waylon noted that "there wasn't anything about a Nashville Rebel in the movie" (Jennings, *Waylon: An Autobiography,* p. 139).

70. Ibid., pp. 209, 222–24.

71. Willie Nelson, with Bud Shrake, *Willie: An Autobiography* (New York: Simon and Schuster, 1988), p. 169.

72. The first description of the Austin music scene was Reid, *Improbable Rise of Redneck Rock.* He later lamented the decline of the phenomenon in "Who Killed Redneck Rock," *Texas Monthly* 4 (Dec., 1976): 112–13, 209–16. The best assessments of the Austin musical era, though, are Archie Green, "Austin's Cosmic Cowboys: Words in Collision," in *"And Other Neighborly Names": Social Process and Cultural Image in Texas Folklore,* ed. Richard Bauman and Roger D. Abrahams (Austin: University of Texas Press, 1981), pp. 152–94; Nicholas Spitzer, "Bob Wills Is Still the King: Romantic Regionalism and Convergent Culture in Central Texas," *JEMF Quarterly* 2, part 4, no. 4 (Winter, 1975): 191–97; Barry Shank, *Dissonant Identities: The Rock'n'Roll Scene in Austin, Texas* (Hanover, N.H.: Wesleyan University Press, 1994); and Clifford Endres, *Austin City Limits* (Austin: University of Texas Press, 1987).

73. Douglas Kent Hall, "Mr. Bojangles' Dance: The Odyssey and Oddities of Jerry Jeff Walker," *Rolling Stone,* Dec. 19, 1974, pp. 9, 20; John Morthland, "Jerry Jeff Rides Again," *Country Music* 6, no. 6 (Mar., 1978): 28–32; Chet Flippo, "One Week in the Life of Kinky Friedman," *Rolling Stone,* Oct. 11, 1973; Kaye Northcott, "Kinky Friedman's First Roundup," *Texas Monthly* 1, no. 4 (May, 1973): 95–96; Bryan Edward Stone, "'Ride 'Em, Jewboy': Kinky Friedman and the Texas Mystique," *Southern Jewish History* 1 (1998): 23–43. "They Ain't Makin' Jews like Jesus" can be heard in *Kinky Friedman* (Varese Vintage CD VSD-5488), while "Sold American" and "Ride 'Em Jewboy," are in *Sold American* (Vanguard VMD 79333). The most interesting collection of Friedman music is the tribute CD that Kinky produced himself—*Pearls in the Snow: The Songs of Kinky Friedman* (Kinkajou 669291181821). The collection includes performances by Friedman, Willie Nelson, Dwight Yoakam, Lyle Lovett, and others. I interviewed Kinky in Medina, Tex., Sept. 3, 1999.

74. Waylon Jennings, *Lonesome, On'ry and Mean* (RCA LSP-4854), and *Ladies Love Outlaws* (RCA LSP-4751); *Wanted: The Outlaws* (RCA APLI-1321). Blackburn's comment was made in an article, "Execs: Country Music World Hit by Drug, Alcohol Abuse," *Tyler* (Texas) *Courier-Times,* Sept. 3, 1984. Jennings's quotes are in *Waylon: An Autobiography,* pp. 112, 147, 239.

75. Erik Philbrook, "Best Frynds," *Country Guitar* 2, no. 5 (Dec., 1994): 45–51, 119. Country singers have recorded tribute albums to the Eagles, *Common Thread: The Songs of the Eagles* (Giant 924531-2), and to Lynyrd Skynyrd, *Skynyrd Frynds* (MCAD 11097).

76. Chet Flippo, "Getting By without the Allmans," *Creem* 6, no. 6 (Mar., 1974): 34–37, 75.

77. Ted Ownby, "Freedom, Manhood, and White Male Tradition in 1970s Southern Rock Music," in *Haunted Bodies: Gender and Southern Texts*, ed. Anne Godwyn Jones and Susan V. Donaldson (Charlottesville: University Press of Virginia, 1997), pp. 369–88.

78. Joe Nick Patoski, "Charlie Daniels' Rowdy, Southern, Swinging Music," *Rolling Stone*, Oct. 7, 1976, pp. 20–21; Russell Shaw, "Charlie Daniels: The Pride of Tennessee," *Country Music* 5, no. 6 (Mar., 1977): 42, 45.

79. Hank Williams, Jr., with Michael Bane, *Living Proof* (New York: Dell, 1979); John Eskow, "Oedipus Rocks: The Fall and Rise of Hank Williams Jr." *New Times* 10, no. 11 (May 29, 1978): 39–50; Chet Flippo, "Hank Williams Jr.'s Hard Road," *Rolling Stone*, June 1, 1978, pp. 8, 17; Bill Bell, "Hank Williams Jr. Is Breaking Away from Ghost of His Father," *Houston Post*, July 2, 1982, p. 15 E.

80. Hank Williams, Jr., "If the South Woulda Won" (Warner/Curb 27862); "Dixie on My Mind" (Elektra/Curb 47137).

81. Hank Williams, Jr., "A Country Boy Can Survive" (Elektra/Curb 47257); "Attitude Adjustment" (Warner/Curb 29253).

82. Hank Williams, Jr., "All My Rowdy Friends Are Coming Over Tonight," in *Major Moves* (Warner/Curb 1-25088); "All My Rowdy Friends Have Settled Down," in *The Pressure Is On* (Elektra SE 535).

83. Hank Williams, Jr., "A Family Tradition" (Elektra/Curb 46046).

84. An item in *Country Weekly* in July, 1998, noted that Hank had recorded the video introduction for ABC-TV's NFL broadcasts for nine consecutive seasons (5, no. 30 [July 28, 1998]: 3).

85. Lesley Sussman, *Yes, Lord, I'm Comin' Home! Country Music Stars Share Their Stories of Knowing God* (New York: Doubleday, 1997), p. 66.

86. Waylon Jennings, "Don't You Think This Outlaw Bit's Done Got out of Hand" (RCA 11390); "Hank Williams Syndrome" appeared on the CD *Too Dumb for New York City, Too Ugly for L.A.* (Epic EK 489820).

87. The songs were released in 1999 on a CD produced by Bobby Bare and called *Old Dogs* (Atlantic 83156-2). The song performed by Waylon Jennings is "I Don't Do It No More."

88. "Don't Give Your Heart to a Rambler" was written by Jimmie Skinner. One of the better recordings of the song was by Jimmy Martin, heard on *You Don't Know My Mind* (Rounder CDSS-21). Travis Tritt and Marty Stuart, "The Whiskey Ain't Working," in *It's All about to Change* (Warner Brothers 26589-2). The quote about old outlaws is in "Outlaws like Us," Travis Tritt, *Ten Feet Tall and Bulletproof* (Warner Brothers 45603-2).

89. Confederate Railroad, "Trashy Women," in *Confederate Railroad* (Atlantic 782335-2).

90. It is impossible to give a precise definition of "alternative" country music

because it encompasses a range of widely divergent styles. They are linked to each other, however, because the participating performers sing from outside the Top 40 milieu and are generally in rebellion against it. Many of the alternative acts, such as the "insurgent" performers who are identified with the Bloodshot label in Chicago, exhibit a strong rock influence or attitude. The alternative country music world is chronicled in *No Depression* (a magazine published in Seattle, Washington), which typically describes itself as an "alternative country music (whatever that is) bimonthly." The journal is a marvelous compendium of information about every style of country music that lies outside the Nashville establishment. David Goodman's *Modern Twang: An Alternative Country Music Guide and Directory* (Nashville: Dowling Press, 1999), is an encyclopedic source that every student and fan of country should own.

91. This song was included in Fulks's CD *South Mouth* (Bloodshot BS 023).

92. Jon Langford, notes to *For a Life of Sin* (Bloodshot BS 001).

93. *Straight Outta Boone County* (Bloodshot BS 019); *The Pine Valley Cosmonauts Salute the Majesty of Bob Wills* (Bloodshot BS 029). The transcriptions were released under the aegis of a subsidiary imprint called "Bloodshot Revival." The first releases have been Rex Allen, *The Last of the Great Singing Cowboys* (Bloodshot 801); Spade Cooley, *Shame on You* (Bloodshot 802); Hank Thompson, *Hank World* (Bloodshot 803); Pee Wee King, *Hoedown* (Bloodshot 804); Jimmie Davis, *Louisiana* (Bloodshot 805); Johnny Bond, *Country and Western* (Bloodshot BS 807); and Hank Penny, *Crazy Rhythm* (Bloodshot 806).

94. Bloodshot Records brochure on Split Lip Rayfield (no date; 912 W. Addison, Chicago).

95. Steve Earle, *Guitar Town* (MCA MCAD-5713). Helpful discussions of Steve Earle include Jay Cocks, "The Color of Country," *Time*, Sept. 8, 1986, p. 84; Patrick Carr, "Steve Earle Flat Out," *Southern Magazine* 3, no. 8 (May/June, 1989): 39–42, 82; Harold DeMuir, "The Hillbilly Boss," *Pulse!* no. 85 (Aug., 1990): 65–68; Peter Blackstock, "Steve Earle: Can't Keep a Good Man Down," *No Depression* 1, no. 3 (Spring, 1996): 33–37; Grant Alden, "Bring the Family," *No Depression*, no. 20 (Mar.–Apr., 1999): 56–65.

96. Steve Earle and the Del McCoury Band, *The Mountain* (E-Squared 1064-2).

Chapter 6: "Stay All Night, Stay a Little Longer; Dance All Night, Dance a Little Longer"

1. Billy Ray Cyrus, "Achy Breaky Heart," *Some Gave All* (Mercury 314-510635-2).

2. Brooks and Dunn, "Boot Scootin' Boogie" (Arista 12440); Guy Garcia, "Scoot Your Booty!" *Time*, Mar. 15, 1993, pp. 60–61; Lydia Dixon Harden, "Put on Your Dancing Shoes," *Music City News* 29, no. 8 (Feb., 1992).

3. Earl Spielman, "Traditional North American Fiddling: A Methodology for

the Historical and Comparative Analytical Style Study of Instrumental Musical Traditions" (Ph.D. diss., University of Wisconsin at Madison, 1975), p. 194.

4. Percy Scholes provides the best corrective to the old assumptions in *The Puritans and Music in England and New England: A Contribution to the Cultural History of Two Nations* (New York: Russell and Russell, 1962).

5. John Fitzhugh Millar, *Country Dances of Colonial America* (Williamsburg, Va.: Thirteen Colonies Press, 1990), p. 2.

6. Richard Nevell, *A Time to Dance: American Country Dancing from Hornpipes to Hot Hash* (New York: St. Martin's Press, 1977), p. 24.

7. Ibid., p. 26.

8. S. Foster Damon, "The History of Square Dancing," *American Antiquarian Society, Proceedings of the Annual Meeting* 62, no. 1 (Apr. 16, 1952): 80–81.

9. Ibid., p. 81.

10. Cecil Sharp, *The Country Dance Book* (London: Novelle and Co., 1918), part 5.

11. W. Eugene Hollon and Ruth Lapham Butler, *William Bollaert's Texas* (Norman: University of Oklahoma Press, 1956), p. 27.

12. Wheeler is mentioned in James E. Marks III, *America Learns to Dance: A Historical Study of Dance Education in America before 1900* (New York: Exposition Press, 1957), p. 25.

13. Charles Lanman, *Adventures in the Wilds of the United States and British American Provinces,* vol. 1 (Philadelphia: John W. Moore, 1856), p. 441; Frederick Gerstaecker, *Wild Sports of the Far West* (London: Routledge, 1856), p. 174.

14. For example, see Charles Read Baskervill's discussion in *The Elizabethan Jig* (Chicago: University of Chicago Press, 1929), pp. 12–13, 16.

15. Isaac Goldberg, *Tin Pan Alley: A Chronicle of American Popular Music* (New York: Frederick Ungar, 1961), p. 48. Goldberg lists Charles Queen and George McAuley as "minstrel clog dancers" (p. 52).

16. Augustus Baldwin Longstreet, *Georgia Scenes,* 2d ed. (1835; New York: Harper & Brothers, 1859), p. 15.

17. Isaac, *Transformation of Virginia,* p. 86. The banjo is presumed to have been of African slave origin, but the question of how it got into the hands of rural southern whites has been vigorously debated. Robert Winans believes that the instrument was popularized throughout the rural South by white touring minstrel entertainers ("The Folk, the Stage, and the Five-String Banjo in the Nineteenth Century," *Journal of American Folklore* 89 [Oct.–Dec., 1976]: 407–37). William Tallmadge and Cecelia Conway, on the other hand, present evidence that rural whites learned directly from blacks: Tallmadge, "The Folk Banjo and Clawhammer Performance Practice in the Upper South: A Study of Origins," in *The Appalachian Experience: Proceedings of the Sixth Annual Studies Conference,* ed. Barry M. Buxton (Boone, N.C.: Appalachian Consortium Press, 1983); Conway, *African Banjo Echoes in Appalachia: A Study of Folk Traditions* (Knoxville: University of Tennessee Press, 1995).

18. See Malone, *Singing Cowboys and Musical Mountaineers,* pp. 32–37.

19. *Spirit of the Times,* Sept. 2, 1843, p. 30.

20. Frederick Law Olmstead, *A Journey in the Back Country,* vol. 1 (1860; New York: G. P. Putnam's Sons, 1907), p. 160.

21. "Breakdown is a term from across the Atlantic and refers to the final rout before the breakup of a free and easy dancing party," *Jacobs' Orchestra Monthly* 2, n. 4 (Apr., 1911), p. 23. "Hoedown" had a similar meaning and may have meant literally the dancing celebration that followed the putting down of hoes or the end of harvest. Breakdown and hoedown could refer to a fiddle tune, a dance step, or a frolic.

22. Mortimer Smith, *The Life of Ole Bull* (Princeton, N.J.: Princeton University Press, 1943), p. 56. J. Olcutt Sanders has an anecdote about two fiddling brothers from Texas and Louisiana, Lon and Dan Williams, who journeyed to New Orleans to hear Ole Bull; see "Honor the Fiddler!" in *Texian Stomping Grounds,* Texas Folklore Society Publications, no. 17 (Austin: Texas Folklore Society, 1941), pp. 78–90. Gene Wiggins, convincingly demonstrates the popularity of ragtime melodies and other popular tunes among early hillbilly fiddlers ("Popular Music and the Fiddler," *JEMF Quarterly* 15 [Fall, 1979]: 144–52).

23. Good descriptions of the hornpipe are found in W. Chappell, *Popular Music of the Olden Time,* vol. 2 (London: Cramer, Beale, and Chappell, 1859), pp. 534, 539, 544–46; Gaston Vuillier, *A History of Dancing: From the Earliest Ages to Our Own Times* (New York: D. Appleton and Co., 1898), pp. 420–21; Baskervill, *Elizabethan Jig,* p. 16; A. W. Franks, *Social Dance* (London: Routledge and Kegan Paul, 1963), p. 83; and W. G. Raffe, *Dictionary of the Dance* (New York: A. S. Barnes, 1964), p. 228.

24. I first learned about this contest through an article written by Richard Hulan, "The First Annual Country Fiddlers' Contest," *Newsletter of the Tennessee Valley Old-Time Fiddlers' Association* 8 (Mar. 15, 1969): 15–18. The contest had been announced in the *Virginia Gazette,* Nov. 26, 1736, p. 4.

25. I found references to fiddling at Confederate reunions in scattered and varied sources such as *The Confederate Veteran; Billboard* 13, no. 3 (June 2, 1900), p. 6; and the *New Orleans Times-Democrat,* Jan. 24, Mar. 10, and Apr. 5, 1909.

26. Wayne Daniel, "The Georgia Old-Time Fiddlers' Conventions," *Bluegrass Unlimited* 17, no. 2 (Aug., 1982): 42–47; Guthrie Meade, "From the Archives: 1914 Atlanta Fiddle Convention," *JEMF Quarterly* 5, no. 13 (Spring, 1969): 27–30; Wayne Daniel, "Old Time Fiddlers' Contests on Early Radio," *JEMF Quarterly* 17, no. 61 (Fall, 1981): 159–66.

27. Kevin Fontenot is my source for material on Henry Gilliland. His information, in turn, came from the Henry Gilliland File at the Bernice Ford-Price Memorial Reference Library, Museum of the Western Prairie, Altus, Oklahoma. This material included a twenty-two page undated memoir (probably from 1915) written by Gilliland—*Life and Battles of Henry C. Gilliland for Seventy Years.*

He makes a few references to fiddle contests in the late nineteenth century and to fiddlers like Matt Brown, whom he describes as "the best fiddler on earth" (p. 19). Kevin Fontenot, New Orleans, to author, Nov. 2, 1997. For information on Eck Robertson, see Peter Feldmann's notes to the LP *Eck Robertson* (Sonyatone STR-201), which contains a complete discography; Peter Blanton, "Eck Robertson," *Old-Time Herald* 3, no. 5 (Fall, 1992): 20–25, a condensation of notes that accompanied field recordings made of Robertson in 1963 (County LP 202); and Charles K. Wolfe, "Whatever Happened to Country's First Recording Artist?" *Journal of Country Music* 16, no. 1 (1993): 33–41.

28. Guthrie Meade, who until his death in 1991 was the leading authority on southern fiddling, first told me about the early barn-dance programming on WBAP in Fort Worth (Guthrie Meade to author, Feb. 21, 1967). At his suggestion, I checked the newspaper's radio logs from late 1922 to May, 1923. See *Country Music, USA* (1st ed.), pp. 36–37.

29. George C. Biggar, "The WLS National Barn Dance Story: The Early Years," *JEMF Quarterly*, no. 23 (Autumn, 1971): 105–12.

30. C. Wolfe, *Good-Natured Riot*, p. 10. The best account of Fiddlin' John's discovery is Archie Green, "Hillbilly Music: Source and Symbol," p. 209. Fuller discussions of the early hillbilly radio scene in Atlanta, though, can be found in Wiggins, *Fiddlin' Georgia Crazy,* and Wayne Daniel, *Pickin' on Peachtree.*

31. "Fiddling to Henry Ford," *Literary Digest* 88, no. 1 (Jan. 2, 1926): 33–34, 36, 38. Ford's dance booklet was *"Good Morning." After a Sleep of Twenty-Five Years, Old-Fashioned Dancing Is Being Revived by Mr. and Mrs. Henry Ford* (Dearborn, Mich.: Dearborn Publishing, 1926). See Pete Sutherland, "Beware of Old-Time Music Revivals! The Henry Ford Story," *Old-Time Herald* 2, no. 7 (Feb.–Apr., 1991): 33–37; Art Menius, "Our Ford: Old Time Fiddling and Dancing," *Bluegrass Unlimited* 26, no. 8 (Feb., 1992): 36–39; Estelle Schneider and Bob Norman, "The Henry Ford Dance Movement: Fiddling While the Crosses Burned," *Sing Out!* 25, no. 4 (Nov.–Dec., 1977): 24–27; Don Roberson, "Uncle Bunt Stephens: Champion Fiddler," *Old-Time Music,* no. 5 (Summer, 1972): 4–6.

32. Dave Freeman, through his County record label, has documented many of the best fiddle and string band recordings of the 1920s and 1930s. These include *Mountain Fiddle Music* (County 503); *Old-Time Fiddle Classics* (County 507); *Old-Time Fiddle Classics,* vol. 2 (County 527); *Hell Broke Loose in Georgia: Georgia Fiddle Bands, 1927–1934* (County 514); and *Texas Farewell: Texas Fiddlers, 1922–1930* (County 517). The Skillet Lickers' version of "Soldier's Joy" is heard on *The Skillet Lickers* (County 5060) and on *The Smithsonian Collection of Classic Country Music.* Norm Cohen provides full and discerning notes about the band's career and repertoire in Malone and McCulloh, *Stars of Country Music,* pp. 27–34.

33. Interview with Sam McGee, Franklin, Tenn., Aug. 14, 1973.

34. *Old Time Get Together with Lew Childre* (Starday SLP 153); *On the Air* (Old Homestead OHCS-132).

35. Damon, "History of Square Dancing," p. 95. Burchenal's *Dances of the People* (New York: G. Schirmer, 1913) and *Twenty-Eight Contra-Dances, Largely from New England* (1918) were galvanizing forces behind the movement during the postwar era. The important roles played in the reinvigoration of country dancing by Cecil Sharp and Berea College in Kentucky (with its Christmas Country Dance School) are discussed by John Melville Forbes, "The Music Program of Berea College and the Folk-Music Heritage of Appalachia" (Ph.D. diss., University of Michigan, 1974).

36. Whisnant, *All That Is Native and Fine*, pp. 183–252.

37. Loyal Jones, *Minstrel of the Appalachians: The Story of Bascom Lamar Lunsford* (Boone, N.C.: Appalachian Consortium Press, 1984), pp. 40–50.

38. Ibid., p. 59. Phil Jamison is the premier student of dances popular in the Appalachians; see "In the Old Time Days: The Beginnings of Team Clogging," *Old-Time Herald* 1, no. 2 (Winter, 1987–88); "A Jubilant Spirit within Me . . . Breakdown, Flatfoot, or Clogging," ibid. 4, no. 2 (Winter, 1993): 14–15, 51.

39. Edward King, *The Great South* (Baton Rouge: Louisiana State University Press, 1972). For the sketch, see *Scribner's Monthly* 6, no. 3 (July, 1873): 285.

40. Nick Tosches found the 1894 reference in an Oklahoma newspaper, the Feb. 24 edition of the *Daily Ardmoreite* (*Country: The Biggest Music in America*, p. 24). Tad Jones, an authority on the music of New Orleans, told me about references to early honky-tonks in that city; see *New Orleans Times-Democrat,* Oct. 31, 1900; *New Orleans Daily-Picayune,* Jan. 21, 1905.

41. Al Dexter's "Honky Tonk Blues" (Vocalion 3435) is not the same song that Hank Williams later recorded (Al Dexter, Denton, Tex., to author, Sept. 21, 1973, and telephone interview with Dexter, Denton, Tex., Aug. 26, 1973).

42. References to a "honky-tonk style" of country music may have been in oral circulation, but the designation is not found in the music trade journals until the late sixties or even later. "Taproom" songs were sometimes mentioned. *Billboard* magazine, for example, described "You Are My Sunshine" as "the taproom and tavern classic of the year" (53, no. 34 [Aug. 23, 1941]: 13).

43. Hank Williams, "Honky Tonking" (MGM 10171); "Honky Tonk Blues" (MGM 11160).

44. The earliest discussion of honky-tonk culture and music was in my doctoral dissertation (1965), and then in the first edition of my book, *Country Music, USA* (1968), pp. 162–67, 200, 217. The best discussions of western swing and its pioneers are Townsend, *San Antonio Rose,* and Cary Ginell, *Milton Brown and the Founding of Western Swing* (Urbana: University of Illinois Press, 1994). A good inside account of Bob Wills's Tulsa years is provided by his piano player, Al Stricklin, with Jon McConal, *My Years with Bob Wills* (San Antonio: Naylor Company, 1976).

45. McAuliffe's quote comes from Townsend, *San Antonio Rose,* p. 38. Stricklin's recollections are from his book, *My Years with Bob Wills*, p. 32.

46. Jean A. Boyd argues that the western swing entertainers were jazz musi-

cians and not country at all; see *The Jazz of the Southwest: An Oral History of Western Swing* (Austin: University of Texas Press, 1998).

47. In the program notes to his appearance at the Hollywood Bowl in August, 1998, fiddler Mark O'Connor described Grappelli's contribution as "monumental," and called him "the greatest natural violinist in the world" (p. 45).

48. Susan Chadwick wrote an excellent explanation of the dance, "The Texas Two-Step," for *Texas Monthly*, Aug., 1985, p. 128. See also Betty Casey, *Dance across Texas* (Austin: University of Texas Press, 1985), esp. pp. 72–132.

49. See Haslam, *Workin' Man Blues*. Good samplings of West Coast country swing can be heard in *Swinging West* (Krazy Kat KK CD 15), *Swing West!* vol. 1: *Bakersfield* (Razor & Tie 7930182197-2) and, of course, Spade Cooley, *Shame on You* (Bloodshot 802).

50. Quoted in Nat Hentoff, *Listen to the Stories: Nat Hentoff on Jazz and Country Music* (New York: HarperCollins, 1995), p. 168.

51. Outstanding CDs that illustrate the Ray Price beat of the 1960s are his tribute to Bob Wills, *San Antonio Rose* (Koch KOC-3-7917, originally released on Columbia), and *The Essential Ray Price, 1951–1962* (Columbia/Legacy CK 48532).

52. Buck Owens in *Music City News* 2, no. 9 (Mar., 1965): 5.

53. Owens's contributions are discussed throughout Haslam, *Workin' Man Blues*, but especially on pp. 207–16. Harlan Howard described Owens's music as "hydromatic" in Dawidoff, *In the Country of Country*, p. 243.

54. Haslam, *Workin' Man Blues*, pp. 267–71.

55. The best discussion of Tommy Jackson is by Charles Wolfe, *The Devil's Box: Masters of Southern Fiddling* (Nashville: Country Music Foundation Press and Vanderbilt University Press, 1997), chap. 14. The Grand Ole Opry Square Dancers are discussed in *Music City News* 14, no. 9 (Mar., 1977): 18, 22. A short obituary of Ben Smathers is in *CMA Close Up* 25, no. 10 (Oct., 1990): 25.

56. Cosy Sheridan, "Deep in the Heart of Texas," *Acoustic Guitar* 9, no. 10 (Apr., 1999): 50–53.

57. Pat J. Ahrens, *Union Grove: The First Fifty Years* (privately printed by Pat Ahrens, 1975); Ahrens, "The Season Started Right at Union Grove," *Muleskinner News* 1, no. 3 (June, 1970): 2–3; Ahrens, "The Hub of the Universe: The Union Grove Old Time Fiddlers' Convention," *Muleskinner News* 2, no. 2 (Mar.–Apr., 1971): 12–13, 18; Fred Burton, "The Galax, Virginia, Old Fiddlers' Convention," *Bluegrass Unlimited* 18, no. 9 (Mar., 1984): 12–17; Jim Dodson, "Just Fiddlin' Around," *Atlanta Journal and Constitution Magazine*, June 10, 1979, pp. 34–35, 38.

58. Phil Jamison contributed a column to the *Old Time Herald* called "The Dance Beat." Since the mid-sixties, Mike Seeger had emphasized vocal and instrumental music in his concerts and in his role as folklorist and producer, but by the late eighties had begun to campaign for recognition of the vital role of dancing in folk music. He produced an important video called *Talking Feet, Solo*

Southern Dance: Buck, Flatfoot, and Tap (Flower Films, El Cerrito, Calif., 1989). Anne Johnson with Susan Spalding produced a video *Step Back, Cindy* (Appalshop, Whitesburg, Ky.).

59. Ray Price had recorded a superb album of Bob Wills's songs in 1961, *San Antonio Rose* (Columbia CL 1756, and as a CD, Koch KOC-3-7917) that featured the irresistible shuffle beat made famous by Price.

60. Haggard, *Sing Me Back Home*, p. 111.

61. Ibid.; Townsend, *San Antonio Rose;* Haggard's tribute album was called *The Best Damn Fiddle Player in the World* (Capitol ST-638); the reunion album, produced by Tommy Allsup, was entitled *Bob Wills and His Texas Playboys: For the Last Time* (United Artists UA-LA 216-J2); Benson and Asleep at the Wheel have recorded two important tributes to Wills, both featuring an array of guest artists: *A Tribute to the Music of Bob Wills and His Texas Playboys* (Liberty, 1993), and *Ride with Bob* (Dreamworks DRMD 50117).

62. Waylon Jennings certainly held no illusions about the liberality of his family's church, the Church of Christ. Speaking of it, he said "there was no room for grace; it was all hell-fire and brimstone" (*Waylon: An Autobiography*, p. 369).

63. Spitzer, "Bob Wills Is Still the King"; Alabama, "If You're Gonna Play in Texas (You Gotta Have a Fiddle in the Band)" (RCA 13840); Waylon Jennings's "Bob Wills Is Still the King" was first recorded in 1974 for an album, *Dreaming My Dreams* (RCA APL 1-1062).

64. Chet Flippo, "Willie Nelson," *Rolling Stone,* July 13, 1978, pp. 45–49; Roy Blount, Jr., "Wrasslin' with This Thing Called Willie Nelson," *Esquire,* Aug., 1981, pp. 78–80, 83–87; William C. Martin, "Growing Old at Willie Nelson's Picnic," *Texas Monthly* 2 (Oct., 1974): 94–98, 116–24.

65. Latham, "Ballad of the Urban Cowboy."

66. "Cotton-Eyed Joe" has been performed and recorded in several different versions. The Texas version of the song had been recorded by such musicians as Bob Wills and Adolph Hofner and His San Antonians long before the movie was ever made. Hofner's recording of 1941 (Columbia 37658) was apparently the performance that did most to popularize the song. See Ron Young, "Adolph Hofner: Sweet South Texas Swing," *Country Sounds* 2, no. 3 (Mar., 1987): 10, 48. Willie Nelson's movie, *Honeysuckle Rose,* which included a brief singing appearance by Kenneth Threadgill, was a much better representation of the Texas music scene in the late seventies and early eighties than was the movie *Urban Cowboy.*

67. Travis Tritt is usually credited with the term "hat act," a description that was not designed to be complimentary.

68. Quoted in Dan Daley, *Nashville's Unwritten Rules: Inside the Business of Country Music* (Woodstock, N.Y.: Overlook Press, 1999), p. 311.

69. Brooks and Dunn, "Boot Scootin' Boogie" (Arista 12440); Tim McGraw, "Indian Outlaw" (Curb 76920); Tracy Byrd, "Watermelon Crawl" (MCA 54889); Mary Chapin Carpenter, "Down at the Twist and Shout" (Columbia

73838). "Country Dancing Takes Giant Steps Forward," *Country Weekly* 3, no. 3 (Aug. 13, 1997): 10–13.

70. Barry Ancelet, *The Makers of Cajun Music* (Austin: University of Texas Press, 1984); *French Dance Tonight* (El Cerrito, Calif.: Flower Films, 1970), one of Les Blank's great musical documentary films.

Chapter 7: *"How-dee, I'm Just So Proud to Be Here"*

1. Interview/discussion with the Goose Island Ramblers on my radio show (WORT-FM, Madison, Wis., June 9, 1999). The Ramblers have recorded several cassettes and one CD, *Best of the Goose Island Ramblers* (Cuca KCD 1100).

2. Bob Murphey practiced law and was district attorney in Nacogdoches, Texas, but often regaled audiences with his humor as an after-dinner speaker. Justin Wilson has long been the most popular purveyor of Cajun humor. Jerry Clower will be discussed later at some length.

3. Even though the question of origins is of interest only to scholars, since "regular folk" don't care where a joke comes from as long as it conforms to their social and aesthetic needs, it is useful to know that country humor draws upon a large body of venerable comic traditions. See William Jensen Smyth, "Traditional Humor on Knoxville Country Radio Entertainment Shows" (Ph.D. diss., UCLA, 1987), esp. pp. 103–31.

4. Vance Randolph collected a large body of this material, some of which is found in his *Pissing in the Snow and Other Ozark Folktales* (Urbana: University of Illinois Press, 1976; reprint, New York: Avon Books, 1977), and some in *Roll Me in Your Arms: "Unprintable" Ozark Folksongs and Folklore,* vol. 1: *Folksongs and Music,* ed. G. Legman (Fayetteville: University of Arkansas Press, 1992). Guy Logsdon collected a similar body of material from cowboy culture, *"The Whorehouse Bells Were Ringing" and Other Songs Cowboys Sing* (Urbana: University of Illinois Press, 1989).

5. The adoption of burlesqued rural images by country entertainers is reminiscent of the phenomenon described by Jane Kramer in *The Last Cowboy* (New York: Harper & Row, 1977), a book first serialized in the *New Yorker.* Kramer's chief character was a real Texas cowboy who bemoaned the fact that his life did not conform to that of Hollywood actor Glenn Ford.

6. *Variety,* Mar. 4, 1925, p. 12.

7. Even though Lulu Belle Wiseman, in the mid-1930s, was groomed to be a tart-tongued comedienne in the mold of Elviry Weaver, she actually inaugurated a new phase of comic "sweetness" among comediennes even as they preserved the rural garb of their predecessors.

8. John Edwards, "A Discography of Columbia Rural Drama Records," *Caravan,* Jan., 1960, pp. 36–37; "A Bee Hunt" and "Hog Killing Day" can be heard on *A Day at the County Fair: Early Country Comedy Featuring Gid Tanner, Clayton McMichen, Riley Puckett, and Others* (Old Homestead OHCS-145). "A

Corn Licker Still in Georgia" is documented on an LP with the same name (Voyager Recordings VRLP 303). Other important humor recordings include *A Day in the Mountains, 1928: Old-Time Music and Humor* (County 512) and Uncle Dave Macon's *Keep My Skillet Good and Greasy* (Old Homestead OHCS-148), which includes "Uncle Dave's Travels," parts 1–4. The Jimmie Rodgers/Carter Family skits were originally recorded on June 12, 1931, and were issued on Victor 23574 and Bluebird B-6762.

9. Bouchillon's recording of "Born in Hard Luck" appeared on Columbia 15151-D. "Talking Blues" appeared on Columbia 15120-D in 1926. His songs have been reissued on an LP, *Chris Bouchillon, "The Original Talking Blues Man"* (Old Homestead OHCS-181), notes by Charles Wolfe.

10. Tubb seems not to have recorded his version, but he did perform it frequently on radio and personal appearances. Lyrics can be found in the *Ernest Tubb Song Folio*, no. 3 (Hollywood: American Music, 1943), p. 34.

11. Quoted by Hay in *Story of the Grand Ole Opry*, p. 37.

12. "Talking Dust Bowl Blues" was recorded for Victor on May 3, 1940, but was released in 1964 on *Dust Bowl Ballads* (Folkways FH 5212); Happy Traum, "The Art of the Talking Blues," *Sing Out!* 15, no. 6 (Jan., 1966): 53–59.

13. Day began his career as a comedian on WDZ in Tuscola, Illinois, when he substituted one night for a newscaster and musically ad-libbed the day's headlines. See Byron Crawford, "Lazy Jim Day Spoke Very Slowly, but He Sang Rhythm and News," *Louisville Courier Journal*, Nov. 13, 1981. Day also recorded a song, "Jim Day's News" (King 6160).

14. Gene Sullivan, "Please Pass the Biscuits" (Columbia 40971).

15. "What It Was, Was Football," parts 1 and 2 (Capitol 2693). "Tarheel Tale Spinner: 'Deacon' Andy Griffith," untitled account in *Cowboy Songs* 1, no. 34 (June, 1954): 22. The recitation is printed in its entirety in the same magazine, p. 25.

16. One of Landers's recordings, "Before You Call," climbed to number ten on the country charts in July, 1949 (MGM 10427). Terry Fell, best known for "Truck Driving Man," recorded an item called "Hillbilly Impersonations" (GE 5084).

17. Ferlin Husky, "Country Music Is Here to Stay" (Capitol 4073).

18. Arleigh Duff, "Y'all Come" (Starday 104); Bradley Kincaid, "The Little Shirt My Mother Made for Me" (Bluebird B-5321); Billy Edd Wheeler, "Ode to the Little Brown Shack Out Back" (Kapp 617).

19. "Take an Old Cold 'Tater and Wait" (Columbia 20548); "Country Boy" (Columbia 20585); "A-Sleeping at the Foot of the Bed" (Columbia 20644); "Out behind the Barn" (Columbia 21247); "Galvanized Washtub" (Columbia 20835).

20. "From the Archive: 'The Arkansas Traveler,'" *JEMF Quarterly* 6, part 2, no. 18 (Summer, 1970): 51–57, a reprint of an article in *Century Magazine*, Mar., 1896. Sarah Brown, "The Arkansas Traveller: Southwest Humor on Canvas," *Arkansas Historical Quarterly* 46, no. 4 (Winter, 1987): 348–75. The earliest

hillbilly recording of the Arkansas Traveler skit was probably Gid Tanner and Riley Puckett's 1924 version (Columbia 15017-D).

21. The Stanley Brothers updated the song in 1960, recording it as "How Far to Little Rock" (King 5306). In their version the city slicker says that "there ain't much between you and a fool," and then receives the rejoinder, "No, only that microphone."

22. Best known as "I Wish I Had Stayed in the Wagon Yard," the song was recorded by several people including Peg Moreland (Victor V-40008), but I have used the version performed by Lowe Stokes in *A Collection of Mountain Songs* (County 504).

23. The 1951 version is Grandpa Jones, "Fifteen Cents Is All I Got" (King 1069). Grandpa recorded it again in 1969 on Monument SLP-18138.

24. Roy Acuff, "Stuck Up Blues" (Okeh 06300), and in his LP, *Fly Birdie Fly* (Rounder SS 24). Printed in Horstman, *Sing Your Heart Out, Country Boy*, p. 260.

25. Tex Ritter, "Old Shorty," in *Hillbilly Heaven* (Capitol SM-1623); Grandpa Jones, "Old Rattler" (King 668); Jimmie Dickens, "Bessie the Heifer" (Columbia 20786). "Ole Slewfoot" is in Johnny Horton's *Honky-Tonk Man* (Columbia CS-8779), but Porter Wagoner had the biggest recording of the song (RCA 11441).

26. Buster Carter and Preston Young, "A Lazy Farmer Boy" (Columbia 15702-D, and in *Anthology of American Folk Music*); Stanley Brothers, "He Went to Sleep and the Hogs Ate Him," in *Folk Concert* (King 834); Lonzo and Oscar, "Charming Betsy" (Decca 46393); Merle Travis, "Fat Gal" (Capitol A 40026); Blue Sky Boys, "Cindy," in *A Treasury of Rare Song Gems from the Past* (Starday SCD 205); Gene Autry and Jimmie Long, "That Cross-Eyed Gal" (Victor 23622); Henry Whitter, "The Old Maid and the Burglar" (Okeh 45063).

27. Wenatchee Mountaineers, "I Like Mountain Music" (Melodeon M 12782); Esmereldy, "Slap Her Down Again, Pa" (Musicor 524); Dorothy Shay, "Feudin' and Fightin'," in *Dorothy Shay Sings* (Columbia C-119); Esmereldy, "I Didn't Know the Gun Was Loaded" (MGM 10413). Al Capp, the creator of Li'l Abner, had in fact been inspired to create his comic strip after having seen some vaudeville hillbillies; see Edwin T. Arnold, "Al, Abner, and Appalachia," *Appalachian Journal* 17 (Spring, 1990): 266.

28. The American literary exploitation of the simple but innately wise bumpkin dates from at least 1787 when Royall Tyler published a play called *The Contrast*. But it was foreshadowed by tales in European literature.

29. Greg Baum, "Jethro Burns," *Pickin'* 6, no. 11 (Dec., 1979): 23–33. Jethro's quote is from an interview with Bob Claypool in *Houston Post*, Nov. 25, 1979, p. 8AA. "The Battle of Kookamonga" (RCA 7585); "Baby, It's Cold Outside" (RCA 0078). The quoted lyrics were part of Homer and Jethro's "How Much Is That Hound Dog in the Winder" (RCA 5280).

30. Ben Colder, "Almost Persuaded, No. 2," MGM 13590.

31. "I'm My Own Grandpa" (Victor 20-2563); "Moving On, no. 2," *Traces of Life* (GRC 1006). Neil Pond, "Lonzo and Oscar Press on 35 Years," *Music City News* 17, no. 10 (Apr., 1980): 10; Douglas Green, "Lonzo and Oscar Join the World of Bluegrass," *Bluegrass Unlimited* 14, no. 10 (Apr., 1980): 14–19.

32. Representative samples of their work can be heard in *Pinkard and Bowden: PG-13* (Warner Brothers 1-25299).

33. Interview with Sam Allred, Austin, Tex., May 30, 1997. Examples of the Geezinslaws' humor and music can be heard on *I Wish I Had a Job to Shove* (Step One Records SOR 0082) and *The Geezinslaws: Blah, Blah, Blah* (Step One Records SOR 0105).

34. David McCarn, "Everyday Dirt" (Victor V-40274) and on *Singers of the Piedmont* (Folk Variety FV 12 505-2). "Our Goodman" has shown up in various forms in country music, with the best version being that of the African American singer Coley Jones, who recorded it as "Drunkard's Special" (*Anthology of American Folk Music*). Earl Johnson had one of the earliest hillbilly versions, "Three Nights Experience" (Victor 45092-B). Blue Sky Boys, "Hang Out the Front Door Key" (Bluebird B-8110-A); Merle Travis, "Divorce Me, C.O.D" (Capitol 290); Jerry Reed, "She Got the Gold Mine" (RCAS 13268).

35. Loretta Lynn, "Don't Come Home a-Drinkin'" (Decca 32045); Loretta Lynn, "Fist City" (Decca 32264); Nat Stuckey, "Sweet Thang" (Paula 243); Hank Williams, "Dear John" (MGM 10904); "Move It on Over" (MGM 10033); "Mind Your Own Business" (MGM 10461).

36. Robbie Fulks, "Fuck This Town," in *South Mouth* (Bloodshot BS 023) is as graphic an example as one can find, although Kinky Friedman's "They Ain't Making Jews like Jesus Anymore" might run it a close second (*Kinky Friedman,* Varese Vintage CD VSD-5488). Other reminders of the loosening of standards in country music is the language used on stage and on records by Steve Earle, or in the promotional literature used by the Bloodshot record label in Chicago.

37. Bill Callahan, "Rattlesnaking Daddy" (on a variety of labels, including Columbia 37634; it can also be heard on the CD collection *White Man's Blues*); Hawkshaw Hawkins revived the tune in the early 1960s (King 944).

38. Bob and June Lambert, a popular husband and wife team from Louisiana, perform a song called "Too Old to Cut the Mustard" with a verse that describes the man's rejuvenation since he began taking Viagra. Their routines are presented at the Piney Woods Opry in Abita Springs, Louisiana.

39. Lefty Frizzell, "I'm an Old, Old Man" (Columbia 21034); Merle Haggard, "I'm an Old, Old Man" (in *The Way It Was in '51,* Capitol SW 11839); The Carlisles, "Too Old to Cut the Mustard" (Mercury 6348); Maddox Brothers and Rose, "Sally, Let Your Bangs Hang Low" (4-Star 1398, and on the CD *Maddox Brothers and Rose, 1946–1951* (Arhoolie 391); Hank Cochran, "Sally Was a Good Old Girl" (Liberty 55461); Jeannie C. Riley, "The Girl Most Likely" (Plantation 7); Del Reeves, "Girl on the Billboard" (United Artists 824); Tennessee Ernie Ford, "The Shotgun Boogie" (Capitol 1295) and "Blackberry Boogie" (Capitol 2170).

40. Grandpa Jones, "Mountain Dew" (King 624); George Jones, "White Lightning" (Mercury 71406); Osborne Brothers, "Rocky Top" (Decca 32242); Jay Lee Webb, "She's Looking Better by the Minute" (Decca 32430); Dixon Brothers, "Intoxicated Rat," in *The Dixon Brothers, Vol. 1* (Old Homestead OHCS-151); Johnny Bond, "Ten Little Bottles" (Starday 704), "Love Song in 32 Bars" (Columbia 20671), "Sick, Sober and Sorry" (Columbia 20808), and "Three Sheets in the Wind" (Starday 649); Tex Ritter, "Rye Whiskey" (Capitol A 40084).

41. Red River Dave McEnery apparently recorded "Watergate Blues" on Reveal, a small San Antonio label (number unknown). Red Patterson and the Piedmont Log Rollers, "Battleship of Maine" (Victor 20936); Roger Miller, "Private John Q" (Smash MGS 27049); Uncle Dave Macon, "On the Dixie Bee Line" (Vocalion 15320); Jerry Reed, "Lord, Mr. Ford" (RCA 0960).

42. Blind Alfred Reed, "Why Do You Bob Your Hair, Girls?" (Victor 21360); Lester Flatt, "I Can't Tell the Boys from the Girls," in *Sixty Years of the Grand Ole Opry* (RCA CPL 2–9507); Ray Stevens, "The Streak" (Barnaby 600); Tex Williams, "Smoke! Smoke! Smoke!" (Capitol A 40001), and "Smoke! Smoke! Smoke! 1968" (Boone 1069).

43. Interview with Benny Ford in Nashville, Tenn., Aug. 16, 1973. Ford made the same claim elsewhere; see press releases in the Duke of Paducah file, Country Music Foundation, Nashville. Pat Buttram also commented on the "science" of joke-telling in "Serious Side of Humor," *Stand By* 3, no. 51 (Jan. 29, 1938): 3.

44. Material that I have found useful for the humor of the Southwest includes Mody Boatright, *Laughter on the American Frontier* (New York: Collier Books, 1942); Hennig Cohen and William F. Dillingham, *Humor of the Old Southwest,* 2d ed. (Athens: University of Georgia Press, 1964, 1975); T. Clark, *Rampaging Frontier;* and Arthur Palmer Hudson, ed., *Humor of the Old Deep South* (New York: Macmillan, 1936).

45. Denman Thompson, who played the role of Uncle Josh Whitcomb, was the subject of numerous articles. These include Charles R. Sherlock, "Where Vaudeville Holds the Boards," *Cosmopolitan* 32 (Feb., 1902): 411–20; "A Play That Ran for Thirty Years," *World's Work* 22, no. 2 (June, 1911): 14439–40; Benjamin A. Heydrick, "The Drama," *Chautauquan* 65, no. 1 (Dec., 1911): 25–48, and "The Significance of Joshua Whitcomb," *Current Literature* 50, no. 6 (June, 1911): 648–50. Cal Stewart's recording career is discussed by Jim Walsh in "Cal Stewart: Favorite Pioneer Recording Artists," *Hobbies,* Feb., 1951, pp. 20–25. Norm Cohen also provides a short biography of Stewart, along with a recorded example of his humor, in *Minstrels and Tunesmiths.*

46. Buttram, "Serious Side of Humor"; interview with Benny Ford, Nashville, Tenn., Aug. 16, 1973; Archie Campbell said that he had 7,800 jokes and comic stints filed away in his office; see "Nobody Likes a Big Shot," *CountryStyle* no. 40 (Feb., 1979): 18; Bonnie Bucy, "Archie Campbell: What's So Funny about Country Humor?" *Country and Western Music* 1, no. 2 (June, 1970): 28–29, 54, 56.

47. The literature on blackface minstrelsy is large and growing larger. Of use

to me have been Toll, *Blacking Up;* Donald Lee Nelson, "Uncle Tom Collins: Minstrel Man," *JEMF Quarterly* 8, no. 26 (Summer, 1972): 70–72; Robert Cogswell, "A Discography of Blackface Comedy Dialogs," *JEMF Quarterly* 15, no. 55 (Fall, 1979): 166–78; and Theodore Wallace Johnson, "Black Images in American Popular Song, 1840–1910" (Ph.D. diss., Northwestern University, 1975).

48. See Dan Harmon, "Snuffy, Pappy and Greasy," *Pickin'* 3, no. 3 (Apr., 1976): 16–18; Wayne Erbsen, "Tommy Millard: Blackface Comedian, Blue Grass Boy," *Bluegrass Unlimited* 20, no. 11 (May, 1986): 22–25, and Ivan Tribe, "Kentucky Slim," *Bluegrass Unlimited* 16, no. 5 (Nov., 1981): 20–22.

49. J. E. Mainer's Mountaineers were performing blackface skits as late as 1965. They did a skit entitled "Sambo and Liza: What Happened on Washday," described by Archie Green in *JEMF Quarterly* 7, no. 22 (Summer, 1971): 73–75.

50. G. Carson, *Roguish World of Dr. Brinkley.*

51. Brooks McNamara, *Step Right Up: An Illustrated History of the Medicine Show* (Garden City, N.Y.: Doubleday, 1976); Floyd M. Clay, *Coozan Dudley LeBlanc: From Huey to Hadacol* (Gretna, La.: Pelican Publications, 1973). Tommy Scott was a veteran country entertainer who had performed everything from blackface comedy to traditional hillbilly music. In the 1950s he had a hit recording of a song called "Rosebuds and You" (Macy's 116).

52. I had the good fortune to interview a genuine "Toby," Hank Jones, at his home in Hammond, La., May 28, 1993, and by telephone on May 19, 1993. The photos of Childre and Stover are on page 94 of Clifford Ashby and Suzanne DePauw May, *Trouping through Texas: Harley Sadler and His Tent Show* (Bowling Green, Ohio: Bowling Green University Popular Press, 1982). I found abundant references to Jimmie Rodgers's tent show involvement in issues of *Billboard* magazine during the late twenties and early thirties, as did Nolan Porterfield in his biography of Rodgers (*Jimmie Rodgers*). Gene Sullivan spoke of his partner Wylie Walker's tent show days in a telephone interview with me (from Oklahoma City, Jan. 26, 1982). In addition to Ashby and May's account of Harley Sadler, other studies of tent-repertoire theater include W. L. Slout, *Theatre in a Tent: The Development of a Provincial Entertainment* (Bowling Green, Ohio: Bowling Green University Popular Press, 1972); Robert Dean Klassen, "The Tent-Repertoire Theatre: A Rural American Institution" (Ph.D. diss., Michigan State University, 1970); Larry Dale Clark, "Toby Shows: A Form of American Popular Theatre" (Ph.D. diss., University of Illinois, 1963); and Jere C. Mickel, "The Genesis of Toby: A Folk Hero of the American Theater," *Journal of American Folklore* 80, no. 318 (Oct.–Dec., 1967): 334–40.

53. Slout, *Theatre in a Tent,* pp. 90–92.

54. Loyal Jones, the onetime director of the Appalachian Center at Berea College in Kentucky, has been working on a study of country music humor. Debby Gray, also from Berea, Kentucky, has long been compiling material on the Na-

tional Barn Dance. She made available to me typed transcripts of comic dialogue between Lulu Belle, Red Foley, Scott Wiseman, and other Barn Dance personalities. The only book-length study of humor in country music is William Jensen Smyth's 1987 dissertation "Traditional Humor on Knoxville Country Radio Entertainment Shows." My other impressions of country humor come from a lifetime of listening to and observing people like Bob Shelton and Minnie Pearl.

55. My information on the Weaver Brothers and Elviry comes from articles written by Reta Spears-Stewart in *Springfield! Magazine*. She and Gordon McCann, an authority on the music of the Ozarks, graciously made copies available to me: 10, no. 8 (Jan., 1989): 34–39; 10, no. 9 (Feb., 1989): 61–64; 10, no. 10 (Mar., 1989): 50–53; 10, no. 11 (Apr., 1989): 50–53; 10, no. 12 (May, 1989): 34–35, 72–75; 11, no. 1 (June, 1989): 32–35, 59; 11, no. 2 (July, 1989): 40–43; 11, no. 3 (Aug., 1989): 43–45; 11, no. 4 (Sept., 1989): 42–44; 11, no. 5 (Oct., 1989): 22–23; 11, no. 6 (Nov., 1989): 46–49; 11, no. 7 (Dec., 1989): 36–37.

56. Lightfoot, "Belle of the Barn Dance," p. 8. Interview with Minnie Pearl, Nashville, Tenn., July 28, 1972.

57. Interview with Harry Mullins, Mt. Vernon, Ky., Aug. 18, 1973.

58. "Sarie and Sallie See the City," *Stand By* 3, no. 21 (July 3, 1937): 3, 15.

59. Lee White's 1932 appearances on WSM are noted in *Broadcasting* 3, no. 7 (Oct. 1, 1932): 17. Information on Jamup and Honey was garnered from "Southland's Favorite Minstrel Men," *Purina's Grand Ole Opry and Checkerboard Fun-Fest Souvenir Album* (published by the Purina Company, circa 1944), p. 5, and David Wilds, "The Wilds, the Innocent, and the Grand Ole Opry," *No Depression* 1, no. 4 (Summer, 1996): 48–55.

60. Childre's musical style and effervescent personality were documented on at least two record albums, one of which contained valuable performances taken from his many radio transcriptions: *Old Time Get Together with Lew Childre* (Starday SLP 153) and *On the Air, 1946* (Old Homestead OHCS-132), with notes by Charles Wolfe. Childre can also be seen on some of the Al Gannaway television productions of Grand Ole Opry performers.

61. Telephone interview with Hank Penny, Chatsworth, Calif., Jan. 17, 1981. Sunny Ciesla, "Hank Penny," *National Hillbilly News,* Mar.–Apr., 1948, p. 7.

62. "Lester Alvin Burnette," in Linnell Gentry, *A History and Encyclopedia of Country, Western, and Gospel Music,* 2d ed. (1961; Nashville: Clairmont Corp., 1969), p. 385.

63. George Biggar to author, Mar. 18, 1967.

64. Buttram, "Serious Side of Humor."

65. Interview with Benjamin Francis Ford, Nashville, Tenn., Aug. 16, 1973. See also Arlie Kinkade, "The Duke of Paducah," *National Hillbilly News* 3, no. 3 (Jan.–Feb., 1948): 21; Melodie Nash, "MCN Spotlight," *Music City News* (May, 1986): 7, 15; Bob Millard, "Whitey Ford Dead," *Country Sounds,* Sept., 1986, p. 33. Recorded samples of Ford's comedy routines can be heard on a series of reissued Roy Acuff radio programs, e.g., *The RC Cola Shows,* vol. 1 (RME Music, Goodlettsville, Tenn.), sixty minutes of transcribed music and comedy.

66. I am indebted to Bob Pinson, who supplied me with photocopies of scripts from several Prince Albert Shows, including the repartee between Brasfield, Foley, and Minnie Pearl: Jan. 7, 1950; July 14, 1951; Dec. 27, 1952; July 11, 1953; Dec. 19, 1953; July 3, 1954. Useful biographical and interpretive sketches of Rod, Cyp, and Sap Brasfield include Douglas B. Green, "Rod Brasfield: Funny," *Music City News* (Dec., 1975): 13; and "The Brasfields: Aunt 'Sap' and Uncle 'Cyp,'" *Rustic Rhythm* 1, no. 4 (July, 1957): 10–13. Additional information about Rod Brasfield was obtained from an interview with Minnie Pearl in Nashville, Tenn., July 28, 1972.

67. Basic biographical information on Minnie Pearl came from an interview with Sarah Ophelia (Colley) Cannon in Nashville, Tenn., July 28, 1972. Other useful material includes her autobiography, written with Joan Dew, *Minnie Pearl: An Autobiography* (New York: Simon and Schuster, 1980); Don Rhodes, "Minnie Pearl: Grand Ole Opry's Lady Remembers," *Pickin'* 5, no. 9 (Oct., 1978): 35–46; Sue Thrasher, "The Woman behind Minnie Pearl: She's My Best Friend," *Southern Exposure* 11, no. 4 (Winter, 1975): 32–40; and two profiles in *Music City News:* Bill Littleton, "Country Comedy and Minnie Pearl" (13, no. 9 [Mar., 1976]: 4, 18), and Lee Rector, "Cuzzin' Minnie Pearl Is Still in 'Early Flirties'" (19, no. 8 [Feb., 1982]: 16–17).

68. The William Esty Company insisted on the change, a departure that Sarah thought was unnecessary and detrimental.

69. Sarah Ophelia Cannon sometimes expressed the wish that she possessed the character traits of Minnie Pearl. She actually did, and was well known as a humanitarian and civic leader in Nashville.

70. Audrey Winters, "CBS Debuts 'Hee-Haw' TV Show on June 15," *Music City News* 6, no. 12 (June, 1969): 1, 14; "The Corn Is Still Green," *Time*, May 8, 1969, p. 59; John Fergus Ryan, "Press a Button and Out Comes Hee Haw," *Country Music* 2, no. 1 (Sept., 1975): 28–33. Further information on the show can be garnered from Roy Clark, with Marc Eliot, *My Life in Spite of Myself* (New York: Simon and Schuster, 1994), pp. 120–41 and passim; and Grandpa Jones's autobiography, *Everybody's Grandpa*.

71. John Duggleby, "Hold On to Your Ears, Homer and Jethro Are Back!" *CountryStyle*, no. 5 (Oct., 1976): 52; Baum, "Jethro Burns," p. 32.

72. Archie Campbell, with Ben Byrd, *Archie Campbell: An Autobiography* (Memphis, Tenn.: Memphis State University Press, 1981).

73. Roy Clark, *My Life in Spite of Myself*.

74. Grandpa's story is well told in his autobiography, *Everybody's Grandpa*.

75. Genevieve J. Waddell, "Stringbean," *Country Music World* 3, no. 1 (Jan.–Feb., 1974): 41–44; Alanna Nash, "Asa Martin: A Guiding Light for Rural Music," *Louisville Courier-Journal*, July 31, 1977, pp. 1, 7, sec. C; Charles Wolfe, "String," *Bluegrass Unlimited* 16, no. 11 (June, 1982): 45–51; Hay, *Story of the Grand Ole Opry*, pp. 61–62.

76. Clower, *Ain't God Good!* Hazel Smith, "Jerry Clower," *Country Sounds*, Oct., 1986, p. 43; Don Rhodes, "Clower Power Is Humor, Not Comedy," *Mu-

sic City News 13, no. 4 (Oct., 1975): 14; Caleb Pirtle III, "Confessions of a Mississippi Coon Hunter," *Southern Living* 8, no. 4 (Apr., 1973): 122–30; and John Pugh, "Jerry Clower: The Funniest 'Billy in the World," *Country Music* 3, no. 9 (June, 1975): 38–44.

77. Junior Samples's dialogue with the game warden was recorded as "World's Biggest Whopper" (Chart 1460). John Fergus Ryan provides good anecdotes about Junior in "Press a Button and Out Comes Hee Haw."

78. The quote concerning Shakespeare was taken from Bill Klasne, "Hee Haw Gagman Swaps Cosmetics for Corn," *CountryStyle*, no. 2 (June, 1976): 10. The young revivalist band mistakenly put the dash in the wrong place, consequently becoming known as BR 5-49.

79. Michael Bane, "20 Questions with Jeff Foxworthy," *Country Music* no. 183 (Jan.–Feb., 1997): 4–5; "One Redneck Equals a Million Laughs for Jeff Foxworthy," *Music City News* 32, no. 11 (May, 1995): 20; Craig Peters, "Jeff Foxworthy: Comedy's Platinum-Plated Redneck," *CountryBeat*, Aug., 1995, pp. 38–41. Representative CDs of Foxworthy are *You Might Be a Redneck If* (Warner Brothers 9 45312-2) and *Games Rednecks Play* (Warner Brothers 9 45856-2). Lola Scobey, "Ray Stevens Thrives on Constant Changes," *Music City News* (June, 1976): 6B. Shawn Williams, "Ray Stevens Is Serious about Being Funny," *Music City News* 23, no. 12 (June, 1986): 6–8. Stevens's funniest routines are on *Get the Best of Ray Stevens* (MCA MSD 35085).

80. Bruce Williams's ad was in *Music City News* 25, no. 9 (Mar., 1988): 9. Other information on Williams and Ree came from their Internet Web site. Eugenia Snyder, "Ron Thomason: Looking for the Roots of Humor," *Bluegrass Unlimited* 30, no. 1 (July, 1995): 46–51; Sharon Wright, "The Dry Branch Fire Squad," *Bluegrass Unlimited* 14, no. 7 (Jan., 1980): 12–16.

81. Interview with the Austin Lounge Lizards, Madison, Wis.

82. The Austin Lounge Lizards: *Lizard Vision* (Flying Fish FF 70569); *Highway Cafe of the Damned* (Watermelon 1001-CD); *Paint Me on Velvet* (Flying Fish FF 70618); *Small Minds* (Watermelon 1034); *Employee of the Month* (Sugar Hill SHCD-3874).

83. The Statler Brothers, *Alive from Johnny Mack Brown High School* (Mercury SRM 1-708).

84. Al Glassner, "Backstage with Red Knuckles and the Trailblazers," *Frets Magazine* 8, no. 4 (Apr., 1986): 20–25. Pete Wernick has a brief account of the Trailblazers in *How to Make a Band Work*, rev. 3d ed. (Niwot, Colo.: Peter Wernick, 1997), p. 101.

85. Doug Green, Fred LaBour, Woody Paul, with Texas Bix Bender, *Riders in the Sky* (Salt Lake City, Utah: Gibbs Smith, Publisher, 1992), contains biographical information, jokes, radio scripts, photos, and song lyrics. Bill Malone, notes to *Always Drink Upstream from the Herd* (Rounder CD 0360).

86. This kind of reunion, linking old and new performers to each other in a contrived but informal session, was anticipated by the Nitty Gritty Dirt Band's

highly touted album of 1972, *Will the Circle Be Unbroken* (EMI E22V-46589), which combined the talents of this young country-rock band with those of such veteran entertainers as Roy Acuff, Maybelle Carter, and Merle Travis. Johnny Cash and Willie Nelson, *VH1 Storytellers* (American CK 69416).

Chapter 8: "We Still Wave Old Glory down at the Courthouse"

1. Merle Haggard, "Okie from Muskogee" (Capitol 2626).

2. For a discussion of how the Democratic Party preserved its hegemony in the South after the Civil War, see Woodward's classic study, *Origins of the New South.* After the African American vote was effectively stifled, Republicanism in the South tended to be most strongly concentrated in the Appalachians. See Gordon B. McKinney, *Southern Mountain Republicans, 1865–1900: Politics and the Appalachian Community* (Chapel Hill: University of North Carolina Press, 1978). Woodward is also the best guide on Populism, especially in his biography, *Tom Watson: Agrarian Rebel,* but much profit can be gained also from Goodwyn, *Democratic Promise,* and Robert C. McMath, Jr.'s *Populist Vanguard,* and *American Populism: A Social History, 1877–1898* (New York: Hill & Wang, 1992).

3. James Gregory's discussion of "plain folk Americanism" in *American Exodus* is centered around the Okie migration to California but is nevertheless a brilliant analysis of the political thought of poor white southerners (pp. 139–72).

4. The historical literature on southern Jews is small but growing. Eli Evans, *The Provincials: A Personal History of Jews in the South* (New York: Atheneum, 1973) is the best place to begin to understand this important component of the South, but Harry Golden, *Our Southern Landsman* (New York: Putnam, 1974), and Leonard Dinnerstein and Mary Dale Palsson, eds., *Jews in the South* (Baton Rouge: Louisiana State University Press, 1973) can also be read with profit.

5. Charles Sydnor, *American Revolutionaries in the Making: Political Practices in Washington's Virginia* (New York, 1952).

6. T. Clark, *Rampaging Frontier,* p. 267. Daniel Dupre, "Barbecues and Pledges: Electioneering and the Rise of Democratic Politics in Antebellum Alabama," *Journal of Southern History* 60, no. 3 (Aug., 1994): 479–512.

7. Noah Ludlow described the incident in *Dramatic Life as I Found It* (St. Louis: G. I. Jones, 1880). Jimmie Driftwood based his famous "Battle of New Orleans" (RCA 7534) on the tune, and in 1959 Johnny Horton recorded a huge-selling version of it (Columbia 41339).

8. Reuben Davis, *Recollections of Mississippi and Mississippians* (Boston: Houghton, Mifflin & Co., 1890), p. 68.

9. *Spirit of the Times,* Apr. 22, 1837, pp. 78–79.

10. Hamilton W. Pierson, *In the Brush; or, Old-Time Social, Political, and Religious Life in the Southwest* (New York: D. Appleton & Co., 1861), pp. 154–55.

11. Leah Atkins, "Williamson R. W. Cobb and the Graduation Act of 1854," *Alabama Review* 28, no. 1 (Jan., 1975): 18.

12. Pierson, *In the Brush*, p. 144. Lewis Collins gives the details of Boyd's legislative service in *History of Kentucky* (Covington, Ky.: Collins and Co., 1882), vol. 1, pp. 67–69, 81, 350–51, and vol. 2, pp. 84–85.

13. Alf Taylor's quote is from Paul Deresco Augsburg, *Bob and Alf Taylor: Their Lives and Lectures* (Morristown, Tenn: 1925). Biographical information came from Augsburg and from Daniel Merritt Robison, *Bob Taylor and the Agrarian Revolt in Tennessee* (Chapel Hill: University of North Carolina Press, 1935). Bob Taylor's enshrinement as a backwoods folk hero began with an article by a Tennessee local colorist, William Allen Drumgoole, "Fiddling His Way to Fame," *Arena* 2 (Nov., 1890): 719–31. Additional information came from Roger L. Hart, *Redeemers, Bourbons, and Populists: Tennessee, 1870–1896* (Baton Rouge: Louisiana State University Press, 1975), pp. 84–107.

14. References to fiddling or music-making appear in Woodward, *Tom Watson: Agrarian Rebel*, pp. 34, 37, 41, 102, 105, 232, 444. Fiddlin' John Carson, "Tom Watson Special" (Okeh 40050); Vernon Dalhart, "Thomas E. Watson" (Columbia 15053-D).

15. Charlie Oaks, "The Death of William Jennings Bryan" (Vocalion 15094).

16. Fiddlin' John Carson, "The Little Old Log Cabin in the Lane" and "The Old Hen Cackled and the Rooster's Going to Crow" (Okeh 4890). The best discussion of this recording session is still Archie Green, "Hillbilly Music: Source and Symbol," pp. 208–11.

17. The best biographical account of Carson, including a complete discography, is Wiggins, *Fiddlin' Georgia Crazy.*

18. Uncle Dave Macon, "Buddy, Won't You Roll down the Line" (Brunswick 292, and in the *Anthology of American Folk Music*). Woodward discusses the labor conflict in *Origins of the New South.*

19. Fiddlin' John Carson, "The Farmer Is the Man That Feeds Them All" (Okeh 40071) and "The Honest Farmer" (Okeh 40411). The history of "The Wabash Cannon Ball," and a listing of its many recordings, are in Norm Cohen, *Long Steel Rail*, pp. 373–81. McClintock's songs are included on an LP, *Hallelujah! I'm a Bum* (Rounder 1009), which includes a booklet containing several detailed letters written by him.

20. Flynt, *Dixie's Forgotten People*, pp. 66–69.

21. The Bentley Boys, "Down on Penny's Farm" (Columbia 15565-D, and in the *Anthology of American Folk Music*). The lyrics to many of the songs in this historic Folkways collection were printed in a book of the same name, edited by Moses Asch, Josh Dunson, and Ethel Raim (New York: Oak Publications, 1973).

22. "Eleven Cent Cotton" was recorded by its composer, Bob Miller, under the name of Bob Ferguson (Columbia 15297-D) and by Vernon Dalhart (Victor V-40050). Blind Alfred Reed, "How Can a Poor Man Stand Such Times and Live" can be heard in an anthology of his songs (Rounder 1001). The most influential recordings of "Wish I Had Stayed in the Wagon Yard" included Peg Moreland (Victor V-40008) and Lowe Stokes (Columbia 15557-D). The Carolina Tarheels,

"Got the Farmland Blues" (Victor 23611A and *Anthology of American Folk Music*).

23. Donald Mathews, *Religion in the Old South* (Chicago: University of Chicago Press, 1977), p. 20.

24. Ibid., p. 38.

25. Blind Alfred Reed, "Why Do You Bob Your Hair, Girls" (Victor 21360 and Rounder 1001).

26. The Foreman Family, "The Dying Nun" (Victor V-40165). Nelstone's Hawaiians, "The Fatal Flower Garden" (Victor V-40193, and *Anthology of American Folk Music*). Some versions of "Sir Hugh, or the Jew's Daughter" that were collected in the South did refer to Jews. For example, see Foster B. Gresham, "'The Jew's Daughter': An Example of Ballad Variation," in Dinnerstein and Palsson, *Jews in the South,* pp. 201–5.

27. Rosa Lee Carson, "Little Mary Phagan" (Okeh 40446). The Little Mary Phagan tragedy, and Fiddlin' John's relationship to it, are discussed in Wiggins, *Fiddlin' Georgia Crazy,* pp. 23–44. See also D. K. Wilgus and Nathan Hurvitz, "Little Mary Phagan: Further Notes on a Native American Ballad in Context," *Journal of Country Music* 4, no. 1 (1973): 17–26. The best accounts of the Little Mary Phagan murder itself are Harry Golden, *A Little Girl Is Dead* (Cleveland: World Publishing Co., 1965); Leonard Dinnerstein, *The Leo Frank Case* (New York: Columbia University Press, 1968); and Woodward, *Tom Watson: Agrarian Rebel.*

28. Examples of racially stereotyped music include Gid Tanner and His Skillet Lickers, "Watermelon on the Vine" (Columbia 15091-D); The Happy Chappies, "My Pretty Quadroon" (Columbia 2252-D); Blue Sky Boys, "Away Down on the Old Plantation" (Bluebird B-8128-B); Blue Sky Boys, "Sweet Allalee" (Bluebird B-6854-B); Fiddlin' John Carson, "Little Old Log Cabin in the Lane" (Okeh 4890); Milton Brown and the Musical Brownies, "Yellow Rose of Texas" (Decca 5273); and Vernon Dalhart, "Bully of the Town," parts 1 and 2 (Columbia 15302-D). Contemporary news items about music at Klan rallies tended to be similar to the one carried in a 1923 issue of the *Fort Worth Star-Telegram,* where the Klavalier Quartet was described as having performed a group of popular and classical numbers. James H. Dorman discusses the coon songs in "Shaping the Popular Image of Post-Reconstruction American Blacks: 'The Coon Song' Phenomenon of the Gilded Age," *American Quarterly* 40, no. 4 (Dec., 1938): 450–71. The Klan of the 1920s is discussed by Charles Alexander, *The Ku Klux Klan in the Southwest* (Lexington: University Press of Kentucky, 1965) and Kenneth Jackson, *Ku Klux Klan in the City, 1915–1930* (New York: Oxford University Press, 1967).

29. Although Norm Cohen presents an overly narrow perspective in his reference to mountain folk, his article, "Scopes and Evolution in Hillbilly Songs," is nevertheless the best discussion of the Monkey Trial and its impact on musicians (*JEMF Quarterly* 6, no. 20 [Winter, 1970]: 174–81).

30. All of these songs are mentioned in Norm Cohen's article (ibid.): Uncle Dave Macon, "The Bible's True" (Vocalion 15322); Vernon Dalhart, "The John T. Scopes Trial" (Columbia 15037-D); Dalhart, "Bryan's Last Fight" (Columbia 15039-D); Charles O. Oaks, "Death of William Jennings Bryan" (Vocalion 15094).

31. The New Lost City Ramblers anthologized a good sampling of songs about drinking, pro and con, in *American Moonshine and Prohibition* (Folkways FH 5263).

32. Vernon Dalhart, "The Drunkard's Hell" (Okeh 40565); Riley Puckett, "The Drunkard's Dream" (Columbia 15035-D); Blue Sky Boys, "Father Dear Father Come Home" (Bluebird B-8522-B); Allen Brothers, "Jake Walk Blues" (Victor V-40303); Blind Alfred Reed, "How Can a Poor Man Stand Such Times and Live" (Victor V-40236 and Rounder 1003); Uncle Dave Macon, "Governor Al Smith" (Brunswick 263); Bill Cox, "Franklin D. Roosevelt's Back Again" (Okeh 05896). The line about passing around "the long neck bottle" comes from "Wild Bill Jones" (recorded by many people).

33. Studies of southern violence, such as those by Edward Ayers, Bertram Wyatt-Brown, John Shelton Reed, and Elliott Gorn, are noted in the chapter on rambling. Fascination with southerners' alleged propensity for violence still persists; see the *New York Times,* July 26, 1998.

34. Red Patterson and the Piedmont Log Rollers, "The Battleship of Maine" (Victor 20936); Charlie Oaks, "Just before the Battle, Mother" (Vocalion 15345); Buell Kazee, "Faded Coat of Blue" (Brunswick 206); Riley Puckett, "Just as the Sun Went Down" (Columbia 240-D); Vernon Dalhart, "Take the News to Mother" (Bell 364); Richard Harold, "Mary Dear" (Columbia 15426-D); Mac and Bob, "When the Roses Bloom Again" (Vocalion 5027).

35. Tindall, *Emergence of the New South*

36. The best introductions to Brinkley and the border stations are G. Carson, *Roguish World of Doctor Brinkley,* and Fowler and Crawford, *Border Radio.*

37. C. L. Douglas and Francis Miller, *The Life Story of W. Lee O'Daniel* (Dallas: Regional Press, 1938); Seth S. McKay, *W. Lee O'Daniel and Texas Politics, 1938–42* (Lubbock: Texas Technological College Research Funds, 1944); Townsend, *San Antonio Rose,* pp. 69–76; and Ginell, *Milton Brown and the Founding of Western Swing,* pp. 44–65, 213, 221, 225–26.

38. *Broadcasting and Broadcast Advertising,* Sept. 15, 1938, p. 17.

39. *Dallas Morning News,* Mar. 24, 1943, sec. 1, p. 7.

40. Gus Weill presents a completely uncritical account of Davis in *You Are My Sunshine: The Jimmie Davis Story* (Waco, Tex.: Word Books, 1977). Readers looking for a more balanced treatment should consult Ross Yockey, "The Sunshine Governor," *Louisiana Life* 9, no. 1 (Mar.–Apr., 1989): 33–38, 81–84; and Kevin Fontenot's forthcoming biography of Davis.

41. A good sampling of this material can be heard in the New Lost City Ramblers, *Songs from the Depression* (Folkways FH 5264). This influential record-

ing should be reissued on compact discs. Some of the songs are also printed in *The New Lost City Ramblers Song Book* (New York: Oak Publications, 1964).

42. O'Daniel's Hillbilly Boys, "My Million Dollar Smile" (Vocalion 02975); Jimmie Rodgers, "No Hard Times" (Victor 23751); Goebel Reeves, "Hobo's Lullaby" (Vocalion 02828); Jimmie Rodgers, "Hobo Bill's Last Ride" (Victor 22421); Jimmie Rodgers, "Hobo's Meditation" (Victor 23711); Jimmie Rodgers, "Waiting for a Train" (Victor V-40014).

43. Slim Smith, "Breadline Blues" (Victor 21406); Carter Family, "No Depression in Heaven" (Decca 5242). Escott, with Merritt and MacEwen, tells the story of "WPA Blues" in *Hank Williams: The Biography*, p. 17.

44. *These Are Our Lives*, interviews collected and written by members of the WPA Federal Writers' Project, pp. 210–11; Fiddlin' John Carson, "The Honest Farmer" (Bluebird B-5742).

45. Bill Cox, "NRA Blues"(Conqueror 8392)

46. Roy Acuff, "Old Age Pension Check" (Vocalion 05244); Sons of the Pioneers, "Old Age Pension Check" (Decca D 5082).

47. Bill Cox, "The Democratic Donkey Is in His Stall Again" and "Franklin D. Roosevelt's Back Again" (ARC 7-02-61 and other labels). Lily May Ledford talks about the White House concert in *Coon Creek Girl*. For insights about the White Top Festival, see Whisnant, *All That Is Native and Fine*.

48. The cultural nationalism of the New Deal era is discussed by Charles Alexander, *Nationalism in American Thought, 1930–45* (Chicago: Rand McNally, 1969); Jerre Mangione, *The Dream and the Deal: The Federal Writers' Project, 1935–1943* (Philadelphia: University of Pennsylvania Press, 1983); Peter Thomas Bartis, "A History of the Archive of Folk Song at the Library of Congress: The First Fifty Years" (Ph.D. diss., University of Pennsylvania, 1982); Archie Green, "The Archive of American Folk-Song," *JEMF Quarterly* 10, part 4, no. 36 (Winter, 1974): 157–64; Archie Green, "A Resettlement Administration Song Sheet," *JEMF Quarterly* 11, no. 38 (Summer, 1975): 80.

49. Debora Kodish, *Good Friends and Bad Enemies: Robert W. Gordon and the Study of American Folksong* (Urbana: University of Illinois Press, 1986); Porterfield, *Last Cavalier.*

50. While the Lomaxes hinted at the varieties of folklore that lay outside the domain of rural culture, George Korson probably did most to document the rich lode of industrial culture; see *Songs and Ballads of the Anthracite Miner* (New York: Frederick H. Hitchcock, 1927) and *Minstrels of the Mine Patch* (Philadelphia: University of Pennsylvania Press, 1938).

51. More often, the academic folklorists hewed closely to the canons established earlier by Francis James Child and Cecil Sharp, and looked askance at those who posited theories of folk process based on economic determinism or class struggle. The dissenters, including both academic and amateur collectors as well as singers of folksongs, cast their nets far and wide for folk material, and sometimes utilized the songs of the commercial hillbillies. But these sources were almost never

acknowledged, and hillbilly music as a whole remained outside the pale of respectability, rejected by the literary folklorists because it did not conform to the conventionally accepted dictates of aesthetics and good taste, and ignored by the socially conscious exploiters of folk material because it was the commercial reflection of a conservative culture.

52. *Time*, Nov. 23, 1962, p. 60.

53. The best discussion of American radicals' discovery of folk music is Richard A. Reuss, "American Folklore and Left-Wing Politics: 1928–1957" (Ph.D. diss., Indiana University, 1971). See also R. Serge Denisoff, *Great Day Coming: Folk Music and the American Left* (Urbana: University of Illinois Press, 1971); Jerome L. Rodnitzky, *Minstrels of the Dawn: The Folk-Protest Singer as a Cultural Hero* (Chicago: Nelson-Hall, 1971); and Joe Klein, *Woody Guthrie: A Life* (New York: Alfred A. Knopf, 1980).

54. John Greenway compiled the first book-length survey of radical songmaking in the United States, *American Folk Songs of Protest*. Julia S. Ardery edited *Welcome the Traveler Home: Jim Garland's Story of the Kentucky Mountains* (Lexington: University Press of Kentucky, 1983). *Kentucky Folklore Record* published a memorial issue dedicated to Aunt Molly Jackson (8, no. 4 [Oct.–Dec., 1961]). She has also been the subject of a master's thesis by Carole Murphy, "Aunt Molly Jackson: The Making of a Hero" (Wesleyan University, 1981), and a biography by Shelly Romalis, *Pistol Packin' Mama: Aunt Molly Jackson and the Politics of Folksong* (Urbana: University of Illinois Press, 1999). The unsigned notes attached to her record album are also good, *Aunt Molly Jackson* (Rounder). Sarah Ogan Gunning's biography and songs are skillfully interpreted by Archie Green; see *Sarah Ogan Gunning: Girl of Constant Sorrow* (Folk-Legacy Records FSA-26). Loyal Jones commemorated the life of Florence Reece in "Florence Reece: Against the Current," *Appalachian Journal* 12, no. 1 (Fall, 1984): 68–72, and Guy Carawan and Candie Carawan wrote an affectionate obituary, "Florence Reece: Labor Anthem Composer," in *Sing Out!* 32, no. 2 (Fall, 1986): 47–48.

55. Margaret Larkin, "Ella May's Songs," *Nation* 129 (Oct. 9, 1929): 382; and "The Story of Ella May," *New Masses* 5, no. 6 (Nov., 1929).

56. The best biography of the Okie balladeer is Joe Klein, *Woody Guthrie* (New York: Alfred A. Knopf, 1980), but no one should ignore the work done by Richard Reuss: "Woody Guthrie and His Folk Tradition," *Journal of American Folklore* 83, no. 329 (July–Sept., 1970): 273–303, and *A Woody Guthrie Bibliography* (New York: Guthrie Children's Trust Fund, 1968).

57. *Etude* 62, no. 1 (Jan., 1944): 54. Invidious distinctions between "folk" and "hillbilly" based on economic-political considerations were largely confined to singers and musicians of "folk music." Most academic folklorists clung to the older Child-literary canons and rejected both hillbilly and protest music. It was not until 1952 that John Greenway in *American Folksongs of Protest* (an extension of his doctoral dissertation at the University of Pennsylvania) became the

first folklorist to argue that protest material could also be folk music. Greenway also recognized the folk legitimacy of hillbilly songs, but both he and Alan Lomax, one of the few earlier folklorists to value hillbilly music, saw Woody Guthrie as the ideal folk composer.

58. Lomax's enthusiastic "discovery" of Woody is described in Klein, *Woody Guthrie,* pp. 143, 149–50.

59. Carson Robison, "1942 Turkey in the Straw" (Bluebird 11459); Sons of the Pioneers, "Old Man Atom" (Victor 20-0368).

60. Jimmie Dickens, "They Locked God outside the Iron Curtain" (Columbia 20905); Elton Britt, "The Red We Want" (Victor V 21-0381); Lulu Belle and Scotty, "I'm No Communist" (Mercury 6400); Cactus Pryor, "Point of Order" (Four Star 1661); Jimmie Osborne, "A Tribute of Robert A. Taft" (King 1268); Jimmy Renfro "Estes Is Bestes" (Rich-R-Tone 1036); Larry Dean, "Estes Is Bestes" (Rich-R-Tone 1039); Prairie Ramblers, "Have a Heart, Taft-Hartley" (Mercury 6051); Smokey Stover, "The Ballad of Jimmy Hoffa" (in *Work's Many Voices,* JEMF 110 and 111).

61. Harry Choates, "Korea, Here We Come" (Macy's 141); Jimmie Osborne, "Thank God for Victory in Korea" (King 908); Roy Acuff, "Douglas MacArthur" (Columbia 20822); Gene Autry, "Old Soldiers Never Die" (Columbia 39405); Jimmie Osborne, "God Please Protect America" (King 843); Happy Fats LeBlanc, "Dear Mr. President" (Reb Rebel 501); The Dixie Guys, "Old Uncle Joe" (Conservative Label 139); Colonel Sharecropper, "Move Them Niggers North" (Reb-Time 1861); The Coon Hunters, "Nigger, Nigger" (Reb-Time 1862); Johnny Rebel, "Kajun Klu Klux Klan" (Reb Rebel 504). The racist records were discussed by Neil Maxwell in "The Bigotry Business: Racist Records, Books Are Hits in the South," *Wall Street Journal,* Apr. 26, 1967, and in "Crowley Today," *Blues Unlimited* 47 (Oct., 1967): 4–7. These records were still being sold and defended by David Duke, the notorious Louisiana white power spokesman, as late as 1990; see Tyler Bridges, "Critic Cites Racist Songs in Attack on David Duke," *New Orleans Times-Picayune,* Aug. 9, 1990, p. 10B.

62. Howard Zinn, *The Southern Mystique* (New York: Alfred A. Knopf, 1964); Dan T. Carter, *The Politics of Rage: George Wallace, the Origins of the New Conservatism, and the Transformation of American Politics* (New York: Simon and Schuster, 1995); Egerton, *Americanization of Dixie;* and Applebome, *Dixie Rising.*

63. Ross Yockey, "The Sunshine Governor," *Louisiana Life* 9, no. 1 (Mar.–Apr., 1989): 82.

64. "Country Music to Win Campaign for Alabama's Governor," *Country and Western Jamboree* 4, no. 1 (Summer, 1958): 18. Joseph Kraft captured the mood of many northern workers with his quote from a Ford employee near Detroit: "We're all hillbillies. What Wallace says goes," in "Michigan Apathy," *New Orleans Times-Picayune,* Oct. 20, 1972. The indispensable analysis of Wallace is that of Dan Carter in *Politics of Rage.*

65. A discussion that captures the almost-euphoric idealism of the early folk revival is Cantwell, *When We Were Good.*

66. Some of the urban folksingers, however, such as Phil Ochs, Hedy West, Segle Fry, and Carolyn Hester, came from the South.

67. Interview with Buell Kazee, Stillwater, Okla., Apr. 7, 1972.

68. Paul Hemphill was one of the first writers who talked about the political conservatism of country musicians, in *The Nashville Sound: Bright Lights and Country Music* (New York: Simon and Schuster, 1970). James Gregory, however, provides the analysis of this political posture that Hemphill ignored, particularly in his chapter on "plain folk Americanism" in *American Exodus.*

69. To recover the feeling that many liberals and radicals had about America's capacity for change in the early sixties, read Charles Reich, *The Greening of America: How the Youth Revolution Is Trying to Make America Livable* (New York: Random House, 1970); Cantwell, *When We Were Good;* and Hodgson, *America in Our Time.*

70. Johnny Seay, "Day for Decision" (Warner 5820).

71. Country music's anti-protest and anti-hippie songs inspired a torrent of writing both scholarly and journalistic. One of the most balanced accounts is that of Paul DiMaggio, Richard A. Peterson, and Jack Esco, Jr., "Country Music, Ballad of the Silent Majority," in *The Sounds of Social Change: Studies in Popular Culture,* ed. R. Serge Denisoff and Richard A. Peterson (Chicago: Rand McNally, 1972), pp. 38–55; reprinted as no. 29 in the John Edwards Memorial Foundation series of reprints.

72. Barry Sadler, "The Ballad of the Green Berets" (RCA 8739); Dave Dudley, "What We're Fighting For" (Mercury 72500); Terry Nelson, "The Battle Hymn of Lt. Calley" was published in 1971.

73. Glen Campbell, "Universal Soldier" (Capitol F 5504); Bobby Bare, "God Bless America Again" (RCA 0264); Johnny Cash, "Man in Black" (Columbia 45339); Johnny Cash, "Ragged Old Flag" (Columbia 46028).

74. Alfred G. Aronowitz, "New Country Twang Hits Town," *Life,* May 3, 1968, p. 12; Hemphill, "Merle Haggard," in Malone and McCulloh, *Stars of Country Music,* pp. 357–73; A. Gerrard, "Merle Haggard: 'I Take a Lot of Pride in What I Am.'" John Berlau makes the strongest case for Haggard's conservative consistency in "The Battle over 'Okie from Muskogee,'" *Weekly Standard,* Aug. 19, 1996. Malcolm MacKinnon, on the other hand, concentrates on the singer's libertarian views (including marijuana use) in "Merle Haggard: A Patriot's Song," *Hemp Times* 1, no. 4 (Apr.–May, 1997): 45–47. The writers who have come closest to capturing the essence of Merle Haggard's worldview are Guralnick, "Merle Haggard: In the Good Old Days (When Times Were Bad)"; and Bryan DiSalvatore, "Ornery," *New Yorker* 65, no. 52 (Feb. 12, 1990): 39–77. Haggard's Capitol releases can be heard in the CD box set *Down Every Road,* but the original singles numbers for the songs listed above are "Mama's Hungry Eyes" (Capitol 2383) and "The Fightin' Side of Me" (Capitol 2719).

75. Bill Anderson, "Where Have All Our Heroes Gone" (Decca 32744). Anderson later expressed regrets about writing the song, saying that he had "come down a little too hard" on hippies and young people; see "Bill Anderson Regrets Making Hit Song," *CountryStyle*, no. 5 (Oct., 1976): 5. Rich Kienzle refers to "Ain't I Right" in "Marty Robbins," *Journal of the American Academy for the Preservation of Old-Time Country Music* 1, no. 4 (Aug., 1991): 19. Ernest Tubb, "It's America" (Decca 75222). Ronnie Pugh makes only a few passing references to Tubb's political views in *Ernest Tubb: The Texas Troubadour* (Durham, N.C.: Duke University Press, 1996).

76. Tom Braden made the comments on CBS-TV's "Spectrum" and was quoted in the *National Observer* (Nov. 4, 1972, p. 13); see also Hemphill, *Nashville Sound*; Richard Goldstein, "My Country Music Problem—and Yours," *Mademoiselle* 77, no. 2 (June, 1973): 114–15, 185; and Florence King, "Red Necks, White Socks, and Blue Ribbon Fear," *Harper's* 249 (July, 1974): 30–34. By the seventies scarcely a meeting of the Popular Culture Association, the American Studies Association, the American Folklore Society, or even the Modern Language Association (but almost never any kind of historical convocation) convened without some kind of session devoted to country music. Political eccentricities or attitudes held by country entertainers or conveyed by country songs were clearly the major factors that inspired the attention. Some writers such as Jens Lund saw a continuity of conservative ideology in the history of the music, while others, such as Paul DiMaggio, saw greater diversity in the music's background. Both scholarly and popular interpretations, however, veered between "silent majority" and "working class" positions.

77. Bobby Bare, "Up against the Wall, Redneck Mother"; Jerry Reed, "Redneck in a Rock and Roll Bar"; Vernon Oxford, "Redneck!"; and Johnny Russell, "Rednecks, White Socks and Blue Ribbon Beer" are all included in an album called *Redneck Mothers* (RCA AYL 1-3674). Much of the avant garde interest in good old boys, and the vogue for the term itself, began in 1965 with Tom Wolfe's discussion of Junior Johnson, the champion stock-car driver who had gained his automotive driving prowess as a bootlegger in the North Carolina hills. In an article in the March, 1965, issue of *Esquire*, Wolfe called him "the last American hero." (The essay also appeared in Wolfe's *Kandy-Kolored Tangerine-Flake Streamline Baby*.) Hollywood contributed to the idealization of southern macho figures with movies like *Deliverance, Bonnie and Clyde*, and *Smokey and the Bandit*, which also featured country music as integral parts of the plots or in their soundtracks. Two of television's popular, long-running series, "The Andy Griffith Show" and "The Waltons," downplayed the brawling, boozing, violent side of southern rural life, but they played significant roles in extolling the good life lived close to the soil. These shows and the good old boy movies (which usually starred Burt Reynolds) revealed once again the persistent yearning in American postindustrial culture for a simpler and more basic existence, even if it were satisfied largely in the imagination. See the film review by

Vincent Canby, "Why 'Smokey and the Bandit' Is Making a Killing," *New York Times,* Dec. 18, 1977, p. 13D; and the article by Phil Patton, "Country Movies Are in Tune with the New Patriotism," *New York Times,* Mar. 9, 1980, pp. 1, 21, sect. 2.

78. James Talley, "Are They Going to Make Us Outlaws Again?" The best assessment of Talley is Peter Guralnick, "Mr. Talley Goes to Washington," *Rolling Stone,* Mar. 10, 1977. Good samplings of Talley's music are *James Talley Live* (Bear BCD 15704-AH), recorded in concert at the Lone Star Café in New York and the Great Southeast Music Hall in Atlanta, and *Woody Guthrie and Songs of My Oklahoma Home* (Torreon 1994). Richard Peterson's quote is in an essay called "Class Unconsciousness," in *You Wrote My Life: Lyrical Themes in Country Music,* ed. Melton A. McLaurin and Richard Peterson (Philadelphia: Gordon and Breach, 1992), p. 47.

79. Gregory, *American Exodus,* p. 164.

80. Articles that discuss the mutual affection exhibited by country entertainers and Jimmy Carter include Ed Kiersh, "What's Jimmy Carter Doing in This Magazine Anyway?" *Country Music* 5, no. 3 (Dec., 1976): 41–42, and Russell D. Barnard, "Presidents, Pickers and Politics," *Country Music* 9, no. 3 (Nov., 1980): 50–53. Lee Greenwood, "God Bless the USA" (MCA 52386). An AP report asserted that "Greenwood Captures Spirit of America," *Tyler (Texas) Courier-Times-Telegraph,* Feb. 23, 1986, p. 3, sec. 12. An ad for *Forbes* magazine in the *New Yorker* described an article that spoke of George Bush's "lifelong love affair with country music" 70, no. 16 (June 6, 1994): 37.

81. Tamara Saviano, "Charlie in Charge," *Country Music* no. 198 (June–July, 1999): 72.

82. Charlie Daniels, "Simple Man" (Epic 73030); Hank Williams, Jr., "Dixie on My Mind" (Elektra/Curb 47137); Hank Williams, Jr., "A Country Boy Can Survive" (Elektra/Curb 47257); Hank Williams, Jr., "Don't Give Us a Reason" (Warner/Curb 19542).

83. Neil Pond, "Country Stars, Rockers Unite to Aid Farmers," *Music City News* 23, no. 5 (Nov., 1985): 32. Sheryl Johnston, "Willie's FarmAid Big Success," *Close-Up* 19, no. 11 (Nov.–Dec., 1985): 10–11. Charlie Daniels, "American Farmer" copyright 1985 by Hat Band Music); Charley Pride, "Down on the Farm" (RCA). The occasional defense of industrial workers usually came from "alternative" country singers, e.g., Tom Russell, "U.S. Steel" in *Road to Bayamon* (Philo CD Ph 1116), and Hazel Dickens, "Aragon Mill" in *Hard-Hitting Songs for Hard-Hit People* (Rounder 0126).

84. Steve Earle, "Christmas Time in Washington" in *El Corazon* (Warner Brothers WB 946789-2). The best recorded version of Jean Ritchie's "Black Waters" is by Betty Smith, in *For My Friends of Song* (June Appal 018); the Goins Brothers, "Black Lung Blues," in *Bluegrass Hits Old and New* (REM 1041); Billy Edd Wheeler, "Coal Tattoo," in *Wild Mountain Flowers* (Flying Fish FF 085); John

Prine's "Paradise" won its widest circulation in country music through a recording made by Jim and Jesse McReynolds, in *The Jim and Jesse Story* (CMH 9022); Vern and Ray, "To Hell with the Land," in *Sounds from the Ozarks* (Old Homestead 10001).

85. Songs such as "Nobody's Darling on Earth," "The Orphan Child," "God Have Pity on the Blind," "Hobo Bill's Last Ride," and Stephen Foster's "Hard Times Come Again No More," had expressed sympathy for unfortunate people but had offered no remedies other than individual charity or religious consolation.

86. The Bellamy Brothers, "Kids of the Baby Boom" (Curb 53018); Garth Brooks, "We Shall Be Free" (Liberty 57994); Iris DeMent, "Wasteland of the Free," in *The Way I Should* (Warner 9362-46188-2). Dennis Hunt and Martin McOmbert, "Too Liberal for Garth Brooks' Fans?" *Los Angeles Times,* Oct. 29, 1992, pp. B8–11.

87. The most successful recording of Dolly Parton's "To Daddy" was by Emmylou Harris in 1977 (Warner 8498); Loretta Lynn, "The Pill" (MCA 40358). The mild controversy aroused by Lynn's recording (marked by the song's banning from some radio stations) is discussed by Don Rhodes, "'The Pill' Wasn't Hard to Swallow," *Music City News* 12, no. 12 (June, 1975): 23, 38. The information concerning Lulu Belle's vote in the North Carolina legislature came from the *Chicago Sun Times,* Jan. 16, 1977, pp. 4, 52. Garth Brooks, "The Thunder Rolls" (Capitol 44727). Songs have been plentiful that address the struggle to keep home and marriage together, raise kids, balance careers, and salve the egos of husbands, but since the 1980s "women's songs" express increasingly a yearning for a liberation that does not always include marriage. Songs like K. T. Oslin's "80's Ladies," Deana Carter's "Did I Shave My Legs for This?" and Mary Chapin Carpenter's "He Thinks He'll Keep Her" capture the loneliness, frustration, and anger that have often accompanied freedom.

88. "West Side of Town" and "Joaquin" are included in Tish Hinojosa, *Homeland* (A & M CD 5263), while "Something in the Rain" can be heard on her *Culture Swing* (Rounder CD 3122).

89. I interviewed Hazel Dickens in Washington, D.C., June 18, 1998. The best articles on this great American singer include Alice Gerrard, "Hazel Dickens: As Country as I Could Sing," *Sing Out!* 21, no. 1 (Sept.–Oct., 1971): 2–7; Ron Thomason, "Hazel Dickens: Only a Woman," *Bluegrass Unlimited* 16, no. 8 (Feb., 1982): 23–26; and Len Stanley, "Custom Made Woman Blues," *Southern Exposure* 14, no. 4 (Winter, 1977): 92–94. Dickens's best songs can be heard on *Hard-Hitting Songs for Hard-Hit People* (Rounder 0126) and *A Few Old Memories* (Rounder CD-11529).

90. Iris DeMent, *Infamous Angel* (Philo CD PH 1138); *My Life* (Warner 9 45493-2); *The Way I Should* (Warner 9362-46188-2). I interviewed DeMent in St. Paul, Minn., July 21, 1997. The best discussion of DeMent is Dawidoff, *In the Country of Country,* esp. pp. 261–70.

Conclusion

1. The song is in a CD of the same name by Larry Cordle and Lonesome Standard Time, *Murder on Music Row* (Shell Point 35759-1215-2).

2. Strait's and Jackson's version is in George Strait, *Latest Greatest Straitest Hits* (MCA 088 17 01002)

3. Telephone interview with Eddie Stubbs, Mar. 15, 2000

4. Cash, *Johnny Cash: The Autobiography*, p. 17.

5. James C. Cobb, "Rednecks, White Socks, and Piña Coladas? Country Music Ain't What It Used to Be . . . and It Really Never Was," *Southern Cultures* 5, no. 4 (Winter, 1999): 48.

6. Alan Jackson, "Little Man" in *High Mileage* (Arista 07822); Montgomery Gentry, "Daddy Don't Sell the Farm" in *Tattoos and Scars* (Columbia CK 69156).

7. Dixie Chicks, "Goodbye Earl," in *Fly* (Monument NK 69678).

8. J. C. Cobb, "Rednecks, White Socks, and Piña Coladas?" p. 41.

9. John Prine, *In Spite of Ourselves* (Oh Boy OBR-019).

10. Listen, for example, to the songs in his CD of early 2000: Jimmie Dale Gilmore, *One Endless Night* (Rounder/Windcharger 11661-3173-2)

11. Merle Haggard, with Tom Carter, *My House of Memories* (New York: Cliff St. Books, 1999), p. 5.

12. Good accounts of local country music affairs are Amy Noel Davis, "When You Coming Back? The Local Country-Music Opry Community" (M.A. thesis, University of North Carolina–Chapel Hill, 1998), and Timothy C. Duffy, "Monday Nights at Green Acres: A Case Study of a Grass-Roots Picking Party" (M.A. thesis, University of North Carolina–Chapel Hill, 1990).

13. Tom Alesia, "Ojibwe Radio Available over Internet," *Wisconsin State Journal,* May 12, 2000; the information about Tracy Pitcock came from the liner notes of *Heart of Texas Country* (Neon Nightmare 1002); and the description of Eddie Stubbs's show came from the radio interview on Mar. 15, 2000.

14. Eclecticism, musical versatility, and respect for roots are the hallmarks of O'Brien's music. Compare, for example, his tribute to Bob Dylan in *Red on Blonde* (Sugar Hill SHCD 3853) with *Songs from the Mountain* (Howdy Skies HS 1001), a CD featuring Dirk Powell and John Herrmann, and inspired by the music discussed in Charles Frazier's Civil War novel *Cold Mountain;* and *The Crossing* (Alula 1014), a tribute to the presumed links between Appalachia and the Celtic past. Green's talents are proudly displayed in all of the CDs made by Riders in the Sky, but he has also made a fine solo album, *Songs of the Sage* (Warner Western 9 46497-2). "Night Riding Song" alone is well worth the price of this album.

15. Don Walser has made at least five albums for the Watermelon label in Austin. *Rolling Stone from Texas* would be a good place to begin an introduction to his music (Watermelon CD 1028).

16. Dale Watson recorded "Jack's Truck Stop and Cafe" on *I Hate These Songs* (Hightone HCD 8082). "A Real Country Song" is on *Blessed or Damned* (Hightone HCD 8070).

Bibliographical and Discographical Suggestions

Serious researchers, particularly in the area of old-time country music, will want to visit the major repositories of country music. I spent productive time in several archives, such as the Berea College Archives in Berea, Kentucky, the Barker History Center at the University of Texas in Austin, the Western Kentucky Library in Bowling Green, and the Harris Collection, Hay Library, at Brown University in Providence, Rhode Island, but my strongest debt is to the Country Music Hall of Fame and Museum in Nashville and the Southern Folklife Collection at the University of North Carolina in Chapel Hill. The CMF has vast holdings and is superintended by very knowledgeable people. Paul Kingsbury, John Rumble, Bob Pinson, and Ronnie Pugh have been kind friends and generous advisers to me for many years. The Southern Folklife Collection, housed in the Wilson Library at the University of North Carolina in Chapel Hill, is now the home of what was once known as the John Edwards Memorial Foundation (formerly located at UCLA). Building upon the enormous storehouse of material (recordings, songbooks, printed ephemera) bequeathed to his American collector friends by the young Australian, John Edwards, the Southern Folklife Collection has gone on to become the depository for many of the most important folklorists and historians of country music. Archie Green, D. K. Wilgus, Mike Seeger, Alice Gerrard, Anne Romaine, and Gus Meade are only a few of the authorities whose collections now reside in the library. Archivists Steve Weiss and Amy Davis have worked diligently to make the collections available for the research use of anyone interested in the history or cultural significance of American vernacular music.

The listings included here are not intended as definitive guides. The notes at the end of the book provide the full retinue of sources that have informed my scholarship. What follows is a description of the authorities that have been most useful to me. Specialists in both southern history and country music will immediately think of important works that have been omitted. Their absence sometimes means that I have not read or listened to them, or, more likely, that I have forgotten them.

Southern History

W. J. Cash, *The Mind of the South* (New York: Alfred A. Knopf, 1941), was the book that did most to arouse my interest in the subject. He was the first writer I encountered who sounded like he knew the people I grew up with. Although he wrote with the perspectives and flaws of 1941, his major assertions still ring true. Readers who are only now discovering Cash should read the introduction to the Vintage reprint of 1991 written by Bertram Wyatt-Brown. Cash's chief critic, C. Vann Woodward, also influenced me greatly. In *Tom Watson: Agrarian Rebel* (New York: Macmillan, 1938) and *The Origins of the New South, 1877–1913* (Baton Rouge: Louisiana State University Press, 1951), he informed us of the South's populist tradition and reminded us that change had been a constant in the lives of conservative southerners. That knowledge, of course, gave us hope that even an oppressive system of racial segregation might wither away. Edward Ayers's work has not replaced that of Woodward as the most useful guide to the late nineteenth-century South, but, in *The Promise of the New South: Life after Reconstruction* (New York: Oxford University Press, 1992), he has added significantly to our understanding of that era. His bibliography is rich with suggestions for future reading and research. Other general overviews of southern history that are rich with detail, interpretation, and hints to further research are George B. Tindall, *The Emergence of the New South, 1913–1945* (Baton Rouge: Louisiana State University Press, 1967) and Numan V. Bartley, *The New South, 1945–1980: The Story of the South's Modernization* (Baton Rouge: Louisiana State University Press, 1995).

Howard Odum and Frank Owsley wrote from different ideological perspectives, but they were the first scholars to concentrate on the plain people of the South. Odum, the pioneering sociologist of the South, had great respect for its poor people, black and white. He was one of the first scholars to recognize the role of music in these people's lives, and had almost no predecessor in his use of phonograph records. Odum was a prolific scholar, but *An American Epoch: Southern Portraiture in the National Picture* (New York: Henry Holt, 1930) has been most helpful to me. Frank Owsley's *Plain Folk of the Old South* (1949; reprint, Baton Rouge: Louisiana State University Press, 1982), was the first history of non-elite whites. He recognized their diversity and hunger for independence, discredited the idea that they were all poor and servile, and contributed useful information about their migratory patterns and economic functions. J. Wayne Flynt, though, disclosed in *Dixie's Forgotten People: The South's Poor Whites* (Bloomington: Indiana University Press, 1979) that the region, both old

and new, did have poor whites who had been ignored by both scholars and political activists. Grady McWhiney has been Frank Owsley's most devoted disciple. His *Cracker Culture: Celtic Ways in the Old South* (Tuscaloosa: University
of Alabama Press, 1988) provides a wealth of detail about the lives and habits
of plain whites. His arguments concerning the Celtic origins of southern traits,
however, should be taken with a grain of salt. David Hackett Fischer is much more
convincing in *Albion's Seed* (New York: Oxford University Press, 1989), which
sees the origins of southern plain folk culture in the migrations made by "borderlanders" from the British Isles to the southern colonies. Carl Bridenbaugh,
Vexed and Troubled Englishmen, 1590–1642 (New York: Oxford University
Press, 1968), is also persuasive when he argues that many presumed early American traits first took root in England in the years surveyed by his book. For those
who want to pursue questions concerning plain-folk culture in a more intensive
and localized context, good places to begin are Jeanette Keith, *Country People
in the New South: Tennessee's Upper Cumberland* (Chapel Hill: University of
North Carolina Press, 1995); Durwood Dunn, *Cades Cove: The Life and Death
of a Southern Appalachian Community, 1818–1937* (Knoxville: University of
Tennessee Press, 1988); and Bill Cecil-Fronsman, *Common Whites: Class and
Culture in Antebellum North Carolina* (Lexington: University Press of Kentucky,
1992); Samuel C. Hyde, Jr., ed., *Plain Folk of the South Revisited* (Baton Rouge:
Louisiana State University Press, 1997), presents the views of several scholars,
while J. Wayne Flynt and Dorothy S. Flynt provide guides to further scholarship
in *Southern Poor Whites: A Selected, Annotated Bibliography of Published Sources*
(New York: Garland, 1981).

The economic transformation of the South in the late nineteenth and early
twentieth centuries has been discussed by a broad range of scholars. Edward
Ayers's bibliography is a good place to begin, but that source can be supplemented
by the notes and interpretation provided by James C. Cobb in *Industrialization
and Southern Society, 1877–1984* (Lexington: University Press of Kentucky,
1984). Cobb's work should be particularly helpful to anyone interested in the
evolution of country music because the author is a perceptive student of both
music and economic change. The books that have informed my knowledge and
understanding of the processes that transformed southern agriculture and introduced new ways of making a living include Steven Hahn, *The Roots of Southern
Populism: Yeoman Farmers and the Transformation of the Georgia Upcountry,
1850–1890* (New York: Oxford University Press, 1983); Thomas D. Clark, *Pills,
Petticoats, and Plows: The Southern Country Store* (Norman: University of Oklahoma Press, 1944); Ronald D. Eller, *Miners, Millhands, and Mountaineers: Industrialization of the Appalachian South, 1880–1930* (Knoxville: University of
Tennessee, 1982); David L. Carlton, *Mill and Town in South Carolina, 1880–
1920* (Baton Rouge: Louisiana State University Press, 1980); Jacqueline Hall et
al., *Like a Family: The Making of a Southern Cotton Mill World* (Chapel Hill:
University of North Carolina Press, 1987); Allen Tullos, *Habits of Industry: White*

Culture and the Transformation of the Carolina Piedmont (Chapel Hill: University of North Carolina Press, 1989); I. A. Newby, *Plain Folk of the New South: Social Change and Cultural Persistence, 1880–1915* (Baton Rouge: Louisiana State University Press, 1989); Crandall Shiflett, *Coal Town: Life, Work, and Culture in Company Towns of Southern Appalachia, 1880–1960* (Knoxville: University of Tennessee, 1991); Pete Daniel, *Breaking the Land: The Transformation of Cotton, Tobacco, and Rice Cultures since 1880* (Urbana: University of Ilinois Press, 1985); Jack Temple Kirby, *Rural Worlds Lost: The American South, 1920–1960* (Baton Rouge: Louisiana State University Press, 1987); Lawrence Goodwyn, *Democratic Promise: The Populist Moment in America* (New York: Oxford University Press, 1976); and Robert C. McMath, Jr., *Populist Vanguard: A History of the Southern Farmers' Alliance* (Chapel Hill: University of North Carolina Press, 1975).

The cultural consequences of economic change have been noted in some of the books mentioned above, particularly in *Like a Family*, which talks about the role played by cotton mill families in the making of hillbilly music, and in a perceptive article by Pamela Grundy: "From Il Trovatore to the Crazy Mountaineers: The Rise and Fall of Elevated Culture on WBT-Charlotte, 1922–1930," *Southern Cultures* 1, no. 1 (Fall, 1994): 51–75. Ted Ownby has been acutely conscious of the impact made by economic change in the lives of poor people in general and southern men more specifically. His *American Dreams in Mississippi: Consumers, Poverty, and Culture, 1830–1998* (Chapel Hill: University of North Carolina Press, 2000) suggests that poor people sometimes willingly participated in their transformation. His *Subduing Satan: Religion, Recreation, and Manhood in the Rural South, 1865–1920* (Chapel Hill: University of North Carolina Press, 1990) explores the world lost by white men in the late nineteenth century as well as the role played by evangelical religion in their "taming." Apart from music, few studies have addressed the role of popular culture in the lives of the southern people. Crandall Shiflett describes the allure of cities for rural folk in *Coal Town*. Gregory Waller reveals the kind of work that can and should be done by scholars in his study of Lexington, Kentucky, *Main Street Amusements: Movies and Commercial Entertainment in a Southern City, 1896–1930* (Washington, D.C.: Smithsonian Institution Press, 1995). Henry D. Shapiro discusses the role played by local color writers and ballad collectors in the shaping of public attitudes concerning Appalachia, in *Appalachia on Our Mind: The Southern Mountains and Mountaineers in the American Consciousness, 1870–1920* (Chapel Hill: University of North Carolina Press, 1978). David Whisnant explores the impact made by settlement-school teachers, folk festival entrepreneurs, and other "cultural interventionists" on the culture of the southern mountains in *All That Is Native and Fine: The Politics of Culture in an American Region* (Chapel Hill: University of North Carolina Press, 1983).

The peculiar interrelationship of honor and violence among white southerners is best discussed by Bertram Wyatt-Brown, in *Southern Honor: Ethics and*

Behavior in the Old South (New York: Oxford University Press, 1982), while Elliot Gorn analyzes the more bizarre manifestations among plain whites in "'Gouge and Bite, Pull Hair and Scratch': The Social Significance of Fighting in the Southern Backcountry," *American Historical Review* 90, no. 1 (Feb., 1985): 18–43. Other useful studies include Edward L. Ayers, *Vengeance and Justice: Crime and Punishment in the Nineteenth-Century American South* (New York: Oxford University Press, 1984), and John Shelton Reed, "Below the Smith and Wesson Line: Southern Violence," in *One South: An Ethnic Approach to Regional Culture* (Baton Rouge: Louisiana State University Press, 1982).

My understanding of the role played by religion in the shaping of southern habits and music has been enhanced by many scholars: John B. Boles, *The Great Revival, 1787–1805: The Origins of the Southern Evangelical Mind* (Lexington: University Press of Kentucky, 1972); Rhys Isaac, *The Transformation of Virginia, 1740–1790* (Chapel Hill: University of North Carolina Press, 1982); Dickson Bruce, Jr., *And They All Sang Hallelujah: Plain-Folk Camp-Meeting Religion, 1800–1845* (Knoxville: University of Tennessee Press, 1974); Donald Mathews, *Religion in the Old South* (Chicago: University of Chicago Press, 1977); Christine Leigh Heyrman, *Southern Cross: The Beginnings of the Bible Belt* (New York: Alfred A. Knopf, 1997); Mechal Sobel, *The World They Made Together: Black and White Values in Eighteenth-Century Virginia* (Princeton, N.J.: Princeton University Press, 1987); David Edwin Harrell, *Oral Roberts: An American Life* (Bloomington: Indiana University Press, 1985), and *All Things Are Possible: The Healing and Charismatic Revivals in Modern America* (Bloomington: Indiana University Press, 1975); Charles Reagan Wilson, *Baptized in Blood: The Religion of the Lost Cause, 1865–1920* (Athens: University of Georgia Press, 1980).

The cultural consequences of the migrations made by plain southerners to other parts of the nation are discussed by James N. Gregory, *American Exodus: The Dust Bowl Migration and Okie Culture in California* (New York: Oxford University Press, 1989); Lewis Killian, *White Southerners* (New York: Random House, 1970); Jack Temple Kirby, "The Southern Exodus, 1910–1960: A Primer for Historians," *Journal of Southern History* 49, no. 4 (Nov., 1983): 585–600; Pete Daniel, "Going among Strangers: Southern Reactions to World War II," *Journal of American History* 77, no. 3 (Dec., 1990): 886–911, and "Rhythm of the Land," *Agricultural History* 68, no. 4 (Fall, 1994): 1–22.

We need more good studies of southern rural and working-class women. *Like a Family* is an excellent account of Piedmont cotton mill women; Margaret Jarman Hagood provides a sociological survey of rural women in the Upper South during the 1930s in *Mothers of the South: Portraiture of the White Tenant Farm Woman* (Chapel Hill: University of North Carolina Press, 1939). Although it treats a very narrow slice of Appalachia, the Tennessee mountains near Chattanooga, Emma Bell Miles, *Spirit of the Mountains* (New York: J. Pott, 1905; reprint, Knoxville: University of Tennessee Press, 1975) has a universal ring to it. Her analysis of male-female relations, and the perceived spheres assigned to each, is probably applicable to the entire rural South in the late nineteenth century. My favorite account of the role played by mothers in southern poor white culture is Rick Bragg, *All Over but the Shoutin'* (New York: Pantheon, 1997).

The persistence of southern values has been the cornerstone of John Shelton Reed's scholarship. This leading sociologist of the South has written much on the subject, including *The Enduring South: Subcultural Persistence in Mass Society* (Lexington, Mass.: Lexington Books, 1972; reprint, Chapel Hill: University of North Carolina Press, 1986), *Southern Folk Plain and Fancy: Native White Social Types* (Athens: University or Georgia Press, 1986), and *My Tears Spoiled My Aim and Other Reflections on Southern Culture* (Columbia: University of Missouri Press, 1993). The export of southern values, both positive and negative, to the North has attracted several good writers. John Egerton led the way with *The Americanization of Dixie: The Southernization of America* (New York: Harper's Magazine Press, 1974), but Peter Applebome followed up on that work with his brilliant *Dixie Rising: How the South Is Shaping American Values, Politics, and Culture* (New York: Random House, 1996). Dan Carter concentrated on the political consequences of southernization with *The Politics of Rage: George Wallace, the Origins of the New Conservatism, and the Transformation of American Politics* (New York: Simon and Schuster, 1995). James C. Cobb discussed the reciprocal relations of North and South in *Redefining Southern Culture: Mind and Identity in the Modern South* (Athens: University of Georgia Press, 1999). Jack Temple Kirby argues that some groups in southern society, plain whites and African Americans, have resisted mainstream homogenization; see *The Countercultural South* (Athens: University of Georgia Press, 1995). Charles Joyner has looked behind the ugly facts of racial hostility in the South and has found a common culture of mutual interaction; see *Shared Traditions: Southern History and Folk Culture* (Urbana: University of Illinois Press, 1999). This insight, of course, informs much of the work I have done, as well as that offered by Mechal Sobel in *The World They Made Together: Black and White Values in Eighteenth-Century Virginia.*

Music Bibliography

In about 1970 Archie Green, recognizing the growing interest in American vernacular music, recommended to the University of Illinois Press that a series be inaugurated on the subject. The result was Music in American Life, the first such venture ever by an academic press. Richard Wentworth, director of the press, warmly embraced the idea and was fortunate to have the services of Judith McCulloh, an ethnomusicologist who had a profound appreciation for all grassroots styles and an intimate knowledge of the work being done in the field. R. Serge Denisoff's *Great Day Coming: Folk Music and the American Left* (1971) and Green's *Only a Miner: Studies in Recorded Coal-Mining Songs* (1972) inaugurated the series. Over one hundred books have since been published bearing the imprint of Music in American Life. Whether published by the University of Illinois Press, or by the many other presses that have entered the field since the early seventies, the number of books devoted to American vernacular music have multiplied dramatically.

The suggestions that follow are not comprehensive, but instead constitute some of the works that have been most helpful to me. I will begin with biographies and autobiographies because they put a human face on most of the topics and issues that are discussed in this book. The early commercial manifestations of country music are ably discussed by Gene Wiggins, *Fiddlin' Georgia Crazy: Fiddlin' John Carson, His Real World, and the World of His Songs* (Urbana: University of Illinois Press, 1987); Ivan Tribe, *The Stonemans: An Appalachian Family and the Music That Shaped Their Lives* (Urbana: University of Illinois Press, 1993); David C. Morton, with Charles Wolfe, *DeFord Bailey: A Black Star in Early Country Music* (Knoxville: University of Tennessee Press, 1991); Nolan Porterfield, *Jimmie Rodgers: The Life and Times of America's Blue Yodeler*, rev. ed. (1979; Urbana: University of Illinois Press, 1992); and Kinney Rorrer, *Rambling Blues: The Life and Songs of Charlie Poole* (London: Old Time Music, 1982).

The best biographical introductions to country music during the Great Depression are Joe Klein's *Woody Guthrie: A Life* (New York: Alfred A. Knopf, 1980); Charles Townsend's *San Antonio Rose: The Life and Music of Bob Wills* (Urbana: University of Illinois Press, 1976, 1986); Cary Ginell's *Milton Brown and the Founding of Western Swing* (Urbana: University of Illinois Press, 1994); Nolan Porterfield, *Last Cavalier: The Life and Times of John A. Lomax, 1867–1948* (Urbana: University of Illinois Press, 1996); Louis M. Jones, with Charles Wolfe, *Everybody's Grandpa: Fifty Years behind the Mike* (Knoxville: University of Tennessee Press, 1984); and Ronnie Pugh, *Ernest Tubb: The Texas Troubadour* (Durham, N.C.: Duke University Press, 1996).

Klein's impressively researched book presents a comprehensive and balanced view of Guthrie, and tells us much about the relationship between political radicalism and folk music during the 1930s. Porterfield talks about the folk consciousness that emerged during those years, but we sorely need a biography of Alan Lomax, too. We do get a good insight, though, into the thinking that motivated him during those years in his *The Land Where the Blues Began* (New York: Pantheon, 1993). The fine biographies of Wills, Brown, and Tubb discuss the emergence of the western swing and honky-tonk styles, and remind us that Americans coped with hard times in a variety of ways.

Pugh's biography is also very good on the years of World War II, largely because Ernest Tubb played such a seminal role in country music's popularization and nationalization during those years. Townsend gives a good account of the blossoming of country music on the West Coast, but Jonny Whiteside tells us even more in *Rambling Rose: The Life and Career of Rose Maddox* (Nashville, Tenn.: Country Music Foundation Press and Vanderbilt University Press, 1997). Grandpa Jones's autobiography informs us that he served in the army during the war, and contributed to the music's worldwide popularity as a member of a Special Services unit in Europe.

The burgeoning of country music in the forties and fifties is described in several good biographies. Two of them discuss Eddy Arnold, the first star of the immediate postwar era: Don Cusic, *Eddy Arnold: I'll Hold You in My Heart* (Nashville: Rutledge Hill Press, 1997), and Michael Streissguth, *Eddy Arnold: Pioneer of the Nashville Sound* (New York: Schirmer Books, 1997). Charles Wolfe tells the story of country music's greatest "brother duet" in *In Close Harmony: The Story of the Louvin Brothers* (Jackson: University Press of Mississippi, 1996). The central theme of Daniel Cooper's *Lefty Frizzell: The Honky-Tonk Life of Country Music's Greatest Singer* (New York: Little, Brown, 1995) is presented in the book's title; Wade Hall, on the other hand, pays tribute to a northern entertainer who paved the way for country-pop music in *Hell-Bent for Music: The Life of Pee Wee King* (Lexington: University Press of Kentucky, 1996). Hank Williams has been the subject of much speculation and commentary, including three good biographies: Roger M. Williams, *Sing a Sad Song: The Life of Hank Williams* (Urbana: University of Illinois Press, second ed., 1981); Chet Flippo, *Your Cheatin' Heart: A Biography of Hank Williams* (New York: Simon and Schuster, 1981); and Colin Escott, with George Merritt and William MacEwen, *Hank Williams: The Biography* (Boston: Little, Brown, 1994). Both Escott and Roger Williams include discographies, but the latter has the virtue of being a product of Bob Pinson's labors.

The rock-and-roll revolution is the focus of outstanding biographies written by two of our finest music historians, Peter Guralnick and Nick Tosches. Guralnick's masterful two-volume biography of Elvis Presley, *Last Train to Memphis: The Rise of Elvis Presley* (New York: Little, Brown, 1994) and *Careless Love: The Unmaking of Elvis Presley* (Boston: Little, Brown, 1998), is one of the best accounts yet written of any American musician. However, Jerry Hopkins's biography of "the King" is still worth reading; see *Elvis: A Biography* (New York: Warner Books, 1972), as is Greil Marcus's brilliant essay on Elvis in *Mystery Train: Images of America in Rock 'n' Roll* (New York: E. P. Dutton, 1976; 4th rev. ed., New York: Penguin, 1997). The other southern wild man of rock-and-roll, Jerry Lee Lewis, has received extended treatment, but his best chronicler is Nick Tosches; see *Hellfire: The Jerry Lee Lewis Story* (1982; New York: Grove Press, 1998). Tosches is easily the most wide-ranging writer who has dealt with country music, with biographical treatments that range from the boxer Sonny Liston to the pop singer Dean Martin. He is also preparing a biography of the white minstrel singer Emmett Miller, who was a major influence on such entertainers as Bob Wills and Tommy Duncan.

Bluegrass music, of course, spans several decades of country music history, but glimpses of its power and appeal can be discerned in some biographies. John Wright discusses the lonesome sound of bluegrass in the music's present-day patriarch, Ralph Stanley; see *Traveling the High Way Home: Ralph Stanley and the World of Traditional Bluegrass Music* (Urbana: University of Illinois Press, 1993).

The definitive biography of "the father of bluegrass," Bill Monroe, has not yet been written, but good beginnings have been made by Ralph Rinzler, "Bill Monroe," in *Stars of Country Music,* ed. Bill C. Malone and Judith McCulloh (Urbana: University of Illinois Press, 1975), pp. 202–21; James Rooney, *Bossmen: Bill Monroe and Muddy Waters* (New York: Dial Press, 1971); and Richard D. Smith, *"Can't You Hear Me Callin'": The Life of Bill Monroe, Father of Bluegrass* (Boston: Little, Brown, 2000). Rinzler's interviews with Monroe served as the nucleus of the research that went into the writing of Smith's fine biography.

Academic scholars have not been much attracted to biographical depictions of contemporary country entertainers, but the modern period has been well served by a few autobiographies and an occasional biography written by journalists or freelance writers. The autobiographies, usually written with the assistance of professional writers, tend to be uneven in quality and style. A few of them, like Al Stricklin, with Jon McConal, *My Years with Bob Wills* (San Antonio: Naylor Company, 1976), and Alton Delmore, with Charles Wolfe, *Truth Is Stranger Than Publicity* (Nashville: Country Music Foundation Press, 1977), document earlier periods of country music. Delmore was refreshingly honest about the Grand Ole Opry, himself, and his brother Rabon in an unfinished memoir that Charles Wolfe shaped into an autobiography. The best country music autobiography is still probably Loretta Lynn, with George Vecsey, *Coal Miner's Daughter* (New York: Warner Books, 1976). Hank Snow, however, has many frankly engaging things to say in his autobiography, especially about Elvis Presley and Colonel Tom Parker; see Snow, with Jack Ownbey and Bob Burris, *The Hank Snow Story* (Urbana: University of Illinois Press, 1994). Waylon Jennings (along with Lenny Kaye) was not simply refreshing in his honesty, he was brutal, in *Waylon: An Autobiography* (New York: Warner Books, 1996). The result was an entertaining and informative view of the modern country music business and the responses made to it by freethinking mavericks. Some of the "mavericks" who have produced revealing stories include Johnny Cash, with Patrick Carr, in *Johnny Cash: The Autobiography* (New York: HarperCollins, 1997); Merle Haggard, with Peggy Russell, *Sing Me Back Home: My Story* (New York: Times Books, 1981); Willie Nelson, with Bud Shrake, *Willie: An Autobiography* (New York: Simon and Schuster, 1988); Hank Williams, Jr., with Michael Bane, *Living Proof* (New York: Dell, 1979); and Tammy Wynette, with Joan Dew, *Stand By Your Man* (New York: Simon and Schuster, 1978). Dolly Parton, who literally is in a class by herself, apparently wrote her autobiography without assistance. *Dolly: My Life and Other Unfinished Business* (New York: HarperCollins, 1994) is much like the singer herself, funny, candid, and free-floating.

The South and Country Music

The bibliographical listing of themes and topics that follows addresses books, articles, and record liner notes.

Two of my books discuss the ways in which images of the South shaped perceptions of country music: *Southern Music/American Music* (Lexington: University Press of Kentucky, 1979) and *Singing Cowboys and Musical Mountaineers* (Athens: University of Georgia Press, 1993). The southern music book is now undergoing revision, with the assistance of David Stricklin, and is scheduled for a new publication in 2002. Two evaluations of Stephen Foster describe the influence of that great songwriter on American popular culture: William W. Austin, *"Susanna," "Jeanie," and "The Old Folks at Home": The Songs of Stephen C. Foster from His Time to Ours,* 2d ed. (1975; Urbana: University of Illinois Press, 1988) and Ken Emerson, *Doo-dah! Stephen Foster and the Rise of American Popular Culture* (New York: Simon and Schuster, 1997). Blackface minstrelsy has captured the attention of many scholars, but Robert C. Toll presents a good discussion of the phenomenon's music in *Blacking Up: The Minstrel Show in Nineteenth-Century America* (New York: Oxford University Press, 1974). Hans Nathan discusses one of minstrelsy's greatest musicians in *Dan Emmett and the Rise of Early Negro Minstrelsy* (Norman: University of Oklahoma Press, 1962). Earl Bargainneer provides glimpses of the fascination that the South has exerted over pop songwriters in "Tin Pan Alley and Dixie: The South in Popular Song," *Mississippi Quarterly* 30, no. 4 (Fall, 1977): 527–65. Emma Bell Miles in 1904 wrote the first account of "Appalachian Music" in an essay called "Some Real American Music" (available in her great book *Spirit of the Mountains*) but the book that did most to implant the idea in the minds of Americans, while also reaffirming romantic perceptions of Appalachia, was Olive Dame Campbell and Cecil J. Sharp, *English Folk Songs from the Southern Appalachians* (New York: G. P. Putnam's Sons, 1917). The previously mentioned books by Henry D. Shapiro (*Appalachia on Our Mind*) and David Whisnant (*All That Is Native and Fine*) provide discerning interpretations of the work done by Campbell and Sharp. I explore the concept of "mountain music" in "Appalachian Music and American Popular Culture: The Romance That Will Not Die," in *Appalachia Inside Out: A Sequel to Voices from the Hills,* ed. Robert J. Higgs, Ambrose N. Manning, and Jim Wayne Miller (Knoxville: University of Tennessee Press, 1995), vol. 2, pp. 462–69. Richard A. Peterson and Russell Davis, Jr., define the southern geography of country music in "The Fertile Crescent of Country Music," *Journal of Country Music* 6, no. 1 (Spring, 1975): 19–27.

The relationship between music and work has been a special preoccupation of Archie Green. He wrote an outstanding book, *Only a Miner: Studies in Recorded Coal-Mining Songs* (Urbana: University of Illinois Press, 1972); edited an important collection of essays, *Songs about Work: Essays in Occupational Culture for Richard A. Reuss* (Bloomington: Folklore Institute, Indiana University, 1993); contributed his own original essays in *Wobblies, Pile Butts, and Other Heroes: Laborlore Explorations* (Urbana: University of Illinois Press, 1993); and produced and wrote the notes for a two-volume anthology of recordings dealing with work, *Work's Many Voices* (JEMF 110 and 111). The music that emerged from the southern labor struggles of the 1930s has been discussed extensively, and some of the most pertinent works, such as Joe Klein's biography of Woody Guthrie, have been mentioned previously or will be cited in the material dealing with protest. Marc S. Miller's edited collection, *Working Lives: The Southern Exposure History of Labor in the South* (New York: Pantheon Books, 1974), explores that era of southern history and provides a very good bibliography on labor activities. Discussions of music that issued forth from certain occupations are available in a few articles and books. Archie Green, again, made a distinctive contribution with his notes to Mike Seeger's record album, *Tipple, Loom, and Rail: Songs of the Industrialization of the South* (Folkways FH 5273), and his article "Born on Picketlines, Textile Workers' Songs Are Woven into History," *Textile Labor* 21, no. 4 (Apr., 1961): 3–5. Doug DeNatale and Glenn Hinson contributed an important article to Green's *Songs about Work*, "The Southern Textile Song Tradition Reconsidered," pp. 77–107. Green's protégé, Norm Cohen, concentrated on the songs inspired by the railroad industry. His superbly documented *Long Steel Rail: The Railroad in American Folksong*, 2d ed. (Urbana: University of Illinois Press, 2000), a book whose significance and reach extend far beyond work, is one of the major achievements of American folksong scholarship.

Protest music has prompted several good studies. John Greenway wrote the pioneering study of socially conscious music, *American Folksongs of Protest* (New York: A. S. Barnes, 1953). Other useful studies include R. Serge Denisoff's *Great Day Coming: Folk Music and the American Left* (Urbana: University of Illinois Press, 1971); Jerome L. Rodnitzky's *Minstrels of the Dawn: The Folk-Protest Singer as a Cultural Hero* (Chicago: Nelson-Hall, 1971); Shelly Romalis, *Pistol Packin' Mama: Aunt Molly Jackson and the Politics of Folksong* (Urbana: University of Illinois Press, 1999); Joe Klein, *Woody Guthrie*; Richard A. Reuss, "Woody Guthrie and His Folk Tradition," *Journal of American Folklore* 83, no. 329 (July–Sept., 1970): 273–303; and James Gregory's chapter, "The Language of a Subculture," in *American Exodus*.

Gregory's book, of course, is also a good place to begin a discussion of country music and politics. The subject really began to attract writers, good and bad, during the cultural ferment of the 1960s and early 1970s. Paul Hemphill, *The Nashville Sound: Bright Lights and Country Music* (New York: Simon and Schuster, 1970) equated the music with workingman's politics, while some other writers tended to see only sinister, right-wing content in country lyrics and behavior. Typical of the latter was Richard Goldstein, "My Country Music Problem—and Yours," *Mademoiselle* 77, no. 2 (June, 1973): 114–15, 185. More balanced perspectives include Paul DiMaggio, Richard A. Peterson, and Jack Esco, Jr., "Country Music: Ballad of the Silent Majority," in *The Sounds of Social Change*, ed. R. Serge Denisoff and Richard A. Peterson (Chicago: Rand McNally, 1972), pp. 38–55; and Bill C. Malone, "Country Music, the South and Americanism," *Mississippi Folklore Register* 10 (Spring, 1976): 54–66. Ronnie Pugh, with whom I have often discussed matters of state, usually in a partisan but friendly manner, is working on a general study of the topic, tentatively entitled "the politics of country music."

No good general studies of country music's preoccupation with home exist. The idea of the South as a home to those Americans who long for a land of rustic security and stability is treated in the books mentioned above on Stephen Foster and the southern Appalachians. Nicholas E. Tawa also alludes briefly to that idea in *The Way to Tin Pan Alley: American Popular Song, 1866–1910* (New York: Schirmer Books, 1990). The early emphasis on home, mama, and morality in country music is treated by Loyal Jones, *Radio's Kentucky Mountain Boy: Bradley Kincaid* (Appalachian Center: Berea College, 1980); John Atkins, "The Carter Family," in *Stars of Country Music;* William E. Lightfoot, introduction to the reprint of Scott G. Wiseman, *Wiseman's View: The Autobiography of Skyland Scotty Wiseman,* in *North Carolina Folklore Journal* 33, nos. 1 and 2 (1985–86); and Harry S. Rice, "Renfro Valley on the Radio, 1937–1941," *Journal of Country Music* 19, no. 2 (1997), 16–25. Cecelia Tichi devotes a chapter to "Home" in *High Lonesome: The American Culture of Country Music* (Chapel Hill: University of North Carolina Press, 1994), 19–51. Country music as home or community is the subject of Curtis W. Ellison, in his important *Country Music Culture: From Hard Times to Heaven* (Jackson: University Press of Mississippi, 1995). Charles Wolfe also touches upon that topic in *A Good-Natured Riot: The Birth of the Grand Ole Opry* (Nashville: Country Music Foundation and Vanderbilt University Press, 1999).

A very large percentage of the early country songs that dealt with Mother and home came from nineteenth-century popular music, both before and during the golden age of Tin Pan Alley. Several sources have proved helpful in my quest for the pop origins of southern folk and country songs. Sigmund Spaeth, usually with tongue in cheek, compiled two delightful books of mostly sentimental songs, *Read 'em and Weep* (New York: Doubleday, Page, 1926) and *Weep Some More My Lady* (New York: Doubleday, Page, 1927). Nicholas E. Tawa has covered the same ground and more, but with considerably more academic rigor and seriousness, in *Sweet Songs for Gentle Americans: The Parlor Song in America, 1790–1860* (Bowling Green, Ohio: Popular Press, 1980) and *The Way to Tin Pan Alley: American Popular Song, 1866–1910.* I have always enjoyed, and learned much from, one of the veteran tunesmiths of Tin Pan Alley, Edward B. Marks, who contributed his memoir, *They All Sang* (New York: Viking Press, 1934). Gene Wiggins wrote a good article on the popular songs that became fiddle tunes, in "Popular Music and the Fiddler," *JEMF Quarterly* 15, no. 55 (Fall, 1979): 144–52. Norm Cohen, however, has done the most impressive studies of the pop origins of folk music. Examples of his scholarship include "Tin Pan Alley's Contribution to Folk Music," *Western Folklore* 29, no. 1 (1970): 9–20; "The Folk and Popular Roots of Country Music," in *The Encyclopedia of Country Music,* ed. Paul Kingsbury (New York: Oxford University Press, 1998), pp. 188–92; "Ragtime in Early Country Music" (with David Cohen), in *Ragtime,* ed. John Edward Hasse (New York: Schirmer Books, 1985), pp. 296–301; and the extensive notes to the record album produced for the John Edwards Memorial Foundation, *Minstrels and Tunesmiths: The Commercial Roots of Early Country Music* (JEMF-109). I also have written on the pop origins of country music in chap. 2 of *Singing Cowboys and Musical Mountaineers* and in "William S. Hays: The Bard of Kentucky," *Register of the Kentucky Historical Society* 93, no. 3 (Summer, 1995): 286–306.

The relationship between religion and country music has been often noted, but not much written about. I wrote an essay on the relationship, "The Gospel Truth: Christianity and Country Music," in *The Encyclopedia of Country Music,* pp. 218–21. The white gospel quartet tradition (now commonly known as "southern gospel") has elicited little scholarly attention, although Lois S. Blackwell has compiled a short account called *The Wings of the Dove: The Story of Gospel Music in America* (Norfolk, Va.: Donning, 1978). It and all other studies will soon be superseded by the work of James Goff, at Appalachian State University in Boone, North Carolina, who is completing a history of that genre, tentatively entitled "The Gospel Jubilee." Jack Bernhardt, at Elon College in Elon, North Carolina, is working more specifically on country music and religion (particularly Pentecostalism and the music of Jerry and Tammy Sullivan). Loyal Jones has contributed a highly regarded study of religion in Appalachia, *Faith and Meaning in the Southern Uplands* (Urbana: University of Illinois Press, 1999), which contains a good section on the role played by music in the mountain churches. Other studies that I have found particularly illuminating include Howard Odum, *An American Epoch;* George Pullen Jackson's landmark *White Spirituals in the Southern Uplands* (1933; Chapel Hill: University of North Carolina Press, 1965); Jo Lee Fleming, "James D. Vaughan, Music Publisher" (S.M.D. diss., Union Theological Seminary, 1972); Richard Hulan, "Camp-Meeting Spiritual Folksongs: Legacy of the 'Great Revival in the West,'" (Ph.D. diss., University of Texas, 1978); Dickson Bruce, Jr., *And They All Sang Hallelujah;* Archie Green, "Hear These Beautiful Sacred Selections," reprinted from the 1970 *Yearbook of the International Folk Music Council* (Los Angeles: JEMF, 1970), pp. 28–50; and Charles Wolfe, "Frank Smith, Andrew Jenkins, and Early Commercial Gospel Music," *American Music* 1, no. 1 (Spring, 1983): 49–59.

General discussions of the rambling impulse in country music are also rare. Discussions of rambling types, though, do exist: Nolan Porterfield, *Jimmie Rodgers;* Clifford Kinney Rorrer, *Rambling Blues: The Life and Songs of Charlie Poole;* Hank Williams, Jr., with Michael Bane, *Living Proof;* Waylon Jennings, with Lenny Kaye, *Waylon: An Autobiography;* and the various books and essays, such as Dave Hickey's "In Defense of the Telecaster Cowboy Outlaws" (*Country Music* 2, no. 5 [Jan., 1974]: 90–95) and Michael Bane's *The Outlaws: Revolution in Country Music* (New York: Doubleday, 1978), dealing with people like David Allan Coe and the other musicians who gathered around Willie Nelson.

The Los Angeles phase of country outlawry is well told by Ben Fong-Torres in *Hickory Wind: The Life and Times of Gram Parsons* (New York: Pocket Books, 1991).

The rambler spirit showed up in the personas and musical styles of the rockabillies. Good introductions to those musicians are Colin Escott and Martin Hawkins, *Good Rockin' Tonight: Sun Records and the Birth of Rock 'n' Roll* (New York: St. Martin's Press, 1991). Robert K. Oermann and Mary A. Bufwack, "Rockabilly Women," *Journal of Country Music* 8 (May, 1979): 65–94; Nick Tosches, "Rockabilly," in *The Illustrated History of Country Music*, ed. Patrick Carr (Garden City, N.Y.: Doubleday & Company, 1979), pp. 217–37; Craig Morrison, *Go Cat Go! Rockabilly Music and Its Makers* (Urbana: University of Illinois Press, 1996); Michael Bertrand, *Race, Rock, and Elvis* (Urbana: University of Illinois Press, 2000), and of course, the biographies of Elvis Presley and Jerry Lee Lewis.

The most respectable manifestation of the rambler, the cowboy, is richly documented, but his relationship to country music still awaits definitive treatment. The place to start, of course, is John A. Lomax, *Cowboy Songs and Other Frontier Ballads* (New York: Sturgis & Walton, 1910). For the full context in which Lomax worked, see Porterfield's biography. An interesting study that shatters some illusions about the origins of the cowboy songs is John White, *Git Along, Little Dogies: Songs and Songmakers of the American West* (Urbana: University of Illinois Press, 1975). The best collections of cowboy songs, both "traditional" and "Hollywood," are Jim Bob Tinsley, *He Was Singin' This Song* (Orlando: University Presses of Florida, 1981) and *For a Cowboy Has to Sing* (Orlando: University of Central Florida Press, 1991). A shorter but useful collection is Don Edwards, *Classic Cowboy Songs* (Salt Lake City: Gibbs-Smith, 1994). The best study of rodeo songs is "I Ain't Rich but Lord I'm Free: The Rodeo Cowboy in Country Music," in Michael Allen, *Rodeo Cowboys in the North American Imagination* (Reno: University of Nevada Press, 1998), pp. 131–54. The cowboy's impact on the American popular consciousness has been ably discussed by Stephen Ray Tucker in "The Western Image in Country Music" (M.A. thesis, Southern Methodist University, 1976), and by Douglas B. Green in "The Singing Cowboy: An American Dream," *Journal of Country Music* 7, no. 2 (May, 1978): 4–62. Green, better known as Ranger Doug, is working on a full-scale history of western music.

Despite their importance to the definition and vitality of country music, neither humor nor dancing (which I have called "the frolic tradition") have attracted much attention from students of country music. Douglas Green was virtually alone among scholars in 1976 when he wrote a chapter called "Comedy" for *Country Roots: The Origins of Country Music* (New York: Hawthorn Books, 1976), pp. 65–87. Short autobiographies of various comedians and brief articles on humor have appeared since that time, but a comprehensive study is still to be written. Representative autobiographies include Jerry Clower, with Gerry Wood, *Ain't God Good!* (Waco, Tex.: Word Books, 1975), and Minnie Pearl (Sarah

Ophelia Cannon), with Joan Dew, *Minnie Pearl: An Autobiography* (New York: Simon and Schuster, 1980). Willie Smyth did a study of humor on Knoxville radio stations, "Traditional Humor on Knoxville Country Radio Entertainment Shows" (Ph.D. diss., UCLA, 1987), and Loyal Jones, who has long been interested in Appalachian humor—see Loyal Jones and Billy Edd Wheeler, *Laughter in Appalachia: A Festival of Southern Mountain Humor* (Little Rock, Ark.: August House, 1987)—is also compiling a study of country music humor.

The classic exposition of country dancing is S. Foster Damon, "The History of Square Dancing," American Antiquarian Society, *Proceedings of the Annual Meeting* 62, no. 1 (Apr. 16, 1952). Richard Nevell has compiled a short overview in *A Time to Dance: American Country Dancing from Hornpipies to Hot Hash* (New York: St. Martin's Press, 1977). The centerpieces of the country dances, house parties, and frolics were the fiddlers. The greatest scholar of fiddle tunes, Samuel P. Bayard, presented examples of his pioneering work in *Hill Country Tunes: Instrumental Folk Music of Southwestern Pennsylvania,* Memoirs of the American Folklore Society, no. 39 (Philadelphia: American Folklore Society, 1944), and *Dance to the Fiddle, March to the Fife: Instrumental Folk Tunes in Pennsylvania* (University Park: Pennsylvania State University Press, 1982). His work dealt primarily with Pennsylvania, but should nevertheless be of interest to scholars of southern music because so much of this music migrated south. Students searching for these and other tunes will most likely find them in the massive collection of Guthrie Meade, housed in the Southern Folklife Collection at the University of North Carolina at Chapel Hill. Earl Spielman exhibits impressive research in "Traditional North American Fiddling: A Methodology for the Historical and Comparative Analytical Style Study of Instrumental Musical Traditions" (Ph.D. diss., University of Wisconsin at Madison, 1975). Verbatim transcripts of some of Spielman's interviews with Georgia Slim Rutland and other fiddlers are on deposit in the Southern Folklife Collection. Some of the best fiddlers are chronicled in Charles Wolfe's *The Devil's Box: Masters of Southern Fiddling* (Nashville: Country Music Foundation Press and Vanderbilt University Press, 1997). Joyce Cauthen has contributed a very good study of Alabama fiddling in *With Fiddle and Well-Rosined Bow: Old-Time Fiddling in Alabama* (Tuscaloosa: University of Alabama Press, 1989). Although fine critiques can often be found on album liner notes, we are sorely in need of other state and regional studies. An indication of the role played by dance music in the reshaping of music in the Southwest can be discerned from Townsend's and Ginell's biographies of Bob Wills and Milton Brown, respectively. The most useful contemporary articles on country dancing that I have seen were written by Phil Jamison for the *Old-Time Herald.* What we need most is an exploration of the Texas two-step, and the cultural context that nourished it.

Bluegrass music has been the most carefully documented genre of country music. Contributors to the style's principal journal, *Bluegrass Unlimited,* often discuss musicians and songs that predate the bluegrass style. Ivan Tribe and Wayne

Daniel, for example, write often about the hillbilly musicians of the late thirties and forties, and consequently provide information that can be found nowhere else. The leading historian of the music, Neil Rosenberg, strikes a good balance between popular appeal and academic rigor in *Bluegrass: A History* (Urbana: University of Illinois Press, 1985, 1993). It is still the best and most comprehensive study, but it begs for revision and expansion. Robert Cantwell's *Bluegrass Breakdown: The Making of the Old Southern Sound* (Urbana: University of Illinois Press, 1984), on the other hand, is a brilliant study that is aimed only at music and cultural specialists.

Barn dances and local or regional centers of country music activity are discussed in a number of sources. Charles Wolfe has documented the early years of the most important radio show in *A Good-Natured Riot: The Birth of the Grand Ole Opry*. The Louisiana Hayride is chronicled in Stephen Ray Tucker, "The Louisiana Hayride, 1948–1954," in the *North Louisiana Historical Association Journal 8*, no. 5 (Fall, 1977): 187–201; and Horace Logan, with Bill Sloan, *Elvis, Hank and Me: Making Musical History on the Louisiana Hayride* (New York: St. Martin's Press, 1998). Reta Spears-Stewart compiled a short account of the show that featured Red Foley in the 1950s, *Remembering the Ozark Jubilee* (Springfield, Mo.: Stewart, Dillbeck & White, 1993). The story of the Renfro Valley Barn Dance is told anecdotally and informally in a memoir by one of its longtime participants: Pete Stamper, *It All Happened in Renfro Valley* (Lexington: University Press of Kentucky, 1999). Harry Rice has supplied good stories about the early days of that show in "Renfro Valley on the Radio, 1937–1941," *Journal of Country Music 19*, no. 2 (1977): 16–25, and Wayne Daniel has surveyed the whole story in such articles as "The Renfro Valley Barn Dance—The First Fifty Years," *Old Time Country 8*, no. 3 (Fall, 1992): 4–8. Daniel is also working on a larger and more comprehensive study of the Kentucky show. His *Pickin' on Peachtree: A History of Country Music in Atlanta, Georgia* (Urbana: University of Illinois Press, 1990) is a further reminder that Nashville did not always have a monopoly on country music (nor does it today). Amy Noel Davis, in fact, informs us that country music is still alive and well on local barn dances throughout the South and Midwest. She gives an extensive list but concentrates on two local "oprys" in Nortonville, Kentucky, and McLeansville, North Carolina, in "When You Coming Back? The Local Country-Music Opry Community" (M.A. thesis, University of North Carolina–Chapel Hill, 1998).

A few good studies of statewide country music activity also exist. Ivan Tribe concentrates on the power exerted by WWVA and other radio stations in West Virginia in *Mountaineer Jamboree: Country Music in West Virginia* (Lexington: University Press of Kentucky, 1984). Charles Wolfe discusses the music of two other states in *Tennessee Strings: The Story of Country Music in Tennessee* (Knoxville: University of Tennessee Press, 1977) and *Kentucky Country: Folk and Country Music of Kentucky* (Lexington: University Press of Kentucky, 1982). Gerald W. Haslam, however, has written the most significant of the state studies: *Workin' Man Blues: Country Music in California* (Berkeley: University of California Press, 1999). The book is important because California witnessed many of the most important innovations in country music history, but nevertheless has been often ignored by scholars and other writers. Someone needs to do a similar study of the important Texas country music scene. Local studies with a Texas setting, however, have been written: Alan B. Govenar and Jay F. Brakefield, *Deep Ellum and Central Track: Where the Black and White Worlds of Dallas Converged* (Denton: University of North Texas Press, 1998); Joe Carr and Alan Munde, *Prairie Nights to Neon Lights: The Story of Country Music in West Texas* (Lubbock: Texas Tech University Press, 1995); Jan Reid, *The Improbable Rise of Redneck Rock* (Austin: Heidelberg Press, 1974); Clifford Endres, *Austin City Limits* (Austin: University of Texas Press, 1987); and Nicholas Spitzer, "Bob Wills Is Still the King: Romantic Regionalism and Convergent Culture in Central Texas," *JEMF Quarterly* 2, part 4, no. 4 (Winter, 1975): 191–97. If anyone writes a general history of the great Texas music scene, it will probably be Kevin Coffey, who has been compiling useful interviews and rare research data on the subject for many years.

Studies of songs and songwriters are rare, but a few good ones exist. Dorothy Horstman's *Sing Your Heart Out, Country Boy* (3d ed. [Nashville: Country Music Foundation Press, 1996]) is a very useful book because it provides lyrics to many of country music's most important songs as well as explanations (usually given by the writers themselves) about why they were written. Jimmie C. Rogers's *The Country Music Message: Revisited* (Fayetteville: University of Arkansas Press, 1989) is an ambitious study, arranged by categories, of the lyrics of fourteen hundred songs that were popular in the years between 1960 and 1987. Rogers reaffirms the centrality of love in country lyrics but shows that its many manifestations were expressed through the lives of working people.

Challenges to the white male dominance of country music, and reminders that the music was always more eclectic in origin than its masculine personnel suggested, have been addressed by a growing number of writers. Women now play prominent roles in country music, and of course were present in distinctive ways from the beginnings of the music's history. But they still have not been given their due. The first significant study was that done by Joan Dew, *Singers and Sweethearts: The Women of Country Music* (Garden City, N.Y.: Doubleday, 1977). Based heavily on interviews, the book told the stories of Loretta Lynn, Tammy Wynette, June Carter, Dolly Parton, and Tanya Tucker. Helpful information on women can be found in the previously cited autobiographies of Lynn, Wynette, and Minnie Pearl, and in Whiteside's biography of Rose Maddox (references to the women of Top 40 country will be made toward the end of this bibliographical essay). The indispensable guide to bluegrass women is Murphy Henry's newsletter, *Women in Bluegrass,* issued monthly since September, 1994. The best overview is the comprehensive work done by Mary Bufwack and Robert Oermann, *Finding Her Voice: The Saga of Women in Country Music* (New York: Crown, 1993).

Harry Smith was just about the first person to recognize that the southern folk music culture was one shared by both blacks and whites, an insight that appeared in the choices made for his famous *Anthology of American Folk Music*. Tony Russell, though, was the first writer who directly addressed the issue, in *Blacks, Whites, and Blues* (New York: Stein & Day, 1970). Since the publication of Russell's book, much attention has been given to the African American string band tradition, and particularly to the role played by black banjo players. Karen Linn addressed the latter topic in *That Half-Barbaric Twang: The Banjo in American Popular Culture* (Urbana: University of Illinois Press, 1991, 1994), and Cecelia Conway proposed the provocative thesis that black banjo players had introduced what is perceived as "the mountain style," in *African Banjo Echoes in Appalachia: A Study of Folk Traditions* (Knoxville: University of Tennessee Press, 1995). African American participation in country and western music is discussed in the notes written by Bill Ivey, Claudia Perry, Bill C. Malone, and John W. Rumble for the CD anthology, *From Where I Stand: The Black Experience in Country Music* (Warner Brothers 9 46428-2). David Morton, with Charles Wolfe, told the story of country music's first African American star in *DeFord Bailey: A Black Star in Early Country Music*. Wolfe, with Kip Lornell, wrote a biography of the great African American folk singer, Huddie "Leadbelly" Ledbetter, who often exhibited a knowledge of and affection for "white" music: *The Life and Legend of Leadbelly* (New York: HarperCollins, 1992). Michael Harris has written the best biography of "the father of black gospel music," *The Rise of the Gospel Blues: The Music of Thomas Andrew Dorsey* (New York: Oxford University Press, 1992). Dorsey's songs, such as "If You See My Saviour" and "Peace in the Valley," moved often into the repertoires of country singers. The best overall study of black music (and more) is Lawrence Levine, *Black Culture and Black Consciousness* (New York: Oxford University Press, 1977).

The literature of country music contains a large, and ever-growing, array of articles and books that present general surveys of the music, or that provide special interpretations or personal points of view. Some of the best of these works appear in formats not immediately available to country music fans, such as Tony Scherman's "Country," in *American Heritage* 45, no. 7 (Nov., 1994): 38–58; Bryan DiSalvatore, "Profiles: Merle Haggard," *New Yorker* 65, no. 52 (Feb. 12, 1990): 39–77); Peter Applebome's "A Southern Throb in a Northern Heart," *New York Times,* June 25, 2000, sec. 2, pp. 1, 26; or in Nat Hentoff's columns in the *Village Voice.* Jack Hurst, who was writing newspaper columns about country music long before anyone else was, does have a wide readership for his syndicated columns in the *Chicago Tribune* and other newspapers, and country music Web sites make information available for anyone who has a computer. The best journalistic sources for country music fans, however, lie in the music trade magazines. *Bluegrass Unlimited,* as noted earlier, is a valuable source for bluegrass and traditional country fans. The *Old-Time Herald* is more restricted in approach, and is directly largely toward the fraternity of musicians and fans who grew up in or were influenced by the stringband revival of the sixties. The *Journal of Country Music* has coverage of both old-time and modern country entertainers, but the quality of its articles is uneven. *Country Music* magazine is a slick journal that is generally breezy in tone and oriented heavily toward that which is currently popular (although it does have an insert that presents historical profiles of older and more traditional performers). *No Depression* magazine is the best of the journals devoted to country music. Its articles and reviews concentrate on alternative performers, but each issue usually has material on such traditional musicians as Ralph Stanley and Doc Watson. The information carried in the magazine is staggering in its variety and detail. These journals have been the chief forums for much of the best and most readable writing done on country music. Dave Hickey (from the days when *Country Music* magazine was a good and hard-hitting journal), Patrick Carr, Chet Flippo, Bob Allen, Alanna Nash, Joan Dew, Geoffrey Himes, Bill Friskics-Warren, Jon Weisberger, Kevin Coffey (the best and most energetic chronicler of Texas country music), and Don Rhodes are only a few of the first-class researchers and writers who have documented the world of country music. Samples of their work can be found in the magazines listed here and in CD and album liner notes, and sometimes they appear as co-writers of country autobiographies. Don Rhodes, however, is one of the very few who has assembled an anthology of his own writings, a body of newspaper columns entitled *Down Country Roads with Ramblin' Rhodes* (privately printed by Don Rhodes, 1982). It would be good to see other anthologies of the writings of, say, Patrick Carr, Joan Dew, or Chet Flippo.

Much can be learned about the modern country music scene by reading three books that present widely divergent points of view: Nicholas Dawidoff, *In the Country of Country: People and Places in American Music* (New York: Pantheon Books, 1997); Bruce Feiler, *Dreaming Out Loud: Garth Brooks, Wynonna Judd, Wade Hayes, and the Changing Face of Nashville* (New York: Avon Books, 1998); and Laurence Leamer, *Three Chords and the Truth: Hope, Heartbreak, and Changing Fortunes in Nashville* (New York: HarperCollins, 1997). Leamer presents a generally positive but sometimes cynical view of contemporary country, and provides excellent vignettes of such entertainers as Reba McEntire and Patty Loveless. Dawidoff is respectful of "traditional" country music and hostile toward Top 40; his discussions of such people as Iris DeMent, Merle Haggard, Doc Watson, and Ralph Stanley are sensitive and beautifully written. Feiler, on the other hand, is contemptuous of older styles of country music (although his tone tends to moderate as his book progresses) and almost rhapsodic in his praise of the music ushered in by Garth Brooks and his contemporaries. Feiler's discussion of the "business" of country music is excellent, and he presents probably the best defense of modern country that we are likely to get.

Several books harbor no discernible point of view, but instead give general accounts of country music or serve as forums for contrasting approaches. John Lomax III, a direct heir to the most famous family in folk music scholarship, presents a casually written, insider's point of view of modern country music in *Nashville: Music City U.S.A* (New York: Harry N. Abrams, 1985). Patrick Carr rounded up some of the best contemporary observers of country music, such as Doug Green, Nick Tosches, and Charles Wolfe, to write the essays for *The Illustrated History of Country Music.* The chapters written by Carr on the decades since the seventies are exceptionally good. Melton A. McLaurin and Richard A. Peterson edited and contributed essays to *You Wrote My Life: Themes in Country Music* (Philadelphia: Gordon and Breach, 1992). The essays by Peterson on "class unconsciousness in country music" and James C. Cobb on "country music and the economic transformation of the South" are excellent analyses that should be useful to both students of the South and country music. Cecelia Tichi's *High Lonesome: The American Culture of Country Music* argues that country music is American, rather than southern, because it addresses the ambiguities of the American soul as expressed in such themes as the yearning for home and the open road. Tichi also edited a book of essays for a special issue of the *South Atlantic Quarterly: Readin' Country Music: Steel Guitars, Opry Stars, and Honky Tonk Bars* (Durham, N.C.: Duke University Press, 1995). The range of articles, extending from Teresa Ortega's "'My Name Is Sue! How Do You Do?': Johnny Cash as Lesbian Icon" to Curtis W. Ellison's "Keeping Faith: Evangelical Performance in Country Music," suggests the breadth that now characterizes country music scholarship, as well as the expanding horizons of the music itself. Paul Kingsbury contributed another wide array of articles with his edited volume, *The Country Reader: Twenty-Five Years of the Journal of Country Music* (Nashville: Country Music Foundation Press and Vanderbilt University Press, 1996). While *The Country Reader* comes from inside the country music establishment, David Goodman's *Modern Twang: An Alternative Country Music Guide and Directory* (Nashville: Dowling Press, 1999) surveys, in a wonderfully comprehensive fashion, the interesting realms of music that lie outside of Nashville. Add this book to your library, along with *The Encyclopedia of Country Music: The Ultimate Guide to the Music,* edited by Paul Kingsbury (New York: Oxford University Press, 1998). Don't be misled by the statement on the latter's title page, averring that the book was "compiled by the staff of the Country Music Hall of Fame and Museum." The biographies and articles were written by a large group of people like myself who have never had any kind of official affiliation with that organization (as exemplary as it might be). Together, however, these books provide just about all that you need for quick reference to the world of country music.

Discographical Suggestions

Eventually, students and fans of pre–World War II country music will have available to them two valuable guides to the recordings of that era. Tony Russell and Guthrie T. "Gus" Meade apparently worked independently of each other compiling information on every known phonograph recording made in the two decades before the war. Russell's project, which has been in preparation for many years, will be published by Oxford University Press. It will list the recordings by label, providing details about session date and place, master and release numbers, performing musicians, and instruments played. Meade, who was best known as an authority on southern fiddling, was similarly ambitious in his aims. Up until his death, he painstakingly assembled his "annotated discography," listing songs according to categories—such as "mother and home," "war and patriotism," and so on—and then assembled every known recording of the songs, along with the composers of the pieces, references to books that either included or referred to the songs, and pertinent recording session data. This massive labor of love will be completed by Richard Spottswood and Doug Meade (Gus's son), and will be published by the University of North Carolina Press.

Until those books are published, researchers will have to be content with a variety of published discographies devoted to specific record labels or individual performers. Greenwood Publishing Group, for example, has printed a large number of discographies that run the gamut from classical to country. A complete listing can be found in the Greenwood Web site <http://www.greenwood.com>. Some of those that are particularly pertinent to country music are Cary Ginell, *The Decca Hillbilly Discography, 1934–45* (Westport, Conn: Greenwood Press, 1987); Brian Rust and Tim Brooks, *The Columbia Master Book Discography,* vols. 1–4 (Greenwood, 1999); Michel Ruppli, *The King Labels* (Greenwood, 1985); Michel Ruppli and Ed Novitsky, *The Mercury Labels* (Greenwood, 1993); Michel Ruppli and Ed Novitsky, *The MGM Labels* (Greenwood, 1998). The ledgers (or copies of them) kept by Arthur E. Satherley, who supervised many of Columbia's historic country recordings, are also available at the two repositories, the Country Music Hall of Fame and Museum in Nashville and the Southern Folklife Collection at the University of North Carolina in Chapel Hill.

The most popular country recordings since World War II (as judged by their presence on *Billboard*'s charts) have been compiled by Joel Whitburn. The most recent that I have seen is *The Billboard Book of Top 40 Country Hits, 1944–1996* (New York: Billboard Books, 1996). Tom Roland, in *The Billboard Book of Number One Country Hits* (New York: Billboard Books, 1991), takes a different approach that should be appealing to country fans. He presents profiles of 848 songs, in no particular order but strictly from the 1960s on, with descriptions of the song's contents, writer, sessions producer, and length of time on the charts.

Once a recording is identified, it of course still needs to be heard. Researchers who go to the Country Music Library or Southern Folklife Collection should not expect to browse through the old recordings. "Listening copies" will be provided. If desired recordings are unavailable, the serious researcher's next recourse is to tap into the network of private collectors, most of whom are generally predisposed to be helpful.

Most people who are interested in the old recordings, however, are fans rather than historians or collectors. Some of them will hunger for mint copies of old 45 or 78 rpm disks or LPs. Most will hope to find versions that have been rerecorded on CDs. The discussion that follows is designed for those listeners. We must first understand, though, that most commercial recording companies are biased toward recent recordings, and they tend to be very repetitious in what they present. Consequently, the very early recorded material is seldom reissued (except by European or small American labels). Unless they come from Moe Asch's Folkways catalogue (material that is now being released by the Smithsonian Institution), CDs also tend to go out of print rapidly. The collections listed here may not be available by the time you read this book.

A few printed guides to country music on CDs are available. Paul Kingsbury, ed., *Country on Compact Disc: The Essential Guide to the Music* (New York: Grove Press, 1993), presents reviews of over two thousand CDs by twenty-six writers (who are described, curiously, as "the Country Music Foundation"). Bob Allen, ed., *The Blackwell Guide to Recorded Country Music* (Oxford: Blackwell, 1994), organizes its collections by topics, such as "Bluegrass," "Western," and "Alternative," which are discussed by various experts. Interested listeners, though, would be just as well off to peruse the listings of Amazon.com, the computer holdings of Barnes & Noble, or any record store or, better yet, the resources of County Sales in Floyd, Virginia (the most important source of bluegrass and old-time country music).

Anthologies or Recorded Series

Harry Smith's *Anthology of American Folk Music* (Smithsonian Folkways FP 251-253; originally released in 1952 on LPs, but newly produced on CDs in 1997). If you are beginning to fashion a library of country music, this should be your first purchase. The eighty-four recordings found here were important documents of the folk revival, and dramatic evidence of the multiracial dimensions of southern folk culture. The large booklet that accompanies the Smithsonian Folkways reissue contains several excellent articles, the most noteworthy being that written by Greil Marcus (Marcus's essay is based largely on the research of Mike Seeger—a potent combination of intellectual resources).

Alan Lomax's *Sounds of the South* (Atlantic 7 82496-2) is a boxed collection of four CDs containing 105 recordings made "in the field." The full panoply of southern grassroots styles, from Cajun and hillbilly to gospel and blues, is here. The collection is a testament to Lomax's passion for the music of the working people and an introduction to the still-living roots of the most important vernacular styles.

The *Smithsonian Collection of Classic Country Music* (Smithsonian Institution, 1981). I am admittedly biased toward this collection because I chose the selections and wrote the notes for it. No other boxed collection was quite like it, in that its 148 recordings ranged from early hillbilly performers through Willie Nelson. For reasons unknown to me, this collection was discontinued and replaced in 1990 by a revised edition (also organized and annotated by me). The revised edition (*Classic Country Music,* RD 042) is available on four CDs but includes only eighty-four songs, few of which are old-time or bluegrass.

Sony Music 100 Years: Soundtrack for a Century (Sony JXK 65750) is one of the most ambitious projects ever undertaken by a commercial recording corporation. This boxed collection, inspired by the coming of the new millennium, includes a large book of history and annotations, and twenty-six CDs composed of historic recordings (from classical to jazz) made by Columbia and other labels now owned by Sony. The country CDs include twenty-four songs, ranging from Fiddlin' John Carson to the Dixie Chicks, and can be purchased separately.

The Smithsonian Institution purchased Moe Asch's Folkways catalogue. Taken collectively, these recordings encompass a major slice of country music history, particularly since the folk revival of the early 1960s. The Harry Smith collection was listed above; other Smithsonian Folkways items will be described throughout the discographical notes that follow.

Altamont: Black Stringband Music from the Library of Congress (Rounder CD 0238). A reminder of the rich musical culture that southern blacks and whites once shared.

American Banjo: Three-Finger and Scruggs (Smithsonian Folkways CD 40037). Formerly Folkways 2314.

American Fiddle Tunes (Rounder 18964-1518-2). Library of Congress, Archive of Folk Culture.

American Yodeling, 1911–1946 (Trikont US-0246-2). 26 songs, annotated in German and English by Christoph Wagner.

Anglo-American Ballads, vol. 1 (Rounder CD 1511). An album of 13 songs originally edited by Alan Lomax and issued in 1942 by the Archive of Folk Song in the Library of Congress.

Are You from Dixie? Great Country Brother Teams of the 1930s (RCA Heritage Series 8417-2-R).

Back in the Saddle Again: American Cowboy Songs (New World NW 314/315-2). A historical anthology of the recordings of a variety of cowboy singers.

Bluegrass at Newport (Vanguard VCD 121/122). Recorded at the Newport Folk Festival in the early sixties.

The Bristol Sessions (Country Music Foundation CMF-011-D). 2 CDs. The historic recordings supervised by Ralph Peer in July and August, 1927.

Crossroads: Southern Routes (Smithsonian Folkways SFCD 40080). A sampling of the major southern vernacular styles.

From the Vaults: Decca Country Classics (MCAD 3-11009). 60 songs, spanning the period from 1934 to 1973.

From Where I Stand: The Black Experience in Country Music (Warner Brothers 9 46428-2). 3 CDs of African Americans performing country music, from the 1920s to the present.

Hard Times Come Again No More: Early American Rural Songs of Hard Times and Hardships, vols. 1 and 2 (Yazoo 2036 and 2037).

Heart of Texas Country (Neon Nightmare 1002). A very good anthology of such Texas honky-tonk singers as Johnny Bush, Claude Gray, and Darrell McCall.

Hillbilly Fever! vol. 2: *Legends of Honky Tonk* (Rhino 71901A).

Honky Tonk Heroes (Columbia CK 46030).

Mama's Hungry Eyes: A Tribute to Merle Haggard (Arista 07822-18760-2). Performances by leading country singers. Should be compared with *Tulare Dust,* listed below.

Masters of the Banjo (Arhoolie CD 421). A showcase for the varying ways in which the banjo has been played. Produced in conjunction with a tour sponsored by the National Council for the Traditional Arts.

Mountain Music Bluegrass Style (Smithsonian Folkways 40038). Originally recorded in 1959.

Music from the Lost Provinces: Old-Time Stringbands from Ashe County, North Carolina and Vicinity, 1927–31 (Old Hat CD 1001).

My Rough and Rowdy Ways: Early American Rural Music, vols. 1 and 2 (Yazoo 2039 and 2040). An anthology of songs from the "wild side of life," performed by white and black musicians.

Okeh Western Swing (CBS Special Products A 37324).

Old-Time Mountain Ballads, 1926–29 (County CD-3504). 18 recordings, from Clarence Ashley to Uncle Dave Macon.

Prayers from Hell: White Gospel and Sinners Blues, 1927–1940 (Trikont US-0267). Excellent collection of songs by such musicians as Dock Boggs, the Monroe Brothers, and Byron Parker's Mountaineers.

Ragged but Right: Great Country String Bands of the 1930s (RCA Victor 8416-2-R).

Rebels and Outlaws: Music from the Wild Side of Life (Capitol 72435-20014). Despite the title, this is a relatively tame collection of songs about murder and other illicit activities. Produced by Colin Escott.

Rhythm Country and Blues (MCA MCAD 10965). Duets by white and black singers, recorded in 1994.

Roots 'n' Blues: The Retrospective, 1925–1950 (Columbia/Legacy 47911). Outstanding collection of 107 blues, hillbilly, gospel, and western swing songs.

Silent Witness: A Tribute to Country's Gospel Legacy (Columbia CK 66974). Includes Ricky Skaggs, Marty Stuart, Johnny Cash, and others.

Something Got a Hold of Me: A Treasury of Sacred Music (RCA Victor 2100-2-R).

Swing West! vol. 1: *Bakersfield* (Razor & Tie 7930182197-2). West Coast country music.

Texas Folks (K-Tel 3741-2). Jerry Jeff Walker, Nanci Griffith, Guy Clark, Jimmie Dale Gilmore, Townes Van Zandt, Joe Ely, Alvin Crow, Robert Earl Keen.

True Life Blues: The Songs of Bill Monroe (Sugar Hill SHCD-2209). Recordings made by various bluegrass performers.

Tulare Dust: A Songwriters' Tribute to Merle Haggard (Hightone HCD 8058). 15 recordings by "alternative" country singers.

White Country Blues, 1926–1938: A Lighter Shade of Blue (Columbia/Legacy C2K 47466). 48 songs annotated by Charles Wolfe.

Working Man's Blues (Hip-O-40046). Anthology of songs by Alan Jackson and others.

World's Greatest Country Fiddlers (CMH 5904). 36 songs.

Individual Acts

The following list is in no sense definitive. It merely provides a sampling of many of country music's varied performers and styles.

Roy Acuff: Columbia Historic Edition (CK 39998); *The Essential Roy Acuff* (Columbia Legacy CK 48956).

Eddy Arnold: The Tennessee Plowboy and His Guitar (Bear Family BCD 15726 E1). The "complete" Eddy Arnold collection.

Jimmy Arnold, *Southern Soul* (Rebel CD-1621). The best country concept album.

Charline Arthur, *Welcome to the Club* (Bear Family BCD-16279 AH). Good recordings by a neglected Texas country and rockabilly singer.

Gene Autry: Blues Singer, 1929–1931 (Columbia/Legacy CK 64987); *Gene Autry Columbia Historic Edition* (Columbia CK 37465E); *The Essential Gene Autry, 1933–1946* (Columbia/Legacy CK 48957); *The Last Roundup* (Living Era CD AJA 5264); *Sing Cowboy Sing: The Gene Autry Collection* (Rhino R 272630).

Moe Bandy, *Greatest Hits* (Columbia CK 38315).

Blue Sky Boys, *On Radio* (Copper Creek CCCD-0145); *Farm and Fun Time Favorites*, vol. 1 (Copper Creek CCCD-0125); *In Concert* (Rounder CD-11536).

Dock Boggs, *Country Blues: Complete Early Recordings, 1927–1929* (Revenant CD 205).

Cliff Bruner, *Cliff Bruner and His Texas Wanderers* (Bear Family BCD 15932).

The Byrds, *Sweetheart of the Rodeo* (Columbia CK 09670). The first significant country-rock album.

Cliff Carlisle, *Blues Yodeler and Steel Guitar Wizard* (Arhoolie Folklyric 7039).

The Carter Family, *Country Music Hall of Fame* (MCA MCAD 10088); samplings from their Decca years. The complete Carter Family collection is now available on the Bear Family label (BCD 15865), edited and annotated by Charles Wolfe and Richard Weize.

Johnny Cash, *Sun Years* (Rhino R 270950); *Johnny Cash at Folsom Prison and San Quentin* (Columbia CGK 33639); *American Recordings* (American 9 45520-2).

Ray Charles, *Modern Sounds in Country and Western Music* (Rhino R 2 70099). A major document in the national popularization and acceptance of country music.

Charles River Valley Boys, *Beatle Country* (Rounder). One of the earliest "northern" bluegrass bands, and probably the earliest country "cover" of Beatles' material.

Bill Clifton, *The Early Years, 1957–58* (Rounder CD-1021).

The Patsy Cline Collection (MCA MCAD 4-10421).

Dudley Connell and Don Rigsby, *Meet Me by the Moonlight* (Sugar Hill SUG-CD-3897). Outstanding duet performance of classic country songs.

Larry Cordele and Lonesome Standard Time, *Murder on Music Row* (Shell Point 35759-1215-2).

The Country Gentlemen, *Country Songs Old and New* (Smithsonian Folkways SF 40004); *Folksongs and Bluegrass* (Smithsonian Folkways SF 40022).

J. D. Crowe and the New South (Rounder CD 0044).

Jimmie Davis, *Country Music Hall of Fame* (MCA MCAD-10087).

Iris DeMent, *Infamous Angel* (Philo CD PH 1138); *My Life* (Warner 9 45493-2); *The Way I Should* (Warner 9362-46188-2).

Hazel Dickens, *A Few Old Memories* (Rounder CD-11529); *Heart of a Singer* (Rounder 0443). Trio album performed with Ginny Hawker and Carol Elizabeth Jones.

Jimmy Dickens, *Take an Old Cold Tater & Wait* (Richmond NCD-2131).

Dixie Chicks, *Fly* (Monument NK 69678); *Wide Open Spaces* (Monument NK 68195).

Steve Earle, *Guitar Town* (MCA MCAD-31305); *El Corazon* (Warner Brothers WB 946789-2).

East Texas Serenaders, 1927–1937 (Document DOCD-8031).

Brother Claude Ely, *Satan Get Back* (King Ace CDCHD 456). Wonderful examples of Pentecostal singing, recorded at Kentucky revivals.

Joe Ely, *Honky Tonk Masquerade* (MCA MCAD-10220).

Everly Brothers, *Songs Our Daddy Taught Us* (Rhino R 2-70212); *Cadence Classics* (Rhino R 2-5258); *The Classic Everly Brothers* (Bear Family BCD 15618).

Flatt and Scruggs, *The Mercury Sessions,* vols. 1 and 2 (Rounder CDSS-18 and CDSS-19); *The Complete Mercury Sessions* (Mercury 314512 644-2); *Blue Ridge Cabin Home* (County CCS-CD-102); *Foggy Mountain Banjo* (Sony A-23392).

Red Foley, *Country Music Hall of Fame* (MCA MCAD-10084).

Tennessee Ernie Ford, *Sixteen Tons of Boogie* (Rhino R 2 70975).

Lefty Frizzell, *The Best of Lefty Frizzell* (Rhino R 2 71005); *American Originals* (Columbia CK-45067).

Robbie Fulks, *South Mouth* (Bloodshot BS 023).

Jimmie Dale Gilmore, *After Awhile* (Elektra/Nonesuch 9 61448-2); *One Endless Night* (Rounder/Windcharger 11661-3173-2).

Vern Gosdin, *Chiseled in Stone* (Columbia CK 40982).

Grayson and Whitter, 1928–1930 (County CO-CD-3517).

Nanci Griffith, *Other Voices, Other Rooms* (Elektra 61464-4).

Woody Guthrie, *Dust Bowl Ballads* (Rounder CD 1040); *The Asch Recordings* (Smithsonian Folkways): vol. 1: *This Land Is Your Land* (40100-2); vol. 2: *Muleskinner Blues* (40101); vol. 3: *Hard Travelin'* (40102).

Merle Haggard, *Capitol Collector's Series* (Capitol CDP 7 93191 2); *Down Every Road, 1962–1994* (Capitol 7 2438 35711 2).

Tom T. Hall, *Greatest Hits* (Mercury 824 143-2).

Emmylou Harris, *Pieces of the Sky* (Reprise 2284-2); *Elite Hotel* (Reprise 2286-2); *Luxury Liner* (Warner Bros. 3115-2); *Angel Band* (Warner Bros. 9 25585-2).

Emmylou Harris, Dolly Parton, Linda Ronstadt, *Trio* (Warner Bros. 25491-2).

Tish Hinojosa, *Taos to Tennessee* (Watermelon 1008); *Homeland* (A & M 5263).

Mike Ireland, *Learning How to Live* (SubPop 31021-2). Songs by one of the very best young alternative country singers.

Alan Jackson, *Here in the Real World* (Arista ARCD-8623). A Top 40 singer with real soul and working-class identification.

Wanda Jackson, *Rockin' the Country* (Rhino R 2-70990). The premier woman rockabilly singer.

Waylon Jennings, *Collector's Series* (RCA 07863-58400-2); *Dreaming My Dreams* (CD DCC,AAD 75).

Johnnie and Jack (Bear Family BCD 15555). 6 CDs.

George Jones, *The Classic Mercury Years* (Mercury 314522279-2); *Sings the Hits of His Country Cousins* (Razor & Tie RE 2064); *Sings like the Dickens* (Razor & Tie (RE 2071); *Best of George Jones* (Rhino R 2 70531).

Grandpa Jones, *Hall of Fame Series* (MCA MCAD-10549).

Alfred Karnes (and Ernest Phipps), *Kentucky Gospel, 1927–28* (Document DOCD-8013). Outstanding collection of early recorded religious music. Few singers were as good as Karnes.

Kris Kristofferson, *Singer Songwriter* (Sony A2K 48621). 2 CDs.

Doyle Lawson and Quicksilver, *Rock My Soul* (Sugar Hill SH-CD-3717).

Jerry Lee Lewis, *Original Sun Greatest Hits* (Rhino R 2-70255).

Lilly Brothers, *Early Recordings* (Rebel CD 1688).

Louvin Brothers, *Tragic Songs of Life* (Capitol 37380); *Songs That Tell a Story* (Rounder CD 1030); *In Close Harmony* (Bear Family BCD 15561 HI) is the complete collection of Louvin recordings. *Tragic Songs of Life* gets my vote as the greatest country album of all time (wonderful choice of songs and spine-tingling harmonies).

Loretta Lynn, *Country Music Hall of Fame Series* (MCA MCAD-10083); *Coal Miner's Daughter* (MCA MCAD-936).

Uncle Dave Macon: Country Music Hall of Fame (MCA MCAD-10546).

Rose Maddox, *The Maddox Bros. and Rose*, vol. 1 (Arhoolie CD 391).

Jimmy Martin, *You Don't Know My Mind* (Rounder CDSS-21).

Roger Miller, *Golden Hits* (Smash 826 261-2).

Bill Monroe, *Mule Skinner Blues* (RCA Victor 2494-2-R); *The Essential Bill*

Monroe and His Blue Grass Boys (Columbia C2K 52478); *Country Music Hall of Fame* (MCA MCAD-10082).

Nashville Bluegrass Band, *To Be His Child* (Rounder CD-0242); *Waitin' for the Hard Times to Go* (Sugar Hill SH-CD-3809).

Willie Nelson, *Red Headed Stranger* (Columbia CK 33482); *To Lefty from Willie* (Columbia CK 34695); *Who'll Buy My Memories* (Sony 22323).

New Lost City Ramblers, *The Early Years, 1958–1962* (Smithsonian Folkways SF CD 40036). 26 songs from 12 different albums.

The Nitty Gritty Dirt Band, *Will the Circle Be Unbroken* (EMI E22V-46589).

Tim O'Brien, *Oh Boy! O'Boy!* (Sugar Hill SHCD-3808); *Red on Blonde* (Sugar Hill SHCD 3853); *Songs from the Mountain* (Howdy Skies HS 1001); *The Crossing* (Alula 1014).

Tim and Mollie O'Brien, *Take Me Back* (Sugar Hill SHCD-3766).

Molly O'Day and the Cumberland Mountain Folks (Bear Family BCD 15565). The complete Columbia collection.

Buck Owens, *The Buck Owens Collection* (Rhino R 2 71016).

Gram Parsons, *GP/Grievous Angel* (Reprise 9 26108-2).

Dolly Parton, *The Grass Is Blue* (Sugar Hill 3900). A Grammy award winning collection of songs done in the bluegrass style.

Johnny Paycheck, *The Real Mr. Heartache* (CMF 023D).

Webb Pierce, *King of the Honky Tonks* (CMF 019D).

Charlie Poole and the North Carolina Ramblers, *Old Time Songs* (County CO-CD 3501); *Old Time Songs,* vol. 2 (CO-CD 3508).

Elvis Presley, *Elvis Country* (RCA 6330-2-R); *How Great Thou Art* (RCA 3758-2-R).

Ray Price, *The Essential Ray Price, 1951–1962* (Columbia/Legacy CK 48532); *San Antonio Rose* (KOC-3-7917, originally recorded on Columbia CL 1756).

John Prine, *In Spite of Ourselves* (Oh Boy OBR-019).

Don Reno and Red Smiley, *The King Collection* (King KBSCD-7001).

Tony Rice, *Church Street Blues* (Sugar Hill SHCD-3732); *Manzanita* (Rounder CD-0092).

Lesley Riddle, *Step by Step* (Rounder CD 0299). The African American man who contributed music to the Carter Family, recorded by Mike Seeger in the years from 1965 to 1978.

Riders in the Sky, *Best of the West* (Rounder CD-11517).

Tex Ritter, *Capitol Collector's Series* (Capitol CDP 7950362); *Country Music Hall of Fame* (MCA MCAD-10188).

Jimmie Rodgers, *The Singing Brakeman* (Bear Family BCD 15540). The complete collection on 6 CDs, edited by Nolan Porterfield.

Mike Seeger (Rounder CD 0278). Superb performances by one of country music's greatest researchers and collectors.

Seldom Scene, *Scene 20: 20th Anniversary Concert* (Sugar Hill SH-CD-2501/02).

Jean Shepard, *Honky-Tonk Heroine* (CMF 021-D).

Ricky Skaggs, Waitin' for the Sun to Shine (Epic EK 37193); *Highways and Heart-aches* (Epic EK-37996).

Skaggs and Rice (Sugar Hill CD-3711 and SH-CD-3711). One of the great duet albums of all time.

Carl Smith, *The Essential Carl Smith: 1950–56* (Columbia/Legacy CK 47996).

Connie Smith, *The Essential Connie Smith* (RCA 66824-2).

Hank Snow, *I'm Movin' On and Other Great Country Hits* (RCA 9968-2-R); *The Yodelling Ranger* (Bear Family BCD 15587), 5 CDs.

Sons of the Pioneers, *Country Music Hall of Fame* (MCA MCAD-10090).

Larry Sparks, *Sings Hank Williams* (Rebel CD-1694).

Ralph Stanley, *Bound to Ride* (Rebel REBCD-1114); *Clinch Mountain Country* (Rebel REB-5001). 2 CDs of duets with other country singers.

The Stanley Brothers, *Rich-R-Tone. Earliest Recordings* (Revenant 203); *The Complete Columbia Sessions* (Col 53798); *Angel Band: The Classic Mercury Recordings* (Mercury 3145251912); *Long Journey Home* (Rebel CD-1110).

Gary Stewart, *Out of Hand* (HighTone HCD 8026). Recorded originally for RCA, this is one of the greatest honky-tonk country albums ever recorded.

George Strait, *Does Fort Worth Ever Cross Your Mind* (MCA MCAD-31032).

Marty Stuart, *This One's Gonna Hurt You* (MCA MCAD-10596); *The Pilgrim* (MCA-70057).

Jimmie Tarlton, *Steel Guitar Rag* (HMG 2503); *Darby and Tarlton: On the Banks of a Lonely River* (County CD-3503).

Hank Thompson, *Capitol Collector's Series* (Capitol C21Y-92124).

Floyd Tillman, *The Country Music Hall of Fame* (MCA MCAD-10189).

Aaron Tippin, *You've Got to Stand for Something* (RCA 2374-2-R).

Merle Travis, *Guitar Rags and a Too Fast Past* (Bear Family BCD 15637 E1).

Randy Travis, *Storms of Life* (Warner Bros. 9 25435-2).

Travis Tritt, *Greatest Hits* (Warner Brothers 946001-2).

Ernest Tubb, *Country Music Hall of Fame* (MCA MCAD-10086).

Tanya Tucker, *Greatest Hits* (Columbia CK 33355).

Uncle Tupelo, *No Depression* (Rockville Rock 6050-2).

Don Walser, *Rolling Stone from Texas* (Watermelon CD 1028); *Down at the Sky-Vue Drive-In* (Watermelon CD 31017).

Dale Watson, *Blessed or Damned* (Hightone HCD 8070); *I Hate These Songs* (Hightone HCD 8082); *The Truckin' Sessions* (Koch KOC 8018).

Doc Watson, *The Doc Watson Family* (Smithsonian Folkways CDSF-40012); *The Essential Doc Watson* (Vanguard VCD 45/46); *Doc Watson* (Vanguard VMD-79152); *The Vanguard Years* (VNGD 155/58), 4 CDs with 64 songs; *Southbound* (Vanguard VMC-79213); *My Dear Old Southern Home* (Sugar Hill SHCD-3795); *Down South* (Sugar Hill SHCD-3800); *Docabilly* (Sugar Hill SHCD-3836); *Third Generation Blues* (Sugar Hill SHCD-3893).

Gene Watson, *Greatest Hits* (MCA MCAD-31128); *Greatest Hits* (Curb/CEMA D21K-77393).

Kitty Wells, *The Country Music Hall of Fame Series* (MCAD-10081); *Greatest Hits*, vol. 1 (Step One SOR-0046); *Release Me* (Classic 7568).

The Whitstein Brothers (Rounder CD 0264). The best surviving examples of the brother duet tradition.

Hank Williams, *The Original Singles Collection* (Polydor 847 194-2); *Health and Happiness Shows* (Mercury 314 517 862-2); *Rare Demos: First to Last* (Country Music Foundation CMF-067-D); *The Complete Hank Williams* (Mercury 314536077-2), 10 CDs.

Hank Williams, Jr., *Family Tradition* (Warner Bros. 194-2); *Whiskey Bent and Hellbound* (Elektra 237-2).

Lucinda Williams (Chameleon 61387-2); *Car Wheels on a Gravel Road* (Mercury 3145583382).

Bob Wills, *Anthology: 1935–1973* (Rhino R 2 70744); *Columbia Historic Edition* (Columbia CK-37468E); *The Tiffany Transcriptions*, vols. 1–9 (Rhino 71469-71477); classic Wills's recordings made during the late 1940s.

Mac Wiseman, *Early Dot Recordings*, vol. 3 (MCA-County CCS CD 113).

Tammy Wynette, *Anniversary: 20 Years of Hits* (Epic EGK 40625); *Tears of Fire: The 25th Anniversary Collection* (Epic E3K 52741).

Dwight Yoakam, *Guitars, Cadillacs* (Reprise 9 25749-2); *Hillbilly Deluxe* (Reprise 9 25567-2).

Faron Young, *Live Fast, Love Hard* (CMF 020-D).

General Index

Kingston Trio, 83
Kirby, Beecher (Bashful Brother Oswald), 192
Kirwan, Albert, 270 n. 5
Klavalier Quartet, 325 n. 28
KNEL (radio station), 259
Knippers, Otis J., 289 n. 11
Knuckles, Red, 207
Koehler, Violet, 69
Korean War, 236
Korson, George, 231, 327 n. 50
Kristofferson, Kris, 107, 110, 111, 141, 296 n. 64
KRLD (radio station), 98
Ku Klux Klan, 27, 111, 212, 221, 237, 325 n. 28
KVOO (radio station), 162
KWKH (radio station), 76, 283 n. 51

Labor unions, 42, 49, 212, 232. *See also* Industrial Workers of the World
LaBour, Fred "Too Slim," 207–8
Ladies Love Outlaws (Waylon Jennings), 143
Lair, John: Benny Ford and, 195; and country's rustic image, 62, 69, 281 n. 34; Homer and Jethro and, 181; and humor, 192, 193; and Karl and Harty, 72; and religious songs, 100; and "Sunday Morning Gathering," 78–79
Lambert, Bob, 317 n. 38
Lambert, June, 317 n. 38
Landers, Dave, 175–76, 315 n. 16
Land of Many Churches (Merle Haggard), 115
Landon, Alfred, 224
Lane, Christy, 107
lang, k. d., 249
Lange, Daisy, 69
Langford, Jon, 147
Lanman, Charles, 154
Larkin, Margaret, 233
Lasses White and Honey Wilds, 193
Last Real Medicine Show, 190
"Laugh In," 198
Lawson, Doyle, 114, 297 n. 76
Leary, Jim, 269 n. 46
LeBlanc, Dudley, 105, 189–90
LeBlanc, Happy Fats, 237
Ledbetter, Huddie "Leadbelly," 137–38, 270 n. 8
Ledford, Lily May, 69
Ledford, Rosie, 69
Led Zeppelin, 256
Lee, Johnny, 168
Lefty Lou, 233

Leno, Jay, 204
Lester "Roadhog" Moran and His Cadillac Cowboys, 206–7
Letterman, David, 204
Levine, Lawrence, 266 n. 23, 267 n. 30
Lewis, Jerry Lee, 79, 135, 136, 284–85 n. 59, 303 n. 53
Lewis, Laurie, 260
Lewis, Little Roy, 113
Lewis Family, 113
Liberace, 203
"Life Gets Teejus, Don't It," 175, 180
Life magazine, 243
Light Crust Doughboys, 162, 225–26, 228
Lightfoot, William E., 70, 192
Like a Family, 33
Lillie, Margaret. *See* Aunt Idy
Lilly Brothers, 83
"Lily May, the Mountain Gal" (comic strip), 69
Lincoln, Abraham, 17, 79, 100
Lindbergh, Charles, 242
Line dancing, 169, 258
Little, William, 92
Loar, Lloyd, 282 n. 40
Lomax, Alan, 231, 234–35, 327 n. 50
Lomax, John, 130–31, 231, 327 n. 50
Lonesome, On'ry and Mean (Waylon Jennings), 143
Lonesome Cowboy, 131
Long, Huey, 215, 227
Longstreet, A. B., 155
Lonzo and Oscar, 182
Louisiana Hayride, 9, 77
Louvin Brothers, 76, 105, 107, 283 n. 48
Louvin (Loudermilk), Charlie, 37, 103–4, 183
Louvin (Loudermilk), Ira, 37, 101, 102, 103–4
Love, Bob, 160–61
Loveless, Patty, 255
Lowry, Reverend Robert, 279 n. 13
Ludlow, Noah, 213
Luke the Drifter, 283 n. 47
Lulu Belle and Scotty. *See* Wiseman, Myrtle Eleanor (Lulu Belle); Wiseman, Scott
"Lum and Abner," 176, 188, 201
Lumber industry, 35
Lunn, Robert, 174
Luns, Jens, 331 n. 76
Lunsford, Bascom Lamar, 70, 160, 239
Lynn, Loretta, 88; and feminism, 249; and politics, 333 n. 87; and war between the sexes, 183, 184; and working people, 48, 86

Index of Song Titles

BILL C. MALONE is emeritus professor of history at Tulane University in New Orleans. He currently lives in Madison, Wisconsin, where he writes and does research on southern forms of grassroots music. He is also the host of a radio show, "Back to the Country," a three-hour program of classic country music that runs each Wednesday morning from 9 to 12 on WORT-FM in Madison.

Music in American Life

Composed in 10/13 Sabon
with Caflisch Script display
by Jim Proefrock
at the University of Illinois Press
Designed by Dennis Roberts
Manufactured by Thomson-Shore, Inc.

University of Illinois Press
1325 South Oak Street
Champaign, IL 61820-6903
www.press.uillinois.edu